The McGraw-Hill Handbook of Commodities and Futures

OTHER BOOKS BY MARTIN J. PRING

How to Forecast Interest Rates: A Guide to Profits for Consumers, Managers and Investors (1981)

International Investing Made Easy (1981)

Technical Analysis Explained: An Illustrated Guide for the Investor (1985)

The McGraw-Hill Handbook of Commodities and Futures

Edited by

Martin J. Pring

McGraw-Hill Book Company

New York St. Louis San Francisco Auckland
Bogotá Hamburg Johannesburg London Madrid
Mexico Montreal New Delhi Panama Paris
São Paulo Singapore Sydney Tokyo Toronto

Library of Congress Cataloging in Publication Data

Main entry under title:

The McGraw-Hill handbook of commodities and futures.

Bibliography: P.
Includes index.
1. Commodity exchanges—Handbooks, manuals, etc.
2. Financial futures—Handbooks, manuals, etc. I. Pring, Martin J. II. McGraw-Hill Book Company.
HG6046.M374 1985 332,64'4 84-29617
ISBN 0-07-050915-8

1234567890 DOC/DOC 898765

ISBN 0-07-050915-8

The editors for this book were William Sabin, Christine Ulwick, and Georgia Kornbluth; the designer was Jules Perlmutter; and the production supervisor was Teresa F. Leaden. It was set in Melior by University Graphics, Inc.

Printed and bound by R. R. Donnelley & Sons, Inc.

Figures 40-1–40-7, 40-9–40-10, 40-12–40-14, 40-16, 40-18, 40-20–40-22, 40-24–40-25, 40-27, 40-29–40-30, 40-32–40-33, 41-1–41-15, 43-1–43-4, 44-2–44-8, and 45-1 from *Technical Analysis Explained* by Martin J. Pring, © 1980 by McGraw-Hill, Inc. Used with permission.

NOTE: Although masculine pronouns have been used with such terms as "investor" and "analyst," they are intended to cover both sexes. McGraw-Hill policy is not to discriminate on the basis of gender.

CONTENTS

To Kiril Sokoloff

About the Editor

Martin J. Pring, one of the most respected names in the field of forecasting financial markets, is editor of *The Pring Market Review*, a technically oriented forecasting publication covering commodities, currencies, and the U.S. stock and bond markets. He is also president of The International Institute for Economic Research, and investment consulting editor to *The Bank Credit Analyst*, *The International Bank Credit Analyst*, and *The Interest Rate Forecast*. He is the author of three highly acclaimed McGraw-Hill publications: *Technical Analysis Explained*, *International Investing Made Easy*, and *How to Forecast Interest Rates*. He has lectured in Europe and North America on global financial markets. (Chapters 1, 2, 4, and 38 to 46)

Contributors

Thomas Bell, Associate Secretary General International, Cotton Advisory Commission (Chapters 10, 20, 21, and 37)

Richard T. Coghlan, Editor, *The Financial Economist* (Chapters 5 and 22)

Amos Cohen, President, Cohen Research, Inc. (Chapter 50)

Alan Davison, Research Analyst, Shearson American Express (Chapters 29, 30, and 32 to 35)

Giles Evans, Analyst, of Tropical Products, Refco (London) (Chapter 17)

Steven Gilson, Statistical Analyst, Cotton Advisory Commission (Washington) (Chapters 10, 20, 21, and 37)

Richard Grace, Fund Manager/Analyst, Drexel Burnham (London) (Chapter 18)

Reid Hampton, Technical Analyst, Prudential Bache (Chapters 3 and 49)

Michael Hinebaugh, Vice President of Research, Blunt Ellis Lowe (Milwaukee) (Chapters 6 to 8 and 12 to 14)

James Leatherberry, Director, of Currency Trading, Chicago Corp. (Chapter 27)

Alan London, Market Monitor, Oilseeds, Refco (Chicago) (Chapters 9 and 11)

Paul McAuliffe, Research Analyst, Continental Grain (Chapter 19)

Robert Menzies, Director of Research, Refco (London) (Chapter 28)

Richard Newbury, Account Executive, Refco (Vancouver) (Chapter 36)

John Parry, Managing Director of Trading, Capital Commodities (London) (Chapter 51)

Marc Rivalland, Floor Trader, LIFFE (London) (Chapter 31)
Brian Singer, Analyst, Interest Rates, Refco (Chicago) (Chapter 37)
J. R. Stevenson, Technical Analyst, Prudential Bache (Chapter 48)
Geraldine L. Szymanski, Account Executive, Dean Witter (Chapters 23 to 26)
Phillip E. Tiger, Account Executive, E. F. Hutton (Washington) (Chapter 52)
Thomas V. Tully, Private Consultant (Chapter 2)
Jack R. Weaver, Analyst, Refco (Chicago) (Chapters 15 and 16)
David Weis, Editor, *Elliott Wave Commodity Letter* (Chapter 47)

How to Use This Book

This book is intended to be used as a reference work by a broad spectrum of investors and speculators, ranging from beginners to those very knowledgeable and experienced. With this in mind, the book has been divided into seven main parts. Part 1 discusses introductory topics for those unfamiliar with the futures industry, and includes some pointers on general trends in commodity prices. Parts 2 to 5 describe the fundamentals of the main commodity and financial-instrument contracts. At the end of many of the fundamental chapters a section has been included on sources of information. Part 6, the technical part, explains how commodity traders study the action of the market itself to help them make their decisions. Any investor who wishes to adopt the technical approach is advised to study all the material presented on technical analysis because a balanced and comprehensive understanding is necessary to achieve success. Part 7 consists of a glossary and a bibliography.

While every effort has been made to furnish as much information and background for trading futures as possible, explaining the basic material is telling only half the story. The other half concerns the psychological makeup of the individual trader. All the knowledge in the world is of little help to the trader who lacks discipline, patience, and humility. The following fourteen precepts should help traders maximize their gains and minimize their losses.

1. *Don't try to go too fast or you may never get to your financial destination.* Given the tremendous leverage associated with futures, it is natural for a trader to become as fully margined as possible. As a result, if the market moves adversely, there is a very good chance that a substantial portion of the equity in the account will be wiped out. Similarly, if the trader is taking on too much risk, the significance of any minor price movement will be greatly magnified psychologically, leading to emotional rather than rational trading decisions.

2. *Don't make a trade unless you know where you are going to get out.* If a position is taken and the trader has not decided where to get out if the market moves adversely, the trader is not assessing the risk-to-reward ratio of the trade. Under such circumstances there is a tendency to hang on and let losses run.

3. *Set a loss limit and profit objective before taking a new position.* If these points are reached, stick with your original game plan by liquidating or by taking profits. Only in the most exceptional circumstances does a reevaluation justify running the position.

4. *If the market goes against you, liquidate your position and look for a better opportunity elsewhere.* If such a development takes place, chances are your judgment was incorrect. It is always hard to take a loss, but small losses have a habit of turning into big ones.

5. *Never answer a margin call.* A margin call usually results either from an unexpected adverse market move or from having too many positions. Either way it means that developments have not gone according to plan. Liquidation is the only sensible solution, for throwing good money after bad rarely works.

6. *Try to maintain some cash reserves at all times.* While cash will never earn such a high return as a fully invested futures position, it is always a good idea to maintain some reserves since an outstanding buying opportunity may arise at a time when it is inconvenient to liquidate other positions.

7. *Diversify as much as possible.* Even the best-laid plans can fail to bring success, so it is a good idea to diversify into several different markets. In case luck goes against you in one area, good judgment will save you elsewhere.

8. *Do not assume that you have to be active at all times.* There are often periods when it is not clear which way the markets are going, or when the trader is not in tune with the markets. In such cases you will make more money by being idle than by being active. Psychologically you will be in a stronger position to recognize the next major move, since you will be far more objective emotionally.

9. *Always wait for a near-perfect situation.* In most markets important long-term buying or selling junctures come two to four times a year. Given the plethora of futures markets, it does not involve a tremendous amount of patience to wait out such situations until either the technical or fundamental signs (or, better still, both) look favorable for a long or short position. There is always risk in any situation, but if the trader can isolate and minimize such risks, the chances of success are much greater.

10. *Do not overtrade.* This rule is a natural extension of the previous one. Overtrading indicates that the trader is not really sure what to do. The trader is often trying to pick the minor moves, which tend to be random anyway, and may become so involved that he or she fails to see the big picture.

11. *Avoid counteractions to the main trend.* If traders think they have determined the direction of the main trend, they should stick to that trend and not attempt to play the counteracting corrective movements to that trend by reversing positions. This is because intermediate corrective movements are notoriously difficult to predict and, by definition, are of smaller magnitude than intermediate movements of the main trend.

12. *Never commit more than you can afford to lose.* If you cannot afford to lose the money at risk, and the market goes against you, chances are that you will be "psyched out" of the position for no reason at all and you will be unable to ride out any unexpected setbacks.

13. *Do not let success go to your head.* If you find that your positions are continually making profits, it is time to move some of those profits out of the account. In no case should you pyramid your positions by taking on a lot of additional contracts as your equity expands. Pyramids are slow to build up but can come down awfully fast. After a good run it is often better to withdraw from the markets for a few weeks. Since nobody is in tune with the markets at all times, chances are that you are about to hit a losing streak—and there is nothing like newly won profit to breed complacency. One of the largest problems facing professional traders is not in making money, but in avoiding giving a substantial portion back. Therefore it is best either to take money out of the account, and drastically reduce trading activity, or to temporarily withdraw altogether.

14. *Listen to the opinions of others, but only take action based on your own assessment of the situation.* If you are managing your own account it is you, not others, who have to bear the loss if things go wrong. Only by forming your own conclusions can you hope to have the psychological fortitude to outlast temporary setbacks.

The guidelines given above are purely commonsense, but it is amazing how many of us can start off with good intentions and then fall into bad habits. If you find that things are going against you, it is a good idea to analyze where you have been going wrong and make a definite effort not to make the same mistakes again. It also makes sense, after a cooling-off period, to try again by using a much, much smaller portion of your risk capital until confidence and good judgment return. Even if your temporary withdrawal causes you to miss a major opportunity, you should always remember that another one lies just around the corner.

Acknowledgments

This book would not have been possible without the hard work of all the contributors. I would like to thank Bob Schulman, who was formerly vice president and head of research at ContiCommodity Research Division and who now heads his own economic consulting firm, for his help and encouragement, and Dan Martin and David Weis for their cooperation in creating many of the charts.

Special thanks are also due to Kathy McCrae and Kathy McCreavy for their work in coordinating the material, and to Ginette Boyle in the ContiCommodity London office for her very enthusiastic and diligent help in coordinating the efforts of the British contributors.

The original idea for this book came from Kiril Sokoloff, editor and publisher of *Street Smart Investing*, and from Larry Ladner. These people all deserve special mention, as do Eddie Read, Cindy Bissell, and my wife Danny, for all their help and encouragement over the years.

The McGraw-Hill Handbook of Commodities and Futures

PART 1

General Introduction

CHAPTER

1

The Nature and Mechanics of the Futures Markets

Martin J. Pring

The futures markets have always been viewed as a highly speculative area—and no place for the faint of heart. In recent years the increasing volatility of all financial markets, and the need of individuals to find some kind of hedge against the inflation of the 1970s and early 1980s, have led to a tremendous growth in the volume of existing contracts and to a plethora of new vehicles. The increasing volatility not only attracted a wider base of speculators but also encouraged commercial users to hedge more actively against violent price swings. The greatest expansion in new contract options has taken place in the area of financial instruments. This includes currencies, interest-rate futures, and stock market index futures. Consequently the futures industry, which used to be concerned solely with physical commodities, now embraces many more areas.

As a result of this widening base of futures participants and the general trend toward global financial instability, the futures industry has become a more widely utilized financial vehicle by the general public and the financial establishment.

MAJOR MARKET PARTICIPANTS

In any futures market there are essentially three types of participant. Those who are risk-averse and use the markets for hedging, therefore reducing risk; those who undertake the risk; and those who buy or sell to take advantage of temporary price aberrations. Those in the first category may be loosely termed "hedgers" whose business is usually involved with the actual commodity traded. Thus a copper producer may feel that copper prices are at a temporary high. Since the company knows that it will be producing a certain amount of copper in the future it can take advantage of this situation by selling that production for a future delivery date. Similarly a copper consumer, such as an industrial manufacturer, knows of the need to buy copper at specific dates in the future. If prices are attractive this company will buy copper contracts for delivery at a specific date rather than waiting for that time to make the purchase, because later prices may be significantly higher.

The same type of hedging could be transacted by a pension fund manager in either the bond or equity market. Suppose for example that the manager knew the fund was going to receive an injection of a substantial amount of cash at some future date and also felt that the stock or bond market had reached a major low. If the investment was planned in any case, the fund would be better off buying some futures contracts and taking delivery. In the case of stocks this would represent a cash settlement, but financially it would amount to the same thing.

Another possible situation would involve an individual who owned some bonds which showed substantial paper profits. If he or she had owned the bonds for less than a year the gain would be subject to tax at ordinary rates, or a maximum of 50 percent. By selling some futures contracts against this cash position the individual could hold onto those profits until the year was up. Even if the bonds returned to the original purchase price, there would still be a gain, since the profits on the futures contracts would be taxed at a maximum of 32 percent.

A hedger therefore uses the futures markets to lessen the risk of price fluctuations, and in this way is able to both plan ahead and reduce costs.

The second major participant is the speculator who takes on the risk that the hedger would normally bear. If the speculator's judgment is correct, the reward can be substantial.

To the speculator in futures relative to equities or other financial markets the essential attraction is leverage, for it is possible, with the leverage available in futures contracts, to make (or lose) a considerable amount of money very quickly. Another advantage of futures trading is that commission costs are far lower than for any other type of market. Thus if a mistake is made, and the trader quickly realizes it, the cost of getting in and out is less than in other markets.

While the speculator tends to come from the ranks of the general public, there are also a large number of professional traders, known as "locals," on the floors of the exchange. These individuals, who might trade for their own or for a company account, greatly add to the liquidity of the markets. Commercial institutions that would normally be transacting business as hedgers also speculate on occasion. This is because these entities have a substantial knowledge of the commodity or financial instrument in which they are dealing on a day-to-day basis. Consequently, if they feel that prices have gotten out of line with the fundamentals, many of them try to profit from such abnormalities by speculating in the markets.

The third broad type of market participant is the arbitrager. "Arbitrage" is defined as the process of profiting from the price differential between futures contracts which are purchased or sold virtually simultaneously in different markets. Thus if the copper price in London rises more than that in New York (allowing for currency fluctuations, delivery costs, and so forth), an arbitrager would sell London copper and buy New York copper, reversing the transaction when the prices returned to their normal relationship. Another form of arbitrage could occur in the Treasury-bill (T-bill) market. Suppose, for example, that the price of T-bill futures rose well ahead of the equivalent maturity in the cash market. Then an arbitrager would sell the futures and buy the cash. Since the profit margin of an arbitrage transaction is usually very small, such operations are carried out by brokers who have virtually no commission costs, who are well financed, and who are on the spot to perform both sides of the transaction simultaneously.

DEFINITION AND MECHANICS OF FUTURES CONTRACTS

A futures contract is essentially a regulated contract covering the purchase or sale of a commodity or financial instrument for delivery or cash settlement at a specified date in the future. The contract specifically states the quantity, quality, and delivery condition of the item concerned. Some contracts, such as stock index futures, are settled by cash on both sides rather than by the delivery of the actual commodity or financial instrument in question.

When the general public buys or sells contracts it deals through a futures merchant (broker), who is a member of an exchange and who will charge a commission for such services. The broker is responsible for the fulfillment of the contract if the broker is a clearing member of the exchange, as is Conti-Commodity. If he or she is not a clearing member, such trades must be cleared by a clearing member. A clearing member is one who deals directly with the clearing house, which is a subsidiary of the exchange. At the end of the day the clearing house assumes one side of all open contracts. Thus, if a broker is long, the clearing house assumes a short position. The house guarantees its members the performance of both sides of all open contracts. Thus brokers do not actually deal with those on the other side of the trade but with the clearing house itself.

THE MECHANICS OF THE EXCHANGE

The basic function of the exchange is to provide facilities where members can transact futures contracts. This not only involves a physical building but also the means of settling contracts, regulating trading, and so forth. Trading generally takes place in a pit or the outside of a ring. All orders received by members are sent to the exchange floor for execution and are filled according to the bids and offers by open outcry. Usually only one commodity is traded in a pit, and for active contracts trading in the same delivery month occurs in the same area of the ring or pit so the broker with an order can find the proper market as quickly as possible. If volume is particularly high and price changes are rapid, it is not uncommon for different prices to be quoted for the same delivery month in different parts of the pit. Under such conditions it is possible to get executions at prices that are never officially recorded. Similarly an order might be marked "unable" even though the price of the order was well within the trading range of that commodity.

Once a transaction has been made it is reported to the pit recorder, who is a representative of the exchange. The report includes the commodity traded, the delivery month, the price, and the time of sale; it does not record the volume, since this would delay the execution of orders in active markets. This information is then sent to a quotations room from which it is transmitted to the outside world. The broker transacting the order will of course relay a report to a telephone clerk on the exchange floor, who in turn will report to the account executive whose customer originally placed the order. It can be appreciated that because of the speed of commodity price movement, execution of orders is not so precise as those of stocks and shares. Nevertheless, if an account executive feels that customers' orders have not been properly executed, he or she can do a "time and sales" study to ascertain what trades took place at what time. If there is a dispute involving a settlement following the time and sales study, the matter will be taken up with the exchange, which will mediate the dispute.

Some markets begin with an open outcry in which all contract months are traded simultaneously all day. Others, such as cotton, heating oil, and so forth, open and close with a call, which means that each contract is called in turn until all orders currently on hand for that contract are filled.

The total of contracts outstanding at any one time is called the "open interest." Anyone who is long a contract during a delivery month meets the obligation either by selling the contract or by taking delivery. If this contract is sold to someone who is also long, the open interest is unchanged. On the other hand if it is sold to someone who has had a short position, then the open interest declines by one contract. The size of the open interest position and the total volume of activity in a contract indicate the overall liquidity level.

As well as providing physical trading facilities, the exchanges also set rules as to the permissible price limits to which a commodity may move during the day. Nearby contract months are often free to trade without limit. If a contract moves the daily limit for 2 days, the limit is usually expanded on the third day. These limits, which are usually set for a considerable period of time, are changed when the price of a commodity moves away from its previous "normal" level or when price fluctuations become abnormally volatile. It is usual therefore to raise trading limits when prices rise into a new trading range and vice versa. An exchange will typically change margin requirements under similar circumstances. "Margin" is in effect a deposit required by the exchange to cover any adverse movement against the holder of a contract position, be it long or short. Consequently the higher prices move or the more volatile they become the greater will be the margin requirement. For example, even though U.S. Treasury bonds fell sharply in early 1980, thereby reducing the value of the contract, the increased volatility of prices associated with this decline persuaded the exchange to actually raise margin requirements. While the exchange sets margin requirements, these are minimum amounts. Commodity brokers can, and often do, want added protection, for if their customers find themselves in bankruptcy and cannot pay, it is the broker who is responsible to the exchange for the debt.

OPENING AN ACCOUNT AND TRANSACTING BUSINESS

The selection of a broker and the placement of orders are covered in a later chapter, but it is worthwhile at this point to discuss briefly the financial arrangement between broker and client. When opening an account the broker will require the client to send in a sum of money to establish some kind of net worth. The opening balance can range from $5000 to $15,000. Once this money has been deposited and the customer has furnished the broker with other financial data, including a signed statement accepting liability for any possible losses over and above the amout deposited with the broker, the customer may begin trading. Given the tremendous leverage available in the commodity markets, it is sensible to start off in a small way. If the initial trading is successful and the client makes some money, the equity in the account will rise. At this point the customer may take the excess equity out of the account if the trader wishes, since the margin adequately covers his or her position. This is very different from investments such as stocks or bonds, where paper profits cannot be realized without a sale (or purchase in the case of a short sale). If the investor is really lucky or well-heeled, with equity over $15,000 or $20,000, Treasury bills may be bought and these can be used as margin. In this way the trader is able to obtain a return not only on the futures contracts that are bought and sold but also on a substantial portion of the money on deposit with the broker. A trader must always be careful not to put too much money into T-bills, for if his or her equity declines in value the broker will have to put up more cash at the exchange clearing house, and in turn will request the investor either to send in more money or liquidate the T-bills, which will involve some transaction costs.

LONDON MARKETS

The principles of trading commodities in London are basically the same as in the U.S. markets but there are some important differences. First, metals traded on the London Metal Exchange (LME) are traded for a prompt date, usually 3 months from the date of initiation of a transaction. Thus if I buy 3-month copper today I must either take delivery or sell the copper within 90 days. Unlike the U.S. market, London metals are not traded by specific contract months but continuous "prompt" dates into the future. This does not preclude the speculator from getting out of a position before the prompt date, but unlike the U.S. markets no actual money changes hands until the prompt date falls due. Usually the metals markets are a carrying charge market; that is, the 3-month price will be higher than the cash price. This is because there are certain carrying charges associated with holding a metal in storage, for example, interest and storage insurance. The premium, or "contango" as it is called, offsets these costs in the price differential between the cash and forward prices. The further out in time the delivery date, generally speaking, the higher the contango. Thus if I buy a 3-month copper contract today with, for example, a £20 contango and then decide to sell it 6 weeks later, the contango will be approximately £10, assuming it is still £20 for a 3-month contract. For this reason the broker to whom I sell the copper contracts adjusts the price downward for my prompt date. Since settlement does not take place until the prompt date I cannot realize cash from my profits until that date arrives. This is unlike the situation in the United States, where cash can be physically removed from the account even before the transaction is closed out. While a contango is the normal situation in a metals market it is possible, during a period of shortage for the physical metal, to see the cash price rise above that of the 3-month contract. This situation is known as a "backwardation." In this case the speculator is actually being paid to hold the commodity. In the case of the copper transaction described above, in a backwardation situation the price adjustment would be an upward one. Without becoming too complicated it should be noted that the backwardation or contango is not necessarily spread evenly over the period between the cash and 3-month dates. For example, if market participants perceive that a metal shortage is only going to last for 2 or 3 weeks they will bid up the nearby settlements, thus putting most of the backwardation for nearby prompt dates. The other major metal traded in London, but not on the LME is gold. Gold is traded on a spot basis, so investors who purchase gold pay a daily interest rate linked to the short-term eurodollar rate. This interest is payable when the transaction is closed. Those who sell short, on the other hand, receive interest based on the selling price. This also is tied to short-term eurodollar rates and paid when the transaction is closed out. There are no daily price limits either on the LME or among the gold bullion dealers.

Other major markets in London include cocoa, coffee, sugar, gasoil, rubber, foreign currencies, and interest-rate futures. Most of these markets have limits which are usually much wider than those in New York. Business is transacted for a specific contract month, as it is in the United States. However, while cash changes hands at the time each transaction is closed (unless the commodity is delivered), the speculator is not able to withdraw cash from the account before the position is closed out, even though there may be a considerable paper profit.

CHAPTER

2

Selecting a Broker and Learning the Language

Thomas V. Tully and Martin J. Pring

Most newcomers to the commodity markets pay very little attention to the choice of a broker. The decision is usually made on the basis of a friend's recommendation, the carrot of cheaper commissions, or a promising advertisement. The process of broker selection, however, is a critical one. An inexperienced trader will require recommendations from the broker, so if the account executive (AE) is incompetent or more interested in commissions than making money for his client, the odds are against the trader right from the start. Even with more experienced traders used to making independent decisions, and AE's failing to call at the right time, or getting an order mixed up, can be crucial.

Since most people trade commodities because of the leverage available, it only takes a few poor trading recommendations or a little general incompetence by the broker to wipe out your equity.

If you are planning to trade commodities for the first time, proceed with the same caution and humility you would use to learn a new sport at 30, 40, or 50 years of age. Failure to do so will not result in strained muscles, but will probably produce a strained bank account.

Say you were going to take up golf on a serious basis. You would probably do three things. You would seek a pro for lessons. And, not knowing the game, if you happened to be left-handed, you might look for a left-handed pro. Then, on the pro's recommendation, you would buy equipment. And, finally, you would certainly take the time to learn the rules and language of the game.

Your approach to entering the markets should not be much different, except that you should already have the equipment: money. You need a pro, preferably one compatible with your expectations and investing philosophy. And you need to learn the rules and the language of the markets.

The pro is, of course, the *broker*—a term used interchangeably to mean both a brokerage firm and an AE who works for that firm. From your point of view, they represent two separate decisions and their relative importance depends on the type of account you plan to open.

If you participate in a limited partnership, or open a managed account with a commodity trading advisor (CTA) represented by the AE, the AE is relatively unimportant. The AE is functioning as an equity raiser and you should focus your emphasis on the track record of the CTA, the commission and fee structure, and the order execution performance of the brokerage firm.

Your selection of a brokerage firm and an AE take on added importance if you open a personal or, as it is often called, a trading account. There are basically three types. In the first, you call the signals. You make the trading decision on the basis of your own knowledge. This is usually unwise for the new trader unless you limit your trades to commodities related to your business, where you have a particular expertise.

The second type is the most frequently employed. You make the decisions based on recommendations from the brokerage house and/or your AE. The third is known as a discretionary account. It is similar to the managed account but with two exceptions. Trading decisions are usually made by your local AE rather than an outside CTA, and you are charged on a straight commission basis rather than on a combination of fees and performance incentive.

CHOOSING A BROKERAGE FIRM

Your initial contact with any brokerage firm will be with an AE. The AE will attempt to sell you on his or her talents. And that's important for reasons we'll discuss later. But remember this: there are many more good AEs than there are good brokerage firms, and an AE is rarely more effective than the firm providing the support. Make sure you are as sold on the brokerage house as you are on the AE's qualifications.

You should evaluate a brokerage firm in five areas. The first is information. Most traders simply have neither the access nor the time to acquire the information needed to trade commodities successfully. While judging the firm's ability to provide data, look for access to information needed to trade commodities successfully. Both of the above are true whether you are calling the trades or your AE is making the decisions. As well as access to information, try to evaluate the firm's analyses, especially in regard to depth and quality.

The second area is execution. How much time is required to fill an order from an AE's desk in Dallas or Los Angeles until it is traded in a hectic trading pit in Chicago, New York, or London? And, assuming you are satisfied with the quality of the executions, does the firm back them up with timely confirmations?

The third measurement is the firm's ability to provide timing on trades. It is a function of both information and execution. Timing is the knowledge of the price at which a trade should be made and the ability to execute at, or near, that point.

The firm's history of performance is an important consideration. As in any business relationship, you want to do business with a firm that has a history of integrity and stability. How do you assure stability? Be sure the firm is a member of the clearing houses of all major exchanges. Members are audited by the Commodity Futures Trading Commission (CFTC), the clearing house, and the exchange.

Finally, does the firm provide accurate monthly statements? That may seem like a small consideration, but you won't feel that way if there are errors in your account following a month of heavy trading.

Naturally, commission charges must also be figured into the equation. But when you compare dollars, be sure you also compare services and factor in your need for those services. When you're satisfied with the brokerage firm's competency, you can begin to make judgments regarding the selection of an AE.

CHOOSING AN ACCOUNT EXECUTIVE

Federal regulations require the AE to take a close look at your financial suitability. It's in your best interest if the AE also probes your investing personality and goals. In fact, if you are not interviewed in this manner, you should question whether the AE is sincerely interested in helping you achieve your goals.

Nowhere is it written that interviews are a one-way street. While the AE is qualifying you, you should be qualifying the AE. Here are some questions you might ask. How many accounts do you have and how large are they? Will the size of my account be important to you? Have you made money for your clients? Will you provide the names of other traders so I can verify your qualifications?

Those are hard questions and may be unfair. A relative newcomer with a small clientele may work harder on your behalf than will a veteran with many large accounts. For example, a newcomer may be more willing to help you learn the mechanics of trading. But there are other, equally important ways of judging an AE's competency. Do you have compatible money-management philosophies? If one of you likes to go for broke, and the other is conservative, one of you had better have the sense to admit the relationship will never work.

What about the AE's trading philosophy? Is it logical? Equally important, can it be applied to accounts in your equity bracket? Is it designed to produce results which meet your expectations?

Is the AE a commodity specialist or are the futures markets just a sideline? At least one of you had better know what you're doing, especially if you are just getting started.

What if the AE fails your test? (Incidentally, you may fail the AE's test.) Find another one. It's your money, but it is tough enough to succeed in the futures markets without the handicap of an investor-AE relationship which lacks mutual confidence, respect, and goals. In short, don't sign the papers or write the check until you have established a comfortable "fit" with an AE.

MONITORING AN ACCOUNT EXECUTIVE

When you have chosen an AE half the battle is over, but it is still important to monitor his or her attitudes and to help in managing your account. At this stage it is also important to establish some ground rules so that both you and your AE understand what you expect of each other. The most successful AE will place the growth of your equity as top priority. He or she will realize that this is the only way in which reward, in the form of commissions, can accumulate. It is a fact that 80 percent of newcomers to the commodity markets do not last for more than 12 months. If you can make it past that point, your chances of success in the markets are greatly enhanced. A shortsighted AE will overtrade your account with a possibly fatal effect on your equity. The AE will have earned a substantial amount in commissions over a short period of time but neither of you will gain over the long term. The AE who introduces you to the market slowly is able to get a better feeling for your relationship, and in the process will be more likely to select recommendations more carefully. If you are lucky enough to earn some profits, both you and the AE should agree on a program to take some of those profits physically out of the account. In this way the temptation to overleverage those profits, to which all of us succumb, will be drastically reduced. The farsighted AE will see this as a sensible way for you to build up your equity, and will realize that a successful client will keep coming back. If your AE is reluctant to go along with this process, it is a red flag and you should question his or her motives very carefully.

As you begin your relationship, you should make it quite clear whether you or the AE is to generate the trading ideas, or whether you are expecting a combination of both. Whichever way you decide, make sure you explain your reasons for each trade and at what price or under what conditions you would close it out. Always be completely frank and open with your AE. In this way the AE is totally informed about your ideas, and is in a far better position to call or advise you if something unexpected should happen. If you find your AE unapproachable or unable to explain things, you probably made a mistake and should look for another one. At the same time, if you are not doing very much business you cannot expect your AE to spend a lot of time with you. If you are in any doubt over this point, ask. If there is a problem of this nature, the AE will be happy to have the opportunity to "open up." If you think his or her position is reasonable, say so, make fewer demands, and chances are your relationship will improve.

It is very important to make sure that your AE is comfortable handling your account. It is hard trying to make the right decisions in the commodity markets and if the AE has to worry about your attitude, the task is made still more difficult. If a few recommendations go sour, continue to give encouragement and he or she will have greater confidence in making recommendations in the future. Everybody goes through a bad patch when nothing seems to work. Try to look at the longer-term trend in your equity position. If the overall picture is satisfactory, some short-term encouragement will help your AE to feel more confident. Obviously, if you continue to get poor recommendations some reexamination of the whole situation is in order and some remedial action should be taken.

AN INTRODUCTION TO TERMINOLOGY

You've brought the equipment and you've selected a pro. The next step is to learn the language of the game. If you had played tennis for 10 years, you wouldn't expect the jargon to be transferable to golf. And you shouldn't expect all terms used in other forms of investment to have the same meaning in the commodity markets.

The most basic parts of a commodity order are the commodity and the quantity. In most cases, they are entered in a straightforward manner. For example, 5 Gold means five gold contracts. The exception is in grains, where most are traded in 5000-bushel contracts and an abbreviation of the number of bushels is written on the order. Thus an order reading 50 corn means 50,000 bushels or 10 contracts, rather than 50 contracts of corn. The two other important parts of the order are considerably more involved. One is the time element, such as a day order. The other is the price element, the most popular being the market order. From these two variations, the Futures Industry Association lists more than thirty types of orders. Some reflect specific strategies and are never used by most traders, while others are not accepted by all exchanges or brokerage firms. Still, it is important to know your alternatives in markets which move as quickly as commodity trading pits. The following is a glossary of the most common types of orders:

Market Order

Example: BUY 1 Jan 1985 Orange Juice MKT

The market order is to be executed immediately by the floor broker at the best possible price.

Limit Order

Example: BUY 1 May 1985 Copper 93.60
SELL 1 Jan 1985 Sugar 15.62

The limit order specifies a limit price. In this example, the broker may fill the buy order on copper at or below $93.60. The sell order on sugar can be executed at or above $15.62.

Stop Order

Example: SELL 5 Sept 1985 T-bonds 67-14 Stop
BUY 2 Feb 1985 Hogs 55.60

The sell-stop order can be filled only if the contract trades, or is offered, at or below the stop price. The buy-stop takes effect when the contract trades, or is bid, at or above the stop price. In either event, the stop-order becomes a market order to be filled immediately at the best possible price, even if the price rebounds in the adverse direction. The sell-stop is used to limit losses on long positions and the buy-stop to limit losses on short positions.

Stop-Limit Order

Example: BUY 1 May 1985 Orange Juice 149.95 Stop Limit
SELL 10 March 1985 Soybean Meal 238.70 Stop Limit 238.20

This is similar to a stop-order except that execution is restricted to the limit price or better. Thus the buy order above can be filled only at $149.95 or less. In the second order, the floor broker must try to sell at $238.70, but cannot execute at less than $238.20. The problem with this type of order is that a fast-moving market may move beyond the stop-limit price before the order can be filled. Thus, the stop-limit order offers less protection against an adverse move.

Around Order

Example: SELL 5 June 1985 Gold around 544.00

This order gives the floor broker limited flexibility regarding the fill price. The extent of the latitude is established by the brokerage firms. Around orders can only be filled if the market trades through the specified limit. This type of order is not accepted at the Chicago Board of Trade or the Chicago Mercantile Exchange.

Basis Order

Example: If Dec 1984 Cattle trades at 67.00 or higher, BUY 10 June cattle

This is also called a contingent order. It's a strategy employed when the trader believes one contract is an indicator of probable price action on another. It cannot be used trading silver futures on the Chicago Board of Trade.

Cancel Former Order

Example: BUY 5 April 1985 Hogs 56.05 CFO #_____ to
BUY 5 April 1985 Hogs 55.25 entered (Date)

Also indentified as CFO, this order allows the trader to cancel former orders. It is usually written when a customer wishes to change an existing buy or sell price limit. The important thing about CFO orders is to make sure the new order includes complete indentification of the order to be cancelled.

Closing Order

Example: BUY 5 Nov 1985 Soybeans MKT on close

The trader may wish to hold a position throughout the trading day and close it out just as the market closes. No price is specified, and, although the floor broker is not required to fill on the exact closing price, the execution should fall within the closing range of prices on the day specified.

Conversion Spread Order

Example: Spread BUY 50 Jan 1985 Soybeans
SELL 9 Jan 1985 SBO (Soybean oil)
SELL 12 Jan 1985 SBM MKT (Soybean meal)

At one time, the above example of a soybean crush spread was used almost exclusively by soybean processors. They used the markets to lock in profitable margins for their crushing business. In recent years, speculators have made increasing use of the same formula in an attempt to earn futures profits.

Conversion Spread Order (Limit Price)

Example: Spread BUY 50 Jan 1985 Soybeans
SELL 9 Jan 1985 SBO
SELL 12 Jan 1985 SBM, 4½¢ premium the products

In this case, the trader wishes to employ the crush only if the combined value of the oil and the meal produce a yield value of at least 4½¢ per bushel over the cost of soybeans. Because such spreads are more difficult to execute than outright trades, some brokerage firms employ floor brokers who specialize in the most frequently used spreads. Since spreads qualify for lower commission rates, the word "spread" should precede the command portion of the order.

Conversion Spread Order (Reverse Crush)

Example: Spread BUY 9 March 1985 SBO
BUY 12 March 1985 SBM
SELL 50 Jan 1985 Soybeans MKT

Obviously, when the value of soybean oil and meal does not exceed the cost of a bushel of soybeans, it is unprofitable for the processor to crush beans. When this circumstance prevails, the processor may elect to close down the crushing operation temporarily and seek profit in the markets. This trader buys oil and meal and sells soybean futures in the proper ratio in the expectation that prices will return to the normal margin. The limit-price technique, utilizing a specified premium as shown in the previous example, can also be employed in the reverse crush.

Day Trade Order

Example: BUY 5 Feb 1985 Pork Bellies MKT DAY TRADE

The day trade specifies that both sides of the transaction are to take place the same day.

Discretionary Order

Example: BUY 5 June 1985 Hogs 57.90 with 10 pts. discretion

The discretionary order is intended to allow a limited degree of flexibility for the floor broker. In this example, the broker can provide a fill as high as $58.00. Had this been a sell order, the trade could have been executed at $57.80 or above. While not as loose as a market order, it does enhance the likelihood of a fill in a fast moving market.

Enter Day Stop Order

Example: SELL 25 March 1985 Wheat MKT
ENTER DAY STOP 4.95

This type of trade is also known as an EDS. The potential problem is that if the order is misunderstood and the stop is executed instead of the command, you own five wheat contracts on the wrong side of the market. To avoid the problem, the EDS instruction should be shown on a separate line. There are several contracts and exchanges where EDS orders are not accepted.

Enter Open Stop Order

Example: BUY 10 Dec 1984 Corn MKT
ENTER OPEN STOP 3.66½

Known as an EOS, this is a protective device inserted at a price point below a buy order, or above a sell order. As with the EDS order, the EOS is unacceptable on some contracts. And, since special handling is required on the floor, most floor brokers will accept an EOS only on a "not held" basis, meaning the broker cannot be held responsible for failure to execute the "stop" part of the order.

Exchange for Physicals

Example: SELL 5 Jan 1985 Feeder Cattle 68.25
EX-PIT to ACME Company vs Cash

In all likelihood, you'll never use this order. It is one of two which can be executed legally on the trading floor without competitive bidding. An ex-pit order (i.e., an order executed outside the exchange) usually involves two commercial entities, a supplier and a customer, and is the result of prior negotiation. It must, however, be reported to, and approved by, exchange officials.

Fill or Kill Order

Example: SELL 10 March 1985 GNMA 65-19 FOK

A fill or kill (FOK) order means "fill it immediately or cancel it." An FOK may, however, be filled on a partial basis if a report on the part filled is completed immediately. In this case, for example, five GNMAs might be sold and five cancelled.

Intermarket Trade

Example: SPREAD BUY 50 Chgo May 1985 Wheat
SELL 50 KC May 1985 Wheat
5¢ premium KC

An intermarket trade is a spread on contracts for the same commodity as offered on two different exchanges. As is always the case, the key to the spread is the difference in price rather than absolute prices. The fill for this order requires communication between pit brokers at the two exchanges in question. The optimum execution is to place both orders simultaneously. If not, the difference must be at least 5¢ premium to Kansas City wheat as specified by the customer.

Limit or Market on Close Order

Example: BUY 20 Jan 1985 Soybeans at 7.90 or MKT on close

With this order, the trader hopes to buy soybeans at $7.90 per bushel at some point during the day. If the price never dips to $7.90, the floor broker is instructed to execute at the most favorable price available on the close. On this order, "or MKT on close" should be included on the same line as the buy or sell command so that it is not overlooked by the floor broker.

Market if Touched Order

Example: SELL 5 Oct 1984 Broilers 50¢ MIT

Commonly called an MIT or "board" order, this instruction tells the pit broker to sell if the price reaches 52¢ even if light volume makes it impossible to execute at exactly that figure. The advantage is that if the price does reach 52¢, the trader will receive a fill at close to the desired price. Since a seller would establish an MIT above market price, and a buyer below it, this type of order provides a price advantage over a market order if the price is reached.

Not Held Order

Example: SELL 10 Feb 1985 Hogs 55.90 NH

This order allows the floor broker to take advantage of his location in the pit. For example, as hogs approach $55.90 in a strong market, the pit broker may feel he can better that price. This order gives him the discretion to try for the higher price, but does not hold him responsible for the $55.90 fill if the market turns and he must accept a lower price.

One Cancels the Other

Example: SELL 5 Oct 1984 Cattle 63.50 or 61.50 Stop OCO

This is an either/or order. In this example, the trader may issue the sell instruction to take a profit at $63.50. If the price is reached, the fill is executed and the second sell order cancelled. If the market turns before it reaches $63.50, the alternative sell price of $61.50 serves as protection and the first order is cancelled.

Opening Order Only

Example: BUY 10 Sept 1984 Corn 3.66 OPG only

This is an attempt to lock in the opening price. If the pit broker cannot fill at the opening price, the order is cancelled. Without the "OPG only" designation, the broker could fill the order at any price within the opening range.

Retender Order

Example: SELL 25 Nov 1984 Soybeans
MKT AND RETENDER

This is an order you don't want to place. It usually means a contract has lapsed and the trader has received 25,000 bushels of unwanted soybeans. To avoid that he enters "and retender" on the second line of the order. This instructs the pit broker to sell and issue a redelivery notice, on the customer's behalf, to another buyer. There are some markets in which retender orders are not allowed.

Scale Order

Example: BUY 10 Jan 1985 Feeder Cattle 68.25 and 10 each 50¢ lower, Total 50, GTC

This is a form of contingent order. The GTC designation means "good until cancelled." The pit broker will fill the first ten contracts at $68.25, the second ten at $67.75, the third ten at $67.25 and so on. It is an attempt to spread an order and avoid a mistake on a large trade. It can accomplish the same objective during liquidation. Variations include the use of a limit price, for example $68.50 on the purchase of the first ten contracts.

Spread or Straddle Orders

Example: SPREAD BUY 25 May 1984 Oats
SELL 25 March 1985 Oats, 6¢ or less premium the May
SPREAD BUY 10 Dec 1984 Wheat
SELL 10 Dec 1984 Corn, 90¢ premium wheat

Earlier we discussed intermarket spreads and three commodity relationships such as the soybean crush. The examples above illustrate two other forms. The first is the intramarket spread where both legs are in the same commodity and exchange. In this order, the trader expects the gap between the nearby and distant months to widen. The second example is an intercommodity spread—different commodities offered on the same exchange. The trader doesn't care whether prices rise or fall, but he expects December wheat to gain on December corn. Incidentally, if you are confused about the difference in meaning of "spread" and "straddle," don't worry about it. "Spread" is used largely for CBT orders and "straddle" is the term usually applied for markets other than grains.

On all spread orders, pit brokers are directed to execute both ends as nearly simultaneously as possible.

Switch Order

Example: SWITCH BUY 2 Dec 1984 Silver
SELL 2 Sept 1984 Silver 70 pts. premium or less the Dec

A switch order is used to move an existing position from one delivery month to another or from one market to another. While the switch order closely resembles the spread or straddle, there is one major difference. A switch order is not entitled to the reduced spread commission rate. Hence the prefix "switch" on the order.

Time Order

Example: AT 11 am CHICAGO TIME BUY 20 Dec 1984 SBO MKT
BUY 5 Feb 1985 Cattle 66.00 GTC
SELL 10 March 1985 Corn 3.78 GTW (or GTM)
BUY 1 Sept 1985 GNMA 64.20 GT Aug. 15, 1984

Unless specified to the contrary, all commodity futures orders expire the day of, or the day following, the placement. There are, however, techniques for specifying the length of the life of the order. We've reviewed two types, those instructing buys or sells "on the opening" or "on the close." The four examples shown above provide further flexibility in defining the life of the order.

The first instructs the pit broker to buy soybean oil at 11 A.M. on the date the order is placed. The other three make use of the GT designation which means "good through." The GTC means "good till cancelled," meaning the broker can buy the cattle contract at $66.00 at any time until a cancelling order is received.

The GTW designation on the corn order means the contract can be sold at $3.78 at any time through the week during or following that in which the order is placed. The GTM is the first cousin of the GTW. It defines the life of the order as the month during or following the placement. The final variation instructs the floor broker to buy one Ginnie Mae contract if the price reaches $64.20 on or before August 15.

SUMMARY

In this chapter we've touched on some of the basics required to enter the commodity markets. Select a brokerage house with services to match your needs. Choose an account executive who understands your goals and is sincerely interested in helping you achieve them. Finally, don't assume that the jargon used in other investments has the same meaning in futures trading. If you don't understand a term, ask for clarification.

CHAPTER

3

Speculation: Risk and Money Management

Reid Hampton

WHAT IS RISK?

Risk is the variability of an income stream, or the degree of instability in returns. In commodity speculation, this is present to a considerable degree because of the very nature of the speculative vehicle. Low margins create a highly leveraged situation in which a small percentage change in the price of the actual commodity is magnified as a much larger percentage change in account equity. A look at a theoretical account equity growth curve, Figure 3-1, gives a clearer picture of this concept of risk.

The dotted line is an average of mean return (growth rate) for the account, and fluctuations around it, both above and below, are what is considered income variability, or risk. At any given point in time, the relationship could be expressed as shown in Figure 3-2. The dotted line bisecting this curve is the same dotted line as in Figure 3-1, the mean return, represented by *X*. Along the *X* axis is the rate of return, and along the *Y* axis is the probability of getting a certain return. Since any variability, or risk, to the right of *X* is increased return, we are obviously not worried about reducing that risk. The chief concern of the commodity trader is to reduce chances of losses to the left of point *X*, especially those beyond −50 percent, which could be considered devastating in which at least one-half of the original margin is lost. The purpose of this chapter is to increase the trader's awareness of the ways that this risk may be reduced in speculations, and to also bolster the trader's knowledge of the concepts that make up risk theory.

Risk Capital

This term refers to those funds that are not required by the trader to meet obligations, and should be plentiful enough to survive some equity erosion. These funds should also be intended solely for the purpose of speculation, as their withdrawal at any time would be self-defeating unless these funds are profits not needed in the trader's equity base.

Why Take Risk?

People assume risk for many different reasons, the foremost and possibly most rational of these being to make money. Others risk their money either for fun and games, such as gambling, or for some subtle form of self-punishment. We are not concerned here with the masochist or the gambler, but with the investor; more specifically, with the speculator in commodities.

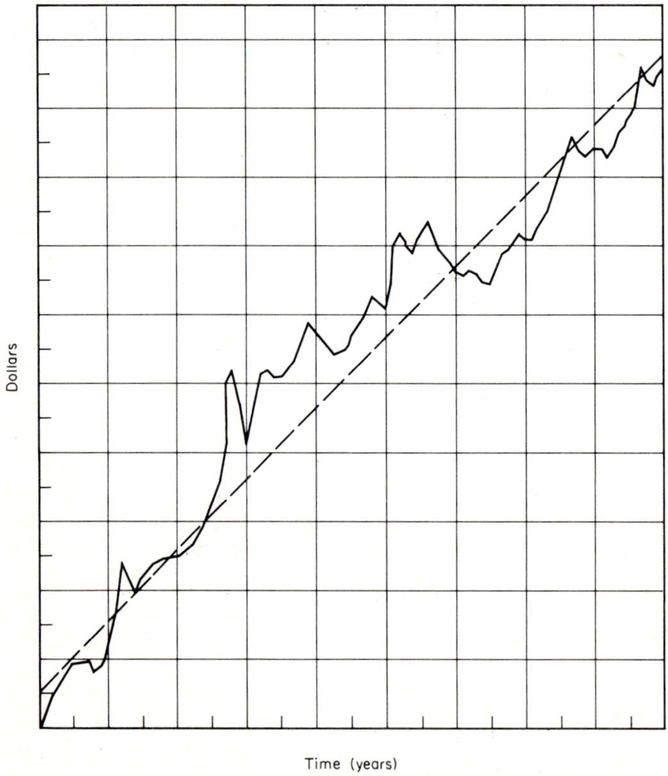

Figure 3-1 Equity growth curve. *(ContiCommodity Research Division)*

RISK AVERSION

All investors are basically risk-averse. Risk aversion refers to the amount of risk that the speculator is comfortable with, or the risk-to-return ratio that is sought in trading. There are many variables that have an influence in the determination of this risk-aversion level. Age, sex, income, capital position, education, and even marital status are all factors that mold the attitudes toward risk of the potential investor.

The older the investor the more conservative he or she generally is, in that financial security is sought rather than high returns. The assets that have been accumulated over a lifetime are generally not risked. A younger investor, fresh out of college, is less likely to have any major responsibilities or commitments, and is in a much better position to risk it all. A large loss at such a point in time would be less devastating to this individual than to an older one, despite the fact that a large portion of his or her net worth might be lost.

Better-educated people are generally less risk-averse than the less-educated segments of the population. This is not only because higher education usually brings a larger mean income, but also because it often brings an increased potential for dealing with complex risk situations, such as those found in commodity futures trading. Income level and net worth are important as well, regardless of education. An individual who truly has risk capital, that which can be lost without financial disaster, is more likely to get into a high-risk situation, for example, than an individual who has to second-mortgage a house to generate funds.

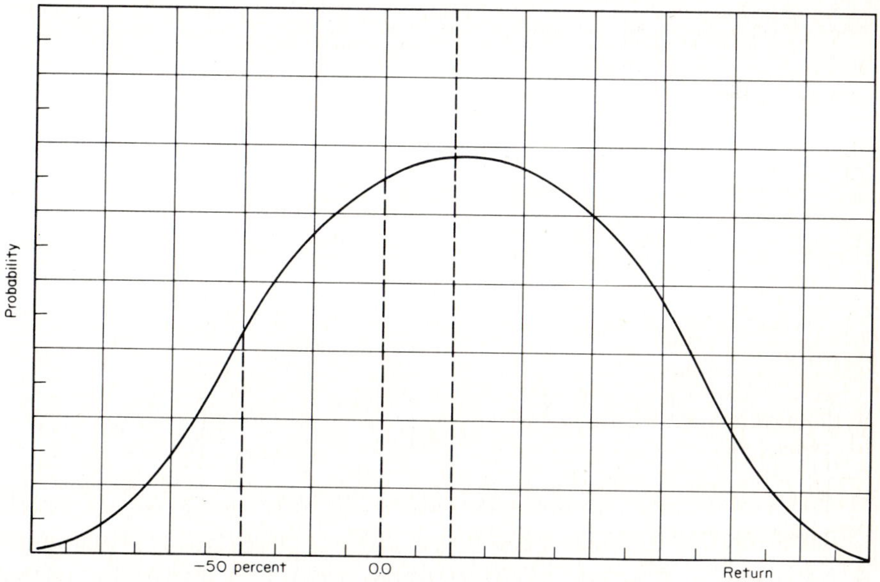

Figure 3-2 Expected return. *(ContiCommodity Research Division)*

To lesser degrees, occupation and religious and cultural factors are also determinants of an individual's risk aversion. These tie in with income and education to a great extent, and, on the bottom line, it seems that risk capital and the investor's aversion to risk are the two main factors in determining what risk-to-return ratio will be sought by the speculator in commodity futures. This relationship is illustrated in Figure 3-3.

The Risk Preference Curve

An individual with no tolerance for risk would place his or her funds at the first point in Figure 3-3, the risk-free investment, approximated in the real world by Treasury bills, which is the closest thing to a risk-free investment vehicle that is yet available. Through point *A*, a slightly less risk-averse investor could take on another unit of risk and be rewarded with another unit of return. At points *B* and *C*, investors wanting more return would have to assume an entire additional unit of risk for each one-half unit of return. An investor with very little risk aversion, that is, one with a high risk tolerance might invest at point *D* or *E*, assuming considerably more risk, three units in this example, for one additional unit of return. It is at this point that we find the commodity speculator, although this graph does not reflect the highly leveraged position that is possible due to the low margins required for such trading.

The purpose of this brief overview of risk theory is to arrive at the conclusion that the commodity speculator must realize both what is involved, in terms of

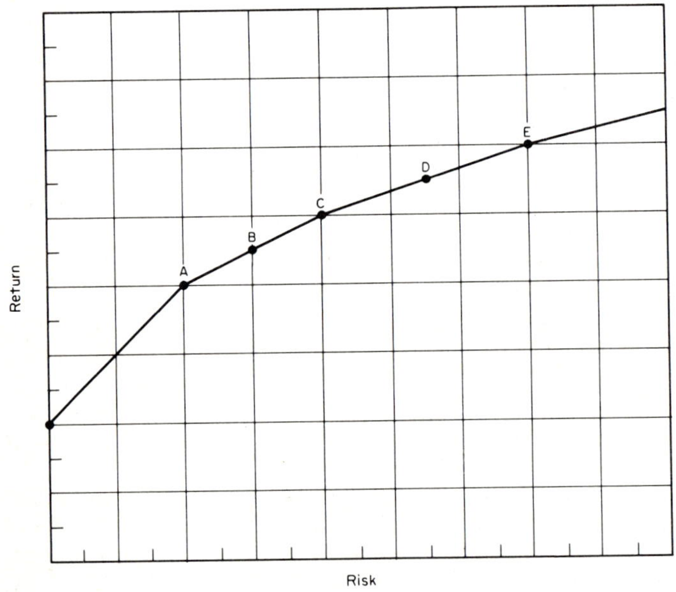

Figure 3-3 Risk preference curve. *(ContiCommodity Research Division)*

risk, and where along this risk-to-return curve he or she would like to be positioned.

In fact, somewhere well beyond point E there is presumably a point where risk and return both approach infinity; but one can see that this is a diminishing marginal relationship, where greater and greater amounts of risk must be taken on for a higher expected return. It has also been theorized that this curve flattens out somewhere well beyond point *E*, which carries with it the implication that there is a point where, despite assuming more risk, more return is not possible.

Relating Risk Aversion to Trading

Given that trading commodity futures is a risky business, there are still wide variances in the risk associated with trading different commodities, and selection of which commodities one should trade should be determined by the amount of equity in one's account and by the relative risk aversion of the trader. The two best gauges of the risk of trading a given commodity are the margins required to trade that commodity and the average daily range in dollars. The latter must be computed but may very well be a more accurate gauge. For example, the margin for a 5000-bushel contract of corn may be $500, and for oats only $400. This might lead one to believe that oats may be less risky to trade. Glancing at recent activity in these markets, one would see that 2½¢ is the approximate average range for corn, or $125, whereas the range for oats is slightly over 4¢, or $200. Since risk is considered the variability of an investment, the oats market, with its wider swings, must be considered to be the riskier of the two. The relationship between one afternoon's closing price and the next day's opening must also be considered. Any markets susceptible to political actions and rumors, such as the currencies and financials, are quite prone to wide gaps from one afternoon's closing price to the next morning's opening one. It is not unusual for the Japanese yen to open anywhere from 20 to 50 points away from the previous close, a value of $250 to $625, which could be devastating to the trader, especially if the market already closed very near to a stop, jumping it on the open. Be assured, this can and will happen.

After the relative riskiness of the various commodities has been determined to one's satisfaction, the funding and risk attitudes of the trader must then be incorporated into the selection of those commodities that the trader will then begin watching with intent to trade. A less than well-funded speculator has no business entering trades with high margins and wide daily swings, despite the fact that this trader may feel a very low aversion to risk. (In Figure 3-3, this trader would be out near point *E* or beyond.) Equity, then, could be said to override risk preferences in those instances where trading capital is limited. When equity is no problem, the risk attitudes of the trade would take precedence. A good general rule to follow is to risk no more than one-third of one's equity as margin for any one trade, and even more conservative margin-to-equity ratios are recommended. Preservation of capital is at least as important as the basic analysis, because once one's risk assets are gone, the sidelines is the only position that can be taken until new trading capital is generated. It is quite important not to divert funds from obligations in this or any other situation. In other words, never trade with what may be considered "bread money."

CAPITAL PRESERVATION STRATEGIES

In any discussion of risk and capital, certain strategies that relate to the preservation of one's trading capital should be included. The first two of these concern the number of positions taken. Doubling-up, or taking more than one position in a contract, must be governed by the rules previously discussed concerning the margin-to-equity ratio. In situations where multiple positions are taken, and the position begins to show a profit, the trader will probably consider adding more positions. Each group of positions added should definitely be smaller than the previous group, so that the net position of the trader is based on those positions with the greatest profit. This is known as pyramiding, and diagramatically appears as follows:

Proper Method of Pyramiding		*Improper Method*
X	Last positions	XXXX
XX	Next positions	XXX
XXX	First additions	XX
XXXX	Original positions	X

The inverse of this should never be done (right side of example). If a one- or two-contract position shows a profit, it is unwise to then take more positions than were previously held, as this position would not be built on a strong base. An acceptable alternative would be a one-to-one approach to adding positions.

Diversification between commodites is considered by many to be an effective means of reducing trading risk, but caution must be used in the implementation of such an approach. A common error in trading is for a speculator to try to trade in more markets than is feasible. Depending on the time available and the trader's analytical abilities, a number of markets that fit the previously developed risk criteria can be found. For most traders, anywhere from three to six markets are plenty to try to watch and trade in regularly. A corollary to this concept is the importance of not overtrading. This refers to the time between the taking of positions in any one market more than to the diversification just mentioned, but it certainly is quite possible to overdiversify and try to watch too many markets. A certain amount of time is required by most traders for analysis to be reconsidered and for the biases and emotions from the previous position to be forgotten.

There are other practices that should also be avoided if the trader is to preserve speculative capital. The first of these concerns is meeting margin calls. Any trader that meets a margin call has probably fallen in love with that position and is being blind to the fact that, if a position deteriorates that far, the analysis has broken down and the trade has gone bad and should be closed out. If one's analysis allows for such a large adverse move, then it would be wise to put up more margin in the beginning. In this situation, though, it is probable that an entry point could have been chosen that would have minimized the risk of such adversity. Another poor practice is the use of a straddle to lock in a loss. This is usually accompanied by the rationalization that the straddle may be taken off when prices return to the level where it was put on. It is unlikely that this would work because few traders are patient enough to wait for this to occur or nimble enough to take advantage when it does. Then there is the strong possibility that the price will not return to that level before contract expiration. Loss-avoidance techniques such as these rarely work and should be shunned. The speculator should face the fact that a trade is not working out as anticipated, and take the loss before it consumes valuable trading capital.

Obviously every trader is different but, to varying degrees, all have the same common tendencies. It has been found that the rules previously described will benefit all traders if strictly adhered to, because they will eliminate most of the irrational, emotionally generated decisions that undermine most speculative activities.

STOP AND STOP-LOSS ORDERS

If a trader's analysis is proven wrong, he or she would obviously wish to close out any positions taken on the merit of that analysis. The rational trader would also wish to minimize any losses taken. Through the use of stop-loss orders both of these objectives can be accomplished. The chartist knows at what point in any adverse market action that a previous analysis breaks down, either from penetration of a support or a resistance level, or from a change in trend. By entering a stop immediately after taking a position, any second-guessing or rationalization will be eliminated. With a stop order resting in the market, the speculator will not be as likely to postpone taking a loss, a situation which stems from the human tendency to avoid dealing with the negative. Using the stop-loss order upon entry into a trade, then, is an effective means of not only limiting potential losses, but also forces the trader out of any soured trades and frees capital for new ones.

After a trade is beginning to show a profit, the speculator may determine that there is a new point or area (support-resistance or trend-changing price) where the technical picture would change. By bringing the stop-loss order closer to current price action, paper profits can be protected, and a minimum profit level is more or less locked in. Of course, no technique is perfect, as in thin markets stops may be hit without really changing the picture. Care should also be taken to ensure that stop-loss orders are not brought too close to the action too quickly. Many trades that could have become highly profitable have been closed out prematurely by poor stop placement. Even though this discussion has been in technical terms, the use of stop-loss orders is recommended also for those traders oriented to fundamentals. It is realistic to consider the possibility of a situation in which a market could do serious damage to a trader before any change in fundamentals comes to light. This second use of stop orders also minimizes risk to the speculator by protecting profits, as opposed to limiting losses.

There is a third use of the stop order, and although not as obvious as the first two described, it minimizes the trader's exposure to risk as well. Using a stop to enter a position qualifies the trade, or makes the market conform to the expectation of the trader, allowing one to avoid premature entry into a position. With this technique, a speculator can buy on strength or sell on weakness, after the market shows that it is, indeed, going to move in the anticipated direction. Figure 3-4 illustrates all three of the potential ways in which stop orders can be used by the trader to limit exposure to risk.

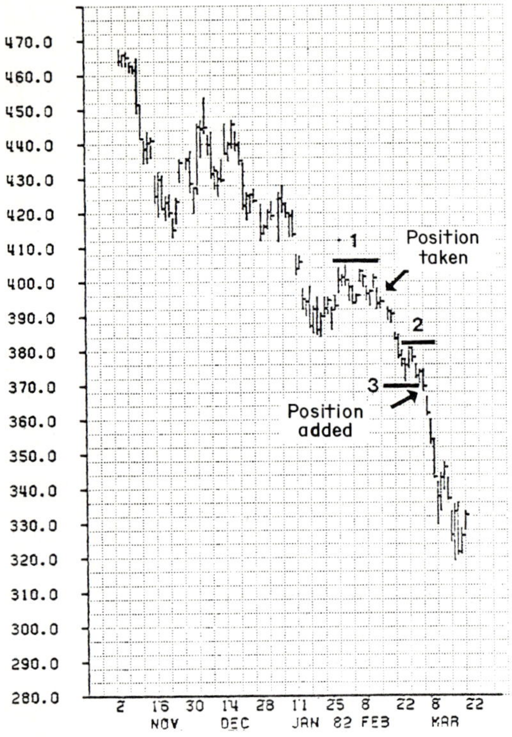

Figure 3-4 Use of stop-loss orders. (1) If a short position was taken in this congestion area, a stop-loss order could be placed just above this level, as there is heavy resistance above $400. (2) Assuming this short gold had been held from around $400 down to $375, when the market turns back down from this small congestion area, the stop-loss order is brought to just above the heaviest resistance, just over $380, to protect profits. (3) This fictional trader has now a good profit in one position and wishes to add another, but only if there is reasonable certainty that gold will sell off further. By using a sell-stop below the February 23 low, a position can be added, selling on weakness, as new contract lows are made by this penetration. *(ContiCommodity Research Division)*

MEASURING PERFORMANCE

It is important for anyone in any field to be able to judge how well they are performing. A baseball pitcher might have an earned run average, and a basketball player a field goal percentage, as qualitative, not quantitative, measures of performance. One might say that profit or loss is this measure, but that is a quantitative measure and does not adequately reflect the quality of trading decisions. The number of profitable trades versus losses, the average size of profitable trades versus that of losses, the number of losses in a row, and the average profit or loss for all trades are all factors which give a deeper insight into the trading performance of an individual than does net profit alone.

Recently in the trade magazines there has been a flood of advertisements for different trading systems that use some or all of these factors to tout their performances. Someone, then, does consider measures other than the bottom line profit or loss to be critical in gauging trading performance. It should be equally important for an individual trader to know where he or she stands, despite the fact that it is not with the intent of selling a system.

The standard measures of performance for investment vehicles do not seem especially well-suited to gauging the results of speculation in commodities. A brief look at a couple of the academic world's favorites will perhaps bring this to light. It should be noted that these measures are based on and developed for individuals with a higher aversion to risk than the typical commodity speculator, and so reflect more traditional risk concepts, making them of questionable value to the trader of commodities.

Two composite measures of investment portfolio performance are the Treynor measure and the Sharpe ratio. Both of these use the risk-free asset concept introduced previously as well as another concept, a risk index called "beta," which can be thought of as nothing more than the slope of the line in Figure 3-3. Looking back at this graph, one can see that between the first point and *A*, beta equals 1.0, which is equivalent to the market yield. Between *A* and *B*, beta equals 0.50, and between *C* and *D* it has a value of 0.33. Remember that Figure 3-3 is purely hypothetical and is in no way an attempt to reflect the real world, as a beta coefficient or slope greater than one is common as well. The higher the beta, which represents volatility of returns as a risk surrogate, the riskier the asset in terms of downside potential. A high-beta investment vehicle carries with it the potential for greater profitability also, however. This discussion of beta, while seemingly unrelated to commodities, has been undertaken so that the reader might better understand the mathematical formulation of the Treynor measure, which is as follows:

where $T = Ri\text{-}Rf/Bi$

Ri = average rate of return during any period i

Rf = rate of return, approximated by T-bills

Bi = volatility of returns, beta, representing risk

For this measure, a higher T is a superior investment performance, regardless of the investor's risk attitude. Questions as to the validity of applying this measure to commodities crop up, however. First, should rate of return be computed based on margins or on the actual value of the contract being traded? Should the beta, or volatility of returns, be computed from the returns for each trade, or for increments of time, as it would be for conventional investment vehicles, or does it have any meaning at all when applied to commodities?

Although the Sharpe ratio is quite similar to the Treynor measure, it has found somewhat wider use in the evaluation of commodity trading. It, too, may be suspect for such a purpose, however, The formula for this appears identical to the Treynor with the substitution of the standard deviation of returns for beta as a risk factor. Without going into a statistics lesson, standard deviation can be considered to be the average difference for each return from the average for the entire set of returns, or *Ri* in the formula presented earlier. Again we face the question of how to calculate these individual rates of return. Are they for units of time, or for each trade? Although the Sharpe ratio measures the relative smoothness of equity increases over time, which are those fluctuations around the straight line in Figure 3-1, it is rather unwieldy for the average investor to work with, in addition to the questionable factors given earlier. We are still, then, looking for an adequate composite test of commodity trading performance.

A composite performance measure that is very well suited to gauging the commodity trader's ability is the profit factor. Any trader has at his or her disposal all the information necessary for this computation. The only information required is the individual trading results and the number of trades taken. It can be computed for any time period, and equates short- and long-term traders through its use of a double-indexing type of formulation. From this data set one merely computes the percentages of trades that are both profitable and unprofitable, and the average sizes of both profitable and unprofitable trades. A profit factor of 1 is a break-even profit level. A value of 2 would indicate that the trader or system accumulates profits twice as fast as it incurs losses. If, for example, over a certain period of time, a trader had five profitable trades and five losing trades, but the average profitable trade was twice the size of the average loss, the profit factor would equal 2. On the other hand, if profits and

TABLE 3-1 Performance Measures

Total of losing trades	−9898.38
Number of losing trades	25
Gross profit	25711.59
Commissions ($80 per trade)	3600.00
Net profit	22111.59
Total number of trades	45
Average profitable trade	1874.21
Average losing trade	−395.94
Maximum drawdown (worst run)	−4940.22
Percentage of profitable trades	42.22
Percentage of losing trades	55.56
Profit per trade (total trades)	571.37
Profit factor*	3.60

$$\text{*Profit factor} = \frac{\text{average profitable trade}}{\text{average losing trade}} \times \frac{\text{percentage of profitable trades}}{\text{percentage of losing trades}}$$

losses were equal in size on the average, but there were eight losses and sixteen profitable trades, profit factor would again equal 2. This index could then be said to be unbiased toward the various styles of trading because of this double-indexed formulation. Table 3-1 illustrates not only this computation, but also several others that measure certain specific phases of performance worth looking at. Profit per trade for all trades, equity erosion, number of losses incurred consecutively, and extremes of both profit and loss size should all be considered in any evaluation of one's trading record.

Trading performance is perhaps the best measure of the types and amount of risk that one is exposed to in commodity speculation, because a good index of performance takes into consideration those factors that compose risk. Although the risk-reduction strategies mentioned earlier are of prime importance to each trade, without some gauge of one's performance on an after-the-fact basis, the trader cannot judge how well those strategies have been carried out.

BIBLIOGRAPHY

1. Barnes, Robert M., *Taming the Pits: A Technical Approach to Commodity Trading*, Wiley, New York, 1979.
2. Reilly, Frank K., *Investment Analysis and Portfolio Management*, Dryden Press, Hinsdale, Ill., 1979.
3. Gold, Gerald, *Modern Commodities Futures Trading*, Commodity Research Bureau Inc., New York, 1959.

CHAPTER

4

The Long-Term Trend of Commodity Prices

Martin J. Pring

While price inflation has been a persistent characteristic of the postwar period, history shows that for long periods of time prices have actually declined. The experience of anyone under 45 years of age has therefore been one of inflation. People generally have become accustomed to prices going up, whereas a wider view of history shows that falling prices are almost as normal.

THE 50- to 54-YEAR CYCLE IN COMMODITY PRICES

These long-term price trends have been analyzed by several economists, the most notable of whom were Joseph Schumpeter* and Nicolai Kondratieff. The latter has gained more prominence in recent years with the popularization of his wave theory. Kondratieff discovered his theory as part of a study authorized by the Russian government in the 1920s to prove that the capitalist system was self-destructive. After considerable research however, Kondratieff satisfied himself that the level of business activity, prices, and interest rates were subject to a 50- to 54-year cycle, and that far from exhibiting self-destructive tendencies the capitalist system, through the process of boom and bust cycles, was actually

*Joseph Schumpeter, *Business Cycles*, McGraw-Hill, New York, 1939.

self-cleansing. For this clearly astute but politically devastating discovery Kondratieff was exiled to Siberia.

He observed that since the late eighteenth century the economies of Europe and the United States have undergone three distinct waves of long-term cycles, each lasting, from trough to trough, approximately 54 years. In his analysis he noticed that a complete cycle comprised three parts—an upwave lasting for about 20 years, a downwave which covered a similar amount of time, and a third period lasting about 7 years which separated the upwave from the downwave.

The upwave consisted of four or five business cycles in which the level of economic activity, prices, interest rates, and social tensions became progressively higher. The separation, or "plateau" period as it is known, was one of relative calm in terms of price inflation and social tension. The downwave was one of actual price deflation and lower business activity in successive business cycles. The 20-year downwave was therefore the classic period of panics, crises, and depression.

The Upwave

Kondratieff noted that the U.S. economy had been subject to three long waves in its history, as shown in Figure 4-1, and that each low point of the cycle seemed to correspond with a major war. These were the War of 1812, the Mexican-American War, and World War II. The war acted as a catalyst to get economic activity on the upswing and to use up a substantial amount of economic and financial slack that had developed through the two decades of weak economic activity. Normally wars are associated with high rates of price inflation, but given the very depressed levels of business activity, these "trough" wars, as they have been called, caused hardly a ripple on the inflation front.

The war either turned the situation around or acted as a catalyst to economic activity which had already turned. Either way Kondratieff noted that the trough war set the scene for the long period of growing prosperity. The next two decades were therefore marked by higher levels of economic activity in succeeding business cycles and, unfortunately, higher levels of price inflation and interest rates. At first the higher prices were regarded as a positive factor, especially by farmers and other groups that had suffered an extreme squeeze in profit margins during the deflationary period. However, as the upwave progressed prices accelerated to an uncomfortable level as price inflation set one group against another, each demanding what they considered to be a fair share of the economic pie. Such periods were therefore characterized by increasing social and political tensions and were exacerbated by a "peak" war. Unlike the trough war, the peak war put tremendous pressure on economic and financial capacity which by this point was overextended in any case. The interaction of the peak war and the distorted business structure resulted in a huge increase in price inflation. The Civil War, which was the peak war in the nineteenth century, provides a classic example both in terms of its social and political roots and the huge inflationary bubble that accompanied it.

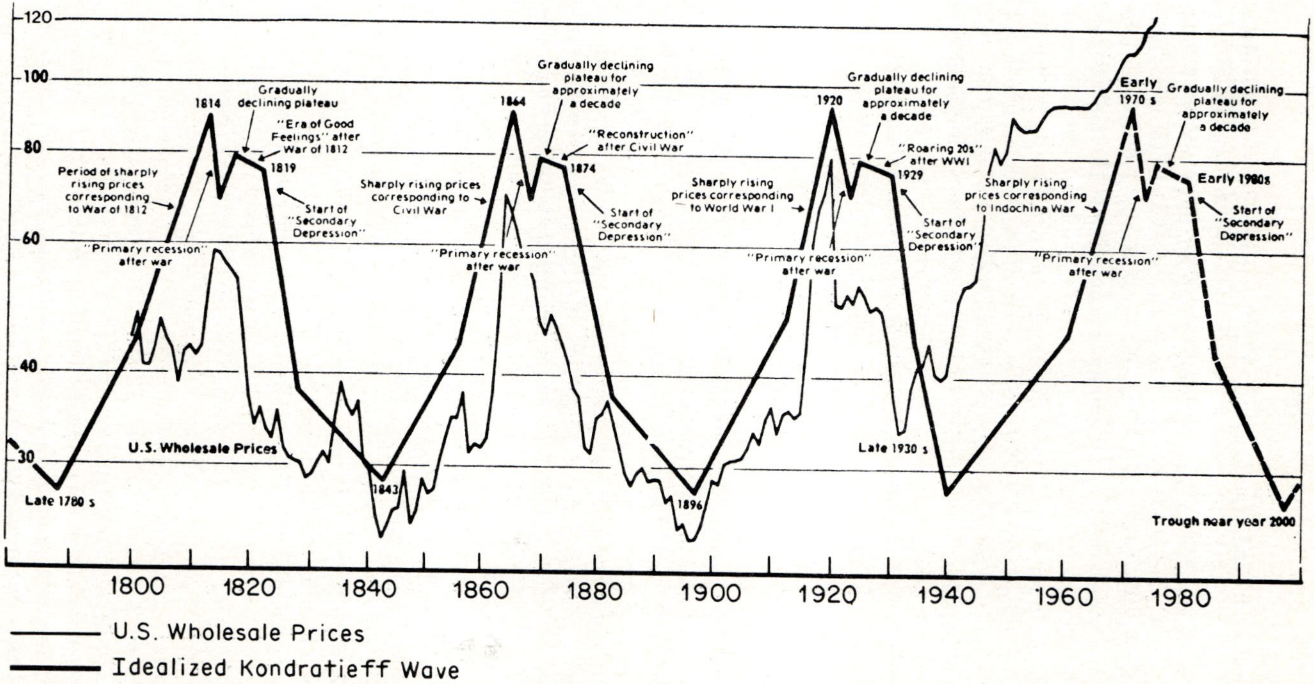

Figure 4-1 The Kondratieff wave, based on annual averages with a ratio scale of 1967 = 100. (*From* The Media General Financial Weekly, *June 3, 1974*)

The Transition or Plateau Period

After this traumatic period associated with the termination of the upwave the next phase, known as the plateau period, was relatively calm and lasted from 7 to 10 years. Price inflation was relatively subdued, interest rates fell, and people generally felt good about things. The era of good feelings in the nineteenth century or in the roaring twenties, another plateau period, gives a good indication of the economic and social climate of such times. The plateau period has also traditionally been a good time for stock market investors as some of the best equity rallies on record have developed at such times. Another contrast between the plateau period and the final years of the upwave has been the fact that the more conservative plateau period has been associated with a balancing or surplus in the federal government's budgetary position compared to an inflationary deficit which accompanied the dying throes of the upwave.

At first sight it might appear that the plateau period was able to deliver the economy from its inflationary sins in a relatively painless way, but this was not the case since the inflationary period of the upwave caused many dislocations in the economic and financial structures. Many people, for example, built their spending and investment plans around the assumption of continuing and accelerating price inflation. As a result businesses that earned considerable profits from higher prices expanded aggressively, so that when prices failed to accelerate at expected levels such businesses and individuals were caught in a profit squeeze. Similarly many businesses borrowed money for capital expansion during the peak war. However, not only did the volume of business decline for these corporations during the plateau period but also the expansion had often been financed over a long period at very high fixed levels of interest which, while appropriate for the high levels of price inflation during the upwave, were extraordinarily high for the period of relative price stability associated with the plateau phase.

At the same time others, who were not locked into an inflationary environment and who could adapt to the changing price structure, felt pretty good about the whole thing and their sectors of the economy were very prosperous. As a result the business-cycle recoveries during the plateau periods looked to be quite good on the surface. But underneath, those sectors which could not adapt to the changing economic environment were barely able to survive during the recoveries, and actually began to go bankrupt during the recessions. Just as these "inflation-hedge" businesses overexpanded during the upwave there was a tendency for other businesses to overexpand in the plateau period. For example, in the 1920s the U.S. automobile industry increased plant capacity to 8 million cars per year, but even in the best year up to that point sales had only reached 5.4 million cars per year. Clearly there were some pretty optimistic projections built into industry forecasts. Thus at the termination of the plateau period the potential for economic decline came from three fronts. First, the inflation-oriented businesses and others who had borrowed at high rates of interest were under pressure. Second, the prosperity industries that emerged or were climaxing in the plateau period overexpanded as a result of the change from a war to a peacetime economy. Third, through its new-found conservatism, the government tended to run a deflationary budget surplus rather than an inflationary deficit.

In a global context there was also a tendency toward protectionism as each country set up tariff barriers to protect its struggling industries. This decline in world trade exacerbated the problem. Thus, the economy turned into the downwave phase of the cycle as the deflationary forces picked up momentum.

The Downwave

The downwave consisted of several successive business cycles which were relatively weaker in the recovery phase and more pronounced on the downside than those business cycles experienced during the upwave. This resulted first from the fact that the excess capacity, built up during the previous two phases, had to be worked off so that supply could once again be brought back into balance with demand. Hence it was not a good period for capital investment. Second, the debt accumulated previously had to be liquidated by being paid off or forgiven or eliminated through foreclosure or other means. Gradually the excesses would be worked off and interest rates would fall to the level that attracted money out of savings into productive investment and a new cycle would begin.

The Relevance of the Cycle Today

It can be argued that the current cycle began during the 1930s with World War II being the trough war. The facts appeared to support this theory in the early 1970s, given the peak Vietnam War in the late 1960s and the substantial run up in commodity prices in the years 1972 to 1974. The persistent government deficits for much of this time and the social tensions of the late 1960s also seemed to set the scene for a plateau period in the 1980s. However, the late 1970s and the beginning of the next decade found a continuation of budget deficits and high rates of price inflation. These facts raise the question of whether Kondratieff's theory is still relevant.

The answer probably lies in a somewhat grey area, in that Kondratieff's ideas should be looked at as a framework for considering inflationary and deflationary forces rather than as an actual forecast of price trends. In this way Kondratieff's wave may still be considered to be operating since the deflationary forces sowed by the inflation of the 1970s are still at work.

The inflation of the 1970s was due to the fact that governments moved to counteract the deflationary forces through monetary and fiscal stimulus. This can be seen not only from the fact that government stabilization policies coupled with demand for more federal services have left the public sector with a much greater share of the economy than in previous cycles, but also by the fact that governments themselves have run large budget deficits and expanded the money supply to finance them. In this respect Figures 4-2 and 4-3 show global fiscal and monetary stimulus in the 1970s and early 1980s.

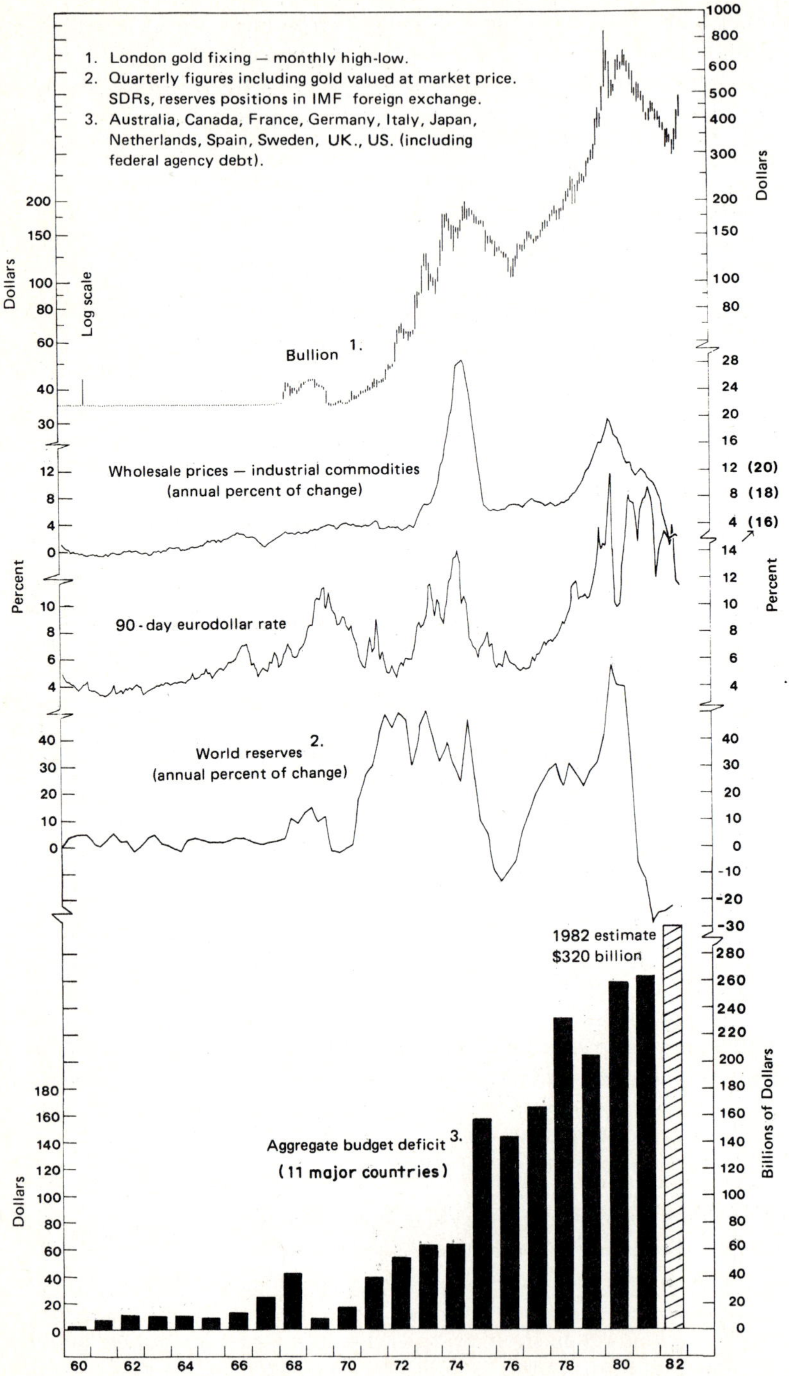

Figure 4-2 International financial barometers. *(The Financial Economist)*

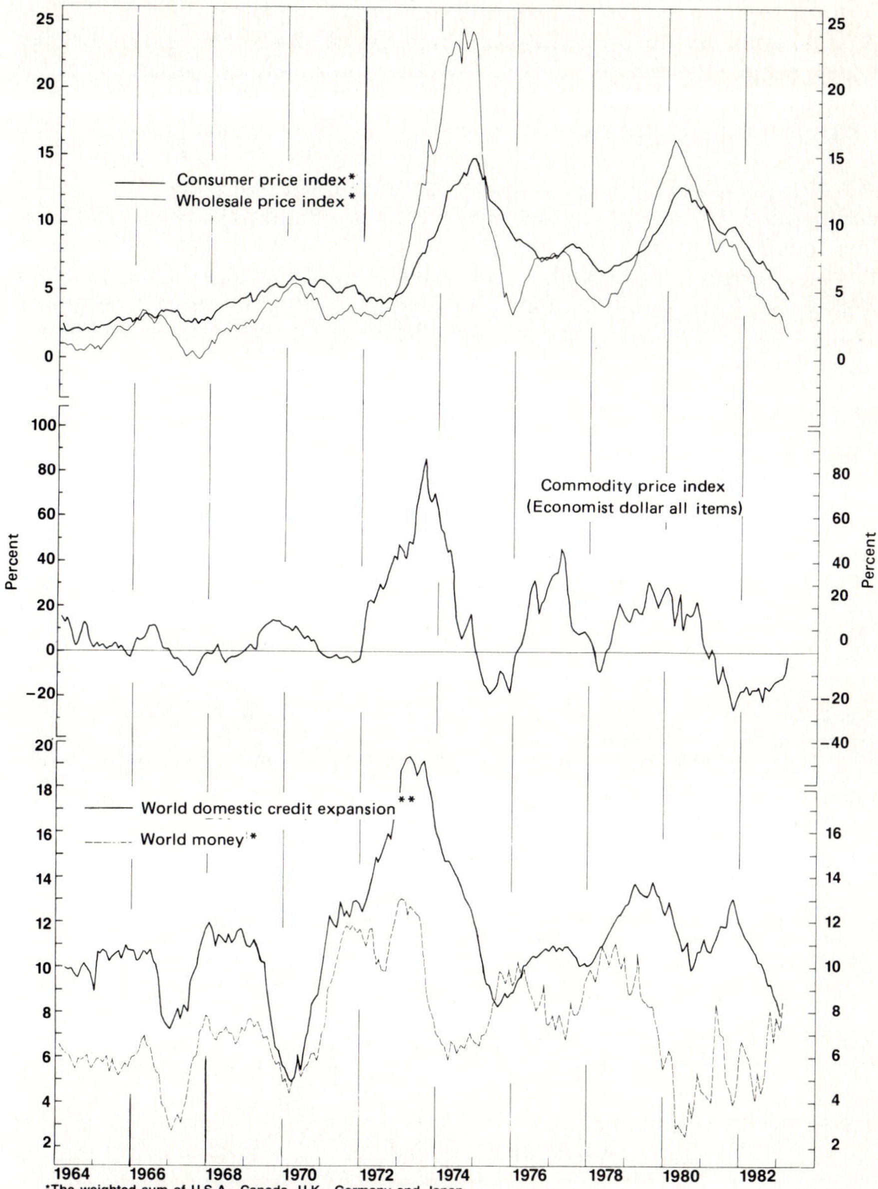

*The weighted sum of U.S.A., Canada, U.K., Germany, and Japan.
**The weighted sum of U.S.A., Canada, U.K., Germany, Japan, France, and Italy.

Figure 4-3 World inflation. *(© 1983, The Bank Credit Analyst)*

The degree to which governments have been willing to run budget deficits to offset deflationary forces can be seen from the bottom of Figure 4-2. It shows that aggregate global budget deficits have risen, in a more or less uninterrupted trend, from virtually zero in 1960 to an estimated $320 billion for 1982.

Figure 4-3 shows the degree of monetary expansion which took place on a global basis in the same period. It is worth noting that during the period from 1929 to 1932 the money supply actually contracted. However, the fact that commodity prices fell sharply in the 1980 to 1982 period despite the massive stimulus demonstrates the substantial deflationary forces which were prevalent at this time. (Figures 4-4 through 4-7 illustrate the price swings during the years 1969 to 1983.) The question might be raised as to what the result would have been for commodity prices and the global economy if such stimulation had not taken place.

Figure 4-4 Monthly CRB index (1967 = 100). *(ContiCommodity Research Division)*

Figure 4-5 Monthly CRB, index, imported. *(ContiCommodity Research Division)*

Figure 4-6 Monthly CRB index, grains. *(ContiCommodity Research Division)*

Conclusion

While a discussion of the long wave has taken us a long way from the day-to-day trading of commodities it is nevertheless important to have some basic framework from which to work. The Kondratieff cycle should not be taken too literally, but it does provide a useful model of inflationary and deflationary forces. The lesson for the 1980s is that the prevailing forces are likely to continue to be on the side of deflation, but that governments will seek to combat this trend through monetary and fiscal stimuli, especially when the readjustment process becomes excessively painful in terms of unemployment, bankruptcies, and so forth. In such an environment it is likely that, in general, commodity bull markets based on the business cycle will be more restrained than in the 1970s and early 1980s, while primary uptrends in interest-rate futures and in equities will be far more pronounced.

Figure 4-7 Monthly CRB index, industry. *(ContiCommodity Research Division)*

CHAPTER

5

Cyclical Fluctuations in General Commodity Prices

Richard T. Coghlan

This introductory chapter deals with general commodity prices as measured by a composite index of the main traded commodities. It will be left to later chapters to discuss the special factors affecting the price of each particular commodity. Naturally the construction of such a composite index requires bringing together many diverse commodities, and it might be supposed that there are sufficient "special factors" in each case to make a combined total meaningless. In fact that is not the case. There are certain powerful cyclical influences which are so strong that they tend to outweigh the effect of the weather and other individual influences.

Of particular importance are the forces causing broad, cyclical swings in prices, and it is these which are the focus in this chapter. The main emphasis here is placed on the forces creating inflation, and the best ways of identifying these at an early stage. There are long-term secular forces that affect commodity prices reflecting such things as resource limitations and the pressure of an ever-growing world population, but these generally change only gradually and are not included as part of this discussion.

The first section shows how commodity prices in general follow the basic inflation cycle. This is followed by a discussion of the underlying causes of inflation and what early danger signs to look for. At that point it is time to examine some of the more obvious indicators that might be used to detect cyclical movements in commodity prices.

COMMODITY PRICES AND INFLATION

Figure 4-3 (page 4-7) shows the rate of change of commodity prices together with two indexes of world inflation. These last two indexes have been specially constructed for use in the *Financial Economist* and employ the two most popular measures of inflation: the consumer price index (CPI) and the wholesale price index (WPI). The world indexes are based on inflation as measured in the United States, Canada, the United Kingdom, West Germany, Japan, France, and Italy and are weighted by the economic size of each country relative to the total.

It will be noticed that the relationship between world inflation as measured by world CPI or WPI is very close, but that the wholesale price index tends to be more variable, rising higher and falling lower than the CPI. Moving on to the commodity price index we can see that again the rate at which prices change follows the same broad pattern as in the other two indexes but in this case the volatility is even more pronounced. For example, when the rate of increase for all these indexes peaked in the 1973–1974 cycle, the commodity price index reached 86 percent, the WPI reached 24 percent, while the CPI managed only 15 percent. There is also a noticeable difference in timing. Commodity price inflation demonstrates a clear tendency to change direction ahead of the other two series, with the WPI second and CPI inflation bringing up the rear.

This pattern of behavior in the three series is explicable in the nature of the series themselves. The relative magnitudes and timing can be expected to continue into the future, suggesting that the movement in commodity price inflation may provide a guide to what will happen to the broader indexes, but that the behavior of these other indexes will not be any help in forecasting the rate of change of commodity prices. In general that is true, but there have been cases, and no doubt there will be again, when the WPI and CPI inflation have provided a clue to the future. For example, during 1980 the rate of commodity inflation held up at a high level while WPI and CPI inflation fell, more clearly reflecting the deflationary environment. In drawing such a conclusion it is obviously necessary to take other available information into account, and the other pieces of the jigsaw will be put together below. For the moment it is sufficient to recognize that even though WPI and CPI inflation lag behind the turning point of commmodity price inflation, there will be occasions when these series will at least provide supporting evidence in forecasting the likely rate of change of commodity prices.

But why should commodity prices be more volatile than wholesale and consumer prices, and why should the turning points come earlier? To recap, in terms of degree of movement and timing, commodity prices come first, then wholesale prices, then consumer prices. This relationship is summarized in Table 5-1.

All of the series are subjected to the same broad cyclical influence, but the speed and magnitude of the response depends critically on the extent to which prices are determined within a free market. To the extent that a market can be cornered this will prevent prices from moving to reflect the normal competitive forces of a free market. In many countries trade unions have succeeded in cor-

TABLE 5-1 Comparing the Magnitude and Timing of the Cyclical Movements of Different Measures of Inflation

	Commodity price index (%)	Wholesale price index (%)	Consumer price index (%)
1971–72 trough	−5.7 (Sept. 1971)	+3.0 (Apr. 1972)	+4.0 (June 1972)
1973–74 peak	+85.5 (Aug. 1973)	+24.4 (July 1974)	+14.8 (Oct. 1974)
1975–76 trough	−19.8 (May 1975)	+3.2 (Nov. 1975)	+7.4 (Oct. 1976)
1977 peak	+46.8 (Mar. 1977)	+8.0 (Mar. 1977)	+8.4 (June 1977)
1978 trough	−7.9 (Mar. 1978)	+3.9 (Apr. 1978)	+6.3 (Apr. 1978)
1979–80 peak	+31.3 (July 1979)	+16.3 (Feb. 1980)	+12.6 (Apr. 1980)
1981–83 trough	25.9 (Oct. 1981)		

nering large sections of the labor market, but only with government support for their jobs (at least in the short term). In other countries pressure groups have effectively cornered certain parts of the economy with the aid of dependent politicians. Through brand names and advertising many companies have carved out sections of the market, and for extended periods often act as if they did not face significant competition. This type of behavior is particularly noticeable within the government and its agencies. In many, if not most, cases full protection is granted through the conferring of absolute monopoly powers.

As a result of this institutional structure the prices of manufactured goods and services are set periodically by contract rather than flexibly through the unconstrained operation of free-market forces. The pricing structure is such that it is slow to adapt to changing circumstances, while the cost structure, particularly for labor, is extremely rigid. Workers have typically come to expect continuing increases in real wages even when economic conditions warrant a significant decline in real wages if jobs are to be preserved. Wages are often seen as the major cause of inflation. That, however, is rarely true, though it would be wrong to say never. Wages typically follow inflation, and cause inflation to become entrenched, making it difficult to bring down. This is the true significance of wages, and explains why unemployment tends to lag behind the cycle. It is at this point in the cycle that real wages rise the fastest. Prices start to come down, and final demand falls, but wages are based on expectations derived from the inflationary past, so that profits become squeezed. Commodity prices in the free market react quickly to these pressures but workers do not. And if prices won't change, then the quantity must, so layoffs increase and unemployment rises.

The net result is that price declines are slowed. This is an expected result of strongly organized trade unions and pressure groups generally. These influences are felt most strongly in the prices of the products making up the consumer price index, slightly less in the components of the wholesale price index, and least in the commodity price index. It is these structural, institutionalized forces which account for the main difference in timing and volatility between the three series.

The same forces can also be seen at work in the prices of different commodities. The overall Economist dollar index employed here excludes oil and gold, and it is instructive to compare the index against these two commodities since they represent the extremes in market structure. Since 1970 the gold price has very much been determined in a free market, between the virtually unrestricted forces of supply and demand. The main producing countries have tried to counteract the trend when the pressure has been strongly downward, and both South Africa and the Soviet Union reduced their sales significantly during 1980. These actions certainly succeeded in slowing the trend but were not able to reverse it. The market is too big with too many different buyers and sellers. Because of its size and diversity the gold market remains as close to a perfectly free market as we are likely to find. The basic underlying influence has been inflationary expectations, related to actual inflation and the growth of the world money supply; these influences are discussed in detail below. On top of this, political uncertainty has played a role, but has its main impact at times of greatest uncertainty over inflation. At such times an escalation of international tensions has been capable of accelerating the gold price increases, and accounting for sharp peaks, as in January 1980 when gold ran up in a final convulsive move to $850 an ounce. When the inflationary trend has been clearly downward, international crises have had very little, if any, real effect.

The price of gold has responded very quickly to inflationary expectations, if anything exaggerating these expectations. The gold price has moved more quickly and further than commodity prices in general, as shown in Figure 5-1. The oil price, on the other hand, has tended to move later and more abruptly. This pattern of behavior results from the fact that the price is more nearly controlled by decree (from OPEC), although even OPEC has been unable to ignore market forces, as is becoming increasingly apparent as we move into the 1980s.

A widely held view is that OPEC set alight and fueled the inflation that exploded in the 1970s. While that would be convenient for politicians to believe, enabling them to pass off the blame, it is not true. Certainly OPEC, as a large obligopoly, can influence prices to some extent, but it is limited in its actions by the laws of economics, as are all others. Under normal circumstances OPEC will act as profit maximizers do, and react to the forces of demand and other sources of supply. In the event of natural catastrophe or war or revolution, normal economic forces may be suspended for a while and a major disruption created. However, in that respect oil is no different from any other commodity which might be hit by frost, drought, storm, or political disruption. The Middle East, with its concentration of oil and its political instability, is a special cause for concern, but has so far not been a major independent inflationary force.

The oil price held remarkably steady through the 1960s into the early 1970s as did commodity prices in general; this is shown in Figure 5-1. The first major oil price increase came only in late 1973, but when it did come it was truly dramatic, an increase of 400 percent in less than 6 months. The manner and form of the increase did depend on the existence of OPEC, and the increase was all the more disruptive as a result. However, OPEC was not the cause of the troublesome inflation that became endemic during the 1970s. General commodity prices (excluding oil) had risen by more than 100 percent over 1972 and into 1973, from an index figure of 44.4 at the end of 1971 to over 100 by July 1973, and the price of gold had risen by more than 200 percent over the same period. During this period the price of gold in terms of oil, shown at the bottom of Figure 5-1, rose by nearly the same percentage, representing a major depreciation of the value of OPEC's oil reserves.

It is hard, therefore, to avoid the conclusion that the oil price was responding to the inflationary excess demand that had already been created. The combination of the OPEC cartel plus the low substitutability of other energy sources for oil did increase the rise in the price of oil when it came. However, as demand conditions stabilized over the next few years so the price of oil stabilized.

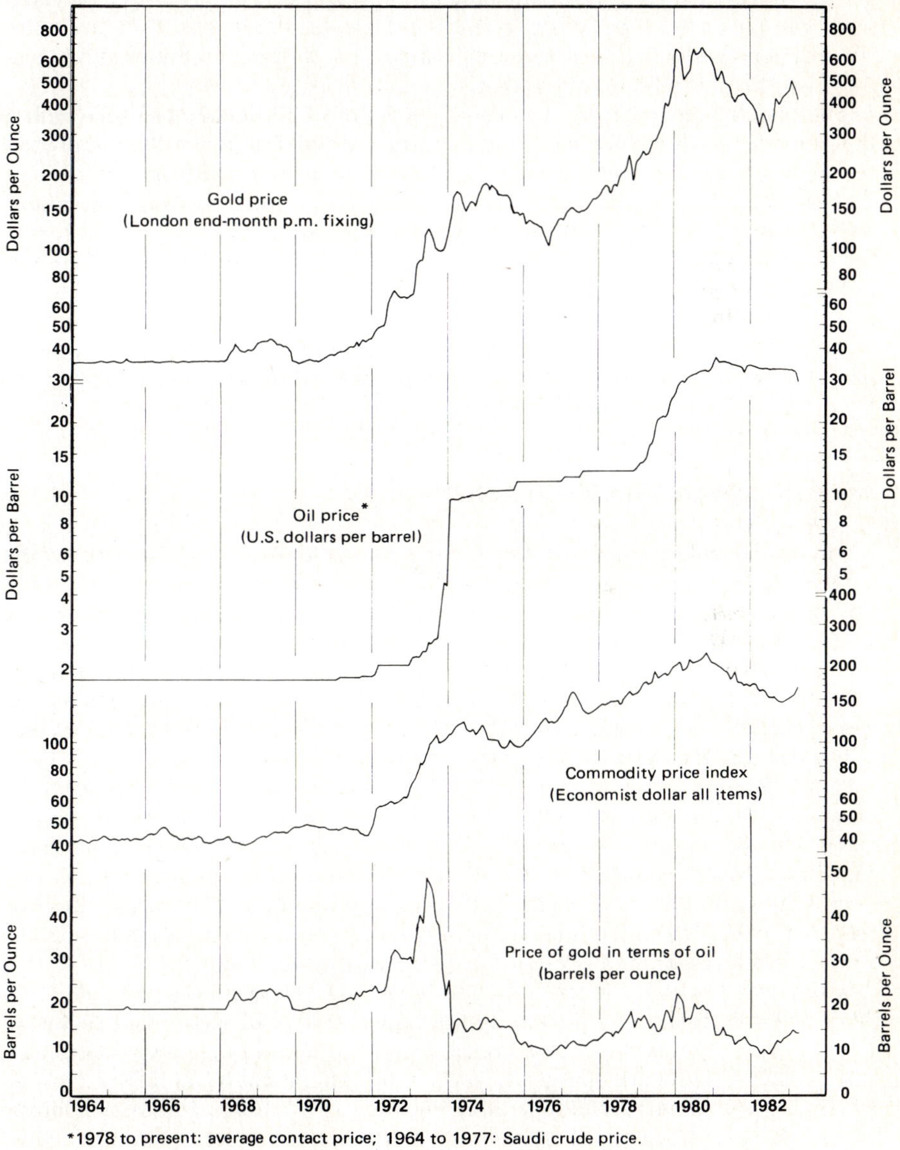

Figure 5-1 Commodity prices. *(© 1983, The Financial Economist)*

At the time of the second oil price explosion, inflationary pressure was less than during the earlier episode, and the rise in oil prices in 1979 and into 1982 was exaggerated by the political and economic chaos in Iran. However, the basic pattern was the same. The oil price increases lagged behind the general inflationary spiral, but not by nearly as much as in 1973, and the rise was not quite so sharp when it came. This time the inflationary blow-off was followed by much greater deflationary forces. These were first reflected in the prices of gold and other commodities, but a slight fall in oil prices followed in 1981 and even greater downward pressure on oil prices was evident in 1982 and 1983. The price increase this time contained more of a political premium and therefore had the potential to fall further.

The conclusion must be that oil prices follow inflationary pressure rather than lead it, but that downward momentum and the strength of the nonmarket forces has been sufficient to put a temporary floor under prices and prevent them from falling, at least as fast as they otherwise would do. The effect is similar to that created by trade unions who find it easier to justify, and achieve, real increases in wages than real cuts. So even with the need to halt inflation it becomes difficult to get real wages to increase more slowly. These forces do not necessarily cause inflation but they certainly produce substantial inertia against a decline once the process is under way. The blame for inflation is not easy to pinpoint, since the pressure can come from many directions, summarized by the catchall phrase "excess demand."

EXCESS DEMAND AND INFLATION

Inflation and balance of payments deficits on current account are both symptoms of the same problem—an excess of domestic demand above domestic supply. It is important to recognize that it is not simply increases in demand that cause inflation, but increases in demand relative to supply. Therefore, events or policies that reduce the domestic supply potential can be just as inflationary as events or policies that increase demand. Good policy will be a question of achieving an even balance. Unfortunately, there frequently is extreme uncertainty and disagreement as to how this might be achieved.

Excess demand can have many causes. All that is required is that some group in society demand more of the total economic pie without adding an equal amount to total output. In effect they are demanding a change in relative prices. The most obvious source of these additional demands is the government, but inflationary pressure can also come from groups of workers or workers in general, certain industries or the corporate sector as a whole, or from actions abroad or outside human control, for example, the weather.

When faced with an increased claim over and above productive potential, this will either result in a decline in the relative share of some other sector of society, or, if all relative shares are protected, in continuing or even accelerating inflation. How disruptive any particular claim might be, and the extent to which it is inflationary, will depend on how large the claimant group is relative to the rest of the economy. For example, an exceptionally large claim by a few highly specialized athletes or actors will have a minimal direct effect on inflation (although there may be an effect through its influence on the behavior of the majority). Alternatively, an additional small claim by any group representing 25 percent or more of the economy is likely to have a significant effect on inflation.

The initial increased claim on resources could come from the private sector, the public sector, or from abroad. It could be generated by the most noble of sentiments, for example, a desire to increase the real income of old-age pensioners, or to improve medical conditions for the poor and needy. However, if the additional claims are not accepted by the rest of society, inflation will be the result. In a static economy relative improvements in living standards for old-age pensioners would require the loss of real income for some other group. In a growing economy it means passing on some of the productive gains in one sector to another sector. Sometimes this is just as difficult to achieve as an actual reduction in income.

There are many competing demands within society—between the private sector and the public sector, profits and wages, workers and the unemployed, the young and the old, the healthy and the sick. There are no easy solutions to these conflicts. In a perfectly free market the swift will prosper and the slow will not. There will be high returns available but also high risks, which are unknown now, of real and absolute collapse on a mammoth scale. There will inevitably be a large amount of human suffering. In a democracy human suffering on a large scale is unacceptable. Government must bow to the will of the majority and the majority will not take high risks.

Governments play a major role in the inflationary process in two ways. First, they make their own demands upon resources. They run many services such as fire, police, defense, education and, often, health. In nearly every country governments directly employ a vast army of workers to staff these services and their own giant administrative bureaucracy. Second, modern governments have a major impact on inflation through their control over the disbursement of money and distribution of income. Governments (at all levels) are major puchasers of goods and services from the private sector. In addition, governments have increasingly attempted to improve health care, pensions, unemployment pay, education, and social welfare, even where the main service is not directly administered by the government. In many cases these entitlements have become index-linked to compensate for inflation. When growth is low or negative, this makes it increasingly difficult to bring inflation under control, since it means the cuts in living standards must come somewhere else, which is probably unacceptable to the other groups in society.

Wherever the initial inflationary pressure comes from, there can be no doubt that government has played a major role in sustaining it. In many cases the government has clearly been responsible for setting the fires alight in the first place, and stoking them along the way. Whatever the cause, government must take the blame for continuing inflation, since it has the responsibility for managing the economy, and persistent inflation is a ringing condemnation of the job it is doing.

The economic cycle is closely related to the creation of credit. As will be seen below, the growth of real bank credit is closely related to the performance of the economy. This in turn is significantly influenced by the monetary policy which determines the cost of credit, and fiscal policy which provides the major independent means of government control over aggregate credit demands. Government policy in the postwar period has been one of excessive budget demands and excessive monetary ease, with some constraint shown only when inflationary pressures have built up to excessive levels, and at that point creating the downturn in the cycle.

Government economic management has not succeeded in eliminating cyclicality. Over the postwar period economic fluctuations have on average been reduced from the swings experienced during the previous 100 years. However, the cyclical pressures were not eliminated, only suppressed, and more recent experience from the 1970s and early 1980s suggests that it is getting harder and harder to sustain the economy. This is because inflation has now come to be expected, and stimulatory policies have less potential for bringing about real growth and more potential for causing inflation.

MONEY, MONETARY POLICY, AND INFLATION

So far inflation has been discussed with little mention of the money supply. A popular myth has grown up that inflation is caused by the supply of money. That is not true. Inflation is caused by the forces creating excess demand as discussed above. However, these excess demands do need to be financed, and that generally will require an increase in credit. The stock of money, consisting of the main liabilities of the banking system (and often including the liabilities of related institutions), will to a large extent reflect this credit expansion.

Money, therefore, becomes a measure of potential inflation without necessarily being the direct cause of it. The one time that money can be said to directly cause inflation is under a gold standard when there is a massive new discovery of gold which adds significantly to the existing circulating currency. Under a fiat money system money comes into existence either in direct payment for government services or in exchange for other forms of debt, usually longer-term government debt. If these actions are inflationary, it is either because of excess government expenditures or because the cost of credit (the price of money) is being held too low. Those are the responsibility of the government, directly or indirectly through the monetary authorities who in a democracy must ultimately be responsible to elected representatives.

The originating pressures may, however, lie elsewhere. It may be that the government is trying to stimulate growth either through Keynesian demand-management policies, which are paradoxically often referred to now as supply-side policies, or by following an easy money policy, or both. But it may also be the case that the government is responding to excess demand pressures from the private sector. There is, in fact, a large degree of interdependence between direct government action, as the government sees it, and private sector behavior. For example, as already pointed out, a demand for a greater share of the cake (whether growing or not) by one sector can only be satisfied if some other sector gives up an equal share. The government, for one, is unlikely to give up its growth. The history of the postwar period has been one of ever-increasing real demands from the public sector, greatly increasing its relative share in the economy. Very recently there have been belated and so far unsuccessful attempts to slow down or even reverse the growth rate.

It is not necessary to debate the social, political, moral, or economic desirability of these changes in order to recognize that they are potentially extremely inflationary unless the rest of society is prepared to make the required transfer of resources. And for the purposes of the present discussion that is all that matters. The crucial point to note is that given these varied and wide-ranging objectives of government, the politicians have found themselves forced to finance the additional demands of each new group in order to prevent other groups from losing out in the struggle for shares in the national pie. To some extent additional finance can be made available without increasing the supply of money, by raising the velocity of circulation of the existing money supply, but any sustained expansion will almost certainly require an increasing supply of money.

Inflation, an increase in the general price level, as opposed to a change in relative prices, will require a broad increase in aggregate excess demand. The chief clue is some broadly defined money measure, one that picks up the increase in these overall financial demands. Picking a narrow group of bank liabilities will not necessarily be very helpful. One of the more useful and comprehensive measures is domestic credit expansion (DCE), which sounds complicated but is really quite simple. It is designed to measure the extent to which the banking system is increasing credit to all sectors of the domestic economy.* Instead of measuring total domestic bank deposits of all kinds (equal to a broad definition of money) it measures total domestic bank lending (including securities purchased). It is quite simply the other, the asset, side of the banks' balance sheet. It is, therefore, a more direct measure of the new effective demand being created.

Of course, there is still the supply side to be taken into account before arriving at "excess" demand. Obviously the greater the supply response the less any demand increase will have on excess demand. Ideally some direct measure of supply potential would be preferable, but one thing is certain, supply is unlikely to grow very much above its historical average without setting up inflationary pressures. Growth potential can be increased but it is most improbable that it can be increased very quickly. In fact, the disruptions of recent years in terms of the *relative* increase in the price of oil, and general inflation raising inflationary expectations, have had the effect of lowering the growth potential of the industrialized countries. And this has happened despite the electronic revolution that is under way, which would otherwise be raising the growth potential.

In the United States and many other countries it is common to emphasize narrow measures of money (M_1 of one form or another), give much less emphasis to broad measures of the money supply, and pay no attention at all to DCE. Narrow money is typically a good measure of the stance of monetary policy,

*This view of the world is discussed in detail in Richard Coghlan, *Money, Credit and the Economy*, Allen & Unwin, New York and London, 1981.

although that will be less true in the future given the widespread and increasing use of interest-bearing checking accounts. This development has the effect of distorting the M_1 series over the transition period, and in the longer term reduces the interest rate sensitivity of the demand for transactions balances (i.e., narrow money).

Control of M_1 is achieved by moving along a demand schedule. There is no separate, independent supply of M_1, as there is for a broad money measure. In technical terms the supply of M_1 is infinitely elastic at any given interest rate. From the demand side the short-term interest rate on alternative liquid assets provides a measure of the income foregone by holding non-interest-bearing (or low-interest-bearing) deposits for the convenience of making immediate payment; it is the price of holding transactions balances, and has a negative influence on the demand for M_1. The higher the price the less that will be demanded and vice versa.

The other important influence, in this case positive, comes from the level of income. In most studies the influence of real income is rather less than changes in the price level which are generally assumed, or estimated, to be fully compensated for by changes in the money supply, thereby keeping real money balances unchanged. Higher income will, therefore, result in higher money growth while lower income will result in a reduction in the demand for money. In addition, inflation should be expected to have a more pronounced effect on money growth than will changes in real income.

These basic relationships with income, prices, and interest rates are further complicated by the fact that the effects are not immediate, but take some time to be completed. In particular, the effect of interest-rate changes is complicated by the fact that it will also influence income and prices and thereby feed back onto the demand for money that way.

The Federal Reserve is trying to fine-tune the demand for money (on a transactions definition) by moving up and down a demand relationship which is subject to other influences and experiences long lags between cause and effect. These difficulties are compounded by less than complete understanding of the exact relationships existing between these variables, particularly when it comes to precise timing. But then no demand relationship is understood that well. When it comes to human behavior perfect knowledge is impossible.

Problems for control and interpretation are further compounded by the natural and unnatural evolution of the financial system. Natural evolution is to be expected and need not cause unnecessary difficulties. The unnatural variety is more worrisome. This results from past and present distortions, and, like the damming of a river, can result in unpredictable flows around the edges. These distortions are generally created with the best intentions, but nonetheless can be extremely disruptive.

Some economists give overwhelming emphasis to bank reserves when trying to measure monetary policy. Reserves are certainly important but not in the way normally suggested. The importance of bank reserves is not that there is a separate supply of M_1 which might somehow result in a lower growth for M_1, without the annoying inconvenience of high interest rates. There is no magic control mechanism between bank reserves and the money supply, no separate supply determined stock of M_1 which can be achieved without putting pressure on the money markets and interest rates.

It is through its control over the supply of bank reserves that the Federal Reserve can control the liquidity of the banking system and the liquidity of the financial system in general. It is this mechanism which in turn allows it to control interest rates in order to move up and down the demand schedule for M_1.

If the only effect of changing interest rates was to change the demand for money, then the task of monetary policy would be very simple and would not touch on sensitive political nerves. However, neither would it be of any use. The problem arises because interest rates that are high in real terms have an impact on the real side of the economy and create a recession. But it is no use criticizing monetary policy for creating a recession, for that is precisely how it will help to bring about a reduction in inflation and inflationary expectations.

There is, in fact, no direct causal relationship between M_1 and inflation, although some correlation should exist because of the influence of a third factor, the level of real interest rates. That is the true policy weapon. The growth of M_1 is simply a measure, a reflection, of the tightness or ease of monetary policy. This distinction is absolutely crucial to a proper understanding of monetary policy.

Monetary policy works by changing the price of money in real terms. It will limit inflation only to the extent that it limits total demand. It is not a decline in the growth of bank liabilities as measured by some arbitrary standard which will reduce excess demand and, therefore, inflation. Rather, it is the high cost of money implied by a tight money policy that will bring down inflation, but only by reducing demand in total and necessarily producing a recession. Changes in the growth of M_1 can be used to gauge the tightness or ease of policy, but do not themselves form part of the transmission mechanism through which monetary policy works.

The time has now come to fit this brief discussion of monetary policy into the broader context of overall inflationary pressure, and in the process return to the causes of inflation listed earlier. It should be clear, although it frequently is not, that monetary policy is not the sole, nor necessarily the main, influence on inflation. Inflation, as has been emphasized here, is caused by excess demand, not by monetary policy, and that is an important distinction. Monetary policy is just one potential source of inflation-y pressure. In a free-market environment this occurs when the real rate of interest is kept too low. The correct solution in such a case is a tighter monetary policy. Under other circumstances tight money will have extremely harmful effects on industry without necessarily resolving the underlying inflationary pressure.

Over the long term it is reasonable to argue that for inflation to persist monetary policy must be accommodative. It is less obvious but equally true that fiscal policy must also be accommodative.

INDICATORS OF INFLATION

This discussion of money, monetary policy, and inflation has necessarily been brief, but it does suggest a number of indicators which should provide useful information regarding prospects for future inflation. It should also be clear, however, that the process is highly complicated, and it would be naive to expect any very simple relationship. Moreover, past relationships will be changed as the expectations of inflation take a firm hold and change people's behavior, causing them to react to the indicator in an attempt to anticipate the expected inflation.

The first indicator to consider is some measure of the new short-term credit created to finance additional demand. This, it has been argued, is best represented by DCE, which captures the expansionary pressures financed through bank credit coming from all sectors of the economy and not just one particular corner. In order to measure such inflationary financing as it might influence commodity prices in general it is necessary to have an indicator which reflects excess demand on a global scale. This can be achieved through the construction of a world DCE series based on the main five countries for which data are available quickly. This is shown in Figure 4-3, page 4-7, along with three measures of inflation. Naturally, any such measure will be affected by financial innovation. Although DCE is clearly the best single indicator, it is not possible to ignore what else is going on in the world. As is the case with all of these measures, DCE is only a guide to future inflation. There is no unwritten law which dictates a certain relationship irrespective of all social, political, and economic changes.

The second indicator included here is the rate of growth of M_1, used in order to pick up the influence of monetary policy. A world index has been constructed on the same basis as world DCE and is also shown in Figure 4-3. With relatively free credit markets, and particularly with floating exchange rates, the effects of monetary policy are still wide-ranging. By keeping monetary policy is just one potential source of inflationary pressure. In a free-market environan approach can result in extreme instability. This instability has been apparent over the early 1980s, but there is nothing unexpected or unusual about it.

If excess demand is being financed through excess bank credit creation as illustrated by rapid growth of DCE, it is possible for the symptoms of high inflation to be suppressed through the maintenance of a tight money policy, resulting in a low or even negative growth of M_1. However, the process is similar to depressing a powerful spring. If the pressure is taken off, inflation will accelerate sharply. Therefore, monetary policy cannot be relaxed until the excess demand has been eliminated—and that could take a long time. There is, therefore, always the risk that the monetary authorities will ease up too soon and unleash the pent-up inflation on an unsuspecting world.

If we deduct the rate of inflation from the nominal growth of DCE and money it is possible to get some idea of the potential for real growth in the economy. These "real" measures of DCE and money for the world are shown in Figure 5-2. It will be seen that the historical relationship between these real-world financial series and world industrial production has been very close. Once an inflationary momentum has been built up, as in the early and late 1970s, this will usually be capable of carrying inflation to new highs even as the economy turns down. This is the final spurt before the peak and gradual easing of inflation. However, it is hard to get a sustained acceleration in inflation when the world economy is depressed. In fact, it is reasonable to assume that an economic recovery will be a precondition to getting into a situation of accelerating inflation, in which commodity prices in general increase in a regular and sustainable fashion.

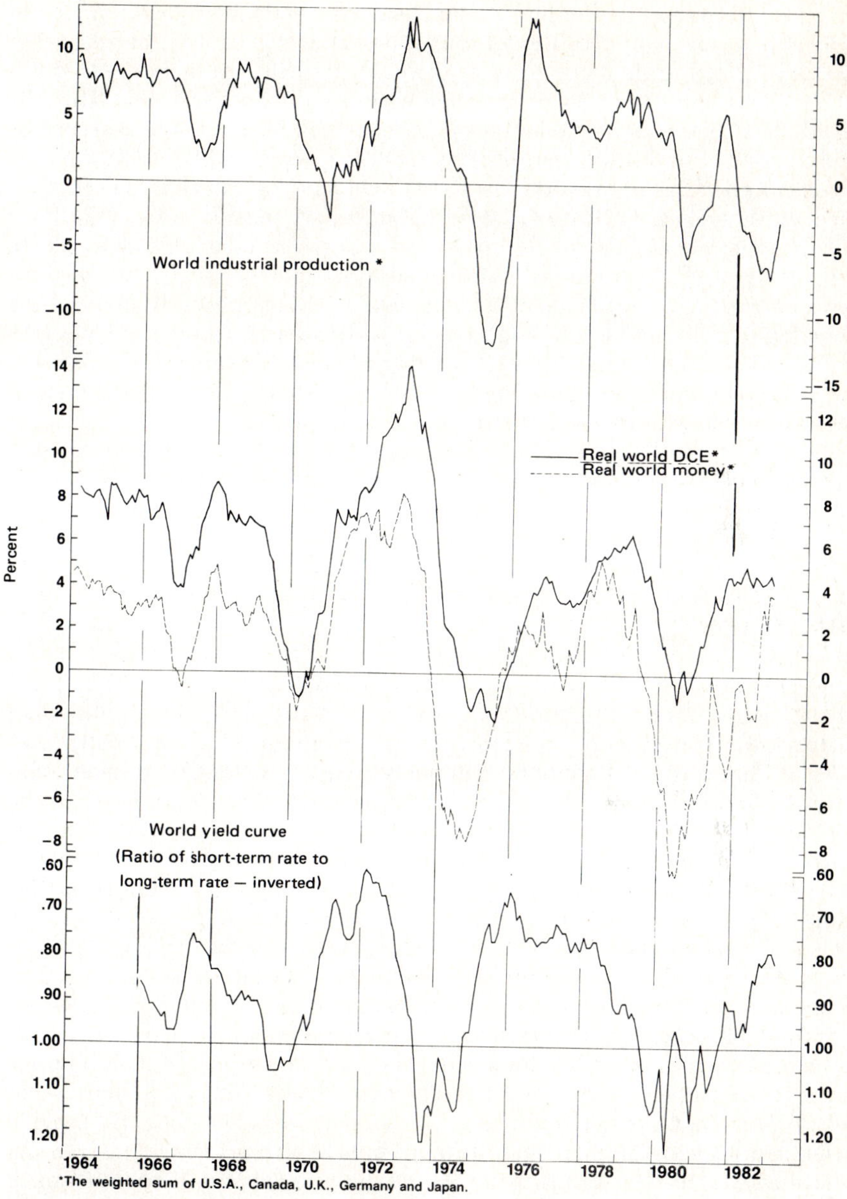

Figure 5-2 World production, real money, and the yield curve. *(© 1983, The Financial Economist)*

It is also necessary to monitor in other ways the actions of government and the central bank, as opposed to what they *say* they are or are not doing. For monetary policy the yield curve, as measured by the differential between short- and long-term interest rates, provides an extremely useful indicator. This historically has been well correlated with the growth of M_1 as can be seen in Figure 5-2. And as more and more of M_1 comes to consist of interest-bearing deposits of one kind or another, the yield curve may well have to be relied on almost exclusively to indicate the stance of monetary policy.

Fiscal policy should also be watched closely to see whether real attempts are being made to reduce the growth of expenditures and the level of the government's borrowing requirement. This does not mean that expenditures and the borrowing requirement are falling each and every year. However, if it appears that the government is persistently claiming increasing shares of the national cake, it is clear that it will soon run up against resistance from some groups in society, and this will almost certainly prove inflationary.

Look also at the strength of the dollar, for this is often an indicator of inflationary pressure—actual or impending. And related to that is the price of gold. Gold is traded in what closely approximates a free market, and the price of gold quickly comes to reflect inflationary expectations.

CONCLUSION

There have been clear cyclical patterns over the postwar period with inflation lagging behind the behavior of the economy. More recently the amplitude of the fluctuations in inflation has grown considerably and become easily forecastable. That could not continue without leading very quickly to hyperinflation. It cannot be assumed that the inflationary cycle will continue as in the past; that would be too easy. Cycles will not disappear, that is clear, but a very determined attempt will be made during the 1980s to bring down the long-run trend. It will take real political and economic skill to do that without turning recession into depression, and a strong nerve to see it through. At present the jury is still out, and only time will tell which way the verdict will go.

In trying to explain changes in general commodity prices we are in effect discussing the worldwide forces determining inflation. Although it is misleading to think of the supply of money as the cause of inflation, money in one form or another will be required to finance the excess demands that lie behind price increases and current account deficits. The broad money supply, or more accurately, DCE, in conjunction with the growth of narrow money, M_1, will provide the single most valuable indicator of future inflationary pressure. However, in a complicated and ever-changing world it would be naive to expect too much from any one indicator, and it is necessary to look elsewhere for confirmatory evidence of actual and potential inflationary pressure. The state of the real economy will be important, and real DCE and money will provide valuable indicators. Monetary policy will also be reflected by the behavior of the yield curve. In addition public sector policy, in the form of total expenditure and the borrowing requirement, should be monitored closely in order to determine the extent of the government's contribution to excess demand. Finally, the strength of the U.S. dollar should provide some confirmatory evidence of any build-up in inflationary pressures.

The investment outlook in the 1980s is far more uncertain than it has been for a long time. The old cyclical pattern, with a strong government bias toward inflationary policies, has become too predictable and can no longer be relied upon to continue into the future. The attempt to turn around the old, ingrained policies and end the deteriorating trend is bound to create great instability and large risks. There can be no guarantee that such policies will persevere, thereby adding to present uncertainty. However, it is reasonable to expect the longer-term trend of inflation to move irregularly down. The volatility will make the outcome uncertain and will make it difficult for investors to anticipate the benefits of lower inflation. It will take some time before the smoke finally clears, and the discovery is made that inflation did after all come down.

PART

2

Agricultural Commodities— Grains and Meats

CHAPTER

6

Wheat

Michael Hinebaugh

INTRODUCTION

Wheat has been grown for thousands of years and can be produced amost anywhere, unlike many other grains, which are geographically limited by climate constraints.

Wheat and rice are the major world-food grains. While rice is consumed primarily in the area where it is grown, wheat accounts for the vast bulk of total world-food-grain trade. Wheat also contains more calories and protein per pound than rice does.

The world price for rice usually commands a premium over wheat; thus there is little incentive to plant wheat in areas where rice and wheat compete for acreage. Also, rice is preferred over wheat in Asian diets. Most developing countries grow wheat in regions of drier climates and during their dry season (for example, during the winter as opposed to summer); rice is grown under paddy conditions, which require much more water and adequate monsoon conditions for maximum production.

The higher world price for rice means that wheat is the preferred substitute in Asia when imports of food grains are necessary or must be increased because of crop failures. Very little of the world's rice production enters into foreign trade channels; the United States, for example, presently is the second largest world exporter of rice (and soon may become the leading world exporter) despite having only 1 to 2 percent of total world production. The rice crop failures in Asia in the 1973 to 1974 crop year preceded the surge in world wheat demand and the escalation of wheat prices to a record high. World rice production, particularly in Asia, must be watched closely in order to assess prospective wheat demand (and therefore prices) more accurately.

TYPES OF WHEAT

Hard Winter Wheat

Hard winter wheat is by far the most important class of wheat grown in the United States; it approximates 50 percent of total U.S. wheat production on average. Production, as noted in Table 6-1, is centered in the central and southern plains states; Kansas alone normally accounts for around 40 percent of U.S. hard winter wheat production.

Hard winter wheat is used primarily for bread, rolls, and sweet goods because its protein content ranges from 10 to 15 percent. (Protein content in wheat is a measure of its gluten content, which in turn measures its baking quality.) Exports are a key factor in prices for hard red winter wheat because domestic milling demand is relatively stable. More hard red winter wheat is exported on average than all other classes combined (in recent years, however, the sharp surge in exports of soft red and soft white wheats pushed total exports of other classes above those of hard winter for the first time—and combined exports of the soft wheats almost reached those of hard red winter wheat).

The level of hard winter exports, especially as related to ending carry-over supplies of this class, is very important to Kansas City futures prices. Kansas City prices are very sensitive to cash basis fluctuations in the export market. The existence of a strong Gulf "basis," or cash premium, to move wheat into export channels exerts strong influence on Kansas City futures. (It also tends to reflect in a stronger premium for cash wheat over the nearby, or maturing, futures contract and thereby lessens the likelihood of deliveries of cash wheat against futures because of the strength in commercial values. This in turn tends to cause more relative firmness in the nearby futures contract with a resultant narrowing of spread—i.e., the price relationship between various contract months.

The Kansas City futures market has been long identified closely with the basic fundamentals in wheat because of its close association with export demand and its relatively high percentage share of total U.S. wheat exports, plus the much smaller share of speculative participation in Kansas City futures. Commitment of Traders reports over the years have shown small trader long positions in Kansas City futures to make up little more than 30 percent of the total open interest and small trader short positions to account for less than 10 percent of the total (both figures are on an average annual basis). These reports are compiled monthly.

Soft Red Winter Wheat

Soft red winter wheat has increased its proportionate share of total U.S. winter wheat production in recent years, primarily because the wheat acreage can be double-cropped with soybeans in the south and some midwestern areas. (Double-cropping is the practice of planting another crop on the same land imme-

TABLE 6-1 Major U.S. Wheat-Producing States
(State rankings by class of wheat; 1980 production listed in million bushels)

	1978	1979	1980	1981	1982	1982 production
			Winter wheat*			
Kansas (HRW)	1	1	1	1	1	462
Oklahoma (HRW)	2	2	2	3	2	227
Washington (SW)	3	4	3	4	4	125
Texas (HRW)	7	3	4	2	3	144
Nebraska (HRW)	5	5	5	6	5	101
Colorado (HRW)	6	7	6	10	6	84
Missouri (SRW)	14	6	7	5	8	76
California (HRW)	11	11	8	8	9	70
Illinois (SRW)	12	10	9	7	11	67
Oregon (SW)	8	12	10	11	12	60
Ohio (SRW)	9	8	11	12	13	55
Montana (HRW)	4	9	12	9	7	80
Indiana (SRW)	13	13	13	14	16	46
Idaho (HRW & SW)	10	14	14	15	14	52
Michigan (SRW)	16	15	15	17	21	25
			Spring wheat†			
North Dakota	1	1	1	1	1	214
Minnesota	2	2	2	2	2	121
Montana	3	3	3	3	3	93
Idaho	5	5	4	5	5	58
South Dakota	4	4	5	4	4	42
			Durum‡			
North Dakota	1	1	1	1	1	112
Arizona	4	3	2	2	4	7
California	3	5	3	3	2	12
Montana	2	2	4	4	3	10
South Dakota	5	4	5	5	5	3
Minnesota	6	6	6	6	5	3

*These states produce around 90 percent of total U.S. winter wheat production. The letters in parentheses next to the states identify the type of wheat grown: HRW = hard red winter, SRW = soft red winter, SW = soft white.

†These five states account for over 90 percent of the total U.S. spring wheat production.

‡These six states account for all of U.S. durum wheat production.

diately following the harvest of the first crop.) Wheat is also more of a "cash crop" in those areas, that is, it is sold to meet cash flow needs rather than stored, as corn, soybeans, or cotton often are, or as hard winter wheat must be in the southern plains areas because there it may be a farmer's basic crop.

Soft red wheat ranges in protein value from 8 to 11 percent; its primary use in the United States is for milled flour for chemically leavened products such as cookies, crackers, cakes, doughnuts, and pies. Exports of soft red wheat formerly had been relatively small, as production ranged from 50 to 100 million bushels annually. But soft red winter exports escalated sharply when production did; soft red winter exports approximated 90, 150, and 300 million bushels, respectively, for the 1978, 1979, 1980 crop years—recent U.S. Department of Agriculture (USDA) projections estimated soft red winter exports during the 1981 to 1982 crop year at an astounding level of close to 500 million bushels. The price of soft red winter wheat relative to hard red winter wheat is a very important market consideration. Soft red winter prices should provide a sufficient discount to stimulate purchases by those countries to whom price is more important than protein (e.g., China). Export prices in years of large soft red winter production and total U.S. wheat production must be "cheap" relative to other classes in order to stimulate increased exports. This is due primarily to the fact that government price-support programs are that much less important to soft red winter producers; they make less use of support programs because these farmers usually produce soft red winter as a cash crop, and because less of the crop is eligible for government programs, with which soft red winter producers generally do not comply. In fact, soft red winter production increased sharply in the years following acreage decontrols.

Soft red winter exports often run into competition from the European Economic Community (EEC). High EEC domestic subsidies almost always produce annual surpluses, particularly in France. These surpluses comprise inferior qualities of wheat and, in turn, require heavy subsidies to dispose of them. Imports of higher-quality (higher-protein) wheats for baking needs continue to be required. Australia also is a major competitor, especially in good production years; soft white wheat composes most of Australia's wheat exports although that country does grow hard spring varieties (most of which are retained at home for domestic needs).

The existence of large stocks in terminals that are in a better export position than Chicago can have a bearing upon Chicago futures prices—especially if Chicago-Toledo deliverable stocks are large also. At such times, the composition of open interest in the Chicago futures market also becomes increasingly significant. (Generally, if speculative long open interest—identified in Commitment of Traders reports—is higher than usual and soft red wheat demand is satisfied without recourse to tapping Chicago stocks, then liquidation in speculative long positions can result. A long-term annual average for the small trader long position has been around 45 percent of the total; short small trader positions average around 35 percent of total commitments.)

Spring Wheat

Spring wheat is a high-protein wheat, generally ranging from 12 to 18 percent in protein content. It produces a superior bread flour. Countries which grow low-protein soft wheat often import high-protein spring wheat to blend with domestic wheat to produce better flour.

The Minneapolis futures market is a relatively small, highly professional market. Small traders (who usually are identified with the "speculative" element in markets) generally have accounted for 25 percent of the total open interest in Minneapolis wheat futures. Minneapolis-Kansas City and Minneapolis-Chicago wheat spreads sometimes have shown the general trend of overall wheat prices; more often than not, however, they have followed overall developments among specific classes and have reflected basic spring wheat fundamentals rather than other wheats.

Soft White Wheat

Soft white wheat is the most important subclass of white wheats. Its percentage of the total U.S. wheat production also has been increasing. Protein content in soft white wheats averages the same as in soft red wheats, roughly 8 to 11 percent. Soft whites compete domestically with soft reds, primarily in the northwest. Exports are a major consideration for this class of wheat because prohibitive rail rate structures inhibit an eastern flow. Far East destinations are the primary export customers.

Durum Wheat

Durum wheat accounts for a very small percentage of total U.S. wheat production and no more than 10 percent of total domestic use of wheat for food; the primary use is for macaroni and spaghetti. The small production, rapid disappearance, and lack of a futures market results in little interest in durum on the part of wheat traders, other than those associated with commercial interests.

GROWING CONDITIONS

Wheat often is referred to as a "weed" because it is harder to kill than most other grains. Similar to a weed, the wheat plant can snap back and recover from a period of adverse conditions. However, this obscures the fact that wheat actually is highly sensitive to variability in weather factors—perhaps even more so than corn or soybeans. Winter wheat production is particularly affected by the variable factors in spring and early summer weather. Year-to-year variations in wheat yields in individual states can be tremendous; these sharp swings are attributed to weather. (In fact, some weather factors which promote excellent wheat yields in one area may not be favorable in another area.)

In general, relatively cool temperatures are desirable during the main growing period following wheat's emergence from winter dormancy. This is particularly true during the heading stage of development; cool temperatures at that time permit heads to develop more slowly, which benefits the filling process and therefore maximizes yields. In the United States, above-normal moisture during the fall and winter in the western wheat belt is favorable, but below-normal precipitation is preferable in eastern areas, such as Illinois and Indiana. Normal rainfall in those areas appears to be excessive for optimum wheat yields. Wheat in Illinois gets a boost from good rainfall in April, at the start of the main growing season, but below-normal rainfall in May and June is desired. Above-normal rainfall in both April and May is beneficial in western areas. These are broad generalizations, though; the potential yields from various combinations of variable weather actually fall all over the map, a fact which again stresses how sensitive wheat yields are to variability in weather.

Acreage Planted

The amount of acreage planted to wheat in the United States has varied considerably over the years; this can be attributed mostly to the impact of government programs, particularly acreage diversion programs and loan-target price-support programs. These land-retirement programs were initiated during the 1950s and 1960s in an attempt to manage supply. They were unsuccessful because farmers generally idled marginally productive land and increased the application of technology on the remaining land to maximize production. The high prices during most of the 1970s brought an end to permanent acreage retirement programs and a temporary end to annual diversion programs. Loan rates and target prices also rose sharply during the late 1970s (government programs are outlined fully in Chapter 14). Planted acreage increased steadily during the 1970s. The successful implementation of double-cropping has encouraged an expansion of wheat acreage in southeastern and midwestern areas in recent years. The most usual practice in these areas is to follow wheat with soybeans. (As a result, double-cropped soybeans have sharply increased their proportionate share of total soybean acreage planted.)

WHEAT DISAPPEARANCE

Domestic Usage

Exports account for the largest portion of total disappearance of wheat in the United States. Domestic utilization mostly involves food, primarily bread, cereals, cookies, and the like. Fairly large amounts of wheat sometimes have been used for feeding purposes. However, this practice has been limited in recent years because of the sharp increase in wheat loan rates compared to those of feed grains; this tends to support wheat prices at higher relative prices. (The existence of the grain reserve and the much higher release prices for wheat also tend to support much higher price relationships than formerly existed; for a description on how the grain reserve affects prices, refer to Chapter 14.) For example, wheat loan rates from 1965 until the mid-1970s had been fixed at $1.25 per bushel, which was not much higher than the loan rate for corn; this often allowed wheat and corn prices to trade close to each other for extended periods of time, particularly during the summer when wheat harvest pressure is heaviest but corn prices often are at their highest level. Wheat is favored over corn when price differentials are narrow because wheat has a higher protein level. Table 6-2 shows some of the important variables in the amount of wheat fed and annual statistics from 1960 to 1978. However, wheat loan rates escalated sharply relative to corn during the late 1970s; for the 1982–83 season, the national average loan rate for wheat was $3.65 per bushel and the corresponding loan rate for corn was $2.65.

Exports

U.S. wheat exports usually exceed total domestic consumption by a wide margin and approximate 65 to 68 percent of total U.S. wheat disappearance. The

TABLE 6-2 Wheat: Quantity Used for Livestock Feed in June-May Year and Related Variables, United States, 1960-1961 to 1979-1980

Year beginning June 1	Quantity of wheat fed June–May, million bushels	Cattle on feed July 1 in 7 western states, thousand head	Price ratio* of fed cattle (annual) to wheat (May–September)	Price ratio* of fed cattle to wheat (May–September)	Price ratio* of sorghum to wheat (May–September)
1960–61	30.3	2,165	8.73	8.79	.53
1961–62	43.9	2,158	8.33	7.78	.56
1962–63	34.6	2,472	7.83	7.98	.52
1963–64	28.5	2,807	7.30	7.65	.57
1964–65	54.8	2.959	9.67	9.32	.74
1965–66	145.9	3,377	11.93	11.93	.86
1966–67	100.5	4,014	0.94	9.36	.67
1967–68	36.5	4,210	10.78	10.71	.81
1968–69	156.3	4,208	13.60	13.03	.84
1969–70	187.7	5,390	14.59	15.41	.92
1970–71	192.6	5,648	13.89	13.86	.88
1971–72	262.3	6,392	15.10	14.52	1.01
1972–73	199.5	7,716	16.28	15.07	.82
1973–74	125.1	8,030	8.26	8.87	.62
1974–75	34.9	6,057	6.14	6.40	.66
1975–76	34.0	5,173	7.57	8.38	.74
1976–77	68.4	6.146	7.24	7.22	.79
1977–78	183.3	6,024	12.69	11.57	.81
1978–79	183.0	7.019	12.74	11.53	.74

*Pound for pound.

SOURCE: United States Department of Agriculture.

relative share of total wheat disappearance accounted for by exports has been increasing over time; during the 1960s, for example, wheat exports accounted for roughly 54 to 59 percent of total U.S. wheat disappearance. This underscores the increasing importance of food in world trade channels and the impact of the burgeoning world population.

Table 6-3 shows the main U.S. export destinations. The United States is by far the largest world exporter of wheat despite the fact that it is not the largest world wheat producer. Figure 6-1 shows the proportionate share of total world wheat exports accounted for by major exporting countries for selected years. The U.S. share has tended to slacken recently as export competitors have become more aggressive, especially given the substantial export subsidies provided by the EEC.

The leading world wheat producers are listed in Table 6-4 for specific years; the growth in total world wheat production and the developments in main producing countries can be seen easily through the data (the numbers in the parentheses identify the ranking of each producing country for that particular year). It also shows the increasing trend of world production among major world importers of wheat (e.g., Soviet Union, People's Republic of China, India) and the decreasing proportionate share of total world wheat production accounted for by some major exporters (e.g., Canada, Australia, and Argentina). Most world producers do not export wheat or, at best, export relatively insignificant

TABLE 6-3 Major U.S. Export Destinations by Class* ***(Whole grain, million bushels)***

	Hard winter			Spring			Soft red			Soft white			Durum			Total wheat		
	1978	1979	1980	1978	1979	1980	1978	1979	1980	1978	1979	1980	1978	1979	1980	1978	1979	1980
Brazil	63	78	80	—	—	—	—	—	—	—	—	—	—	—	—	63	78	80
Other—North and South America†	98	129	137	34	49	42	6	8	9	—	4	7	3	3	3	147	192	203
EEC	10	10	17	58	53	50	2	2	5	—	—	—	22	23	25	92	88	97
Other—Western Europe	15	22	19	4	5	3	9	11	13	—	—	—	7	9	5	35	47	40
Eastern Europe	12	58	10	—	—	—	9	44	27	—	—	6	2	2	2	23	104	44
Soviet Union	94	163	110	—	—	—	—	—	—	—	—	—	—	—	—	94	163	110
Japan	53	44	50	28	31	33	—	1	2	40	40	45	2	2	1	123	118	131
People's Republic of China	57	15	53	15	2	5	23	29	212	—	14	29	—	—	—	95	60	309
Other—Asia and Mideast‡	90	90	102	69	65	39	13	8	5	135	114	110	—	—	—	307	276	251
Egypt	31	14	1	4	—	—	20	26	12	—	7	46	—	—	—	55	47	60
Other—North Africa	50	60	58	8	9	7	7	21	13	—	4	11	25	33	12	90	127	101
Total U.S. wheat exports	573	683	647	220	204	179	89	149	296	175	183	258	67	81	54	1124	1300	1437

*June–May crop years.

†Scattered various countries including Chile, Peru, and Venezuela.

‡Scattered various countries, predominantly Korea.

SOURCE: ContiCommodity Research Division

amounts. Table 6-5 shows the world wheat and flour trade for recent years. One interesting trend is the increase in imports by major world producers such as China and the Soviet Union. Developing countries in many other areas also have been increasing wheat imports.

FOREIGN PRODUCERS

The Soviet Union

The Soviet Union is the world's largest wheat producer. Soviet wheat production in normal years usually has approximated 25 percent of total world wheat production. The long-term trend of Soviet wheat production is an upward one. It received a large boost from the New Lands development program during the 1950s in Kazakhstan and parts of Western Siberia, which sharply increased spring wheat acreage; increasing yields have maintained the upward trend in wheat production since that time. Figure 6-2 shows the major wheat-producing areas in the Soviet Union.

Increased fertilizer applications primarily are responsible for the growth trend in yields. The influence of fertilizing on Soviet wheat yields is witnessed by three important changes: average winter wheat yields in the Soviet Union

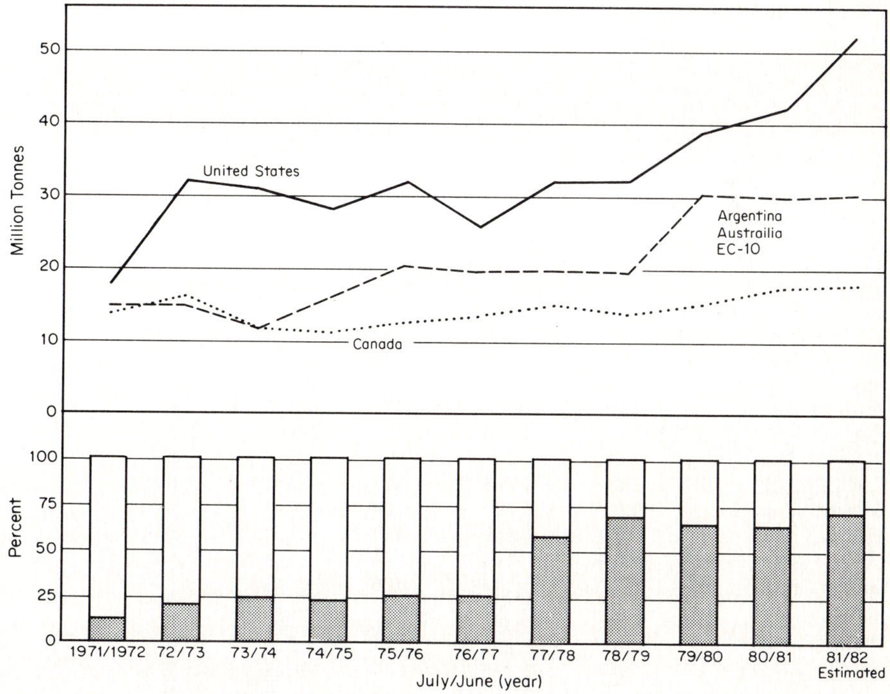

Figure 6-1 (*a*) United States and competitor wheat exports. (*b*) Percent of U.S. production exported.

TABLE 6-4 Leading World Wheat Producers*
(Million bushels, selected years)

Country	1960-61†	1966-67	1971-72	1978-79	1979-80	1981-82
Soviet Union	1700 (1)	2939 (1)	3628 (1)	4438 (1)	3314 (1)	2939 (1)
United States	1355 (2)	1312 (2)	1616 (2)	1774 (3)	2135 (3)	2799 (2)
People's Republic of China	NA (4)	764 (4)	882 (3)	1984 (2)	2296 (2)	2189 (3)
Canada	518 (3)	827 (3)	529 (6)	775 (5)	632 (6)	911 (5)
France	405 (5)	415 (6)	564 (5)	772 (6)	687 (5)	841 (6)
India	377 (6)	394 (7)	874 (4)	1165 (4)	1304 (4)	1333 (4)
Australia	274 (7)	462 (5)	316 (9)	665 (7)	592 (7)	599 (7)
Turkey	260 (8)	301 (9)	393 (7)	489 (8)	478 (8)	485 (8)
Italy	240 (9)	346 (8)	367 (8)	338 (9)	323 (9)	327 (9)
Argentina	150 (10)	234 (10)	209 (10)	298 (10)	298 (10)	297 (10)
World total	8185	10276	11850	16408	15504	16481
Percent of world total produced by above countries	64.6%†	77.7	79.1	77.4	77.8	77.2

*Individual rankings for specific years in parentheses.

†People's Republic of China not included in 1960.

SOURCE: U.S. Department of Agriculture and ContiCommodity Research Division.

TABLE 6-5 World Wheat and Flour Exports
(One thousand metric tons; July–June years)

	1977-78	1978-79	1979-80	1980-81	1981-82
United States	31,538	32,311	37,298	41,936	49,100
Canada	15,860	13,459	15,000	17,000	17,820
Argentina	2,600	3,300	4,750	3,900	4,300
Australia	11,081	6,700	14,950	10,620	11,040
EEC	5,243	8,765	10,433	14,000	15,500
Western Europe	1,064	709	716	2,004	938
East Europe	2,285	2,208	1,085	2,455	2,150
Soviet Union	1,000	1,500	500	500	500
Turkey	1,256	1,896	440	530	337
India	536	643	819	0	0
South Africa	162	140	130	15	0
Subtotal	72,625	71,631	86,021	92,960	101,685
Other countries	341	384	493	655	515
World trade total	72,966	72,015	86,514	93,615	102,200

SOURCE: U.S. Department of Agriculture.

doubled between 1960 and the late 1970s, Soviet production and utilization of fertilizer expanded dramatically during that same period, and the initial priority was allocated to winter wheat acreage. The Soviet Union recently experienced several consecutive years of poor weather, which depressed yields below their previous trends.

Winter wheat and spring wheat combined (including durum) account for around one-half of total Soviet grain production. The relative importance of the winter wheat crop has been increasing in recent years. The proportionate share of total wheat acreage that was planted to winter wheat formerly approximated only 25 to 28 percent because the acreage planted to spring wheat alone was around 2½ times larger than winter wheat acreage (this is the reverse of the situation in the United States, where acreage planted to winter wheat greatly exceeds spring wheat acreage). The higher yields for winter wheat plus the increasing needs for feed grains in the Soviet Union have resulted in steady changes over time (see Table 6-6). Winter wheat acreage has expanded by around 25 percent, or 12 million acres, since the early 1970s while spring wheat acreage has declined. Winter wheat acreage has replaced winter rye acreage in many areas, and barley and oats acreages have increased at the expense of spring wheat. Winter wheat acreage approximated 37 percent of total wheat acreage by 1980 and also accounted for almost three-fourths of the total acreage planted to winter grains. The production of winter wheat now surpasses that of spring wheat, despite the fact that spring wheat acreage still exceeds winter

Figure 6-2 Wheat-growing areas in the Soviet Union. *(ContiCommodity Research Division)*

TABLE 6-6 Soviet Wheat Acreage, Yield, and Production
(In million acres, bushels per acre, million bushels)

	1966–70 average	1971–72	1972–73	1973–74	1974–75	1975–76	1976–77	1977–78	1978–79	1979–80	1980–81	1981–82
						Winter wheat						
Area	45.1	51.1	37.0	45.3	45.9	48.4	42.6	51.1	57.1	46.2	55.7	50.1
Yield	29.1	34.3	29.1	40.1	35.7	27.8	38.5	37.2	42.4	30.4	32.8	32.2
Production	1318	1755	1079	1816	1642	1346	1638	1909	2425	1409	1830	1616
						Spring wheat						
Area	121	107	107.5	110.7	101.5	104.7	104.3	102	98.3	96.2	96.0	96.3
Yield	16.5	17.5	19.3	20.0	14.5	10.4	18.4	14.4	20.5	19.8	18.4	15.2
Production	1995	1873	2080	2217	1440	1086	1921	1477	2013	1904	1773	1469
						Total wheat						
Area	166.1	158.1	144.5	156	147.4	153.1	146.9	153.1	155.4	142.4	151.7	146.4
Yield	19.9	22.9	21.8	25.8	20.8	15.9	24.2	22.0	28.5	24.2	24.7	22.0
Production	3313	3628	3159	4033	3082	2432	3559	3385	4438	3455	3755	3231

SOURCE: U.S. Department of Agriculture and ContiCommodity Research Division.

TABLE 6-7 Soviet Wheat Imports and Exports
(In million bushels)

	1968	1969	1970	1971	1972	1973	1974	1975	1976	1977	1978	1979	1980
Imports	41	12	18	128	573	165	92	371	169	253	190	445	588
Exports	187	246	265	213	48	184	147	18	37	37	55	18	18

SOURCE: U.S. Department of Agriculture and ContiCommodity Research Division

wheat acreage by over 70 percent. This is a substantial change from the old rule of thumb which had always placed spring wheat and winter wheat production in the Soviet Union in a ratio of 60 to 40 (i.e., spring wheat and winter wheat in the Soviet Union accounted for 60 percent and 40 percent, respectively, of total Soviet wheat production).

Spring wheat production in the New Lands often provides a hedge against a national wheat crop failure; poor weather in the winter wheat growing areas of the Soviet Union frequently is offset by good growing conditions in spring wheat areas, and vice versa. Not all of the loss in one wheat crop can be made up entirely by a good harvest in the other wheat crop; the difference in production between good and bad years still can be enormous.

Most of the Soviet wheat production is composed of bread wheat varieties. However, less than one-half is needed for bread and other related consumer food items and for seed requirements.* Historically, the Soviet Union has also exported wheat, primarily to the Socialist states of Eastern Europe, with whom it has a common trade pact. In recent years, due to the rising internal needs of the Soviet Union, not as much wheat has been made available to Eastern European trading partners.† As can readily be seen from Table 6-7, the Soviet Union formerly imported very little wheat, and actually was a major exporter—but in recent years, a complete reversal has occurred.

More wheat actually is fed to livestock than is processed for food purposes.‡ The reason wheat is grown for animal feed (instead of more feed grains, for example) is, in part, the limitations of climate. It also involves the Soviet Union's desire to ensure adequate supplies of wheat for bread-making purposes; the substantial swings in weather necessitate two wheat crops for insurance against a disaster in one of the main growing areas (quality factors also are involved). Excess lower-milling-quality wheat then is used for feed. Conversely, since much of the Soviet wheat crop is used for animal-feeding purposes, replacement imports in years of poor production are predominantly in the form of feed grains, which normally are much cheaper.

Winter wheat production is concentrated in western areas of the Soviet Union, because it can withstand the winter conditions there. The western areas also have greater soil moisture and more reliable rainfall—this latter aspect

*This refers to net usable production (that is, after deduction of excess waste, and so on). About one-third of the Soviet wheat crop is used for food.

†In fact, the existing trade protocol apparently wasn't even discussed in the mid-1970s, let alone signed.

‡The Soviet Union reports that some milled flour also ends up being fed to animals.

determines the fertilizer allocations, because of the policy of concentrating fertilizer in predominantly moist areas.* Spring wheat, on the other hand, is grown predominantly in the more arid eastern regions, where it is too cold for winter grains.† The generally dry conditions prevailing in the spring wheat belt have limited fertilizer allocation in those areas. Thus, winter wheat yields have benefited from increased applications of fertilizer, whereas spring wheat, which receives little or no fertilizer, has not. This is apparent in the diverging yield trends.

There appears to be very little potential acreage which could be brought into wheat production, unless wheat replaces other crops. Winter wheat acreage increases have been responsible for a reduction in rye acreage, but there is a limit to the amount of substitution possible there, because of the long-standing Russian taste for rye bread, plus the fact that there is not that much acreage devoted to the production of rye. Also, increased feed requirements have already been responsible for reducing spring wheat acreage in western regions. While land in some areas awaits reclamation and/or irrigation projects, that land probably would be devoted to production of other crops, particularly forage crops. (In fact, these projects may not be fully developed on account of financial and technological difficulties.)

Hence, further increases in wheat production in the Soviet Union depend primarily upon increased yields. Additional production and use of fertilizer has been able to benefit yields; however, it is doubtful that these methods will provide similar results in the future. Diminishing returns would be seen eventually in western growing areas, where much of the winter wheat acreage already is fertilized, and the semiarid spring wheat areas are unlikely to receive increased fertilizer allocations, since fertilizer represents a valuable capital resource. Soviet research estimates that yields could be boosted substantially in Kazakhstan and other eastern areas (possibly by as much as 25 to 30 percent) if the practices of using fallow for at least one-third of the grain area and complete stubble mulch tillage were followed. However, more fallow land would remove land from current production; this runs counter to both established Soviet policy (which is to keep the amount of fallow land to a minimum), and present increasing grain requirements. Thus that alternative also would appear to be predicated upon additional land development in those areas. Again, such a project is not likely to occur for a long time, if at all.

The People's Republic of China

The People's Republic of China vies with the United States for the position of the second largest world producer of wheat. China's production of wheat has tripled over the past 15 to 20 years. This has been accomplished almost entirely through increased yields; acreage devoted to wheat has remained virtually the

*Moisture is necessary in order for fertilizer to produce any substantial benefit. A similar pattern exists in the United States. For example, more than 90 percent of the wheat acreage in the Great Lakes area receive fertilizer as opposed to only half of Nebraska's relatively dry wheat acreage.

†Most of the spring wheat acreage is located east of the Volga.

same. Increasing use of newer seed varieties that are more responsive to fertilizer has aided yields, but Chinese wheat yields still remain below those of the United States. China's deficiency in fertilizer appears to be the primary factor. Figure 6-3 shows China's wheat production and yields in recent years.

Winter wheat accounts for the largest part of total wheat production; winter wheat makes up around 90 percent of the total, with spring wheat around 10 percent. The east central (or "great plains") area of China accounts for most of the wheat crop; spring wheat is grown mostly in northeastern areas, extending into the Manchurian Plain. One of the most important winter wheat-producing areas is located just south of Peking and on both sides of the Hwang-Ho river. Major winter wheat provinces are: Honan, Shantung, Hopei, northern Kiangsu and northern Anhwei (see Figure 6-4).

Multiple-cropping is important to Chinese grain production; it results in a

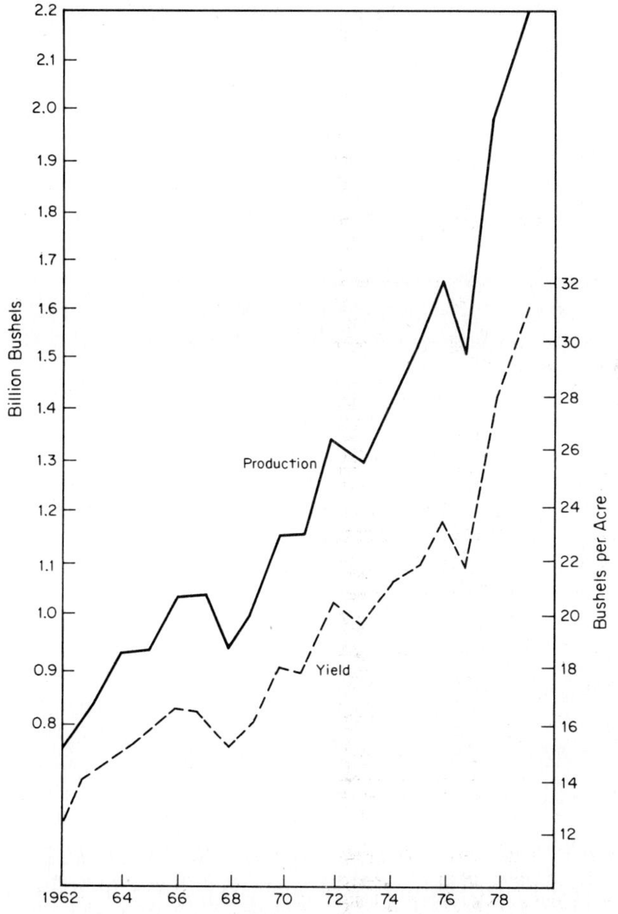

Figure 6-3 People's Republic of China wheat production and yield. *(United States Department of Agriculture)*

higher sown acreage than the cultivated area could provide. The difference between multiple-cropping and single-cropping on the same acreage provides a seeded acreage to grains that is 40 to 45 percent higher than the cultivated acreage could provide for a single crop. Table 6-8 shows an example of multiple-cropping in the Nanking area where three successive crops follow each other. Transplanting by hand often is employed to facilitate multiple-cropping.

Growing conditions in many areas of China are quite similar to those prevailing in the western U.S. wheat belt, where dryness tends to be the rule, rather than an exception. There is drought in northern China virtually every year, differing only in degree. The seasonal wind patterns in China carry cold, dry air from the center of Asia across to the coast during winter. Because of its location between the Pacific Ocean and the great arid Asian land mass, China is subject to monsoon conditions—rain and warm sea breezes in the summer but relatively cold and dry conditions in the winter. Thus reports of dry conditions in China's winter wheat belt should not be considered something out of the ordinary, nor should such reports be given the import they often receive (e.g., that a crop failure in China may be imminent). Wheat is more responsive to and dependent upon moisture at certain periods in the spring than at other times during the crop cycle. Also, much of the acreage in the northern China plains is irrigated; up to 200,000 new wells a year reportedly have been developed in recent years, mostly in the north. Spring wheat is grown in an area similar in climate to North Dakota.

China began to import wheat in 1961 despite fairly consistent annual increases in domestic production. Annual imports have fluctuated widely over the years, but usually ranged between 100 and 250 million bushels a year in former years. China recently began to increase wheat imports, which currently approximate 450 million bushels. China's wheat imports sometimes appeared to be strictly oriented to the level of its own grain production, while at other times China has appeared to be taking advantage of wide disparities between world prices for wheat and rice in order to increase its total grain supplies. Rice exports increased in some years in direct proportion to the increase in wheat imports; the export of rice can help cover the expense of increased grain imports because of the premium prices rice commands. An exchange of this sort also achieves a greater total grain supply and increased nutritional value.

Canada, Australia, and Argentina formerly were the traditional suppliers of

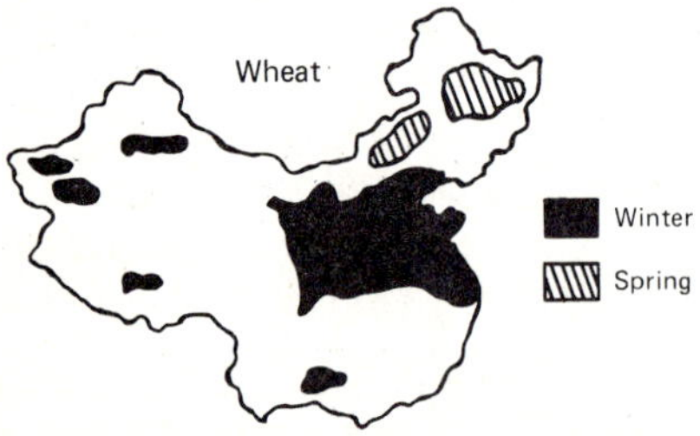

Figure 6-4 Wheat-growing areas in the People's Republic of China. *(ContiCommodity Research Division)*

TABLE 6-8 Example of Multiple Cropping in the Nanking Area

Crop	Plant	Harvest	Yield*
Rice	May	July	4,500
Rice	July	October	3,750
Wheat	October	May	2,350
Total			10,600

*Current estimates, kilograms per hectare.

wheat to China; the United States was relegated to the position of a residual supplier, mostly in years of unusually high Chinese import requirements when other suppliers were unable to perform (either because of quantity or quality problems). Political changes, including the establishment of diplomatic relations between the United States and China and changes in internal leadership in the late 1970s apparently led to a more pragmatic attitude on the part of Chinese leaders. Trade increased between the two countries and numerous consultations about large-scale ventures within China were held with both U.S. government officials and private U.S. businesses. Wheat purchases from the United States increased markedly during the 1978 and 1979 crop years. The United States and China presently have a long-term grain agreement which permits China to purchase up to 8 million tonnes of grain annually without consultation; wheat constitutes most of the U.S. grain sold to China.

China's economic plan identifies increased grain production to meet the basic needs of an expanding population as one of the two most important problems that China faces (the second is the lack of iron and steel for industrial development). The goal is to achieve an annual average increase in agricultural production of 4 to 5 percent, or around double the previous rate of increase. To some extent, the previous average annual rate of increase may not be a true barometer, since the 1970s generally have been a period of above-normal dryness. Thus, better weather, combined with the recent technological advances in fertilizer production, mechanization, and so on, resulted in some fairly sharp year-to-year advances in the beginning of the plan period. The major question is whether or not such advances can be sustained over the longer term; the answer to that rests largely upon the amount of political stability which develops. Given the absence of turmoil, which disrupts basic production, and a continuation of policies to modernize agriculture, a significant increase in agricultural output could be achieved.

At the minimum, China should be able to meet her food production needs and sustain basic self-sufficiency, barring extreme natural disasters. However, it appears probable that there may not be much improvement in the standard of living, and continued food rationing is likely. The crucial element in China's food problem continues to be one of a race between the growth in food production and the growth in population.

Per capita consumption of wheat in China approximates that of other Asian countries but is less than half that of the United States. Government campaigns have been initiated to try to convince the people that bread is more nutritious than noodles and some other starchy components that make up a large part of the current diet, particularly in northern areas, which are more industrial. The Chinese leaders evidently now accept the fact that bread is more adaptable to the pace of life needed to create a more industrialized and modernized society. The effort to "sell" the people on leavened bread and thereby create a profound revolution in the diet of millions of people has not been ignored in the western grain trade. A major point to consider is, if China were to increase the per capita consumption of wheat by only 2 ounces per day, the resulting demand would cause an increase greater than Canada's entire annual production of wheat. (Hence, even if Chinese wheat production does increase according to planned goals, what will happen in poor crop years if the present bread promotion succeeds?)

India

India is the fourth largest producer of wheat in the world and its total grain production averages around 7 percent of total world production. The main wheat-producing areas are located in the northern part of the country; the most productive areas are just south of New Delhi in the fertile Ganges valley. The states of Rajasthan, Madhyqa Pradesh, Uttar Pradesh, Punjab, and Haryana, combined, account for over 80 percent of total Indian wheat production; they make up the surplus production area in India.

Wheat is the main winter grain; the spring harvest in April and May is known as the *rabi* crop, which accounts for around 35 percent of total Indian grain production. The fall, or *kharif*, crop consists mainly of rice, sorghum, millet, and corn and represents the largest share of total grain production.

India is highly dependent on reliable monsoons in order to maximize grain production. Recurrent droughts, which are common, have stimulated an expanded irrigation network. Government canals are the backbone of the system; however, the water flow is not controllable, nor is the timing and quantity of water flow very reliable. Thus, recent efforts have placed greater emphasis on wells and storage reservoirs in order to decrease the reliance upon highly variable water flows, which mostly originate from melting mountain snows.

India was the highly-publicized example of the "green revolution" in Asia in the middle-to-late 1960s. The introduction of newer hybrid wheat varieties, which are more responsive to fertilizer and have a potential for higher yields, resulted in a rapid spurt in grain production; the "green revolution" was expected to be the solution to food problems in that part of the world. However, continued rapid population growth and technological problems have offset this solution. The high-yielding wheat varieties, for example, require good irrigation (and/or rainfall), fertilizer, and pesticides to maximize output. But much of the canal irrigation lacks control over water flow, and shortages of diesel fuel and electricity to power wells have occurred. India also lacks sufficient fertilizer. India's huge population is growing at an estimated 2 percent annually, the equivalent of an additional 14 to 15 million people every year. India plans to increase grain production by expanding multiple-cropping, irrigation facilities, and chemical fertilizer consumption. Wheat imports were renewed by India again recently because of stagnating production, an inability to meet target goals, and reduced government stocks.

Western Europe

Wheat production in Western Europe has increased substantially since the early 1960s; the expanded output has been entirely due to increased yields because the acreage planted to wheat actually has declined over the same period. The EEC accounted for almost all of the increase in wheat production; France alone accounted for one-half of the total increase in the EEC and accounts for around 35 percent of total Western European wheat production. As noted in Table 6-4, France is one of the leading wheat producers in the world.

The expansion in EEC grain production has been motivated by substantial increases in domestic price supports, which have maintained domestic prices well above world price levels. This also has resulted in higher variable levies, or taxes, applied to grain imports, which have had a dampening effect upon grain imports. Although wheat imports are required because of deficits in hard varieties for baking and durum needs, the level of wheat imports essentially has stagnated around the level of the early 1960s, when the General Agreement on Trade and Tariffs (GATT) accord was signed and import tariffs were introduced.

Soft winter wheat varieties are the primary source of wheat production in the EEC; durum production has increased but quality problems persist. Thus, insufficient amounts of good baking-quality wheat are produced and huge surpluses of soft wheat accumulate. These surpluses cause problems and disputes in almost every year of good growing weather. These disputes often center around requests by France—the leading agricultural producer with the strongest agricultural lobby—for higher export subsidies and increased amounts authorized for export. Every year export subsidies are necessary because the internal price is well above world market prices; EEC export subsidies have amounted to over one-half of the world price for wheat during some disposal ("dumping") periods. The subsidies have been criticized by other world wheat exporters; the United States in particular has accused the EEC of dumping wheat into world markets, especially since the export subsidies periodically have been set at levels that are higher than the difference between domestic prices and world prices in order to offer a price below world values and thereby dispose of surpluses more easily.

The problem of continual surpluses has been compounded by the high support price, which insulates domestic production from the effects of world prices and maintains the amount of planted acreage, and by the use of new high-yielding wheat varieties with low baking qualities. The EEC began to address the situation by differentiating among the varieties of wheat and adjusting support prices accordingly; the support price for feed-quality wheats, for example, was placed closer to the support price for feed grains. It was hoped that this would discourage any further rapid expansion in the production of high-yielding varieties with poor baking qualities. But the production of wheat will not be curtailed easily because feed-wheat yields compare very favorably with feed grains, and even approach corn yields in some areas; moreover, the effect of an umbrella price protection is provided for feed wheat by the consistently high threshhold prices for all wheat. (EEC grain price-support mechanisms are covered in the section dealing with the EEC in Chapter 7.)

France accounts for about 75 percent of total EEC wheat exports, which have increased over five times since the early 1960s. EEC imports of wheat generally have remained around 1960 levels, except in poor crop years. Hard red winter and spring varieties make up most of the U.S. wheat exports to the EEC; durum sales to the EEC have constituted almost one-half of total U.S. durum exports, primarily because of the demand for pasta in southern Europe.

Argentina

Argentina is listed as one of the major world wheat exporters. (It is counted with Canada and Australia in Figure 6-5.) However, its share of total world wheat trade has declined significantly in recent years (Table 6-9).

Wheat acreage has tended to fluctuate sharply from year to year, much more so than for any other Argentinian grain. The relationship of cattle prices to wheat prices appears to have a significant influence on wheat acreage in Argentina; the acreage planted to wheat in the year following a sharp change in wheat-to-beef price ratios tends to change accordingly (i.e., wheat acreage increases if the wheat-to-beef ratio increases and decreases if cattle prices strengthened relative to wheat prices). Government price support policies have sometimes tended to encourage corn and sorghum production at the expense of wheat. Wheat acreage recently became more stable because of the increase in soybean production; roughly 75 percent of the total Argentine soybean production is double-cropped with wheat.

Wheat yields have shown little tendency to increase. This stagnation is due

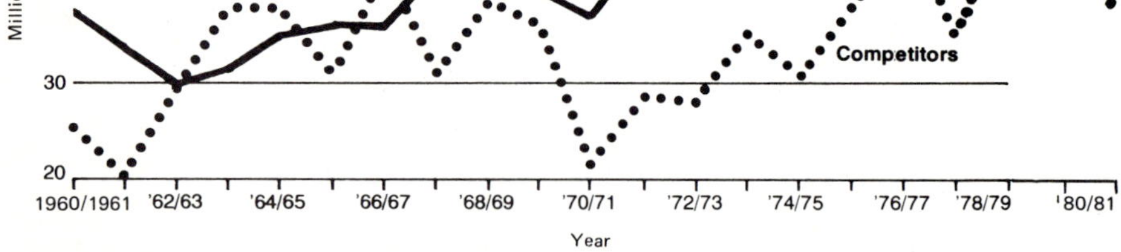

Figure 6-5 United States and competitors' (Canada, Australia, Argentina) wheat production for crop years 1960 to 1961 through 1978 to 1979. *(United States Department of Agriculture)*

TABLE 6-9 Argentine Wheat Exports
(Million bushels)

Year	Export	Year	Export
1960	40	1972	117
1961	100	1973	59
1962	68	1974	66
1963	128	1975	117
1964	230	1976	217
1965	204	1977	66
1966	81	1978	151
1967	83	1979	176
1968	90	1980	143
1969	84	1981	158
1970	31	1982	300
1971	59		

to the lack of application of more modern technology, especially the use of fertilizer, which is extremely important to the success of the newer high-yielding wheat varieties. The record yield of Argentina, for example, stood for almost 20 years before it was surpassed in 1983. Annual yields can fluctuate sharply because of weather, which can change widely in Argentina from year to year and even among different growing areas in the same year. The percentage of wheat acreage actually harvested for grain also can vary widely; it has ranged anywhere from 78 percent to over 90 percent of the planted acreage, depending on weather conditions.

Argentina is one of the world's heaviest per capita consumers of wheat and wheat products, although per capita consumption has tended to decline in recent years. Most domestically consumed wheat is used for milling and seed purposes (very little is used for animal feeding); the balance is exported. Average annual domestic needs approximate 4 million tonnes.

Argentine wheat from some producing zones had enjoyed a preference over U.S. wheat because it was judged to be closer to Canadian wheat in quality (Canadian spring wheat usually commands a premium because of protein content and baking qualities). This helped to offset the fact that Argentine freight costs to Western Europe are higher than freight rates from the United States and Canada. Competition among the United States, Canada, and Argentina for the market in Western Europe has tended to be intense for many years. Western Europe has been a major market for Argentine wheat. South American destinations generally have been important only in years when Argentina has exportable surpluses and world supplies are large, particularly in the United States and Canada. Eastern Europe and China also are important destinations in some years; total Argentine shipments to those areas occasionally would surpass those to Western Europe or the total shipments to South American destinations.

The long-term Argentine–Soviet trade pact diminishes the importance of South American destinations to Argentina in most years. Argentina has had a number of special trade agreements in South America which specified some form of preference for Argentine wheat over wheat from other countries.

Around 60 percent of Argentine wheat exports went to South American destinations in the mid-1970s; however, the agreement with the Soviet Union may drain Argentina's exportable surplus in years other than record production years. During the U.S. embargo against the Soviet Union, for example, other South American countries had to turn to the United States for supplies because of the absorption of Argentine supplies by the Soviet Union. In fact, it may be necessary for Argentina to import wheat in some future years of poor production because of its firm annual commitments to the Soviet Union and other agreed allocations. Imports have been necessary in some prior years, even in the absence of such large commitments to the Soviet Union, simply in order to cover domestic requirements.

Canada

Canada is the second largest world exporter of wheat, after the United States. However, Canada's relative share of total world wheat exports also has declined since the surge of world demand during the 1970s. Table 6-10 depicts the situation very clearly.

Canadian wheat exports have for the most part been relatively stagnant since the 1960s, despite the sharp growth in world wheat trade (the world wheat trade volume, for example, increased over 70 percent during the past nine years). Canadian wheat exports achieved a new record level in the 1980–1981 crop year, finally surpassing the previous record levels established in 1963. Canada made a commitment in the early 1980s to boost wheat exports. The results began to show up in 1982.

Canadian production has not been able to respond proportionately to the same forces that unleashed the productive capacity of the United States. This

TABLE 6-10 Canadian Wheat Exports*
(Million bushels)

Year	Export	Year	Export
1960	353	1972	577
1961	358	1973	422
1962	331	1974	411
1963	595	1975	444
1964	399	1976	474
1965	585	1977	588
1966	515	1978	481
1967	336	1979	584
1968	306	1980	624
1969	347	1981	653
1970	434	1982†	753
1971	504		

*August–July crop year.

†Estimate.

SOURCE: Foreign Agricultural Service.

is partly due to the greater facility of the United States to increase planted acreages; but the predominant reason is the stifling effects of government domination of the wheat industry in Canada. Figure 6-6 shows the trend of Canadian grain exports.

In the United States, the grain trade was relatively freer to respond to the economic forces of demand. Escalating export requirements meant that vastly improved transportation facilities would be needed to handle the increased flow of grain to export channels; increased handling facilities at various locations would also be needed. The prospects of increasing participation in the higher volume and earning unlimited profits stimulated private investment and development of those projects in the United States, the number of large hopper cars and commercially owned "unit trains" increased substantially because increased volume of flow meant more profits. The U.S. government (taxpayers) did not have to expand the transportation system because the private trade did it. Modernization of grain-handling systems also increased grain-flow capacity.

In contrast, the Canadian transportation and grain-handling network is a huge bottleneck to the flow of grain to export channels. This limits the ability of Canada (and the Canadian farmers) to share in the increased export demand. In fact, export contracts have had to be cancelled or deferred in some years because of the shipping bottlenecks. (Canada's principal ports for grain exportation are compared in Figure 6-7.) Canadian farmers lost an estimated $1 billion in the 1977–1978 and 1978–1979 marketing years because of transportation snags. Opportunities for new sales also were lost because the Canadian Wheat Board, unable to assure delivery, declined to bid on export contracts.

Saskatchewan and Alberta are the two leading wheat-growing provinces in Canada. They both are prairie regions, similar in both ecology and climate to North Dakota and eastern Montana. Spring wheat is the major wheat grown,

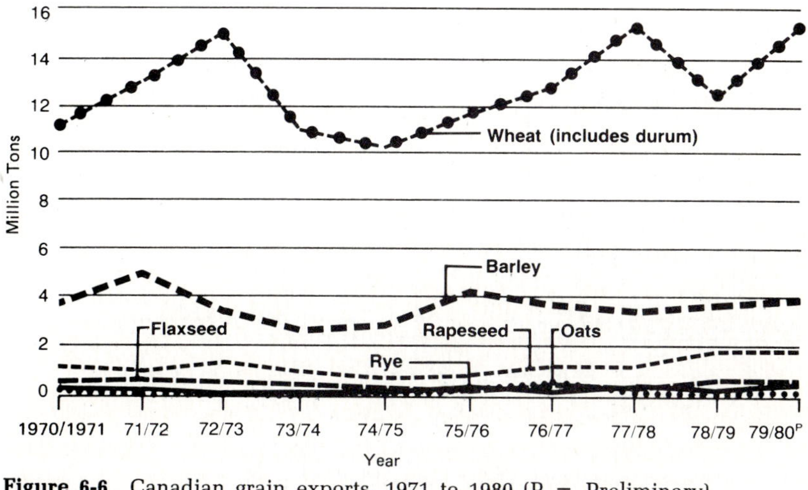

Figure 6-6 Canadian grain exports, 1971 to 1980 (P = Preliminary). *(Canadian Grains Council Statistical Handbook and Canadian Grain Commission)*

although winter wheat acreage has been expanding slightly. (Winter wheat could be a more viable economic alternative in some areas of Canada because wheat prices normally are at their highs in early winter, the crop can be hedged successfully at that time, and winter wheat yields can exceed those of spring wheat. The combination of these three factors would suggest that more experimentation with winter wheat will occur in the future.)

Australia

Acreage planted to wheat in Australia has increased steadily during the 1970s. Wheat is almost always grown in rotation with other crops or in combination with grazing activities. Legume pastures in rotation with wheat are common; they not only afford excellent pasture but in many areas of the country are also the sole source of nitrogen for subsequent crops.

Climatic conditions vary widely but most wheat is grown in a zone with an annual rainfall of between 250 and 650 millimeters and most precipitation occurs between May and October (wheat generally is planted in May and June and harvested in November and December). Most of Australia is either arid or at least seasonally arid, which severely restricts the amount of arable land (see Figure 6-8). Only around 30 percent of the total land area receives sufficient rainfall for arable agriculture; some of this lies in northern Australia, which is unsuitable for crops. Fallowing is used in some areas to increase water storage, but it generally is ineffective in marginal areas (such as interior regions)

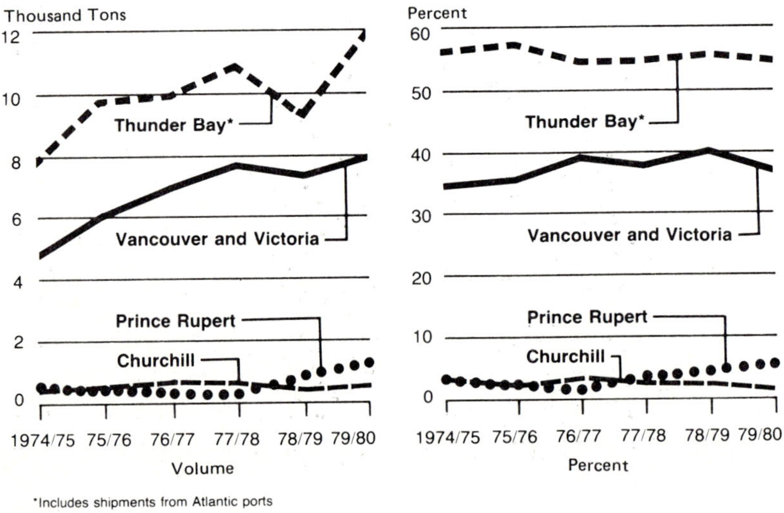

Figure 6-7 Exports of principal western Canadian grain by port. *(Canadian Wheat Board Annual Report, various years and Canadian Grain Commission Grain Statistics Weekly)*

because of the soil characteristics and extreme evaporative conditions. Australian soils, in general, are relatively poor in fertility. Wheat cannot be grown at all in some parts of western Australia without extensive top-dressing with superphosphate.

The notoriously unreliable and relatively scarce rainfall causes extremely high fluctuations in yields; this is a striking characteristic of Australian wheat production. The wide fluctuations tend to obscure the fact that average wheat yields have shown little overall improvement during the past 30 years. The average yield per acre between 1950 and 1959 was around 16½ bushels, 18 bushels between 1960 and 1969, and 18½ bushels between 1970 and 1979 (as shown in Figure 6-9). Problems of soil erosion, disease, and insect damage also hamper yields.

New South Wales traditionally has been the largest wheat-producing state. While acreage in western Australia exceeds that of New South Wales by around 25 percent, production in New South Wales may be as much as 70 percent greater. Consistently higher yields in New South Wales account for the difference in production between the two states.

Average yields in Victoria are also among the highest. Queensland has the

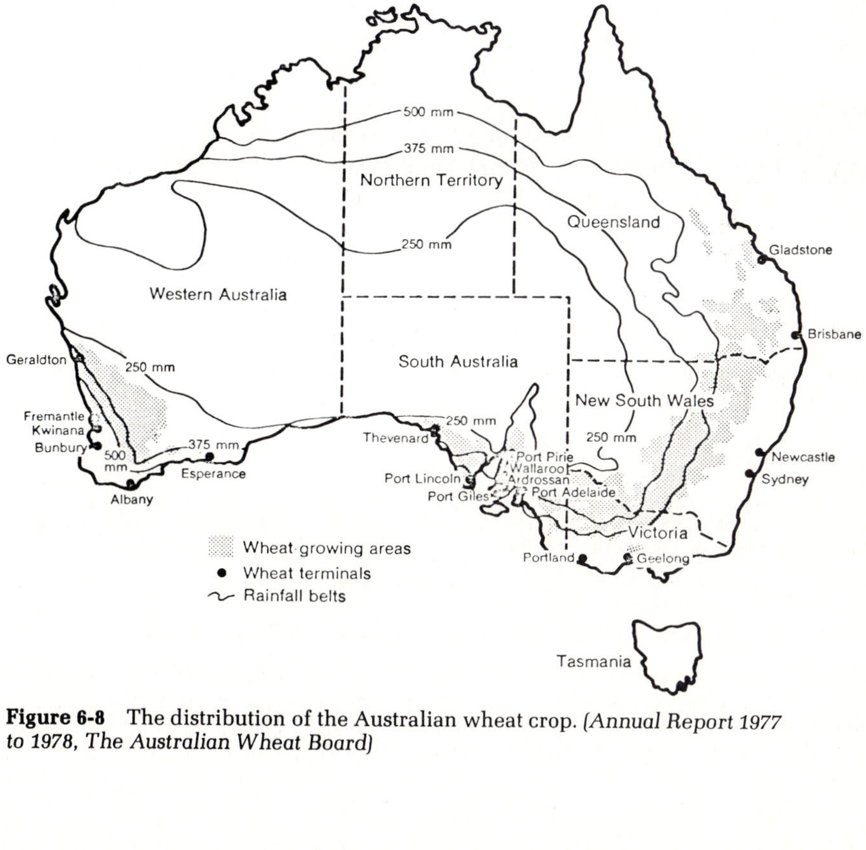

Figure 6-8 The distribution of the Australian wheat crop. *(Annual Report 1977 to 1978, The Australian Wheat Board)*

smallest wheat area and the terrain is such that expansion beyond the southern black soils is unlikely. Acreage in south Australia has been increasing, primarily into areas of lighter rainfall. The largest potential for expanded acreage exists in western Australia, where acreage already has almost doubled over the past 10 years. However, the limitations of rainfall generally restrict plantings to alternate areas in western sections and every third or fourth year in even drier inland areas; long fallowing periods are necessary to restore soil moisture reserves.

Most of Australia's wheat production goes to the export market, since its population is too small to accommodate a large domestic use. Australian wheat production, and hence export capabilities, can vary considerably from year to year because of sharp swings in weather, particularly rainfall (Table 6-11). Wheat yields are notoriously unstable because of the very fickle weather conditions.

Subsidies to increase wheat exports have been suggested periodically by farm groups but the government has steadfastly opposed such measures. The Australian government advocates liberalization of trade and also fears that providing subsidies to promote exports would expose Australian farm products to trade retaliation. Australia already is concerned about the U.S. import barriers, particularly on dairy products, meats, and wool and also about similar barriers in the EEC and Japan.

The Australian Wheat Board (AWB) has statutory control of the entire marketing system for wheat in Australia. The AWB was founded in 1939 to control food supplied during World War II, but was given exclusive authority in the purchase and marketing of all Australian wheat after the War, including both domestic use and exports.

The AWB has been criticized for a lack of flexibility in negotiating the terms on wheat export sales. This has been a weak point in the AWB's capacity as an exporter. Important export customers have included China, Egypt, the Soviet Union, Japan, and other mideastern and far eastern destinations. The Soviet Union and Eastern Europe have accounted for an increasing share of total Australian agricultural exports in recent years.

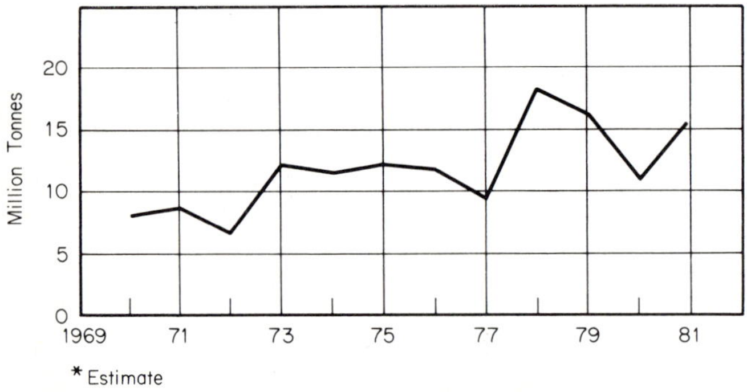

Figure 6-9 Australian wheat production, 1970 to 1980. *(Australia Bureau of Statistics and United States Department of Agriculture)*

TABLE 6-11 Australian Wheat Exports*
(Million bushels)

Year	Export	Year	Export
1960	237	1972	158
1961	182	1973	198
1962	226	1974	301
1963	256	1975	290
1964	270	1976	312
1965	180	1977	408
1966	314	1978	430
1967	208	1979	485
1968	237	1980	389
1969	297	1981	604
1970	336	1982†	257
1971	286		

*December–November crop year.

†Estimate.

SOURCE: Foreign Agricultural Service.

FACTORS INFLUENCING MARKET PRICES

General

The supply-and-demand balance for specific classes of wheat must be looked at following an assessment of the total wheat situation, particularly if nothing as clear as the bullish outlook of 1973–1974 or the bearish 1977 summer outlook can be projected. The discussion of various wheat classes earlier in this chapter should serve as an aid in considering individual classes and wheat markets; the coverage of planting and harvesting periods, weather factors, uses, export markets, and developments in foreign countries of importance should help in placing news in perspective and in evaluating both overall wheat prospects and individual classes. The following will be geared toward an assessment of overall supply-and-demand fundamental balances.

Supplies

The USDA estimates winter wheat acreage in December and also applies a tentative production estimate. But this tentative figure has little market impact, generally, because it is unable to take into account future spring weather conditions, which are the primary determinant of yields. The planted acreage estimate is the important figure; if it is large, for example, then poor yields must be "proven" in average years before any bearish overtures can be removed and vice versa. Sufficient planted acreage usually is a precursor to a normal seasonal decline in prices during the winter and spring.

Adverse weather during the winter, such as no snow cover to protect the dormant wheat crop, alternative thawing and heaving of soils (which can be detrimental by uprooting plants), blowing soils, and so forth, can spark "crop-scare" rallies. But they are unlikely to last or to grow to major proportions because of the importance of spring weather to winter wheat yields. Close attention is paid to weather during the spring growing season after wheat's emergence from dormancy. The amount of influence that spring weather has upon prices is directly proportionate to overall fundamental balances (e.g., demand, prospective carryover, and free supplies) and new crop prospects relative to prospective disappearance.

The wheat supply base also includes the amount of "free" supplies which exist to cover marketing needs; free supplies constitute that portion of the total wheat supplies which are not under the shelter of government programs. Here again, the amount of free supplies may vary greatly among different classes of wheat and thereby affect spread relationships, if not outright market prices. Hence, government farm programs should be examined carefully; also, entries of wheat into government loan and grain reserve programs should be watched (these reports are published weekly and monthly by the USDA). Wheat supplies can be tightened severely if producers enter too much wheat into the grain reserve program; this is because the minimum trigger, or release price, of the grain reserve is way above market values. The artificial tightening of supplies through government programs (equivalent to artificial demand) can cause some tremendous price surges; this has occurred previously, since the creation of the grain reserve in the 1977 Farm Bill, and is certain to occur again. The existence of the grain reserve helps to support prices at much higher relative levels,

Figure 6-10 Monthly continuation, Minnesota wheat. *(ContiCommodity Research Division)*

thereby distorting "price signals" to producers; at times, however, the existence of the grain reserve also creates prices much higher than ordinarily would exist.

A trader should be aware of specific information about government programs, including what the basic price supports are. Particularly relevant in surplus years, basic price supports provide a floor under market values and a bottom to price declines. Another important piece of knowledge is where the grain reserve trigger prices are. Trigger prices can influence a rally from lower price levels; they can also halt bullish price advances in years when grain is needed to cover marketing flow requirements to feed domestic and export channels, but too much grain is tied up in the grain reserve. (The 1980–1981 crop year in corn is a prime example—the corn reserve was "called" through a rampant price surge to record high price levels, not because total supplies were nonexistent or "short" but because too much was locked up in the grain reserve and therefore only accessible at much higher prices.) Figures 6-10, 6-11, and 6-12 graph the wheat prices from 1960 to 1982 at three centers. It can be seen that wheat followed the spiraling price lead of corn.

Demand

Exports are the most relevant factor in both U.S. and world total wheat supply-and-demand evaluations. Constant attention must be given to export shipments

Figure 6-11 Monthly continuation, Chicago Board of Trade wheat. *(U.S. Department of Agriculture)*

from the United States and other exporting countries and to the rate of bookings (published weekly by the USDA for U.S. exports). Domestic milling demand varies very little from year to year.

Relative consumption trends in wheat are important; they can become more important when related to individual classes. For example, the consumption trend of hard red winter or soft red winter threaten to exhaust free supplies for that class of wheat. A major question to ask is, how does wheat disappearance compare to supplies? A general rule of thumb is that wheat can withstand two consecutive years of disappearance exceeding the crop size and therefore drawing down stocks; however a third consecutive year results in a major bull market. The last time this occurred was in 1973–1974, when wheat prices skyrocketed to record levels.

Ending supplies also should be related to disappearance. Low ending stocks relative to disappearance increase the importance of new crop production in the United States and the world. It is particularly important that new crop production be sufficient to cover demand in cases when ending stocks are relatively low as related to disappearance.

Harvesting of large crops in Argentina, Australia, and Canada and/or aggressive export sales programs by those countries can provide pressure to wheat prices at various times but the influence of these countries has declined in

Figure 6-12 Monthly continuation, Kansas City Board of Trade wheat. *(ContiCommodity Research Division)*

recent years (Figure 6-5) on account of the predominance of the United States. "Fire sales" by the EEC to dispose of surplus soft wheat stocks in the spring, prior to the harvest of the new crop, often occur; these moves also can affect prices, particularly for the soft red wheat class. The EEC's attitude toward providing subsidies to increase wheat exports should be monitored.

Wheat production has escalated sharply in developing countries during the past 20 years but still is insufficient to cover demand. In other areas, such as the Soviet Union and China, wheat imports have increased despite strong gains in production. Such trends also should be watched closely to assess future U.S. export potential. The assessment also should include an evaluation of the ability of various world areas to pay for imports, including such factors as credit availability. Many developing areas will find their resources for internal development projects increasingly drained by expenditures for food imports unless their domestic production can increase more rapidly in proportion to population growth than it has during the past 5 years, or unless world grain prices cease their upward trend (which is another reason for becoming thoroughly familiar with U.S. government farm programs and policies).

SUMMARY OF MAJOR FACTORS TO MONITOR

1. U.S. supplies
   a. Carryover stocks and projected carryover
   b. Planted acreage
   c. Weather during the growing season, primarily after the emergence from winter dormancy
   d. U.S. Department of Agriculture crop estimates
   e. Free supplies
2. Foreign supplies and production, particularly among the export competitors of Canada, Argentina, Australia, and the EEC
3. U.S. disappearance, particularly relative to total supplies, and mainly:
   a. Exports
   b. The amount fed to livestock
4. Government farm programs
   a. Basic loan rate
   b. Amount eligible for price support
   c. Grain reserve release prices
   d. Acreage reduction provisions
   e. Government policies and decisions
5. Total world supplies and consumption
6. Asian rice production and supplies (wheat is the chosen substitute for rice in Asia)

7. Seasonal factors
8. Cash market trends
9. World economic conditions

Commodity	Exchange(s)	Contract size	Limit moves
Wheat	Chicago Board of Trade	5000 bushels	20¢
	Kansas City Board of Trade	5000 bushels	20¢
	Minneapolis Grain Exchange	5000 bushels	20¢
	Mid-America Commodity Exchange	1000 bushels	20¢

CHAPTER

7

Corn

Michael Hinebaugh

The corn plant is one of nature's greatest multipliers. A single kernel of planted corn, which weighs about one one-hundredth of an ounce, yields an average of 800 kernels weighing 8 ounces. Wheat, by comparison, will produce around a fifty-fold yield per seed planted. The proportions of corn harvested to the number of acres planted each year are shown in Figure 7-1. Corn is grown principally as a feed grain in order to produce livestock and poultry to increase the protein in human diets, although corn still is grown for human consumption in some areas of the world.

PRODUCTION AND CONSUMPTION IN THE UNITED STATES

Production

The United States is by far the world's largest producer of corn. The vast bulk of U.S. corn production occurs in an area vaguely defined as "the Midwest." This fails to isolate the fact that just two states, Iowa and Illinois, account for almost 40 percent of U.S. production. Iowa and Illinois together produce as much corn as Minnesota, Nebraska, Indiana, Ohio, and Wisconsin combined. (In other words, what happens in only two states can be critical to both U.S. and world prices.) The Midwest accounts for such a large share of U.S. corn production because of its excellent soils and favorable climate. That combination is unique in the world; the fabled *chernozem*— or black soils—belt in the Soviet Union, for example, does not have a similar climate.

Table 7-1 presents the leading corn-producing states in the United States for 1978, 1979, 1981, and 1982 when yields and production achieved record levels, and for 1980, when severe drought plagued the crop. The fifteen states listed in Table 7-1 usually account for around 93 percent of U.S. corn production.

The most important factors in corn production are the following: weather during the main growing season, trends in technology, the profitability of growing corn, corn prices (ratios) related to those of other competitors for planted acreage, and government programs. Many of these factors are interrelated. For example, government programs can affect profitability, and technological developments affect both profitability and yield trends associated with weather conditions.

Weather. Optimum corn yields are associated with normal "preseason" moisture ("preseason" is September through June), normal to slightly below normal summer temperatures, and above-normal summer rainfall. Normal precipitation during the 10 months which precede the midsummer growing period is optimum for corn because it provides an adequate subsoil moisture reserve. Corn requires access to more water during its main growth period than is usually provided by rainfall. The production capacity of midwestern soils is large, given an adequate subsoil moisture reserve and normal summer rainfall. Low preseason moisture creates a necessity for exceptionally high summer rainfall to maintain good yield prospects. However, it should be noted that moisture during the fall-through-spring period is a relatively minor factor as compared to the main summer growing period. Corn yields primarily are determined by summer growing conditions, particularly during July.

Corn enters its "grand growth" period in July. Plant development is excep-

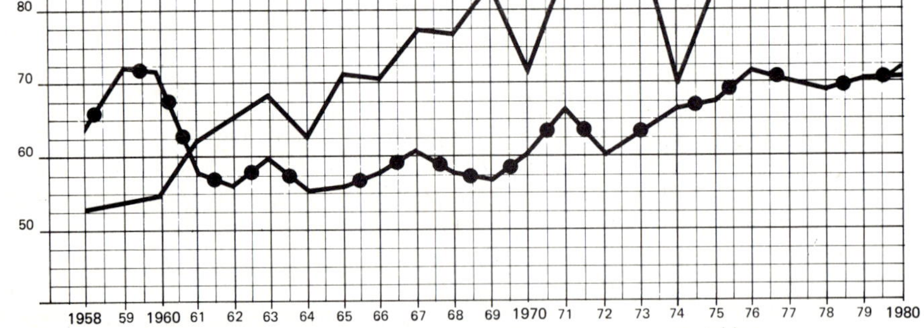

Figure 7-1 Harvested corn acreage versus yield. *(ContiCommodity Research Division)*

TABLE 7-1 Leading U.S. Corn-Producing States

	Rank of individual states in corn production					Actual corn production, millions of bushels				
	1978	1979	1980	1981	1982	1978	1979	1980	1981	1982
Iowa	1	1	1	1	1	1478	1664	1463	1759	1591
Illinois	2	2	2	2	2	1240	1414	1066	1454	1525
Nebraska	3	3	4	3	4	763	822	603	791	770
Indiana	4	4	5	5	3	669	675	602	654	815
Minnesota	5	5	3	4	5	644	606	610	745	734
Ohio	6	6	6	7	6	379	417	441	360	475
Wisconsin	7	7	7	6	7	294	317	348	378	362
Missouri	8	8	12	9	9	200	240	110	213	205
Michigan	9	9	9	8	8	194	237	247	274	307
South Dakota	10	10	9	10	10	177	211	122	180	193
Kansas	11	11	11	12	13	153	172	116	148	140
Texas	12	13	10	15	15	144	132	117	127	120
North Carolina	13	14	13	13	11	121	128	104	141	165
Kentucky	14	12	14	11	12	120	132	103	149	158
Pennsylvania	15	15	15	14	14	116	121	96	134	126

tionally rapid; hence the old farmer's tale of being able to hear corn grow at midnight. At this time, total available moisture (that is, soil moisture reserves plus actual rainfall) becomes a crucial factor (see Figure 7-2). July rainfall itself is one of the most critical weather variables for corn yields. Deficit summer rainfall can be offset to some extent by access to good subsoil moisture reserves. However, maximum yields still are lost if July rainfall is below normal. Even excellent soil moisture reserves have not prevented large crop losses during severe droughts in July (although much of the loss from the droughts in July has been caused by the high temperatures that usually are associated with drought conditions). The years 1975 and 1977 are good examples of the adverse effects on corn yields from subnormal rainfall during most of July, despite relatively cool temperatures. Yields in both years were well below average trend yields associated with good growing conditions.

Table 7-2 shows average moistures and temperatures for the main corn-producing states. (Temperatures are listed only for June, July, and August, the only months when temperatures are significant.)

High temperatures during the prime growing period cause excessive plant respiration; this places plants under stress and spurs rapid plant development. Because plants then do not have time to develop normally, reduced yields result. In July, high temperatures can also curb pollination, which determines the number of kernels on the ears. (The number of kernels and the size and weight of the kernels determines the yield.)

High temperatures during the pollination period reduce the number of kernels on each ear by (1) delaying the emergence of silk on the ears (which receives the falling pollen) and (2) drying out the pollen to the point where the pollen from corn tassels either falls prematurely or else cannot sufficiently fertilize the silk. High temperatures in August cause stress at the time of kernel filling, and so diminish kernel weight, and therefore, yield. August heat also reduces the photosynthate storage capability of kernels, and that factor lowers yields, too. In August, rainfall is not as important as temperatures; good rainfall does aid the filling process, but corn still can do well in a relatively dry August if temperatures remain sufficiently cool.

Global weather trends are important to watch because they offer valuable clues to future probabilities regarding average annual weather in many important areas. Although these shifts may appear to be very slight, they have drastic effects upon local weather and, consequently, grain production; relatively small changes in overall temperatures have caused major climatic shifts. (For example, variations in temperatures of only a few degrees Celsius separate an ice age from a mild period.) Changes in hemispheric climate involve movements of tremendous amounts of energy; these global fluctuations in climate affect the temperatures of land and ocean surfaces for years, conveying extremely complex local effects.

The northern hemisphere is presently in an abrupt cooling trend. This has brought average temperatures back to the level which existed around 1880. North Atlantic ocean temperatures have cooled around 2°F since 1950. The gulf stream has shifted farther south. A shift in wind patterns has occurred which has created sharper dips in the jet stream. Our surface wind patterns on earth

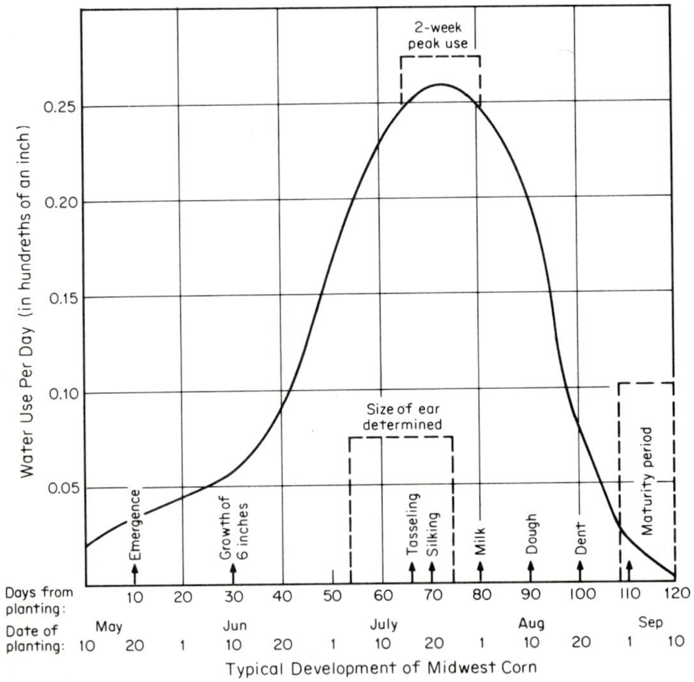

Figure 7-2 Corn water usage during growing season. *(CGC-Research)*

TABLE 7-2 Average Moisture and Temperatures in Main Corn States
(Moisture in inches; temperatures in degrees Fahrenheit)

	Average monthly moisture												Average temperature (maximum and minimum)		
	Preseason									Main growth					
	Sept.	Oct.	Nov.	Dec.	Jan.	Feb.	Mar.	Apr.	May	June	July	Aug.	June	July	August
Des Moines, Iowa	3.4	2.4	1.6	1.2	1.1	1.1	1.9	2.9	4.2	4.7	3.3	3.7	81–61	87–66	84–63
Chicago, Ill.	3.8	2.2	2.1	2.0	1.7	1.3	2.7	3.7	3.2	4.1	3.4	3.1	79–58	83–63	82–62
Springfield, Ill.	3.4	2.7	2.4	2.1	2.0	2.1	3.1	3.6	4.1	4.0	3.1	3.0	83–63	88–67	85–65
Lincoln, Neb.	3.0	1.9	1.2	.8	.7	1.0	1.5	2.5	3.8	4.3	3.6	3.4	83–62	89–67	87–65
Indianapolis, Ind.	3.2	2.7	3.2	2.9	3.0	2.5	3.8	3.9	3.9	4.1	3.8	3.2	82–62	86–66	84–64
Minneapolis, Minn.	2.9	2.0	1.3	.9	.8	.9	1.5	2.1	3.4	4.1	3.4	3.2	78–58	83–63	81–61
Columbus, Ohio	2.6	2.2	2.7	2.6	2.9	2.5	4.1	3.2	3.6	3.7	3.7	3.2	81–60	85–64	83–62
St. Louis, Mo.	3.2	2.6	2.6	2.2	2.2	2.3	3.3	3.7	4.1	4.1	3.3	3.0	84–66	89–70	87–68
Aberdeen, S. Dak.	1.6	1.2	.7	.5	.6	.6	1.1	2.0	2.4	3.4	2.6	2.0	79–54	87–59	86–57
Kansas City, Kan.	4.3	3.0	1.8	1.4	1.4	1.4	2.6	3.4	4.7	4.8	3.8	4.0	84–65	89–70	88–68
Wichita, Kan.	3.3	2.4	1.5	1.0	.8	1.1	1.8	2.9	4.2	4.4	3.5	3.0	86–65	91–69	90–68

are governed by high altitude wind patterns; changes there can create more blocking ridges which limit moisture in many areas. The duration of sunlight also has been decreasing; this affects the number of heat units received in a given area, which determine the length of the growing season. The reduction in heat units over the past 15 years in the Midwest, for example, has had an effect equivalent to placing the Midwest at a higher latitude (approximately 100 miles farther north). Europe has seen the length of its growing season decline already.

The future impact of the cooling trend upon growing seasons and corn production boundaries depends on future developments in average annual temperatures. Initially, the cooling trend should be considered beneficial; however, it would become detrimental if it extends.

Cooler temperatures have been associated with higher yields during recent history (partly because of the fact that these cooler temperatures usually are accompanied by increased rainfall). The optimum daily average temperature for corn in the U.S. corn belt during the summer is around 72°F. Summer temperatures during the past 50 years have averaged 76 and 74°F for July and August, respectively, along a line from Des Moines, Iowa to Indianapolis, Indiana. The maximum daily temperatures should not exceed 86°. The summers of 1961 to 1973 were as cool as the summers of 1900 to 1911 and corn yields accelerated during the 1960s. (Computer regression models show that corn yields during the early 1900s would have been as high as corn yields during the 1960s if the same technology had existed.) The yields achieved on experimental farms have long suggested that corn yields in Illinois and Iowa can reach 130 bushels per acre whenever excellent growing conditions occur (both above-average rainfall and relatively cool temperatures). The yield in Illinois exceeded 130 bushels per acre in 1983.

Cooler world temperatures also are associated with a higher degree of variability in weather, which means that yield prospects also fluctuate more. Thus higher variability in both weather conditions and yield prospects should be expected to continue. U.S. national average corn yields should range from 105 to 115 bushels per acre in years when favorable weather prevails. In years when government programs reduce planted acreage the range can be from 115 to 125 bushels per acre.

A *prolonged* decline in average world temperatures would have a significant impact on grain production in future years. A southward shift in grain production boundaries could become necessary; this would entail shifting more production to areas of poorer soils as well as limiting total land resources available for crop production in some major world areas. Most of the productive land areas in the Soviet Union, Canada, and northern Europe lie at latitudes where a shortened growing season would have a major adverse impact. The southern land areas in the Soviet Union, for example, basically are deserts. A southward shift in the United States even could produce problems; average soils in Arkansas, for example, are far less fertile than average soils in Iowa and, therefore, yield prospects are lower even with the same weather. A continuation of the present cooling trend could therefore lead to disastrous results in world food production.

Technology. "Technology" primarily refers to the direct application of nitrogenous fertilizers; nitrogen is an extremely important factor in corn yields. The sharp increases in corn yields over the past 30 years directly paralleled the dramatic increase in fertilizer use, which began in the 1940s and accelerated rapidly during the 1960s.

Figure 7-3 depicting Illinois corn yields and the amount of fertilizer applications, shows the correlation very clearly. Spiralling world petroleum prices boosted fertilizer prices sharply during the 1970s. However, corn production has been generally quite profitable during that period and fertilizer use has continued to increase to record levels.

Technology also encompasses farm equipment. Farm machinery has improved substantially over the years and this too has benefited corn yields. Because corn planting takes far less time, adverse weather is less likely to delay planting. Also, harvesting can be accomplished more quickly and with reduced field losses.

Developments in research are also important. The development of hybrid seed varieties was an important factor in achieving much higher yields. No significant breakthroughs have been achieved in recent years, though. Research developments could become very important within 10 to 20 years because of the continued growth in world population. Currently, however, yields on experimental farms are still well above national average farm yields. Farm

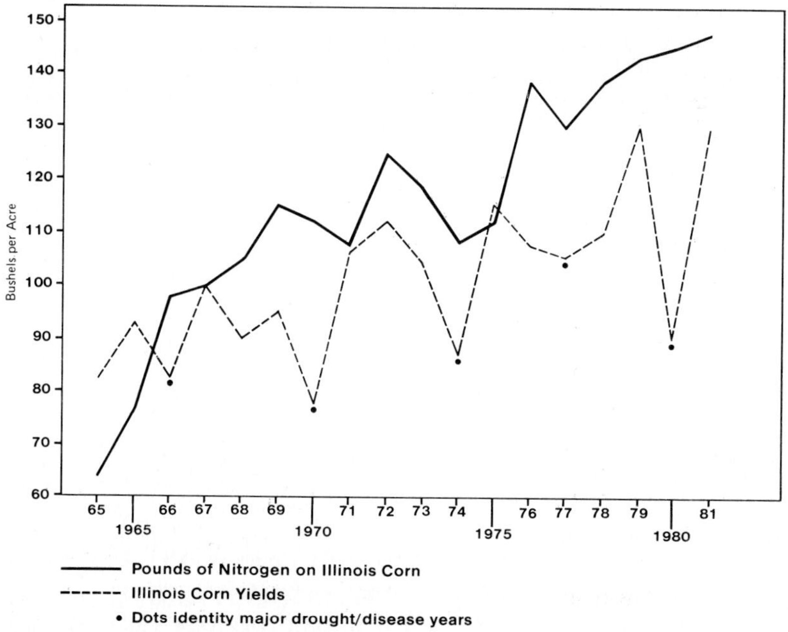

Figure 7-3 Illinois corn yields and fertilizer application. *(ContiCommodity Research Division)*

yields tend to rise towards the level achieved by experimental farms as the technology filters down and is absorbed by basic agriculture. National average yields should continue to rise during the short term.

Yield Trends. Average trend yield increases associated with normal weather formerly could be depicted in a straight linear equation. The decade of the 1960s was a period of highly favorable weather and very little year-to-year deviation in summer weather patterns; a rapid escalation in the amount of fertilizer used also occurred. But that trend changed in the 1970s and became more parabolic in nature, as depicted in Figure 7-4. The reasons for this are:

1. More marginal lands—those with poorer soils and a relatively lower productive capacity—were brought back into cultivation after 1974. (Government programs since 1933 had been devoted to retiring increasing amounts of acreage from production, especially from 1950 to 1970 when yields began to escalate and production increased despite the reduced acreage; this is outlined in Chapter 14.) The urbanization of suburban areas almost everywhere has resulted in paving over soils that are better-producing than some of the lands recently brought into cultivation; thus the more marginal lands include some which are even poorer in production capacity than the acreage that had been retired because of government programs (land reclamation projects in Idaho and other areas are good examples). The high prices that have prevailed during the last decade stimulated the cultivation of lands which never usually would be planted to anything except grass or forage crops.
2. The rate of increase in fertilizer applications has slowed compared to previous years; the sharp escalation in fertilizer prices and the idea that fertilizer use has reached optimum levels on much of the acreage is responsible. It is also uncertain, though, whether or not the former rate of increase in fertilizer use would provide similar results in yields; in other words, it is

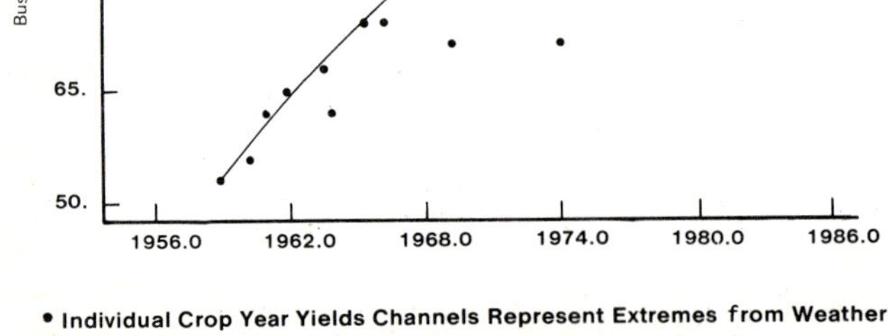

Figure 7-4 Average trend yields. *(ContiCommodity Research Division)*

not really known whether there is a maximum level of fertilizer use beyond which yields would not increase. However, increased applications of fertilizer on more marginal soils undoubtedly would increase yields on that acreage. The escalating price of fertilizer and the leveling off in fertilizer use is, therefore, an important factor in average trend yields.

3. The variability in weather patterns has been increasing, which means that highs and lows of extremes can be reached more frequently. This can result in the more median average of annual yields being achieved less frequently during the 1980s than previous experience would have indicated. Corn yields may fluctuate much more widely on an annual basis now. (We are in a "regime of extremes," according to meteorologists; a good example of this was the spring and summer of 1981—record low temperatures followed record high temperatures and vice versa within days of each other, and record rainfall followed a period of prolonged dryness.)

The average annual trend increase in corn yields presently appears to be around 1½ bushels per acre; formerly, with normal weather, it had approximated 3 bushels per acre per year. The sharp decline in planted acreage because of the 1983 farm program is expected to return average yields to a higher linear trend level. The removal of marginal lands from production leaves the best soils in production. An extension of the linear trend that existed in the 1960s would reach 128 bushels per acre by 1985.

Profitability. Profitability can be influenced by government programs in terms of both the amount of acreage planted and the prospective yields. When farming is very profitable, farmers tend to increase technological inputs in order to maximize yields. Corn also competes with soybeans for planted acreage in the Midwest. So when corn prices are more favorable than soybean prices, acreage planted to corn almost always increases relative to soybean acreage. Conversely, acreage planted to soybeans always increases when soybean prices are more profitable. (This does not necessarily mean that corn acreage will decrease; more acreage may be brought into production, especially in years of high prices. The above comments refer to relative shifts in acreage patterns.)

The relative profitability of corn and soybeans can be shown through the use of simple ratios. These are obtained by dividing the price of soybeans by the price of corn. A ratio of 2.35 to 1 generally is considered to be a break-even area. Table 7-3 shows that shifts of acreage out of soybeans into corn usually occur when soybean-to-corn ratios average below 2.2 to 1 during the winter preceding spring planting. (The aberration which occurred in 1975 was due to a large shift of cotton acreage into soybeans in the South; soybean acreage in the Midwest, however, did decline.)

Consumption

Domestic and export markets determine the demand for corn. U.S. corn exports have been increasing in importance but domestic disappearance still accounts for about two-thirds of total U.S. corn consumption.

TABLE 7-3 Percentage of Change in Acreage

Calendar year	JFM soybean-to-corn ratio*	Soybeans	Corn
1972	2.6	+ 8	−9½
1973	3.5	+21	+7½
1974	2.1	− 6	+8
1975	2.0	+ 2	+1
1976	1.8	− 8	+7½
1977	3.0	+17	0
1978	2.6	+ 9	−3
1979	3.0	+11	0
1980	2.2	− 2	+3
1981	2.1	− 3	0
1982	2.35	+ 6	−3

*The JFM ratio refers to the soybean-to-corn ratio prevailing during the January-to-March period *before* the planting of the crops in April and May.

Animal Feeding. Animal feeding comprises the largest component of domestic disappearance. Corn is relatively high in carbohydrates, which provide the basic energy value in feeding rations. Cattle account for the largest proportionate share of corn consumption; hogs, too, are an important corn-feeding group. Table 7-4 provides the amount of grain consumed by individual animal classes in recent years.

The proportionate share of feed use accounted for by specific animal groups varies according to the changes in animal populations, which fluctuate with the profitability of animal feeding. Dairy cattle numbers show very little change because milk prices are supported by specific government subsidies. But herd sizes of both cattle on feed (as differentiated from cattle on pasture) and hogs can fluctuate greatly in response to economic changes in feeding profitability. Poultry numbers have the most rapid turnaround time because of shorter breeding periods. Hog numbers tend to increase over time when favorable margins exist; periods of marked unprofitability spur sharp liquidation of hog

TABLE 7-4 Total Corn Fed Accounted for by Animal Class
(Percent)

Year	Hogs	Cattle on feed	Dairy	Poultry	All other
1974–75	32	20	19	19	10
1975–76	33	23.5	17	18	8.5
1976–77	36	20.5	17	19	7.5
1977–78	34	22.5	17	19	7.5
1978–79	37	19.5	15	19.5	9
1979–80	38	18.5	16	20	7.5
1980–81	36	17.5	17	22	7.5
1981–82	34	17	18	23	8

numbers. Table 7-5 shows the recent history of grain consuming animal numbers in the United States.

It is interesting to note that animal numbers in the United States only recently recovered to levels that had existed at the beginning of the 1970s. This is a direct contrast to the sharp expansion in animal numbers in the Soviet Union during the same time period. There may be some correlation between the decline in U.S. animal numbers and the rapid gain in U.S. corn exports as a proportionate share of total U.S. corn disappearance. The increase in the relative importance of exports puts more pressure on domestic feeding margins in the absence of excess crop production. Government programs which maintain high grain prices despite excess production help to achieve the same result. Consumer resistance in the United States increases as meat prices advance. Consumer disposable income has been cut during recent years because inflation has outpaced wage increases. Thus meat prices have not been able to maintain an increase proportionate with the rise in grain prices, a basic cost in livestock production. (The only way to return animal production to a profitable level if grain prices remain high is to reduce animal numbers, which eventually creates higher meat prices because of the reduction in supply.)

Feed use is not a figure which can be measured as precisely as exports. The amount officially listed as feed disappearance is not necessarily accurate, either. Feed use is simply a residual category derived from stocks reports. Food and industrial use are added to exports; their combined total disappearance then is subtracted from the corn stocks and the resulting residual amount is assumed to have been fed to animals. Large discrepancies can exist between calculated feed use and the residual figure in stock reports which subsequently becomes the amount officially approved for the feed-use category in U.S. Department of Agriculture Supply/Demand reports. These "shocks" can result in sharp price moves as the market adjusts to new data; (this is why grain stocks reports are some of the most important reports of the season). The residual category known as feed disappearance is used to "tidy up" supply-and-demand balance sheets.

Feed disappearance can vary quite sharply on an annual basis depending upon whether or not animal numbers are in a buildup or liquidation phase. Other domestic use, however (food, seed, and industrial use), has been steadily increasing (see Table 7-6). This aggregate component of demand had been relatively stable because the use of corn for food purposes formerly had increased at a fairly slow rate. But the escalating production of corn sweeteners as a sub-

TABLE 7-5 U.S. Grain-Consuming Animal Units
(Million head)

	1971	1972	1973	1974	1975	1976	1977	1978	1979	1980	1981
Cattle on feed	21.1	22.0	20.8	15.4	19.8	19.2	20.4	20.1	18.8	17.8	16.6
Hogs	21.7	20.5	20.0	17.6	17.5	19.4	21.1	21.5	23.8	22.2	20.4
Poultry	18.5	18.0	18.0	17.2	18.1	18.3	18.8	20.1	21.1	21.5	21.9
Others	18.9	18.8	19.7	19.6	19.6	19.0	18.8	18.4	18.6	18.9	18.9
Total	80.2	79.4	78.5	69.8	75.0	75.9	79.1	80.1	82.3	80.4	77.8

SOURCE: United States Department of Agriculture, ContiCommodity Research Division.

TABLE 7-6 Usage Balance Sheet for Corn*
(Million bushels)

	1962–69†		1973–74		1979–80		1981–82	
Item	Bushels	Percent of total	Bushels	Percent of total	Bushels	Percent of total	Bushels	Percent of total
Milling								
Food and industry	271.7	6.0	350.4	5.9	557.5	7.2	715.3	10.6
Alcoholic beverages	74.6	1.7	80.1	1.4	72.0	1.0	76.8	1.1
Total milling	346.3	7.7	430.5	7.3	629.5	8.2	792.1	11.7
Seed	12.3	0.3	17.7	0.3	20.1	0.3	19.4	0.3
Feed	3607.0	80.1	4204.8	71.3	4544.0	59.0	4079	59
Export	535.6	11.9	1243.1	21.1	2432.6	32.6	1980	28.8
Total usage	4501.2	100	5896.1	100	7453.1	100	6870	100

*Year beginning October 1.

†Average.

SOURCE: Feed Situation Reports, United States Department of Agriculture.

stitute for sugar has escalated the rate of increase in annual demand from the FSI (food, seed, and industry) component. Recently the use of corn for gasohol production also has accelerated the demand from this sector.

Corn Milling. The corn refining industry accounts for practically all of the demand listed as "food" use. Both "wet" milling and "dry" milling processes exist (these refer to the technological processes involved); "wet" milling plants far exceed "dry" milling operations.

Corn oil has been an important element in the manufacturing of margarine because of its low cholesterol content. The average annual increase in demand for corn by the food industry formerly had been relatively small. The escalating demand for corn sweeteners, produced by the conversion of the starch content of corn into sugar, changed that picture. The corn milling industry presently utilizes around 500 million bushels of corn annually; demand is increasing by 40 to 50 million bushels a year because production capacity is expanding and because the substitution of sugar with corn sweeteners is still well below maximum levels. The growth rate in production of corn sweeteners has been dramatic, as Figure 7-5 shows.

The demand for corn in the production of sweeteners accelerated after sugar prices spiraled to record high levels in the early 1970s. (Consumer resistance and a search for substitutes by industrial users always develops when the price of any commodity escalates sharply.) The large annual increase in world population and the limited growth in world production of centrifugal sugar indicate that substitutes for sugar will be demanded to the maximum extent possible for the foreseeable future. The U.S. cane and sugar beet industries lack the capacity to increase output substantially; part of this is due to the continued growth in the production of cheaper sweeteners derived from corn. Increased use of high-fructose corn syrup continues to reduce both consumption of sugar by industrial users and overall per capita consumption of sugar.

The soft drink industry has accounted for a large portion of the increase in demand for corn sweeteners. Corn sweeteners can be used in any product which utilizes sweeteners. The present breakdown of various corn sweetener derivatives by shipments is listed in Table 7-7.

Presently the capacity to produce corn sweeteners is lower than demand for the product. The maximum level of substitution of sugar by corn sweeteners in the soft drink industry approximates 50 percent. Thus the present level of production is well below the potential demand, despite the continued expansion in output. The profitability of sweetener production should lead to increased plant capacity.

Gasohol. Gasohol is a mixture of 10 percent ethanol and 90 percent unleaded gasoline. Ethanol is an alcohol which can be produced from a variety of plant materials (termed "biomass"). Grain is usually the material distilled to produce ethanol. One bushel of corn produces 2.6 gallons of ethanol. Corn currently composes around 84 percent of the biomass used to produce ethanol. Ethanol production takes the conversion process used to produce sweeteners one step further; the starch is turned into sugar, which is then fermented to produce alcohol. Ethanol production in 1980 approximated 150 million gallons. The near-term goal of the Carter administration was to increase ethanol production to close to 1 billion gallons by 1982 (almost seven times higher than 1980 production) and to 4 billion gallons by 1985. The long-term goal of 10 billion gallons of ethanol production was targeted for the 1990s. But gasohol production is not feasible without direct government subsidies. The Carter administration provided a special 20 percent investment tax credit for alcohol fuel plants, direct tax breaks equal to around $1.04/bushel corn price, a 4¢ excise tax exemption, and 1.4 billion dollars of loans and loan guarantees for gasohol projects. Most states also offer additional incentives; these usually involve state sales-tax exemptions.

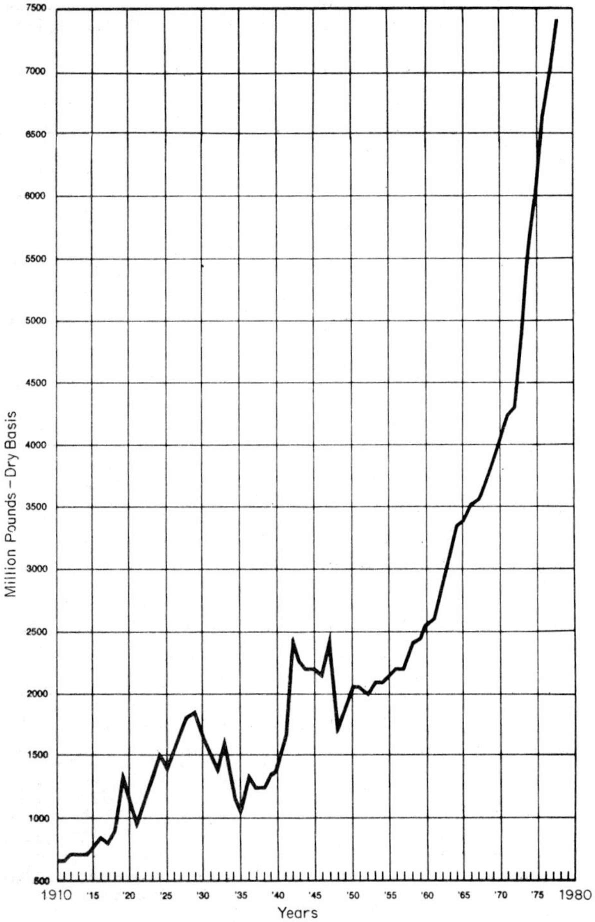

Figure 7-5 Corn sweetener shipments. *(United States Department of Agriculture and Saul Kolodny, "Economic Factors Affecting Future Sweetener Consumption," American Chemical Society Centennial Meeting, Sweetener Symposium, April 1976)*

TABLE 7-7 Corn Sweetener Use*
(Million tons)

	1980	1981
High fructose content (HFC)	2.1	2.5
Glucose	2.05	2.1
Dextrose	.42	.45

*Calendar years.

The rationale offered to the taxpayers was that the United States could cut its dependence on foreign oil and thereby decrease expenditures for imported oil. However, the idea of using food to produce fuel is coming under increasing attack.

Production of 10 billion gallons of ethanol would require 100 million tons of corn based on the current breakdown of biomass substances used for gasohol production. That amount of corn is equivalent to one-half of the record 1979 crop and over 60 percent of the 1980 crop. The near-term goal of 2 to 3 billion gallons of ethanol would require 1 billion bushels of corn; that approximates 15 percent of current corn production and is around ten times more than current demand from the gasohol industry.

Gasohol production at those projected levels could have an adverse impact upon U.S. corn exports; U.S. export revenues could decline sharply. The increased demand also would require higher livestock prices in order to maintain profitable feeding margins. Land could be switched from other crops in order to increase corn supplies, but that would cause economic disruption in other markets. For example, a sharp reduction in soybean acreage would upset both the U.S. and world fats and oils markets.

The gasohol program should be watched closely because, if the program is continued, it is potentially highly inflationary for prices in future years.

Exports. Corn exports have increased sharply as a percentage of total disappearance. Table 7-8 shows that corn exports have more than doubled their proportionate share of total disappearance during the past 10 years. This can be mainly attributed to the sharp increases in imports by Communist bloc countries, particularly the Soviet Union. In fact, the combined increase in U.S. corn shipments to the Soviet Union, Eastern Europe, and the People's Republic of China equals the total increase in U.S. corn exports from the mid-1970s to the 1978–1979 crop year.

Soviet grain imports have grown steadily in response to the government's commitment to expand herds and flocks. The expansion in animal numbers has resulted in a huge increase in feed requirements that can be met only through expanded imports. Over 50 percent of total Soviet grain supplies, including imports, are used for feeding purposes.

The complete turnaround that has occurred in the Soviet grain situation cannot be overemphasized. The Soviet Union formerly was a net exporter of grains. There was almost a net zero balance between Soviet exports and imports even as recently as 1974. Previously, increases in Soviet grain produc-

TABLE 7-8 Corn Exports as a Percent of Total U.S. Corn Disappearance

Year	Percent
1969	12.7
1970	11.4
1971	15.3
1972	20.9
1973	21.1
1974	24.0
1975	29.5
1976	29.1
1977	31.3
1978	30.8
1979	32.6
1980	32.6
1981	28.6

SOURCE: ContiCommodity Research Division.

tion had been able to keep pace with the expansion in animal numbers, except in disaster years. But a subtle shift has been occurring over time when correlated with livestock production goals. It has reached the point where high annual grain imports will be necessary even in years of good Soviet grain production if their livestock goals are maintained.

The EEC formerly had been the largest corn customer of the United States. The Netherlands alone was one of the largest individual customers. However, recent changes in world trade patterns and the trade barriers represented by the EEC levy system have combined to reduce their share of U.S. corn exports (see Table 7-9). Japan, individually, currently imports more U.S. corn than the total EEC bloc. The combined U.S. corn exports to the Eastern bloc, including the Soviet Union now surpass those to the EEC, too.

WORLD PRODUCTION AND CONSUMPTION

General Trends

Corn accounted for over 70 percent of all coarse grains (including barley, sorghum, oats, rye, millet, and mixed grains) traded on international markets in 1975; barley and sorghum accounted for 16 percent and 12 percent, respectively. In 1960, corn made up only half of total coarse grain imports. Because it is the leading world exporter of other coarse grains as well, the United States dominates the market in total world exports of all feed grains (see Figure 7-6).

The United States currently accounts for around 80 percent of total world corn exports (see Table 7-10). Corn's percentage of total world coarse-grain exports has also steadily increased. These trends are due to the United States' large productive capacity for corn, compared to other countries.

The United States has been able to increase its share of total corn exports because most other major competitors in the world coarse-grain market lack

TABLE 7-9 U.S. CornExports by Country of Destination
(Million bushels, selected years and countries)

Destinations	1967–68	1971–72	1976–77	1978–79	1979–80	1981–82
Bel-Lux and France	22	15	95	83	77	78
West Germany and Denmark	54	56	214	59	70	46
Netherlands	120	103	184	90	84	56
Italy	79	91	94	74	106	26
United Kingdom and Ireland	65	55	118	80	73	43
Greece	8	7	37	48	44	29
Total EEC	348	327	742	434	455	278
Spain	33	38	80	112	157	226
Portugal	NA	18	64	74	99	87
Total other Western Europe	33	56	150	191	216	325
Bulgaria	—	—	—	9	20	32
Czechoslovakia	2	3	14	21	29	14
East Germany	9	12	11	39	110	61
Poland	—	11	46	59	101	16
Romania	—	7	5	40	41	17
Yugoslavia	—	16	—	42	1	15
Total Eastern Europe*	11	49	78	210	302	445
Soviet Union	0	136	124	422	197	301
Total Eastern Bloc†	11	185	202	632	499	446
China	0	—	—	108	70	44
Japan	102	111	301	353	441	417
Taiwan	—	9	46	85	84	68
Korea	—	17	49	105	84	106
Mexico	0	—	57	25	152	22
Brazil	0	—	—	50	68	0
Total above	102	137	453	726	899	657
Other	69	81	137	150	319	123
Total U.S. corn exports	613	786	1684	2133	2433	1980

*Excluding the Soviet Union.

†Including Eastern Europe.

the ability to increase planted acreages and/or suffer from infrastructural deficiencies. South Africa, France, Thailand, and Australia, for example, lack additional open areas suitable for growing corn. Argentina and Canada suffer from limitations on their marketing systems and transportations structures (in contrast, the "relatively free" U.S. system was able to respond more directly to the changes which occurred during the 1970s).

The decline in some countries in the proportionate share of total world exports (as shown in Table 7-11) does not imply reduced production. But acreage and technology in those areas are limited. Corn production in Thailand, for example, is relatively stable. Future increases in corn production in Thailand would require an escalation in fertilizer use to increase yields because the prospects of further land expansion are limited. The burgeoning growth in world demand for feed grains did, however, unleash the productive capacity of the United States.

In many parts of the world acreage is planted to coarse grains other than corn primarily for climatic reasons. The Soviet Union is a good example of this; it is the largest world producer of barley yet it also is one of the leading importers of corn (most countries which grow barley do so for domestic feeding purposes rather than for export purposes).

The world's leading corn producers are shown in Table 7-12.

Most countries grow corn only for domestic consumption. Even the People's Republic of China, Brazil, and Romania, which are the next three largest producers of corn following the United States, are not major exporters of corn; indeed, they have had to import corn from time to time. In fact, an interesting development in recent years has been the increasing trend of corn imports by most of the producing countries listed above.

The leading importers of corn are shown in Table 7-13, along with their individual rankings according to their proportionate share of total world corn imports. Those rankings fluctuate annually; Table 7-14, however, clearly por-

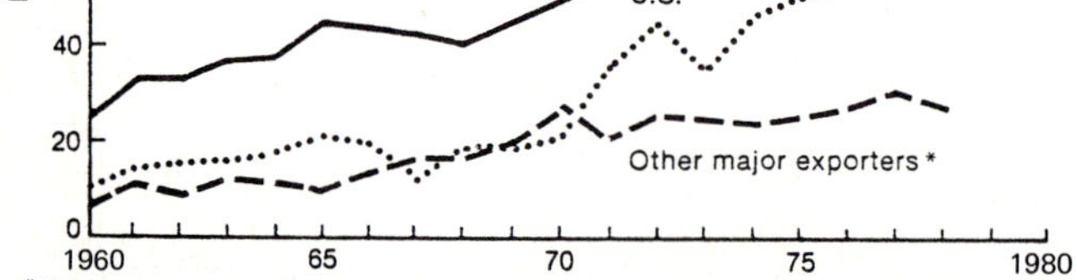

* Other major exporters include Argentina, South Africa, Thailand, Canada, France, and Australia. July-June years.

Figure 7-6 World coarse grain exports. *(United States Department of Agriculture)*

TABLE 7-10 Volume Share of Total World Corn Exports by Selected Exporters to Selected Destinations *(Percentage amounts)*

Destinations	United States	Argentina	South Africa	Thailand	France	Netherlands	Bel-Lux
Canada	100						
Mexico	100						
Total Caribbean	78	22					
Total North America	97	3					
Brazil	100						
Chile	64	36					
Peru	100						
Total South America	94	6					
Bel-Lux	73	1			25	2	
West Germany	60	1.5			20	17	1.5
Italy	72	22	3		3		
Netherlands	58	1.5	0.5		23		17
United Kingdom	67	1	5		24	1	2
Total EEC	63	5	2		19	4	7
Greece	100						
Portugal	100						
Spain	90	10					
Total other Western Europe	95	5					
Total Eastern Europe	100						
Soviet Union	80	20					
China	100						
Taiwan	86						
Japan	89		8	2			
Korea	100						
Total Asia	85		7	8			
Total Africa	85	4	2.5	6	2.5		
Total Oceania	100						
Unidentified	5	10	85				
Total world	82	5	3.5	2.5	4.5	1	1.5

TABLE 7-11 Percentage of Total World Corn Exports by Leading Exporters*
(July–June, selected years)

World crop year	United States	Argentina	South Africa	Thailand	Others
1960	50	15	8	4	23
1971	50	14	8	6	22
1972	69	6.5	7.5	2.5	14.5
1973	67.5	10	1	4	17.5
1974	59	12	7	4	18
1975	70	4.5	2.5	4	19
1976	71	7.5	4.5	3.5	14.5
1977	72.5	9.5	4.5	2	11.5
1978	74	9.5	4	3	9.5
1979	82	5	3	3	7
1982	82	7.5	5	3.5	2

*Figures rounded to the neartest ½.

trays the declining trend in corn imports by EEC countries and the increasing trend elsewhere.

Japan is one of the major importers of corn because of the sharp escalation in its meat production to improve diets. This coincides with the economic boom which Japan has enjoyed. Japanese feed grain production is insignificant. Rice is principally used for human consumption. However, recent policy measures to encourage the use of rice for feeding purposes could affect the future rate of growth in Japanese feed grain imports because Japan often has a surplus of rice.

Eastern Europe had been a growing market for corn in recent years because former government policies had emphasized development in the livestock sector. Also, with the exception of Yugoslavia, those countries subsidize consumer food prices, particularly meat. Food prices in Eastern Europe are held at levels well below the actual cost of production. Rising livestock numbers and stagnation in crop developments led to a necessity for increased feed grain imports. The future market potential in Eastern Europe is uncertain, however, for various reasons:

1. Present policies emphasize faster growth in the crops sector in order to change the present imbalance between production and demand; the present attempts to increase crop production could affect future imports.
2. There is evidence that suggests part of the "explosion" in feed grain imports by Eastern Europe may have been in response to the U.S. embargo on grain shipments to the Soviet Union. There was no embargo against Eastern Europe; therefore, grain could be imported by East European countries and transhipped to the Soviet Union. Thus recent grain imports by Eastern Europe may not have been an accurate indicator of true demand from that area. Indeed, imports slipped dramatically by 1982.
3. The sharply increasing debt structure has limited the ability of many countries in Eastern Europe to pay for needed grain. (One of the largest importers in Eastern Europe, Poland, is in serious financial difficulties and even

TABLE 7-12 Leading World Corn Producers
(Million bushels)

	1975	1976	1977	1978	1979	1980
United States	5841 (1)	6289 (1)	6505 (1)	7268 (1)	7939 (1)	6648 (1)
People's Republic of China	1401 (2)	1889 (2)	1948 (2)	2200 (2)	2362 (2)	2244 (2)
Brazil	704 (3)	740 (3)	535 (3)	641 (3)	795 (3)	901 (3)
Romania	364 (4)	455 (4)	397 (5)	401 (4)	490 (4)	393 (6)
South Africa	287 (6)	381 (6)	401 (5)	326 (7)	417 (5)	433 (5)
France	322 (5)	220 (10)	334 (7)	374 (5)	409 (5)	374 (7)
Mexico	366 (4)	377 (6)	381 (6)	401 (4)	362 (7)	393 (6)
Soviet Union	288 (6)	400 (5)	432 (4)	352 (6)	330 (8)	307(9)
Yugoslavia	370 (4)	358 (7)	388 (6)	298 (8)	393 (6)	358 (8)
Argentina	230 (7)	326 (8)	381 (6)	354 (6)	251 (10)	503 (4)
Hungary	279 (6)	202 (11)	233 (9)	262 (9)	291 (9)	244 (10)
Italy	209 (8)	205 (11)	252 (8)	244 (10)	244 (10)	252 (10)
India	285 (6)	250 (9)	233 (9)	244 (10)	219 (11)	236 (11)

*Figures in parentheses indicate the ranking in corn production for each individual country in that particular year. Equal rankings are given when production of a country does not vary by more than 10 million bushels from that of other countries. The combined production of the countries listed normally accounts for around 80 percent of total world corn production.

TABLE 7-13 Main World Corn Importers*
(Million bushels)

	1975	1976	1977	1978	1979	1980	1982†
Japan	310 (2)	349 (1)	382 (2)	430 (1)	467 (2)	547 (1)	570 (1)
Soviet Union	484 (1)	197 (2)	427 (1)	378 (2)	573 (1)	441 (2)	325 (3)
Spain	126 (6)	147 (6)	181 (3)	169 (3)	174 (3)	177 (3)	170 [5]
Netherlands	173 (3)	208 (3)	142 (4)	126 (6)	145 (4)	122 (6)	56
Italy	171 (4)	175 (4)	114 (7)	165 (4)	134 (5)	153 (5)	46
Mexico	57	51	67	52	108 (7)	173 (4)	256 [4]
United Kingdom	130 (5)	166 (5)	141 (5)	128 (5)	114 (6)	102	33
Taiwan	71	71	83	103	96	102	110 [7]
South Korea	39	55	71	114 (7)	90	106	158 [6]
West Germany	117 (7)	145 (7)	117 (6)	105	97	96	39
Portugal	47	63	71	77	95	103	105
Bel-Lux	63	106	83	98	102	94	68
East Germany	70	92	51	48	102	79	50
Poland	67	49	71	67	107	107 (7)	18
People's Republic of China	—	—	—	118	77	59	85
Percent of total world corn by the above countries	88	84	82	81	81	81	81

*The numbers in parentheses indicate the ranking of the top seven corn importers for each year.

†Estimated.

TABLE 7-14 Volume Share of World Corn Imports

	Total Western Europe	(EEC only)	Japan	Soviet Union	Asia excluding Japan	Eastern Europe	Latin America	Africa
1960	67.9	(60.2)	12.9	1.0	2.9	4.3	1.4	0.7
1962	67.1	(57.7)	12.3	.0	4.3	4.7	2.3	1.5
1965	68.4	(55.5)	10.5	.1	1.6	4.3	1.0	2.8
1966	70.9	(57.9)	14.8	.7	2.5	2.6	1.0	1.8
1970	60.7	(50.7)	17.4	.9	4.8	5.2	4.1	1.4
1973	47.5	(35.8)	15.7	9.2	9.1	3.7	5.2	2.1
1975	40.1	(30.1)	13.9	21.7	6.6	8.5	4.0	2.1
1976	50.2	(38.9)	15.3	8.6	7.5	8.4	4.6	2.1
1977	39.8	(26.8)	16.0	17.8	8.3	7.1	5.2	2.4
1978	35.9	(24.5)	16.1	14.1	14.3	7.6	6.3	2.4
1979	31.0	(21.0)	14.8	18.7	10.8	11.7	7.2	2.7
1982*	21.5	(10.0)	23.2	9.1	14.2	3.0	15.0	4.2

*Preliminary

SOURCE: Foreign Agricultural Service, United States Department of Agriculture.

lacks the ability to pay for shipments already received.) There also are concerted efforts by some countries to reduce financial credit dependency upon the West.

All of the above suggests that grain imports by Eastern Europe will develop a more negative growth trend.

One factor could alter that assessment: future developments in the Soviet Union. If the gaps between Soviet grain production and the requirements to feed escalating livestock numbers continue to widen and surpass Soviet port capacity, then Eastern Europe may serve to help alleviate the logistical burden through transhipments of grain.

Argentina

Argentina is the second leading exporter of corn following the United States.

Argentine corn production normally approximates the level of many other countries which do not export any corn; it usually produces the same as or less than many countries which actually *import* significant amounts of corn. The reason Argentina accounts for such a high proportionate share of world corn exports is because coarse grains are not utilized significantly for feeding purposes in Argentina, even though it is one of the world's largest beef producers. Traditionally, cattle in Argentina have been raised on pasture because of the philosophy that "grass is cheaper." Feedlot operations are virtually unknown there.

There always has been speculation that the situation will change. Large tracts of land exist which could be converted to grain production if even a relatively small percentage of cattle were removed from pasture and raised in feedlots. Certain factors are likely to prevent the removal of cattle from pasture for grain production; for one thing, the taste preferences of Argentine consumers favor present beef-production methods. Argentine beef has a very distinctive flavor; in contrast, cattle raised in feedlots have a much blander flavor. (The difference is similar in nature to the "gamey" flavor of hunted animals.) The farm structure in Argentina also limits the ability to change.

The tenure system in the Argentine farm structure is very restrictive to structural changes. Early colonial and national land policies in Argentina produced a land tenure system dominated by large land holdings; it is very restrictive to structural changes. Hired labor is common, with relatively few tenant or sharecropping agreements such as those which exist in the United States. (Workers who share in profits according to productivity produce better results than those simply paid wages). Absentee landowners (many of whom reside overseas) are a major impediment, reducing the incentive to increase productivity in Argentina. Ownership of large tracts of land traditionally has been a "prestige" symbol in Argentina. This is quite different from the concept of owning land to "do" something with it; for example, the U.S. farmer buys more land not to let it lie idle, but rather to increase grain production. Approximately 5 percent of the landowners in Argentina hold almost 75 percent of total private agricultural land.

The pampa region is the heart of Argentine agriculture; a map of this area superimposed on a map of the United States, would overlap a west-to-east band through southern Arkansas and central Alabama. Around two-thirds of the pampa region is under natural, temporary, or permanent pasture. About 20 percent of the pampa land area is devoted to cereals; that, however, can understate the predominance of cattle production because barley, oats, and rye often are grown for grazing purposes. The pampa land area accounts for 99 percent of Argentina's total wheat production, 90 percent of corn production, and 95 percent of sorghum production. The primary grain-production areas fan out about 400 miles to the northwest, west, and southwest of the city of Buenos Aires.

Grain yields in Argentina are comparatively low and have increased rather slowly. The low yields are usually blamed on the highly variable weather conditions. Weather is an important factor and can fluctuate widely from year to year and from region to region. Argentine yields are influenced greatly by the following weather factors: (1) rainfall varies significantly throughout the area; (2) moisture also varies widely from month-to-month; (3) damp years produce abundant weed growth (milk thistle and musk thistle can be a big problem); and (4) insect damage is often high.

Low fertilizer use, however, is the main contributing factor to the relatively low yields in Argentina. Argentine corn farmers use little or no fertilizer; time-honored cultural practices are slow to change. Fertilizer applications to grain acreage in Argentina are substantially lower than the average rate in South America—and the average rate of fertilizer use in South America itself is less than 25 percent of the rate of fertilizer use in North America, by comparison. Fertilizer use in Argentina is also unlikely to increase much because costs are comparatively high.

Argentina lacks grain storage capacity; the shortage is estimated to be around 15 million tonnes. Both on-farm storage capacity and country elevator storage capacity are limited (country elevators as known in the United States are a rarity in Argentina). Farmers in Argentina also want to acquire immediate cash from harvest production. This all combines to produce a rapid flow of supplies into export channels at harvest. (A comparison of price quotations in Rotterdam shows that Argentine prices have fluctuated widely relative to U.S. prices during the periods immediately preceding and immediately following the grain harvests in Argentina.)

Seventy percent of all grain moves by trucks; this slows down the average rate of grain flow and causes logistical snarls. Three different railroad gauges exist; transferring grain from one gauge to another increases handling costs. Port congestion can become very severe, especially in years of large harvests. The depths at all ports limit the ability to receive large ocean vessels. The Plate River is relatively shallow; the river depths also fluctuate according to the seasonal changes in rainfall, reducing draft depths at Buenos Aires during the season of minimum rainfall. Boats which load at upriver ports cannot be loaded completely because of the restrictive draft depths; they must "top off" (complete loading) in Buenos Aires. The largest ports, ranked in order according to size of elevator capacity, are Rosario, Buenos Aires, Bahia Blanca, Neocochea, and Santa Fe. Rosario leads in corn exports, followed closely by Buenos Aires.

Soviet Union

The lack of geoclimatic conditions similar to those existing in the U.S. corn belt places severe limitations on corn production in the Soviet Union. Climatic conditions are analogous to Canada. Temperatures in the Soviet Union generally are too cool and rainfall generally is too erratic and inadequate for optimum corn development (see Figures 7-7 and 7-8).

Much of the corn sown in northern areas of the Soviet Union fails to mature and is harvested for silage or for green fodder; less than 20 percent of the acreage planted in the Soviet Union actually produces fully matured grain. Most corn acreage is located in the Ukraine; the Donets Dnepr region in the southern Ukraine is the largest-producing region of corn for grain.

Extreme weather swings exist in the Soviet Union. Very distinctive biannual weather cycles can be noted: "good" years and "bad" years alternate with high regularity (see Table 7-15). Poor production years are often caused by the infa-

Figure 7-7 Zone of agriculture in the Soviet Union. *(ContiCommodity Research Division)*

mous *sukhovei* winds. Those winds combine hot temperatures with very low relative humidities and can dessicate crops quickly.

Corn yields are low by U.S. standards. Most of the corn acreage in the Soviet Union is fertilized; plans exist to increase the amount of fertilizer allocations to corn. However, a slowdown in the rate of growth in fertilizer production has been a limiting factor. About 15 percent of Soviet corn production is from irrigated land. But Soviet farms use irrigation mainly as a preventive measure against drought rather than as a method to increase yields. Irrigated corn yields in the Soviet Union are only one-third higher than the average yield for all corn production. (In contrast, grain yields on irrigated lands in the United States produce yields far above dryland yields in the same area; different farming practices are responsible.) Corn production accounts for only 5 percent of total Soviet grain production.

The Soviet Union reports crop production on a bunker weight basis (U.S. crop reports, in contrast, project a net usable crop). Excess moisture prior to drying and even high weed content and other admixtures are counted in Soviet crop reports; Soviet crop reports also exclude the normal losses which occur from postharvest handling. No production reports have been issued since 1980.

Corn imports represent a large part of total Soviet grain imports. The Soviet appetite for grains has increased at a dramatic rate over recent years, as Table 7-16 illustrates. Climatic conditions limit the ability of grain production to keep pace with the increased livestock numbers in the Soviet Union. The amount of grain fed to animals in the Soviet Union has increased by around 70 million

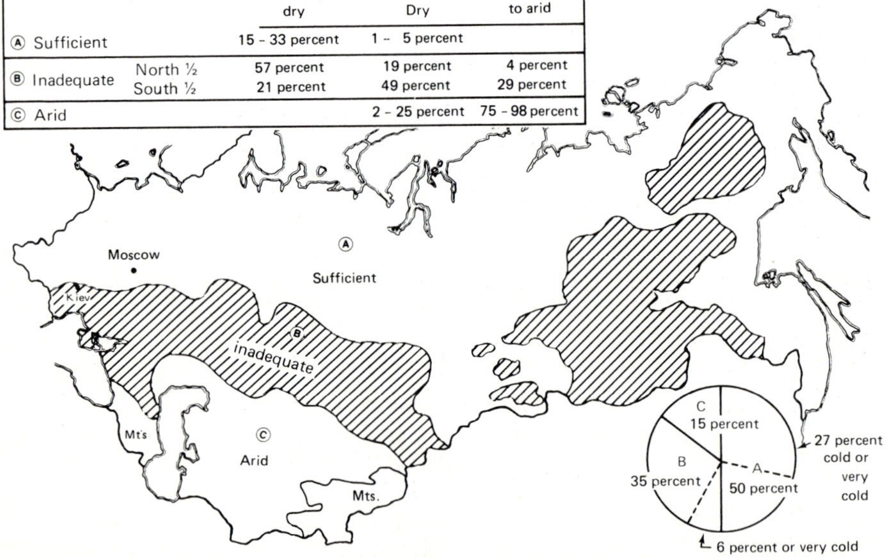

		Probability that any year will be:		
		Moderately dry	Dry	Semiarid to arid
Ⓐ Sufficient		15 - 33 percent	1 - 5 percent	
Ⓑ Inadequate	North ½	57 percent	19 percent	4 percent
	South ½	21 percent	49 percent	29 percent
Ⓒ Arid			2 - 25 percent	75 - 98 percent

Figure 7-8 Moisture supply in the Soviet Union. *(ContiCommodity Research Division)*

TABLE 7-15 Soviet Corn Acreage, Yield and Production ***(Million acres, bushels per acre, and million bushels)***

	Area	Yield	Production
1966–70 average	8.7	43.3	376
1971	8.2	41.0	338
1972	9.9	38.8	387
1973	9.9	52.2	520
1974	9.8	48.5	476
1975	6.5	43.6	288
1976	8.1	48.7	399
1977	8.3	51.9	432
1978	6.3	56.5	354
1979	6.5	50.0	333
1980	7.4	52.0	384

SOURCE: Foreign Agricultural Service.

tons over the past 20 years; this amounts to almost 3 billion bushels on a corn-equivalent basis and constitutes the largest increase in grain feeding in the world during that time period. There appears to be no reversal in this trend because established government policies committed to upgrading consumer diets by rapidly increasing herds and flocks have been unwavering since the late 1960s.

The Soviet Union has done everything possible to maintain animal numbers despite severe reductions in crop production in both 1979 and 1980 and the U.S. embargo; this proves that the commitment to increase meat production is very strong. The Soviet Union formerly would decrease livestock numbers in years of disastrous crop losses. However, liquidation of animal numbers reduces the size of the base upon which future increases can be built. The maintenance of herd sizes allows a more rapid increase in animal numbers to occur when feed supplies allow it. Meat prices in the Soviet Union are heavily subsidized; retail meat prices virtually have been held constant since the early 1960s. But wage increases continually have been larger than planned goals. This combination produces a high demand for meat because the production of other consumer items has not kept pace with the growth in consumer incomes. Thus the gap between meat supplies and consumer demand continues to widen despite the increase in meat supplies that has occurred over the past 15 years.

Soviet-planned livestock-production goals for 1985 would require total grain production of 266 to 276 million tonnes, depending on the level of dockage that should be applied in that particular year. That represents crop production 30 to 40 million tonnes higher than the record crop to date. Average annual Soviet grain production during the past 5 years only averaged 191 million tonnes because of poor growing weather. The ambitious goals to increase meat production underline the Soviet Union's addition to world demand. Simply stated, the gap between feed energy requirements and the availabilities from domestic production is widening, despite increased average annual production over time.

TABLE 7-16 Soviet Union Coarse Grain Imports by Source*
(Million tonnes)

	1972–73	1973–74	1974–75	1975–76	1976–77	1977–78	1978–79	1979–80	1980–81
United States	4.2	5.2	1.3	9.9	4.5	9.2	8.3	11.3	5.0
Argentina	0.1	0.3	1.1	0.2	0.2	1.6	1.4	3.1	8.3
Canada	0.9	0.2	—	1.3	0.2	0.2	0.1	1.3	1.8
Australia	—	—	0.1	0.8	0.1	—	—	1.3	0.4
EEC	1.2	0.5	0.1	0.5	0.2	0.2	0.2	0.2	1.0
Others	0.5	0.2	0.1	2.6	0.3	0.6	—	1.2	0.6
Total	6.9	6.4	2.7	15.6	5.7	11.7	10.0	18.3	17.1

*July–June crop year. Totals may not add because of rounding. Rice and pulses excluded.

SOURCE: Foreign Agricultural Service.

People's Republic of China

The People's Republic of China is the world's second largest producer of corn. Corn production has more than doubled over the past 20 years, primarily because of increased acreage; yield increases have been relatively moderate. Open-pollinated corn varieties are quite common in China, similar to the varieties used in U.S. farming technology prior to the development of more prolific corn hybrids. Corn production formerly was limited to the northeast and east central areas of China; however, it now is grown more extensively in southern

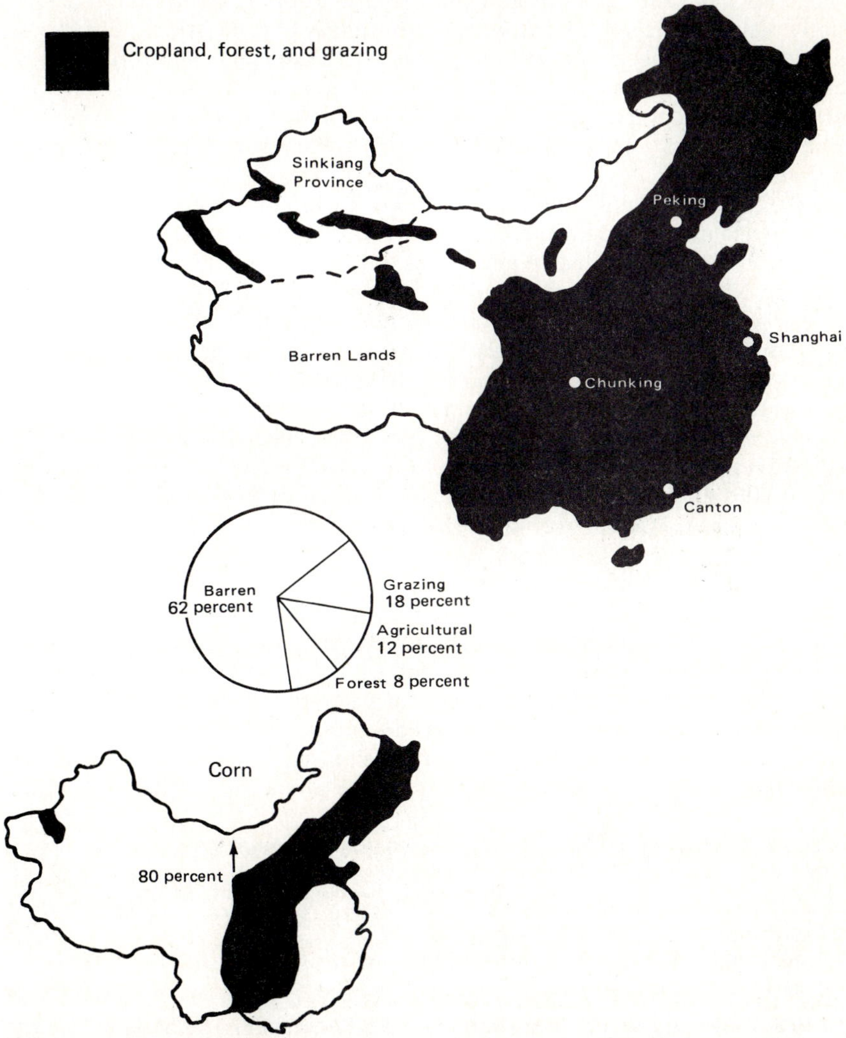

Figure 7-9 Corn-producing areas in the People's Republic of China. *(ContiCommodity Research Division)*

areas, also. Approximately 80 percent of corn production in China occurs in the belt north and east of the arrow drawn in Figure 7-9.

The cultivated land in China is lower than that in the United States, despite the fact that the total Chinese land area is larger than that of the United States (see Table 7-17). China has very little additional acreage which could be cultivated because around 88 percent of its land consists largely of forests, deserts, mountains, wastelands, and urban centers. However, the percentage of sown (planted) land to cultivated (prepared) land is higher than in the United States or any other country. The Chinese multiple-cropping practices result in a higher acreage sown to grains than the cultivated area could provide; the difference between multiple-cropping and single-cropping on the same acreage usually results in a seeded acreage to grains that is 40 to 45 percent higher than the cultivated acreage could provide. Table 7-18 shows an example of multiple-cropping in the Nanking province. Transplanting by hand often is used to facilitate multiple-cropping. (Intercropping also is used to intensify land uses in China—two crops—corn and soybeams or soybeans and millet are grown together.)

China depends heavily on monsoon rains during the summer. Chinese soils generally are not considered to be very favorable; nitrogen deficiency is common. Chinese soils are rated 30 percent fertile, 40 percent ordinary, and 30 percent poor. Most of the undeveloped land in China is considered to be nonarable. The ratio of arable land in China relative to population is well below that in the United States, but China has to feed a population over four times larger than in the United States—and increasing rapidly.

Yields in China are well below the levels achieved in the United States. Differences in the utilization of chemical fertilizers, insecticides, seed varieties, and mechanization account for much of the discrepancies in yields. The average annual output of grain per farm worker in China approximates only 1000 kilograms—as opposed to over 50,000 kilograms per farm worker in the United States.

Organic fertilizers historically have been the source of nutrients for crops in China—both animal and human wastes plus vegetative material have provided the largest portion. China recently began to increase the utilization of chemical fertilizers and has become the world's largest importer of nitrogen fertilizers. Thirteen large "turn-key" fertilizer plants were purchased from the West in the mid-1970s to boost domestic fertilizer production.

Corn consumption patterns in China differ greatly from western patterns. Corn is used mainly for human consumption in China, rather than as a source

TABLE 7-17 Land Area: United States and People's Republic of China*

	United States	People's Republic of China
Total land mass	1900	2404
Cultivated land	386	270
Sown area	287	377

*In million acres; excludes crop land used only for pasture, which does not fit Chinese definition of cultivated land.

SOURCE: United States Department of Agriculture.

TABLE 7-18 Example of Multiple Cropping in the Nanking Area

Crop	Plant	Harvest	Yield*
Rice	May	July	4,500
Rice	July	October	3,750
Wheat	October	May	2,350
Total			10,600

*Current estimates, kilograms per hectare.

of animal food; for example, about 70 percent of China's grain output goes to human consumption as opposed to around 25 percent in the United States. Livestock products account for only 15 percent of the protein intake in China, but account for 70 percent in the United States. Cattle are used primarily for draft purposes as opposed to raising them for meat and dairy purposes; cow-calf operations are virtually unknown in China.

China recently has shown an interest in developing modern large-scale hog-raising and processing plant operations. This could lead to a drastic change in corn consumption patterns. The plans to improve food availability in the major northeastern industrial centers could increase corn imports. Corn imports began in the early 1970s; they have been contained at relatively low annual average levels. China's search for new seed varieties from western sources implies that it may try to accommodate increased demand through domestic production. However, the accelerated increases in population may thwart that intention; China is considered to be almost self-sufficient in food production—but it requires severe food-rationing measures. China's per capita consumption of fats and oils and protein is exceptionally low compared to western standards.

The race between the growth in food production and the growth in population continues to be the crucial element in China, since its population continues to expand at a prodigious rate.

Western Europe

Western Europe is a major world importer of corn, despite sharp increases in production of coarse grains during the past 20 years. Most of the increase in corn production has been due to increased yields; France is the only country in Western Europe where corn acreage has increased appreciably. France, Spain, and Italy combined account for 85 percent of total Western European corn production. France alone produces about half of total Western European output; it is the only Western European country that has become self-sufficient. Around 80 percent of French corn moves directly off the producing farms; this is in direct contrast with other Western European countries, where corn generally is consumed on the farm where it is grown. France accounts for the vast bulk of the intra-EEC corn trade.

Corn accounts for the largest share of total grain imports by Western Europe. Western Europe's corn imports rose sharply into the 1970s, but have declined since then. Western Europe's share of total world corn imports has declined markedly over the past 15 years (as depicted in Table 7-14). This has resulted from the more rapid increase in corn imports in other world areas and also from the effects of the Common Agricultural Policy (CAP) which was adopted by the Common Market (EEC) countries in 1967.

The EEC guarantees a very high price for domestic grain production through a complex maze of subsidies. Domestic grain prices in the EEC are maintained well above world market prices. The basic minimum support price is called the intervention price. Government agencies normally are required to buy all grains grown in the EEC which are offered to them at the intervention prices. Intervention prices are increased monthly to provide a subsidy to cover producers' storage and interest costs and to encourage them not to market all of their crop at harvest.

Import taxes are imposed on grain imports to insulate domestic prices from the effects of world grain prices. This tax is called a levy. The levy is calculated daily on the basis of the lowest Cost Insurance Freight (CIF) price at Rotterdam. This price is then compared against the threshold price, which is the minimum import price allowable. The threshold price is derived by subtracting the combined total of transhipment costs at Rotterdam, freight costs between Rotterdam and interior points, and an importer profit margin from an established target price. The target price is the price which the government hopes to be able to guarantee producers will receive (in other words, it is much higher than the basic intervention price and, therefore, more of a goal than an actual guarantee). The threshold price also increases monthly during the crop season just as the intervention price does. The system is known as "the variable levy" system because the calculated levy, or import tax, changes according to fluctuations in world market prices. Obviously, the lower world prices are, the higher the calculated levy is, and vice versa. The import tax levy amounts to a substantial portion of the total cost of imported corn when world prices are relatively low (see Table 7-19). To enforce the levy system, all grain imports must be licensed.

Subsidies are required to export grain surpluses because EEC domestic prices are so much higher than world values. The subsidies are termed "restitutions"; they are paid to exporters in an attempt to move surpluses into world markets. The subsidy rate is established after considering the domestic supply situation and the difference between domestic and world prices. The amount of the subsidy often varies by destination to encourage exports to specific coun-

TABLE 7-19 Example of Variable Levy Changes*

	1981	1980
Price of U.S. corn†	369.90	241.85
EEC import levy	158.24	232.09
Total cost of corn	528.14	473.94

*Prices in Deutschmarks/tonne, mid-May comparisons.

†Rotterdam.

tries or geographic areas. Subsidies periodically have been set at levels higher than the difference between EEC domestic prices and world prices to attempt to dispose of ("dump") a particular surplus—this particularly applies to wheat, which is constantly a surplus burden.

The sharp increase in prices since the adoption of CAP has tended to dampen consumption over time. The entry of other Western European countries into the Common Market (e.g., Greece, Spain, and Portugal) eventually will have an adverse effect upon the rate of growth in grain imports, compared to the present trends in those countries particularly regarding corn imports. Western Europe should continue to decline in the proportionate share of total world corn imports, except in years of poor crop production.

South Africa

South Africa is a major producer of white as well as yellow corn. White corn is used in the manufacture of specialty food items. Because South Africa is the largest world exporter of white corn, its production can have a large impact upon white corn prices.

The South African share of the world coarse grain trade has declined sharply. The amount of new land which could be brought into cultivation is limited. South African corn production has not increased significantly, and future increases would depend upon increased yields. Recurrent droughts also plague South African corn production.

Internal corn prices in South Africa currently are well above world market levels. This means that any corn sold for export is sold at a loss. Producer prices are set at high levels by the Maize Board to encourage corn production sufficient to cover domestic needs. The Maize Board also restricts corn exports in years of poor production to maintain favorable domestic consumer prices. The Maize Board regulates the amount of corn allowed to be exported and also is responsible for both the distribution of corn throughout the country and shipments to ports for exports.

South Africa generally has become a relatively less important factor to world markets in recent years, with the exception of white corn.

Brazil

Brazilian corn production has increased sharply since 1950 mainly because of increased corn acreage rather than improved yields. Low fertilizer applications are responsible for the slow growth in Brazilian corn yields. Modern technological inputs also are deficient in mechanization and seed varieties. However, government plans exist to improve technology on a consistent basis.

Around 25 percent of Brazilian corn production is consumed as food; this generally occurs in areas where a low standard of living exists. The balance of production is used for animal feeding; hogs account for the largest proportionate share of feed use. The mixed feed industry has grown steadily in importance during the past 10 years. Brazil formerly had exported corn; that amount approximated 10 percent of production, except in poor production years. Japan and Western Europe traditionally accounted for about 75 percent of Brazilian corn exports; the Soviet Union was a major customer in 1975. Brazil currently exports little or no corn but plans to resume larger exports eventually.

Domestic demand increased sharply in recent years because of increasing hog and poultry numbers. Heavy cow slaughter occurred in 1977 because of low beef prices; this resulted in a sharp escalation in beef prices and consumers shifted demand to cheaper meats, pork and poultry. The rise in poultry production has been particularly dramatic. (The decline in cattle numbers did not have any offsetting adverse effect upon feed demand because cattle are raised mostly on grasslands in Brazil.)

The sharp escalation in feed demand outstripped increases in domestic corn production and required Brazil to import corn in the early 1980s. However, Brazil's basic policy is one of reducing imports whenever it is possible because of an unfavorable balance-of-payments position. Consistent large corn imports are unlikely for the foreseeable future; imports will vary proportionately with domestic corn production—however, exports of corn should be expected to resume in years of excess production.

Mexico

Mexico is another major corn producer which recently began to import corn. Corn is the basic staple in the Mexican diet; it accounts for 75 percent of total acreage harvested for grain and about 60 percent of total grain production. The government has adopted programs to attempt to increase corn acreage; these measures primarily involve increased support prices, credit provisions, technical assistance, programs to assist with fertilizer and seed, and so on. Mexico's corn production is hindered by low technological inputs and erratic weather patterns; both climate and soils are not particularly favorable for corn production. Corn yields are quite low, approximately 20 bushels per acre.

Mexico's agricultural sector has suffered from a low growth rate for many years. Meanwhile, rapid population growth, rising per capita incomes, and an increasing demand for meat and other higher-income foods have combined to increase both food and feed demand substantially above former levels. This has resulted in a sharp increase in imports because of the government policy to improve diets; revenues from petroleum production helped to finance the escalation in imports, along with other domestic farm programs. (However, it should be noted that Mexico normally has a net surplus in agricultural trade because of exports of coffee, feeder cattle, vegetables, and the like. The United States is Mexico's main export market for agricultural commodities). Mexico's imports of agricultural commodities from the United States escalated sharply in 1979 to 10.4 million tonnes; corn accounted for around 45 percent of total U.S. agricultural shipments to Mexico. The total tonnage severely strained Mexico's port and rail facilities; around 45,000 U.S. and Canadian railcars became stranded in late 1980 because of the severe backlogs in unloadings.

The future level of Mexican grain imports beyond the next few years is uncertain. The rising imports and the decreased favorable trade balance in agricultural commodities sparked the initiation of an ambitious farm and food development program in 1980. This is known as the Mexican Food System (Sistema Alimentario Mexicano). The goal was to achieve self-sufficiency in corn and beans by 1982, which has so far not occurred, and in other crops by 1985. The main thrust is to increase production in areas of better rainfall through the infusion of more credits, technical assistance, and more technological advances (primarily increased fertilizer and insecticide use). Producers also now are permitted to pool their resources and to create larger, more efficient production units; these larger units also would have easier access to credit. (This, in effect, is tantamount to a reversal of the Mexican agrarian reform policy which had been adhered to closely since the 1930s; that policy advocated subdivided landholdings in an attempt to provide land for every peasant farmer.) Owners of idle lands now are penalized, production of forage crops on grazing lands now is encouraged (this previously would have provided a basis for the expropriation of those lands) and the division of properties into units of less than 5 hectares (12 acres) is discouraged.

Massive injections of money are intended to make all the various farm programs work as planned. But weather will remain a major factor in Mexican crop production and a high proportion of land in Mexico cannot be cultivated. While the goal of self-sufficiency cannot be ruled out, rising incomes could frustrate the government's efforts to achieve this goal. (The history of the past 12 years in the Soviet Union can serve as a good example of a widening gap between consumers' incomes and desires and a government's ability to keep pace with it, once the wheel has been set in motion.)

The 1981 agreement between the United States and Mexico essentially continued the bilateral process begun in 1980; it provides Mexico with the opportunity to purchase between 6.15 and 8.18 million tonnes of grains, oilseeds, and vegetable oils. The continued growth in Mexico's population and the rising per capita incomes probably will result in continued U.S. grain exports of similar quantities over the near future. However, U.S. exports to Mexico are unlikely to continue to expand at the high rates experienced recently because the heavy agricultural investments by the Mexican government should result in some increase in productivity. Mexico is also experiencing severe problems in repayment of its huge foreign debt, which may provide a restraint on future credits for food purchases.

MAJOR INFLUENCES ON PRICES

Supply

Important supply factors include the amount of acreage planted to corn in the spring, the actual production from that acreage, and carry-over stocks. Weather during the growing season is extremely important to supplies and prices.

Production. All production information is published in regular USDA reports. A survey of farmers' acreage intentions is taken in the late winter and usually released in either February or March (the dates are changing for budgetary reasons). The actual planted acreage can vary from what had been "intended" because of weather at planting time and other factors; hence the plantings intention report is normally not a significant price influence. Weather during the growing season is by far more important, because that determines yields. Very adverse growing conditions, such as drought, can cause sharp price increases, especially if a prolonged drought occurs. Both actual daily weather and forecasts of up to 30 days in advance are public information made available by the U.S. weather service. The USDA issues estimates of what they project the corn crop will be at monthly intervals, beginning in August. The crop estimates can have very important influences upon market prices; however they also can be only temporary in nature.

Weather determines the crop size and, therefore, weather conditions must be followed closely throughout the entire growing season. Also, a USDA crop estimate can be (and often has been) far removed from the actual crop size for various reasons; this is especially true with some of the early crop estimates because of the methodologies used. Thus a given USDA crop estimate may be a "surprise" to the market but result in only a temporary influence because it is the *reality* of any given situation which is important, not what any *projection* claims that reality to be.

Carry-over Supplies. Ending stocks carried into the next season are added to crop production and become part of total beginning supplies. The carry-over at the end of the season helps to cover the demand at the start of the new season. October 1 marks the beginning of the new crop year, although very little of the crop normally is harvested by that date. The adequacy of the ending carry-over to help provide sufficient supplies for marketing needs can become an important factor. Table 7-20 shows the carry-over related to the disappearance of

TABLE 7-20 Ending Carry-Over Related to Consumption
(Expressed as a percent of use and the number of days it would cover at current disappearance rate)

Crop year	Percentage of use	Number of days' use
1966	20	72
1967	26	94
1968	25	91
1969	21	76
1970	15	54
1971	22	79
1972	12	43
1973	8.5	30
1974	7.5	27
1975	7	25
1976	15	55
1977	18	64
1978	18.5	67
1979	21.5	77
1980	14.5	52
1981	33	121
1982*	48	177

*Estimate.

each crop year since 1966 and the number of days' usage the stocks would cover at the prevailing rate of disappearance.

Currently, ending carry-over supplies are considered to be very "tight" if they fall below 600 million bushels; that amount is equivalent to around 30 days at the recent rate of disappearance. The actual timing of the harvest becomes more important when carry-over stocks are relatively low.

When demand is strong enough to "threaten" existing supplies, the carry-over is used to portray the threat to supplies. (For example, market reports will cite the number of days' usage which the projected carry-over will cover.)

Stocks reports are issued four times a year by the USDA. These reports are important for corn because they disclose very relevant data regarding both domestic disappearance and available supplies for the balance of the season. Corn stocks reports are issued in October, January, April, and June; the October stocks figure represents the carry-over from the previous season.

Demand

The most important factors in the demand side are the quantities needed for feeding purposes and exports. Of the two, exports are relatively more significant because their proportionate share of total disappearance has been increasing. Corn used for feed has been declining as a share of total consumption. Reports of cattle, hog, and poultry numbers are issued periodically throughout the year by the USDA; estimates of feed use (in Feed Situation Reports); and supply-and-demand projections. The amount estimated to be consumed for feed is a derived residual taken from each stocks report. Projections of future feed use are made by taking present and past history, applying lagged feeding profitability, current feeding profitability, and estimating a given feeding intensity.

Exports are issued weekly by the USDA and monthly by the Commerce Department. New export sales bookings also are reported on a weekly basis by the USDA; thus one always has up-to-date actual export data at hand plus the trend of new sales. The sales data are broken down by country of destination. Data on foreign countries are reported on constantly by news services and periodically by the USDA.

Price Impact

All of the various factors, whether supply- or demand-oriented, should be watched most closely on a *relative* basis. In other words, it should be noted how big the crop is in relation to disappearance, not in comparison to the previous year or some other year. The progress of disappearance should be compared to total supplies, not to disappearance in some other year. (For example, the corn crop may be a "record"; however, if demand is large enough to exceed the crop size, then the fact that production set a record is virtually irrelevant. Also, consumption may increase sharply compared to the previous year but supplies may be so large that there simply is no threat to supplies despite the increased consumption; conversely, consumption in a given year may actually be smaller

TABLE 7-21 Statistical Data Comparisons

Crop Year	Carry in as a percent of previous season's disappearance	Crop size vs. previous year's disappearance, in percent	Disappearance this year vs. previous year, in percent	Ending carry-over as percent of this season's use	Loan rate	Futures harvest low	Percent of loan rate	Season's national average cash farm price	Percent of loan rate
Surplus years									
1967	20	+16	+ 8	26	$1.05	$1.12	+ 9	$1.03	− 2
1968	26	− 2	0	25	1.05	1.05	0	1.08	+ 3
1969	25	+ 4	+ 6.5	21	1.05	1.15	+ 9	1.15	+ 9
1971	15	+24	+15	22	1.05	1.10	+ 5	1.08	+ 3
1977	15.5	+11	+ 7	18	2.00	1.80	−10	2.02	0
1978	18	+14	+11.5	18.5	2.00	2.10	+ 5	2.25	+12.5
1979	18.5	+13	+ 8	21.5	2.10	2.60	+20	2.52	+20
1981	13	+13	− 5	33	2.40	2.40	0	2.50	+ 4
Threat years									
1973	12	− 6	− 2	8.5	1.05	2.24	+113	2.55	+143
1974	8	−20	−18	7.5	1.10	3.25	+195	3.02	+175
1975	7.5	+21	+20	7	1.10	2.60	+136	2.54	+131
Intermediate years									
1970	21	−13	− 6	15	1.05	1.40	+ 33	1.33	+ 27
1972	22	+ 7	+16	12	1.05	1.32	+ 26	1.57	+ 50
1976	7	+ 8	− 1	15	1.50	2.30	+ 53	2.15	+ 35
1980	21.5	−13	− 3	13	2.25	3.35	+ 49	3.11	+ 38

SOURCE: ContiCommodity Research Division.

than the prior year's disappearance—but related to supplies it may be "too large," and therefore demand price rationing.) There are a number of statistical relationships which are useful in evaluating price balances. Table 7-21 shows a few of them which may be used to distinguish between various types of crop years. Figure 7-10 depicts the progress of corn prices from 1959 to 1982.

Relative consumption trends are among the most important factors in determining price direction. These trends can be used to project various probabilities which in turn can influence prices significantly. The formulae and methodologies vary, especially according to the individual analytical model involved and the proven percentage of reliability. There are many examples; as one, it generally is true that first-quarter feed use normally approximates one-third of total season feed disappearance. However, there are almost as many examples of potential distortions which also have to be considered in order to fine-tune the analyses of trends and projections to prevent large errors; just a 2 percent error in the validity of the stocks report used to derive first-quarter feed use given above could provide an error of 300 million bushels in projected feed use. Thus, many factors must be coaligned to reduce the size and probability of errors; it is impossible to fully delineate all of the interrelationships and methodologies. But again, relative consumption trends dominate price direction; when strongly established, they have to change before price direction can change for more than a brief period.

Seasonal factors also should be monitored; as a *broad generalization*, sea-

Figure 7-10 Monthly continuation, Chicago Board of Trade corn. *(Conti-Commodity Research Division)*

sonal lows in corn futures tend to coincide with harvest pressure in the fall, and seasonal highs tend to occur in April and/or July. (Thus one should be wary of buying corn in late July, for example, because a strong seasonal influence for lower prices exists because of the approaching harvest and increased availability of supplies.) It is prudent to be aware of seasonal tendencies because there are solid reasons for their occurrence; however, strict adherence to them is inadvisable because fundamental developments can sometimes outweigh normal seasonal factors and cause contra seasonal price movement.

Government programs are one of the key factors that can affect corn prices. Information regarding the rules of government programs, plus data about participation in such programs, is published periodically by the USDA. On a regular basis, details are included in feed situation reports and weekly reports of crops placed under loan. But all of this is outlined fully in Chapter 14, which explains why government programs must be watched closely and how they affect grain prices.

A full list of all government publications can be obtained from the USDA in Washington, D.C.

SUMMARY AND TRADING CONSIDERATIONS

1. U.S. corn supplies
   a. Ending or projected carry-over stocks
   b. Planted acreage
   c. Summer growing weather
   d. Estimated production in U.S. Department of Agriculture crop reports
2. The amount of free supplies available to the market (total supplies minus the amount in government price-support programs)
3. Government farm programs
   a. Basic loan rates
   b. Amount of crop eligible for price supports
   c. Release levels of grain reserve
   d. Acreage restriction programs
   e. Government policies and decisions
4. Demand, particularly exports and feed-residual disappearance
   a. U.S. feed profitability and animal numbers
   b. Rate of actual exports and new sales
5. Relative consumption trends
6. Seasonal factors
7. Total world coarse grain production and consumption
8. South American production, particularly in Argentina, which is export-oriented and competes with United States

9. Cash market trends
10. World economic conditions

Commodity	Exchange(s)	Contract size	Limit moves
Corn	Chicago Board of Trade	5000 bushels	10¢
	Mid-America Commodity Exchange	1000 bushels	10¢

CHAPTER

8

Soybeans

Michael Hinebaugh

INTRODUCTION

Soybeans are an ancient crop which only recently became commercially important. They have been grown in China for at least 5000 years and are used there principally for food purposes. They were not accepted as a field crop in the United States until the early 1900s. Soybeans actually restore nitrogen to the soil; other crops, such as corn, remove nitrogen from soil. Thus soybeans originally were used as a rotation crop with corn; the soybean field crop was used mostly as fodder for animals. Acreage planted to soybeans in the United States remained extremely low until the 1940s. U.S. soybean production doubled between the late 1930s and the early 1940s; farmers discovered that soybeans were more important than a mere forage crop for animals. However, U.S. soybean production in the mid-1940s still approximated only 200 million bushels. The growth in U.S. soybean production was accelerated by the switch from butter to margarine. (Vegetable oils are the base for margarines.) It also was found that using protein in feeding rations improved the efficiency of the feed; this latter discovery is the principal factor behind the revolutionary developments in soybean acreage—particularly as other areas of the world began to develop more efficient and modern feeding industries. (Acreage planted to corn in the United States, for example, even after the increase in the 1970s, approximated the same level that existed in the 1950s; however, U.S. soybean acreage has skyrocketed since that time.) (See Table 8-1.)

Soybeans are still valued mainly as a food item in Asia, which formerly had accounted for almost the entire world production. But the value of the soybean

TABLE 8-1 U.S. Soybean Acreage *(Selected years, million acres)*

Year	Acreage	Year	Acreage
1958	25.3	1978	64.4
1963	29.6	1979	71.5
1968	42.2	1980	70.3
1971	43.5	1981	67.8
1974	53.5	1982	72.1
1977	58.7		

products is responsible for the dramatic increase in soybean production in the United States and other world areas that has occurred over the past 30 years. Crushing soybeans in processing plants yields 47 to 48 pounds of soybean meal and around 11 pounds of soybean oil per bushel. The use of protein in animal feeding rations has escalated dramatically because of the push in many areas to improve diets; this requires improved efficiency in animal feeding. Grazing animals on pasture or feeding them inferior rations, for example, results in a longer growing period and/or inferior meat quality. (Dairy cattle in Western Europe, for example, now produce more milk per cow than previously because of the improved feeding rations. Ironically, this has caused problems in the European Economic Community, or EEC, because subsidized dairy surpluses have continued to mount despite reductions in dairy herd numbers.)

Soybeans yield a protein by-product that contains around 80 percent of the weight of the original soybean. This is a much higher percentage than any other oilseed renders. Fishmeal formerly constituted an important source of protein in world markets; fishmeal is much higher in protein content. However, the production of fishmeal has stagnated and has not been able to keep pace with the rising world demand for protein. The disappearance of anchovies off the coasts of Peru in 1972–1973 created virtual panic in world markets and was one of the key factors behind the explosion in soybean prices to record levels during that crop year.

Soybeans presently account for over half of the total world production of oilseeds, including cottonseed, peanuts, sunflower seed, rapeseed, sesame seed, safflower seed, flaxseed, castor beans, copra, and palm kernels. In terms of protein equivalent, soybeans account for around two-thirds of total world production of protein meals; this proportionate share is higher because the meal fraction contained in soybeans is much higher than the oil fraction. In terms of edible oil production, world production of soybeans accounts for around one-third.

U.S. PRODUCTION

The United States is by far the world's primary producer of soybeans; U.S. production has been declining as a percentage of total world production because of faster growth in other world areas. China, which had been virtually the only producer of soybeans for centuries, also has seen its production represent a lower percentage of total world production.

Producing Areas

The major soybean-producing states in the United States are located primarily in the Midwest. Illinois and Iowa, usually the two dominant states, account for 30 to 34 percent of U.S. soybean production, while the southeastern states of Arkansas, Louisiana, and Mississippi (which encompass an area known as the "Delta") usually account for approximately 15 percent of total U.S. production.

Table 8-2 shows the leading U.S. soybean-producing states; the numbers represent the comparative ranking of each state for the crop years 1978 through 1982. Those fifteen states, combined, usually account for over 90 percent of U.S. soybean production. U.S. soybean production is affected by weather during the growing season, crop yields, government programs, and any factors that influence the amount of acreage planted to soybeans; government programs which influence the amount of acreage planted to corn, a major "competitor" for acreage, can, in turn, affect soybean acreage.

Corn-Soybean Price Relationships

Price relationships between corn and soybeans are an important factor in determining soybean acreage; price relationships between cotton and soybeans also are important in the Southeast. Soybeans compete with corn for acreage in the main midwestern producing areas. Acreage planted to soybeans always increases when soybeans are highly profitable in comparison with corn; conversely, acreage planted to corn almost always increases relative to soybean acreage when corn prices are more favorable than soybean prices.

TABLE 8-2 Leading U.S. Soybean-Producing States*

State	1978	1979	1980	1981	1982
Iowa	2	2	1	2	2
Illinois	1	1	2	1	1
Indiana	5	5	3	4	4
Minnesota	4	4	4	5	5
Missouri	3	3	5	3	3
Ohio	6	6	6	6	6
Louisiana	9	9	7	10	10
Arkansas	7	7	8	7	7
Mississippi	8	8	9	9	8
Nebraska	11	12	10	8	9
Tennessee	10	10	11	11	12
Kentucky	12	13	12	12	14
North Carolina	12	15	13	14	15
Alabama	14	14	14	13	13
Michigan	18	18	15	17	17

*The top five states usually account for close to 60 percent of total U.S. soybean production.

The relative profitability of corn and soybeans can be shown through the use of simple ratios. These are obtained by dividing the price of soybeans by the price of corn. A ratio of 2.35 to 1 generally is considered to be a break-even area. Table 8-3 shows that shifts of acreage out of soybeans into corn usually occur when soybean-corn ratios average below 2.2 to 1 during the winter preceding spring planting. (The aberration which occurred in 1975 was due to a large shift from cotton acreage to soybean acreage in the south; soybean acreage in the Midwest, however, did decline.)

Growing Conditions

The optimum temperature requirements for soybeans during the growing season are similar to those of corn; namely, above-normal temperatures are deleterious and daily average temperatures in the mid-70s are preferred. August is a critical weather period for soybeans, both negatively and positively. Soybeans can continue to form pods in August; thus they can recover from stress conditions in July and still produce a good crop if August weather is favorable. (For those who wish to study this factor more thoroughly, refer to the growing conditions during the summers of 1975 and 1976. The year 1975 offers a good example of a July drought followed by beneficial growing conditions, which subsequently produced a good soybean yield. Conversely, adverse August weather depressed yields in 1976.)

Soybean yields depend on the number of flowers produced and pods that mature, along with the size of the seeds in the pods. Adverse weather conditions which cause flowers and pods to drop off the plant reduce ultimate yields; high temperatures in late July and August can cause such shedding to occur. Peak moisture requirements for soybean plants occur in middle-to-late July, when rapid vegetative growth occurs, and late August, when the seeds are filling. A prolonged drought during either of these two periods can severely depress yields, particularly if accompanied by high temperatures—especially

TABLE 8-3 Percent Change in Acreage

Calendar year	JFM soybean-corn ratio*	Soybeans	Corn
1972	2.6	+ 8	−9.5
1973	3.5	+21	+7.5
1974	2.1	− 6	+8
1975	2.0	+ 2	+1
1976	1.8	− 8	+7.5
1977	3.0	+17	0
1978	2.6	+ 9	−3
1979	3.0	+11	0
1980	2.2	− 2	+3
1981	2.1	− 3	0
1982	2.35	+ 6	−3

*The JFM ratio refers to the soybean-corn ratio prevailing during the January–March period *before* the planting of the crops in April and May.

in August. The relationship of midsummer precipitation to soybean yields actually can be represented by a straight linear equation. Optimum soybean yields are associated with normal to slightly above normal preseason precipitation, and normal to above-average summer moisture.

Technologically, soybean yields have benefited from the residual effect of the sharp increase in fertilizer applications to corn acreage because of their usual rotation with corn. The direct application of fertilizer to soybean acreage is not a widespread practice, although leaf applications have been increasing. Some tests reportedly have shown that fertilizer could boost soybean yields; however, that also has been disputed. At any rate, it probably would take a prolonged period of relatively favorable prices for soybeans before any significant change in the fertility management of soybeans would occur. Improved varieties and cultural practices presently are the only significant technological factors associated with soybean yields.

WORLD PRODUCTION AND DISTRIBUTION

The United States normally produces around 65 percent of total world soybean supplies. The U.S. share of total world production formerly had been higher but the advent of Brazil as a major world soybean producer has limited the ability of the United States to account for an increasing proportionate share of total world production, despite steadily increased production (Table 8-4).

Other areas also have been increasing their share of production. China, which still is the third largest world soybean producer, has been steadily declining in its proportionate share of total world production. The major importers of soybeans have shown little or no increase in soybean production; the reasons are either an inability to bring more acreage into production or climate. Specific areas of the world that are important to world soybean trade are examined below.

People's Republic of China

Soybeans make up the largest share of total oilseed production in China; however, production has been neglected for a long time because of low yields and

TABLE 8-4 World Soybean Production Comparisons*
(Percentage of total world production)

	1976	1978	1979	1980	1982
United States	57	66	66	60	65
Brazil	19	13	16	19	16
China	17	10	8	9	9
Argentina	—†	5	4	5	3
All others	7	6	6	7	7

*Crop year beginning September 1 of each year.

†Negligible; Argentina is included in "all others" for 1976.

Note: 1976 and 1980 were major drought years in the United States.

the heavy state emphasis on food-grain production. (See Figure 8-1.) Acreage devoted to soybeans in China actually declined from the peak years of the mid-1950s. But China still is the third largest soybean producer; China's soybean acreage is second only to that of the United States. The main soybean producing areas are located in the north and northeast.

Acreage planted to soybeans in the south has increased in recent years. Figure 8-2 shows that soybean acreage exists in a long north-to-south band in eastern China; however, the greater intensity of development in northeastern areas can be shown by the fact that two-thirds of total soybean production occurs north of a line which falls between Peking and Shanghai.

Government policy statements have recently included soybeans for the first time in many years. Production units have been asked to stop neglecting soybeans and to place more emphasis upon increasing soybean yields. This is an indication that soybean production may receive a higher priority in future years. However, it does not automatically translate into a large increase in soybean production; arable land is limited in China and the necessity to produce basic foodstuffs restricts the ability to shift acreage into soybeans. The emphasis will be upon improving yields; and that should be a very slow process.

Domestic consumption in China primarily is for human food purposes (as opposed to crushing to produce a protein for animal feeding purposes and exports for the same purpose, as in the United States, Brazil, and Argentina). Soybeans also formerly were an important source of export revenues; although annual bushel amounts were small, they were steady at an annual rate of around 20 to 25 million bushels a year. (China was the second largest soybean exporter in the world, prior to the surge in Brazilian production; but that was due to the fact that the United States was the only real source of soybeans in the world.) Japan has been a traditional export customer, importing over

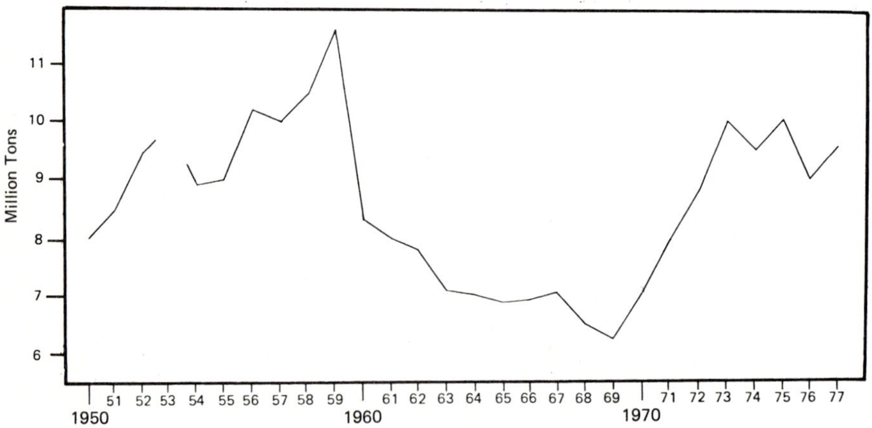

Figure 8-1 Production of soybeans by the People's Republic of China. *(ContiCommodity Research Division)*

100,000 tons annually for food purposes; small amounts also formerly were shipped annually to Eastern Europe and Finland. China's soybean exports in recent years have been confined to small amounts to traditional Asian customers, such as Japan and Hong Kong.

Table 8-5 shows that China actually has tended to become a net importer of soybeans in recent years, despite its own large production. This is because domestic oilseed production has failed to keep pace with the rate of population increase and the government desires to maintain at least minimal per capita consumption levels. Per capita consumption of soybean, cottonseed, peanut, and rapeseed oils has been estimated at only 7 to 8 pounds per person. China also has increased imports of edible oils in recent years, including soybean oil—which never was imported in former years. Small amounts of palm oil and coconut oil traditionally had been imported in the past; however, the quantity of those imports has tended to increase in recent years.

There is no question that China has the capacity to become an increasing force in world edible-oil markets. The Chinese per capita consumption of vegetable oils is very low, large increases in domestic oilseed production are very unlikely, and the population still is expanding sharply each year. To increase per capita consumption even to the relatively low level of India, for example, would require an increase in domestic production and/or imports of two million tons, equivalent to about *4 percent of total world consumption.* China can become an increasing force in world markets over time even without improving per capita consumption of vegetable oils; just the sharply expanding population base and little increase in domestic vegetable oil production could accomplish that. Domestic production has barely been able to keep pace with the population growth. One has to take into account the fact that the Chinese population has an enormous capacity to absorb any quantity that their political leaders permit them to have; thus, when China does anything the world commercial trade pays attention.

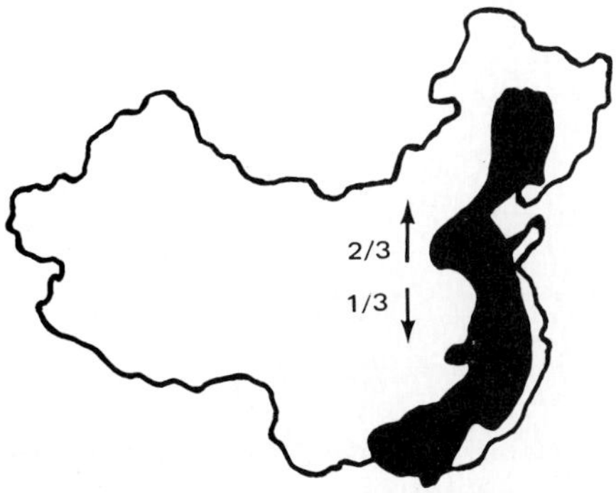

Figure 8-2 Soybean-growing areas in the People's Republic of China. *(Conti-Commodity Research Division)*

TABLE 8-5 Annual Soybean Exports and Imports ***(Thousand tonnes)***

Year	Exports	Imports
1966	550	—
1967	565	—
1968	571	—
1969	488	—
1970	424	—
1971	460	—
1972	370	2
1973	310	255
1974	340	619
1975	330	36
1976	180	25
1977	115	362
1978	325	261
1979	132	810
1980	151	560
1981	160	510

Brazil

Growing Areas. Most of Brazil's soybean acreage is located at or below the Tropic of Capricorn, which represents the transition from tropical to subtropical conditions. The average rainfall around the Tropic of Capricorn ranges between 43 and 60 inches per year. The total annual rainfall is comparable to the Mississippi delta in the United States; however, most of the rainfall around the Tropic of Capricorn occurs during the summer growing season, which is higher than the normal summer amounts in the United States. Temperatures in Brazilian growing areas are more similar to those around Memphis, Tennessee.

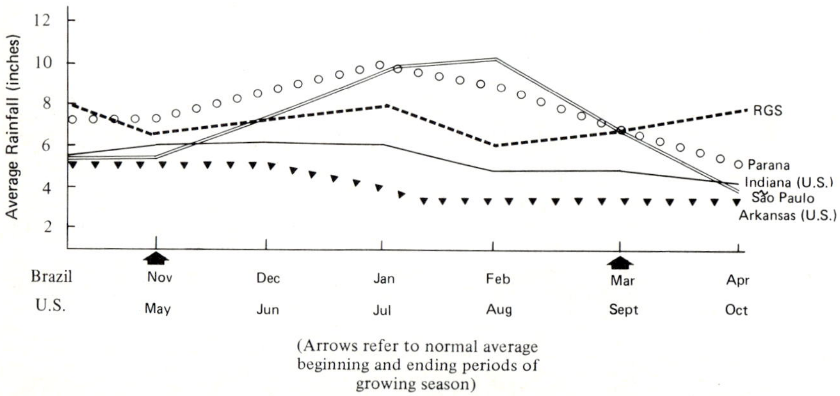

Figure 8-3 Comparison of rainfall during the growing season. *(Conti-Commodity Research Division)*

The actual latitude of the Tropic of Capricorn is at a level equivalent to central Mexico; but winds sweep freely from the Andes mountain chain along the western coast of South America all the way across into southern Brazil, which can bring lower temperatures than are normally equated with such latitudes. Rainfall during the peak growing period for soybeans in Brazil normally is much higher than it is in the prime growing areas of the United States. (See Figure 8-3.) Low soil fertility is the main limiting factor of Brazilian yields.

In years of good growing weather Brazil usually produces around 16 percent of world soybean production; acreage planted to soybeans in Brazil approximates 16 percent of total world acreage. Government programs during the 1960s aimed at achieving self-sufficiency in food production. The programs stimulated a rapid expansion in wheat acreage, despite the fact that wheat was a marginal crop at that time; a high government support price for wheat and the fact that it could be double-cropped with soybeans encouraged an expansion in acreage of both crops. The early statistics showed a direct correlation between acreage planted to wheat and soybean acreage. The importance of double-cropping with wheat to the growth in soybean production also is apparent in the fact that Brazilian soybean production mostly had been concentrated in just two states, Rio Grande do Sul and Paraná; these two states also are the major wheat producers, accounting for around 88 percent of total Brazilian production.

Many commentators state that Brazilian soybean production is the result of the brief U.S. embargo on soybean sales in the summer of 1973. That is false. Government reports called for an increase in production as early as the mid-1960s. Figure 8-4 shows the sharp increase in soybean acreage that began prior to the 1973 embargo and continued long afterwards.

The pre-1973 expansion in soybean production was largely due to the price

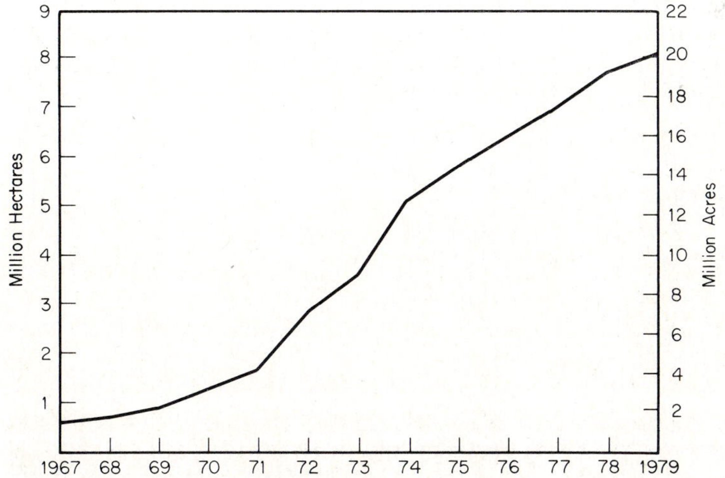

Figure 8-4 Brazilian soybean acreage harvested. *(United States Department of Agriculture)*

support system for wheat; but high world prices during the mid-1970s motivated a sharp expansion in soybean acreage independent of wheat. Government programs were designed to stimulate a rapid expansion in soybean production to increase export earnings by taking advantage of high world prices and also what was termed the inevitable "world food crises." (Brazil also had planned to export 100 million bushels of corn annually, although this so far has never materialized.) It was hoped that the increased export revenues would offset the bill for imported petroleum and thereby solve the serious balance of payments deficit; but the OPEC price increases have negated that plan.

Rio Grande do Sul and Paraná are still the leading soybean-producing states. But most of the expansion in soybean acreage in recent years has come from the conversion of pasture and timberland into acreage for the production of soybeans in northern states such as Mato Grosso. There no longer is a precise correlation between wheat acreage and soybean acreage. Soybean acreage also gained at the expense of other traditional crop acreage as remuneration increased for soybeans relative to those crops. In addition, the disastrous 1975 frost caused extreme damage to coffee trees in Paraná and São Paulo; many of these trees were pulled out and the land was replanted to crops with a lower risk, notably soybeans. Recent changes in soybean production by region are shown in Table 8-6.

The trend of increasing production outside of past traditional growing areas is certain to continue because of government programs for land development in the vast Cerrados area. Acreage expansion there has been so rapid in recent years that the state of Mato Grosso is now considered to be a regular producing state, in contrast to 8 to 10 years ago, when it produced practically no soybeans at all. Acreage expansion in Mato Grosso should continue on a consistent annual basis because of the continued development of rice and pasture in that area; land is first planted to rice or pasture as it is cleared—soybeans, which are more expensive and hence a greater risk in early land development, are not planted until 2 to 3 years later.

The sharp increase in both world food prices and petroleum prices (Brazil imports most of its petroleum needs) in the early 1970s stimulated various government actions to boost agricultural output. One of the actions was a study of

TABLE 8-6 Growth in Soybean Production by Area
(Percent shares of total)*

	1970	1972	1975	1979	1981
Rio Grande do Sul	67	57	45	37	40
Paraná	22	26	40	36	35
São Paulo	4	7	7	7	6
Santa Catarina	4	5	4	5	5
Mato Grosso	1	2	2	10	10
All others	1	3	2	5	4

*Table shows percent share of total Brazilian production for selected years.

SOURCE: ContiCommodity Research Division.

land resources. The study indicated that close to 500 million acres in the vast undeveloped western areas of Brazil could have good potential for cultivated crops without irrigation. These areas were identified as having good terrain and adequate rainfall; they are located mostly in the vast savannah (or grassland) area known as the Cerrados. The Cerrados (outlined in Figure 8-5) covers most of Goiás, a large part of Mato Grosso, and Minas Gerais, plus smaller portions of other states. But the report also stated that advanced technology must be applied to maintain any productive outlook. The soils there are relatively poor; they are highly acidic and low in phosphate. The remedy requires heavy and consistent inputs of lime and fertilizer; otherwise, whatever soil fertility that exists would be depleted rapidly. The remedy presupposes a necessary infrastructure for transportation and other elements that would be vitally necessary

Figure 8-5 Map of Brazil with main soybean-growing areas. *(ContiCommodity Research Division)*

for any massive expansion and would pose the question of costs versus returns. But the government is committed to ambitious plans to develop the Cerrados area.

The land resource study also indicated that an additional 500 million acres of less desirable soils could be brought into cultivation if advanced technology were used. Much of this acreage is located in the vast Amazon region; the Amazon region is larger than all of Europe but more thinly settled than the Sahara. A variety of government programs have been initiated to develop agriculture in that area also, despite the very low soil fertility and dense forest cover that exists. The Amazon has been touted as a major future growth area but that potential has to be questioned. Experience shows that crop yields there decline sharply after the first harvest; large quantities of fertilizer are needed simply to maintain average yield prospects. This appears to be economically unfeasible. And because soils in the traditional growing areas of Brazil could also benefit from fertilizer applications, it would appear more feasible to apply fertilizer to the "better" soils in Brazil than to allocate the massive quantities needed in the Amazon (actually, even soils in the traditional, or better, growing areas in Brazil suffer from low fertility, which depresses yields). The same soils in the Amazon which support the lush vegetation and tropical forests simply are not fertile. Conditions also appear ripe for the development of plant pathogens that attack foliage and roots. There is also a valid concern about what will happen in the future after the lush jungle area is cleared; it appears that the heavy rainfall of the area would be likely to cause serious erosion problems. Conversely, some scientists believe the rains may cease if the massive jungle vegetation is removed. (The history of the Mayans is often cited in support of this thesis; evidence suggests that the ancient Mayan civilization cleared jungle areas to cultivate crops and that the cropland eventually failed.)

Many large government subsidies have existed for the purpose of promoting crop production. These have included subsidized credit terms for crop production and machinery purchases, subsidized fertilizer costs, and so on. Thus future developments may depend upon the extent to which these policies are continued.

The subsidized financing of production costs was recently reduced for large farmers. Small farmers still can receive the subsidized credit rate to finance 100 percent of their production costs, but large farmers are now eligible to receive the subsidized rate to cover only 40 percent of their total production costs. Large farmers now have to cover 60 percent of their production costs by their own means. The difference between the subsidized rate for agriculture and the open market rate of interest is considerable. This leads some observers to expect a decline in the growth trend for soybean acreage in southern areas of Brazil; however, soybean acreage should continue to expand in the areas of land development projects in northern Brazil. Policies can and do change frequently and rapidly. Although this particular program may not last long, it illustrates the necessity to watch government policies carefully.

Exports. Much of Brazil's soybean production formerly was exported. The importance of soybean exports to Brazil's foreign exchange can be measured by the fact that soybean export revenues surpassed those of coffee and sugar in

1975 and took over the number one spot in export earnings. The ports of Rio Grande and Paranagua rank first and second, respectively, in export shipments. Western Europe traditionally accounted for most of Brazil's soybean and soybean meal exports; in the mid-1970s, for example, 84 percent of Brazil's soybean exports went to Western Europe while the Soviet Union and Japan accounted for the other 16 percent. Western Europe still is Brazil's largest customer; however, the Soviet Union signed a long-term contract with Brazil for annual shipments of soybeans and soybean products which also will make the Soviet Union an important outlet on a continued basis. Exports have a pronounced seasonal trend, as depicted in Figure 8-6. Brazilian soybean exports pick up sharply immediately following harvest; the peak normally is reached around July or August and exports taper off quickly afterwards (1979 was a poor crop year; exports peak much earlier in years of low supplies).

Brazil's soybean exports have leveled off as product exports have become more important. Domestic crushings have grown at a much faster rate in terms of total soybean consumption than exports have. This is because Brazil sought to maximize export earnings by retaining more of the value of the soybean at home, to help economic growth. Crushing capacity was expanded rapidly throughout the 1970s. Domestic crushings approximated only 23 million bushels in 1969; reached 210 million bushels by 1975, and by the early 1980s had reached almost 500 million bushels.

Domestic utilization of soybean meal increased sharply during the late 1970s because of a rapid expansion in poultry and hog numbers; however, the level of consumption per animal unit remains low. The export market is the most important outlet for soybean meal production; roughly 70 percent of soybean meal production is exported at the present time. Western and Eastern Europe are the major customers for Brazilian soybean meal; the United States is their replacement supplier in years of low Brazilian production. Brazil constantly

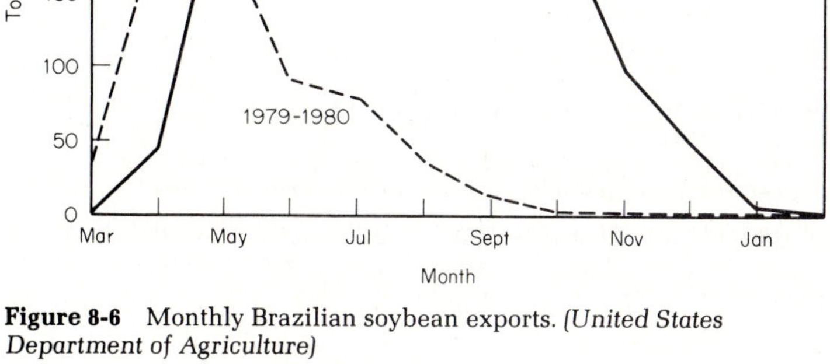

Figure 8-6 Monthly Brazilian soybean exports. *(United States Department of Agriculture)*

TABLE 8-7 Soybean Meal Exports of Brazil and the United States*
(Million tonnes)

	1975	1976	1977	1978	1979	1980	1981
Brazil	3.1	4.4	5.3	5.4	5.2	6.6	7.6
United States	4.6	4.1	5.5	6.0	7.2	6.1	6.7

*Calendar year basis for Brazil, crop year basis for United States.
SOURCE: United States Department of Agriculture, ContiCommodity Research Division.

can undercut U.S. values because of repeated devaluations of Brazil's currency; Brazil maximizes exports through such devaluations. Purchases of Brazilian soybean meal by the Soviet Union make headlines in commodity news columns; however Europe remains by far the largest customer. Brazil recently became the leading world exporter of soybean meal for the first time in 1980, surpassing the United States; this was repeated in 1981. The future outlook suggests that Brazil will continue to be the leading world exporter of soybean meal except in years of poor crop production; expanded crushing facilities and the use of currency devaluations to promote exports will assure that outlook. The relative importance of Brazil as an exporter can be seen in Tables 8-7 and 8-8, where Brazil's soybean meal and soybean oil export tonnage are compared to that of the United States.

As Table 8-8 shows, Brazil has also become the leading world exporter of soybean oil. The early expansion in crushing capacity was used to improve per capita consumption of soybean oil, which increased dramatically during the early 1970s (from around 4 to 14 pounds per person in just 4 years). Domestic subsidies were used to accomplish that objective; domestic prices were insulated from world market values. This insulation from world prices was discontinued in 1981, which should increase the quantity available for export. Most Brazilian soybean oil exports go to the Mideast and Far East, penetrating a former major U.S. market; Iran usually is Brazil's number one customer for soybean oil.

Argentina

Acreage devoted to soybeans in Argentina was negligible until the mid-1970s; in fact, acreage planted to all oilseeds had been relatively stable for years—this includes sunflower acreage, which has been Argentina's predominant oilseed

TABLE 8-8 Soybean Oil Exports of Brazil and the United States*
(Thousand tonnes)

	1975	1976	1977	1978	1979	1980	1981
Brazil	263	453	487	487	534	744	1050
United States	443	703	934	1055	1220	700	900

*Calendar year basis for Brazil, crop year basis for United States.
SOURCE: United States Department of Agriculture, ContiCommodity Research Division.

crop (although soybean acreage and its value of production are rapidly catching up to sunflowers). High vegetable oilseed prices in world markets during the mid-1970s stimulated a rapid expansion in the amount of acreage devoted to oilseeds. Total planted acreage in Argentina has not increased dramatically over the years, but the proportion planted to various crops has tended to shift according to relative profitability. Soybeans have accounted for most of the expansion in acreage planted to oilseeds. For example, soybean acreage in 1977 was almost three times as large as in 1975 and over five times larger than in 1973.

Most of the soybean production is exported (estimated at around 75 percent of total production). Thus domestic consumption statistics are virtually ignored in Argentina and this may be responsible for the lack of reliable data. There is a significant disparity among various estimates of total oilseed-crushing capacity. The USDA estimates crushing capacity in Argentina to be much lower than private Argentine sources indicate it to be. However, lower USDA estimates of Argentine crushing capacity probably are closer to being correct for the following reasons: (1) the USDA estimates are based on a 300-day work year for *effective* crushing facilities, while Argentine estimates are based on a 330-day annual working basis; this contributes largely to the 2- to 2 1/2-million-ton distortion in estimates; (2) the existing capacity includes some old, inefficient plants which may not be utilized to the maximum extent; (3) newer processing facilities have roughly offset the closing of old plants, in terms of bushel capacities; (4) a lot of the crushing capacity had been geared to flaxseed, which cannot really be switched to something else; (5) many crushing statistics over recent years would indicate that an extremely low percentage of existing crush capacity has been utilized (which is unreasonable). All these considerations lend credibility to the fairly low USDA estimate of *effective* Argentine processing capacity.

Most of the soybean-crushing capacity is located in the province of Santa Fe because Santa Fe is the largest soybean-producing area in Argentina. The total crushing capacity in Buenos Aires is greater than that of Santa Fe; however, more sunflower and flax are crushed in Buenos Aires.

Western Europe

This area represents the major world demand center for imports of soybeans and soybean meal. Rapeseed is the most important oilseed produced in Western Europe; it accounts for close to 90 percent of total oilseed production. France accounts for most of the production of rapeseed in the EEC. Domestic rapeseed production is highly subsidized, in accordance with the overall EEC policies of supporting domestic grain production by fixing prices for internal production well above world market values. Subsidies also occasionally are paid to EEC crushers for the purchase of domestic oilseeds. (Most oilseed imports enter the EEC duty-free under General Agreement on Trade and Tariffs, or GATT, trade commitments established in 1961–1962, prior to the adoption of the Common Agricultural Policy of the EEC.)

Soybeans are not extensively grown in Europe because growers in France have demanded a high subsidy in order to increase production. Most other agricultural commodities in Western Europe are highly subsidized; soybeans are not, because of the GATT treaty which allows free access of U.S. soybeans with no extra duty charges. France has required, reportedly, a subsidy equivalent to $10 per bushel to increase soybean production. Soybeans still are grown only experimentally in Europe because of the high subsidies that would be necessary to stimulate increased production. The EEC Commission has promised to examine all marketing arrangements that could increase production of soybeans.

Western Europe represents the major world-demand center for soybeans and soybean meal and accounts for the major share of total U.S. exports of soybeans and soybean meal, despite the inroads made by Brazil in recent years; the United States has maintained its proportionate share of the market because of the escalation in European requirements—which have offset the growth in Brazilian production. Western Europe is the major market for Brazilian soybeans and soybean meal, too.

The level of European demand for soybeans and soybean meal would change dramatically if the GATT trade agreement were changed. That agreement specifies that soybeans and soybean products are allowed entry into EEC markets free of any import tariff. It also helps European consumers because soybeans cannot be grown as cheaply in Europe as they are in the United States. But the GATT agreement also means that soybean meal often is cheaper than corn in Western Europe; this is a dramatic reversal of the situation in the United States, where soybean meal always is more expensive than corn, but the relationship varies according to free market principles. Soybean meal should always be more expensive than corn. It has not been the case in the EEC because their maze of subsidies has served to maintain grain and meat prices well above the average world price level; meanwhile, imported protein trades at lower world values. Import taxes applied to corn raise corn prices substantially. If the GATT agreement is changed and import duties are applied to soybeans and soybean products, then soybean and soybean meal demand would drop sharply; historical price relationships (e.g., meal-corn ratios) would have to be modified accordingly. Western Europe is a large market; changes in price relationships there would bring *major* repercussions.

The EEC has threatened to revoke the GATT trade agreement and impose import duties because gasohol production is subsidized. Gasohol production produces a protein by-product. This would alter the price level of soybeans and soybean products and also would make soybean meal more expensive in feeding rations. History has shown that the rate of growth in imports by the EEC of feed grains and wheat tended to slacken after import tariffs were placed on those commodities; import duties on soybeans and soybean products would be likely to cause a similar effect.

Soviet Union

The Soviet Union raises very few soybeans, but it is the largest world producer of sunflower seed. Sunflowers are valued for their high oil content but they produce relatively small amounts of meal. Total Soviet production of soybeans approximates only 20 to 30 million bushels; most production is located in the Far East. Any significant expansion in soybean production is very unlikely because acreage would have to be diverted from other important crops. Also, irrigated acreage would be required for development of domestic soybean production because of climatic factors; but irrigated acreage presently is inadequate and is highly prioritized in Soviet crop plans (cotton is high in priority).

Soviet oilseed-processing capacity is estimated to be close to 10 million tonnes; approximately one-half is for sunflower seed, about 5 percent for soybeans, and the rest is for cottonseed. More capacity is scheduled to be built in the near future. It is unknown how much of the present capacity is composed of older plants that are scheduled for replacement, but Soviet oilseed-crushing capacity is in need of modernization.

The Soviet Union began to increase soybean imports moderately during the middle-to-late 1970s. This mostly was in response to the depressed production of sunflower seed and the resultant negative effect upon domestic supplies of vegetable oils. However, there also is a correlation with the declining proportion of protein in mixed feeds. Although the Soviet Union has been expanding the production of mixed feeds, oilseed protein supplies have not been able to keep pace with the expansion in mixed-feed output. Table 8-9 shows the history of concentrate balances between 1965 and the late 1970s. The expanding Soviet production of mixed feeds requires increased protein imports in order to sustain even a minimal level of protein in mixed-feed rations.

It often is expected that the Soviet Union will become a far larger market for soybeans and/or soybean meal. This is because of the ambitious plans to expand livestock production. It is correctly pointed out that feeding rations in the Soviet Union are greatly deficient by western standards and that improving rations by adding protein would greatly increase their efficiency (i.e., increased efficiency of feeding rations could "stretch" grain supplies). But several factors appear to militate against this option:

1. Soviet feeding rations generally are deficient in *both* energy and protein contents. Of these two items, energy is by far the most important basic element. A leading Soviet poultry specialist, for example, reported in 1977 that the caloric content of the mixed feeds in the poultry industry often were critically low; the average kilocalories of energy per kilogram of feed reportedly dropped below 2700 units on occasion, or well below the recommended Soviet rate of 3100 units. The feed energy gap also has been widening; the generation of sufficient feed is a basic element that is intrin-

TABLE 8-9 Composition of Soviet Concentrates
(Percent of total)

	1965	1970	1975	1976	1977
Grain	82.4	85.0	85.2	85.4	85.9
Milling by-products	12.9	11.1	9.2	8.5	8.7
Oilseed meal	4.5	3.0	3.0	3.0	2.6
Alfalfa and grass meals	.2	.9	2.6	3.1	2.8

sic to the entire livestock expansion program. This has necessitated a concentration upon grain imports and supplies as opposed to allowing development of programs to improve feeding efficiency to a significant degree.

2. The Soviet mixed feed industry is still at a fairly rudimentary level in terms of adequate mixing facilities, trained personnel, and handling equipment. This suggests that huge quantities of soybean meal may not be efficiently useable. The vast logistical difficulties involved in handling soybean meal and spreading it out uniformly throughout the country where and when needed suggest that the protein deficit in feeding rations will not be addressed first.
3. The calculated annual protein deficit in Soviet feeding rations has been estimated to be the equivalent of 500 million bushels of soybeans, using present animal numbers. In terms of meal, the calculated annual protein deficit approximates 12 to 14 million tons of soybean meal, which is almost equal to the total combined annual soybean meal exports of the United States and Brazil. The price implications that imports of that amount would have for the Soviet Union should be obvious.

Soybeans are in a relatively more "finite" supply status as compared with grains. Any attempt by the Soviet Union to correct the protein deficiency in feeding rations with massive imports of soybean meal (raw soybeans are an impossibility because the crushing facilities do not exist) would cause a greatly accelerated price response and a significant hard currency cost for the Soviet Union.

The Soviet Union so far has steadfastly refused to address the dilemma of protein deficiency in feeding rations, but minimal protein levels are maintained. They have continued to focus attention on the feed energy problem, especially in view of the widening gap between existing feed energy supplies and the requirements for reaching livestock production goals. Nonetheless, imports of 4 million tonnes annually of soybeans and soybean meal should become fairly common because of the expansion in mixed-feed output. Soviet imports of soybeans and/or soybean meal should be expected to increase over time; but it is unlikely that they will exceed 4 million tonnes on an annual average basis over the foreseeable future. (To place that figure in perspective, Japan's annual import of soybeans alone exceeds what would be the equivalent of 6 million tons of soybean meal.)

Japan

Japan is the world's leading importer of soybeans. Soybeans are used for both food and feed (crushed to provide soybean meal) purposes in Japan. The rapid expansion in animal numbers to improve human diets and the equally rapid development of a modernized feeding industry by this technologically conscious nation have resulted in a steadily increasing demand for protein.

Land is a restricted resource in Japan; other crops, such as rice, are too valuable to allow acreage to be switched. Thus Japan must rely on imports to satisfy the demand for protein (soybeans and soybean meal). The Japanese market is *highly* important to U.S. agricultural exports.

U.S. DISAPPEARANCE

Figure 8-7 shows a history of U.S. soybean disappearance since 1960. Formerly, the annual consumption trend nearly paralleled a straight linear trend. The accelerated annual increase which began around 1970 can be identified in the graph, despite several year-to-year declines. This was caused by an increasing world demand for protein, which improves the efficiency of feeding rations; soybean meal is a preferred source of protein because it provides a good balance of amino acids. A large expansion in crushing facilities has occurred in both the United States and Western Europe over the past 15 years in response to the increased demand for protein. Consumption of soybean meal in Western Europe skyrocketed during that period.

Exports

Exports are the primary influence on U.S. soybean prices. A good example of this relationship developed in the 1980–1981 crop year. U.S. soybean exports began to fall sharply below the level of the previous season during the fall of 1980; forward purchases of U.S. soybeans, as presented in the weekly export commitments report, also had stagnated around fairly low levels. Soybean prices plunged throughout the winter, despite the fact that domestic crushings had held up at high levels during the first quarter of the season. Crush activity is slower to change and the increments build up over a longer period; exports, on the other hand, can change much more quickly.

Exports have increased sharply as a percentage of total soybean disappearance. Table 8-10 shows that exports in 1981 approximated 45 percent of total soybean disappearance, but that basically fails to reveal the even more dramatic growth in actual bushel amounts. For example, soybean exports in 1955 approximated 18 percent of total disappearance when the soybean crop was only 370 million bushels; soybean exports currently are over 40 percent of total

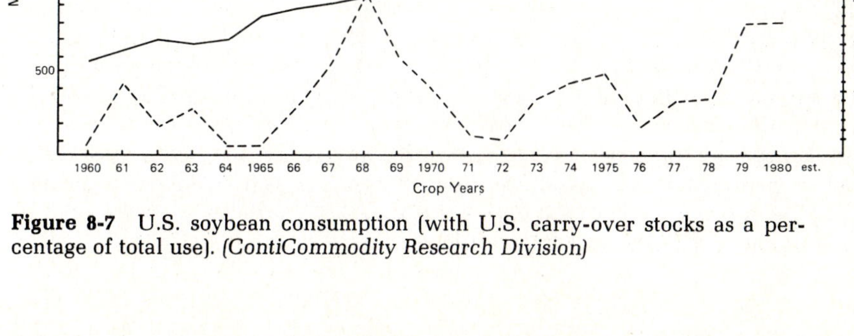

Figure 8-7 U.S. soybean consumption (with U.S. carry-over stocks as a percentage of total use). *(ContiCommodity Research Division)*

TABLE 8-10 U.S. Soybean Exports and Production*

Crop year	Exports (percent)	Production (million bushels)
1955	18.1	373
1960	23.3	700
1965	29.7	845
1970	34.5	1127
1975	37.2	1547
1978	40.4	1843
1979	42.0	2268
1980	40.0	1792
1981	45.2	2000

*Exports expressed as a percent of total disappearance.

disappearance when production has increased over time in excess of 2000 million bushels.

U.S. soybean exports have tended to increase at an average annual rate of 10 to 11 percent. This is depicted in Figure 8-8. Some large annual fluctuations do occur, which also can be noted in the graph; soybean prices can be influenced dramatically by those unusually large aberrations. One of the most important trends is the pace of exports during the fall. Soybean exports are at their highest level during the fall because prices at harvest usually are expected to be the lowest of the season and pipeline inventories normally have been depleted in anticipation of lower harvest prices. It is extremely unlikely that soybean exports can reach a high level if movement during the early part of the season

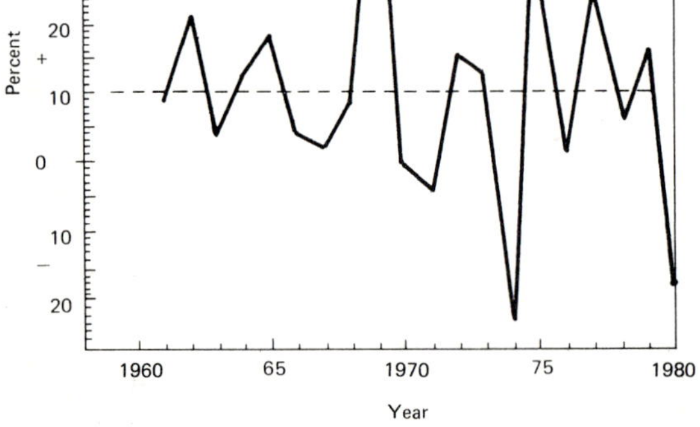

Figure 8-8 Annual percentage changes in season-to-season exports. *(ContiCommodity Research Division)*

TABLE 8-11 Exports from October to December Compared to Previous Season

Year	Million bushels	Percent change
1981	278	+35
1980	206	−28
1979	285	+8.5
1978	260	+17
1977	222	+20.5
1976	184	+5.5
1975	174	+27
1974	137	−23
1973	179	+8.5
1972	165	+30

has been relatively poor; in fact, an old corollary states that early season exports "make or break" the total season outlook. Exports during the October–December period normally approximate around one-third of total season exports. Table 8-11 compares exports during October–December in recent years with those of each previous year.

Western Europe and Japan are by far the most important customers for U.S. soybeans. The United States was essentially the only world supplier of soybeans in former years; thus the United States used to supply around 97 percent of Western Europe's requirements. High world prices stimulated soybean production in South America, though, resulting in a decline in the proportionate share of U.S. soybean imports by Western Europe. However, U.S. shipments to Western Europe so far have remained a fairly consistent percentage of total yearly U.S. soybean exports because of continued expansion in soybean imports by Western Europe (Table 8-12).

TABLE 8-12 U.S. Soybean Exports to Western Europe *(Selected years, million bushels)*

Crop year	Western Europe	Total U.S. exports	Exports to Western Europe as a percent of U.S. total
1970–71	239	434	55
1972–73	260	479	54
1973–74	329	539	61
1974–75	251	420	60
1975–76	339	555	61
1978–79	400	753	53
1979–80	410	875	47
1980–81	382	724	53
1981–82	570	929	61
1982–83*	545	905	60

*Estimate.

The sustained expansion in total soybean imports by Western Europe is threatened by the recent discussion in the EEC of ways to limit oilseed and oilseed product imports.

Crushing

Domestic crushings of soybeans vary according to the margin that exists. This "crush margin" is defined as the difference between the cost of the physical soybeans and the value of the end products (soybean meal and soybean oil). A margin of 40¢ generally is considered to be a typical break-even level. However, it really is impossible to set a fixed crushing margin that would apply to all facilities because many differences exist. There are differences in plant ages, costs, and efficiencies, and some very significant differences in accounting practices. Crushers do not discontinue operations just because margins may be below calculated costs; fixed costs remain even if plants are shut down, so operations normally continue as long as fixed costs are covered.

Crushing activity normally is spread fairly evenly from October through the balance of the season, with some seasonal decline in late spring and summer. Table 8-13 shows the percentage of the total season crush which has occurred during the October–March period in recent years. (September is omitted because it is a transition period while users wait for the availability of harvest supplies and therefore it tends to be inconsistent with the basic trend. A general rule of thumb is that crushings during September will follow the trend of the previous season; however, they are no barometer of the new season.) The table clearly shows that crushings during the October–December period usually approximate around 26 percent of the total season and October–March crushings normally represent about 50 to 52 percent of the total season's crush. The

TABLE 8-13 U.S. Crush Data Percentages*

Crop year	OND	JFM	October–March total†	April–August
1969	25	25	50	85
1970	26	25	52	80
1971	25	26	52	80
1972	29	28	56	65
1973	25	27	52	82
1974	26	25	51	80
1975	25	26	51	86
1976	28	28	55	65
1977	27	27	53	77
1978	27	26	52	76
1979	27	27	53	72
1980	28	25	54	71
1981	29.5	26	55	67

*OND (October, November, and December), JFM (January, February, and March), and October–March totals all are expressed as a percentage of total season crush; April–August is a percentage of October–March total crush.

†Figures may not balance because of rounding.

aberrations that can be seen (e.g., 1972, 1976, 1977, 1980) represent abnormal years.

Table 8-13 also shows that the proportionate share of annual U.S. crushings from April through August has been declining sharply since the mid-1970s (the low figure in 1972/73 was caused by the summer embargo and record high prices). This is a result of a consistent sharp increase in exports of soybean meal by Brazil and Argentina since 1975. Soybean crushings are at their peak level in South America from May through July.

IMPORTANT INFLUENCES ON MARKET PRICES

Disappearance Trends

Soybean consumption data is much more highly visible than data for many other agricultural commodities. Domestic feed use in corn, for example, is only derived on a quarterly basis from the grain stocks reports; moreover, there sometimes can be large errors in those residuals, which may not be corrected for a long time. The crushings by National Soybean Processors Association (NSPA) members are published weekly; the members of this association account for almost all of the total U.S. crushings of soybeans. Weekly exports of soybeans also are published by the USDA. The residual factor in total soybean disappearance is a relatively small amount. Thus it is very simple to follow soybean consumption trends—the data is much more clear and there is a minimal time lag. (Monthly reports of production and stocks of soybean meal and soybean oil also are published; these assist in the evaluation of soybean demand.)

Soybean disappearance can serve as a good benchmark for evaluating supplies. The soybean crop sometimes may be underestimated or overestimated by a relatively large amount; this can be important because even variations of only 30 to 50 million bushels sometimes can have a significant impact upon prices. It is relatively easy to calculate what soybean stocks should be in the quarterly stocks report (which is supplied by the USDA); this is especially true in the January stocks report, which is simply a matter of subtracting combined crush and exports from total beginning supplies. A difference of 5 to 10 million bushels between the calculated stocks and those which are officially reported by the USDA is common. However, the difference sometimes can be quite large; this usually is an indication that the crop size is different from what had been estimated. But the crop estimate is never changed until the following season; the error usually must be confirmed by the September stocks report, which is the carry-over for that particular season. If that report shows an imbalance between actual disappearance and supplies, then the previous crop estimate is changed. For example, the actual reported stocks in January 1981 were 29 million bushels below the calculated figure. This was a strong indication that the crop had been overestimated; further, similar discrepancies occurred in later stocks reports. The soybean crop for the 1980–1981 season was reduced by 26 million bushels in September 1981.

Table 8-14 shows a series of comparisons between the calculated stocks for every season and the actual January stocks figures that were released by the USDA. The extremely large negative difference in the 1972–1973 crop year was an indication that the crop had been overestimated; the crop size subsequently was lowered. The situation was reversed in 1978; the crop later was increased after data throughout the season showed that such an increase was warranted. However, later quarterly reports during the 1979–1980 crop year did not confirm the large aberration which showed up in the January report that year.

There is a strong tendency for disappearance to be firmly set during the October–March period and it is difficult to overcome the trend set during that period. Also, the major trend for the entire crop year is usually strongly indicated by disappearance trends during the fall, as mentioned earlier. It also is more important to look at *relative* comparisons rather than just raw bushel amounts. For example, Table 8-15 portrays a series of relevant fundamental data in relative and percentage terms; the carry-over is a particularly good choice to illustrate the above point. A carry-over of 6 to 7 percent is historically on the low side and represents a "threat" to supplies, particularly if it can be projected as that low early in the season; such situations are characteristic of most bull years. The actual bushel amount that represents such a percentage can vary widely over time according to changes in consumption patterns. A carry-over of 125 million bushels was quite "comfortable" just a few years ago (the carry-over in the 1972–1973 season, for example, was 59 million bushels). Now, however, a carry-over of 125 million bushels would approximate only 6 percent of total consumption; it also would cover only around 3 weeks of disappearance at current rates. The carry-over at the end of the 1980–1981 season is large not because it was in excess of 300 million bushels, but because it again approximated 17 percent of disappearance. A further bearish element at the end of the 1980–1981 season was the fact that new crop production for the 1981–1982 season appeared likely to exceed current disappearance needs—in contrast to the previous drought-plagued crop. Carryover stocks declined in 1981 to 1982, but they still amounted to 13 percent of total disappearance, which is relatively large, and record new crop production was likely. Relative comparisons avoid the distortions that bushel figures can provide. An ending carry-over under 200 million bushels now would have bullish implications whereas not too long ago it would have been a bearish factor.

Soybean Product Demand and Prices

The value of soybeans relates directly to the demand or lack of demand for its two products, soybean oil and soybean meal. The two products have totally different uses and demand structures. Soybean meal is a protein supplement for livestock feeding and soybean oil is a high-grade edible vegetable oil primarily used in salad and cooking oils and in margarines. Thus, an evaluation of soybean product demand is primary to the demand base for soybeans—both in the domestic and export markets. Also, demand trends for one of the two end products from crushing soybeans can be predominant at any given time; in such cases, the value of that particular product (meal or oil) simply increases its proportionate share of the total crush value.

TABLE 8-14 First Quarter Soybean Distribution*
(With differences between computed and reported stocks)

	1968	1969	1970	1971	1972	1973	1974	1975	1976	1977	1978	1979	1980	1981	1982
Total supply†	1273	1459	1357	1275	1342	1606	1385	1706	1510	1819	2004	2442	2176	2348	2543
September–December use	336	393	420	394	440	435	398	475	494	537	645	703	620	709	732
January 1 stocks:															
Computed‡	937	1066	937	881	902	1171	987	1231	1016	1282	1359	1739	1556	1642	1811
Reported§	960	1055	945	889	873	1161	989	1246	1026	1309	1393	1771	1527	1631	1826
Difference	+23	−11	+8	+8	−29	−10	+ 2	+15	+10	+27	+34	+32	−29	−11	+15

*In million bushels.

†The total supply for each crop year given in this table is the figure listed each January, utilizing the final crop estimate of that season. On some occasions crop production was changed at the end of the season after the confirmation by subsequent stocks reports. Hence, these total supply figures may not be identical to present official data for certain years where supply data subsequently was revised upwards.

‡That is, *subtracting* September–December total disappearance from total supply.

§Official January stocks report.

TABLE 8-15 Soybean Disappearance

Crop year	Current year disappearance versus previous year, %	Change in last year disappearance versus previous year, %	Previous year's carry-over as % of use	Current year's crop as a % of previous year's use	First quarter disappearance as % of total supplies	First quarter disappearance compared to previous year	Second quarter use as a % of total supplies	Second quarter use compared to last year	Current year's carryover as a % of total use	Planted acreage comparisons, %
1970–71	+2	(+30)	19	− 8	30.7	(+6.8)	21.6	(+3.5)	8	+1
1971–72	−4	(+2)	8	− 6	31.0	(−6.2)	23.4	(0)	6	0
1972–73	+7	(−4)	6	+5.5	32.7	(+11.6)	26.8	(+21.5)	4	+8
1973–74	+12	(+7)	4	+20	26.7	(−1.2)	23.7	(+6.9)	12	+21
1974–75	−16	(+12)	12	−15	28.3	(−8.5)	24.4	(−22.5)	15	−6
1975–76	+24	(−16)	15	+29	28.0	(+19.3)	22.0	(+26.4)	16	+2
1976–77	−4	(+24)	16	−14	32.2	(+4.0)	25.0	(+2.6)	7	−8
1977–78	+19	(−4)	7	+23	28.8	(+8.7)	22.5	(+8.2)	9	+17
1978–79	+9	(+19)	9	+10	31.7	(+19.9)	23.4	(+13.0)	9	+9
1979–80	+12	(+9)	9	+22	28.8	(+9.2)	23.2	(+19.5)	17	+11
1980–81	−12	(+12)	17	−15	24.6	(−25.2)	22.8	(−8.5)	17	−2
1981–82	+12	(−12)	17	+9	30.5	(+14.3)	22.4	(+5.7)	13	+6
1982–83	+2	(+12)	13	+10	29.0	(+3.0)	22.0	(+7.0)	20	−8

*Estimate.

†That is, carry-in supplies for current season, or ending year carryover of previous season.

To some extent the prospective influence of product values on soybeans can be gauged by watching crushing margins both in the United States and overseas. Widening crush margins indicate maximized crushings of soybeans and vice versa. The trend for crushing activity then can be applied to soybeans to develop demand-trend curves and analyses and arrive at a judgement of their future effect upon soybean values.

Widening and narrowing crush margins, however, by themselves do not definitely indicate soybean price direction. A general belief is that crushing margins tend to be wide when large soybean supplies exist (to induce more crushings) and narrow when soybean supplies are short; but crushing margins more accurately reflect demand for one or both products. Therefore, it is more accurate to suggest that wide crush margins occur when demand for one or both products (particularly meal) is strong and vice versa. Indeed, wide crush margins have been seen in years when soybean supplies were large *and* when they were considered short—the opposite also has occurred.

Planted Acreage

Mini-bull supply-scare markets have been created because the acreage planted to soybeans fell below anticipated or "necessary" levels. Such markets, which occur around 20 to 30 percent of the time, are similar to crop-scare markets which occur in the midsummer from drought and such. Naturally if the acreage is not planted the crop cannot grow and supplies are reduced. These violent markets are especially marked in soybeans because of the size of the price moves and the "hidden" nature by which they begin:

1. They typically begin around mid-May, right at the height of corn plantings. Reliable sources are needed for confirmation of what is going on, but soybean-corn price ratios usually are an early tip-off during the late winter and spring of what to expect.
2. Reports of actual plantings in late May may be able to say only: "they aren't planting the corn," or vice versa.
3. Typically, a soybean-corn ratio of 2.1 to 1 or lower (and especially under 2 to 1) will reduce soybean acreage; a ratio above 2.6 to 1 should increase soybean acreage.

"Acreage bull markets" (so named because the acreage planted to soybeans was too low) typically are over by the time the actual statistical data is released. The USDA releases its survey of spring-planted acreages in late June; by that time, the price move has ended and subsequent price developments depend upon growing weather during July and August, along with demand trends.

South American Competition

South American soybean production has increased proportionately as a share of total world production. Brazil, particularly, has increased its proportionate share of product exports in recent years. Thus, South American crop prospects have become an increasingly important influence upon world values. Brazilian production prospects, particularly, must be watched closely for their prospective impact on world supplies—and especially relative to existing world demand. Growing weather in January and February should be watched closely to assess probable South American production. Good crop outturns in South American grain production traditionally have had a depressing effect upon prices by early February because of the approach of harvest and added supplies in those areas (e.g., Brazil exports soybeans and soybean products, Argentina exports feed grains, wheat, soybeans, and soybean products). Conversely, droughts in South America can increase prices; the magnitude of the effect depends upon world demand and the relative quantity of U.S. supplies. (For example, the price response is magnified in soybeans if U.S. supplies are relatively low and world demand is exceptionally strong when Brazil suffers drought conditions.)

World Economic Situation

There are times when turmoil in the world economic situation, particularly involving inflation and significant weakness in the U.S. dollar vis-à-vis foreign currencies can create upward price trends in soybeans and soybean products (particularly soybean oil, which is storable). These situations are relatively rare in terms of number of occurrences; however, in times of world economic turbulence and uncertainty, food commodities in a relatively greater finite supply balance are used as a storehouse of value for money.

Depressionary trends in world economics also have a negative influence on commodity prices, such as the inability of many countries to pay for grain imports.

Government Programs

Government programs that affect corn prices also have an impact on soybeans indirectly, because of the intertwining price relationships between corn and soybeans. The intrinsic fundamentals of corn and soybeans determine their price relationship in each year—but anything that affects corn affects soybeans.

REASONS FOR SOYBEAN PRICE VOLATILITY

Soybean price movements are often very volatile. The reasons are:

1. Supplies proportionately are much smaller, related to consumption, than most other major agricultural commodities. That places soybeans in a more "finite" supply status, in comparison to other commodities.
2. Variations as small as 50 million bushels in supply-and-demand balances can have a significant impact upon prices (that bushel amount is equivalent to about 200 million bushels in corn). This is particularly true when carryover supplies are less than 10 percent of disappearance.

3. There is a high elasticity of demand which can create some unusual consumption patterns.
4. The United States is the major world soybean supplier; the situation in the United States alone can drastically affect prices. Brazil also can have a major effect upon soybean prices, despite the fact that Brazil accounts for a much smaller share of total world production, because there really are only two world suppliers of soybeans and soybean products—the United States and Brazil. In contrast, low feed-grain production in Argentina (a major world supplier) or a drought in the Soviet Union (a major world importer) may not have much effect upon world coarse grain values.
5. Storable commodities in a relatively more finite supply status are the chosen vehicles to protect money in periods of economic turmoil. Food always will have a value—money may not. (Soybean oil, for example, always has been a "harbor" for money ships during periods of inflationary buying.)

Small changes in soybean supply-and-demand balances can create extremely volatile price swings. (Figure 8-9 traces the recent history of soybean prices.) Soybeans, unlike wheat, for example, cannot be grown successfully worldwide, and it is a specialty crop. A brief description of the 1972–1973 crop year will explain how a tightening supply-demand situation can have a dramatic effect on prices.

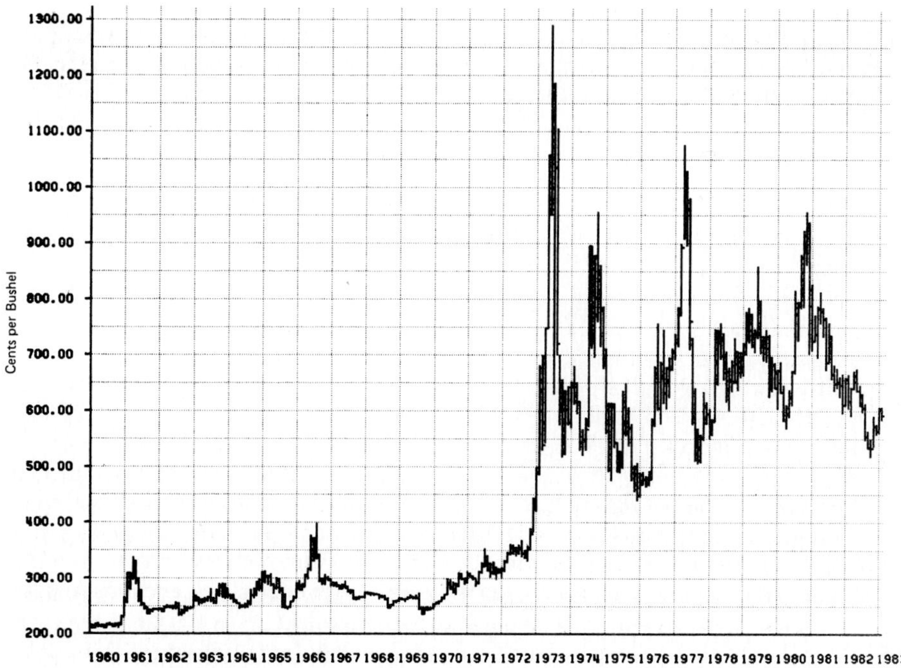

Figure 8-9 Monthly continuation, Chicago Board of Trade soybeans. *(Conti-Commodity Research Division)*

THE 1972–1973 SEASON

The fundamentals of the 1972–1973 season can be most easily understood by referring to Table 8-15. As can be seen in the second column of the table, consumption during the previous two seasons had been constrained at levels which represented below-average annual increases—there had been some sharp increases during previous seasons that are not listed in the table. Part of this was because both the 1970 and 1971 crops were small, relative to disappearance, as noted in column four. Carry-overs in both 1970 and 1971 were relatively low. In other words, there was pent-up demand during the seasons preceding the 1972–1973 crop year; prices had reached the $3 to $3.50 level, which was much above the average annual price of the previous 5 years. Prices remained at relatively high levels; summer crop production had to be "proven" because of a relatively low ending carry-over that amounted to only 6 percent of total use. A year-to-year decline in soybean consumption is unusual and normally indicates one of two things: (1) above-normal consumption the following season if production is large or (2) problems if production is not large.

The 1972 season began with a relatively rare reduction in season-to-season consumption during the previous year; crop production was 5 percent above the 1971 disappearance, but still only slightly higher than 1969 and 1970 actual disappearance.* Moreover, demand from the 1971 season had been "delayed," due to the anticipation of lower fall harvest prices; this provided a built-in, latent demand factor and meant that pipeline inventory supplies would be replaced (at equivalent prices).

Furthermore, factors such as the surprising downturn in South American production of fishmeal (an important source of world protein) occurred during the course of the 1972 crop season. This factor added an accelerated replacement demand for soybean meal, since fishmeal contains considerably higher protein. Additionally, very early November snows "locked in" a large number of unharvested fields because of the late spring plantings and the consequent late plant maturity. This prospectively cut production prospects (indeed, the January stocks report appeared to confirm this, despite the lack of confirmation in official crop reports).

The increase in total beginning supplies was relatively small and early-season consumption was huge. Disappearance during the initial September–December period was almost 33 percent of total supplies; that in itself was sufficient to outline a bullish scenario for the 1972 season, since carry-in stocks were a relatively low 6 percent—certainly not sufficient to cover any robust increase in demand. But even more bullish developments occurred.

However, in January 1973, the stocks report was almost 30 million bushels below the calculated figure from supplies minus September–December consumption indicating the crop had been overestimated. This increased the importance of any marginal increase in demand. Moreover, usage continued to run at an exceptional pace; final second-quarter totals showed second-quarter

*That is, crop production only barely kept pace with the pared consumption requirements of recent periods.

consumption at almost 27 percent of total supplies. This not only was well above the normal JFM (January, February, and March) rate of use, but also meant that disappearance since the start of the season totalled an astounding 60 percent of available supplies.

There was, therefore, a very realistic danger of a complete exhaustion of soybean stocks. Although weekly export commitments were not published at that time, private export projections by major exporting firms had revealed that potential since early January. In fact, adding actual total disappearance through December to projected January–August crush and exports, and subtracting the total from the official January stocks figure left a balance of zero, even at that early period. It is a logistical impossibility, of course, to reduce supplies to a zero level because of the widespread locations of stocks plus pipeline requirements, and so on. But it is also the reason why, when carry-over supplies become "threatened," price is the element that has to "ration" the available supplies.

However, during the course of the 1972 season, even record high prices did not succeed in reducing demand sufficiently. Cash prices serve as a good barometer of what was occurring; by the spring of 1973, the gulf cash price had reached a level $1 higher than Chicago futures. That was unprecedented. Spiraling cash price carried futures into a runaway price move. There really was no way to depict what the actual price of soybeans should be, because demand had outstripped supply and that demand was not abating sufficiently.

Soybean prices reached the statistical high of $12.90 that season. However, the price move was only halted by a partial export embargo finally imposed by the government in late June. That embargo also ultimately created the ending carry-over in 1972, which had been statistically nonexistent. Indeed, the threat to ending carry-over can be seen by the fact that, despite the limitation of shipments by the embargo, the ending carry-over for 1972 still was only around 4 percent of total beginning supplies. Historically, that level even without an embargo has been "too low," resulting in sharp price escalations due to the threat to supplies.

SUMMARY AND TRADING CONSIDERATIONS

1. U.S. soybean supplies:
   a. Planted acreage in spring
   b. Growing weather during summer
   c. Total crop production in USDA late
   d. Ending carry-over stock summer–fall crop estimates
2. Disappearance trends, particularly related to supplies and projected carry-over stocks.
3. Estimated carry-over.
4. Does the particular crop year qualify for a bull or bear price scenario fundamentally?

5. Soybean product demand and prices, particularly for meal.
   a. Domestic and foreign feeding margins
   b. The rate and trend of both actual exports and new sales
   c. Crushing margins
6. The level of deliverable stocks in Chicago and Toledo.
7. Trends in cash markets.
8. South American production, which is the measurement of competition for U.S. soybean and product exports.
9. World economic situation and the value of the U.S. dollar versus other currencies.
10. Government farm programs.
11. Soybean-corn price ratios.

Commodity	Exchange(s)	Contract size	Limit moves
Soybeans	Chicago Board of Trade Mid-America Commodity Exchange	5000 bushels 1000 bushels	30¢

What factors predict major bottoms:

1. Corn futures are at or below price-support levels.
2. Soybean-corn price ratios are low.
3. Export buying is high.
4. Relative consumption trends have turned strong.
5. In the summer, a sudden or severe threat to crop production from drought.

What factors predict major peaks:

1. Relative consumption trends turn very weak.
2. Ending carry-over can be projected well above the level commonly believed and forecast.
3. In spring, a large increase in planted acreage occurs.
4. A heavy, drought-breaking rain occurs during droughts, and more is forecast.
5. Even your local barber recommends buying soybeans (this may appear funny but actually is more common than one may think).

CHAPTER

9

Barley, Oats, and Sorghum

Alan London

BARLEY

U.S. Production

Barley is well adapted to the less temperate regions in the United States. Its production is concentrated in the northern plains and Pacific coast states where other grains cannot adapt as well to the climate. Barley competes with spring wheat and oats for much of the acreage used to produce it; therefore, government programs have a direct effect on barley acreage.

Barley is fourth among major feed grains grown in the United States, falling behind corn, sorghum, and oats. Increasing production of wheat, corn, and soybeans has had an adverse impact on the acreage planted to barley. Future increases in barley acreage, to levels in excess of the 10.8 million acres planted in 1977, depend on government barley price support programs and to a large degree on government programs affecting spring wheat.

Barley is grown under different cropping systems in various parts of the United States. In the northern great plains it is seeded in the spring on land that had been fallowed the prior spring. Barley varieties used for malting may be grown on irrigated land to control protein content. Feed barley usually has a higher protein (protein content is not a favorable characteristic for malting). Malt barley commands a premium because its use is primarily for human consumption. Producers generally plant malting varieties in anticipation of selling high-quality malt barley at a premium price. However, not all barley produced as malting quality makes the grade.

The quality standards for malting barley are much stricter than ordinary feed barley. Specifications are set for size, plumpness, and protein. The reason for strict standards is the need for uniformity in sprouting and quality control for beer. Mallsters usually prefer 80 percent plump barley kernels; barley with more than 15 percent thin kernels cannot be classified as malting quality under U.S. barley standards.

U.S. Consumption

There are three components to demand for U.S. barley; exports, feed, and malting (see Table 9-1). Domestic use of it is mixed between feed and malting. The quantity of barley in beer production has been relatively constant over the recent past. The quantity of barley used for malting includes distilling and brewing. The amount of barley used in distilled spirits is quite small compared to brewing. The U.S. Department of Agriculture (USDA) has estimated that distilling use of barley now averages less than 4 million bushels per year. Barley use in brewing has not increased with increased consumption of beer. Brewing technology has led to a reduction in the amount of barley malt per barrel of beer produced.

Feed is the major domestic use for barley. Roughly half the barley used for feed is used on the farms where it is grown. The balance is used in processed feed. Feed use of barley depends primarily upon the availability of feed barley as well as its price relative to other feed grains. Barley's value as a feed grain is nearly equal to corn as a cattle feed, only 90 percent of the value of corn as a hog feed, and 80 percent of the value of corn as a poultry feed. Thus, in areas where barley is available, its use as a feed grain depends to a large degree on its price relative to other feed grains. Variations in barley prices from 1971 to 1982 are shown in Figure 9-1.

Export demand for barley has been fairly variable over the past several years. Exports during 1975–1976 were just under 24 million bushels and exceeded 100 million bushels in the 1981–1982 marketing year but dropped to 45 million bushels in 1982. The average for exports over the past 7 years is 61 million bushels per year, which is very close to the annual average for exports during the 1970s. Barley competes with other feed grains in foreign markets. There is only a minimal amount of U.S. barley that is exported for malting purposes. Therefore the amount of barley that is exported is a function of its price and availability relative to other feed grains in the United States and the importing country. Since most of the U.S. barley that is exported goes into live-

TABLE 9-1 U.S. Barley Demand
(Million bushels)

	1976	1977	1978	1979	1980	1981	1982
Exports	66	57	26	55	77	100	45
Feed	171	178	218	204	174	202	240
Malting	132	133	148	151	155	155	158

SOURCE: United States Department of Agriculture.

Figure 9-1 Monthly continuation, Winnipeg barley. *(ContiCommodity Research Division)*

stock feed, the number of importing countries is limited to those with a more developed livestock economy. Another factor in determining U.S. barley exports is the profitability of the importing nation's livestock economy.

Overseas Production

World barley production is generally centered in northern latitudes, where climatic and economic conditions are suited for its production. Most of these barley-producing countries have encouraged production of barley to support expanding livestock economies. While world barley production is less concentrated than wheat or corn production, Europe accounts for a very significant percentage of total world production. Table 9-2 shows the world's major barley producers. Five of the largest barley-producing countries are members of the European Economic Community (EEC).

The price of barley in world markets is a function of the supply of and demand for barley as well as other feed grains. Barley prices vary more than corn, primarily because exports are not concentrated in one supplier as they are in the corn market. Use of French soft wheat in European feed rations keeps its price fairly close to barley prices. Generally, in times of surplus supplies, grain prices approach their relative feeding values. This is true in world markets, as it is true for livestock and poultry feed in the United States.

Contract Data

The only futures market for barley is in the Winnipeg Commodity Exchange. The barley contract in Winnipeg is for domestic feed barley. It is traded in job lots of 20 tons and board lots of 100 tons. Barley is traded in Canadian dollars per ton, with minimum fluctuations of 10¢/ton and a daily limit of $5/ton.

TABLE 9-2 World Barley Production
(Million tonnes)

	1977	1978	1979	1980	1981
Soviet Union	52.7	61.1	45.5	57.2	41.9
France	10.3	11.3	11.2	11.2	10.2
Canada	11.8	10.4	8.5	11.0	13.4
United States	7.2	8.2	9.8	9.1	10.4
United Kingdom	10.5	9.8	9.6	9.6	10.1
West Germany	7.5	8.6	8.2	8.7	8.7
Spain	6.7	8.6	6.2	7.1	4.7
Denmark	6.1	6.3	6.7	6.3	6.3
China	6.9	6.7	6.8	7.2	7.4
World total	104.5	182.0	157.0	172.0	160.4

SOURCE: United States Department of Agriculture.

OATS

Introduction

Oats represent a very different sort of futures market contract. Compared to wheat and corn very limited general information on oats is available to the public. The cash oats market has far fewer participants than other grains. The reason for the small cash market is because a much higher percent of the oats crop is consumed on farms where it is produced. Oats are a bulky commodity and have relatively high transportation costs.

Oats have a 6¢/bushel daily price limit, less than the 10¢ in corn, 20¢ in wheat, or 30¢ in soybeans. Despite limited information, less public knowledge, and the air of secrecy surrounding oats, they have attracted both the large trader as well as the weak of heart.

There are only three other crops in the world—wheat, rice, and corn—that are planted on more acres than oats. For a long time in the United States, oats acreage ranked fourth behind wheat, corn, and soybeans. However, in recent years oats acreage has dwindled, and now oats rank fifth, following sorghum.

U.S. Production

The bulk of U.S. oat production takes place in the northern plains. Table 9-3 summarizes recent U.S. oat production by major regions. Oats in these major producing states are planted early in the spring and harvested by the latter half of August.

A very important trend in the oats market has been a steady decline in oat acreage, and consequently in the level of production. The 1981 oat crop according to USDA records, while 11 percent greater than the drought-reduced crop of 1980, was the second smallest production since 1881. Because of the bulkiness of the crop, a large portion of oat consumption takes place close to the point of production. Thus the decline in the production of oats is directly related to the decline in the number of horses and mules employed as work animals.

TABLE 9-3 U.S. Oat Production
(Million bushels)

	1979	1980	1981
Minnesota	84.9	82.7	90.1
South Dakota	94.0	66.0	70.5
Iowa	63.0	62.0	70.5
Wisconsin	55.9	58.7	52.6
North Dakota	37.0	13.5	44.2
U.S. total	526.6	458.3	508.1

SOURCE: United States Department of Agriculture, 1981 Crop Production Summary.

U.S. Consumption

The principal use for oats is as an animal feed grain. Oats are usually priced very competitively with corn as a feed grain on a pound-for-pound basis. Nutritionally, oats and corn are very close substitutes. The USDA has estimated that roughly 85 percent of annual oat consumption goes to animal feed.

Cattle feeding accounts for about one-third of all feed consumption of oats. The feed value of oats is 10 percent greater for dairy cattle than for beef cattle. Oats are valued in dairy feeds for their palatability and energy content. The on-farm use of oats as a dairy feed grain is particularly high in Wisconsin.

Nearly 20 percent of oats used as a feed ingredient goes into hog feeds. Oats are used in feed rations for sows during gestation because of their nutritional value and ease of digestion. Feeder pig rations also include oats for basically the same reason. Feeder pigs and sows are sensitive to digestive problems. At their respective stages of development, it's very important that each animal consume a nutritious and palatable diet.

The major use of oats for feed is for horses and mules. Horse owners prize high-grade feed oats for their palatability. An important point regarding horse-feed demand for oats is that it is a relatively constant number; the size of the horse herd does not vary much from year to year. The total number of horses and mules in the United States has dropped dramatically in the past 55 years, from roughly 27 million head in 1927 to approximately 3 million head in 1982.

The food use of oats is limited to about 6 percent of all oats consumption. Breakfast cereals claim about 40 million bushels per year. Oat consumption per

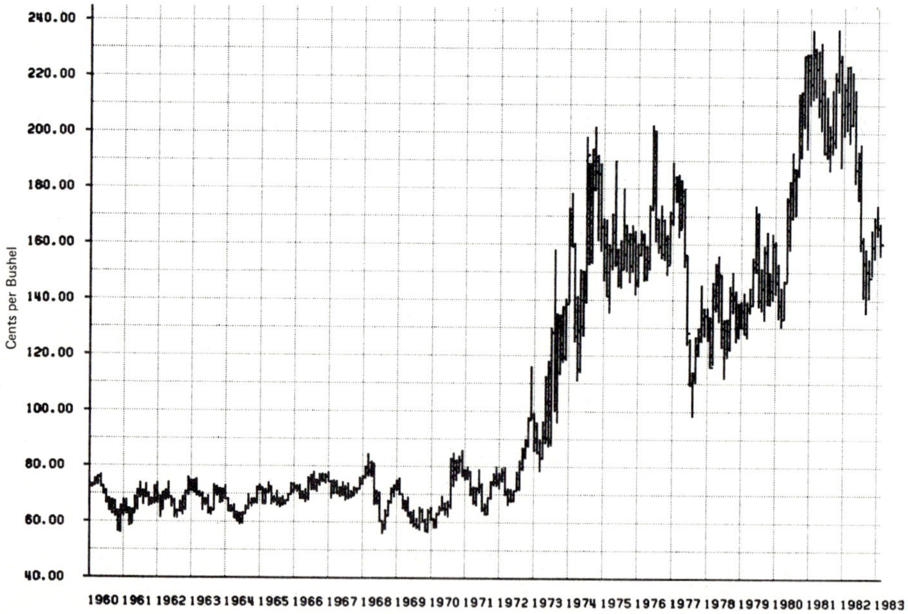

Figure 9-2 Monthly continuation, Chicago Board of Trade oats. *(Conti-Commodity Research Division)*

capita is very low, roughly 5 pounds per year, compared to nearly 120 pounds per year for wheat. Per capita consumption of oats has been constant for sometime and it is unlikely that consumers will alter their tastes or preferences to a degree that will lead to increased oats usage.

The most important point regarding oat consumption is that the demand for quality oats is rather inelastic in price. Specialty feed manufacturers (producing pig starters and horse feeds) as well as cereal manufacturers have very few substitutes available. Their demand for oats, therefore, does not vary as the price of oats changes. Given a relatively constant base demand for oats, the market price will have to be high enough to pull oats off the farm into commercial channels when the supply of quality oats is low. It is this inelastic demand structure that keeps the oats market viable for futures contracts. Were it not for the specialized uses of oats as a feed and food grain, the futures market for oats would have long since gone the way of rye futures, which died from lack of interest over 20 years ago.

Given that a high percentage of oats are used on the farm, the oats that enter the commercial market are meeting a very inelastic demand. Because of high transportation costs and quality factors, higher prices would not necessarily lead to more oats leaving the farm to enter commercial channels. (See Figure 9-2 for oats prices from 1960 to 1982.)

For feed purposes, oats and corn are nearly perfect substitutes. Theoretically, the price of oats, therefore, should be equal to corn on a pound-for-pound basis. Oats weigh 32 pounds per bushel, while corn weighs 56 pounds per bushel. As an example, if oats were $1.60 per bushel, then corn would be $2.80 per bushel if the two cost the same amount per pound. Therefore in theory, oats should cost 57 percent of the price of corn.

It has been shown that the price of oats between November and May averages 59.7 percent of the price of corn per bushel. This is only a guideline, which can vary dramatically, especially in years of a large corn yield and a relatively small oats crop. The inelastic demand for commercial oats will make the price of oats high in relation to the price of corn in those years of high corn production.

Contract Data

Oats at the Chicago Board of Trade are traded in 5000-bushel contracts and, as previously mentioned, there is currently a 6¢ daily trading limit. Because the volume of trade in oats is low compared to trade in other futures markets, the market is not the most liquid. There are few local scalpers that ply their trade in the oat pit. Therefore large orders must be entered with care to obtain the most efficient execution.

SORGHUM

Sorghum is a major feed grain for livestock and poultry feed. It is grown primarily in climatic regions which are too dry and too warm for corn. The United States is a major sorghum producer and exporter. There are two other sorghum exporting nations—Argentina and Australia. The other main producing nations are the People's Republic of China, India, Nigeria, and Mexico.

U.S. Production

Production of sorghum in the United States is concentrated in the southern plains states where the crop is well adapted to the limited moisture and high temperatures. The states of Texas, Oklahoma, Kansas, and Nebraska account for nearly 80 percent of production.

Production in the United States has fluctuated quite dramatically in the past. It experienced a sharp increase in production in the 1950s, acreage reduction in the 1960s offset by increased yields, and wide ranges of production during the 1970s. The swings in production were due to poor weather, improving technologies (seed and fertilizer), and changes in various government programs.

The acreage planted to sorghum in Nebraska, Kansas, Oklahoma, and Texas has an inverse relationship to the acreage of other crops. Sorghum competes for acreage with wheat, cotton, and corn. Thus the profitability of alternate crops and the impact of government programs have a strong effect on the amount of sorghum planted in these major producing states.

The sorghum belt provided the cattle feeding industry with a source of feed and a favorable operating climate. The growth in sorghum production coincided with the increase in cattle feeding in the southern plains states. Fed cattle marketing had a large annual increase from 1955 to 1972 when marketings leveled off in these main producing states (Table 9-4).

Sorghum competes with corn in feed rations, especially in beef cattle rations. They are to a large extent interchangeable in beef rations; price and availability are the decisive factors. The USDA has estimated that sorghum's value in feed rations for beef cattle is 92 percent of the value of corn. Sorghum was found to have 95 percent of the value of corn for all forms of livestock in the United States.

U.S. Consumption

The trend toward increased meat consumption in the United States and other more developed economies helped spur the increase in sorghum consumption. The demand for more meat and poultry meant that more concentrate was

TABLE 9-4 Fed Cattle Marketed *(Million head)*

	1955	1972	1981
Texas	0.3	4.3	4.0
Kansas	0.5	2.4	3.0
Nebraska	1.3	4.0	4.1

SOURCE: United States Department of Agriculture.

needed in livestock rations. Grain use also increased, helped in part by favorable feed-livestock price relationships.

The feed-mixing industry implemented least cost technology and was in a position to take advantage of favorably priced feed substitutes. Thus switching from corn to sorghum became a profitable exercise for mixers, whenever the price of sorghum relative to corn was below the feed value of sorghum relative to corn.

Domestic uses of sorghum are extremely limited. Feed use accounts for over 97 percent of domestic sorghum use. The remainder is scattered between industrial and seed usage. Feed use is by far the largest single use for the U.S. sorghum crop.

The second largest use for sorghum comes from the export market. Sorghum is used as human food in the developing areas of Asia and Africa. However U.S. exports of sorghum are used primarily in the more developed nations of the world. The United States and Argentina account for the overwhelming majority of exports, averaging over 85 percent of the world's exports in the past few years.

U.S. exports of sorghum are concentrated among a fairly small number of buyers. The main importers of U.S. sorghum are Japan, Mexico, Israel, and to a lesser degree Taiwan, Venezuela, Portugal, and Spain. These countries make their importing decisions in a fashion similar to a feed mixer considering relative prices of substitute grains, domestic production of feed grains, availability of feed grains, profitability of livestock production, and size of the livestock herd.

Japan's use of sorghum is a result of the Japanese government's emphasis on improved diets. The Japanese government has devoted substantial resources to the development of its livestock and poultry industries.

The EEC, on the other hand, has not been a major importer of sorghum because of restrictive import policies. Grain prices in the EEC are based on a price set by a commission. The basic price is called the target price. The target price becomes the basis for the threshold price, which is the importer's cost and includes the variable import levy. The variable import levy is the difference between the threshold price and a seller's asking price for grain delivered in a European port. The effect of the variable levy becomes evident if the EEC

TABLE 9-5 World Grain Production
(Million tonnes)

	1979	1980	1981
Wheat	402.9	439.2	453.2
Corn	423.3	404.8	438.8
Rice	368.6	395.9	410.8
Barley	160.1	167.6	171.3
Sorghum	67.3	64.3	69.7

SOURCE: United States Department of Agriculture.

TABLE 9-6 Major Sorghum-Consuming Nations
(Million tonnes)

	China	U.S.	India	Japan	World
1977	14.6	12.2	11.3	5.0	67.2
1978	14	13.5	12	4.8	68.3
1979	15	12.9	12.4	4.9	69.8
1980	8	8.8	10.7	3.3	59.4
1981	8	11.2	11	3.6	67.4

SOURCE: United States Department of Agriculture.

offers its feed grains at a lower price in order to undersell external suppliers. If the price of the imported grain falls, the levy will be increased, offsetting the price drop in an attempt to maintain the threshold price.

Sorghum is the fifth most widely grown grain crop in the world (Table 9-5). The more developed countries use most of their sorghum and other coarse grain crops for livestock and poultry feed. The lesser-developed nations use sorghum for human consumption, and this accounts for more than half of the world's production.

China is the world's largest sorghum consumer, although their use has remained relatively static. U.S. consumption of sorghum has risen from the early 1960s because of increases in use for livestock feeding. India is the third largest sorghum consumer, and like China uses sorghum mainly for food. Japan is another major user of sorghum as a feed grain (Table 9-6).

There had been a sorghum contract at the Chicago Mercantile Exchange but it is no longer in existence. It was rarely used by hedgers and therefore could not attract any speculative participation. Whatever use commercial sorghum users make of a futures market is in the corn pit at the Chicago Board of Trade. Because corn is a close substitute for sorghum as a feed grain, corn has been a reliable cross hedge.

CHAPTER

10

Rice

Thomas Bell and Steven Gilson

INTRODUCTION

First grown in India almost 5000 years ago, rice is now the primary food for over one-half the world population. In the United States, it has been actively cultivated since the late seventeenth century, and is today a major crop. Rice represented less than 1 percent of U.S. cropland acreage in 1977, but it ranked sixth in production value of all major field crops. The United States produced only 1.2 percent of world production in 1978 (Table 10-1), but 61 percent of that crop was exported to over 100 countries. The 2,300,000 tonnes accounted for about 25 percent of all rice in international trade that year (see Table 10-2).

Domestic consumption of rice is distributed to all fifty states, where in addition to its primary value as food, the grain and its by-products find applications in many other industries, such as brewery, livestock feed, leather treatment, and such diverse manufacturing processes as soap, synthetic rubber, rayon, and other textiles.

Rice grown in the United States is probably the finest quality available. Modern cultivation methods have been developed to such a degree that the typical U.S. rice farm is the most scientifically operated and highly mechanized operation in the world. For example, American rice growers use less than 2 worker-days of labor per acre for all cultivation and harvesting operations, compared to more than 400 worker-days in other rice-growing nations. The efficiency has been achieved through the use of specialized machinery in all phases of the production process. Airplanes are used for the seeding and fertilization of the crop, and for insect, grass, and weed control. Powerful tractors, combines, and

TABLE 10-1 Percentage of World Production of Rice by Country *(Rough basis)*

	1979–1980	1980–1981	1981–1982
China	37.49	35.19	34.86
India	17.42	20.18	19.74
Indonesia	7.02	7.50	7.98
Bangladesh	5.02	5.25	4.89
Thailand	4.22	4.67	4.70
Japan	3.98	3.08	3.12
Burma	2.64	3.28	3.31
Other foreign	20.57	19.17	19.75
Total foreign	98.35	19.17	97.96
United States	1.65	1.67	2.04
World total	100.00	100.00	100.00

automatic loading machinery all contribute to a complicated production scheme that provides the consumer with the finest quality rice possible. (The volume of rice production from 1976 to 1982 can be seen in Table 10-3.)

RICE PRODUCTION*

Area planted to rice in the United States since 1950 has varied from a low of 1.4 million acres in 1957 to 3 million acres in 1978. Acreage expanded rapidly after World War II until production controls and marketing quotas were imposed for the 1955 crop. Plantings were restrained by government programs from 1955 to 1973 to prevent large surpluses.

Marketing quotas were suspended in 1974 and subsequent years, resulting in a sharp rise in national acreage. Rice acreage expanded dramatically in some regions with the suspension of marketing quotas, while others changed very

TABLE 10-2 Percentage of Total Exports of Rice by Country *(Milled basis)*

	1980	1981	1982
Australia	2.53	2.66	4.28
Burma	5.32	5.18	5.70
Pakistan	7.63	8.68	7.33
China	8.30	4.62	4.89
Thailand	21.29	23.48	28.52
All others	31.44	32.22	25.66
Total foreign	76.52	76.89	75.37
United States	23.48	23.16	23.67
World total	100.00	100.00	100.00

*This section draws heavily upon unpublished papers by D. W. Parvin, Jr., Mississippi State University, and articles by Shelby Holden in the USDA *Rice Situation*.

TABLE 10-3 U.S. Rice Supply and Usage (rough equivalent)
(Million hundredweight)

	1976–1977	1977–1978	1978–1979	1979–1980	1980–1981	1981–1982
Beginning stocks	36.9	40.5	27.4	31.6	25.7	16.5
Production	115.6	99.2	133.2	131.9	146.2	185.4
Imports	0.1	0.1	0.1	0.1	0.2	0.3
Total	152.6	139.8	160.6	163.6	172.1	202.2
Domestic use	46.5	39.6	53.3	55.4	64.2	71.2
Exports	65.6	72.8	75.7	82.5	91.4	82.1
Total	112.1	112.4	129	137.9	155.6	153.3
Ending stocks	40.5	27.4	31.6	25.7	16.5	48.9
Demand ratio	0.73	0.8	0.8	0.84	0.90	0.76

little. From 1973 to 1978, acreage more than doubled in northeast Arkansas and more than quadrupled in the Mississippi river delta. A moderate decrease occurred in the Grand Prairie of Arkansas, and the Sacramento Valley of California had a 25 percent increase. Southwest Louisiana and the coast prairie of Texas had the least change.

Producing Areas

Rice production in the United States is largely confined to six major production areas contained in five states: Arkansas, Mississippi, Louisiana, Texas, and California. The six areas where the growing takes place—the Grand Prairie and northeast areas of Arkansas, the Mississippi River Delta, southwest Louisiana, the coast prairie of Texas, and the Sacramento Valley of California—accounted for about 99 percent of U.S. production in 1978. Rice is grown under flood irrigation. All operations are highly mechanized and require substantial capital investment in irrigation facilities and farm machinery.

Grand Prairie, Arkansas. The Grand Prairie is located in east-central Arkansas, and includes the counties of Arkansas, Lonoke, and Prairie. Rice competes with soybeans here for land and water, and is grown in rotation with the soybeans. Total water supplies can sustain only about 200,000 acres of rice. Larger acreages have resulted in serious drawdowns of the underground water supply. Further expansion of rice acreages in this area is impossible under present conditions.

Northeast Arkansas. Located between Crowley's Ridge on the east and the White and Black rivers to the southwest and west, this area includes parts of fifteen counties. A much wider range of soil conditions occurs here than in the Grand Prairie. Irrigation water is supplied mainly from underground strata at levels of 50 to 75 feet. No serious drawdown of the underground water level has been observed except in the extreme eastern side of the area. An estimated 668,000 acres of rice, or 50 percent of the cropland suitable for production, could be sustained. However, institutional constraints such as farm size make additional expansion doubtful.

Mississippi River Delta. This is the most extensive major rice growing area in the United States. It includes all or part of forty-three counties in southeast Arkansas, northeast Louisiana, Mississippi, and southeast Missouri. Rice acreage is scattered throughout the Delta, but is concentrated in southeast Arkansas and the central Delta counties of Mississippi. Total Delta cropland suited for rice production is estimated at 6.9 million acres. About 3.4 million acres, made up of clay and mixed soil with impervious subsoils, are suited to rice. Recent expansion has occurred principally on these soils. An additional 800,000 acres of noncropland could be converted into rice production fairly rapidly.

Irrigation water is supplied from shallow underground strata and from surface streams. Water supplies could irrigate much larger acreages in the Delta, but agronomic restrictions in the area impose practical limits on potential acreage to about 2.1 million acres annually planted to rice.

Southwest Louisiana. This area comprises 2.2 million acres of cropland in the eight parishes in the southwestern area. Some 1.8 million of these acres are physically suited for producing rice, with soil characteristics ranging from fine-textured, poorly drained clay soils near marsh areas along the coast to coarser-textured, moderately well-drained soils along the northern and eastern fringes of the area. Soybeans and pastureland for beef cattle compete with rice in this region. Both are also grown in rotation with rice.

Irrigation water is split about evenly between surface and groundwater. Some of the water used to produce rice in southwest Louisiana as well as in Texas and California is supplied by canal companies (sometimes referred to as "waterlords"). Hydrological studies indicate that groundwater levels are relatively static, but salt water intrusion does occur in periods of drought.

The U.S. Department of Agriculture (USDA) estimates a potential annual acreage of 897,000 for this region, with a possibility of about 400,000 additional acres. However, institutional constraints in this region restrict expansion to only about 100,000 acres. For producers to increase their rice acreage, they must own or lease suitable acreage and make arrangements for irrigation water. Farm size is small in this region, which makes the leasing of economically efficient tracts difficult. The scarcity of suitable new land for lease with available water seriously limits expansion in this region. Industrial expansion is competing for land and water. Acreage in the area has actually been declining, and is currently significantly below allotment levels.

Coastal Prairie, Texas. Located along the eastern gulf coast of Texas, this area encompasses all or part of seventeen counties. Beef cattle is the main competing enterprise. Soils in this area include dark clay, clay loams, light loams, and sandy loams. The heavier clay soils are found near coast marshes, while light and sandy soils are to the north and west of the heavier soils. Water for 60 percent of the acreage is supplied from irrigation canals and the balance from wells. Potential annual acreage is estimated at 596,000, but it seems to have stabilized at 600,000 in 1980. Because of increasing industrial and urban competition for water, this area is probably operating at its maximum potential.

With expected population increases, this region will probably have to reduce rice production.

Sacramento Valley, California. Rice is grown here in rotation with small grains, sorghum, and safflowers. Currently, competition from these and other crops is limited due to the high returns from rice. Potential rice producers have about 660,000 acres of cropland, all suited to rice. Most rice here is grown on alluvial clay and clay adobe soils. Rice producers not supplied by irrigation districts pump water from streams, drainage canals, and irrigation wells. The estimated long-term potential acreage for rice, a little over 500,000 acres, represents three-fourths of the cropland. Much more acreage than this, it is thought, could not be sustained over a long period.

About 10 percent of California's rice crop is produced in the San Joaquin Valley; however, potential rice acreage estimates are not available for this area.

Yields

U.S. rice yields experienced a slow upward trend from 1900–1954 at a rate of increase of about 24 pounds per acre per year. The yield of 1221 pounds per acre in 1900 had been doubled by 1954. Allotments and marketing quotas were imposed in 1955 on that and subsequent crop years. Marginal land was removed from production, and yields increased rapidly to 3061 pounds per acre in 1955 and to a high of 4700 pounds per acre in 1972. Yields for crop years 1969–1978 averaged 4500 pounds per acre.

The growth pattern in yields is similar for each state, but the general level of yield is different. Average yield per acre during 1974–1978 ranged from 3772 pounds in Louisiana to 5544 pounds per acre in California. Per acre yield during this same period averaged 4511 pounds in Arkansas, 4447 pounds in Texas, and 4106 pounds in Mississippi. Several factors contributed to this yield variance, with weather playing a key role.

The exceptionally high yields in California reflect the large percentage of short-grain varieties, which are high-yielding. They accounted for 35 to 60 percent of that state's production during the period 1969–1978. Also, California receives very little rainfall and has excellent sunshine during the growing season. Rainfall increases from the western gulf coast to the east, and yield tends to decline in that direction, because of fewer days of full sunshine and increased disease problems related to moisture.

A longer growing season in the western gulf coast area makes it possible to produce a ratoon, or second crop. Therefore, yields west of Houston are consistently higher.

Growers in Arkansas and Mississippi have fewer problems with disease and insects than those in the gulf coast areas of Louisiana and Texas, but yields in Mississippi are still consistently lower than those in the other major growing areas.

Factors affecting rice yield may be grouped as those affecting yield within a given year, those affecting long-term yield levels, and those affecting yield between areas.

Short-Term Variations

A rice plant experiences three stages of growth development: the vegetative, the reproductive, and the maturative stages. Each stage influences the three components of yield: the number of panicles (heads) per unit of land area, the average number of grains per panicle, and the average weight of the individual grain.

Even with advanced cultivation practices, weather remains a major determinant of yield. Rice requires a fixed number of cumulative temperature units for each stage of plant development and a certain amount of sunlight during the reproductive and maturative stages. Lack of normal sunlight early in the development stages of the rice plant usually does not limit the yield, except under extremely cloudy and cool conditions. Day length, maximum sunlight intensity, cloud cover, and mutual shading among plants all influence total sunlight available to the plant. Day length and maximum sunlight intensity are predictable factors, and can be compensated for by timing the planting dates accordingly. Cloud cover for a specific area and time, however, is difficult to predict. Alternative management strategies may be used under such conditions, such as reducing the second nitrogen application under heavy cloud cover conditions. The rice plant's response to nitrogen is related to how much leaf surface is exposed to light.

Rainfall distribution is also an important influence on rice yield. Yield is adversely affected when rainfall delays optimum seeding rate. Ill-timed rainfall can also delay maturity and harvest. The heavy rains and strong winds associated with hurricanes can have a devastating effect on rice yields, but this problem has been lessened in the gulf coast by the use of short-season varieties which shift harvest slightly ahead of the primary hurricane season.

Drying and Storage

The advent of the combine harvester created the need for artificial drying, since rice must be stored at moisture levels of 13 percent but is normally harvested at moisture levels of 18 to 25 percent. Dryers are either farm or commercial. Commercial dryers receive, dry, store, and load out rough rice on a fee basis. The percentage of rice dried on the farm ranges from 10 percent in California to 75 percent in Mississippi, with increases expected, although commercial drying will probably continue to dominate.

On-farm drying and storage costs range from 29¢/bushel for 80,000-bushel facility to 50¢/bushel for 15,000-bushel facility. Cooperative commercial dryers dominate Arkansas and California. The capacity of noncooperative commercial dryers has been increasing; better than 60 percent have storage capacities exceeding 540,000 hundredweight and average costs of 60¢/hundredweight for various capacities.

Milling

Major milling centers are located at Stuggart, Arkansas; Sacramento, California; Cromley, Louisiana; and Houston, Texas with approximately forty mills in total, ten of which mill two-thirds of the crop. Volume ranges from 40,000 to 9 million CWT. Costs range from $1.50 to $2.00 per CWT.

The rice-milling process begins when the rough rice is cleaned before it reaches the huller. A disk sheller then removes the hull from the rice kernel, yielding brown rice with the bran layer intact. The next step, accomplished by pearlers, converts the brown into white by an abrading action that removes the bran layer.

Sizing is then accomplished by screen and disk separation that removes head from "brokers." Brokers include second heads (large broken kernels), screenings (medium broken kernels), and brewers (small broken kernels). Second heads and screenings are usually blended with heads to achieve the brakers allowance in each rice grade.

Marketings

Cooperatives handle most of the rice in California (80 percent), and Arkansas (70 percent). Mississippi is mixed. Texas and Louisiana rice is marketed by private interests. The Texas, Louisiana, and Mississippi rice may be sold green, and if handled through cooperatives is sold in negotiated sales through private mills. Arkansas co-ops use a second pool concept; California co-ops make advance payments, monthly advances, equalization payments, monthly advances, and a final payment.

CONSUMPTION

Domestic

Domestic food use falls into three major categories: (1) direct food use (64 percent), (2) processed-food use (14 percent), and (3) beer (22 percent). Direct food

TABLE 10-4 U.S. Supply and Usage of Rough Rice Only
(Million hundredweight)

	1976–1977	1977–1978	1978–1979	1979–1980	1980–1981	1981–1982
Beginning stocks	31.3	33.4	21.1	25.1	20.1	9.8
Production	115.6	99.2	133.2	132.0	146.1	185.4
Total	146.9	132.6	154.3	157.1	166.2	195.2
Seed	3.2	4.3	4.3	4.8	5.1	4.4
Exports	0.9	4.1	2.8	1.7	—	5.8
Mill use	105.7	101.2	118.0	124.3	141.2	131.9
Unaccounted	3.7	1.9	4.1	6.2	9.7	11.8
Total	113.5	111.5	129.2	137.0	156.4	153.9
Ending stocks	33.4	21.1	25.1	20.1	9.8	41.3
Demand ratio	0.77	0.84	0.84	0.88	0.91	0.78
Average farm price	7.02	9.49	8.16	10.50	12.80	9.25
Loan	6.19	6.19	6.40	6.79	7.12	8.01
Target	8.25	8.25	8.53	9.05	9.49	10.68

TABLE 10-5 U.S. Supply and Usage of Milled Rice
(Million hundredweight)

	1976–1977	1977–1978	1978–1979	1979–1980	1980–1981	1981–1982
Beginning stocks	3.9	5.1	4.3	4.6	4.0	4.9
Production	76.2	70.1	83.4	89.8	103.0	95.1
Imports	0.1	0.1	0.1	0.1	0.2	0.3
Total	80.2	75.3	87.8	94.5	107.2	100.2
Food	20.9	16.5	23.8	23.9	28.0	30.6
Brewers' use	7.5	6.9	7.9	8.1	8.0	9.1
Exports	46.6	47.6	51.6	58.5	66.4	55.0
Total	75.0	71.0	83.3	90.4	102.4	94.7
Ending stocks	5.2	4.3	4.6	4.0	4.9	5.5
Demand ratio	0.94	0.94	0.95	0.96	0.96	0.95

use includes regular milled rice (81 percent), parboiled rice (11 percent), and precooked rice (6 percent). Processed-food uses include cereal, soup, baby food, package mixes, and so forth.

An examination of consumption by type indicates that long-grain rice captures over 60 percent of the domestic food market, medium grain roughly one-third, and short-grain the remainder. Long-grain rice mixes primarily into direct food use. Medium and short grains are used for cereal. Beer processors use either brokens or whole grains which are granulated prior to use. Tables 10-4 and 10-5 show the uses of rough and milled rice over the past few years.

Exports

Exports are extremely important to the U.S. rice industry. Because of varietal differences and taste preferences in rice, exporters and importers are fairly well distributed. The United States and Thailand are the major exporters, though, and Indonesia and the EEC are the major importers. Europeans favor

TABLE 10-6 World Rice Supply and Usage
(Milled basis; million tonnes)

	1976–1977	1977–1978	1978–1979	1979–1980	1980–1981	1981–1982*
Beginning stocks	19.3	17.7	22.8	27.8	23.4	22.1
Production	234.3	248.8	260.7	254.2	267.2	277.8
Total	253.6	266.5	283.5	282.0	290.6	299.9
Domestic use	235.9	243.8	255.6	258.5	268.4	278.7
Exports*	10.2	9.5	11.5	12.6	13.2	12.4
Total	245.1	253.3	267.1	271.1	281.6	291.1
Ending stock	17.7	22.8	27.8	23.4	22.1	21.3

*Exports do not equal imports for a particular crop year. Consequently, ending stocks are not obtained by subtraction.

SOURCE: ContiCommodity Research Division estimates.

TABLE 10-7 Percentage of Total Rice Imports by Country
(Milled basis)

	1977–1978	1978–1979	1979–1980	1980	1981	1982
Bangladesh	—	5.13	2.63	1.32	.26	8.34
EEC	11.7	8.55	8.77	7.01	8.26	9.65
Hong Kong	3.19	2.56	3.51	2.83	2.77	2.93
Indonesia	19.15	17.09	23.68	16.09	4.18	4.89
Iran	3.19	4.27	3.51	3.94	4.63	4.89
Republic of Korea	—	3.42	6.14	6.48	17.65	4.07
West Malaysia	4.26	1.71	2.63	1.32	2.48	3.26
Saudi Arabia	4.26	4.27	4.39	3.75	3.85	4.07
Singapore	1.06	1.71	1.75	1.47	1.54	1.79
Sri Lanka	2.13	2.56	2.63	1.49	1.35	2.04
All others	50	47.86	39.47	54.29	53.04	59.07
World total	100.00	100.00	100.00	100.00	100.00	100.00

long-grain rice; Asians favor short-grain rice. The United States has averaged selling about 25 percent of its export sales under Public Law 480. Consequently, the sales of nonpreferred varieties is often made under this program. U.S. exports may fall slightly in the years ahead depending on the concessional sales programs. World production, use, and export of milled rice over the past few years are shown in Table 10-6.

Thailand appears to be able to hold roughly 25 percent of the export market, although their export tax, trade embargoes in years of short supplies, and their cheap domestic policies will probably discourage significant production gains or increases in their market share.

The People's Republic of China has not maintained their normal market share (around 10 percent) in the past 2 years but exports could rise in years of production gains as they use rice as a source of foreign exchange.

The Pakistan share may well increase because they produce *basmati* rice, the preferred variety in the Middle East and because of their domestic policy of giving farmers a fair return.

Burma's domestic consumer orientation and simultaneous lack of producer incentives will most likely cause their market share to decline further.

Indonesia will probably remain a major importer of rice for years to come, since their domestic policies favor consumers at the expense of the farmers. The EEC will, it seems, continue at their current levels, while Africa is likely to continue its upward trend. The Korean deficit production years are probably over. (The major world importers of rice are compared in Table 10-7.)

PRICE PROJECTIONS

Figure 10-1 illustrates the relationship which exists between the season's average price of rough rice and the rates established by the government assistance

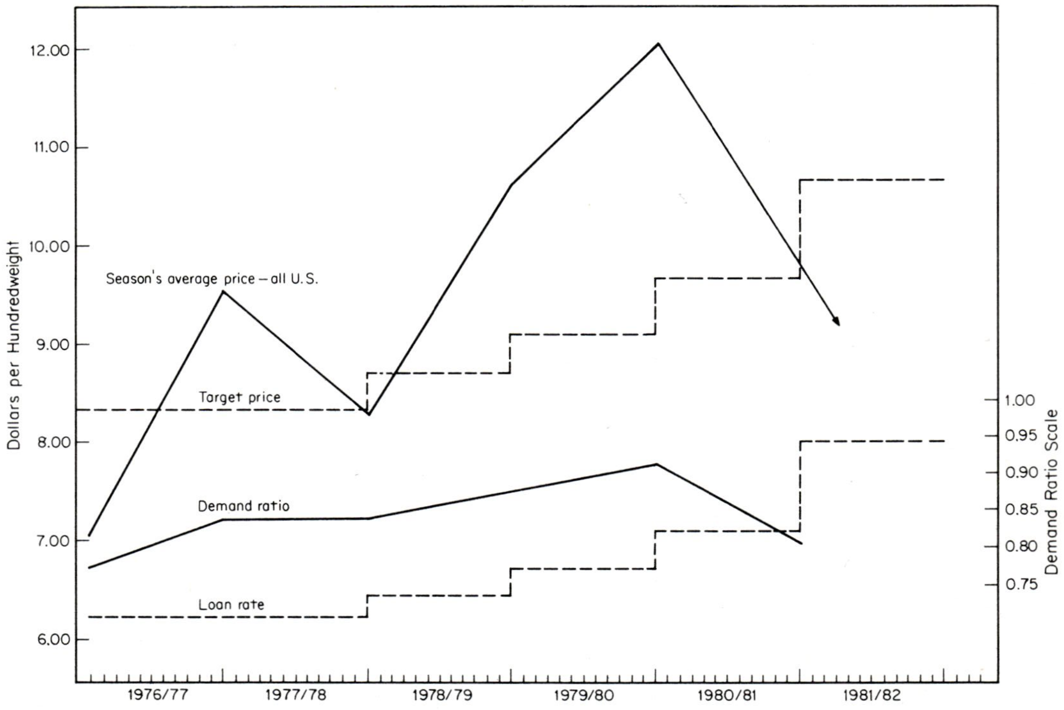

Figure 10-1 Rough rice prices received by farmers, year beginning October 1. Demand ratio = total usage/total supply.

programs through the target price and loan rate. The upper and lower levels defined by these two rates form a type of corridor which can indicate where the price can be reasonably expected to go in a bear market year. In a bull market year the price tends to remain well above the target rate, while in a bear market year the price will probably go no lower than the average of the target price and the loan rate. If the average price does fall to this level, it is most likely the interim bottom. The reason for this is that producers participating in the allotment program (1) will not produce more than their allotment since this would subject them to a penalty (which limits production) and (2) movement of rice will slow down or even cease as the price falls below the target rate, since producers in the program can then afford to place their rice in storage and await higher prices.

The demand ratio, also depicted in Figure 10-1, provides the strongest indication as to the probable direction of prices in a given crop year. This most useful indicator is generated by simply dividing the total usage by the total supply. In reality, it is the percent of supply utilized in a given year. It can be noted that the direction of the average price is in sympathy with the direction of the demand ratio. In short, the higher the demand ratio, the higher the price which can be expected. When the ratio declines, lower prices can be expected. The seasonal variations that occur in the price of rice can be seen in Figure 10-2. Figures 10-3 through 10-6 show recent price trends.

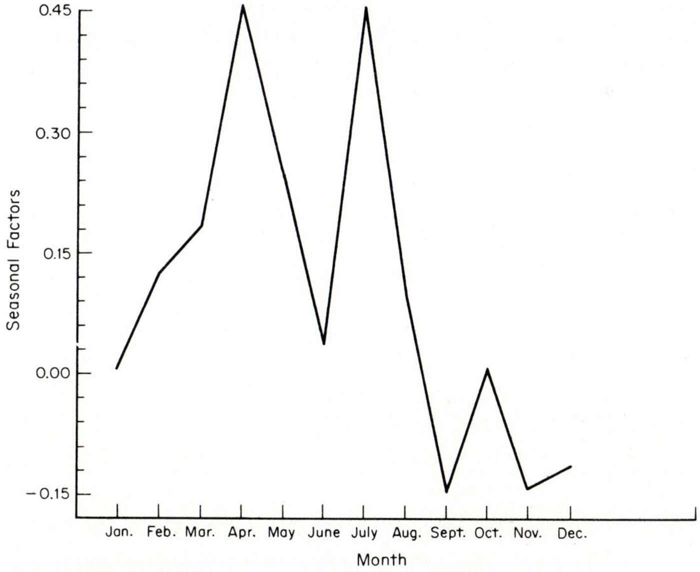

Figure 10-2 Seasonal variations in prices. *(ContiCommodity Research Division)*

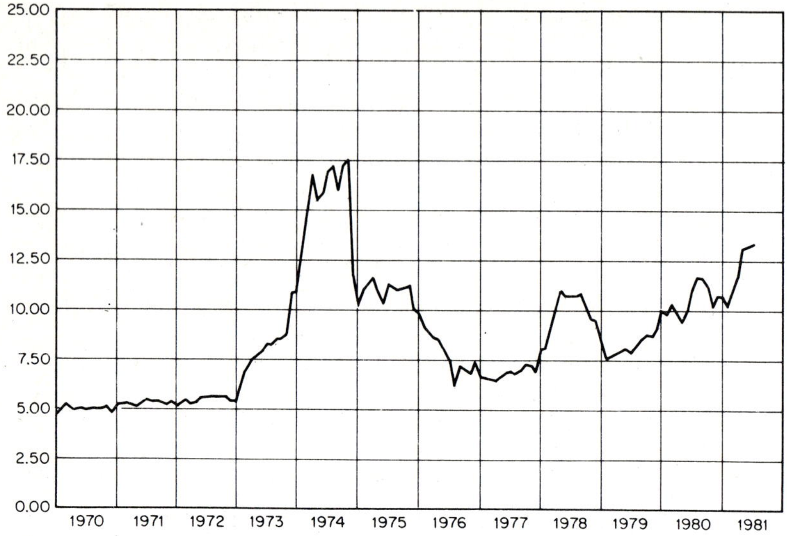

Figure 10-3 Monthly average rough rice prices received by farmers in the United States (dollars per hundredweight). *(ContiCommodity Research Division)*

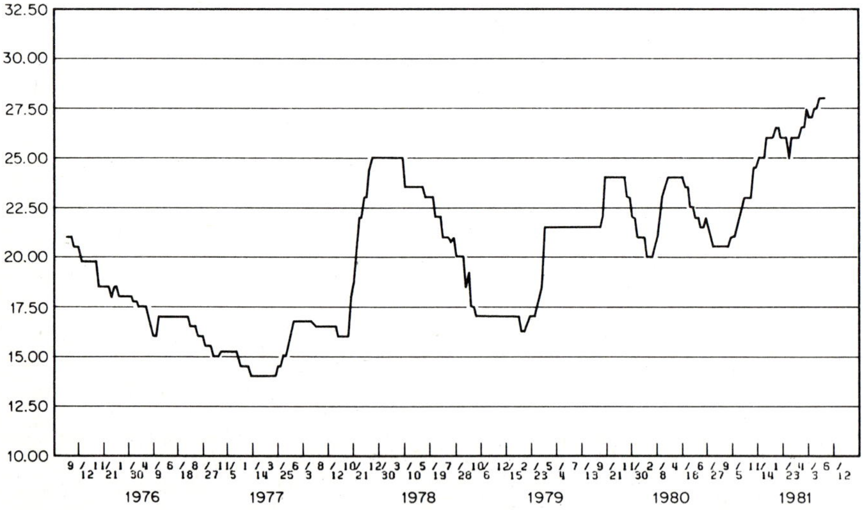

Figure 10-4 Milled rice, long grain, U.S. No. 2 grade, FOB Arkansas Mills. Weekly average price (dollars per hundredweight). *(ContiCommodity Research Division)*

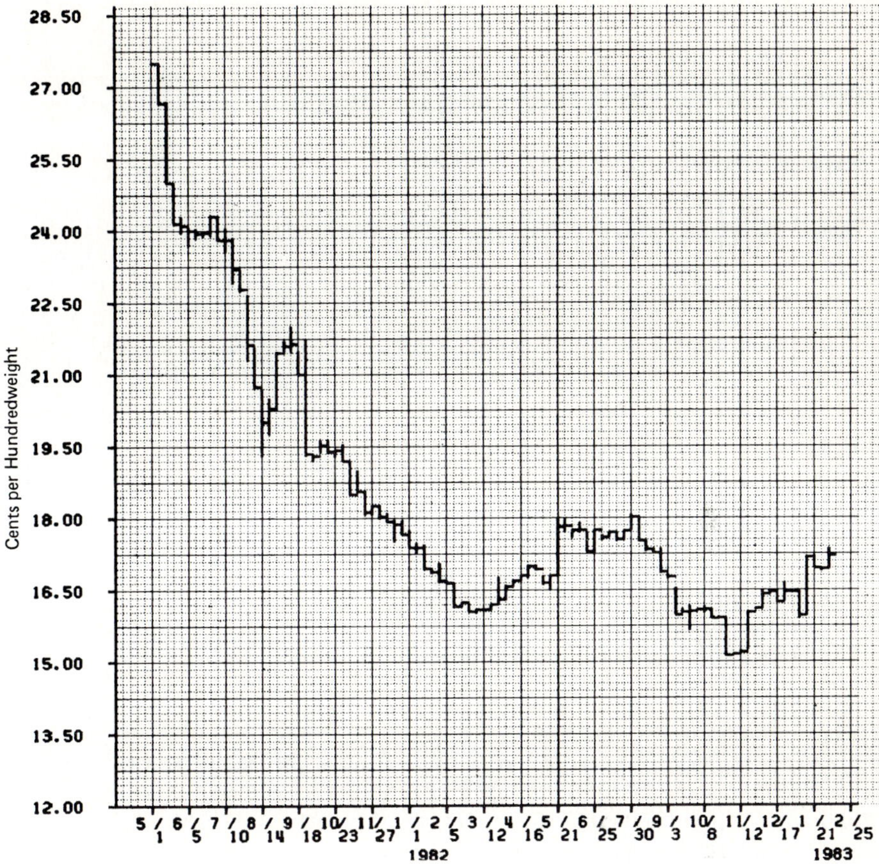

Figure 10-5 Weekly continuation, New Orleans Commodity Exchange milled rice. *(ContiCommodity Research Division)*

CONTRACT DATA

Rough Rice

Grade U.S. No. 2 or better uncoated, milled, long-grain variety rice (unpolished and parboiled is not deliverable), not to exceed 4 percent broken kernels established by standards promulgated by USDA.

Trading unit: 1200 hundredweight (120,000 pounds).

Price increment: 005¢/hundredweight.

Milled Rice

U.S. No. 2 long-grain, established by standards promulgated by the USDA. No other grade is deliverable. Milling yield of 55 percent hard rice not to exceed 15 percent broken kernels. Hard rice over or below 15 percent shall receive appropriate premiums and discounts, broken rice premiums or discounts of 0.5 percent premium, or discount for each percent over or below 15 percent.

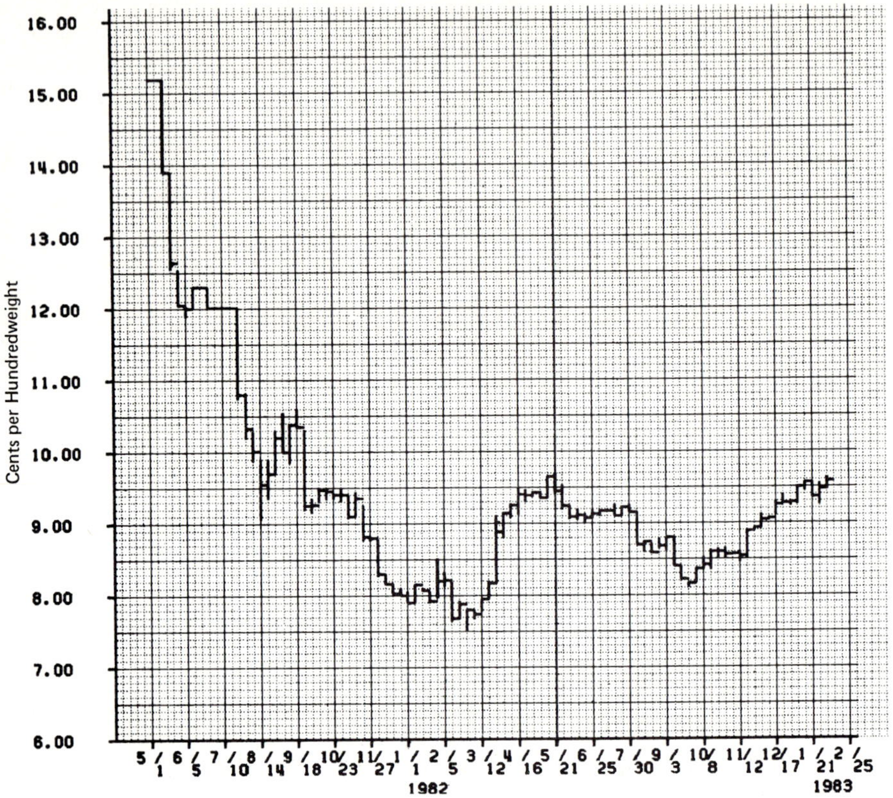

Figure 10-6 Weekly continuation, New Orleans Commodity Exchange rough rice. *(ContiCommodity Research Division)*

Price limits: 50¢/hundredweight with variable limits at certain times or under certain conditions.

Delivery points: Regular designated shipper's facilities in Louisiana, Texas, Mississippi, and Arkansas.

Delivery dates: No later than last business day of delivery month.

Trading unit: 2000 hundredweight (200,000 pounds).

Price increment: 005¢/hundredweight.

Price limits: 30¢/hundredweight with variable limits at certain times or under certain conditions.

Delivery points: Regular board: designated warehouses in Louisiana, Texas, Mississippi, and Arkansas.

Delivery dates: No later than last business day of delivery month.

CHAPTER

11

Soybean Meal

Alan London

INTRODUCTION

Soybeans are grown primarily for their derived products—soybean oil and soybean meal. Soybean meal is used almost exclusively as a protein feed ingredient for livestock and competes with other protein meals for hog, cattle, and poultry feed rations. The extent of soybean meal's use in feed rations is primarily a function of its price relative to substitutes and its price relative to corn.

Soybean meal does not store well for prolonged periods of time, so stocks held in commercial storage are not generally a major price-determining factor. Meal is more of a flow commodity—it tends to move into the pipeline after it is produced. Whenever stocks are low in comparison to nearby demand, soybean processors increase their meal output.

PROCESSING AND PRODUCTION

Processing of soybeans is called "crushing" because of the old practice of actually crushing the beans to remove the oil. Technology has changed this; soybeans are now processed through chemical extraction. The beans are prepared by toasting and flaking and then immersed in liquid hexane. The hexane extracts the oil from the beans. After this process, the beans are dried and ground into a meal. The resulting soybean meal usually has an average protein content of 47.5 to 48 percent. The soybean hulls, removed before the oil is extracted, are ground back into the meal, leaving a product that averages 44 percent protein.

The basic 44 percent protein meal is the most commonly traded cash product in the United States. High-protein soybean meal is also the protein source of choice for domestic poultry producers.

The yield of meal from a bushel of soybeans varies from month to month and crop year to crop year. Generalizations are usually useful, but must be applied with care. Meal yields run about 47.5 pounds per bushel (a bushel of soybeans is 60 pounds). In years in which temperatures during the growing season are considered low for soybeans, meal yields tend to be higher.

There are other factors which affect meal yields directly. The relative profitability of the soybean products provides the economic incentive for crushers to tailor their production for oil or meal. The price of oil is much higher on a pound-for-pound basis than the price of meal. Therefore, when meal prices are strong the profit motive provides the incentive for processors to maximize meal yield per bushel crushed. The yield per bushel also varies somewhat among processing plants. The internal efficiency of the processor has a great deal to do with meal output.

Historically, meal yields are lowest just after the harvest when plants are running at high rates of capacity. The trend is for meal yields to increase into the summer months. Table 11-1 shows the average meal yield for the last few crop years.

MEAL USAGE

Domestic meal consumption is directly related to livestock profitability. When livestock is a profitable industry, feeder operators will use a more efficient ration. The higher the amount of protein in the ration, the more efficient it is in terms of feed conversion. The percentage of soybean meal in feed rations varies with its price relative to other proteins and corn. When livestock prices are unfavorable, feeders tend to "cheat" on rations by using less protein and more carbohydrates.

TABLE 11-1 Soybean Meal Yields
(Pounds per bushel)

	1978–1979	1979–1980	1980–1981
September	47.4	48.0	48.0
October	47.4	47.7	47.6
November	47.7	47.9	48.0
December	47.6	48.0	47.8
January	47.6	47.9	47.8
February	47.7	48.0	47.9
March	47.7	48.1	47.3
April	47.7	47.9	48.0
May	47.5	47.9	47.8
June	47.8	48.4	47.9
July	47.7	48.5	47.9
August	47.8	48.1	47.8
Average	47.6	48.1	47.8

TABLE 11-2 Meal Usage versus the Profitability Ratio

Year*	Meal usage†	Profitability ratio
1973	13.8	0.94
1974	12.5	0.85
1975	15.6	0.96
1976	14.1	0.91
1977	16.3	1.13
1978	17.7	1.29
1979	19.2	1.14
1980	17.6	0.99

*Crop years beginning October 1.

†United States Census Bureau figures in 1000 short tonnes.

Livestock Feed Profitability Ratio

A broad measure of the profitability of livestock is the livestock feed profitability ratio. It is an index of prices based on the prices producers received for livestock divided by the prices paid for feed. The higher values of the index are in years when livestock prices are strong and feed prices relatively low. Larger consumption years for soybean meal occur in years when the livestock profitability index is high. (See Table 11-2.)

Not only is the profitability of the livestock industry a factor in meal consumption, but the absolute size of the livestock sector is also. There are basically two types of livestock, grain-consuming animal units (GCAV) and protein-consuming animal units (PCAV). Grain-consuming animals are those whose basic diet is a lower protein ration—cattle primarily. Poultry and hogs have much more protein in their diets. Poultry consumption of soybean meal accounts for as much as 45 percent of domestic soybean meal usage, while hogs use 30 percent of domestic soybean meal. The balance of meal disappearance is fed cattle 10 percent, dairy cattle 10 percent, and other consumption 5 percent. (See Table 11-3.)

TABLE 11-3 Soybean Meal Usage of Grain- and Protein-Consuming Animals

Year	Total meal usage*	GCAUs†	PCAUs†
1973	13.0	78.5	103.9
1974	12.5	70.3	96.7
1975	15.6	74.6	100.7
1976	14.1	75.9	102.9
1977	16.3	79.0	104.5
1978	17.7	80.0	108.0
1979	19.2	82.3	114.6
1980	17.6	80.6	114.4

*United States Census Bureau figures in 1000 short tonnes.

†In millions.

Increases in domestic meal disappearance are generally associated with increases in PCAUs. This is not an absolute relationship. Increases in use reflect the price of meal relative to corn and its share in the ration. The large amounts of soybean meal in poultry rations are not the only reason that meal usage and PCAUs are directly related. There is a definite increase in poultry consumption in the country. Per capita chicken consumption reached 47 pounds in 1980. Broiler production has a short cycle as well. It takes only 3 weeks from the time eggs are set to place the chicks, and another 6 weeks until the birds are marketed. This short production cycle makes it possible for broiler producers to respond quickly to favorable price situations and consequently cause an increase in meal usage. Naturally, the opposite holds when broiler producers decide to cut production.

Meal-Corn Price Ratio

Another factor influencing domestic meal usage is the soybean meal–corn price ratio. Meal prices are usually quoted in dollars per short ton, while corn prices are quoted in dollars per bushel. To convert the price of corn to dollars per ton, simply multiply the price of corn by 35.714, which is the number of 56-pound bushels of corn needed to make a short ton. Table 11-4 gives the average soybean meal–corn ratio for an entire crop year and the corresponding domestic meal usage figures.

The change in meal consumption from year to year is not necessarily directly related to changes in the soybean meal–corn ratio. The increases in meal usage depend primarily on the profitability of livestock. The soybean meal–corn ratio is more of an intermediate-term indicator of price direction.

Domestic meal usage accounts for roughly 73 percent of all U.S. soybean meal disappearance, so naturally those factors that directly affect domestic usage are extremely important. Although exports account for only 27 percent of disappearance, they, too, have a significant impact on prices.

Exports

Exports of soybean meal go entirely to developed countries with substantial livestock economies. The more developed countries in the world have the

TABLE 11-4 Soybean Meal Usage and the Soybean Meal–Corn Ratio

Year	Total meal usage*	Soybean meal–corn ratio
1973	13.0	1.43
1974	12.5	1.18
1975	15.6	1.50
1976	14.1	2.44
1977	16.3	2.01
1978	17.7	2.10
1979	19.2	1.79
1980	17.6	1.81

*United States Census Bureau figures in 1000 short tons.

TABLE 11-5 U.S. Soybean Meal Exports

Destination	1975–1976	1976–1977	1977–1978	1978–1979	1979–1980
EEC*	2345.5	1863.8	2667.1	2708.5	3595.8
Poland	411.2	232.6	396.2	241.1	437.5
Canada	322.4	306.8	374.3	414.9	330.0
Japan	117.6	221.5	264.6	203.5	208.3
East Germany	281.8	265.2	320.8	547.0	323.3
Total	4777.5	4141.6	5492.2	5918.2	7087.8

*Includes the Netherlands, Italy, West Germany, France, Ireland, Denmark, and the United Kingdom.

resources to support livestock, which consume vegetable protein. Poorer nations do not consume so much meat, milk, or eggs on a per capita basis to import much, if any, soybean meal. The vast majority of U.S. meal exports go to Western Europe (50 percent), Poland, Canada, and Japan (see Table 11-5).

Foreign imports of soybean meal are influenced by the same factors that affect U.S. domestic usage—meat consumption trends, per capita income, livestock population, and livestock profitability.

An emerging factor in world demand for soybean meal (as well as other protein sources) is the Soviet Union. The Soviet Union has a highly developed livestock economy, in both the cooperative and the private sectors. As can be seen in Table 11-6, the size of the Soviet livestock herd has grown in recent years, especially the poultry sector.

The Soviet Union has begun to increase the amount of oilseed meals used in feed rations. This is because of their limited capacity to produce grain. The grain embargo of January 1980, was another factor that accounted for their increased oilseed-meal usage. The Soviet Union, unable to import all the grain it needed, turned to protein meals in an effort to extend its available grain supplies.

TABLE 11-6 Soviet Livestock Numbers*
(Million head)

Year	Cattle	Hogs	Poultry
1973	79.0	54.2	411.2
1974	81.8	56.5	454.0
1975	84.6	49.6	418.8
1976	85.0	49.3	459.3
1977	87.1	54.9	540.5
1978	89.2	58.4	595.1
1979	91.1	54.9	617.5
1980	91.6	54.4	642.8
1981	92.2	55.2	689.7
1982	92.6	54.1	706.7
1983	93.8	56.8	733.3

*United States Department of Agriculture estimates as of May 13, 1983.

The Soviet Union has sharply increased the use of mixed feed and in so doing, has had to increase the percent of oilseed meals in rations as well as the use of grass meals such as alfalfa. As the Soviet Union struggles to maintain its livestock base, it will continue to rely on protein meal to extend its limited grain supplies.

The Soviet Union has recently entered into a long-term agreement with Brazil for soybeans, soybean meal, and compound feed to meet this end. It has also reached agreement with Thailand to import 440,000 metric tonnes of tapioca pellets each year for the next 5 years. Tapioca is a feedstuff rich in carbohydrates, but must be supplemented with protein to make complete feed. Soybean meal is the protein source most commonly used with tapioca.

COMPETITIVE MEALS

U.S. soybean meal competes for markets with other protein meals as well as soybean meal from Brazil.

Soybean meal is by far the most important protein meal in terms of world production. Over the last 5 years it has averaged 63 percent of total world protein-meal production. Cottonseed meal is second in world production, but is considerably less important than soybean meal, accounting for less than 20 percent of world soybean meal production. The other minor meals in world production are fishmeal, rapeseed meal, sunflower meal, and peanut meal (the only minor meal that has consistently expanded production over the past several years). Rapeseed meal offers limited competition for soybean meal. It is lower in protein (36 percent versus 44 or 48 percent for soybean meal), has limited use in feed rations because of high fiber and low fat content, and does not provide the amino acid balance available in soybean meal.

The major source of competition for export soybean-meal markets comes from Brazil. Brazilian soybean and meal production has expanded dramatically over the past 15 years. Brazil has expanded its crushing capacity until it has become a larger exporter of soybean meal than the United States despite the fact that Brazilian soybean production is far less. The reason is that Brazilian domestic needs are much less than those of the United States.

Brazil primarily exports high-protein meal in the form of pellets. The higher protein commands a premium price and the pellets make handling easier. Most importers (especially in the EEC) are highly conscious of the price spread between U.S. 44-percent meal and Brazilian pellets. Generally, when Brazilian meal is less than 8 percent higher in price than U.S. 44-percent meal, the price-conscious buyer will purchase high-protein Brazilian pellets.

SUMMARY AND TRADING CONSIDERATION

There are a number of supply and demand factors that are basic to the determination of the price of soybean meal:

Supply The size of the soybean crop relative to the level demand is a major factor. The larger the size of U.S. soybean supply, the lower meal prices will trade. Another important factor for meal on the supply side is the amount of meal Brazil has to offer the world market.

Demand The larger the size of the livestock herd, the greater the demand for soybean meal to be used in livestock feed. An important determinant of the size of the herd, the potential for expansions, and the amount of meal used in the ration is the profitability of livestock. The percent of soybean meal used in feed rations is also influenced by the soybean meal–corn price ratio and the price of soybean meal relative to other protein meals.

CONTRACT SPECIFICATIONS

Soybean meal is traded at the Chicago Board of Trade. The size of the contract is 100 short tons. A minimum fluctuation is 10¢/contract. The daily trading limit is a $10/ton change from the previous day's settlement; therefore the widest possible range is $20/ton. It is very important to note that during the delivery period the spot option trades without limits. Figure 11-1 shows the variation in soybean meal prices from 1960 to 1982.

The soybean products differ from other contracts at the Board of Trade in the manner in which they open and close. The soybean meal market, like soybean oil, opens and closes on a call rotation. Trading begins in the spot or lead

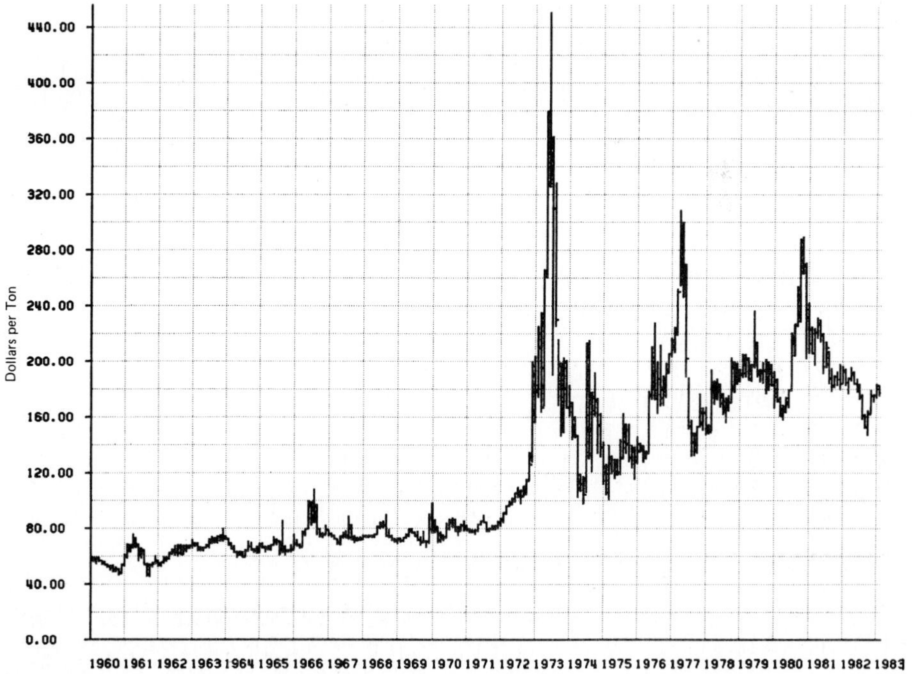

Figure 11-1 Monthly continuation, Chicago Board of Trade soybean meal. *(ContiCommodity Research Division)*

option. As the buy and sell orders are filled, trade begins in the next contract month. Each month begins trading activity only in the month whose turn it is during the opening call. When each month has completed its opening call, trading begins simultaneously in all contract months. The same rotation system is used when the market closes.

SOYBEAN MEAL CONTRACT DATA

Contract size:	100 short tons
Minimum price fluctuation:	10¢/ton
Daily trading limit:	$10/ton
Value of a limit:	$1000/ per contract
Trading hours:	9:30 A.M. to 1:15 P.M., Chicago time
Delivery months:	January, March, May, July, August, September, October, and December
Delivery points:	Registered soybean processors. Consult the Chicago Board of Trade Market Information Department for current list.

CHAPTER

12

Soybean Oil

Michael Hinebaugh

INTRODUCTION

Soybeans are recognized as being a "meal" seed; that is, the proportionate amount of protein meal derived from crushing soybeans is much higher than the amount of oil produced (soybeans yield around 80 percent meal and 18 percent oil per bushel crushed). The oil content of soybeans is much lower than for most other oil-bearing materials; by comparison, copra yields around 64 percent coconut oil, and the oil yields of some varieties of sunflower seed range from 40 to 45 percent. However, soybean oil still accounts for the largest proportion of edible oil production—around one-third of total world edible vegetable oil production. The list of such oils includes peanut, sunflower seed, cottonseed, rapeseed, sesame seed, olive, corn, coconut, palm kernel, palm babassu and soybean oils. Although many other oilseeds contain a much higher oil percentage, there is no other oilseed which presently produces more than 40 percent of the total quantity of world soybean oil production. (This is equivalent to only around 12 to 13 percent of total world production of edible vegetable oils.)

Because soybean oil is the predominant edible oil, any factor which disrupts its production (such as severe droughts in the United States or Brazil, the major soybean-producing and exporting countries) can create a substantial effect upon world prices for edible oil. Such price effects will intensify as the world population continues to escalate because, in areas of uncontrolled population growth, the dietary requirements are the most restrictive. In order to maintain present per capita consumption levels of fats and oils in developing countries, production and imports of edible oils must increase. Thus, raising the per capita consumption would require an even greater increase. In China, for example, to raise per capita consumption to even the relatively low level that exists in India would require an increase in supplies equivalent to *4 percent of total world consumption of fats and oils.*

The following data highlight the per capita availability of edible oils in key world areas. Data are averages for the 5 years from 1976 to 1981 (in thousand tonnes).

	China	India	Soviet Union	United States
Production and imports	3,300	4,593	6,191	17,011
Exports	110	17	237	7,406
Net	3,220	4,576	5,954	9,605
Population (millions)	894	660	264	215
Per capita availability:				
Kilograms	3.67	7.0	22.6	45.7
Pounds	8.1	15.4	49.6	98.3

The range of dietary capabilities is very restrictive in undeveloped large population centers. Even in the Soviet Union, which is classified as more developed, the per capita consumption of fats and oils is still well below the minimum standards recommended by the Soviet Academy for Science and Nutrition; in addition, large quantities of edible oils must be imported to maintain the present Soviet balance.

Table 12-1 shows world production and trends for soybean oil, other vegetable oils, and total fats and oils. This is the framework which influences soybean oil prices. The average annual trend increase for soybean oil since 1960 has approximated 40 percent of the trend increase for all fats and oils. Production above trend results in accumulation of inventories.

The major world producers of soybean oil are, in order, the United States, Brazil, and the European Economic Community (EEC) bloc; combined, these three account for almost 80 percent of total world soybean oil production. Japan and the People's Republic of China account for the bulk of the rest of world production. Although China is the world's third largest soybean producer, more soybeans are domestically consumed directly as human food. By contrast, the EEC processes almost all soybeans for the protein and oil products, and hence produces much more soybean oil than China does (despite the fact that soybean *production* is virtually unknown in the EEC—see Chapter 8). The same three areas, the United States, Brazil, and the EEC, also account for the predominant share of total world consumption of soybean oil; among them, they consume around 57 percent of total world soybean oil disappearance on an annual basis. Since two of the three major world consumers also are the primary producers of soybeans and also predominant exporters of soybean oil, it is easy to see why disruptions in soybean oil or soybean supplies in the United States or Brazil can have major price repercussions. The United States and Brazil, combined, account for around 80 percent of total world soybean production, almost all exports of soybeans, and around 45 percent of total world soybean oil con-

TABLE 12-1 World Production and Exports, All Fats and Oils, with Trends
(Thousand tonnes; industrial taken out)

	Soybean oil						Total world		
Crop year	Actual	Trend	Deviation	Other vegetable*	Palm†	Animal and marine	Actual	Trend	Deviation
1960	3,295	2,150	+1,145	9,495	3,703	11,591	29,561	28,818	+743
1961	3,290	2,638	+652	10,275	3,967	12,000	31,034	30,041	+993
1962	3,850	3,127	+723	10,995	3,770	12,286	32,394	31,263	+1,131
1963	3,810	3,615	+195	10,625	3,880	12,493	32,411	32,486	−75
1964	3,880	4,103	−223	11,565	3,987	12,812	33,942	33,708	+234
1965	3,905	4,592	−687	12,475	3,899	13,138	35,091	34,981	+160
1966	4,585	5,080	−495	12,455	4,041	12,884	35,631	36,153	−522
1967	5,000	5,568	−568	12,995	3,717	13,581	36,899	37,376	−477
1968	5,220	6,057	−837	13,585	3,955	13,631	37,839	38,598	−759
1969	6,092	6,545	−453	13,851	4,036	13,593	38,011	39,821	−1,810
1970	6,270	7,033	−763	14,857	5,522	14,113	40,254	41,043	−789
1971	6,844	7,521	−677	15,738	5,507	13,989	42,178	42,266	−88
1972	7,585	8,010	−425	14,836	5,279	13,784	41,484	43,488	−2,004
1973	9,542	8,498	+1,044	16,077	5,484	14,668	45,779	44,711	+1,068
1974	8,338	8,986	−648	15,724	6,452	14,367	44,881	45,933	−1,052
1975	10,168	9,475	+693	17,166	7,100	14,731	48,165	47,156	+1,010
1976	9,142	9,963	−820	14,894	7,040	15,376	46,452	48,378	−926
1977	11,287	10,451	+836	16,701	7,367	15,695	51,050	49,600	+1,450
1978	12,249	10,940	+1,309	17,891	7,633	15,763	53,536	50,823	+2,713

*Includes cottonseed, peanut, sunflower, rapeseed, sesame, corn, and olive oils.

†Includes palm, palm kernel, coconut, and babassu.

SOURCE: University of Illinois, Champaign-Urbana.

sumption. There are few major world commodities for which one or two nations so totally dominate both supply and demand and price events—especially major food items.

Malaysia, for example, thoroughly dominates palm oil production; but the rapid development of palm oil in Malaysia generally has served only to keep a lid or damper upon soybean oil values in a world of expanding edible oil consumption. What happens regarding soybean oil supplies is of greater significance to palm oil prices than the reverse.

Brazil recently surpassed the United States in soybean oil exports, and assumed the role of the leading world exporter of soybean oil. The EEC bloc ranks second in soybean oil exports if trade among the ten member countries of the EEC bloc is considered; on a specific country basis, however, the United States still would rank second in world soybean oil exports.

Approximately 25 to 27 percent of total world production is imported by a variety of nations, most of which represent large population centers and also depend upon edible oil imports to meet per capita consumption needs; these needs generally are increasing annually because of the growing population base in those world areas (Table 12-2). India is the largest world importer of soybean oil; the percentage of total edible vegetable oil imports by India represented by soybean oil has generally amounted to around 50 percent. A combination of countries in the Mideast and Northern Africa has also tended to increase soybean oil imports; as a bloc, that area is the world's second largest importing area. The EEC is the third largest because of the intra-EEC trade which takes place. Another important bloc is Latin America; soybean oil imports have been increasing there in response to population increases.

U.S. CONSUMPTION

Domestic Usage

The United States is the largest producer of soybean oil because it has the largest soybean crop and soybean-crushing facilities (Table 12-3). Domestic consumption of soybean oil in the United States increased by 60 percent between

TABLE 12-2 Soybean Oil: Gross World Imports ***(Thousand tonnes)***

	1977–1978	1978–1979	1979–1980	1980–1981	1981–1982	1982–1983*
India	510	555	660	653	375	600
Mideast and North Africa	506	544	636	727	776	838
EEC	449	455	492	477	519	503
Latin America	344	328	334	470	467	521
Pakistan	181	260	213	232	308	275
China	184	122	100	80	30	40
Others	425	416	845	826	932	944
Total	2,599	2,680	3280	3465	3407	3721

*Estimated.

SOURCE: Foreign Agricultural Service.

TABLE 12-3 U.S. Production of Soybean Oil *(Million pounds)*

Year	Total
1968–1969	6,531
1969–1970	7,904
1970–1971	8,265
1971–1972	7.892
1972–1973	7,501
1973–1974	8,995
1974–1975	7,375
1975–1976	9,630
1976–1977	8,578
1977–1978	10,288
1978–1979	11,323
1979–1980	12,105
1980–1981	11,270
1981–1982	10,980
1982–1983*	11,705

*Preliminary.

SOURCE: United States Department of Agriculture.

1972 and 1982, while exports have been stagnant in the same period. Soybean oil is the only major U.S. food commodity that has shown a consistent increase in domestic use as a proportionate share of total disappearance.

Soybean oil approximates 60 percent of all food fats and oils consumed in the United States. The preference in fat use began to shift from butter and lard to vegetable oils, particularly soybean oil, in the 1970s; the emphasis in recent years on the use of polyunsaturated fatty acids in diets has benefitted soybean oil. Food products account for over 90 percent of total domestic consumption of soybean oil; major markets are salad and cooking oils, shortening, and margarines. The use of soybean oil in margarines and shortenings has increased only slightly in recent years; the largest growth in domestic consumption has been in cooking and salad oils. (Nonfood uses also have been increasing, albeit slowly.)

Three factors influence the domestic consumption of soybean oil.

1. The production and price of cottonseed oil, lard, and butter affect consumption. For example, increased production of cotton (and, therefore, cottonseed) can increase cottonseed oil's proportionate share of the cooking and salad oils market (and vice versa); increased production of lard can reduce soybean oil's share in shortening (and vice versa).
2. Imports of other edible oils can harm domestic consumption. High-yielding palm oil has posed the major threat in past years because of the continued expansion in palm groves in Malaysia and the fact that it can be imported free of duty. Coconut oil imports also have been an important influence on soybean oil consumption. Changes in import levels are greatly affected by the external value of the U.S. dollar—a falling dollar makes imports more

expensive, thereby discouraging imports, and a rising dollar has the opposite effect.

3. U.S. production of sunflower seed, which has been increasing sharply in recent years, influences domestic consumption. This is largely due to the favorability of sunflower seed returns in comparison to those of spring wheats in some areas. This trend, if continued, could have an important influence on soybean oil consumption patterns (see Figure 12-1).

Exports

U.S. soybean oil exports are sporadic in nature. There is not the sustained growth over time that is very evident in soybean and soybean meal exports. There are two major reasons for this.

1. The sustained growth in the production of other edible oils, particularly Brazilian soybean oil, Malaysian palm oil, and rapeseed, and the ability of export competitors to price their oils competitively (e.g., Brazilian currency devaluations have been used to maintain price competitiveness).
2. The expansion of crushing facilities in Brazil, Malaysia, the EEC and some other world areas. This increases the world production capacity for edible oils, including areas which may not account for much production of a basic oilseed (e.g., the EEC and Japan).

The United States exported approximately 1700 million pounds of soybean oil in the 1970 crop year, which was not exceeded until 1978. Exports fell back sharply again in 1980–1981. Factors which affect U.S. soybean oil exports include the level of international stocks of edible vegetable oils, the annual world production of edible vegetable oils, the amount of soybean oil programmed for export under concessionary programs such as PL 480, and the activity of India. The importance of India to U.S. soybean oil exports can be seen from Table 12-4, which shows the major destinations for U.S. exports.

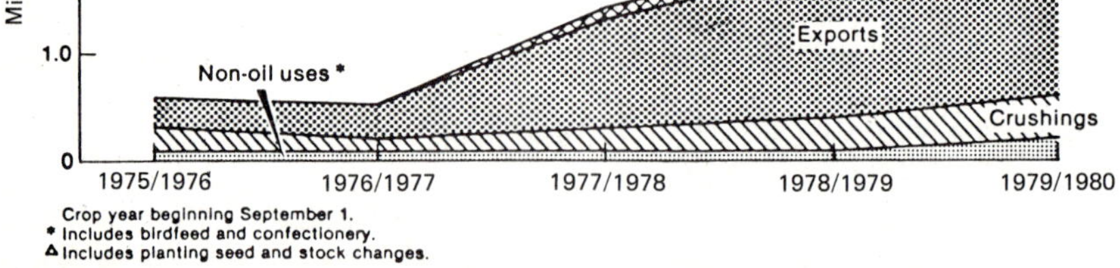

Figure 12-1 U.S. sunflower seed uses. *(United States Department of Agriculture)*

TABLE 12-4 U.S. Soybean Oil Exports
(Million pounds)

	1978–1979	1979–1980	1980–1981	1981–1982	1982–1983*
Western Europe	8	22	6	1	101
Eastern Europe	52	8	92	52	320
Soviet Union	0	54	0	0	0
Total Asia	1504	1636	654	1007	819
India	399	943	136	150	45
Pakistan	360	325	277	573	450
China	130	220	56	0	0
Iran	399	0	0	0	0
Africa	127	115	124	148	100
Total western hemisphere†	642	854	752	869	760
Colombia	185	182	133	171	180
Total U.S. exports	2333	2691	1628	2077	1875

*Estimated.

†The western hemisphere generally includes relatively small amounts scattered among a large number of countries in the Caribbean, Latin American, and South American areas.

SOURCE: ContiCommodity Research Division.

The most important influence on U.S. exports in the future will probably be the direction that per capita consumption trends take in the less developed countries, together with the degree to which the populations of these countries continue to expand.

Table 12-5 shows the shares of total world exports of soybean oil accounted for by the major exporters. It can be seen that U.S. soybean oil exports as a share of the world total are less than one-half of what they formerly had been. This is a result of both increased foreign production and expanded crushing capacity.

OVERSEAS PRODUCERS

Brazil

Brazil was a net importer of soybean oil until 1970, but since then it has been a steadily growing exporter and is now the world's largest (see Figure 12-2). Table 12-6 compares U.S. and Brazilian exports between 1975 and 1981.

Most of Brazil's exports are sent to the mideast, far east, and other South American countries. India, which imported almost all of its soybean oil requirements from Brazil during 1981, is the leading customer for Brazilian soybean oil. In 1981, India accounted for over 50 percent of Brazil's total exports.

India

India is the leading world importer of soybean oil (see Figure 12-3). This is largely because of government policies which have been oriented towards

TABLE 12-5 World Soybean Oil Exports: Volume of Leading Exporters
(Listed as a percentage of total world exports)

Calendar year	United States	Brazil	China	Argentina	Other*
1960	71.1	—†	3.6	—	25.3
1961	69.9	—	0.3	—	30.1
1962	81.6	—	0.1	—	18.2
1963	79.4	—	0.4	—	20.1
1964	79.8	—	0.4	—	19.8
1965	79.2	—	0.3	—	20.5
1966	75.9	—	0.8	—	23.3
1967	76.4	—	0.6	—	23.0
1968	72.1	—	0.5	—	27.4
1969	61.0	—	0.5	—	38.6
1970	60.5	0.3	0.2	—	39.1
1971	60.5	0.5	0.2	—	38.8
1972	53.6	5.4	—	—	41.0
1973	40.7	8.4	—	2.0	48.8
1974	48.0	0.1	—	2.4	49.5
1975	26.1	19.4	—	1.5	53.0
1976	28.0	27.3	—	3.5	41.1
1977	36.6	23.7	—	3.4	20.1
1978	35.8	19.4	—	2.5	42.3
1975–1978 average	31.6	22.5	—	2.7	39.2
1980	31.2	36.2	—	3.0	39.6

*Primarily soybean oil produced in the EEC from imported soybeans and reexported to member countries. Also includes Spain.

†Where no figures appear, only a negligible amount of oil was exported.

SOURCES: *Foreign Agriculture Circular (Oilseeds and Products)*, various issues, Foreign Agricultural Service, United States Department of Agriculture; *Trade Yearbook*, various issues, Food and Agriculture Organization of the United Nations.

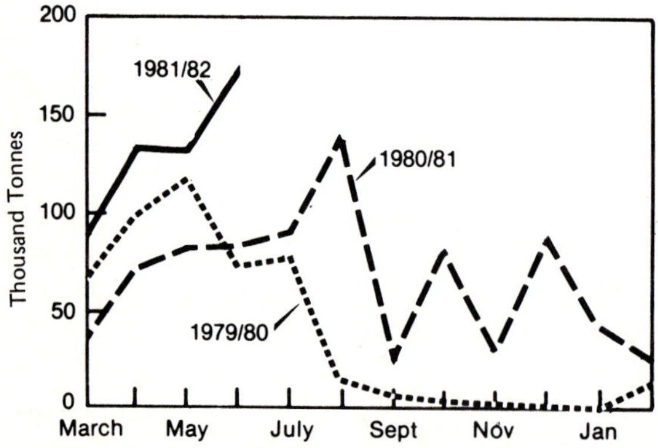

Figure 12-2 Monthly Brazilian soybean oil exports. *(United States Department of Agriculture)*

TABLE 12-6 Brazilian and U.S. Soybean Oil Exports Compared*
(Thousand tonnes)

	1975	1976	1977	1978	1979	1980	1981	1982
Brazil	263	453	487	487	534	744	1050	881
United States	443	703	934	1055	1220	740	942	850

*Calendar-year basis for Brazil; crop-year basis for the United States.
SOURCE: United States Department of Agriculture, ContiCommodity Research Division.

enhancing and ensuring the production of cereals at the expense of oilseed cultivation. Table 12-7 shows the production and imports of major oils in recent years.

The policy of importing large quantities of vegetable oils was begun in 1977. At that time, India had a comfortable foreign exchange position and the choice was made to satisfy growing consumer demand and halt price increases for vegetable oils. However, continued chronic shortages of domestic vegetable oil production have increased the size of the vegetable oil import bill and have led to growing concern over vegetable oil import policies. Vegetable oils are now India's third most expensive import item, behind petroleum and fertilizers.

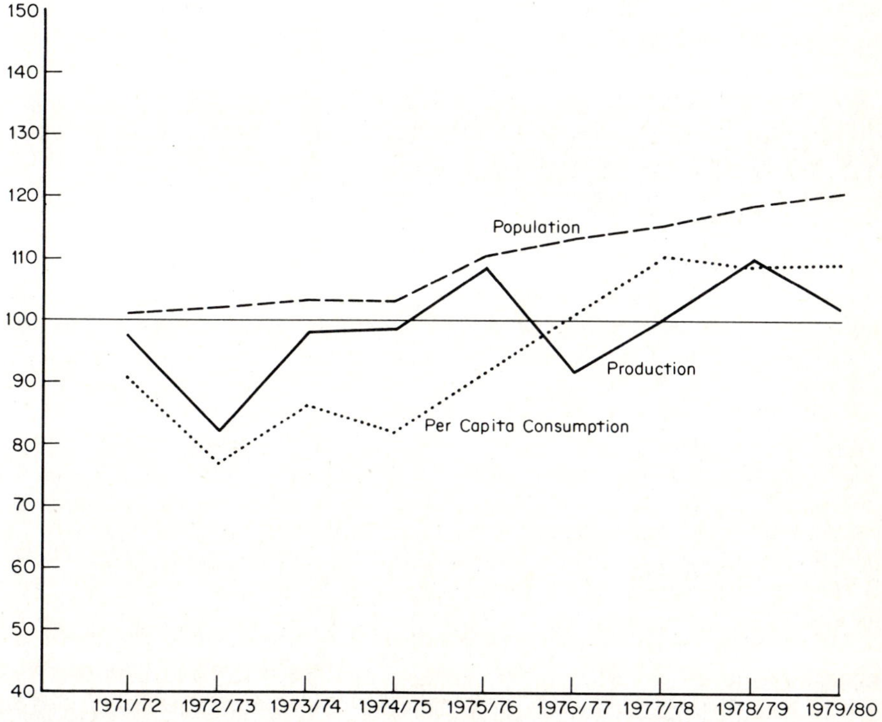

Figure 12-3 Indian domestic oilseed production versus population growth and per capita consumption of vegetable oil. *(United States Department of Agriculture)*

TABLE 12-7 India: Supply and Distribution of Vegetable Oils
(Selected years, thousand tonnes)

	1976	1978	1979	1980
Total oil production	3144	2908	3020	2655
Peanut	1625	1485	1494	1389
Rapeseed	610	520	577	444
Total oil imports	222	1327	1122	1364
Soybean	151	513	555	692
Palm	26	486	396	515
Rapeseed	37	273	138	131

Several initiatives have been introduced to curtail the situation. First, acreage expansion for peanuts, oil palm, and soybeans is being encouraged in various growing areas to attempt to increase production. Funds also have been allocated to improving oilseed technology to try to increase yields, which have been relatively low. Also, a new requirement specifies that the amount of domestically produced oil used in the production of *vanaspati*, an Indian dietary staple, must be increased by 25 percent. This is expected to increase prices for domestic oilseeds and thereby stimulate production. Vanaspati production now cannot contain more than 70 percent of oils that are imported, compared to a 95 percent allowance previously.

Present vegetable oil import policies have not been altered because of the desire to avoid aggravating consumers with higher food prices. Thus no immediate change is likely in India's import position until the results of these initiatives can be more fully assessed.

People's Republic of China

A decline in China's exports of fats and oils and oilseeds has been going on since the late 1960s; this is due to the fact that domestic oilseed production has failed to keep pace with the rate of population increase and the apparent government desire to maintain per capita consumption levels. China has now become a net importer.

There is no question that China could become more of an important force in the world market for vegetable oil even without a significant increase in per capita consumption. Its expanding population coupled with even a marginal increase in per capita consumption (which is low even by Asian standards) would cause a leverage effect on world consumption, and therefore prices, which would be considerable. In light of this, developments in China should be monitored very closely in the 1980s as a possibly very important future price influence.

Soviet Union

Since the mid-1970s the Soviet Union has been increasing imports of fats and oils dramatically due to a discrepancy between falling production (of sunflower seeds) and rising consumption (Table 12-8).

Imports of fats and oils have concentrated upon the cheapest sources. These

TABLE 12-8 Soviet Imports of Soybeans, Protein Meals, Fats, and Oils ***(October to September, thousand tonnes)***

	1978–1979	1979–1980	1980–1981	1981–1982
Protein meals				
Soybean meal	*	281	1,033	1,203
Cottonseed meal	*	9	45	48
Peanut meal	*	52	120	80
Sunflower meal	*	—	11	—
Rapeseed meal	*	—	3	10
Total		342	1,212	1,341
Fats and oils				
Soybean oil	22	72	112	205
Palm oil	109	71	178	290
Coconut oil	54	79	67	83
Butter (fat basis)	111	220	161	159
Linseed oil	79	93	13	107
Tallow and grease	95	103	136	77
Rapeseed oil	5	19	8	6
Olive oil	6	13	12	14
Palm kernel oil	1	12	13	13
Castor oil	46	46	38	44
Tung oil	4	8	5	6
Sunflower oil	—	52	229	234
Cotton oil	—	—	2	—
Total	532	787	1,089	1,239
Soybeans	1,253	1,470	1,476	1,551

*Not applicable.
SOURCE: *Oil World.*

have included subsidized butter from the EEC and Malaysian palm oil; palm oil imports in particular have shown an increasing trend in recent years. Small amounts of soybean oil imports from Brazil have occurred on a semiregular basis; a 5-year trade pact with Brazil requires the Soviet Union to import at least 40,000 tons of soybean oil annually during 1982–1986. Even if sunflower oil production in the Soviet Union can ever return to "normal" (pre-1975 levels) it is still likely that large Soviet imports of fats and oils and oilseeds may continue, since the high-priced sunflower exports would finance the lower-priced fats and oil imports.

The EEC

The ten nations of the EEC form the dominant factor in the total world fats and oils trade. The EEC is the primary world importer of fats and oils other than soybean oil but is an exporter of soybean oil as a result of its processing capacity. Whereas other exporters actually grow the soybeans themselves, the EEC imports them and exports the oil to satisfy intra-EEC trade.

Factors Influencing Market Prices

The factors which influence the price of soybean oil are as follows.

1. Brazilian availability of soybean oil for the export market and Malaysian production and supplies of palm oil are of special importance.
   a. Brazil will be able to export all of the soybean oil it wants to because of currency devaluations.
   b. Large surpluses of Malaysian palm oil result in low palm oil prices relative to soybean oil; also, stronger U.S. dollar values cheapen palm and coconut oil imports for U.S. processors and cut into domestic U.S. soybean oil consumption (and vice versa).
   c. Decreasing supplies of other edible oils increase the demand for soybean oil at equivalent relative price differentials; the impact upon U.S. values depends highly upon Brazilian supplies.
2. Decreasing supplies of the higher-priced oils (e.g., sunflower seed oil). As higher-priced oils decrease in supply, they will increase their prices in world markets and thereby tend to support the values of cheaper oils (e.g., soybean oil). This holds true unless the production of cheaper oils is in large surplus and the price discrepancies have been fairly narrow to begin with.
3. The increasing production of cheaper-priced oils (such as palm oils, coconut oils, and corn oils), which tends to hold down the price of soybean oil.
4. The size of the U.S. soybean crop.

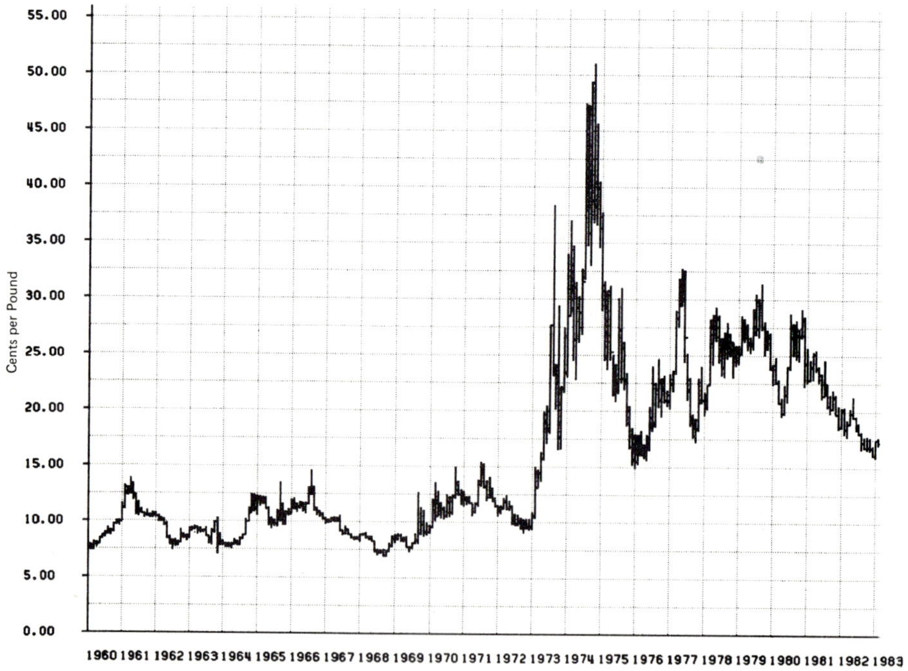

Figure 12-4 Monthly continuation, Chicago Board of Trade soybean oil. *(ContiCommodity Research Division)*

5. The rate of utilization of both soybeans and soybean oil. The proportion of the soybean supply that is crushed can vary widely from season to season and depends largely upon crushing margins. It is generally true that factors that determine soybean meal demand normally influence the rate of crush more than factors in the oil market. Meal is less storable than oil and there is a tendency to crush for meal demand rather than the oil—supplies of oil usually are sufficiently large to be drawn upon if necessary.
6. The level of U.S. soybean oil stocks. Soybean oil stocks of less than 700 to 800 million pounds should spark price advances—especially if soybean crushing margins or soybean supplies are not sufficient to increase crushings to replenish soybean oil stocks.

There are various reports to be watched. The U.S. Weekly Export Sales Report issued by the USDA provides information on soybean oil export sales by destination for the current and next marketing season, and also reports actual export shipments. The Census Bureau releases a monthly crush report around the end of the third week in each month; this lists the crushings of soybeans during the previous month as well as crude soybean oil and soybean meal production for the month. The Census Bureau also releases a report covering factory and warehouse stocks of soybean oil; the U.S. production and stocks of other major fats and oils also are listed. These reports allow a check on the production and distribution of soybean oil.

Figure 12-4 illustrates price trends for soybean oil on the Chicago Board of Trade.

SUMMARY OF MAJOR FACTORS TO MONITOR

1. Size of the U.S. soybean crop
2. Supplies and price trends of other competitive oils, especially:
    a. Brazilian soybean production
    b. Malaysian palm oil production
    c. Total world supplies of all fats and oils relative to consumption
3. The rate of utilization of both U.S. soybeans and U.S. soybean oil
4. The trend of U.S. soybean oil stocks (i.e., whether they are increasing or decreasing)
5. Foreign oilseed crops, particularly in major consuming areas

Commodity	Exchange	Contract size	Limit moves
Soybean oil	Chicago Board of Trade	60,000 pounds	1¢

CHAPTER

13

Other Vegetable Oils

Michael Hinebaugh

Other vegetable oils sometimes used as soybean oil substitutes in the world market include peanut, sunflower seed, cottonseed, rapeseed, olive, corn, sesame seed, coconut, palm kernel, palm, and babassu oils. All tables in this chapter are on a July to June crop-year basis.

SUNFLOWER SEED OIL

The price on world markets of sunflower seed oil is normally well above the value of other edible oils because it is relatively high in oil content (40 to 45 percent oil) compared to other oilseeds, and more preferred in some areas. World production of sunflower seed is spread across a large number of countries; however, 65 to 70 percent of world production is concentrated in just three nations: the Soviet Union, the United States, and Argentina. (See Table 13-1 and Figure 13-1.)

Argentina has slipped from its position as the second largest world producer since more profitable corn and soybean crops have attracted acreage away from sunflower seeds. Acreage and yields have expanded in the United States to place it in a commanding position of second place in total world production. Crushing capacity specifically geared to sunflower seed is increasing rapidly in the United States. This factor, combined with the stagnation in production in the Soviet Union, may enable the United States to replace the Soviet Union as the number one producer during the latter part of the decade. Soviet seed inbreeding has emphasized oil content, but is believed to have weakened the

TABLE 13-1 World Sunflower Oil Production
(Selected years, thousand tonnes)

1970	1972	1974	1976	1977	1978	1979	1980
3576	3637	4493	3737	4724	4710	5609	4724

seed kernel and increased its vulnerability to moisture and disease. Soviet yields have declined severely over the past 10 years. (See Table 13-2.)

In view of the weakening positions of the Soviet Union and Argentina, the most important influence on the price of sunflower seed oil probably depends largely upon future developments in the United States, because the United States is export-oriented and because sunflower seed and oil exports from the Soviet Union have declined substantially. As Figure 13-2 illustrates, the United States already is the foremost world exporter of sunflower seed. (See also Figure 13-3.)

PEANUT OIL

World peanut (groundnut) production remained steady in the 1970s at around 17 million tonnes annually.

The leading world producer is India, which accounts for around one-third of total world peanut production. The People's Republic of China is the second largest producer and the United States is the third. Combined, the United States, China, and India produce around 55 to 60 percent of the world's supply of groundnuts; Senegal, Nigeria, and the Sudan also are important producing areas. (Nigeria and Senegal have been important exporters of peanuts and peanut oil.) The remaining percentage is scattered in small amounts across many countries in South America, Africa, and the Far East.

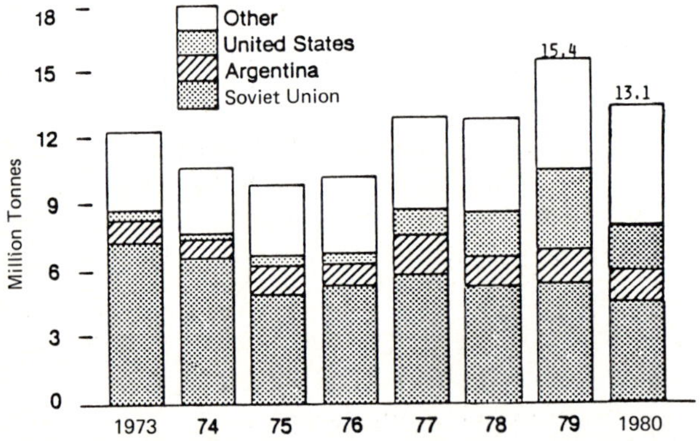

Crop year beginning September 1.

Figure 13-1 World production of sunflower seed. *(United States Department of Agriculture)*

TABLE 13-2 Soviet Production of Sunflower Oil ***(Thousand tonnes)***

1976	1977	1978	1979	1980
1816	2031	1834	1852	1610

World peanut oil production also has stagnated in accordance with the production decline of raw peanuts; this is clearly visible in Table 13-3. Meanwhile, imports of peanut oil by major consuming centers have continued to increase. France is the leading world importer of peanut oil; French imports of peanut oil have increased by almost 40 percent since the late 1960s. Other countries, such as India, have seen production declines result in shortages and increased imports of cheaper edible oils, such as palm, coconut, and soybean oils.

COTTONSEED OIL

World cottonseed production has been able to increase only slightly over the last 15 years, and it has stagnated in recent years. This is due primarily to the lack of any significant growth in production in the major producing countries, the Soviet Union, the United States and China. Together, these three countries account for around 55 to 60 percent of total world cotton production. World cottonseed oil production also has barely increased from levels of the early 1970s (Table 13-4).

The emphasis upon the amount of polyunsaturated fatty acids in U.S. diets

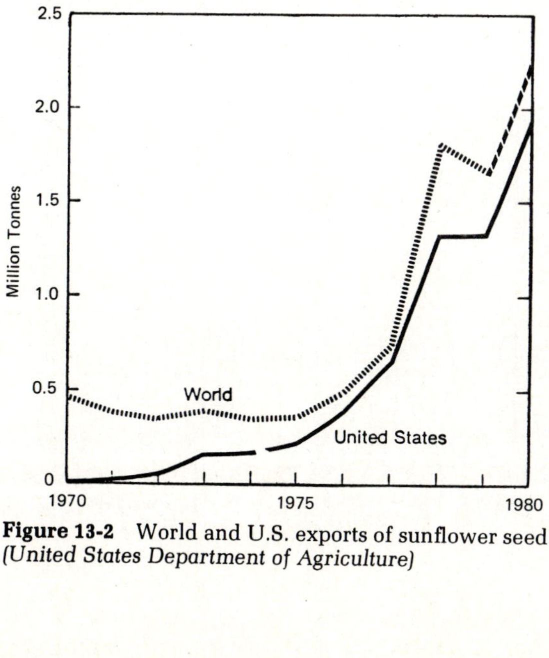

Figure 13-2 World and U.S. exports of sunflower seed. *(United States Department of Agriculture)*

has tended to increase the domestic use of soybean oil as opposed to cottonseed oil; the latter contains a somewhat lower amount of polyunsaturated fatty acids than soybean oil. (Polyunsaturated fatty acids are "fats" but are low in cholesterol.) Cottonseed oil is used mostly in salad and cooking oils and shortening in the United States. However, domestic use decreased sharply in the 1970s; since 1968, consumption fell by 50 percent. U.S. production of cottonseed oil stagnated, during these years, and the resulting surplus has been exported.

PALM OIL

Palm oil production has increased by a factor of 4 since the mid-1960s (see Table 13-5), largely because of the dramatic growth in West Malaysia. One of the interesting aspects about the growth of palm oil production is that palm groves have been financed indirectly by the United States through the World Bank and other similar financial institutions. As a result, the United States has increased export competition for its own products (such as soybean oil).

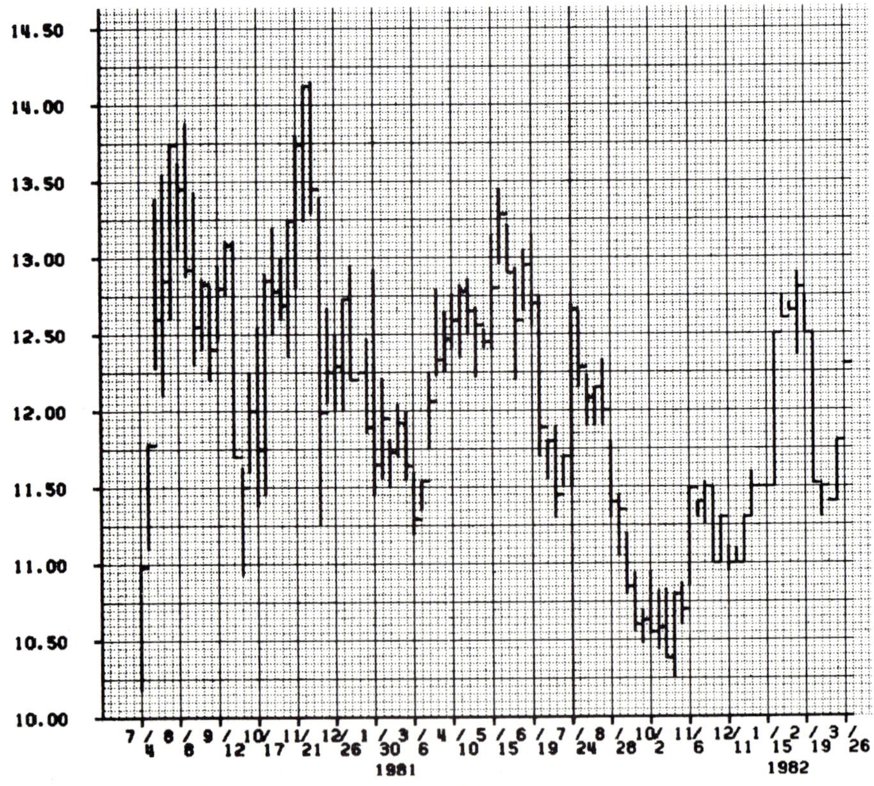

Figure 13-3 Weekly continuation, Minneapolis sunflower seed. *(Conti-Commodity Research Division)*

TABLE 13-3 World Production of Peanut Oil
(Selected years; thousand tonnes)

1970	1972	1974	1976	1977	1978	1979	1980
3271	3519	3023	3192	3147	3422	3128	3111

Malaysia accounts for over 50 percent of total world production. Indonesia and Nigeria are two other major producers, with the rest of world production scattered widely among various countries. Rainfall is an important factor in terms of the production outlook. In Malaysia, the minimum rainfall for successful oil palm cultivation is around 60 inches a year—provided that it is distributed evenly throughout the year and there is no marked and prolonged dry season (which would create the need for higher annual rainfall amounts).

Exports of palm oil also have increased dramatically in line with the increased production; palm oil-producing countries export most of their product. Refined palm oil recently has increased its proportionate share of total export volume relative to crude palm oil. Attempts have been made to assist local economies by increasing local processing. This keeps more of the value of the product at home, because processed products cost more. The escalation in the export of refined palm oil has been most noteworthy in Malaysia.

The European Economic Community (EEC) and the United States were formerly the main markets for Malaysian palm oil. But U.S. palm oil imports slipped in the late 1970s because of the decreasing value of the U.S. dollar, and so imports were no longer competitive. Other markets such as India increased in importance for Malaysian palm oil at the same time because of stagnation in vegetable oil production. Imports of palm oil by the Soviet Union and China also began to increase around the same time. Malaysia alone accounts for approximately 70 percent of total world palm oil exports, which currently are around 3¼ million tonnes.

The large increases in production of palm oil have been a major factor in preventing the stagnating trend in other edible vegetable oils from having a pronounced price impact. The increase in international trade in palm oil relative to production has ended the former problem of recurrent large stocks of palm oil. However, this increase in trade has periodically tightened palm oil prices relative to soybean oil prices to the extent that, at times, the demand for soybean oil also increases. The price spread between palm oil and soybean oil is quite often, therefore, an important barometer for soybean oil demand. (Palm oil formerly had to sell at a *substantial* discount to find a home for its large surplus.)

TABLE 13-4 World Production of Cottonseed Oil
(Selected years; thousand tonnes)

1970	1972	1974	1976	1977	1978	1979	1980	1981	1982*
2621	2860	3149	2814	3172	2996	3200	3169	3575	3339

*Estimated.

TABLE 13-5 World Palm Oil Production
(Selected years; thousand tonnes)

1970	1972	1974	1976	1977	1978	1979	1980	1981	1982*
1715	2143	2605	3371	3784	4295	4812	5155	5929	6110

*Estimated.

COCONUT OIL

The Philippines is the dominant force in the world copra and coconut oil market, and accounts for almost 80 percent of total world exports of coconut oil. Total world production of coconut oil for various years in the past decade is shown in Table 13-6. Total world coconut oil exports (about 37 percent of production) are approximately double the level of the early 1970s but stagnated toward the end of the decade at 1.2 million tonnes. Recent increases in imports of coconut oil by the Soviet Union have been the major development in the world market. U.S. imports of coconut oil also are increasing again, after several declining years. (The United States formerly was the predominant world importer of coconut oil.) Coconut oil prices from 1973 to 1982 are shown in Figure 13-4.

Indonesia recently reemerged as a major exporter of coconut oil following successive years of complete absence from the export market because of production problems. Indonesia implemented a national policy change which substituted cheaper-priced palm oil in domestic consumption; this allows exports of the higher-priced coconut oil, thereby maximizing economic benefits and increasing edible oil supplies for consumers.

The Philippines government recently adopted measures designed to speed up the flow of exports and to cope with mounting stocks of copra, by suspending the export levies on all coconut products. These levies (taxes) had been paid by exporters and were used to fund a growers' price-support program. It is uncertain whether or not the government will fund the support program in the absence of the export levies; however, processors' margins should improve, and it is hoped that a more rapid export flow and a reduction of stockpiles will result from the new policy.

Coconut oil is used in the U.S. primarily in the production of confectionaries.

RAPESEED OIL

World production of rapeseed has increased steadily over the past 10 years (see Table 13-7); large production increases in Canada and China plus EEC policies

TABLE 13-6 World Production of Coconut Oil
(Selected years; thousand tonnes)

1970	1972	1974	1976	1977	1978	1979	1980	1981	1982 est
2135	2792	2100	3115	3171	2829	3093	3150	3087	2980

to increase French production have been largely responsible. Canada, China, and India, ranked in order, are the three main world producers of rapeseed; combined, they account for 65 to 70 percent of total world rapeseed production. Canada not only is the largest producer but also has the largest stock of exportable supplies.

The increasing production in Canada and France has added to world export availability, which has fostered competition in world markets for edible oil. But more importantly for the United States, the increasing French production has increased competition for a share of EEC crushing capacity, and therefore has tended to affect soybeans adversely—particularly right after harvest. French rapeseed may offer larger crushing margins than imported soybeans; EEC crushers often have received subsidies for crushing domestically produced oilseeds.

Rapeseed had fallen into a questionable status because of former high levels of euricic acid content and the reports of adverse effects on human health posed by high concentrations of euricic acid. But plant breeders in Canada and Europe worked steadily throughout the 1970s to manipulate the genetic structure of rapeseed varieties to attempt to eliminate or at least minimize the euricic acid content from rapeseed oil and the glucosinolates (sulfur compounds) from rapeseed meal. These improved oil and meal products have gained increased acceptance as general-purpose edible vegetable oil and protein feedstuffs.

Figure 13-4 Monthly cash coconut oil, CRD PAC CST LB. *(ContiCommodity Research Division)*

TABLE 13-7 World Production of Rapeseed Oil
(Selected years; thousand tonnes)

1970	1972	1974	1976	1977	1978	1979	1980	1981	1982*
1878	2556	2397	2485	2699	3673	3432	3790	4125	5037

*Estimated.

TABLE 13-8 World Production of Olive Oil
(Selected years; thousand tonnes)

1970	1972	1974	1976	1977	1978	1979	1980	1981	1982
1245	1559	1531	1334	1620	1570	1599	1829	1322	1978

TABLE 13-9 World Production of Corn Oil
(Selected years; thousand tonnes)

1976	1977	1978	1979	1980
410	436	445	512	518

TABLE 13-10 World Production of Sesame Seed Oil
(Selected years; thousand tonnes)

1976	1977	1978	1979	1980
598	624	655	626	612

TABLE 13-11 World Production of Safflower Seed Oil
(Selected years; thousand tonnes)

1976	1977	1978	1979	1980
217	274	325	342	255

Most European rapeseed production is from *Brassica campestris L* (turnip rape); this fall-seeded variety outyields those seeded in the spring.

OLIVE OIL

Olive oil production fluctuates widely on an annual basis, as depicted in Table 13-8.

Olive oil is not a major element in the world market for fats and oils, except for countries such as those surrounding the Mediterranean, which prefer olive oil in dietary channels; it is basically a specialty product. Not surprisingly, Italy, Spain, Greece, Turkey, and Tunisia are the largest producers of olive oil; their production, combined, accounts for almost 90 percent of total world production of olive oil. The wide fluctuations in annual production are caused by recurrent droughts in this part of the world.

CORN OIL

Corn oil is not a major factor in the world market for edible oils. As can be seen in Table 13-9, world production of corn oil is relatively small. It could be said to be in its "infancy" stage; whether or not it will ever achieve maturity in terms of large production, rivaling major edible oils, depends on a variety of factors. It is likely that corn oil production will expand over time, albeit slowly, and ultimately account for a greatly increased proportionate share of total world edible oil production. This likelihood is based on a number of factors—the stagnating trends in several important edible oils, the lack of land resources available to dramatically increase production of other edible oilseeds, the increasing world population base (which escalates mathematically at increasing proportions every year) and the financial resources of the United States and other areas to increase facilities and capacities for profitable enterprises.

Corn oil production, despite its present small size, already approximates almost 20 percent of world coconut oil production and 30 percent of world olive oil production. The United States alone accounts for almost 75 percent of world production of corn oil, because of the dominance of the United States in total world corn production. Corn oil prices are geared closely to overall developments in world prices for edible oils; its low production relegates corn oil prices to a role of being a follower and residual supplier rather than a price setter.

SESAME SEED OIL AND SAFFLOWER SEED OIL

In terms of the total world edible oils balance, sesame seed oil and safflower seed oil are very minor. A large part of the total world production of safflower seed oil occurs in the United States, the bulk being used domestically. Tables 13-10 and 13-11 show the total world production of both oils.

Safflower seed production and distribution in the United States have tended to decrease since 1970, despite the fact that its oil content has the highest concentrate of polyunsaturated fatty acids compared to other vegetable oils. The increasing production and availability of soybean oil and the relatively higher price for safflower seed oil are responsible.

CHAPTER

14

Government Farm Programs

Michael Hinebaugh

INTRODUCTION

Government policies and programs have been an important factor for agricultural prices in many years. Farm programs since 1929 have been oriented primarily toward maintaining farm income and attempting to adjust production to fit demand. Most current agricultural programs stem from a series of interrelated laws that began in 1933 in response to the economic crisis of the Great Depression. These programs originally were intended to be temporary measures, designed to help the agricultural sector during the worst times of the depression period. Direct government involvement was not expected to continue beyond the crisis period.

The government programs usually have involved one or more of the following:

1. Nonrecourse price support loans, which presently include a 3-year grain reserve
2. Production restrictions including:
   a. Acreage allotments
   b. Various types of land diversion, or "set-asides"
3. Demand expanders such as:
   a. Food stamp and school lunch programs to increase domestic demand
   b. Public Law 480 and other subsidized credit programs, plus direct export subsidies to aid exports

4. Direct income payments to farmers (e.g., target prices and deficiency payments).

The loan rates are often too high and have interfered with price-setting mechanisms of the markets; currently, grain market economics are highly influenced by the existence of the grain reserve. (This is explained later.) Land diversion programs are expensive and not very effective, because the least productive land is diverted from production. Such programs also have encouraged heavier capital inputs, such as fertilizer applications, in an attempt to continue to maximize production despite the acreage diversion.

Since 1933, government programs have been provided at various times for corn, wheat, cotton, peanuts, rice, tobacco, butterfat and milk, wool, mohair, honey, tung, nuts, barley, oats, rye, sorghum, flaxseed, soybeans, dry edible beans, cottonseed, crude pine gum, sugar, sugarbeets, chickens, eggs, turkeys, flax fiber, hemp fiber, hempseed, castorbean seeds, olive oil, canned fruits, concentrated grapefruit juice, hogs, figs, dates, prunes, raisins, pecans, walnuts, various kinds of hay and pasture seeds, several kinds of winter cover-crop seeds, lamb, mutton, Puerto Rican molasses, and hazelnuts.

A brief outline of some basic elements of price support programs is warranted before the discussion of actual farm programs.

Nonrecourse Loans

Loans are available from the U.S. Department of Agriculture's Commodity Credit Corporation (CCC). The farmer pledges a specific quantity of a commodity, such as corn, as collateral for a loan at the loan rate in effect at the time. The total loan value is the loan rate multiplied by the quantity of corn placed under loan. The producer has a specified time period in which to repay the loan plus interest. The interest rates charged usually are no higher than the level which the U.S. Treasury charges the CCC—that is, well below actual market rates. The producer can redeem the loan at any time by repaying the principal and interest; if the free market price is greater than the sum of the principal and interest, the loan is usually redeemed. But the producer also has the option of delivering the collateral to the CCC instead of selling it; this usually occurs when prices are below the sum of the principal amount of the loan plus interest. In this case both interest and principal are considered paid in full (hence the term "nonrecourse" loan). The CCC then takes title to the stored commodity. The program essentially means that any gain from price increases goes to the borrowers (who then can redeem the loans and sell the grain) and all losses are absorbed by the federal treasury.

Target Prices

The target price is a price which farmers are guaranteed to receive, regardless of actual market values. Target prices theoretically are keyed to the cost of production of the individual crop. Direct cash payments are made to producers when the average market price is less than the target price during the first 5 months of the crop year. These payments are termed "deficiency payments";

they are viewed as income supplements to producers. The payment amounts to the difference between the target price and the average market price unless the average price level has remained below the basic loan rate during those 5 months; in that case the payment would amount to the difference between the loan price and the target price.* The target price also is used as the basis for calculating "disaster payments." Disaster payments are made when natural disasters prevent normal planting operations; they also are paid if natural disasters after the crop is planted cause a reduction in production to two-thirds of "normal" production. (The 1980 summer drought and the 1981 spring frost in the western wheat belt are good examples of natural disasters covered by this subsidy; hail-damaged crops, a frequent occurrence, are also covered.)

The *loan rate* represents a minimum value, or "floor," for prices; the farmer essentially can sell grain to the government at that level, rather than accept a lower actual market value. The *target price* is the price the government wants the farmers to receive.

HISTORY OF GOVERNMENT FARM PROGRAMS

A partial history of basic farm program changes follows.

1932 The federal farm board recommended legislation to regulate planted acreages and/or quantities of grain allowed to be sold.

1933 Direct cash payments to farmers were initiated to encourage their participation in government programs to reduce planted acreage. The first nonrecourse loans were initiated and the CCC was established. ("Nonrecourse" simply means that the producer does not have to pay back the loan but is allowed to turn over the stored commodity to the CCC as full payment.)

1935 The first grain reserve program was proposed but was not fully incorporated as policy.

1936 The soil conservation program was initiated; farmers would be paid for shifting acreage from crops declared to be in surplus to soil-conserving legumes and grasses. The goal of achieving "income parity" for farmers was established. (Parity, a concept which is often misinterpreted, is explained later in this chapter.)

1938 Comprehensive price support legislation was adopted. The loan programs were expanded. Parity payments were authorized in order to provide a return as close to parity as available government funds would permit; the stated goal was to achieve both "price parity" and "income parity." (Crop yields began an upward trend around this time; thus, overall grain production did not decrease despite reduced

*Deficiency payments are based upon a calculated "normal yield" for each farm rather than actual yields in a particular year.

acreages and low prices. In 1939, direct government payments amounted to 35 percent of net farm cash income.)

1939 Food distribution programs were expanded in order to help dispose of surplus grain and meat; school lunch and food stamp programs were added.

1941–1945 Loan levels were set at 85 to 90 percent of parity during the war period to serve as an incentive for crop production for lend-lease and military needs.

1948 to early 1950s Price supports on basic commodities were continued at the high levels that existed during World War II. The formula for determining price parity for producers was changed to add a labor charge to the parity cost index. Public Law 480 was initiated to provide a vehicle for the disposition of surplus products; exports under the PL-480 program subsequently became a major factor in the total annual exports of some commodities during the 1950s and 1960s. The Soil Bank Program enlarged previous acreage diversion programs; the objective was to further reduce the amount of acreage in order to try to adjust supply to fit demand. (This program caused disruption in some farm communities because many farmers placed their entire farms in the conservation reserve and simply "retired.")

Mid-1960s More programs for diverting grain acreage to nonproductive uses were initiated. One program authorized direct cash payments to producers amounting to 40 percent of the value of the crop that would have been produced if it had been planted. (More land was offered for retirement than the government could accommodate because a ceiling had been placed on the authorized expenditures.) A wheat-marketing certificate program was initiated. Price supports for the farmer's share of domestic consumption (around 45 percent of the farmer's crop at that time) were set at higher levels than price supports for the share of production that went into exports (also around 45 percent). The remaining 10 percent of the farmer's production received still lower supports. Price supports in 1964 ranged as follows: domestic portion, $2 per bushel; export portion, $1.55 per bushel; remainder, $1.30 per bushel. A system of direct export subsidies maintained wheat exports; U.S. wheat prices usually were well above world market prices so subsidies were necessary to enable U.S. wheat to compete in world markets.

1970 Specific acreage allotments for individual crops and marketing quotas were discontinued. Farmers were able to plant whatever grain crops they wished to as long as they complied with the required set-aside acreage (if not, the farmer was ineligible to participate in government price support programs). Farm prices were supported through a combination of loans, government purchases, and direct cash payments to producers.

1973 The worldwide crop failures in 1972 and 1973 and record-high grain prices caused a switch from former attitudes of trying to "fine-tune" supply and demand. Policies were reoriented toward full production.

(However, restrictions on planted acreages still continued to exist at the height of the food crisis; set-aside acreages in the 1973–1974 crop year, for example, were 7.4 million acres for wheat and 6 million acres for corn. Unrestricted plantings were not allowed until the 1974 crop year.) Much of the original 1938 price support legislation was retained as a standby authority in case prices fell. The 1973 Farm Bill also introduced a new concept of target prices. Cash payments to farmers would be equal to the amount by which market prices fell below the established "target" price. (This is explained earlier in the discussions under Nonrecourse Loans and Target Prices.) The 1973 legislation also contained a mandate that target prices must be adjusted according to an index of calculated production costs. The formula by which production costs are calculated was devised by Congress. The USDA disagreed with the formula, stating that the congressional formula produces calculations of production costs which are higher than actual costs.

1977 The 1977 Farm Bill authorized set-aside acreage provisions where producers could be required to divert some farm production acreage in order to qualify for direct cash payments under the target-price support program. Authority also was granted to allow cash payments to producers to encourage them to divert a portion of their land from production. A conservation reserve also was authorized but it was not implemented by the USDA. The storage programs were the main features of the 1977 legislation. Long-term loans to producers were initiated for construction of storage capacity sufficient to store at least 2 years of a farm's production. A provision was included for the creation of an international food reserve. (This ran into problems initially because no agreement with other nations about an international reserve system was able to be reached; the receiving nations were not willing to accept the terms of the developed countries for instituting the program. However, the United States finally set up an international reserve supply for donation purposes after the 1980 embargo against additional grain sales to the Soviet Union because of the Soviet invasion of Afghanistan; the CCC purchased 4 million tons of wheat for the reserve in an attempt to support prices.) The most important provision of the 1977 bill was by far the creation of the grain reserve program. This is covered in detail in the following section because of its influence upon grain prices.

THE GRAIN RESERVE

The grain reserve utilizes 3- to 5-year extended loans to farmers (as opposed to the traditional shorter-term nonrecourse loans). The producer holds the grain but is paid an appropriate amount to cover the cost of storage; storage payments currently are 26½¢ per bushel per year for corn and wheat. Interest charges on these extended loans also cannot exceed the interest level which the federal treasury charges the CCC; but the USDA may waive the interest charge as an added incentive to producers to place their grain reserve program. This latter provision has been utilized in recent years to increase farmer participation in the reserve in order to raise prices. It acts as an incentive because the interest-free money received can then be invested at the prevailing market interest rate. Producers are encouraged to keep their grain in the reserve, once it has been entered, through a system of penalties; repayment of all storage payments received and added interest charges would be required if producers redeem their extended loans before a specific level of release price is reached. These price levels are referred to as the "release" price (or "minimum trigger" price) and the "call" price (or "maximum trigger" price).

The trigger prices vary for specific grains; the grain reserve is placed in release status for a particular grain when the national average cash price for that grain reaches the minimum trigger, or release price. The Secretary of Agriculture may discontinue storage payments and charge interest at that point. However, farmers are not forced to sell their grain. If prices reach the higher maximum trigger, or call price, the grain reserve is placed in call status and the reserve ceases to exist. Forceful measures to induce farmer redemptions and sales at that point *had been* contemplated in the original proposals; calling the outstanding loans, requiring the payment of accrued interest, requiring producers to refund storage payments or other charges were among the penalties discussed in the original bill. But the "rules of the game" have been changed many times in actual practice for both the release and call provisions; corn, for example, was called in early January 1981—but producers later were granted an "indefinite" extension of their loans at a fixed interest charge. The most recent changes involve setting both the release and call prices at the same level, but the Secretary of Agriculture exercises the decision of whether or not the reserve actually is placed in call status.

The release price may be set between 140 and 160 percent of the wheat loan rate at the discretion of the Secretary of Agriculture, but it cannot be outside of that range (it currently approximates 145 percent of the wheat loan rate). The release price for corn is subject to the discretion of the Secretary of Agriculture (it currently approximates 125 percent of the corn loan rate). There has been some talk about trying to tie release prices to target prices.

The grain reserve has been used at times to increase prices above the basic economic value of the free market. Government measures announced after the grain embargo against the Soviet Union in January of 1980 because of the invasion of Afghanistan included opening up the grain reserve for entries well in excess of previous intended amounts; interest charges also were waived. This, in combination with other government actions, threatened to reduce free supplies to a very low level and caused a sharp upward price move, particularly in wheat. In other words, the government moved to tighten free supplies, and market prices had to move higher to free them again; supplies are freed by going high enough in price to trigger the grain reserve into release status.

Free supplies are those supplies which are not under any government program shelter such as grain reserve, CCC inventories, basic loan program, or international reserve. Free supplies often can be a more important price factor than the amount of total grain supplies because free supplies must be adequate to cover marketing flow requirements. As an example, let's say total supplies of a grain are 2 billion bushels and marketing flow requirements of this grain are 1 billion bushels to cover export and domestic demand plus minimum pipeline inventories; but 1.5 billion bushels are in government programs. That actually leaves the free market short 500 million bushels of the amount needed to cover demand and would be considered an exceedingly tight free-supply situation. Grain would have to be enticed somehow from various government programs; the process would begin with a rise in price to encourage redemptions from the basic loan program and then a sharper rise to gain access to grain reserve supplies. This, in essence, is what the free market did in the late spring of 1980 when the government measures were "too much" for the free market. The 1982–1983 season is another example of an artificial bull move caused by the grain reserve. Ending stocks were at record highs but free supplies became very tight.

The existence of the grain reserve also has served to maintain prices at a higher level than they normally had been, given equivalent fundamental balances. Harvest lows, for example, in the fall of 1979 were much higher than they were in other years of similar surplus conditions.* Surplus supplies formerly resulted in prices retreating to around the loan rate, or basic support, level. (This was true for both futures and cash prices; cash-basis levels have widened in recent years because of the change.) However, if grain is allowed to be entered directly into the reserve at the time of harvest, and entries into the reserve are large, then prices would have a long way to rise before reaching the minimum trigger of the grain reserve. Free markets are rational creatures; therefore, prices will hover between the basic loan rate and the minimum trigger of the grain reserve when entry provisions are "loose" rather than "restrictive," assuming that compliance with the government farm program is high. ("Loose" refers to immediate entry allowed at harvest or upon the waiver of interest charges; "restrictive" refers to a mandatory placement of grain under the ordinary loan for 9 months before allowing entry into the reserve—and charging interest.) *Government programs can be extremely important price determinants and therefore should be watched closely.*

THE INTERPRETATION OF OFFICIALLY COMPUTED INDICES

Many concepts incorporated into farm legislation are based upon computed indices maintained by the USDA; these include "parity" prices, crop production costs, relative income comparisons expressed as a percentage of the total national economy, and the like. These comparisons are neither statistically nor economically valid. However, to the extent that distortions are allowed to influence the determination of price supports, they are equally likely to affect farming profitability, decisions concerning planted acreages, consumer food prices,

*Harvest lows in Chicago corn futures, for example, were around 20 percent above the loan rate. That was a historical first for any year of a record crop well in excess of consumption requirements and at least sufficient carry-over supplies.

and a host of other interrelated factors. It is essential to understand several of these indices in order to understand the distortions they provide; this is especially true in view of the present attempts to "marry" support prices to the cost of production index and parity index more closely than before. The following discussion of these indices illustrates how they operate and why they are invalid.

Parity

Parity prices are those which would give farm products the same *per unit* purchasing power as that which prevailed in the period of 1910–1914. The concept is based on the assumption that price relationships during that period represent a true equilibrium or parity for both that period and the present and that any disparities can be measured properly. That is a myth; the following three arguments demonstrate how "parity" indices portray a false picture.

1. The original base period chosen to represent "parity" prices for agricultural products actually represents an abnormally high base value for any farm-price series; this also leads to increasing disparities in later years. Figure 14-1 shows the ratio of prices of farm products to prices of nonagricultural products (the prices in both categories are wholesale). The chart discloses that the ratio for the years 1910–1914 was well above previous levels. It is equally possible to say that the years 1900–1905 represented a truer equilibrium, or more normal relationship. The principal disadvantage of any base-period approach is the determination of exactly which period should be used as the base.

   Because of various technological changes, the series data also lack homogeneity. This means that the present situation is not measured accurately

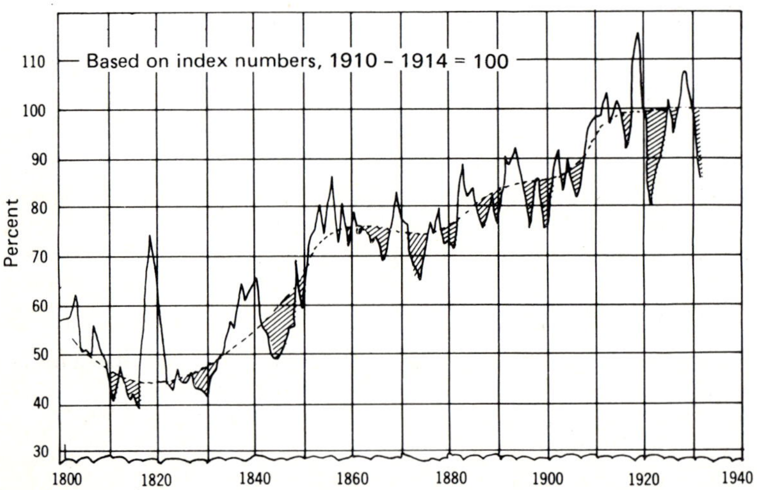

Figure 14-1 Parity, 1800 to 1940. *(ContiCommodity Research Division)*

by such an index. For example, changes have occurred in methods of production and transportation. These changes since 1910 have profoundly affected many manufactured goods in terms of their function, quality, durability, and accompanying services (including the drastic changes that have occurred in the processing and packaging of basic foodstuffs). Because these technological changes are not factored into the parity price index, such comparisons are grossly distorted.

2. The parity price formula also omits any consideration of *quantities* produced on the farm; it ignores completely the gains in productivity which have occurred during the past 70 years. The parity formula simply measures the gross dollar costs for farmers for nonagricultural products against their gross dollar costs of a previous period. Then, however, it compares the price-per-bushel income (or per unit return) that farmers receive against the price per bushel of the earlier period. This greatly obscures reality. Here is a simplified example: Assume that various gross dollar costs doubled between the base period and the present. Thus, if the farmer received $1 per bushel during the base period and still is receiving $1 per bushel now, then the per unit return would be listed as only 50 percent of parity. However, if the farmer's crop yields had doubled during that period, there actually would be twice as many bushels produced per acre, and this would provide a doubled gross return. In other words, a doubled yield at $1 per bushel provides the same gross dollar return per acre as the previous yield would have provided at $2 per acre.

   Comparing gross dollar costs to per unit returns is tantamount to comparing apples and oranges. This is especially true if, in the example above, farm crop yields had tripled, rather than doubled; that would have provided an increase in farm income over costs despite the poor comparison that would be shown by the parity index (see point 3 below). The parity index would show a vastly different picture if gross dollar costs were measured against gross dollar returns (instead of per unit returns) and especially if government payments were included as income.

3. The actual per capita income of the farm population has been above the year's computed parity levels almost every year since 1941. In fact, farm income has averaged 20 to 35 percent above computed parity levels in a number of years (even excluding the years of 1973, 1974, and 1975, when grain prices were at record high levels). This demonstrates vividly that the parity formula used has no solid economic foundation.

Income Comparison Indices

Comparisons of agricultural income to "total national income" or "the share of the consumer dollar" are unrealistic. No reliable index of real incomes of farmers comparable to real incomes of nonfarmers exists. A large proportion of farm production is consumed on the farm, which stretches the farmer's dollar return farther than that of urban dwellers. The computed indices also usually ignore income from nonagricultural sources, which further understates income comparisons. For example, a large number of farm operators farm as a sideline, and earn their main source of income elsewhere (some full-time farmers also do outside work).

Maturing societies and economic progress throughout history have been associated with a decline in the relative importance of agriculture as a share of the gross national product (GNP). Increasing attention and income are devoted to leisure and to an expanding variety of goods and services that are valued by societies as "making life more worth living." The farmer's share of the consumer dollar expended for food has declined largely because an increasing portion of that dollar is being earned by others who are contributing to more elaborate processes for providing foodstuffs to consumers. The food and textile materials which farmers supply constitute a declining proportion of the national consumption of goods and services. Inflation and increasing transportation rates also widen the spread between consumer food expenditures and the farmer's share of those dollars; wage rates move with cost-of-living increases and there now are increased numbers of workers involved in the processing chain from farm to consumer.

The various computed indices also include many uneconomical farm units; these are run by individuals who stay in farming mostly because of a desire for that way of life. These units are included in the calculation of basic support prices but many of the small units do not even participate in the farm program (and thus are not eligible to receive the benefits); these units cannot afford to divert any acreage from production because they are so small. In one recent year, over 50 percent of the price support payments went to less than 10 percent of the farms in the United States.

Cost of Production

Efforts to use *calculated* production costs as the basis for setting farm price subsidies began as long ago as the mid-1930s. The concept was initially defeated. There also were attempts to set the cost of production for farm prices at a level which would assure a return on labor and a return on investment as high as the level obtained by city investments. This latter comparison was attempted in the 1960s; but the study showed that the return on farm investment was higher than the return on investments in common stocks. The cost-of-production concept finally became incorporated into farm legislation in the 1973 and 1977 farm bills.

Support prices now are based on official calculations of production costs. The official formula used includes fees or charges for labor and management; these constitute a farm salary or income base (as opposed to "farming for a profit").

1. The labor fee assumes that all unpaid family labor is equal in quality to hired labor and that the family labor has other employment alternatives. The labor fee is valued at a rate equal to hired labor or the average wage rate in the subregion.*
2. A "return for management" fee is included. This is computed at 10 percent of the estimated variable, machinery ownership, and farm overhead costs.

*This is similar in principle to paying family members for household work. The GNP would rise sharply if such calculations were included.

Variable costs include expenditures for seed, fertilizer, chemicals, custom operations ("custom" means having someone else do the planting or harvesting, for example), labor (e.g., unpaid family labor), fuel, lubricants, repairs, interest, crop drying and miscellaneous charges. Machinery ownership costs include replacement costs, interest, insurance, and taxes. General farm overhead includes costs for record-keeping, utilities, general farm maintenance, and other items that are difficult to allocate to any specific function.

The official formula for calculating production costs includes an allocation for land. The inclusion of land as a true cost item is debatable because a large overstatement of production costs can occur when land is included. The subject of a cost allocation for land has always been quite controversial. Some farmland actually has been passed down through generations and the present owners hold it debt-free. Land historically has been considered an investment or income-earning factor; the financial considerations affecting farmers include both annual income and changes in net worth. The appreciation in farmland values often has appeared to be relatively more important because of the substantial increases in equity it has generated. Some economists feel that an offsetting income factor should be added to the balance sheet if calculated production costs include appreciated land values. Estimates of production costs in the past usually omitted allocations for land.

Land allocations are composite charges; they are computed by weighting owner-operated, share-rented, and cash-rented lands in the proportion listed in the most recent USDA survey. Two different land charges are presented in cost-of-production estimates. The first is based on current land values; the second uses an "average acquisition" value.

Under the first method, the owner-operator land charge is derived from surveys of land costs reported in *Farm Real Estate Market Developments*, a USDA publication. The land value is multiplied by the annual average interest rate charged for real estate loans by the Federal Land Bank, thus arriving at a land cost for the year.

The second method uses an "average acquisition" allocation to provide a comparison because much of the farmland has been owned for a long time; therefore, current land values do not apply to those situations. The average acquisition value uses the average value of cropland during the last 35 years as the basis for calculating the owner-operated portion of the total land charge; however, current interest rates are still used. This allocation also includes a weighted proportion of share-rented and cash-rented lands.

Share rent is estimated using the average share rentals paid for each crop in each state minus the share of costs for seed, fertilizer, chemicals, crop drying, irrigation, and custom work paid by the landlord. Cash rent is estimated by using 1974 data as a base and applying an index of rents reported by the Economics Statistics and Cooperatives Service of the USDA to attempt to reflect current values.

Calculated production costs in the formula presented to Congress for discussion on the farm bills are based on planted acreages. This can overstate production costs for grain production; a large proportion of corn acreage, for example, is harvested for silage purposes rather than for grain.

Many discussions of production costs simply compare gross dollar costs; this excludes any productivity gains and thus can distort true costs and profitability.

For example, corn production costs in terms of dollars per acre increased by 6 percent in 1978; however, the *per unit* cost of production *declined* by 7 to 8 percent because yields per acre rose.

Present farm programs tend to promote inflation of input costs and land costs, particularly when support prices are tied to calculated production costs. Farmers who own the land generally do not consider their land as a true "cost" but rather an investment; hence decisions are not based upon whether or not actual prices are below what the government formally calculates production costs to be. The official formula described above includes a number of items which can distort true costs. Many items calculated as costs are not real costs; for example, minimum tillage rather than full tillage is often practiced, and that reduces planting expenses. Some land expense is valid because of such factors as interest and taxes. It is the capitalization factor used for the cost of owned land which is questionable.

The price support system formerly was used to protect farmers against disastrous price declines. Despite the fact that price supports basically involve subsidies, they were accepted because of a general desire to guarantee the nation a basic supply of food and to give the small farmer something like the income protection that unemployment insurance gives the blue-collar worker. Loan rates served as a minimum, or floor, for farm prices. Now, however, government policies tend to be inflationary and involve different objectives.

Estimated production costs usually are stated as if they were absolute facts when they are presented publicly. But the truth is that no reliable method exists, and the USDA will admit privately that they are overstated. In fact, the 1974 study opened with the sentence "How much does it cost to grow a bushel of wheat? The question has almost as many answers as there are wheat farmers." After a discussion of the difficulties involved in such an evaluation, including the subject of land and the fact that most of the data was provided by farmers, the following statement was made: "The study does not pretend to answer the question simply and finally. There is indeed no simple, final answer."

CHAPTER

15

Cattle

Jack R. Weaver

The cattle industry is a large part of the agricultural and food economy of the United States. Commercial beef production in 1980 amounted to 21.5 billion pounds of carcass weight, and consumers spent 2.27 percent of their disposable personal incomes on beef items. Furthermore, the cattle complex is deeply interrelated with other livestock sectors as a competitor and the grain economy as a large domestic user. It has a direct influence on the pork, poultry, and feed grain industries, and therefore is a key market to watch for impacts on most other traditional agricultural markets.

The objective of this chapter is to lay out the basics of the cattle industry with special emphasis on beef production. This chapter is divided into two sections dealing with physical and economic factors. The first part deals with physical characteristics, production methods and peculiarities, and beef distribution. The second half will look more at market action, price determination, and price relationships.

PRODUCTION

A number of terms used by the cattle industry will be introduced and explained in this chapter. However, a few terms need to be presented before beginning.

Terminology

Bull An intact male animal. Bulls either are castrated and then grown for beef production or allowed to mature intact and used for breeding purposes.

Cow A mature female that has given birth to and weaned a calf.

Steer A castrated male. Castration makes the animal more docile, although it limits the daily rate of weight gain and muscle development.

Heifer A female that has yet to give birth to a calf. A heifer may be placed in the cow herd, or put on feed for beef production. A heifer is known as a cow after her first calf is weaned.

Calves Those animals under one year of age (e.g., heifer calf or steer calf). After one year, they are generally known as yearlings or simply as steers and heifers.

Breeding

In general, there are two breed classifications: dairy breeds and beef-type breeds. Naturally, the dairy breeds are most proficient at milk production while the beef cattle are more suited to meat production. Some common dairy breeds are Holstein, Guernsey, and Brown Swiss. Beef cattle breeds—the main topic here—can be divided into two classes. Some typical "English" breeds are Angus, Hereford, and Shorthorn. English breeds are commonly smaller-framed cattle, while the "exotic" breeds—Simmental, Charolais, and Limousin—are larger-framed cattle. It is a common practice today in commercial cowherds to use crossbreeding to gain the meat quality characteristics of the English breeds along with the large frames and rapid growth of the exotic breeds. Cow herds often consist of crossbred animals, although most bulls used for breeding are purebred.

Cattle production begins with the breeding of the cow herd, which consists of cows and "replacement" heifers, those heifers kept for bearing calves. Breeding takes place by bulls turned in with the herd or by artificial insemination. Artificial insemination (AI) involves manually placing semen collected from bulls in the cervical area of cows during estrus. It has been developed as a management tool to spread the benefits of high performance sires over more cows and more herds. AI requires day-to-day supervision of the herd and facilities to aid in the breeding process, but it has been attractive enough to a number of cattle producers to become a common practice.

Regardless of the breeding method, the following gestation period is 285 days. During the gestation period, the cow herd normally has access to some type of grass pasture or crop residue. Depending on the quality of area grazed, additional roughage, protein, and minerals may be provided to balance out the cows' nutritional needs. The roughage is often hay or silage, and the protein source can be a mixture of dehydrated alfalfa, urea, and/or soybean meal.

Following the 9½ months of gestation, the cows calve and nurse the calves for approximately 6 to 7 more months. The goal for the commercial cow-calf operator or rancher during this period is to produce the greatest number of large, healthy calves as possible, given the size of the cow herd. Therefore, special attention is given to the calving process and to eliminating disease and other health hazards to the calf. Rations may be changed somewhat during this time to meet the needs of the lactating cows, but it is common to leave the cow herd on the same pasture or stalk fields, if possible. Also, the calves may have access to concentrate in creep feeders if the situation allows.

Approximately 200 days after calving, the calves are weaned and enter the "backgrounding" phase of cattle production. This period develops the skeletal frame of the calf so that maximum growth potential and efficiency are achieved when the animals are later placed in a feedlot. At weaning, most calves weigh 400 to 500 pounds, and this period generally increases their weight 200 pounds to 600 to 700 pounds. Backgrounding will take from 4 to 7 months, depending on the ration available to the cattle. The ration may range from simple grazing pasture to one where they receive roughage, protein supplements, and in some cases small amounts of grain. This depends on the time of year and locale of the operation, and also on whether the calves have access to pasture or crop residue or are confined to drylots.

Returning to the terminology, this is the period in which "calves" become "cattle." The end result of this period is the production of "yearlings," "feeder cattle," or simply "steers and heifers." It should be noted that some operations move calves directly from weaning to the feedlot, and these animals are known as feeder calves. This is common in the cornbelt, where large amounts of pasture are not available, and crop residues are available only in the late fall and early winter. Calves of this type are generally placed on a growing ration, which allows them to develop larger frames before beginning to put on large amounts of flesh. This type of ration typically contains 4 to 6 pounds of grain per day, much less than a ration normally fed in feedlots.

At the end of the backgrounding phase, the cattle will generally be 1 year old and weigh 600 to 700 pounds. An animal of this type should have a fairly well-developed frame without an excess of flesh or meat. These cattle are then placed in a feedlot and fed a ration of 12 to 25 pounds of grain per day, along with roughage and high protein supplement to balance out nutritional requirements. This ration is known as a high energy or "hot" ration, because the major part—grain—has a high energy content per pound relative to roughage.

Cattle on feed generally gain from 2.5 to 3.0 pounds each day, and they usually require 5 to 9 pounds of grain in addition to roughage to produce one pound of gain. Cattle are fed for 100 to 180 days depending on the size of the cattle when feeding began and the desired finish characteristics (degree of fatness). Usually, cattle are not fed a hot ration for longer than 5 months, because cattle "burn out" after approximately 5 months of heavy feeding and go off feed (i.e., eat less). A second reason is that the animal's muscle tissue is fully developed by then and additional feeding would produce fat, not meat. It requires more grain to produce a pound of fat than a pound of lean beef, so feed conversion ratios worsen.

At the end of the feeding period, the cattle weigh between 900 and 1200 pounds and are ready for slaughter. Heifers that have been fed will be at the lower end of the weight range because of biological reasons. Steers will be at the higher end, with some crossbred steers weighing well over 1200 pounds. These heavier cattle are usually larger-framed, fast-gaining animals that may not have been placed on feed until reaching at least 800 pounds.

Table 15-1 contains a summary of the time, weights, and rations used in raising cattle. It offers a quick overview of the items covered to this point.

TABLE 15-1 Facts Related to Cattle Production

	Cow-calf	Backgrounding	Feedlot
Time	Gestation 9½ months Cow-calf 7 months	5 months	3–6 months
Ration	Cow: Roughage Protein supplement Calf: Roughage Milk Creep feed	Roughage Grain (small amounts) Protein supplement	Grain Roughage Protein supplement
Weight	400–500 pounds at weaning	600–700 pounds at placement in feedlots	900–1200 pounds at marketing

Feedstuffs and Locations

Before discussing feed items normally used in cattle production, it is important to note that cattle are ruminants (i.e., they possess multiple-chambered stomachs). Their complex gastrointestinal tract allows them to utilize roughage and high cellulose feedstuffs that monogastrics, such as swine and poultry, cannot use. Furthermore, the digestive system of cattle can manufacture certain necessary amino acids from crude forms of protein where monogastrics cannot.

The basic component of any ration for cattle is some sort of roughage. Depending on the location, time of year, and type of animals being fed, roughage types may vary greatly. Cows and calves will generally have access to a natural grass pasture or crop residues remaining after harvest of corn or grain sorghum. Animals kept in drylots or placed on feed will generally receive hay (the type depending on the area) or silage. Silage is usually whole-plant material from hay, corn, or sorghum that has been cut, chopped, and stored in an oxygen-limiting structure. Research has been conducted using high cellulose materials as roughage, such as sawdust or chopped-up newspaper. However, items of this sort have not been used to any significant extent by commercial producers.

The second major component of cattle rations is grain and high-protein concentrate. Corn, grain sorghum, and barley are the most common grains. The most important factor in determining which grain is fed is the locale, in other words, whatever can be grown most efficiently there. High-protein concentrates are used to balance out the nutritional needs of cattle. By virtue of their digestive systems, cattle can synthesize a considerable amount of their protein needs from crude nitrogen sources such as urea. However, some requirements must be met from traditional protein sources such as soybean meal, cottonseed meal, and dehydrated alfalfa.

The location of different phases of cattle production depends on the feed produced in the area. Cow-calf and backgrounding operations are located where there are large areas of pasture. Therefore, most operations are in range areas or locations where crop production is not highly profitable. Feedlots and cattle feeding are found in areas close to grain-producing areas. In the mid-1900s most cattle feeding took place in the cornbelt. In the last 20 years, however, the advent of irrigated feed grain production in the high plains has resulted in a shift of cattle feeding to that area. Most feedlots in these areas are large commercial operations, while cattle feeding in the cornbelt continues to be done in relatively small lots operated by individual farmer-feeders.

BEEF MOVEMENT

After feeding, cattle move into the slaughter-processing and marketing sector of the beef industry. Table 15-2 presents the breakdowns of the types of cattle slaughtered in the most recent cattle cycle. As expected, the major portion of slaughter comes from fed steers and heifers. These cattle are usually 15 to 18 months of age, weigh 900 to 1300 pounds, and produce the highest quality beef. Nonfed steers and heifers are usually younger and lighter cattle that produce lightweight, lean carcasses of slightly lower quality. Often a nonfed animal has received some grain, but not enough to give it the finish characteristics of fed cattle. The cow slaughter classification includes both beef and dairy cows that have been culled from herds. They typically yield smaller amounts of beef, but this beef is extremely lean and can be merchandised by itself or mixed with excess fat trimmings and sold as hamburger. Bulls and stags (male animals castrated after maturity) are a very small proportion of slaughter, yielding large, lean carcasses.

After slaughter, the cattle carcasses are classified or graded by government inspectors in two categories—quality and yield. The quality grades are Prime, Choice, Good, Standard, Commercial, Utility, Cutter, and Canner. Most fed steers and heifers grade Choice or Good. Nonfed beef often grades Good, and cow beef generally grades below Good. The quality grade reflects the tenderness, juiciness, and flavor of the beef, and it is determined by maturity and marbling. Maturity can be evaluated by examination of bone hardness and meat color, while marbling is shown by flecks of fat distributed through the muscle tissue.

Yield grades range from 1 to 5, and they reflect the estimated yield of retail cuts from the beef carcass. Yield grade 1 carcasses have the highest yield of retail cuts and yield grade 5 the lowest. Typically, an average carcass of a given

TABLE 15-2 Percentage Breakdown of Total Commercial Cattle Slaughter by Class for the 1969–1979 Cattle Cycle

	Fed cattle, %	Nonfed steers and heifers, %	Cows, %	Bulls and stags, %
Average for entire cycle, 1969–1979	68.6	8.8	20.6	2.0
Highest proportion of slaughter and year of occurrence	77.3 (1972)	17.2 (1975)	28.3 (1975)	2.7 (1975)
Lowest proportion of slaughter and year of occurrence	51.8 (1975)	2.6 (1973)	16.8 (1972)	1.6 (1970)

grade yields 4.6 percent more in closely trimmed retail cuts than the next lower grade. Yield grades are determined by four measurements: amount of external fat (fat cover); size of the ribeye muscle; quantity of kidney, pelvic, and heart fat; and carcass weight.

Now that the beef is in carcass form, it may take one of several channels to reach the consumer. The traditional method is to ship the carcass to city wholesalers, who deliver these carcasses to individual retail outlets. Some wholesalers also "break" the carcass into primal and subprimal sections and deliver these to local retailers. A different market exists for large retailers, who receive whole carcasses direct from packing plants and break the carcasses in their own back rooms or at centralized facilities. Table 15-3 shows the weight and relative importance of the different sections of a beef carcass. The four major primals are the chuck, rib, loin, and round.

In the past decade, a new processing method called "boxed beef" has grown in prominence, and appears to be the marketing channel that will dominate beef trade in the future. This process generally occurs at the packing plant after the carcass has been chilled to the temperatures of the coolers. The carcass is cut into subprimals, vacuum-packed in a tough plastic film, and packed in boxes. There are a number of advantages to boxed beef, the first of which is handling and transportation. Boxes are cleaner, easier to move, and they save considerable amounts of labor spent in breaking carcasses at the retail level. Second, large amounts of fat and bone normally shipped as part of the carcass are removed and processed on a large scale at the plant. This saves on transportation costs and by-product value, as most retailers cannot utilize the small amounts of fat and bone. Third, the beef stays fresh longer and will have a longer shelf-life in the retail outlet because of the vacuum packaging. Finally, boxed beef gives retailers greater flexibility in merchandising beef items. If a retailer who bought carcass beef wanted to have a sale on chuck items, he would also have to merchandise the other cuts of beef. With boxed beef, he can buy only chucks, and not worry about having extra loins, ribs, and rounds. This aspect of merchandising flexibility is very attractive because retail chain stores

TABLE 15-3 Breakdown of Carcass into Primals and Subprimals by Percent and Weight

Name	Percent of carcass	Weight from 625-pound carcass*
Chuck	26.8	167.5
Rib	9.6	60.0
Loin	17.2	107.5
Round	22.4	140.0
Shank	3.1	19.4
Brisket	3.8	23.8
Short Plate	8.3	51.9
Flank	5.2	32.5
Fat, cutting losses	3.6	22.5
Total	100.0	625.1

*A 1000-pound choice steer yields a 625-pound carcass.

sell proportionately more round and chuck items, while the HRI (hotels, restaurants, and institutions) trade sell loin and rib items (the "middle meats").

CATTLE CYCLE

Before turning to economic factors in the cattle industry, it is necessary to discuss one of the most widely known phenomena about the cattle markets: the cattle cycle. The cycle is caused by a combination of biological and economic factors, and is best illustrated by fluctuations in the total inventory of cattle numbers from year to year. The cycles generally last for 9 to 16 years from peak to peak or from trough to trough. The length of the cycle is caused by biological constraints and economic factors in increasing or decreasing beef production. The variance in the length of the cycle results from upsetting changes in substitutes for beef products and inputs to beef production.

An example of the cyclical nature of the cattle industry can be seen in Figure 15-1. The graph shows the January 1 total inventory of cattle on farms and ranches in the United States from 1896 to 1981. While the most obvious factor is the upward trend in numbers, seven distinct cycles can be seen on a trough-to-trough basis: (1) 1896–1912; (2) 1912–1928; (3) 1928–1938; (4) 1938–1949; (5) 1949–1958; (6) 1958–1968; and (7) 1968–1979.

Causes of the Cattle Cycle

The major cause of the cycle in cattle numbers is biological. Buildup of cattle numbers is encouraged by improved profit pictures facing cattle producers. However, producer response is limited because producing beef takes consid-

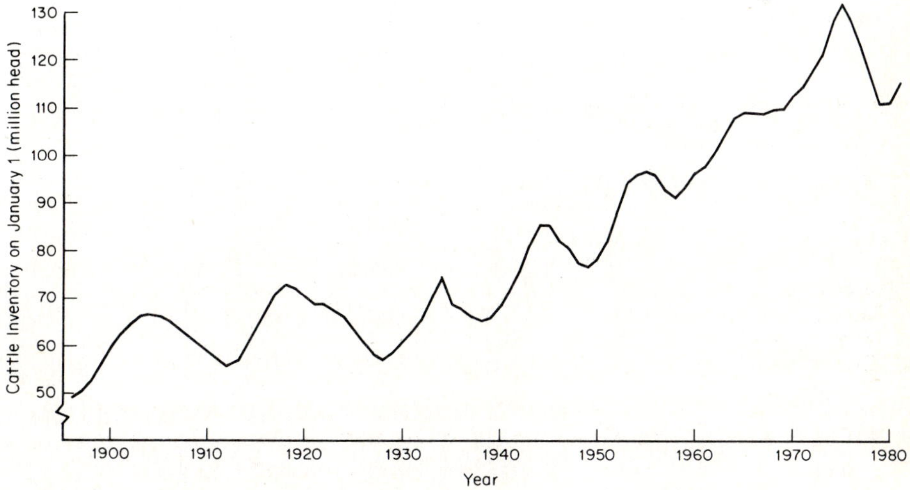

Figure 15-1 Cattle inventory on U.S. farms and ranches, 1896 to 1981.

erable lengths of time. The time lag from rosy profits to increased beef production can be as long as 3 years.

Defined as existing from trough to trough, the cattle cycle begins when inventory is at a relative low. At this point, the profit outlook is good because beef production is low and fed cattle prices are relatively high. The high prices for fed cattle increase the demand and prices for feeder cattle, and thus cow-calf operators are motivated to increase their cow herds and produce more calves. Cow-calf operators can increase their cow herds in two ways. First, they can keep their older cows that normally would be culled and sent to slaughter. Second, they can increase the number of replacement heifers, those kept for breeding and inclusion in the cow herd. Either or both of these actions would begin to increase total inventory and beef cow numbers. However, they also lower the level of beef production in the near term because cow and heifer slaughter drops. This pushes prices higher, causing more producers, in turn, to hold on to cows and keep more replacement heifers. This may go on for several years, as long as price and profit prospects encourage increasing cattle numbers.

Eventually, increased production from larger cow herds will begin to reach slaughter, although this may not occur until 3 years after the beginning of the cycle. Table 15-4 presents the typical time frame required to produce an additional choice slaughter steer, beginning with the decision to increase cow herd numbers. Following the example of replacement heifers, the decision is initially made at weaning of the heifer at 7 months of age. Generally, she must develop frame and scale at least another 8 months before she is ready for breeding. Following is the gestation, cow-calf, backgrounding, and feeding phases that were presented earlier. The total time required to produce an animal ready for slaughter is 34 months, almost 3 years. If the cow-calf operator chooses to keep older cows from slaughter to increase his herd, the time is cut to 26 months, still a considerable lag.

The profit picture facing cattle producers over the first 2 years of the cycle normally remains bright for two reasons: 1) no "new" supplies of fed cattle can reach slaughter, and 2) cow and heifer slaughter has most likely dropped, keeping prices high. About the middle of the third year, the first additional beef supplies from the increased cow herd begin to reach the market. This source of increasing beef supplies grows through the third and fourth years, lowering

TABLE 15-4 Production Time Required to Increase Fed Beef Supplies

	Production time, months	
Activity	Replacement heifer	Cow
Preparation for breeding	8	—
Gestation	9.5	9.5
Calf with cow	7	7
Backgrounding	5	5
Feeding	4.5	4.5
Time to increase fed beef supply	34 (or 2.8 years)	26 (or 2.2 years)

prices and the profit outlook. As a result, the buildup of cow herds slows and cow and heifer slaughter levels begin to increase. This additional supply of beef usually eliminates any profits and the cow herd buildup is eventually stopped. This peak normally comes sometime between the fourth and seventh year of the cycle.

Many of the financial returns to cow-calf operators are now negative, causing them to begin liquidation of cow herds. Cow slaughter thus increases and more heifers are placed on feed rather than being kept for the cow herd. This increases pressure on profit prospects and liquidation continues. The down phase of the cattle cycle lasts from 4 to 7 years, because decisions made 2 or 3 years previously affect current beef production and price levels. The cycle ends when beef production decreases enough to allow prices to buoy the profit picture. This will end cow herd liquidation and stop the decline in the cattle inventory.

Factors Affecting the Cattle Cycle

The length of a cycle is anywhere from 9 to 16 years, and it varies according to economic factors related to the cattle industry. The buildup or liquidation of cattle numbers is related to the profit picture facing producers, especially cow-calf operators. Prices of feeder cattle and calves, however, are derived from prices of fed cattle, which are derived from retail prices of beef. Therefore, changes in the cattle cycle come indirectly from changes in the demand for and supply of beef.

On the demand side, the price and available quantity of other meat supplies have a large influence on beef prices, since these are competitive items. Large quantities of pork and poultry can pressure beef prices, which in turn would slow down the buildup or increase the liquidation of the cow herd. A second demand factor affecting beef prices is consumer income. Changes in the level of real income usually result in a corresponding change in demand for beef. Finally, a long-term factor affecting demand for beef is consumer preferences. In recent years, a number of studies have raised health-related questions about beef as a food. Although the reports have not reached definitive conclusions, there has been some concern in the industry that beef is losing its position as the premier meat in American diets. Such a change in the consuming public might affect the length and timing of cattle cycles to some degree, but it is too early to determine if any changes have occurred.

The major supply-side consideration that would affect the cattle cycle is the cost of feed, particularly grain. Grain is one of the largest costs in producing beef and is fairly representative of other feed item costs. For example, if the price of corn goes up due to short domestic supplies, feeding operations would face tightening margins. This would decrease demand for feeder cattle, which in turn would slow the buildup or speed the liquidation of the cowherd. A second factor affecting the supply side in recent years is interest rates. As rates increase, the incentive to put cattle on feed or to build up inventories of cows decreases. If interest rates are expected to remain volatile, new disruptions in cattle cycles may appear.

FACTORS INFLUENCING PRICES

The basics of the physical process of beef production have been presented. The next step is to translate production numbers into prices. Many factors come into play in the beef market, each of them having a different time frame and severity of price impact. This section will consider the influence of supply and demand on prices.

Supply

In general, prices for cattle are a function of the amount of beef production, consumer income levels and spending patterns, and competing meat supplies and price levels. The variable having the strongest impact on cattle prices is beef production. Simply stated, larger supplies of beef result in lower prices and smaller supplies result in higher prices if all other factors remain unchanged. The supply of beef can be changed as a result of two factors: slaughter levels and slaughter weights of animals.

The number of cattle slaughtered receives the most attention from analysts attempting to forecast beef production. The approach commonly used here is to break total slaughter figures into classes of fed steers and heifers, nonfed steers and heifers, and cows and bulls. Fed cattle slaughter numbers can be projected from reports of cattle numbers on feed and from placement patterns of feeder cattle into feedlots over the previous 6 months. Nonfed steer and heifer slaughter is a function of the size of the feeder cattle pool, placement activity by feedlots, feeder cattle prices, and supplies of hay and pasture conditions. Cow and bull slaughter can be estimated from calf prices, pasture conditions, seasonal factors, and the current position of the cattle cycle. Using these estimates, analysts can project a total slaughter level.

The second part of forecasting beef production is to estimate the average slaughter weight or dressed weight of the animals to be slaughtered. This is important, as weights can vary greatly from year to year and cause errors in beef production estimates that are based on slaughter numbers alone. Table 15-5 contains the average monthly live weights of cattle commercially slaughtered from 1970 to 1980. For any given month, weights exhibit a range of 40 pounds or more, representing a possible 4 percent variation. Estimating weights is a difficult task, because a large part of the variation is due to producer marketing patterns and attitudes. However, a seasonal pattern is shown in Table 15-5, with lows in the summer and highs in the winter. A second factor to be considered is the relative breakdown of slaughter classes. For example, if a large portion of the slaughter mix is made up of cows or nonfed cattle, then average weights will be lower. By using both the seasonal and the class breakdown estimate, weights can be projected. The weight projection can then be applied to estimated slaughter levels to forecast beef production.

Demand

While beef production is solely a supply consideration, three other factors affecting beef prices are demand-related. One factor which includes income

TABLE 15-5 Average Monthly Live Weight of Cattle under Commercial Slaughter, 1970–1980

Year	Jan	Feb	Mar	Apr	May	Jun	Jul	Aug	Sep	Oct	Nov	Dec	Average
1970	1053	1052	1048	1040	1038	1031	1019	1017	1019	1024	1036	1050	1035
1971	1047	1042	1039	1031	1029	1022	1014	1009	1008	1019	1035	1049	1028
1972	1048	1044	1041	1039	1033	1019	1024	1026	1026	1043	1055	1056	1038
1973	1049	1047	1036	1031	1032	1037	1045	1028	1046	1048	1055	1062	1043
1974	1062	1063	1065	1057	1064	1062	1040	1028	1013	1001	1009	1024	1039
1975	1021	1021	1024	1009	1005	987	972	981	974	983	985	994	996
1976	1007	1013	1022	1019	1023	1020	1016	1017	1018	1020	1022	1025	1018
1977	1033	1034	1038	1036	1028	1023	1016	1014	1013	1012	1017	1024	1024
1978	1033	1030	1027	1026	1027	1026	1026	1031	1040	1045	1061	1065	1036
1979	1062	1052	1056	1057	1058	1057	1054	1054	1057	1067	1071	1078	1060
1980	1088	1089	1083	1078	1077	1073	1059	1051	1055	1064	1071	1077	1072

SOURCE: United States Department of Agriculture.

levels and consumer preferences, is demand concerns that are very significant in determining cattle prices. Beef is a highly income-sensitive product, that is, changes in consumer income result in corresponding changes in beef demand. This is especially true in today's marketplace, where consumer dollars are being made smaller by inflation. Related to income level is another consumer demand factor that has long-term implications—preference. For a long time, beef has been viewed as a premier meat by consumers, a staple of American diets. Recent years, however, have seen the development of negative health-related perceptions concerning beef consumption. The impact of these perceptions has long-term implications; it is too early yet to determine if there has been a shift away from beef. Competing meat supplies and prices constitute the other demand factor and can have an impact on price levels of beef, if price differences are great enough to shift consumer spending patterns. The major competitors for beef are pork and poultry.

ESTABLISHING A FRAMEWORK FOR PRICE FORECASTING

In establishing a framework for price forecasting, attention is turned to specifics. The forecasts of consumer income levels and pork and poultry supplies are not considered; the focus is on cattle numbers, beef supplies, and prices. When generating forecasts for these items, consideration must be given to the time frame of the forecast, since certain data will not be available or useful. Therefore, the following discussion will be broken into three time frames.

1. Long term—1 year and beyond
2. Intermediate term—4 to 12 months forward
3. Short term—tomorrow to 3 months forward

Long term analysis (one year or further in the future) is built around the cattle cycle. The major questions to determine are: What is the current position of the cattle cycle and when is the next turn in the cycle coming? To answer the first question, changes in inventory numbers are used to evaluate the cycle. For example, higher numbers of replacement heifers indicate that the inventory cycle is either bottoming or continuing in the buildup phase. Looking at the changes in total numbers helps clarify where the cycle is currently. To answer the second question, beef production numbers must be generated from the inventory totals for the next several years. Using these annual or semi-annual production estimates, prices and break-even levels can be calculated, and potential turning points in the cycle are developed. Long-term projections are difficult to generate and often inaccurate, as many other factors can intervene. However, they provide a framework within which short- and intermediate-term forecasts can be developed.

Intermediate range forecasts (3 months to 1 year hence) are based on the same principles as long-term: Forecasts of future beef supplies are based on cattle inventories. As compared to long-term forecasting, however, more data is available and projections become more complex. Weight breakdowns from cattle on feed reports indiate when fed cattle might be moved to slaughter, and placement patterns of cattle on feed can be used for the same purpose. Secondly, pasture and crop conditions can be taken into consideration as indicators of nonfed slaughter. For example, should a drought occur and hay and grain prices rise, one of two scenarios will develop: (1) feeder cattle will be moved to feedlots as pastures dry up if the grain price increase is small, or (2) feeder cattle will be slaughtered if the grain price rise generates feeding losses. Finally, seasonal factors can be used to forecast beef supplies and certain aspects of demand. Although not extremely seasonal, beef prices tend to be strong in the summer and weak in the winter. One cause of this is the cookout season in the summer and its impact on beef demand. Conversely, winter holidays tend to feature increased consumption of turkeys and hams. Furthermore, cow slaughter is seasonally high in the late fall to early winter, and average slaughter weights of cattle reach highs during this period. These factors add to total beef supplies in the winter, and the opposite is true in the summer period.

Short-term analysis of the cattle markets (tomorrow through several months hence) involves assimilating a large volume of data and transforming it into market "scenarios" or situations. The objective is to take the background of long- and intermediate-term analysis and add fine touches to the picture to clarify the near-term market action. Numbers that can be used here are: daily, weekly, and monthly slaughter; gender breakdowns of slaughter numbers; terminals' receipts and direct trade volumes of cattle and hogs on a daily and weekly basis; average weights of slaughter animals; packer and retail attitudes toward meat; short-run consumer demand levels; futures market attitudes and actions; and weather patterns. These items represent a part of the information to be considered.

There are two significant problems in the analysis of short-term factors. First, certain factors may have varying impacts on the market depending on the total picture. Taking weather patterns as an example, assume that cattle production areas have been receiving heavy rains. This could cause marketings to decrease or increase, depending on the time of year; it could affect weight gains; it might improve or deteriorate feed-growing conditions depending on the present situation; and it might alter producer attitudes. Therefore, each factor cannot be analyzed separately but as a part of the entire picture. The second problem in using these numbers is that they often do not exist. For example, variables such as producer attitudes or consumer demand are not published or easily quantified. As a result, analysis depends upon qualitative factors such as conversations with producers, changes in price bids by packers, and levels of featuring in retail chain stores. It is important to look for "symptoms" of problems and anticipate what will happen, because price moves will already have occurred when the event in question is public knowledge.

INFLUENCE OF DERIVED DEMANDS ON PRICE

Up to this point, cattle prices and beef prices have been used interchangeably. In truth, these two prices represent different products and are not interchangeable, although they are strongly correlated. The cattle industry from cow-calf operation to retail level is linked economically by a series of derived demands and profit margins. Table 15-6 shows a typical breakdown of production phases in the cattle industry along with the most applicable price for the "finished product" at each stage. This breakdown is common, although not correct in all cases.

The price for the "cattle product" at each level depends on the interaction of supply and demand, and the price spreads should be close to the cost of transforming it from one state to the next. Supply begins at the cow-calf level, and due to physical constraints in production is relatively fixed in the near term. This "fixed supply" concept is true in general throughout the entire chain, although some variations may result from pulling product ahead or backing it up in the production channels. On the other hand, demand can change in a much quicker fashion, beginning with increased consumer buying at retail stores. Prices and margins at the various levels are continually adjusting to the changes in demand and the slower, lagged supply response. As a result, margins may often fluctuate between profit and loss.

In terms of market power, most market observers feel the first three stages—farm-level production—are the weakest, while the last three stages possess the most market power. This is a direct result of the amount of time spent in production. Farm-level operations require at least several months to produce their product, lengthening the time of exposure to market risk. The beef processing and distribution phases have a much briefer involvement with their product, normally moving the beef through each phase in one week or less. Therefore, they can respond more quickly to market changes and protect their margins.

Two of these six phases in beef production, feedlot operations and retailing, have received special interest in terms of margins. The margin for feedlot operations has attracted interest because of (1) tax advantages that can be used by investors in feeding cattle, and (2) the existence of futures markets for both the input and output products. The margin is often evaluated in terms of the difference between feeder cattle and fat cattle prices, commonly called the feeder-fat spread, although grain prices and interest rates are also important factors. The feeder-fat spread varies from positive to negative values (i.e., feeder cattle prices above or below fed cattle prices), as supply and demand forces interact. However, as a general rule, the spread is positive at the trough of the cattle cycle and negative at the peak of the cycle. This follows economic logic: when cattle numbers are plentiful, prices are lower for the rawest form of the product (calves and feeder cattle); conversely, prices move higher for raw products when demand chases scarce supplies.

TABLE 15-6 Production Phases in the Cattle Industry

Production phase	Finished product price
Cow-calf operation	300–500 pound calf prices
Backgrounding	500–700 pound feeder cattle prices
Feeding	1100 pound choice cattle prices
Packer-processors	600–800 pound carcasses or boxed-beef cutout values
Wholesaler-processor	Boxed-beef cutout value or individual subprimal prices
Retailers	Retail prices for choice beef

The second area of interest in terms of margins is the retail operation. Given their proximity to the initial demand source—the consumer—retailers can exercise some power over volume of beef sold or general price levels by adjusting their margins. For example, they can constrict or expand the volume of beef sold by setting retail prices higher or lower, and thus adjusting their margins. Also, they can pass on wholesale beef price increases by simply raising retail prices. Should consumers buy less beef in response, retailers buy less beef, forcing the problem of holding inventory onto other market sectors. The only factor keeping retail stores from having too much power is competition with other retailers. This competition is often fierce on a local level, because the lowest beef prices often attract customers who will also buy other groceries and nonfood items.

SOURCES OF INFORMATION

A large amount of information is available for use in analyzing the cattle market, most of which is prepared and published by the U.S. Department of Agriculture (USDA). The emphasis here is not on the specific reports that are published and how often they are released, for these reports change over time as the industry changes. Rather, the focus is on the types of numbers published and how they can be used to forecast market trends. Also, one peculiarity should be noted: Most traders and people involved in the cattle industry evaluate reports on the basis of "percent of year ago" numbers. For example, market watchers in April of 1982 would not say that *13-State Cattle on Feed Report* showed 8.818 million head were on feed. They would not say it was down 210,000 head from the January number of 9.028 million, or up 156,000 head from last April's number of 8.666. They would say that cattle on feed are "102 percent of a year ago" (8.818 million/8.666 million). Actual numbers are used in analysis, but when discussing the markets, percentage figures are normally used.

One major report published in January and July each year has to do with the inventory of cattle and calves on farms and ranches in the United States. It gives a detailed breakdown of both dairy and beef cattle. Currently, it reports the following categories:

1. Total cattle and calves
   Beef cows and heifers that have calved
   Milk cows and heifers that have calved
2. Heifers over 500 pounds for beef cow replacement
   Heifers over 500 pounds for milk cow replacement
3. Heifers over 500 pounds intended for slaughter
   Steers over 500 pounds intended for slaughter
4. Heifers, steers, and bulls under 500 pounds (calves)
   Calf crop (annual estimate)

In general, the numbers in this report are used for analysis of the cattle cycle when comparisons to previous years are made. These numbers, as grouped above, show four areas of possible analysis. The first group can be used to gain a general understanding of the particular stage of the cattle cycle. The second group can be used as an indicator of turning points in the cycle. For example, decreasing numbers of replacement heifers would indicate that the buildup phase is slowing and the peak in the cycle may be near. This set of numbers may also be used to forecast future calf crops and long-term beef supplies. The third category of numbers can be used to estimate beef production over the next 6 to 12 months, while the fourth category can be used to forecast beef supplies more than 12 months ahead.

A second set of reports issued by the USDA are the *Cattle on Feed* reports, issued both on a quarterly and on a monthly basis. The quarterly report covers thirteen states at present and includes a state-by-state breakdown of:

1. Number of cattle on feed
2. Marketings of fed cattle over the past quarter
3. Placements of feeder cattle on feed over the past quarter
4. Weight breakdowns of those cattle currently on feed

This report is very useful in determining near-term supplies of fed cattle. The number of cattle on feed provides a general indication of the level of fed beef supplies available in the next 6 months, while the placement figure can be used to project a little more specifically when some of the cattle will be ready for slaughter. Marketing numbers clarify what has happened and also indicate the situation at present. Perhaps most useful are the weight breakdowns of those cattle presently on feed. These numbers can aid in forecasting when the slaughter might be relatively high or low. For example, if the marketings were low for the past quarter and the weight breakdowns showed a larger number than usual in the heavy categories, the conclusion would be that cattle are "backed up" in the feedlots. Marketings of fed cattle in the next 1 or 2 months would be large, but would taper off 3 to 4 months from the present.

Similar to the quarterly *Cattle on Feed* report is the monthly *Cattle on Feed* report. It covers seven major cattle-feeding states, and it presents the number of cattle on feed along with placements and marketings from the previous month. It is used in the same manner as the quarterly report with two changes. First, the shorter period (1 month) for placements can be better used to forecast marketings 4 or 5 months in the future. Second, the advantage of the shorter time period is offset by the absence of weight breakdowns. It is not as easy to identify whether feedlots are current or backed up in their marketings.

Also used in analyzing the cattle markets are slaughter number reports. These come out in a variety of forms, the least useful of which is the annual summary. It is merely an aggregation of the prior monthly reports, and is useful mainly for analyzing the cattle cycle. The monthly and weekly reports are far more useful. They generally contain breakdowns into steer, heifer, cow, and bull categories, and also provide average weights. These numbers reveal whether feedlots are marketing their cattle well or holding them back and whether cow-calf operators are liquidating their herds. They also provide estimates of beef production on a weekly and monthly basis. The lowest level of aggregation of slaughter reports is the daily report, where the number of cattle slaughtered are estimated. This number is rather simple, but when watched regularly, it can give a general idea of the very near-term beef supply. If the number of head slaughtered drops for several days in a row, it would be reasonable to expect increases in both carcass and live cattle prices.

TABLE 15-7 Feeder Cattle and Live Cattle Futures Contracts: Facts and Figures

Item	Feeder cattle	Live cattle
Exchange	Chicago Mercantile Exchange	Chicago Mercantile Exchange
Contact size	44,000 pounds (approximately 65–70 head)	40,000 pounds (approximately 34–38 head)
Trading hours	9:05 A.M. to 12:45 P.M.	9:05 A.M. to 12:45 P.M.
Trading limits	1.5¢ per pound per day	1.5¢ per pound per day
Contract months	January, March, April, May, August, September, October, November	February, April, June, August, October, December

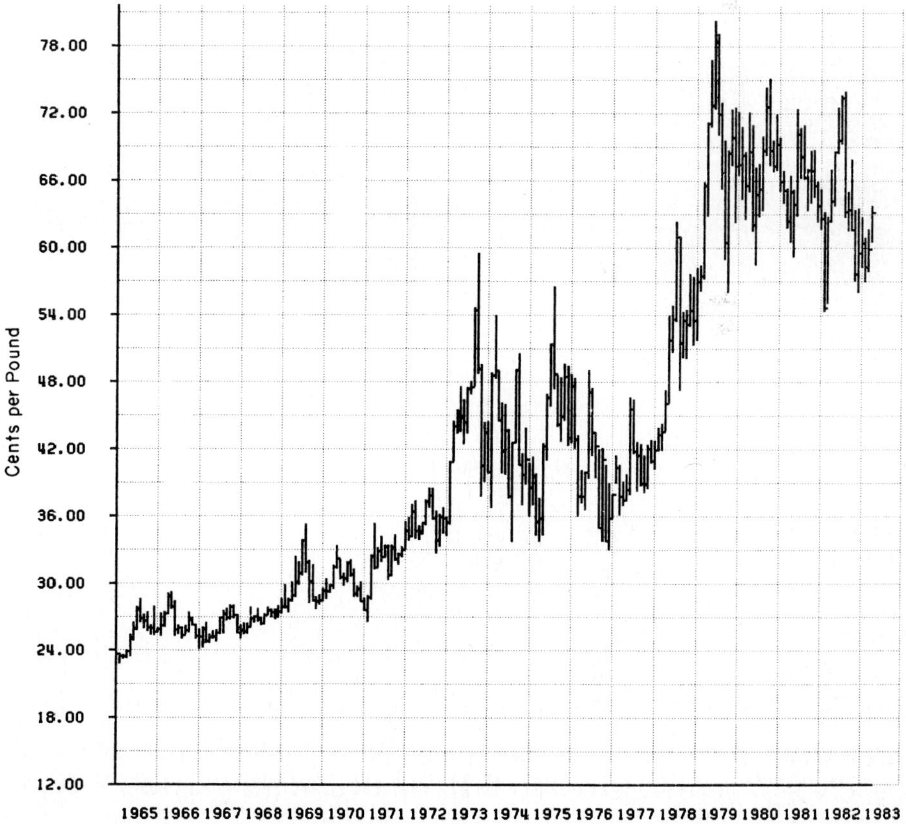

Figure 15-2 Monthly continuation, Chicago Mercantile Exchange live cattle. *(ContiCommodity Research Division)*

FUTURES MARKETS

As a conclusion, it is important to mention the futures markets and their use in the cattle industry. Futures contracts are traded for live cattle and feeder cattle, and various facts and figures are presented in Table 15-7. Figures 15-2 and 15-3 show the price fluctuations over the recent past for live cattle and feed cattle. Unlike the grain futures, the cattle contracts are relatively new—live cattle started in the 1960s and feeder cattle in 1971.

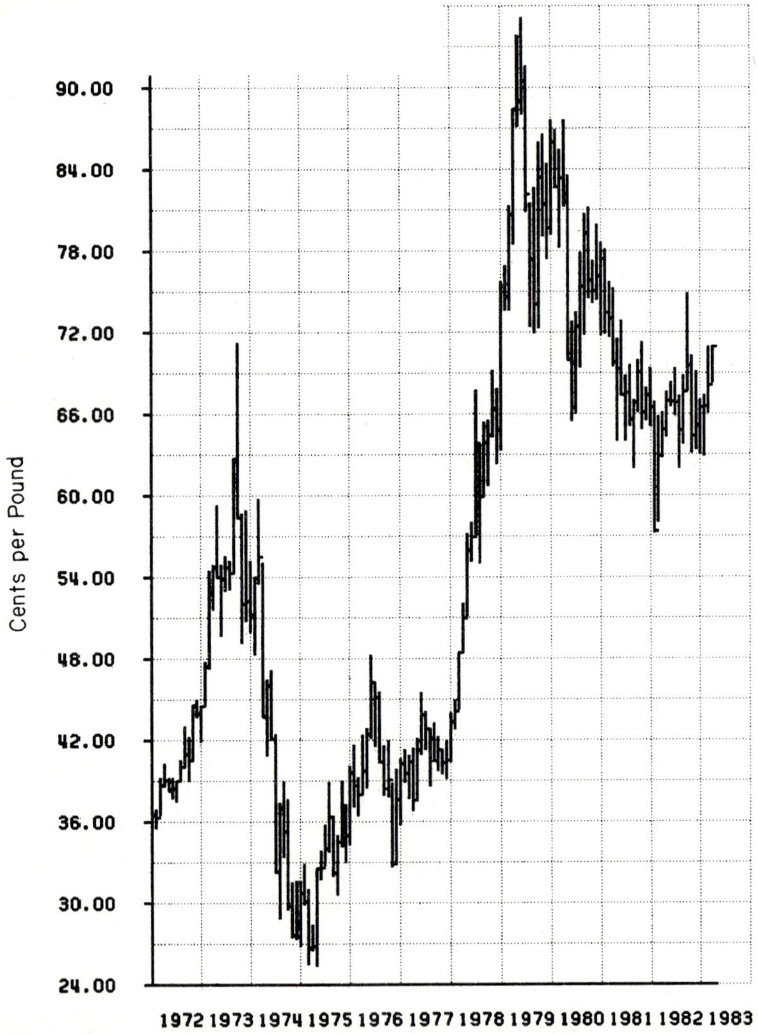

Figure 15-3 Monthly continuation, Chicago Mercantile Exchange feeder cattle. *(ContiCommodity Research Division)*

Cattle futures have yet to reach the level of use by commercial firms that grain futures have, but they are used by a number of packers, feedlot operators, and background and cow-calf operations. While each of these industry sectors do some hedging, the major users are feedlot operations hedging fed cattle. Packers do use the futures to lock in raw material prices (fed cattle) but on a relatively small scale. Packer use of futures may expand in the near future, because farmer-feeders are showing interest in forward contracting of cattle. New futures contracts in the beef industry for carcasses and/or boxed beef have been discussed, but are unlikely for two reasons. One is the diversity of beef products in either carcass or boxed-beef form. The second reason is the expected use and acceptance of such contracts by the beef trade. Most commercial firms that would be potential users show little or no interest in using such a contract at present.

SUMMARY AND TRADING CONSIDERATIONS

Factors Affecting the Cattle Supply and Demand Relationship

Supply:

1. Estimate fed cattle marketings from cattle on feed reports.
2. Estimate nonfed cattle slaughter from yearling feeder cattle supplies and feeder cattle prices.
3. Estimate cow slaughter from position in the cattle cycle and feeder cattle prices.

Demand:

1. Follow consumer income figures closely; changes will affect beef consumption.
2. Farm-wholesale and wholesale-to-retail marketing margins must be watched to translate consumer demand into farm-level prices.

Leading Indicators of Cattle Price Trends

1. Follow closely the average weights of cattle being slaughtered. Increasing weights can indicate cattle backing up and prices beginning a downward trend. Conversely, when marketings of cattle are current, prices tend to move higher.
2. Expect prices to move higher when packers show signs of wanting to accumulate inventories, and expect weakness in prices when they are liquidating inventory.
3. Sharp changes in expected production of pork and poultry indicate direction of cattle prices.

Common Mistakes Made by Investors and Traders

1. Buying when futures are at a premium to cash, and selling when they are at a discount. The relationship of futures to cash is indicative of market sentiment, not good trade potential.
2. Trading in sympathy with movements in financial futures.
3. Being on the right side for the wrong reason. Always evaluate why markets have moved in your favor; if your reason was not correct, market reaction against your position can be swift.
4. For hedgers: not locking-in profits when everyone is bullish.

What To Look for at Bull Market Peaks

1. Packers and retailers show a willingness to hold large inventories.
2. Placements of feeder cattle in feedlots increase.
3. Cattle feeders make significant profits on their operations.
4. Increasing weights of slaughter cattle.
5. If prices back off, producers respond by not marketing and holding on to cattle.
6. The futures markets at significant premiums to cash markets.

What To Look for at Major Troughs

1. Beef supplies in storage and marketing channels are drawn down to low levels.
2. Futures are at a discount to cash.
3. Producer attitudes are negative, resulting in decreased placements.
4. Weakness in prices are met by heavy marketings.
5. Marketing of "short-fed" cattle—cattle that would normally be fed for longer periods of time.

CHAPTER

16

Hogs

Jack R. Weaver

"Hogs Are Beautiful!" was the theme of a recent promotional effort by the swine industry, and this is undoubtedly true to a large number of farmers in the United States today. Pork production is a major component of the U.S. livestock economy and has strong ties to other agricultural commodity markets. Furthermore, pork has an extensive distribution system of wholesalers and retailers and is a major meat item in most consumers' diets. Understanding the basics of the hog and pork industry will aid in analyzing the U.S. agricultural complex and food industry.

PRODUCTION

Physical Characteristics

Before describing price-making forces, it is necessary to understand some basic physical characteristics of hog production. The hog "family" on a typical corn belt hog farm will include boars, sows, barrows, and gilts. Boars are male animals kept for breeding purposes, while sows are females that have farrowed (given birth to) and weaned at least one litter of pigs. Barrows are castrated male pigs grown solely for the purpose of pork production. Castration slows the growth of the male pig and causes him to produce fat tissue at lighter weights, but it is necessary to avoid the strong smell and taste (due to hormones) of pork produced by boars. Gilts are young female animals grown mainly for pork production, although some are held back from slaughter and kept for the breeding herd. The gilt officially becomes a sow after the weaning of her first litter of pigs.

There are a number of different breeds used in the United States, each with its own special characteristics. Some breeds are known for fast rate of gain, some for superior meat quality, and some for their mothering capabilities. As a result, commercial hog production is dominated by crossbreeding. Producers that specialize in purebred operations usually produce breeding stock for other herds.

Most barrows and gilts grown for pork production reach a market weight of 210 to 260 pounds at 5 to 7 months of age. Boars and sows can reach ages and weights in a very wide range, depending on their physical characteristics and productivity. Boars are normally put into service at approximately 8 months of age or older and weigh at least 270 pounds at this time. If kept for several years, a boar will easily reach 400 to 500 pounds, often growing much heavier. Sows reach weights ranging between 350 and 500 pounds, although they may weigh more. They may be kept farrowing for several years or only one, depending on their productivity. On average, sows are farrowed 2½ times before culling, representing a little over 1 year after being bred. (Culling as used here refers to removing the sow from the breeding herd, sending her to slaughter, and most likely replacing her with a gilt.) Gilts held back for the breeding herd are allowed to reach an age of 8 months before breeding, and they normally weigh 260 to 270 pounds at this time.

Breeding

The reproductive cycle of hogs begins with the breeding herd, which consists of boars, sows, and replacement gilts. The sows and gilts are bred, after which comes the gestation period of 114 to 116 days or "3 months, 3 weeks, and 3 days." During this time a breeding herd is kept on a 12 to 14 percent protein ration of grain, protein supplement, and minerals. This ration is normally hand-fed (i.e., limited) to curtail excess weight gains. After farrowing, the amount of feed received by the sow or gilt is increased because of lactation. This is continued until the pigs are weaned, normally at an age of 3 to 6 weeks. The sow is then allowed to return to her normal estrus cycle, and is soon rebred for another litter or culled and sold for slaughter.

Regardless of age at weaning, pigs begin to receive a supplemental creep feed at the age of 2 or 3 weeks. The creep feed starts at an 18 to 20 percent protein formulation and is gradually reduced to 16 percent by the time each pig weighs 30 pounds or is 6 weeks old. Creep feeds usually have high levels of minerals, vitamins, and low-level antibiotics to stimulate growth and thwart disease. As the pig grows, the percent protein in the ration drops so that at market weight, the ration consists of only 13 percent protein. Rations commonly used for hogs are based on grain and high-protein concentrate. The most common grain is corn, and soybean meal is the base for most concentrates. Concentrates are usually 38 to 42 percent protein (soybean meal is usually 44 percent protein) and have a number of minerals and antibiotics added to meet nutritional needs and combat disease. Corn is approximately 8.5 to 9 percent protein.

There are two methods of evaluating rate of gain and feed conversion rates in a farrow to finish operation. The first looks only at the growth of the animal after it has been weaned. In this case, from weaning to market weight, typical barrows and gilts should gain at least 1 pound for every 3.5 pounds of feed consumed. Any feed efficiency rates less than this are indicative of problems somewhere within the operation. A second method of evaluating feed efficiency is to include feed fed to the breeding herd. This gives a feed conversion rate based on the overall hog operation. Studies based on this point of view show that the average farm should produce one pound pork (live weight) for every 4.2 pounds of feed consumed. Again, this method includes feed fed to the breeding herd in its calculation.

It is estimated that 75 percent of all hog farm operations in business today are farrow-to-finish operations—in other words, producers supervise both the breeding and growing phases. Some units do specialize in farrowing or feeding of hogs only, but these are exceptions to the rule.

With the main input to hog production being grain, it is natural that hog producers are mainly grain farmers located in the corn belt. Furthermore, the advent of grain exports is concentrating production in those areas away from points of easy export, such as the Mississippi and Illinois rivers. The cheaper the source of grain, the better the potential for raising hogs. As a result, hog production is concentrated in Iowa, Illinois, Indiana, Minnesota, Missouri, and Nebraska with fewer in those states on the fringe of the corn belt.

In the past two decades, hog production has been undergoing a major structural change. In the period following World War II, hog production was spread over the entire corn belt with almost every farmer having at least a few hogs. Hog operations were labor-intensive, with very little investment in capital equipment such as buildings. However, the past 20 years have seen a significant trend toward specialization in hog production: there are fewer farmers, but they have larger operations. At the same time, hog production units have become more capital-intensive—buildings and automated facilities are commonplace. This change has also brought about a change in the seasonal period normally associated with hogs. Hog slaughter and pork production levels used to peak in the spring and fall, 6 months after the peak farrowing seasons. Farrowings were concentrated in the spring and fall to avoid the heat of summer and cold winters that lowered the number of pigs saved per litter. However, with new confinement operations, farrowing can take place year round, thus removing a significant part of this seasonal pattern.

PRICE-DETERMINING FACTORS

General Factors

As in many other agricultural commodities, the major factor in determining market-clearing price levels is the supply of pork relative to consumer demand. In the long run, consumer preferences and consumption patterns can shift; in the short run, however, it is relatively constant, given certain seasonal factors. Therefore, to forecast or follow price levels, it is extremely important to determine the supply of pork coming into the market.

Several other important factors affecting pork prices include consumer income and quantity and price of competing meats. Red meats in general are very income-sensitive. Thus, any change in personal income levels brings about a shift in the amount of pork demanded at a given price. Other meats such as beef and poultry can also influence price levels for pork. Beef has been generally regarded as a higher-quality or more greatly desired meat. Its price level and available quantity may cause shifts in demand for pork by virtue of consumers shifting purchases to or away from pork. On the other hand, poultry is a lower-cost substitute for pork. In the past decade, poultry has made significant inroads into normal diets and continues to gain in popularity. It can be viewed as a substitute for pork, although some claim that, rather than replacing pork, poultry is filling a new niche in consumer demand. If poultry production continues to expand, it will increase its competition with pork for the consumer's dollar.

Each of these factors is important in estimating pork prices, but the task of

TABLE 16-1 Relationship of per Capita Pork Production and Deflated Hog Prices, 1950–1980

Year	Commercial pork production per capita, pounds carcass weight	Average barrow and gilt price, Omaha, deflated by CPI, dollars per hundredweight
1950	61.7	26.16
1951	65.8	25.36
1952	65.5	22.49
1953	56.0	27.51
1954	54.8	28.15
1955	60.4	19.85
1956	60.9	18.82
1957	55.7	22.18
1958	55.0	23.54
1959	62.6	17.62
1960	60.1	18.93
1961	58.4	19.96
1962	60.2	19.49
1963	62.7	17.65
1964	62.6	17.34
1965	55.3	23.31
1966	56.6	24.68
1967	62.3	20.20
1968	64.1	19.08
1969	63.0	22.48
1970	65.0	20.38
1971	70.8	16.26
1972	64.6	22.31
1973	59.9	29.17
1974	64.3	22.78
1975	53.0	28.56
1976	56.8	24.71
1977	60.2	21.89
1978	60.5	23.29
1979	69.4	18.53
1980	72.2	16.02

forecasting income and other meat supplies belongs elsewhere. The issue to be dealt with here, then, is estimating the quantity of pork production. Table 16-1 shows the consumption per capita of pork compared to price levels for live hogs. To remove the inflationary trend over time, the price has been deflated by the consumer price index for food. It is clear that there is a direct inverse relationship between pork production and price levels.

It should be stated explicitly that pork production and prices are inversely related, but this is not necessarily true of hog slaughter levels and price. The difference stems from the fact that hog weights vary. Table 16-2 contains the monthly average live weight of barrows and gilts at the seven major terminal markets from 1970 to 1980. Although they are relatively consistent, problems caused by weather or producers' marketing patterns can cause average weights to fluctuate within a range of 5 to 14 pounds for a given month. A seasonal pattern does exist in hog weights, but looking at one particular month (e.g., January) from year to year points out this range. Although not very large, such a range can represent a 2 to 5 percent fluctuation in pork production, depending on the slaughter level. Therefore, when analyzing future pork production, it is necessary to keep in mind both slaughter levels and average weights.

Within a year, the largest impact on weight changes is the seasonal factor. Peaks are often reached in the spring and fall, while lows come during the summer and winter. This seasonal variance is tied to slaughter levels: as greater numbers of hogs need to be sold, it is relatively harder to remain current in marketings. The converse is also true. Favorable temperatures also increase weight gains in the spring and fall, causing higher slaughter weights at those times. Another factor that can influence hog weights is the price of feed grains, namely corn. If corn is cheap relative to hog prices, farmers will tend to feed hogs longer and market additional corn through the hogs, increasing average weights. As corn prices rise, farmers become more careful in feeding practices and keep hog weights lower. A final consideration in estimating hog weights has to do with price direction. If prices are declining, farmers tend to hold hogs longer, waiting for prices to recover. This tends to increase weights. However, this scenario only exists for a certain length of time before producers' attitudes

TABLE 16-2 Average Monthly Live Weight of Barrows and Gilts at the Seven Major Terminal Markets, 1970–1980

Year	Jan.	Feb.	Mar.	Apr.	May	June	July	Aug.	Sep.	Oct.	Nov.	Dec.	Average
1970	242	236	238	243	246	243	234	227	230	234	238	237	237
1971	235	231	231	236	241	239	234	230	229	234	239	238	235
1972	238	234	236	240	242	241	234	230	231	237	240	236	237
1973	237	232	233	238	241	240	234	229	232	239	243	243	237
1974	245	243	244	246	249	248	239	234	232	235	238	237	241
1975	239	235	234	237	241	240	234	230	233	240	246	237	241
1976	243	236	235	239	240	238	232	229	231	236	240	233	236
1977	232	229	231	235	238	237	232	229	231	236	238	233	234
1978	232	229	231	237	240	241	238	234	234	239	243	240	237
1979	237	232	234	237	242	242	239	231	232	235	240	238	237
1980	237	233	234	239	241	238	232	230	233	237	242	241	237

SOURCE: United States Department of Agriculture.

turn negative and they market their hogs with reckless abandon, thus correcting the weight problem.

Factors Affecting Slaughter Levels

After discussing one part of the pork production equation, it is now time to turn to the more commonly debated point: hog slaughter levels. In the longer term, hog slaughter levels are determined by cyclic fluctuations caused by economic factors and physiological limitations. The intermediate term (4 to 12 months) of hog slaughter levels is probably most affected by seasonal factors given the relevant position in the hog cycle. Near-term considerations in hog slaughter levels are based on price action, weather, and other factors such as producers' marketing patterns. Each of these matters will be discussed in sequence.

Long Term—the Hog Cycle. First of all, the hog cycle is normally evaluated and predicted on the basis of total hog numbers. The hog cycle, as commonly perceived, is believed to be 4 years long. However, certain economic factors can intervene and make the cycle length 2 to 6 years. Figure 16-1 is a graph of the U.S. inventory of hogs from 1948 to 1981. From this graph, several cycles can be picked out, a few of which are 4 years in length. Aberrations will be discussed later.

The hog inventory cycle is a function of economic factors and the reproductive time frame of hogs. As mentioned earlier, most gilts held back from slaughter for breeding purposes are sorted out at the age of 4 to 5 months. They are allowed to develop frame and scale for another 3 to 4 months before breeding. A gestation period of almost 4 months follows, and then another 6 months for their litters to reach market weights. Therefore, the time from the decision to increase hog numbers to the slaughter of extra hogs is 13 months. If the hog producer decides to increase production by holding onto sows that normally

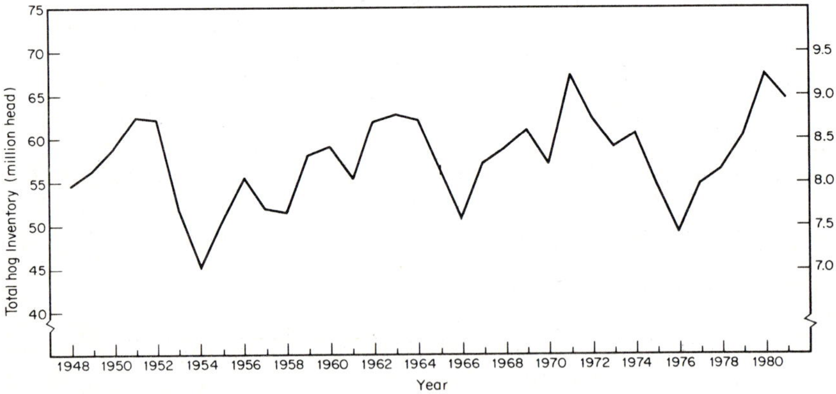

Figure 16-1 Total inventory of hogs on U.S. farms on January 1, 1948 to 1981. (From 1961 on data was from December 1 of the previous year. The post-1961 series is approximately 5 million head higher.) *(United States Department of Agriculture)*

would be culled, the time frame is cut to 11 months. Hog producers usually do both, so a rough average of the length of time between the actual decision and increased production is 1 year. Table 16-3 summarizes this time frame.

The key to beginning and ending points in the hog cycle is the economic environment facing hog producers. High prices stimulate increases in hog numbers, and lower prices encourage liquidation. However, there is not a direct relationship between price levels and inventory level. Prices respond to pork production; pork production follows a pattern from hog inventory levels. Therefore, inventory numbers must be translated into prospective pork production before being used to forecast prices. To illustrate this, a typical 4-year hog cycle will be discussed, an example of which is 1954 to 1958 in Figure 16-1.

For this discussion, the inventory cycle begins with numbers at a low point. With low inventory numbers, slaughter levels are light, pork production is low, and prices are relatively attractive. This favorable profit picture encourages producers to hold back gilts for the breeding herd and to end culling of the sow herd. This action further curtails slaughter levels, cutting pork production. As a result, prices go higher and more producers begin building their breeding herds. This is the beginning of the buildup phase, and it usually lasts about 1 year. During this first year prices are increasing, but increased pork production does not reach the market because of the reproductive time frame. As a result, a price "blow off" normally occurs in this part of the cycle.

The second year of the cycle begins with profits still at healthy levels, but increased production is coming into the market. As a result, prices begin to come under pressure. Hog producers respond by slowing the herd buildup, although the inventory levels are still increasing (at a decreasing rate). By the end of the second year, prices are at levels that have stopped increases in the breeding herd. However, market hog numbers are still increasing as a result of increased farrowings during the second year of the cycle and decreased gilt retention. As the third year of the cycle begins, these increasing numbers of market hogs for slaughter cause profit pictures to turn negative. This prompts the first wave of breeding herd liquidation, usually in the form of increased culling of older sows. This increased source of pork production further pressures prices, and the situation snowballs. Prices break sharply and profit margins drop deeply into the red.

The fourth and last year of the cycle begins with low prices and fairly high levels of hog slaughter and pork production. Breeding herd liquidation during this period results as producers do not hold back gilts to enter the sow herd. However, barrow and gilt slaughter begins to decrease as a result of the breeding herd liquidation in the third year. Prices begin to improve, and the rate of

TABLE 16-3 Reproductive Time Frame of Hogs
(In months)

	Replacement gilt	Sow
Preparation for breeding	3–4	1 (after weaning)
Gestation	4	4
Growth of litter	6	6
Total	13–14	11

liquidation declines. By the end of the fourth year, barrow and gilt slaughter has declined enough to decrease pork production and bring profit margins back to moderate levels. Liquidation of the breeding herd slows, and the inventory cycle is ready to begin again.

The 4-year cycle is a classical case. It largely ignores the impact of outside economic factors such as income levels, prices of other meat items, or prices of feed grains. Income levels of consumers may fluctuate as the economy goes through business cycles. This can result in slight demand shifts for pork, which would alter price levels and producers' actions concerning production decisions. Price levels in other meat items can also affect the hog cycle. If other meats are cheap or expensive, pork prices would be pressured or supported respectively, and the cycle might be altered. Finally, the cost of feed grains, especially corn, is a major factor in profits from hog production. As a result, changes in corn prices relative to hog prices can lengthen or shorten various phases of the cycle.

The past 15 years contain good examples of these outside impacts altering the standard hog cycle (see Figure 16-1). The first example is of a short 2-year peak-to-peak cycle from 1969 to 1971. Low hog prices during 1968 prompted breeding-herd liquidation, causing total inventories to decline during 1969. At the same time, though, the cattle inventory cycle was reaching a low and beef prices were high. The drop in pork supplies in late 1969 along with support from beef prices turned farmers from liquidation to withholding breeding stock. Inventory numbers increased during most of 1970, but the increase was ended late in the year by a sharp drop in hog prices and an increase in corn prices induced by blight. As a result, a new liquidation phase was started.*

An example of a cycle lengthened by economic factors occurred from 1974 to 1980. Farmers had liquidated hogs from mid-1970 to 1972, and then began building their herds. Strong hog prices in 1973 turned the hog cycle up into early 1974, but sharply higher corn prices and large beef supplies shocked the market in 1974 and 1975, causing farmers to decrease swine herds to low levels. By late 1975, hog prices had reached record levels, ending the liquidation phase. From 1975 to 1979, corn prices and beef prices eased because of production and cyclical considerations. As a result, the buildup phase took 4 years (1976 to 1980), making a 6-year cycle.

In summary, hog cycles are normally assumed to be 4 years in length, but this length often varies in response to outside factors. The major outside factors are the cost of production (specifically corn prices) and supplies and prices of competing meat, such as beef. The cycle is not fixed in length and therefore cannot be used for strict price forecasting in the long run. However, following the cycle gives an overall framework for long-term price action, if certain assumptions are made about outside economic factors.

Intermediate Term—Seasonals. Now that the long-term framework has been laid out, the next fundamental price-making factor to be reviewed is the

*Liquidation of breeding stock began in August 1970 as it became apparent that the corn blight had reduced the crop and corn prices rose sharply.

seasonal one. Although seasonal fluctuations are not as severe as in the past, these changes are one of the most dependable factors in pork production from year to year. This dependability arises from the consistency of the source of the seasonal variation—weather.

Before 1960, hog production in general was conducted without large numbers of confinement units or enclosed production buildings. As a result, farrowings, the production phase where favorable weather conditions are most beneficial, were normally scheduled to take place during moderate weather periods. Without buildings, the winter weather is restrictive in its severity, causing winter-quarter farrowings to be low. Sows that are held through the winter period and bred to farrow in the spring, cause the seasonal peak in farrowings. Figure 16-2 shows quarterly farrowings in the fourteen major hog-producing states from 1975 to 1980. The four quarters are December to February, March to May, June to August, and September to November. By figuring an average 6-month lag from birth to slaughter, the seasonality of farrowings can also be translated into seasonal changes in hog slaughter. Then, from expected slaughter levels, pork production and prices can be estimated.

As pork production methods have evolved over the past 20 years to more automation and confinement units, the susceptibility of hogs to weather has decreased. Producers can farrow and raise hogs year round, which allows the producers to better distribute their labor among periods when other farm work is slack. Furthermore, the increased cost of production facilities has given producers incentive to intensify hog production levels, using their facilities year round. Thus technology has dampened the seasonal impact, but the seasonal factor still exists because a number of producers do not use modern confinement systems.

Near Term—Weather, Marketing Patterns, Producer Attitudes. Fundamental factors that affect pork production and hog prices in the near term (less than 1 month) are not as clear as hog cycles or seasonals. Many different factors exist, but only a few will be discussed here. A major factor affecting short-term hog prices is weather. Certain types of weather during different times of the year can either increase or decrease the marketing levels of hogs, thus affecting prices. For example, rainy weather during the spring, summer, or fall may induce increased hog marketings, because farmers are able to get away from their field crop operations. Conversely, long spells of fair weather stimulate field work, and hog slaughter levels may be temporarily depressed. Another example of weather impact arises when extremes in temperature occur. Hog producers may be reluctant to market their hogs during extremely cold, snowy conditions, or as well during extremely hot summer weather. It is important to note that weather effects are only short-term and must be compensated for sometime in the future.

Two other factors that affect near-term market action are marketing patterns and producers' attitudes. These two are interrelated and are best viewed as one factor. Producer attitudes consist of the average producer's outlook on the market and future profit potential. Marketing patterns are the manner in which hog producers sell their hogs. They are a direct function of recent price action and producer attitudes. For example, assume prices have just begun to drop and

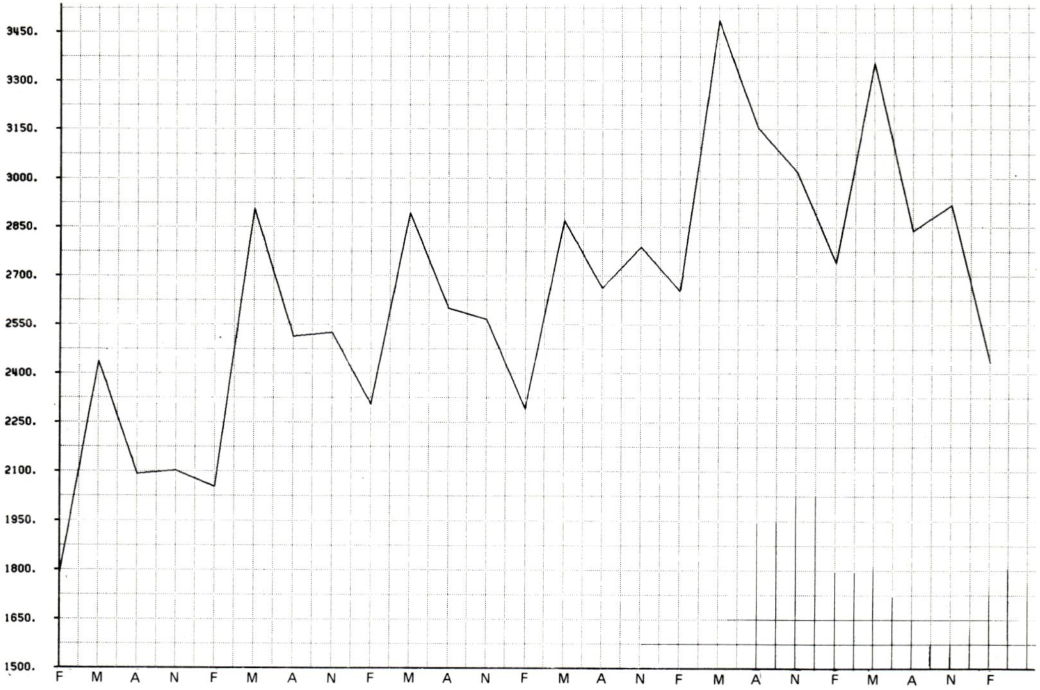

Figure 16-2 Quarterly number of sows farrowing in fourteen states (000 head). *(Conti-Commodity Research Division)*

producer attitudes are bullish. As a result, farmers reduce marketing levels to wait for a return to high prices. Slaughter levels subside and prices may strengthen in the near term. However, market-ready hogs would eventually backlog and prices could break sharply later on. Another example would be when prices begin to fall and producer attitudes are negative. Producers may respond by flooding the market with their hogs to avoid the lower prices they expect later. As a result, prices come under greater pressure than expected in the near term, but will bounce back after farmer marketings dry up. A large number of scenarios involving attitudes and marketing patterns exist; to make proper use of them in fundamental analysis requires close contact with the cash

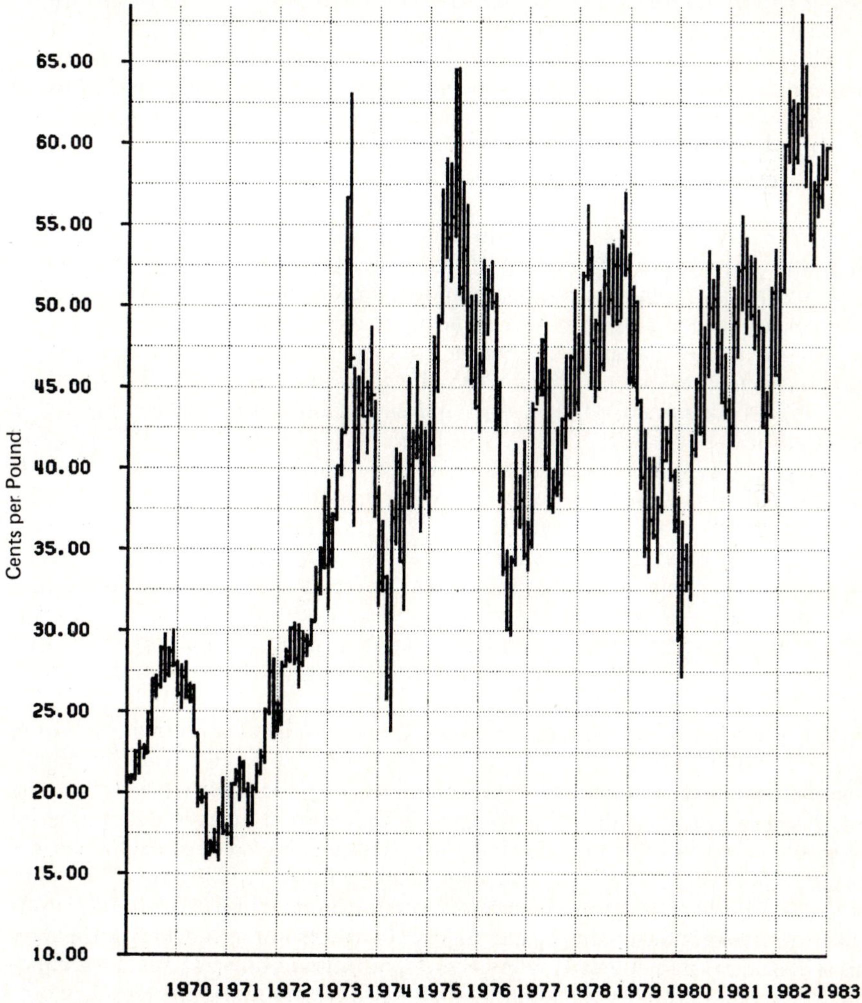

Figure 16-3 Monthly continuation, Chicago Mercantile Exchange live hogs. *(ContiCommodity Research Division)*

markets and producers. (Live hog futures prices from 1970 to 1983 are depicted in Figure 16-3.)

THE PORK TRADE

Much has been said up to this point concerning producer marketings, but little has been explained of pork movement after hogs leave the farm. Hog marketing developed in the early 1900s around a terminal market system. These terminals were located throughout the Midwest in large cities. Packing plants were concentrated at these terminal markets, and producers would ship their hogs by truck or rail to the cities to be slaughtered. Following World War II, rail transportation began to decline and a new system began to develop. Collection points for hogs throughout the country were formed by individual packers and commission agencies. These points were interspersed throughout the Midwest and became known as "interior" markets. Eventually, packing plants also moved away from the terminal markets to interior locations, closer to the source of hogs. Terminal markets still exist today, but carry only a fraction of the hog volume that moves through the interior market system.

Regardless of how hogs reach the packing plant, they are slaughtered and processed into various subprimals at the plant. The major pork items are the ham, loin, picnic shoulder, boston shoulder (boston butt), and belly. All of the slaughter and processing activities of most hog-slaughtering plants come under the scrutiny of government inspectors. In 1980, over 95 percent of the hogs slaughtered in the United States were slaughtered under federal inspection. These inspections ensure that health and sanitation requirements are met in the slaughtering process.

Following slaughter, the pork products move through wholesale and retail market channels to consumers. As the meat goes through a number of hands, various margins are added on. Margins are classified into two general categories: farm-wholesale and wholesale-retail. The farm-wholesale margin represents the cost of slaughtering the hog and processing the carcass into its various cuts. The wholesale-retail spread represents the cost of transportation, further cutting and packaging, and merchandising the retail cuts. Table 16-4 shows the quarterly retail price and marketing margins for pork from 1971 to 1980.

Retail price levels and margins are important factors to watch in determining the level of demand for pork. Hog prices are generated from derived demand; the average consumer does not know what hog prices are, but what pork roasts cost. Therefore, the retail price determines the amount of pork demanded by consumers, not the price level for live hogs. Retailers have considerable market power in that they can pass on increased costs by raising retail prices. They can also adjust to lower quantity demanded by consumers by refusing to buy products from packers at existing price levels. They know the markets intimately and will widen their margins when the opportunity to do so arises. One situation that retailers often take advantage of is backed-up marketings by hog producers. For example, market hogs were backed up in the first half of 1974. Dur-

TABLE 16-4 Quarterly Pork Prices—Retail Price

Year	Quarter*	Retail price, cents/ pound	Farm-wholesale margin, cents/ pound	Wholesale-retail margin, cents/ pound	Omaha barrow and gilt, cents/ pound
1971	J -M	68.7	24.3	14.2	18.29
	A-J	68.3	24.4	14.1	18.25
	J -S	70.8	25.6	12.1	19.79
	O-D	71.4	25.4	11.2	20.65
1972	J -M	79.2	24.5	11.5	25.48
	A-J	79.4	23.8	12.7	25.88
	J -S	85.6	23.7	12.2	29.31
	O-D	87.2	28.3	9.0	29.65
1973	J -M	97.6	27.6	9.6	36.51
	A-J	102.6	25.9	15.4	37.60
	J -S	121.2	30.4	9.5	48.98
	O-D	115.5	28.8	19.0	41.92
1974	J -M	114.8	28.9	23.9	39.61
	A-J	98.9	27.9	25.6	30.04
	J -S	107.0	26.6	21.4	37.87
	O-D	110.6	29.7	18.4	39.89
1975	J -M	114.1	31.5	18.9	40.08
	A-J	122.7	32.7	15.2	47.11
	J -S	148.8	36.4	16.7	59.40
	O-D	152.9	41.3	26.4	53.87
1976	J -M	141.2	34.5	29.1	49.05
	A-J	138.2	33.1	25.3	50.18
	J -S	137.1	33.6	32.6	44.59
	O-D	119.6	36.0	28.1	34.97
1977	J -M	120.5	33.1	25.5	39.88
	A-J	121.7	32.0	25.1	41.75
	J -S	131.0	31.2	30.1	44.38
	O-D	128.2	37.3	24.9	42.40
1978	J -M	137.0	29.7	32.2	48.23
	A-J	142.4	30.1	36.8	48.60
	J -S	144.7	31.2	37.1	49.18
	O-D	150.1	33.5	37.4	51.28
1979	J -M	156.1	32.5	42.3	52.95
	A-J	148.2	32.7	48.1	44.13
	J -S	138.0	32.9	44.6	39.55
	O-D	134.3	36.8	40.2	37.47
1980	J -M	133.9	33.7	43.0	37.05
	A-J	125.3	33.0	43.0	32.06
	J -S	144.2	34.8	36.5	46.96
	O-D	154.3	37.9	43.1	47.11

*The quarters are January to March (J-M), April to June (A-J), July to September (J-S), and October to December (O-D).

ing this time period hog prices fell sharply, but retailers dropped retail prices at a slower rate and widened their margins. This response from retailers has also been observed in the cattle market. When animals are backed up and overweight, meat production swells and retailers back off from aggressive buying. Prices drop sharply at the wholesale and farm level, and retailers reduce retail prices slowly, thus widening their margins.

Another example of the retailer's power is the practice of "featuring" meat items. Retail grocery stores use this as a means of competing and drawing traffic (consumers) into their stores. Meat items often carry top billing in retail chains' advertising of their food prices. When an item is featured, the retailer cuts the price by a certain amount. In addition, the retailer must buy extra tonnage, since specials tend to see larger volumes sold. Seasonally, pork features are strongest in the fall and spring, coinciding with the highs of pork production. Specific pork products also have periods of high demand, such as hams at Christmas and Easter and bellies (bacon) in the summer for the bacon, lettuce, and tomato season. These seasonals are not exclusive, however; when retailers have wide margins and meat supplies are adequate, featuring will occur.

SOURCES OF INFORMATION

A large amount of information is available to the public to aid in analyzing the hog market. The government conducts and publishes a number of surveys regarding hog inventories, slaughter levels, production intentions, and prices. The frequency and scope of these reports change over time. Therefore, comments on the usefulness of various reports will be organized around the general value of their information, not the specific reports published at this time.

Long-term forecasting of the hog markets requires numbers that deal with cyclical variations. These numbers include total inventory, breeding herd numbers, and farrowing intentions. Following total inventory numbers gives a sense of the current position of the hog cycle. Breeding-herd numbers indicate the potential for future pork production, while changes in breeding-herd levels point out the relevant phase of the cycle. Finally, farrowing intentions can be used to forecast pig crops and future pork production. All of these numbers are currently reported in the U.S. Department of Agriculture (USDA) *Hogs and Pigs* reports. Currently, these reports are released on a quarterly basis with the June and December surveys covering the entire United States and reports released in March and September covering only the 10 major hog-producing states.

Intermediate-term forecasting of the hog markets involves the same numbers used in long-term analysis, broken into more specific units of information. Farrowing intentions are useful for forecasting 6 to 12 months in advance. Actual farrowings and pig crops also can be used in forecasting ahead 3 to 6 months. Weight breakdowns of market hog inventories can be used for estimates of slaughter patterns up to 6 months ahead. These numbers are all included in the *Hogs and Pigs* reports mentioned above.

Near-term forecasting takes the base developed by the intermediate and long-term numbers and adjusts it with current market data. Slaughter and pork production levels, weights, retail activity, and prices are very useful here. Slaughter numbers are reported daily and then summarized in weekly and monthly aggregates. In the weekly and monthly forms, a breakdown is given by sex and by states. The breakdown by sex can be used to detect turns in the hog cycle, or short-term aberrations, while the state-by-state breakdown points out regional changes over time. Meat production and weight levels are reported in conjunction with the weekly and monthly slaughter numbers. Many of the weight figures commonly used do not cover all animals slaughtered, but represent benchmark markets that indicate the overall situation. Commodity information reporting services release these numbers on a regular basis; they can also be obtained from two USDA reports: *Livestock Meat and Wool Market News* (weekly), and *Livestock Slaughter* (monthly).

A large number of price statistics are released by the USDA for all phases of the hog and pork production industry. In addition, estimates of retail prices are released by several industry groups. Price action can often be used as an indicator or "symptom" of what is actually happening in the market. In the short run, certain numbers regarding quantities are not available. However, changes in price levels and price spreads, which may be available on a daily basis, may reveal what is actually happening in terms of quantity.

To properly use near-term information, it is necessary to be in close contact with the market on a daily basis. This is true because (1) use of short-term information requires familiarity with both recent and historical levels of the relevant numbers, and (2) much of the information is not easily quantifiable. The second point is especially important, because following and forecasting the markets in the near term often requires an intuitive feeling for the market.

PORK BELLIES

Closely related to the hog market in terms of both supply and demand is the pork belly market. Being one of the pork products, the supply of pork bellies (often called "bellies") is directly proportional to hog slaughter except for changes in belly stock levels. Demand for pork bellies and other pork products is not as closely related, because bacon is merchandised separately from hams, loins, and picnics. The general public believes pork belly price action to be extremely volatile, and the claim is made that fundamental factors do not affect the market. This is a popular misconception, however; fundamentals are extremely important in evaluating this market. (Figure 16-4 shows the price action in pork bellies from 1963 to 1983.)

Pork bellies come from the side or belly of the hog. During the processing of pork carcasses the ham and shoulder cuts are first removed, leaving the middle part of the carcass. Then the loin portion is removed, leaving the "belly" or side of the hog. The belly has the outer skin trimmed off and is cut to a rectangular shape. The belly can then be frozen and stored, or moved into further processing prior to consumption. Bellies have two outlets; they are sliced and sold as bacon, or ground up and used as pork trimmings. Bacon is the more common use for bellies, and the "green" or fresh belly must first be cured and smoked before slicing and retailing the product. Grinding up bellies and using them as

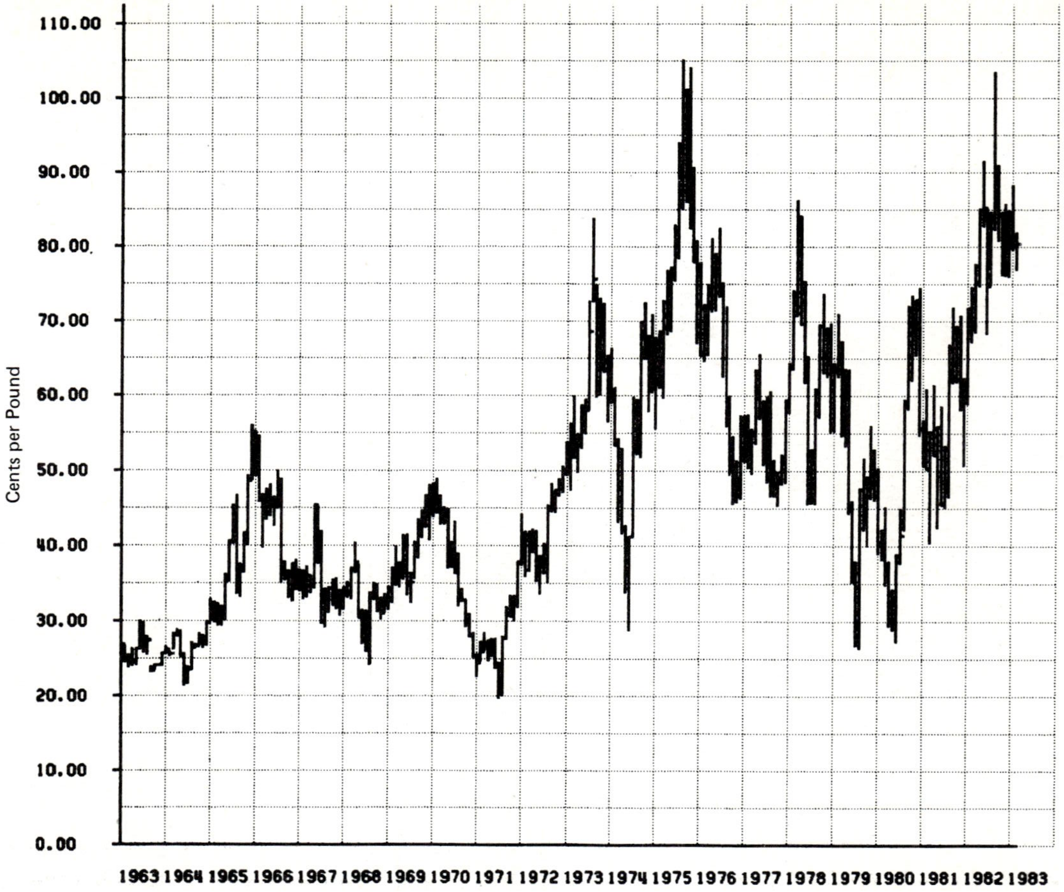

Figure 16-4 Monthly continuation, Chicago Mercantile Exchange pork bellies. *Conti-Commodity Research Division)*

sausage materials occurs at times when belly prices fall to the level of pork trimmings prices. Therefore, trimmings prices are an effective floor for belly prices.

The supply of pork bellies is determined by two factors: hog slaughter levels and belly stocks in cold storage warehouses. As already discussed, hog slaughter levels follow a seasonal pattern with highs in the fall and spring and lows in the winter and summer. Therefore, belly production as a fixed percent of the carcass also follows seasonal patterns. Consumption of bellies (i.e., bacon), also follows a seasonal pattern, with special featuring in the winter and during the "BLT" (bacon, lettuce, and tomato) season in the summer. To balance out the fluctuations in production and consumption, bellies are often frozen and held in warehouses until periods of high consumption demand. If properly handled, bellies can be stored for 6 months or more.

Table 16-5 shows the holdings of pork bellies in cold storage from 1970 to 1980 on a monthly basis. From these numbers the movement of bellies into and out of storage is clear: movement into storage during spring and fall, and movements out of storage during summer and winter. The largest in-movements occur during the spring, and the largest out-movements are during the summer, usually continuing to October.

The storable feature of tbe belly market makes for unique cash and futures relationships. While all other livestock and meat futures contracts are nonstorable commodities, the pork belly market has the added facet of carrying charges in evaluating and forecasting price levels. As a result, the fundamentals of the belly market can be complex as one attempts to integrate hog slaughter levels, stock levels, movements in and out of storage, and consumer demand.

The base for forecasting pork belly supplies is a forecast of future hog slaughter levels (discussed earlier in this chapter). Once this is developed, current stock levels and expected stock level changes are considered to generate an estimate of future belly supplies. Demand for pork bellies is a function of consumer income, recent consumption levels, and seasonal factors described earlier. Recent consumption levels are included here, as bacon is a food that

TABLE 16-5 U.S. Cold Storage Holdings of Pork Bellies
(Forty-eight states, first of month, million pounds)

Year	Jan.	Feb.	Mar.	Apr.	May	June	July	Aug.	Sep.	Oct.	Nov.	Dec.
1970	38.7	37.0	47.1	61.1	74.0	82.1	67.3	39.3	20.4	9.8	21.0	42.1
1971	76.4	81.6	83.0	111.6	131.3	146.1	140.8	105.0	70.5	50.7	53.1	68.0
1972	86.1	84.1	88.1	107.5	130.9	133.0	105.6	69.8	35.7	16.6	22.1	34.2
1973	39.3	32.4	30.8	46.4	50.2	55.0	48.8	26.3	10.2	9.1	15.4	31.6
1974	48.8	48.5	53.1	65.2	78.7	87.3	70.5	39.6	21.8	12.9	22.3	38.4
1975	49.5	40.4	42.8	51.8	65.6	65.5	53.4	23.0	10.1	7.4	17.6	33.5
1976	44.7	37.4	38.5	51.2	60.1	63.8	49.3	25.8	8.7	5.9	9.7	24.9
1977	42.9	38.8	36.4	52.8	69.5	80.7	62.7	29.9	9.6	5.2	4.2	20.6
1978	23.7	19.0	15.7	39.6	71.0	82.3	75.0	44.8	21.0	7.5	20.0	41.0
1979	54.4	39.4	37.2	57.7	69.7	86.1	78.9	53.4	21.8	11.1	17.7	42.2
1980	70.2	69.6	67.9	85.4	98.2	106.9	97.0	68.6	34.4	21.9	42.2	72.1

SOURCE: United States Department of Agriculture.

develops a consumer following; i.e., people who have had bacon for breakfast for the past 6 months will buy it again next month, even if prices rise.

Equating these demand-and-supply factors results in a matrix of current cash and futures prices, and the carrying charge relationships adjust this matrix on a day-to-day basis. For example, futures prices at a $10 premium over cash where carrying charges are $7 over current cash prices will stimulate hedging and in-movement of bellies. Speculators with cash connections will buy cash bellies, hedge, deliver them against the futures contract, and make a profit on the arbitrager basis change. Of course, this action will ultimately realign the price structure. A converse example is one in which futures markets are below cash prices plus carrying charges. This would stimulate out-movements from storage or slow the pace of in-movements until the relationship is brought into line. Because of the seasonality of belly movements, cash-futures price relationships also exhibit seasonal tendencies as prices ration out supplies and control storage levels. Futures prices normally need to be sufficiently premium to cash prices to attract in-movements to storage from October to December and from March to May. Wider premiums increase the size of the in-movement. Cash prices are above futures from June to August to move the product out of storage. January and February are also periods of out-movements.

THE FUTURES MARKET

Futures contracts for both hogs and pork bellies are traded on the Chicago Mercantile Exchange, with a minicontract for hogs also traded on the Mid-America Exchange. Table 16-6 presents the basic information for both of the Chicago Mercantile Exchange contracts.

Users of the hog futures include a mixture of speculators, packers, and producers. Producers from the broiler industry also use the hog futures to an extent for cross-hedging, as pork and broiler prices show a close relationship and the broiler futures are generally illiquid. Perhaps the greatest potential for increased use is for hog producers. As the industry becomes more specialized with larger and fewer producers, more attention will be given to marketing. Also, a number of packers and commission companies are developing forward contracts and basis trading, which will lead to greater use of the futures market by producers. Increased use by packers for procurement is unlikely, unless they change their profit focus from processing to market forecasting. In the pork bel-

TABLE 16-6 Chicago Mercantile Exchange Futures Contracts for Live Hogs and Pork Bellies

Item	Live hogs	Frozen pork bellies
Size	30,000 pounds	38,000 pounds
Daily limits	1.5¢/pound	2.0¢/pound
Trading hours	9:10 A.M. to 1:00 P.M. Central Time	9:10 A.M. to 1:00 P.M. Central Time
Delivery points	Most major cornbelt terminals with varying discounts depending on location	Approved Chicago warehouses, with discounts for locations outside Chicago

lies market, active market participants include speculators, packers, and cash pork traders. Pork bellies have always attracted speculative interest, while packers and cash pork traders use the futures to lock in prices or conduct arbitrage.

SUMMARY AND TRADING CONSIDERATIONS

Factors Affecting the Supply and Demand Relationship

To determine factors affecting supply:

1. Estimate future pork production from USDA *Hog and Pig reports.*
2. Estimate changes in pork stocks in cold storage. This is especially important to the pork belly market.

To determine factors affecting demand:

1. Estimate changes in income.
2. Marketing margins at the wholesale and retail level need to be evaluated to convert retail demand into cash hog prices.
3. Competitive meat supplies (beef and poultry) must be evaluated to show potential pork demand.

Leading Indicators of Hog Price Trends

1. Changes in weight levels apart from the seasonal pattern. Increasing weights indicates that hog marketings are backed up and prices could move down. Conversely, decreasing weights are indicative of uptrending prices.
2. Sharp changes in production of competing meats can trigger changes in price direction for hogs.

Common Mistakes Made by Investors and Traders

1. Buying when futures are at a premium to cash in excess of seasonal expectations, or selling when futures are discounted more than is seasonal. It is common for premiums and discounts in deferred futures prices to not be realized. This comes about as producers watch futures prices to develop price expectations and alter their production and marketing plans accordingly. Therefore, expected price action is preempted.
2. Being right for the wrong reason. It is common that traders take a position and the market immediately moves in their favor. It is extremely important to know that the market moved because of your expectation and not another force. Otherwise profits can evaporate quickly.
3. Believing that spreading hogs against bellies is less risky than an outright position. These markets are related, but a spread between the two is often as volatile as an outright position.

4. Going through *Hogs and Pigs* reports with positions in the market. These reports are famed for their volatility and often result in one or more limit moves. Be very careful about holding futures positions when *Hogs and Pigs* reports are released.

What to Look for at Bull Market Peaks

1. There are adequate stocks in cold storage, and packers and retailers are willing to hold inventories.
2. Hog producers are holding back gilts and increasing the breeding herd.
3. The futures markets at large premiums to cash.
4. Profits are large in the hog industry.
5. Price weakness is met by farmers with skepticism, and producers hold on to their hogs longer and increase average weights.
6. Reports of slow meat movement at retail levels.
7. Retail margins narrowing to unprofitable levels.
8. Price-making surprises such as price controls or consumer boycotts.
9. A sharp drop in corn prices will often signal an end to a bull market.

What to Look for at Major Troughs

1. Large-scale liquidation of the breeding herd has been going on for at least 1 year. Producer attitudes are negative.
2. Futures are discounted to cash prices.
3. Producers respond to price weakness with heavy marketings.
4. Pork supplies in cold storage are drawn down to low levels.
5. Hog production units in rural areas are for sale, and stories about farmer bankruptcy circulate.

PART

3

Agricultural Commodities—Foods and Fibers

CHAPTER

17

Cocoa

Giles Evans

HISTORICAL BACKGROUND

Although cocoa has been consumed as a beverage for many centuries, it was not until the Dutch manufacturer Conrad J. Van Houten manufactured chocolate in 1828 that the industry as we know it today began to emerge. His discovery was that, when ground and pressed, cocoa beans yielded up their fat content, or butter. By adding this "butter" to sugar and the original grindings, Van Houten produced an elementary chocolate—a palatable and solid form of cocoa. Later developments in Switzerland included adding milk to the production process and making a more attractive product which helped stimulate the demand for cocoa beans.

Although indigenous to the Americas, cocoa beans were taken to Ghana (then the Gold Coast) in the latter half of the nineteenth century. From there cocoa spread to other adjacent areas, predominantly Nigeria, the Ivory Coast, and the Cameroons. The African growers expanded quickly to keep up with a growing world demand for chocolate and soon surpassed the output of the West Indies and the Americas during the 1920s. It is significant that quality grades of cocoa, those used to add flavor to products, still come from the Americas, although they constitute only a very small fraction of total world production. The lesser-quality cocoa now accounts for some 80 to 90 percent of world output. In recent years Brazil has emerged as a major producer following a rapid expansion policy during the 1970s, and has now joined the West African countries as a significant partner.

Cocoa consumption, as might be expected, is relatively concentrated in the high-income countries of the developed world with the United States, Europe, Japan, and the Soviet Union accounting for almost 70 percent of total world consumption. Certain European countries, including the Netherlands, Switzerland, the United Kingdom, and West Germany have a long tradition of chocolate manufacture and to this day have the highest per capita consumption.

As a result of the historical development of cocoa production, primarily in Africa, it is not surprising that trade in this commodity is centered upon Amsterdam, London, and Paris—the capitals of the predominant colonial powers of that time. Today "cash" cocoa is actively traded in all three centers. Both London and Paris also developed active "futures" markets to enhance forward trading of cash cocoa although during the 1970s the Paris market ran into severe financial difficulties and now only exists as a minor market for futures. London, however, has assumed a leading role for futures trading under the auspices of the London Cocoa Terminal Market Association since 1928. This market has become highly developed and complements the active trade of cash cocoa in Amsterdam, Paris, and London. Indeed it could be argued that the use of futures trading in the cocoa market represents a greater proportion of annual world trade than exists in almost any other commodity market. While London provides the most liquid market for futures trading, the New York Cocoa Exchange, which was established just before the London market in 1925, deals primarily with cocoa produced in South America. The increasing importance of Brazil as a world producer in the last decade has helped increase the importance of New York as a major world futures exchange. In 1979 the New York Cocoa Exchange merged with the Coffee and Sugar Exchange to become officially known as the New York Coffee, Sugar and Cocoa Exchange.

MAJOR MARKET PARTICIPANTS

As mentioned above, the production of cocoa is concentrated in five countries, Brazil, Ghana, the Ivory Coast, Nigeria, and the Cameroons, and the method by which these countries sell their crops to the world market is very important to understanding the way in which the cash and futures markets operate. All these countries have adopted, to some extent, an institutionalized system for selling their cocoa. This development, as is frequently the case with agricultural products, is designed to protect farmers from the instability associated with sharp fluctuations of world market prices. There are basically two forms of government organization in this respect. First, the government simply buys the cocoa beans from the farmers at fixed prices and assumes the risk of price movement itself. This type of system is operated by both the Ghana Cocoa Marketing Board and the Nigerian Cocoa Marketing Board and it is these two organizations that enter the world markets. Second, an alternative arrangement followed by the remaining major producers incorporates stabilization funds or "Caisses de Stabilisation" as they are known. Under this system the government fixes prices to farmers and to exporters. As world prices fluctuate, the exporters either rebate profits to the fund when world prices are above their fixed prices, or receive compensation when world prices fall below. In this way private exporters can be used to market products while at the same time protecting farmers.

Consumers of cocoa, that is, chocolate manufacturers of the developed countries, only rarely deal directly with marketing boards or exporters in countries of production, since quality and contractual difficulties can create major problems. As a consequence, a dealer network has emerged where private companies, based close to the major world cash and futures markets, specialize in buying and selling cocoa. These are the dealers who are primarily involved in the futures markets and must be considered their most important element. Another group of importance are those manufacturers who produce cocoa products, the end products of the grinding process—butter, cake, and liquor. These products are usually sold as intermediate products for a variety of chocolate-flavored products such as cakes and confectionery. In many instances manufacturers make both chocolate and products but this is not necessarily the case. There is also a keenly developed market for "secondhand" cocoa beans and products—that is, cocoa which is traded between nonproducers. Specialist brokerage firms engage in this market and as a result are actively engaged in futures trading. Finally, mention must be given to speculators who on occasions can be a major element in the London and New York futures markets, particularly when price changes are large, as can often be the case in the international free market for cocoa.

PRODUCTION

Since the end of World War II, cocoa producton has almost trebled. The rate of growth accelerated in the late 1950s and early 1960s and again in the late 1970s and early 1980s, reaching more than 1.7 million tonnes in 1981.* Because production remains in the hands of the "big five," it is instructive to look at these countries in more detail. Table 17-1 breaks down the market share of these countries over the last 15 years.

It is clear from Table 17-1 that Ghana and Nigeria have lost their dominant position to the Ivory Coast and Brazil. In part, this is a result of the average size of plantations. Small farms are by far the most important in Ghana and Nigeria. Brazil and the Ivory Coast, however, have become involved in large-scale cocoa production only in relatively recent times; as a result, they have tended to organize very large and efficient plantations that can quickly take advantage of economies of scale and new agricultural techniques to increase yield and reduce pests and disease. Although not yet large by the standards of the big five, there is a rapid growth of cocoa bean farming in Indonesia and Malaysia. In 1971 these two countries produced only 3000 and 5000 tonnes respectively, but in 1982 their outputs reached 9000 and 60,000 tonnes. The significance of these growth rates is further enhanced by the fact that the lead time between planting and production of cocoa beans is at least 3 to 4 years for modern vari-

*However, production declined in 1982 because of adverse weather conditions.

TABLE 17-1 Market Share of Major Producers as a Percentage of World Production *(Million tonnes)*

	1965	1975	1980	1982
Ghana	34.0	26.0	19.2	12.0
Ivory Coast	9.0	15.3	26.2	22.9
Brazil	12.0	17.1	20.1	20.4
Nigeria	19.5	14.3	9.3	10.6
Cameroons	6.0	6.0	7.2	7.3
Total	80.5	78.7	80.0	73.2
Total world production	1.214	1.495	1.647	1.530

eties, but it can take 10 years to attain full maturity. Consequently, the increase of production in the Far East can be expected to continue, with Malaysia in particular becoming a major producer during the 1980s.

SEASONAL FACTORS IN COCOA PRODUCTION

The crop-year cycle in cocoa is all-important because, with the exception of Brazil, the main crop of the major producers occurs between October and February. Table 17-2 shows the aggregate impact of the crop cycle on the level of purchases from farmers, the rate of exports, and the level of consumer stocks.

These figures show that exports reach a peak during December and January and therefore can be presumed to arrive at consumer destinations during January and February, with consumer stocks reaching a peak during March. Stocks are then depleted during the remainder of the year as the new crop approaches. During the summer months estimates of the new crop begin to emerge from the offices of brokers and dealers in the international markets; these estimates are

TABLE 17-2 Indices of Seasonal Variation

	Purchases	Exports	Consumer stocks
September	0.0	37.0	18.0
October	44.0	46.6	0.0
November	81.4	70.3	7.8
December	100.0	100.0	44.8
January	80.1	94.0	74.0
February	25.8	78.8	88.0
March	6.3	70.9	100.0
April	4.5	44.2	85.2
May	1.9	52.1	71.9
June	1.3	54.5	79.5
July	0.6	46.7	59.1
August	1.3	38.2	39.1

an important part of any analysis of likely price movement during the coming crop year. However, not until the fourth quarter can any real reliance be placed on such forecasts, since it is not until this time that the trend of purchases can be extrapolated. Earlier forecasts are generally based upon sample counts and rainfall measurements.

CONSUMPTION

Cocoa and chocolate are interesting commodities in terms of substitution since there are no products that can be directly substituted for cocoa in chocolate manufacture. Consequently, world consumption trends are primarily a function of price and income alone. Although chocolate might be regarded as a luxury product, and therefore have a high coefficient of elasticity with regard to price, the statistical evidence does not tend to bear this theory out. It appears that consumers are very loyal to chocolate and, indeed, in times of political crisis chocolate has on occasion been used as a form of currency for the purpose of barter. This was noticeably the case during World War II and must indicate the extent to which people are attracted to the product's unique flavor and properties.

The growth of world demand for cocoa followed a relatively stable path during the 1950s and 1960s; not until the mid-1970s did the upward trend show any signs of abating. During the mid-1970s prices increased more than six-fold and consumption dropped from a peak of 1.5 million tonnes in 1972 to just below 1.4 million tonnes by 1977. It is clear from these figures that the price elasticity of cocoa is relatively low. The dramatic price fall between 1977 and 1981 of nearly 70 percent has led to a pickup in demand, and only in 1982 have consumption levels once again reached the peak levels of the early 1970s.

The relationship between price and consumption is subject to various time

TABLE 17-3 Long-Term Real and Actual Price Trends

Year	World price of beans—actual (U.S. cents per pound)	World price of beans—real 1972 prices (U.S. cents per pound FOB)
1971	26	37
1972	24	24
1973	38	35
1974	64	55
1975	62	48
1976	68	50
1977	126	86
1978	146	94
1979	150	86
1980	119	59
1981	85	62
1982	74	35

lags and these are important in any fundamental analysis. From the futures market price peak above £2800 per tonne to the recent lows below £800 the recovery in consumption has been relatively dismal. Two factors should be noted in this regard. First, average manufacturer costs of cocoa inputs are determined by the prevailing price level multiplied by the quantity purchased. Therefore, in 1977 as prices reached a peak, it can be presumed that only a small quantity was purchased. Manufacturers ran down stocks rather than pay up for tight new crop supplies. Table 17-3 shows clearly that even though prices tripled in the bull market of 1976–77, actual average prices paid increased by less than twice. Second, deflating the actual price series to take out the effect of inflation shows that, in real terms, prices did not begin to fall until 1979, some 2 years after the futures price peak. Table 17-3 shows that the price drop in real terms since 1979 has been dramatic. Growth rates have since been retarded to an extent by the world recession, which demonstrates that demand is somewhat responsive to income changes. Given the 2-year time lag associated with real prices and consumption, it can be assumed that cocoa consumption is set for a rapid recovery as we move toward the mid-1980s.

INTERNATIONAL COCOA AGREEMENT

The International Cocoa Agreement (ICA), negotiated in November 1980, called for a target price range to be defended through the operation of a buffer stock, as detailed below.

$1.60/pound ($3527 per tonne) Maximum upper intervention price
No action between $1.50 and $1.10/pound
$1.00/pound ($2205 per tonne) Lower intervention price minimum

If prices rose above the upper intervention price, the buffer stock manager was to sell cocoa; if prices fell below the lower intervention price, the buffer stock manager could purchase sufficient cocoa to raise prices above that level. If purchases were to exceed 100,000 tonnes, the intervention prices would be reduced by 4¢/pound. The buffer stock was limited to 250,000 tonnes and financing was arranged through a levy of 1¢/pound on imports or exports of cocoa.

The history of the ICA is quite simply told. The Ivory Coast, the major producer, and the United States, the major consumer, did not join the agreement. Thus, the agreement was fatally flawed from the beginning. In addition, the fundamentals at that time were very much against the agreement because of several years of surplus production. (No international commodity agreement, not even OPEC, has ever been able to control prices when supply has been sharply out of line with demand.) Prices fell, and by March 1982, the buffer stock manager had exhausted the available funds, having bought 100,345 tonnes. The intervention prices were therefore lowered by 4¢, and the buffer stock has since been sidelined. The levy was increased to 2¢/pound for the 1982–83 year so as to rebuild finances.

Prices fell almost constantly, with the indicator price bottoming below 70¢/pound in November 1982. Since that time, prices have risen because of a production deficit in 1982–83 and a predicted deficit in 1983–84. In June 1983 prices moved back into the ICA price range. This rise in price came about without any help at all from the agreement.

The failure of the ICA has been apparent to all market participants, and efforts are now under way to negotiate a new agreement. A series of meetings, starting in late 1983, will be held to try and reach a concensus, and a new ICA is targeted to begin in October 1984. A promising development is that the Ivory Coast is to take part in the negotiations; however, the position of the United States is more ambivalent. The likely outcome is an agreement similar to the present one but with extra controls, probably including quota limitations on exports. Importing members may also be required to make some sort of commitment which will strengthen the agreement.

If price levels can then be successfully defended in both directions, the ICA will be a dominating market factor and a major influence on the subsequent development of the cocoa and chocolate industry.

STATISTICAL SOURCES

Cocoa statistics are very complete, extend back many years, and are an invaluable guide to anyone involved in the cocoa industry or markets. The most complete source of data is provided by *Gill and Duffus Cocoa Market Report.* The International Cocoa Organization in London also produces the *Quarterly Bulletin of Cocoa Statistics,* though this is less up to date than the Gill and Duffus report. (Table 17-4 summarizes the world supply of and demand for cocoa.)

TABLE 17-4 World Summary of Cocoa Supply and Demand *(Thousand tonnes)*

Crop year	Production	Consumption	End-of-year stocks
1970–71	1484	1399	585
1971–72	1567	1536	616
1972–73	1383	1583	416
1973–74	1434	1512	338
1974–75	1534	1452	420
1975–76	1497	1523	394
1976–77	1325	1442	277
1977–78	1488	1399	366
1978–79	1474	1459	381
1979–80	1606	1489	498
1980–81	1647	1589	556
1981–82	1711	1593	674
1982–83*	1530	1620	584*

*ContiCommodity Research Division estimates.

SOURCE: *Gill and Duffus Cocoa Market Report,* No. 307, May 1983.

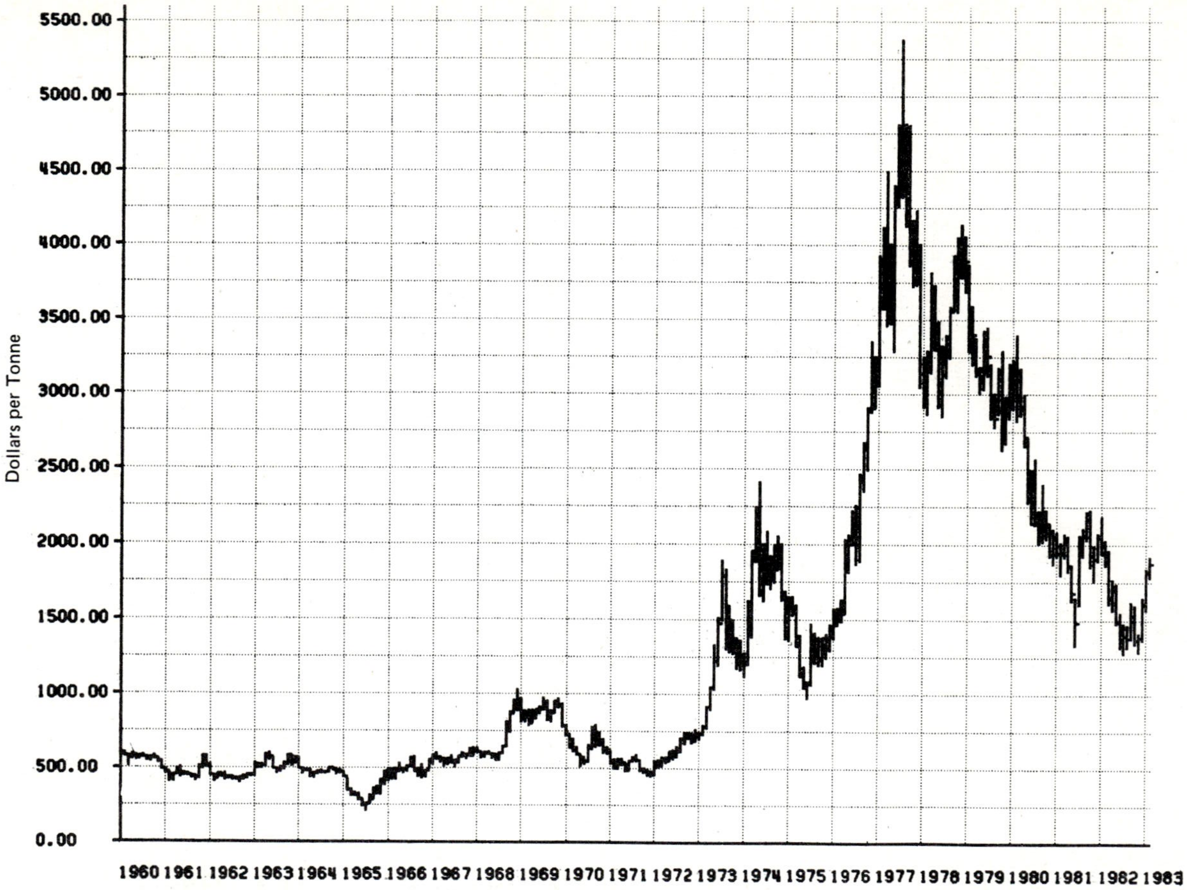

Figure 17-1 Monthly continuation, New York Coffee, Sugar and Cocoa Exchange, cocoa. *(ContiCommodity Research Division)*

TRADING COCOA FUTURES

Because the great majority of the world's cocoa production is contained within only five countries, statistical data is very reliable. Furthermore, the consumption of cocoa as a food product tends to be a stable variable. As a result, estimated crop year surpluses and deficits are generally accurate enough to be of great use when trading cocoa futures. It is generally possible to get a good overall indication of the long-term price trend from this data alone and when a period of successive surpluses or deficits occurs, excellent trading opportunities become available.

During the 1970s, four crop deficits were recorded between 1972 and 1977,

Figure 17-2 Monthly continuation, London Cocoa *(ContiCommodity Research Division)*

culminating in a price move from approximately $500 per tonne to over $5000 per tonne. Subsequently, the market has experienced 5 consecutive years of surplus and prices retracing 65 percent of those gains. In the short term, however, prices are more related to the actions of the five major producers. Because market share is divided among such a small group, any significant change in marketing policy by any individual producer can have a marked price effect. Attempts to stockpile and withdraw from the market can quickly turn into a situation of nearby tightness of physical availability. But if such a policy is contrary to the long-term price trends, it ultimately causes a strong price distortion which will eventually resolve itself by a major corrective move in the direction of the long-term trend. It is because of these distortions and subsequent corrections that cocoa has undeservedly gained a reputation for volatility. (Figures 17-1 and 17-2 show the price variations in recent years at the two major exchanges.)

For the futures trader, the implication of the market concentration in production is that it is very necessary to assess the marketing policy of particularly Brazil, Ivory Coast, and Ghana, within the context of the long-term trend during any particular crop year. Seasonal factors do not come into play since the futures market is highly developed. All cash pricing is related to the futures contracts and any seasonal fluctuations tend to be smoothed out. For forecasting purposes, however, the summer months usually see early—and approximate—estimates of new crop potential. Generally the market has formed a reasonably reliable view of the new crop by about October or November with confirmations in December.

CONTRACT DATA

	London	**New York**
Contract size	10 tonnes (22,046 pounds)	10 tonnes (22,046 pounds)
Price quotation	Sterling per tonne	Dollars per tonne
Delivery months	March, May, July, September, December	March, May, July, September, December
Market hours	10:00 A.M. to 1:00 P.M., 2:30 P.M. to 5:00 P.M. London time	9:30 A.M. to 3:00 P.M. Eastern time
Tenderable growths	Group 1 (at current prices) Ghana Ivory Coast Nigeria Sierra Leone Togo Cameroons Zaire Western Samoa Grenada Five Estates Trinidad and Tobago Jamaica	Group A ($160 premium) Ghana Ivory Coast Nigeria

Group 2 (£25 discount) San Thome Sri Lanka Papua, New Guinea	Group B ($80 premium)
Group 3 (£50 discount) Brazil Ecuador Malaysia	Group C (at par)

CHAPTER

18

Coffee

Richard Grace

INTRODUCTION

Although the coffee plant is indigenous to the African continent, it was not until it was cultivated in Asia and particularly in South and Central America that it became a major commercial product. Initially coffee was introduced into Brazil in 1727, but the real expansion in production did not take place until the nineteenth century. By 1880 Brazil had become a significant coffee exporter and this trend has continued ever since.

Although the trade in coffee was totally dominated by the South and Central American producers until the middle of this century, in the last forty years there has been a considerable growth in production from African countries. During the 1970s Latin American producers accounted for 85 percent of world production whereas today their market share is approximately 60 percent with African output reaching 30 percent. The growth in African coffee production reflects an increasing demand for instant coffee, a sector which benefits from the highest rate of growth of all coffee products.

There is a significant difference between the type of coffee grown in Africa and that grown in Latin America. The two main types of coffee are known as robusta and Arabica. Robusta coffee can be grown in very hot and humid climates, normally close to the Equator. By contrast, Arabicas are grown in cooler climates either further from the Equator than robusta or at higher altitudes. Arabicas are generally further subdivided into "washed" and "unwashed" depending upon the processing immediately after picking. Washed Arabicas are usually referred to as "milds" whereas unwashed are referred to as just Arabicas.

Historically, Arabica coffees have commanded a price premium over robustas for two reasons. First, consumer preferences indicate that Arabicas are more palatable than the somewhat bitter robustas. Secondly, the yield from Arabicas is lower than that from robustas.

In general, robustas are grown in Africa and Indonesia and Arabicas are grown in Latin America. It should be noted, however, that there is a small production of Arabicas in Africa—notably in Kenya—and some robustas are produced by Brazil. Other types of coffee are also grown, but the broad categories of robusta and Arabica are dominant.

ECONOMIC AND STATISTICAL BACKGROUND TO THE WORLD COFFEE MARKET

Historical Production Trends

Table 18-1 gives a breakdown of the world market shares of the major coffee-producing countries. The increasing importance of robusta coffee is clearly shown by the growth of production in Africa and Asia. The reason most usually given for the shift towards robustas is twofold. First, their competitiveness vis-a-vis Arabicas has tended to make them attractive to blenders, particularly so when the general price level of coffee is high. The second and probably more significant reason relates to a change in the way in which coffee is actually consumed by end users. In particular, there has been a dramatic increase in the consumption of instant coffee, for which blending is much less critical than in fresh coffee blends, and this growing market attracts the cheaper grades.

Table 18-1 also illustrates the dominance of Brazil, by far the world's largest coffee producer, even though its market share has declined over the period shown. It is because of the dominance of Brazil that concern over frost during the Brazilian winter is such an important factor on the world market between May and September.

During the 1950s, demand for coffee rose dramatically with prices reaching $1 per pound in 1954. During the following years, these prices triggered a dramatic expansion in output, increasing to around 70 million bags by 1960 from 40 million bags at the beginning of the 1950s. It was this growth in output that set the scene until the severe killer frost in Brazil during the winter of 1975. Throughout the 1960s the coffee market was faced with a massive surplus that kept stocks in excess of 1 year of world consumption. Prices were depressed throughout this period with the New York cash price holding in a range between 30¢ and 50¢ per pound. Toward the end of the 1960s the low price levels had begun to stimulate consumption so that as the next decade began there was a much closer balance between supply and demand. By the time of the Brazilian killer frost, stocks had fallen to a more manageable 50 percent of annual world consumption. These dramatic changes in price can be seen in Figures 18-1 through 18-3.

TABLE 18-1 World Market Share of Coffee Producers
(Percentage)

	1950	1960	1970	1980	1983*
Total South America	67.7	62.9	43.3	51.2	50.4
Brazil	50.5	48.7	26.4	33.4	31.2
Colombia	14.5	11.1	12.1	13.3	15.1
Ecuador	0.8	1.0	1.6	1.8	2.3
Peru	0.3	0.8	1.5	1.5	1.1
Venezuela	1.6	1.2	1.4	1.2	0.6
Total North and Central America	16.2	13.5	18.5	17.2	16.6
Costa Rica	1.0	1.5	2.0	2.0	2.5
Dominican Republic	1.0	0.8	1.0	0.7	1.0
El Salvador	3.2	2.3	3.6	2.8	3.5
Guatemala	2.9	2.3	2.9	2.7	3.1
Haiti	1.6	0.8	0.8	0.6	0.3
Honduras	0.4	0.5	0.9	1.5	1.7
Mexico	3.0	3.0	4.9	4.4	3.1
Nicaragua	0.9	0.6	1.0	1.1	1.4
Total Africa	12.3	18.7	30.7	21.4	23.5
Angola	1.9	3.4	5.1	0.5	0.6
Ethiopia	2.5	4.2	7.1	3.5	2.3
Ivory Coast	1.3	1.8	3.2	5.2	4.7
Kenya	0.5	0.7	1.5	1.6	2.0
Madagascar	1.4	1.2	1.6	1.5	1.6
Tanzania	0.7	0.6	1.3	1.0	1.3
Uganda	1.6	2.8	4.7	2.5	4.0
Zaire	1.4	1.5	1.9	1.3	1.7
Total Asia	3.8	5.0	8.1	10.4	9.5
India	0.9	1.3	2.2	2.4	2.1
Indonesia	2.1	2.5	3.5	6.0	5.3

*Estimates.

The Importance of Brazilian Frosts

It is important to look at the impact of a Brazilian frost in some detail since it is the most important single factor in determining price direction. The 1975 frost was extremely severe and had the immediate effect of nearly doubling prices, but it is the long-term effects that are more significant. The coffee bean is picked during the winter as a berry. Therefore if a frost occurs—particularly in June—it is unlikely that the current crop will be much affected, although quality may fall. However, if the frost is severe enough it can kill the plants themselves, or part of the plants. Given the fact that it takes 3 to 4 years to replace output, the crops during the 2 years following the frost will suffer the greatest production drop. Table 18-2 shows Brazilian production during the relevant period. The severity of this frost can be seen by the fall in production to a disastrous 6.7 million bags. However, because world stocks prior to the frost were so large, prices did not finally peak until the second quarter of 1977, when they reached a high in excess of $3.20 per pound.

The effects of a frost upon a coffee plant is shown in Table 18-3. Temperatures must fall to −2°C if damage is to occur; a frost of −5°C is likely to affect the branches of the trees. To some extent, a frost can be seem coming when a high-pressure cold front moves north up through Argentina. Generally, these fronts tend to move East before reaching Brazil, but when this does not occur a frost is highly probable. The frost season in Brazil runs from late May to August.

Because the full effect of a frost can take 1 to 2 years to materialize, it is the

Figure 18-1 Monthly continuation, New York Coffee, Sugar, and Cocoa Exchange coffee. *(ContiCommodity Research Division)*

world level of producer stocks which is the critical variable that will determine the likely price direction.

The response to the high prices in 1977 was a large increase in production in most of the major coffee-producing countries, particularly Colombia. It now appears that the production of coffee is once again moving to a level well in excess of consumption. To some extent, the frost of 1981, which reduced Brazilian production for the 1982–83 crop to 16 million bags from a prefrost estimate of 32 million bags has disguised this trend although a 2 to 3 year period of frost-free production would almost certainly bring the producers' stocks to over 50 million bags once again. The crucial point, however, is that it takes time for a sharp frost to affect prices, and the extent to which prices are pushed up will be dictated by the level of producer stocks at the time of the frost.

Figure 18-2 Monthly continuation, London robusta coffee. *(Conti-Commodity Research Division)*

Figure 18-3 Monthly continuation, New York Coffee, Sugar, and Cocoa Exchange coffee. *(ContiCommodity Research Division)*

TABLE 18-2 Brazilian Production (*Million bags*)

1973–74	26.9
1974–75*	22.4
1975–76	6.7
1976–77	16.0
1977–78	20.5

*Year of killer frost.

TABLE 18-3 Crop Size Following Frost, by Years

Damage	1	2	3	4
Leaves	Small	Normal	Normal	Normal
Leaves and branches	None	Small	Normal	Normal
Leaves, branches, and trunk	None	None	Small	Normal

World Consumption Trends

World consumption of coffee did grow relatively strongly during the 1960s and early 1970s, reaching a peak of nearly 80 million bags in 1973 (see Table 18-4). Not surprisingly, however, this trend reversed following the rapid price rise of 1975–1977, and has only begun to recover during the last 5 years. The world's largest consumer of coffee, the United States, has experienced a decreasing trend in per capita consumption since 1962, primarily as a result of a shift in consumer preferences to soft drinks and beer. By 1981 daily U.S. coffee consumption is estimated at 1.92 cups compared to 3.12 cups in 1962—a forty-percent fall. However, the total consumption of coffee in the United States appears to remain relatively stable at approximately 20 million bags per annum. By contrast, growth of coffee consumption has been strong in most other areas of the world, particularly Western Europe, although this area too appears to be approaching saturation levels and is unlikely to be able to sustain the growth of the last 20 years. It will require growth within the Eastern bloc and in the Far East if the growth of world coffee consumption is to maintain its long-term trend of 3 percent per annum.

SEASONAL FACTORS IN THE COFFEE YEAR

There is no clearly definable seasonal world tendency in the production of coffee because the crop seasons of the producing countries are staggered. Furthermore, coffee can be stored relatively easily for a considerable period of time (2 to 3 years) before suffering a deterioration in quality. For this reason, stock levels reflect the long-term supply-and-demand balance and therefore tend to obscure what seasonal variation there may be.

There is a sharp seasonal pattern in demand, particularly in the United States, where the fourth and first quarters of the year generally witness a higher

TABLE 18-4 World Coffee Statistics
(Tonnes)

	Production	Consumption	Producer stocks	Stocks consumption ratio, %
1962–63	67.4	61.5	71.2	115.7
1963–64	71.0	68.9	73.3	106.4
1964–65	50.6	55.4	68.5	123.6
1965–66	81.6	62.9	87.2	138.6
1966–67	63.4	66.4	81.4	122.5
1967–68	70.8	70.4	79.4	112.8
1968–69	63.3	70.4	70.6	100.3
1969–70	69.7	71.8	65.2	90.8
1970–71	59.0	70.9	52.6	74.2
1971–72	73.7	76.6	47.8	62.4
1972–73	77.0	79.0	45.4	57.5
1973–74	66.1	76.1	31.7	41.6
1974–75	82.5	74.6	37.6	50.4
1975–76	72.9	74.3	36.5	49.1
1976–77	61.4	70.7	25.4	35.9
1977–78	70.7	68.0	29.4	43.2
1978–79	78.4	78.5	25.0	31.8
1979–80	80.4	80.9	23.6	29.2
1980–81	80.7	82.0	22.3	27.2
1981–82	96.9	82.0	37.2	45.4
1982–83	81.0	84.0	34.2	40.7
1983–84	95.0	84.5	44.7	52.9

*Estimates.

consumption than the warmer spring and summer months. However, this tendency is not distinct enough to cause any seasonal pattern in world prices.

INTERNATIONAL COFFEE ORGANIZATION AND INTERNATIONAL COFFEE AGREEMENT

Since prices fell as low as 80¢/pound during 1981 after reaching over $3 per pound in 1977, it is not surprising that there has been a strong political demand on the part of producing countries to attempt to stabilize and support prices on the world market.

Under the auspices of the International Coffee Organization (ICO), an International Coffee Agreement (ICA) has been negotiated between the majority of the world's producing and consuming countries. The purpose of the agreement is to restrict surplus production from reaching the world market by imposing export quotas on the producing countries. The agreement is to be extended for 6 years starting with the 1983–84 coffee year (October to September). It is likely that the agreement will continue to function similarly to the old system, whereby export quotas have been restricted to about 56 million bags so long as prices remain in the range $1.20 to $1.40/pound. Should prices move out of this range, quotas are adjusted to attempt to defend the range.

SUMMARY AND TRADING CONSIDERATIONS

Because Brazil has such a dominant position in the world coffee market, and because this crop is occasionally prone to frost damage during the winter months (late May through August), the possibility of a frost in Brazil tends to override all other factors for much of the coffee season.

From April onward, roasters consider their inventories and their vulnerability in the event of frost. Also speculative interest is generally awakened around this time. If and when a frost occurs, prices can rally by up to 30 percent in a matter of days, and consequently the New York futures market remains limit up. London, by contrast, has no limits and remains open. However, during such frantic trading in London, business will usually be conducted through the call chairman, one contract month at a time—usually the nearest contract month for most of the time. Price quotes should therefore be regarded carefully since one contract may not have traded while the market may have moved dramatically.

From a longer-term point of view, the effect of a frost can extend for at least 1 and possibly 2 or 3 years into the future, depending on the severity of the frost and the current level of producer stocks at that time. Consequently, anyone trading coffee during a frost-affected period should have this data readily available. Supply, demand, and stock level statistics are available from the U.S. Department of Agriculture (USDA) and the ICO, although the former tends to be more up to date. Estimates of crop damage are usually issued by the USDA and the Brazilian Coffee Institute (IBC) some 3 to 4 weeks following the frost, but at that stage figures are tentative. By November, when the new crop is flowering, a more reliable estimate is available. The forward price structure can usually be relied upon to give a good indication of forward tightness. An inversion across the board following a frost is also extremely constructive. At times, however, large producer groups have entered the market to stabilize prices, particularly when prices are depressed. When this occurs, the forward price structure becomes extremely distorted and it is worth determining whether such an involvement is present before relying on the forward spreads.

During bear markets, prices exhibit a tendency to collapse during the Brazilian winter. Because of this, establishing long positions ahead of the winter can be very costly since, for the most part, the probabilities favor no occurence of frost. At present, however, the International Coffee Agreement appears to be controlling prices in an efficient manner and thus attention should be paid to the various trigger price points of the agreement.

CONTRACT DATA

Coffee futures markets actively trade in London and New York, although there are marked differences in contract specifications. Most notably, London provides a market for robusta coffees, whereas New York trades in washed Arabica coffee (milds).

	London	New York
Contract size	10 tonnes	37,500 pounds
Price quotation	Sterling per tonne	Cents per pound
Delivery months	March, May, July, September, November, January	March, May, July, September, December
Price limit	None	4¢, variable under certain conditions
Market hours	10:30 A.M. to 12:30 P.M., 2:30 P.M. to 5:00 P.M. London time	9:45 A.M. to 2:30 P.M. Eastern time
Deliverable grades	At par	At par
	Uganda	Mexico
	Tanzania	El Salvador
	India	Guatemala
	Ghana	Nicaragua
	Sierre Leone	Kenya
	Nigeria	Tanzania
	Angola	Uganda
	Cameroons	
	Zaire	
	Ivory Coast	
	Madagascar	
	Central African Republic	
	Togo	
	Guinea	
	Others	Others
	Trinidad (£5)	Colombia (+200 points)
	Indonesia (£10)	New Guinea (−100 points)
		Honduras
		Peru (−400 points)
		Venezuela
		Dominican Republic
		Burundi
		Ecuador (−550 points)
		India
		Rwanda

CHAPTER

19

Sugar

Paul McAuliffe

Sugar, the natural sweetener known as sucrose, is obtained commercially in crystalline form from sugar cane and sugar beets. Sugar is made by all green plants in their leaves, but the greatest quantities are in cane and beets.

Nature produces sugar, chemically known as $C_{12}H_{22}O_{11}$, in a process known as photosynthesis. The sunlight acts on water in green plants and carbon dioxide from the air to form sugar in plants. The sugar that comes from beets and cane is exactly the same. In the 1980–81 season, about 63 percent of the world's sugar came from sugar cane and 37 percent from sugar beets.

HISTORY

The history of sugar can be traced back as far as 8000 years ago in New Guinea. In ancient times sugar cane moved from the South Pacific to Southeast Asia, to India and China, but did not reach the Mediterranean until 636 A.D. Sugar was first mentioned by one of Alexander's officers in 325 B.C., because of its importance to human energy needs in an army. Much later Napoleon fostered a beet sugar planting explosion in France.

The western world came to know sugar as a luxury in the thirteenth century. Venice was the world's sugar capital by 1300. The Portuguese and Spanish were the first to develop the production of sugar cane as they discovered new continents and expanded their worlds into new colonies. In the fifteenth century, the Portuguese successfully planted sugar cane on the island of Madeira. They extended this planting into Africa and Brazil. About the same time, the

Spanish had planted sugar cane in the Canary Islands. Columbus brought sugar cane to the Caribbean on his second voyage, and it flourished on Haiti and in the Dominican Republic. In the seventeenth century, France and England established refineries in their own countries to handle the growing supplies of sugar coming from the West Indies.

Sugar beets were also used as a source of sugar in the ancient world but did not become a worldwide commercial sugar producer until the eighteenth century. Some historians believe sugar beets were eaten by Egyptian laborers that built some of the pyramids around 3000 B.C.

Not until 1747 did Europe finally develop a commercial extraction process for sugar beets. Napoleon supported a large increase in French sugar beet production in 1811 for two reasons: both because of this newly discovered economical process, and because the war between Britain and France had suspended Caribbean sugar arrivals. Germany and France became the largest sugar beet producers in Western Europe and remain so today. In the United States, sugar beets developed slowly. After several attempts in 50 years to duplicate the best factories in Europe, the United States finally achieved some success in the sugar beet industry in 1879. The industry experienced good growth in the early 1900s. Today the United States produces over 2.5 million tonnes of beet sugar and 2,474,000 tonnes of cane sugar.

TYPES OF SUGAR

Sugar Beets

Sugar beets are planted every year, unlike sugar cane, and are grown in temperate climates. Like cane, sugar beets need a lot of water (about 15 gallons of water in a growing season of 7 months). Sugar beets are rotated with other crops and grow mainly underground, with the exception of the top leaves. The leaves can be seen above ground, and photosynthesize the sugar which is stored below ground. Unlike cane, the sugar beet roots can grow 8 feet or more below the surface. This enables them to draw on subsoil moisture in times of drought and continue producing sugar in the beets. Very cloudy weather over an extended period of time, however, will inhibit photosynthesis and thereby retard the growth of the sugar content in the beets. This is an important concept to understand, particularly when analysts refer to the growing conditions of the European beet crop grown between April and September, which provides the world with 85 percent of all the sugar produced from sugar beets, and 32 percent of all sugar. After extraction of the sugar, the sugar beet provides by-products which are used to feed cattle, sheep, and dairy herds.

Sugar Cane

Sugar cane is grown above ground and reaches over 15 feet into the air. Cane is a giant tropical grass grown in the tropical and subtropical regions of the world. Sugar cane crops are cut down yearly for their production but grow back like grass unless they are slowed down. Replanting normally occurs when yields fall to low levels, every 2 to 6 years. Sugar cane yields can be severely affected by drought because sugar cane does not have deep roots like sugar beets to draw upon subsoil moisture. Sugar cane also needs large and regular amounts of rainfall to produce its sugar, whch is stored in the cane. About 85 percent of a sugar cane's weight is juice, of which 11 percent is sugar.

THE MAKING OF SUGAR

Sugar Beets

Sugar beets are harvested by machine in the United States and Europe. The average beet weighs 21 pounds and stores up to 14 teaspoons of sugar in its roots. When the plants are taken from the soil, the leafy tops are cut off and used for cattle feed, and the beets are taken to factories for processing. The beets are washed and then sliced into small strips. The strips are treated in hot water to extract the sugar from them. The remaining beet pulp is fed to animals. The sugar beet juice is purified, filtered, and concentrated into white sugar, without stopping at the raw sugar stage as in the case of cane sugar.

Sugar Cane

Sugar cane is grown from sections of the sugar stalk which contain a bud. The growing season lasts from 9 to 36 months. At harvest the cane is cut near the ground by machine or by a machete, and the leaves are stripped from the stalk. The stalks, which are 85 percent juice, are shipped to the mills where they are crushed and shredded. Iron rollers then grind the stalks and extract the juice under heavy pressure. (The remaining ground stalks, known as bagasse, can be used for fuel at the mill or processed into chemical by-products such as paper or wallboard.) The juice containing the sugar is purified and concentrated by boiling. The sugar crystallizes in a centrifuge while the thickened syrup is drawn away. The crystals are the raw sugar; they are light brown in color because they are still lightly coated with molasses. The sugar is then sent to a refinery for processing into white sugar for human consumption.

USES OF SUGAR

Uses of sugar can be divided into two major categories, food and beverages. In food use, sugar goes into the manufacture of bakery and cereal products such as cereal and breakfast foods; confectionery products such as candy, chocolate and gum; processed foods such as canned fruit and frozen juices; and finally dairy products such as ice cream and frozen desserts. In beverage use, sugar goes into the manufacture of soft drinks at the retail level and into the manufacture of syrups at the wholesale level. (See Figure 19-1.)

Table 19-1 shows the uses of raw sugar in the United States in the industrial and nonindustrial sectors. Table 19-2 shows worldwide harvest dates for cane sugar, and Table 19-3 shows worldwide harvest dates for beet sugar.

MAJOR MARKET PARTICIPANTS

The major market participants are the world's major exporters and importers of sugar. Although the world sugar crop is a major crop when compared to coffee or cocoa, most of the sugar is consumed where it is grown. The major participants for sugar then become the major exporters and importers in the world market.

During the past 20 years, the nations consuming the most sugar have been those with the largest per capita consumption coupled with large populations. These per capita consumption levels tend to increase with the standard of living. Currently, developed and developing nations like the United States, Canada, Mexico, Venezuela, Brazil, Australia, and countries in Europe have the higher per capita consumptions in the world. The United States and the Soviet Union are large producers. They are also the two largest importers because of their population sizes and per capita consumptions. An interesting comparison here is the potential demand from the People's Republic of China, which has a very large population coupled with a low per capita consumption. If the standard of living were to increase sharply in China, it would likely cause a sharp

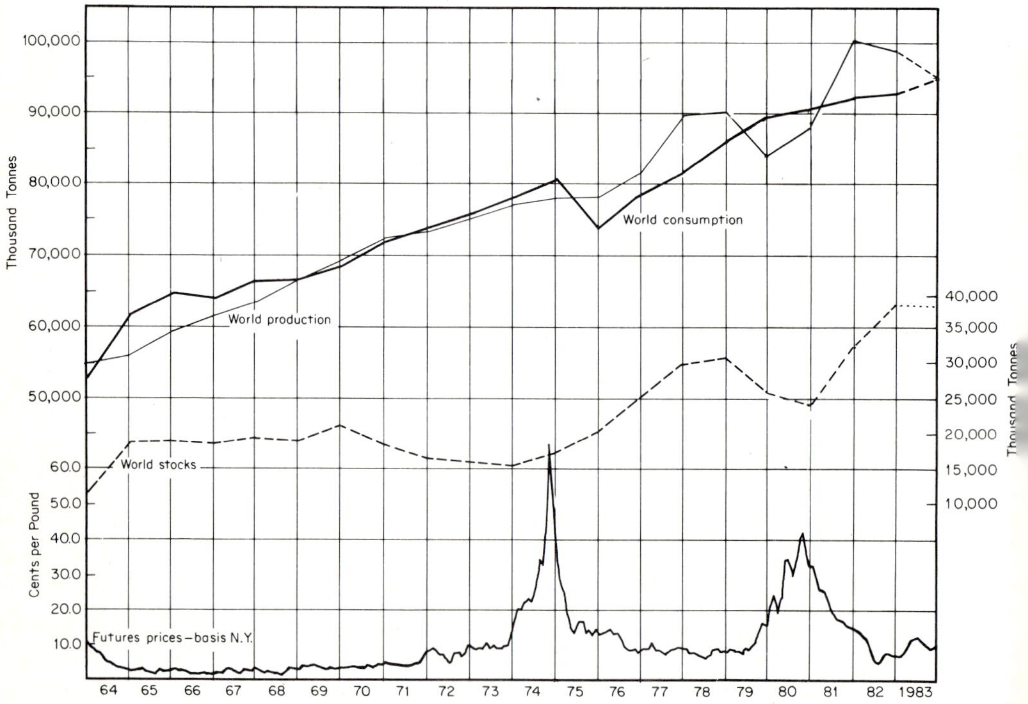

Figure 19-1 World consumption, world production, world stocks, and New York futures prices of the New York number 11 sugar futures contract from 1960 to the present.

TABLE 19-1 U.S. Sugar Deliveries to Industrial and Nonindustrial Users, 1973–1979
(Thousand short tons)

Industrial Users	1973	1974	1975	1976	1977	1978	1979	1980	1981	1982
Food use:										
Bakery and cereal products	1454	1443	1241	1313	1386	1309	1289	1337	1306	1296
Confectionery products	1035	1018	795	915	951	912	911	932	983	940
Processed foods	1025	949	743	737	746	690	681	535	484	450
Dairy products	595	570	511	553	567	550	480	450	459	404
Miscellaneous foods	502	514	486	518	542	413	482	589	581	526
Subtotal	4611	4494	3776	4036	4192	3874	3844	3843	3813	3616
Beverage use	2469	2350	2074	2252	2454	2588	2411	2161	1852	1583
Industrial use	7080	6844	5850	6288	6646	6462	6255	6004	5665	5199
Nonindustrial use	3580	3567	3337	3655	3600	3405	3553	3353	3421	3214
Nonfood use*	111	128	86	101	105	161	126	120	126	106
Total food and nonfood use	10771	10539	9273	10044	10351	10028	9934	9477	9212	8519

*Mainly pharmaceuticals and some tobacco.

SOURCE: Lamborn *Sugar Market Report*, June 4, 1980, based on U.S. Department of Agriculture data in "Sugar and Sweetener Outlook and Situation Report."

TABLE 19-2 Cane Sugar Harvest Dates

Countries	Harvest dates beginning/ending
Europe:	
Spain	Apr./June
North and Central America:	
Cuba	Nov./July
United States	
Louisiana	Oct./Dec.
Florida	Nov./May
Texas	Oct./Dec.
Hawaii	Jan./June
Puerto Rico	Jan./June
Trinidad	Jan./Aug.
Barbados	Jan./Aug.
Jamaica	Dec./June
St. Kitts	Mar./July
Dominican Republic	Nov./Oct.
Mexico	Nov./Sept.
Martinique	Jan./June
Guadeloupe	Mar./June
Haiti	Dec./June
Guatemala	Nov./June
El Salvador	Nov./June
Belize	Dec./July
Honduras	Dec./June
Nicaragua	Dec./June
Costa Rica	Dec./June
Panama	Dec./May
South America:	
Argentina	May/Dec.
Brazil	June/May
Peru	Jan./Dec.
Guyana	Jan./Dec.
Uruguay	May/Nov.
Surinam	Sept./Aug.
Venezuela	Sept./Aug.
Bolivia	May/Nov.
Ecuador	June/Dec.
Colombia	Jan./Dec.
Paraguay	July/Nov.
Africa:	
Egypt	Dec./June
Sudan	Dec./June
Ethiopia	Sept./Aug.
Somalia	June/Apr.
Mauritius	June/Dec.
Mauretania	June/Dec.
Reunion	July/Jan.
Republic of South Africa	May/Apr.
Swaziland	May/Jan.
Mozambique	May/Jan.
Angola	June/Mar.
Kenya	July/June

TABLE 19-2 Cane Sugar Harvest Dates (*continued*)

Countries	Harvest dates beginning/ending
Uganda	July/June
Tanzania	July/June
Madagascar	June/Oct.
Rhodesia	May/Nov.
Malawi	May/Dec.
Zambia	May/Dec.
Nigeria	May/Nov.
Ghana	April/Sept.
Cameroun	Dec./June
Mali	April/Sept.
Madeira	April/June
Asia:	
India	Oct./Sept.
Indonesia	April/Dec.
Pakistan	Nov./May
Nepal	July/June
Burma	Nov./June
Philippines	Sept./Aug.
Taiwan	Nov./June
China	Jan./Dec.
Iran	Oct./April
Iraq	Oct./April
Afghanistan	Oct./April
Bangladesh	Oct./April
Thailand	Nov./Mar.
Japan	Oct./Feb.
Oceania:	
Australia	May/Jan.
Fiji Islands	May/Dec.

increase in their per capita consumption. This would translate into an enormous import demand on the world market. The standard of living has been increasing in many countries for the past decade, which has caused an increase in the per capita sugar consumption. Coupled with rising populations, the higher standard of living has caused several nations to become significant importers and smaller exporters in the world market.

On a continental basis it is interesting to examine the trends of both world per capita consumption and continental per capita consumption. Later we will examine these trends on an individual country basis.

Average world per capita consumption of sugar has increased from 17.3 kilograms in 1963 to 21.1 kilograms in 1979 because of an improved standard of living around the world. The improvement in consumption has been concentrated (as Table 19-5 shows) in America, South America, and Europe. Smaller increases have been seen in Asia and Africa. Declines in consumption have been seen in North America and Oceania. The decline in consumption on a per capita basis has been caused by an apparent saturation of sugar consumption and an increasing use of corn syrup, displacing sugar demand. An aging

TABLE 19-3 Beet Sugar Harvest Dates

Countries	Harvest dates beginning/ending
Western Europe:	
West Germany	Sept./Jan.
France	Sept./Jan.
Belgium-Luxembourg	Sept./Jan.
Netherlands	Sept./Jan.
Italy	Sept./Jan.
Denmark	Sept./Jan.
United Kingdom	Sept./Jan.
Ireland	Sept./Jan.
Austria	Sept./Jan.
Sweden	Sept./Jan.
Spain	July/Mar.
Yugoslavia	Aug./Jan.
Greece	July/Oct.
Switzerland	Sept./Jan.
Finland	Sept./Jan.
Turkey	Aug./Feb.
Eastern Europe:	
East Germany	Sept./Jan.
Czechoslovakia	Sept./Jan.
Hungary	Sept./Jan.
Poland	Sept./Jan.
Albania	Aug./Jan.
Rumania	Aug./Feb.
Bulgaria	Aug./Jan.
Soviet Union	Sept./Jan.
Other Countries:	
United States (excluding California and Arizona)	Sept./Nov.
California (excluding Imperial Valley)	July/Dec.
Imperial Valley and Arizona	May/June
Canada	Oct./Dec.
Uruguay	Nov./Apr.
Chile	Mar./Sept.
Algeria	June/Nov.
Tunisia	June/Oct.
Morocco	May/Aug.
Azores	June/Dec.
Japan	Oct./Feb.
China	Sept./Jan.
Pakistan	June/July
Afghanistan	Nov./Feb.
Iran	Oct./Mar.
Iraq	Oct./Mar.
Israel	May/July
Syria	May/July
Lebanon	June/Nov.
Taiwan	Nov./June
China	Jan./Dec.
Iran	Oct./Apr.
Iraq	Oct./Apr.
Afghanistan	Oct./Apr.

TABLE 19-3 Beet Sugar Harvest Dates (*continued*)

Countries	Harvest dates beginning/ending
Bangladesh	Oct./Apr.
Thailand	Nov./Mar.
Japan	Oct./Feb.
Oceania:	
Australia	May/Jan.
Fiji Islands	May/Dec.

population in the United States also appears to have cut the demand for sugar. Figure 19-1 shows the consumption of caloric sweeteners in the United States by type between 1960 and 1983. As a percentage of total sweetener consumption in the United States, sugar has declined frm 87.8 percent in 1960 to only 66.7 percent in 1980. Sugar supplies less of the American sweetener demand because of increasing consumption of high-fructose corn syrup and glucose corn syrup.

From the producer standpoint, major production of sugar has come primarily from Europe, Central America, South America, and Asia. (Tables 19-4 and 19-5 show breakdowns of continental sugar production and consumption, respectively, between 1963 and 1980.) Major sugar producers in the past 2 decades and their production trends are shown in Table 19-6. The European Economic Community (EEC) and the Soviet Union represent a large portion of European production. Cuba, the Dominican Republic, and Mexico are the major producers in Central America. Brazil is the major exporter in South America. The major exporters of sugar in Asia are India, the Philippines, Thailand, and China. Australia is the major exporter in Oceania. Over the past 20 years or so the major increases in production have come from: Brazil, Cuba, the European Economic Community, and Australia.

TABLE 19-4 Sugar Production
(Thousand tonnes)

	1963	1965	1970	1975	1980	1983*
Europe†	19,254	23,821	24,354	26,810	26,927	27,897
North America‡	3,584	3,915	4,385	4,795	5,462	5,315
Central America§	8,811	11,260	13,055	12,656	13,396	14,041
South America	6,270	8,375	8,943	11,345	13,583	14,390
Asia	8,326	10,759	13,643	16,648	19,128	23,188
Africa	3,230	3,228	4,606	5,170	6,185	6,553
Oceania	3,109	3,511	3,911	4,220	3,785	3,280
World total	52,584	64,819	72,896	81,644	88,466	94,664

*Estimates.

†Includes Western Europe, Eastern Europe, and the Soviet Union.

‡Includes Canada and the United States.

§Includes the Caribbean nations, Mexico, and other Central American countries.

SOURCES: International Sugar Organization, F. O. Licht publications, and Foreign Agricultural Service.

TABLE 19-5 Sugar Consumption
(Thousand tonnes)

	1963	1965	1970	1975	1980	1983*
Europe†	23,889	25,604	29,154	29,988	30,289	31,597
North America‡	10,001	10,170	11,475	10,046	9,864	8,915
Central America§	2,454	2,715	3,508	4,239	5,111	5,515
South America	5,092	5,597	6,592	8,847	10,564	10,787
Asia	9,548	11,306	16,327	18,068	24,352	28,069
Africa	3,023	3,301	4,114	5,081	7,254	8,032
Oceania	876	874	950	1,036	1,020	1,005
World total	54,883	59,568	72,121	77,305	88,454	93,920

*Estimates.

†Includes Western Europe, Eastern Europe, and the Soviet Union.

‡Includes Canada and the United States.

§Includes the Caribbean nations, Mexico, and other Central American nations.

SOURCES: International Sugar Organization, F. O. Licht publications, and Foreign Agricultural Service.

TABLE 19-6 Major Sugar Producers
(Thousand tonnes)

	1963	1965	1970	1975	1980	1983
European Economic Community	6,218	6,772	9,087	10,818	13,001	11,360
Soviet Union	5,976	9,700	8,847	8,200	7,174	8,500
Cuba	3,821	6,082	7,559	6,427	7,542	7,500
Dominican Republic	806	583	1,014	1,170	1,137	1,200
Mexico	1,735	2,121	2,402	2,724	2,518	2,900
United States	3,419	3,767	4,273	4,675	5,355	5,185
Brazil	3,037	4,614	5,019	6,299	8,508	9,400
India	2,497	3,493	4,634	5,048	6,542	8,516
Philippines	1,501	1,659	1,980	2,672	2,373	2,280
Australia	1,799	2,073	2,507	2,930	3,389	3,000
Thailand	125	320	495	1,216	1,676	1,700
China	1,800	2,200	2,900	4,000	3,000	3,882
South Africa	1,294	1,014	1,649	1,968	1,709	1,538
Poland	1,350	1,539	1,542	1,847	1,134	1,978
Other	17,206	18,882	18,988	21,649	23,408	25,725
World total	52,584	64,819	72,896	81,643	88,466	94,664
Beet sugar	22,205	27,286	29,321	32,153	32,931	34,314
Cane sugar	30,379	37,532	43,575	49,490	55,545	60,350
Beets as percent of total	42.23	42.10	40.22	39.38	37.22	36.25
Cane as percent of total	57.77	57.90	59.78	60.62	62.79	63.75

*Included because of increasing importance in recent years.

SOURCES: International Sugar Organization, F. O. Licht publications, and Foreign Agricultural Service.

IMPORTANT FACTORS AFFECTING PRICE

General

It is important to note here that price reacts to the market's perception of supply-and-demand fundamentals. Prices decline as the overall supply relative to demand increases. Prices go up as the overall supply relative to demand decreases. In analyzing this relationship, fundamental analysts create worldwide annual supply-and-demand tables. These tables include the estimated or projected world production, world consumption, world imports, world exports, and ending world stocks. An increase or decrease in the projected ending stocks (production surplus or production deficit) will affect the direction of prices, but the level of ending stocks relative to total consumption (ratio of stocks to consumption) will determine the magnitude of the price change. (See Tables 19-7 and 19-8.)

Sugar consumption has increased steadily in the past because of an increasing world population and an increasing standard of living for much of the world. As families increase their standard of living and increase their consumption of goods above the basic needs of subsistence living, their diets change. They begin consuming processed foods and beverages which contain significant amounts of sugar in comparison to the foods they consumed in their old diets. Worldwide consumption has increased annually in the past 2 decades except in 1963, 1974, and 1980. In each of these years, there was a significant production deficit which caused a major price increase. Consumers reacted to the price increases by cutting back consumption 2.1 million tonnes in 1974 and an estimated 1.8 million tonnes in 1980.

Production of sugar has been growing also, but is more inconsistent than the growth in consumption. Declines in production were seen in 1965, 1970, 1974, 1978, 1979, 1982, and 1983. The inconsistent growth in production has been the major cause of bull markets in recent decades. The unexpected declines in production caused production deficits, which in turn caused prices to rise until either consumption was cut or new production increases reached the market to satiate demand. This is the sugar cycle.

In the past century, there have been five major bull markets. The first, in the Civil War, caused New York spot prices to move from 4¢ to 16¢ per pound. The second bull market was seen in 1915 and lasted until 1920, when prices rose from 3¢ to 20¢ per pound. The third bull market lasted from 1963 to 1964 and carried prices from 2.5¢ to 13.5¢ per pound. The fourth price explosion—and

TABLE 19-7 Comparison of World Growth in Supply of and Demand for Sugar

	Annual growth, percent		
	Production	Consumption	Population*
1960s	4.1	4.3†	2.12
1970s	2.1	2.06	1.98

*World Bank.

†1963 to 1969.

TABLE 19-8 Sugar Supply and Demand, 1963 to 1982
(Thousand tonnes raw value)

Crop year (Sept. to Aug.)	Beginning stocks	World production	World consumption	Ending stocks	Production surplus or deficit	Stocks as percent of consumption
1963–64	10,293	54,745	54,261	11,129	484	20.51
1964–65	11,129	66,880	59,273	18,736	7,607	31.61
1965–66	18,736	62,250	61,989	18,997	261	30.65
1966–67	18,997	63,765	63,855	18,907	−90	29.61
1967–68	18,907	65,626	65,680	18,853	−54	28.70
1968–69	18,853	66,822	66,912	18,763	−90	28.04
1969–70	18,763	72,981	70,590	21,154	2,391	29.97
1970–71	21,154	71,030	73,050	19,134	−2,020	26.19
1971–72	19,134	72,176	74,055	17,255	−1,879	23.30
1972–73	17,255	75,688	75,863	17,080	−175	22.51
1973–74	16,411	78,537	78,718	16,230	−181	20.62
1974–75	16,230	77,956	76,587	17,599	1,369	22.98
1975–76	17,599	81,109	78,219	20,489	2,890	26.19
1976–77	20,489	86,698	82,383	24,804	4,315	30.11
1977–78	24,804	91,256	85,810	30,250	5,446	35.25
1978–79	30,250	90,732	89,951	31,031	781	34.50
1979–80	31,031	84,895	90,802	25,124	−5,907	27.67
1980–81	25,124	88,101	88,940	24,285	−839	27.30
1981–82	24,285	100,575	92,231	32,629	8,344	35.38
1982–83*	32,629	99,900	93,800	38,729	6,100	41.29
1982–84*	38,729	95,000	95,000	38,729	0	40.77

*ContiCommodity Research Division estimates.

SOURCE: F. O. Licht, U.S. Department of Agriculture, and ContiCommodity Research Division.

the largest ever seen—began in 1967 and ended in 1974. Prices rose from under 3¢ to over 66¢ per pound. Finally, the most recent bull market began in 1979 at 8¢ per pound and lasted until late 1980, carrying prices above 45¢ per pound.

The Sugar Cycle: Boom-Bust

The importance of listing the past bull markets in sugar is to show the sugar cycle clearly. The sugar cycle briefly described in the previous section shows the "boom and bust" nature of the business. In the past 20 years, we have seen sugar cycles lasting 5 to 8 years.

Normally, there is ample sugar for world demand and prices tend to be stable for long periods of time. When supplies become burdensome (over 30 percent stocks-consumption ratio) prices decline to below the cost of production. Producers who can switch to other crops to increase the return on their efforts cut back on their sugar production. This cutback and any natural production decline cause a tightening in world supplies and a drawdown in world stocks (also known as a production deficit).

The magnitude of the drawdown in stocks will dictate the magnitude of the rise in prices. The rise in price will cause: (1) consumption to decline as consumers begin to ration supplies; and (2) production to rise if producers perceive the rise in price significant enough to justify their expansion of sugar acreage.

The rise in prices is only half of the sugar cycle—the boom half. The second half of the cycle (bust) is a result of the two responses to the boom cycle cited above. The extent of the bust, or price decline in the cycle is determined by a combination of the extent of the increases in production and decreases in consumption. In the 1970s a new sugar competitor, high-fructose corn syrup, also entered into the sugar cycle. As a result of the enormous price increase in sugar between 1967 and 1974, corn syrup became a cheap substitute in the United States. The growth of this industry affected the sugar cycle in 1975 and again in 1979–80; it has become a major sweetener supplier in the U.S. market. Another area which has had some nonquantifiable effect on sugar production has been the production of ethanol from sugar cane in Brazil. This will certainly influence the supply of sugar in the coming decade. Both of these factors will be discussed later.

The reason for sugar's extreme volatility in times of scarcity and inactivity in periods of oversupply is its high degree of demand inelasticity and supply inelasticity.

Inelastic Demand

Perfectly inelastic demand means consumers tend not to increase or decrease consumption regardless of the change in price. Figure 19-2 portrays a hypothetical situation in which the demand for salt is perfectly inelastic. Consumption remains constant at quantity Q1 regardless of the price.

In reality sugar is not perfectly inelastic, but it did have a very high degree of demand inelasticity from 1967 to 1974 when prices rose from 3¢ to 66¢. This was because (1) consumers spend a relatively small proportion of their incomes on sugar; (2) consumers had no sizable competitive sweetener to turn to; and (3) the major consuming nations were forced to import sugar in the free market when the U.S. quota system and Commonwealth Sugar Agreements ended in 1974.

Since 1974 the inelastic demand for sugar appears to have eased somewhat because of the growth of its competitor—high-fructose corn syrup—and a leveling off of per capita consumption in major developed countries. The shaded area in Figure 19-3 represents the loss in demand when the product price is above 40¢ to 45¢/pound. Consumers resisted at this price, and many switched to high-fructose corn syrup.

Inelastic Supply

Perfectly inelastic supply is seen when producers show a small change in production in response to a relatively large change in price. Sugar producers do not state their planting intentions until they see a relatively large increase in price. Even then, the supplies do not become available until the crop is grown. In the case of beet sugar, the length of time until harvest is considerably long and adds to the "bust" part of the cycle. Sugar cane is not planted every year but rather only planted to meet demand or replanted to improve decreasing yields of an older crop. Sugar cane is harvested annually, although the growing season can last from 9 to 36 months. Once a cane crop is planted, it is only cut down to stumps at harvest. These stumps grow back, much like grass, for a new harvest. Once harvested, a cane crop may yield five to twenty harvests, or ratoons, as they are called. One can easily see why once a cane crop is in place it continues to produce sugar cane annually regardless of an oversupply of

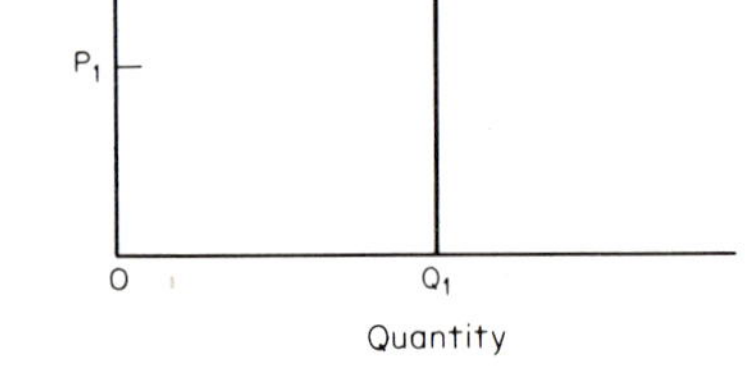

Figure 19-2 Inelastic demand curve for salt.

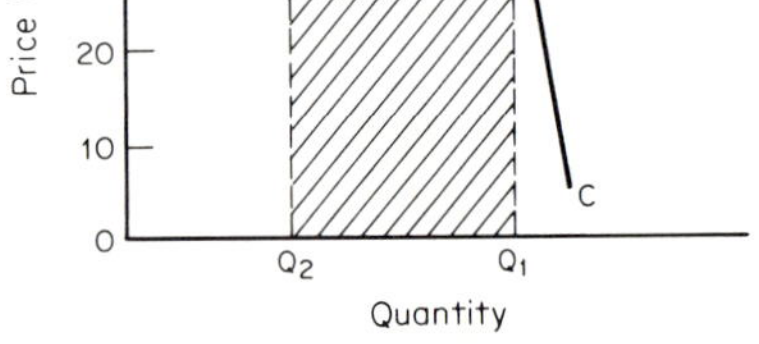

Figure 19-3 Hypothetical demand curve for sugar ($\overline{AC}$). $\overline{BC}$ = almost inelastic demand for sugar; $\overline{AB}$ = kink in demand as it shifts from inelastic to elastic. Hence, as price rises above 40¢, and a shift occurs from 40¢ to 50¢, the quantity demanded falls from Q1 to Q2. The lost demand can be measured as Q1 − Q2.

sugar on the world market. Supplies of cane sugar coming to market are also inelastic because many producing nations fail to pass on or delay passing on any of the increased foreign exchange earnings to the farmer. Hence there is no incentive for the farmer to increase production.

Government Programs Affecting Sugar

In the past 10 to 20 years, there has been a marked tendency for government to become more of a force in the world sugar market. As already mentioned, governments in some producing nations have at times postponed passing on to the farmer the benefits of higher world sugar export earnings. In the United States and the European Economic Community (EEC), there has been a trend to protect the domestic sugar industry or become self-sufficient in sugar. Self-sufficiency has become a reality in the EEC and has caused them to be a major world exporter. This has been accomplished by high subsidies to sugar growers in the EEC. In the United States, the domestic sugar industry is protected by tariffs on imported sugar. In Brazil, the government's Institute of Alcohol and Sugar decides on the amount of sugar and ethanol production annually, thereby dictating the acreage needed to achieve their objectives. The Cuban government established a 5-year plan so that by 1985 they will be producing 10 million tonnes of sugar. The Soviet Union announces 5-year plans and has in the past decade tried to become self-sufficient in many agricultural areas. The governments of India, Thailand, and the Philippines all dictate the amount of sugar exported annually to the world market. Depending on conditions in their domestic markets, their policies on exports can change radically overnight. Domestic pricing policies of the Indian government in the past 10 years have caused a sharp increase in the per capita consumption of sugar in India. Government policies of rationing were instituted in Poland and Iran in 1980, and affected the consumption of world sugar. Governments acting together in the International Sugar Agreement have attempted to keep the price of sugar within a narrow range for the benefit of producers and consumers. U.S. domestic legislation, with government loan programs and import tariffs, support prices above the world market production costs and protect domestic producers of beet and cane sugar.

The International Sugar Agreement

The International Sugar Agreement (ISA) is an agreement between producers and consumers, which has unsuccessfully attempted to keep the price of world sugar between 13¢ and 23¢ per pound by the use of export quotas and stockpiling sugar. In the past decade prices have not been maintained in the range established. A major flaw in the agreement is that the European Economic Community, the world's largest producer, is not in the agreement.

Figure 19-4 shows how the ISA is supposed to work. In a falling market quotas are imposed when the price falls below 16¢ per pound and stockpiling begins when prices go under 13¢ per pound. There is a free market between 16¢ and 21¢. In a rising market the stocks accumulated in the decline under 13¢ per pound are released at 21¢, 22¢, and 23¢ per pound.

Brazilian Ethanol Production

In the past decade, Brazil embarked on an ambitious program of producing ethanol from sugar cane at the expense of sugar production. This was caused by the cheap price of sugar, the increasingly high price of oil, and Brazil's dependence on imports for 90 percent of its oil. In addition, Brazil gives low-interest loans to car owners who convert their cars to run on gasohol. Brazil is also producing vehicles now that run on pure alcohol. Ethanol production in 1979 was 0.61 billion gallons and is forecast to reach 2 billion gallons in 1985.

Ethanol production affects the sugar market because it comes from sugar cane, as does raw sugar. The Brazilian government can produce either 1.71 million tonnes of raw sugar or 0.3 billion gallons of ethanol from 17.1 million tonnes of sugar cane. When sugar prices are low, there is incentive to produce ethanol but as prices rise, cane can be diverted to produce raw sugar at the expense of the Brazilians using ethanol for driving.

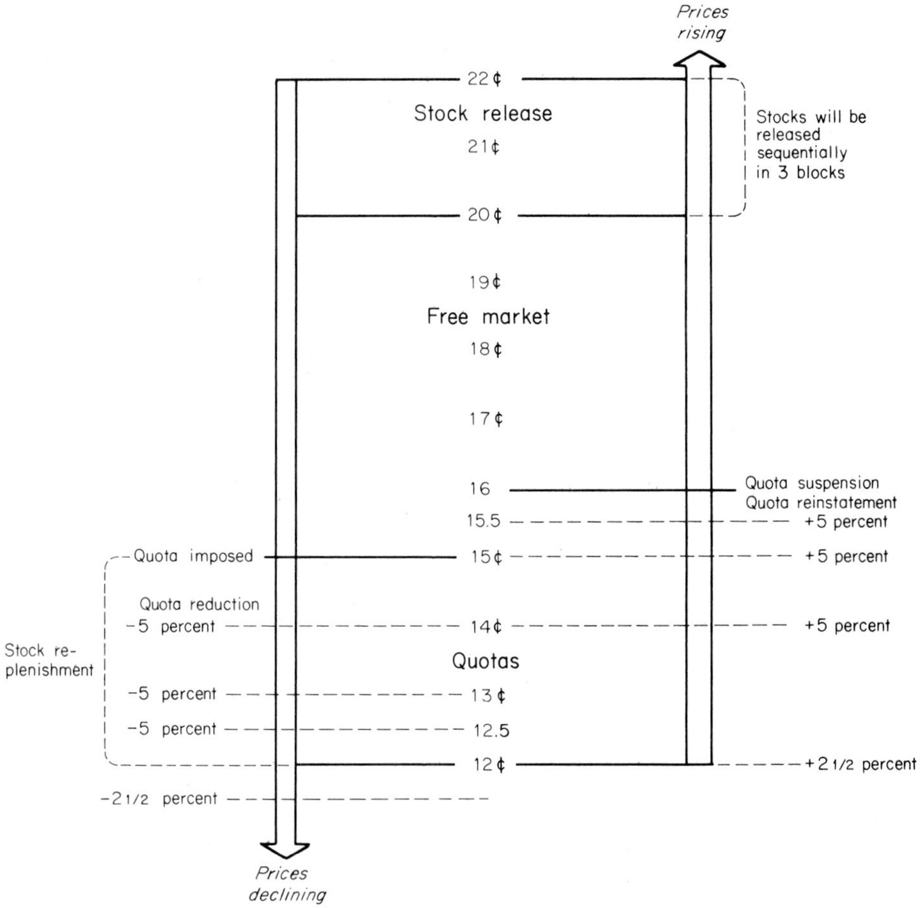

Figure 19-4 International Sugar Agreement. *(F. O. Licht)*

High-Fructose Corn Syrup

World consumption of corn sweeteners has increased in the past decade because of their competitive price advantage over sugar, especially in times of shortage (1974 and 1980). Current world consumption of corn sweeteners is estimated at 8 million tonnes for 1981 which is broken down into 3.6 million tonnes of regular corn syrup, 3.2 million tonnes of high-fructose corn syrup, and 1.25 million tonnes of dextrose. High-fructose corn syrup is a direct competitor with sugar. By 1985 the corn sweetener consumption should reach 11 million tonnes, 5.6 million tonnes of which will be high fructose.

Table 19-9 estimates the current and long-term potential penetration of high-fructose corn syrup by market.

The corn sweetener market has grown mainly in the United States and has displaced a significant amount of sugar demand in the United States. Table 19-10 estimates the U.S. per capita consumption of nutritive sweetener from 1976 to 1980, with forecasts for 1981 and 1982. These estimates show that total U.S. sweetener consumption has tended to increase since 1976, but that demand for sugar declined from 94.7 pounds per capita in 1976 to 85.3 pounds in 1980. This decline has been more than offset by an increase in consumption

TABLE 19-9 High-Fructose Corn Syrup versus Sugar *(Thousand tonnes dry)*

	Sugar	High-fructose corn syrup	High-fructose corn syrup's percent of sweetener market	Long-term theoretical penetration, %
Beverages	1960	1302	40	90
Baking	1135	391	25	25
Canning	405	305	43	60
Dairy products	432	176	29	30
Processed foods	396	101	20	40
Confections	816	11	1	5
Total industrial	5144	2286		

SOURCE: F. O. Licht, April 15, 1981.

TABLE 19-10 U.S. Nutritive Sweetener Per Capita Disappearance, 1976 to 1982

	(Pounds, refined or dry basis)		
Calendar years	Total nutritive sweeteners	All corn sweeteners	Sucrose (cane and beet)
1976	124.0	29.3	94.7
1977	128.7	31.7	97.0
1978	127.4	34.2	93.2
1979	128.6	37.4	91.2
1980	127.3	42.0	85.3
1981	128.4	45.6	82.8
1982	129.0	50.0	79.0

SOURCE: Amstar Corporation estimates.

of corn sweeteners. This corn sweetener demand increased from 29.3 pounds per capita in 1976 to 42.0 pounds per capita in 1980. The projections point to a continuation of this trend.

Dependence of Sugar Exporters on Foreign Exchange

Another problem that some producing nations have is their dependence on sugar as a source of foreign exchange. Some producers have no crop alternative because the soil is only good for growing cane sugar. This is especially true on islands like Cuba, the Philippines, and the Dominican Republic. Because of this, the sugar cycle discussed earlier becomes even harder to change. An additional socioeconomic problem arises for these governments because a large percentage of their society earn their livings in the sugar industry. A cutback in production means their economy will suffer, so political leaders are reluctant to make such a decision. This leads to a prolonged oversupply situation.

SUMMARY AND TRADING CONSIDERATIONS

Supply

1. Estimate the ending stocks for the current and following year. Compare this estimate to consumption and prior stocks-consumption ratios. A good source for this is F. O. Licht; however, their information tends to lag behind general commercial estimates, particularly in bull markets. Consequently, analysis of commercial projections is necessary. Good sources for this type of information are Schnitker Associates, Farr Mann Ltd., Czarnikow Rionda Inc., Woodhouse Inc., Amerop Inc., and the USDA.
2. Study the planted acreage estimates for major producers to determine whether they are expanding or decreasing production, assuming normal weather. This is particularly important in beet-producing countries because beets are planted every year.
3. Study the effect of the government actions on sugar production. The International Sugar Agreement, EEC policies to subsidize sugar production, and the U.S. government policies for support or loan prices to domestic producers can have a major impact on the amount of sugar available.
4. Study the economic justification for major producers altering their sugar production based on the relationship of market price to cost of production.

Demand

1. Estimate the normal consumption growth for the last 10 years in developed and undeveloped countries. F. O. Licht and the USDA are good sources.
2. Estimate the effect of interest rates and economic growth on sugar consumption.

3. Estimate the effect of high world sugar prices and importers that are price-sensitive—i.e., China, India, and Russia.
4. Estimate the effect of high-fructose corn syrup on sugar consumption.

Leading Indicators of Sugar Price Trends

1. In forthcoming bear markets it is a bearish sign when deferred options fail to rise as fast as the nearby contracts (and vice versa).
2. It is a bullish sign when prices fail to decline further in the face of increasing world stocks.
3. Several consecutive years of prices below the cost of production will lead to a rise in prices as a result of producers turning to more profitable crops.
4. A significant increase in acreage expansion by one or more major exporters is a bearish leading indicator.

Most Common Mistakes Made by Traders

1. The initial move in a bull market is commonly fought by the trade because of large existing world supplies. It is more precise to describe this price move as a situation in which the market becomes less bearish than as an outright bullish fundamental situation.
2. Be careful staying with positions when a month is expiring. Sugar typically expires weak and a weak "spot month" will pull the other months down too.
3. Be careful in bull markets—in buying with other commission houses on strength. It is better to buy on weakness where several trade houses are buying aggressively. This information on who is buying and selling is available from competent market monitors and floor brokers.
4. Speculators should not look to trade in and out of the sugar market but rather position trade for large market moves. Because of sugar's inelastic supply and demand properties, once a major trend begins it normally continues, enabling a speculator to trade for sustained moves of 10¢ to 15¢ or 20¢; in other words, do not liquidate a position just because it made a 5¢/pound increase in 2 weeks. A thorough understanding of sugar's fundamentals will give speculators the conviction to trade for large price moves. Figures 19-5 and 19-6 show the price trends in recent years in two sugar markets.

What to Look for at Bull Market Peaks

1. Prices have run up sharply for months and prices are at levels that are very economical for producers to expand production.
2. Talk of rationing in importing countries.
3. Reports of bullish information which fail to move prices higher.
4. An environment where trade houses and speculators are all bullish.

5. Reports of lower consumption, regardless of how much they are "played down" by analysts. Lower consumption forecasts are usually followed by further cuts in consumption estimates.
6. Feature stories of high prices on television and in the newspaper.
7. Defered options trending sideways while nearby options remain in strong uptrends.

What to Look for at Major Troughs

1. Prices are trading at or below the world cost of production.
2. Major producers begin to talk about cutting back acreage to produce other more profitable crops.

Figure 19-5 Monthly continuation; London number 2 raw sugar. *(Conti-Commodity Research Division)*

3. Talk of government action to cut production of subsidized sugar. This is particularly important in the United States and the EEC.
4. Forecasts of surplus production failing to cause a further price decline.
5. Several consecutive years of low stable prices.
6. Deferred options make new contract highs after trading for 4 to 6 months.

CONTRACT DATA

Active Markets

New York Number 11 Sugar Contract—Specifications

Quoted in cents per pound
Size—112,000 pounds
Value of 1¢ move = $11.20; normal limit move = 50¢ (limits can be expanded to $1, $1.50, and $2.00) (Note that the first two options have no limit.)

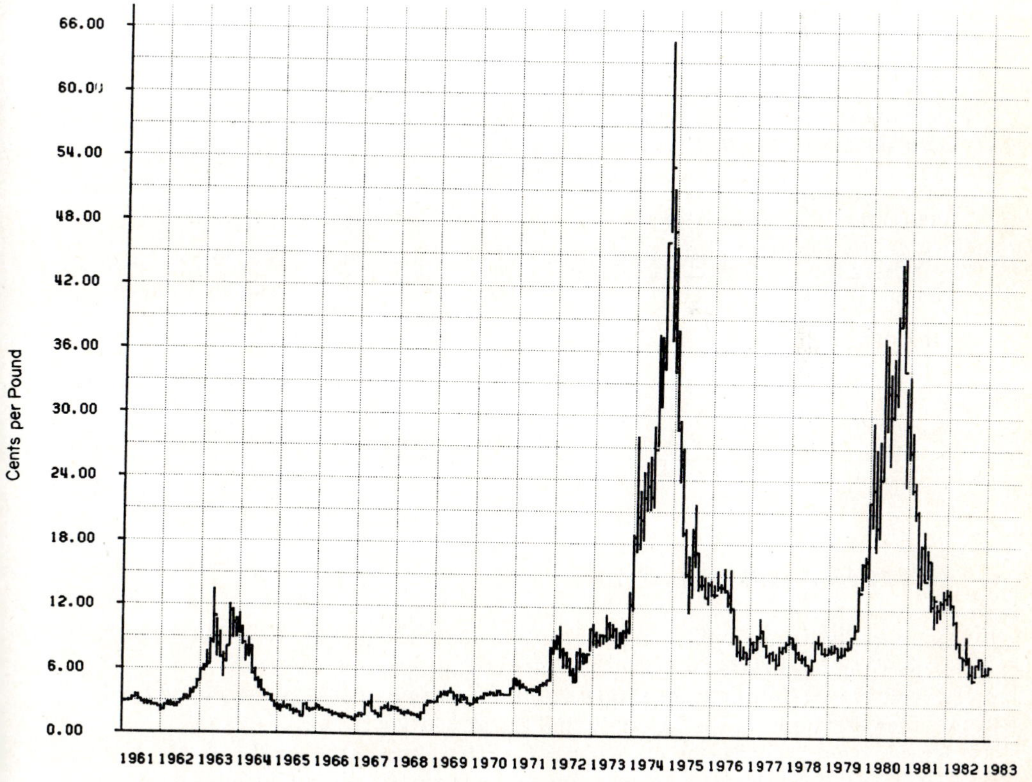

Figure 19-6 Monthly continuation, CSCE number 11 sugar. *(ContiCommodity Research Division)*

Exchange: Coffee, Cocoa and Sugar Exchange, New York
Trading hours: 10:00 A.M. to 1:45 P.M. New York Time
Deliverable raw sugar: Growths from Argentina, Australia, Brazil, Honduras, Colombia, Costa Rica, Dominican Republic, El Salvador, Ecuador, Fiji Islands, French Antilles, Guatemala, India, Jamaica, Mauritius, Mexico, Nicaragua, Peru, Philippines, South Africa, Swaziland, Taiwan, Thailand, Trinidad, and the United States.
A growth or growths may be added to or deleted as deliverable upon recommendation by the sugar committee. Sugar delivered can be made at any of the ports where deliverable growths are produced.
The receiver (buyer) shall provide vessels suitable for carrying the sugar. This is important because, unlike many commodities, sugar buyers must take delivery wherever the seller wants to make delivery. The buyer also has to send a ship to pick up the sugar and instruct the shipping company where to take the sugar.

London Sugar (Number 4 Contract)—Specifications
Quoted in pounds sterling per tonne
Size: 50 tonnes
Value of a £1 move = £50 sterling
Exchange: United Terminal Sugar Association, London
Limit move = 20 pound (Note that the first two options have no limit.)
Trading hours: 10:30 A.M. to 12:30 P.M.; 2:30 A.M. to 5:00 P.M. London Time (a kerb market continues until just after the New York close)

Explanation of the Effect of a Change in Pounds Sterling on the U.S. Price of Sugar

If sterling rises 5¢ from \$2.00 to \$2.05, the price of London sugar will fall relative to the New York price assuming no other economic factors change:

New York sugar price	London price in sterling \$2.00	Sterling \$2.05
11¢ per pound	121.25 per pound	118.30 per pound

Conversion formula:

$$\frac{\text{London price per tonne} \times \text{exchange rate}}{\text{Pounds in a tonne}} = \text{cents per pound}$$

$$\frac{(\text{pound}/121.25) \times (\$2.00)}{2{,}204.67 \text{ pounds}} = 11¢ \text{ per pound}$$

SOURCES OF INFORMATION:

Commodity Research Bureau, "Sugar and Its Shifting Role in the World Economy" and "How to Analyze the World Sugar Futures Market."
Development Center of the Organization for Economic Cooperation and Study, "The Structure of the International Sugar Market," 1976.
Florida Sugar Cane Growers, "Sugar Country" (movie), (813) 983-9151.
F. O. Licht's International Sugar Reports. *Statistical information and studies on the sugar market and high-fructose corn syrup*
Foreign Agricultural Service and U.S. Department of Agriculture "Report on World Sugar Supply and Demand—1980 and 1985."

G. W. Joynson & Co. Ltd., ICCH Commodities Yearbook, 1980–81. *Also contains a directory of commodity traders—commercial and speculative firms*

International Sugar Organization Yearbooks, 1979 and 1980.

Kolodny, Saul, "Corn and Sugar as Energy for Man and Machine." *Seminar speech before the New York Society of Security Analysts, March 1981.*

Massey Ferguson, "A Taste of Energy" (movie), P.O. Box 686, Clewiston, FL 33440.

U.S. Beet Sugar Association, *The Sugar Beet Story*, 1959.

U.S. Department of Agriculture, "Sugar and Sweetener Outlook and Situation."

CHAPTER

20

Frozen Orange Juice

Thomas Bell and Steven Gilson

INTRODUCTION

Frozen concentrated orange juice (FCOJ) was introduced toward the end of World War II, and its popularity has paralleled the growth of the Florida orange industry. Approximately 75 percent of U.S. orange output stems from Florida and more than 90 percent of the country's processed oranges come from Florida. In 1966, futures trading in FCOJ began on the Citrus Associates of the New York Cotton Exchange with the contract specifying delivery to licensed exchange warehouses in Florida. The contract has provided a useful medium for growers, processors, dealers, consumers, and speculators.

PRODUCTION

Florida's orange producing capacity tripled between 1950 and 1970 and has continued to grow as young trees mature. An orange tree normally does not produce marketable fruit for its first 4 to 5 years; it increases in productivity until it is about 10 years old, and continues to bear quality fruit for 30 to 40 years. Improved cultural practices and increasing acreage under irrigation have further benefited production. (Table 20-1 lists U.S. production from 1974 to 1981, along with other major producers.)

In Florida, the peak harvest of oranges consumed as fruit runs from December through June (see Table 20-2). Oranges for the processed product (FCOJ) are brought to a processor where they are halved and crushed. The juice is then

TABLE 20-1 World Orange and Tangerine Production Highlights
(Million pounds)

	1974–75	1975–76	1976–77	1977–78	1978–79	1979–80	1980–81
United States	9,913	183	10,189	9,256	8,888	11,496	11,477
Brazil	5,716	6,596	4,321	8,205	8,665	9,308	—
Japan	3,953	4,234	3,575	3,663	3,300	3,945	3,339
Spain	2,479	2,643	2,441	2,514	2,544	2,597	2,713
Italy	2,097	1,931	2,259	1,942	1,959	2,105	2,160
Argentina	959	972	990	925	917	982	—
Israel	1,016	95	967	949	1,013	962	968
Mexico	1,111	905	1,283	750	1,398	1,810	1,645
World	31,056	32,321	29,967	32,792	30,820		

SOURCE: Estimates based on United States Department of Agriculture *Agricultural Attaches* reports.

subjected to an evaporative process which removes the water from the juice. The product of this process is called "orange solids" and is composed of soluble sugars, citric acid, and vitamin D. It is this product, quoted in pounds of orange solids, which is traded on the futures exchange. Pounds of orange solids are the basis for grower returns from a processor rather than a flat price per box of fruit.

TABLE 20-2 USDA'S Monthly Estimates of Florida Orange Production
(Million boxes and season average yield or gallons per box—early, midseason, valencias, and temples)

Season	Oct.	Nov.	Dec.	Jan.	Feb.	Mar.	Apr.	May	June	July	Final
1960–61	90.5	90.5	89.5	87.5	87.5	88.5	89.5	88.0	87.5	89.0	86.7
1961–62	99.0	99.0	99.0	99.0	96.0	100.0	101.0	104.0	109.0	113.0	113.4
1962–63	118.7	118.7	120.5	84.5	81.0	77.0	74.5	74.5	74.5	74.5	74.5
1963–64	64.5	64.5	64.5	64.0	5.0	65.2	64.2	63.2	60.8	58.3	58.3
1964–65	83.6	83.6	81.6	81.6	80.6	82.2	85.2	85.2	86.2	86.2	86.2
1965–66	91.3	91.3	91.3	94.3	94.3	94.0	95.5	98.5	98.5	100.0	100.4
1966–67	139.4	142.4	142.4	142.4	142.4	142.4	147.0	147.0	146.2	146.2	144.5
1967–68	100.4	100.4	98.4	98.4	98.4	98.4	98.4	101.1	104.0	104.0	105.0
1968–69	129.0	133.0	136.0	130.0	126.5	128.5	133.5	136.5	136.5	135.2	134.2
1969–70	149.0	149.0	140.0	140.0	139.0	139.0	135.2	139.2	139.2	143.0	142.9
1970–71	174.5	174.5	169.5	166.5	165.5	154.5	154.0	150.0	150.2	147.8	147.3
1971–72	137.0	137.0	142.0	142.0	142.0	141.5	141.5	142.0	143.9	142.9	142.3
1972–73	179.0	179.0	173.0	173.0	173.0	173.0	173.3	173.3	175.1	175.1	174.8
1973–74	165.3	165.3	162.0	162.0	167.0	169.0	169.0	169.0	169.0	171.4	171.1
1974–75	179.5	179.5	179.3	173.3	179.3	181.3	181.3	182.9	182.9	180.9	178.6
1975–76	177.5	177.5	177.5	177.5	177.5	177.5	180.3	180.3	183.3	185.3	186.7
1976–77	214.5	214.7	214.7	214.7	186.0	184.5	195.8	195.8	192.8	192.8	190.6
1977–78	169.2	169.2	169.2	171.2	170.7	170.7	172.8	173.2	173.2	173.2	172.7
1978–79	171.8	171.8	171.8	167.8	167.8	167.8	167.7	167.6	167.6	168.6	168.7
1979–80	205.4	205.4	205.4	205.4	205.4	205.4	209.0	209.0	209.0	210.9	212.7
1980–81	208.7	208.7	208.7	208.7	176.5	176.5	175.2	175.2	175.2	175.7	176.0
1981–82	170.2	170.2	170.2	166.2	136.0	136.0	131.0	130.0	128.0	125.8	125.8
1982–83	143.0	—	147.0	147.0	147.0	145.0	145.2	142.2	142.2	140.2	139.5

SOURCE: United States Department of Agriculture Florida Crop and Livestock Reporting Service.

Most of Florida's oranges are unpriced when delivered to the processing plant. Grower cooperatives and participation plans account for about 70 percent of total production. Typically, a growers' co-op would pool the receipts of its members' fruit and return them to its members in the form of dividends after deducting the costs involved in selling the fruit to a processor. Some co-ops have developed their own processing capacity. Growers are assured of a buyer for their fruit, while a processor who enters into an arrangement with the co-op is assured of a supply, barring a crop failure. Growers can also enter into a participation plan with a processor whereby the fruit is not priced when delivered to the plant. Instead, the eventual price paid to the grower is a function of the processor's end product realization or, typically, the average wholesale, or "card," price for a dozen 6-ounce cans. Some processors also maintain their own groves.

Much of the priced fruit is handled by independent dealers or "bird dogs" who make spot purchases of a grower's oranges and then sell to a processor on a per-pound-of-solids basis. This price, called the "delivered-in" price, is closely aligned with the futures market since it represents spot conditions. A grower who sells fruit on a spot basis is at a price risk, as is the dealer who then sells it to a processor for the prevailing market price. Of course, there may be premiums paid for assuming this risk, but a grower or dealer who is involved in spot transactions would normally seek protection by using the futures market. Processors, since they carry inventory, are also at risk and use futures as a risk management tool. It might appear that a processor has very little risk since the processor's major cost, the procurement of fruit, may not be determined until the end of the season. However, the desire of a grower to maximize returns means that the grower will seek out a processor who uses the most efficient management tools, including futures, which result in a better return to the grower. Most retailers are not involved with futures, since processors typically will provide some form of price protection and the wholesale or card price will tend to be fairly static through the season. Dairies or reprocessors that buy bulk orange juice and market a single-strength product do make use of futures.

Weather Impacts

In analyzing the fundamentals of the FCOJ market, one first has to be aware of the potential for a damaging freeze. The Florida citrus belt is located in the central and south-central portions of the state, an area susceptible to freezes. The freeze "season" normally begins in December and ends in the beginning of March. Valencias, due to their late maturity, will be the most susceptible oranges. Their harvest season begins in February, as compared to the early and midseason varieties harvested in September. Recent major damaging freezes have occurred in December 1962, January 1977, and January 1981.* Readings

*Other freezes occurred in 1748, 1766, 1774, 1799, 1828, February 1835, 1850, 1857, December 1870, December 1880, December 1884, January 1886, December 1894, February 1895, February 1899, January 1905, December 1906, December 1909, February 1917, January 1928, December 1934, January 1940, February 1947, December 1957, and January 1971. These dates have led to numerous cyclical projections.

of 28°F to 32°F rarely indicate serious damage. Temperatures below 28°F can cause damage to fruit quality. Two to four hours of 27°F or lower will damage the orange trees' branches and limbs, causing fruit droppage. These conditions are the most severe because subsequent production will be impaired: freeze-damaged trees may take several years to recover their full bearing capacity, while severely damaged trees may have to be uprooted and replanted. After a freeze occurs, much of the fruit can be salvaged (but it then yields considerably less juice than before the cold). Harvesting crews and processors work around the clock in an effort to get as much as possible of the fruit in before further dehydration or rotting renders the fruit useless. Freezes are associated with arctic high-pressure air masses which move southeast from Canada. Snow cover in the Midwest will facilitate movement of the system south towards Florida. A storm moving up the east coast also seems to be a contributing variable in the formation of a freeze. The orange tree is dormant between 35° and 50°F. Consequently, extremely warm nights and high rainfall can both harm fruit quality and increase any damage potential due to a freeze.

Crop Yield

The first official estimate of the Florida orange crop is released by the U.S. Department of Agriculture in October and the market often reacts violently as expectations for the new crop have been building throughout the summer (see Table 20-3). The Florida crop is really two crops: early and midseason varieties (which are harvested from December through February), and the later-maturing Valencia oranges (harvested from March through June). Valencias are sweeter and yield more juice. It is important to recognize that oranges accumulate soluble solids, or juice content, more rapidly as they near maturity. A

TABLE 20-3 USDA'S Monthly Estimates of Season Average Yield *(Gallons per box of FCOJ)*

	Oct.	Nov.	Dec.	Jan.	Feb.	Mar.	Apr.	May	June	July	Final
1970–71	1.30	—	1.32	1.32	—	1.21	1.20	1.20	1.21	1.21	1.21
1971–72	1.28	1.23	—	1.25	1.29	1.31	1.31	1.31	1.29	1.29	1.29
1972–73	1.29	—	1.26	1.33	1.32	1.32	1.32	1.32	1.33	1.33	1.33
1973–74	1.28	—	1.32	1.30	1.30	1.30	1.31	1.30	1.30	1.30	1.30
1974–75	1.29	—	1.29	1.29	1.29	1.29	1.29	1.30	1.31	1.31	1.31
1975–76	1.35	—	1.35	1.34	1.31	1.30	1.30	1.30	1.29	1.26	1.26
1976–77	1.29	—	1.29	1.29	1.17	1.12	1.08	1.07	1.07	1.07	1.07
1977–78	1.28	—	1.28	1.25	1.25	1.24	1.24	1.24	1.24	1.24	1.24
1978–79	1.29	—	1.32	1.33	1.33	1.33	1.33	1.33	1.33	1.33	1.33
1979–80	1.30	—	1.28	1.32	1.33	1.33	1.31	1.32	1.33	1.33	1.33
1980–81	1.37	—	1.37	1.37	1.19	1.19	1.19	1.20	1.21	1.21	1.21
1981–82	1.42	—	1.42	1.41	1.28	1.29	1.28	1.27	1.28	1.28	1.28
1982–83	1.37	—	1.37	1.42	1.43	1.44	1.45	1.47	1.49	1.48	1.48

SOURCE: United States Department of Agriculture Florida Crop and Livestock Reporting Service.

January freeze, therefore, has a much greater impact on the still maturing Valencia crop and its potentially higher juice yield. Juice yield per box is calculated on the basis of brix, or percentage of orange solids by weight in a solution (see Table 20-3). For example, Florida's current* minimum brix requirement is 42° brix which means that 42 percent of the volume is composed of orange solids. At 42 percent brix, 4.2 pounds of orange solids make 1 gallon of FCOJ. A 90-pound box of oranges that yields 5.7 pounds of solids would have a juice yield per box of 1.36 gallons at 42° brix. In an effort to distinguish its product, Florida has in past years maintained a higher brix standard, and a slightly sweeter flavor, than the 41.8° minimum required by the FDA, which is applicable to out-of-state reprocessors. However, Florida has lowered its minimum from the prior 45° minimum, and a move is underway to align Florida with the national minimum. The effect of a lower brix level on a given supply of oranges is to increase FCOJ production (in gallons) since fewer pounds of orange solids will be required to make a gallon of concentrate.

Brazilian Production

In recent years, Brazil has developed its producing and processing capacity to the point that it is the leading exporter of FCOJ in the world. The rising U.S. domestic consumption of orange juice has kept U.S. exports minimal, and Brazil has become a major producer, supplying Canada and western Europe. In times of a domestic supply shortfall—following a damaging Florida freeze, for example—Brazil has been able to make up much of the difference. Even without a supply problem, Brazilian FCOJ, which is slightly more acidic than Florida juice, has found its way into Florida when entrepreneurs perceive a price advantage, and the juice can then be blended with Florida concentrate to achieve the desired taste. A tariff of 35¢/pound of solids is levied on imported concentrates, which, however, can be almost completely retrieved under a duty drawback system whereby a like amount of product is exported within 3 years. The tariff, coupled with transportation costs, generally prices Brazilian juice above the market during a normal supply year.

In recent years Brazilian imports have become increasingly important to the market. Brazil's FCOJ industry grew up after the Florida freeze of 1962. Their major markets are western Europe and Canada, but U.S. consumption of FCOJ dwarfs the rest of the world, to the extent that the Brazilian product has found its way to the U.S. market in increasing volume. During the 1980s Brazil is expected to rival Florida as the leading FCOJ producer in the world. This factor, along with a slowing U.S. population rate, implies a shortage of production over the longer term, with intermediate surges following a damaging Florida freeze. Detailed data on Brazil is given in Tables 20-4, 20-5, and 20-6.

*The new brix requirement as of December 1, 1981 is 41.8 percent, with a maximum tolerance of 0.2 percent.

TABLE 20-4 Estimated Brazilian FCOJ Availability and Movement, 1980 and 1981 Brazilian Production Seasons

	1980		1981	
	Thousand tonnes 65° brix	Million gallons 42° brix	Thousand tonnes 65° brix	Million gallons 42° brix*
Availability				
Beginning inventory	62	21.3	38	13.1
Production	479	165.2	507	174.8
Total	541	186.5	545	187.9
Movement				
Domestic	16	5.5†	15	5.2
Exports	487	167.9	490	168.9
Total	503	173.4	505	174.1
Carry-over	38	13.1	40	13.8

*344.8 42° brix gallons per tonne.

†98 million gallons moved in markets outside the United States.

SOURCE: Department of Citrus, University of Florida; data from USDA, Foreign Agricultural Circular Update on Brazilian Citrus, May 1981. Some values reported have been revised.

TABLE 20-5 Estimated Relationship between Brazilian FCOJ Prices and the Cost of Retail Packed Product Made from Brazilian FCOJ in Florida Processing Plants, 1981–82 Season

Item						
	Dollars per tonne					
FOB price, Santos, Brazil	800	900	1000	1100	1200	1300
	Cents per pounds' solids					
	55.8	62.8	69.8	76.8	83.7	90.7
Transportation cost to Florida port	10.0	10.0	10.0	10.0	10.0	10.0
Cost at Florida port	65.8	72.8	79.8	86.8	93.7	100.7
Tariff	34.0	34.0	34.0	34.0	34.0	34.0
Transportation from port to Florida plant	2.0	2.0	2.0	2.0	2.0	2.0
Florida citrus equalization tax	2.6	2.6	2.6	2.6	2.6	2.6
Total cost at Florida plant	104.4	111.4	118.4	125.4	132.3	139.3
	$/48 6-oz. 42° brix					
Juice cost per case 42° brix 9.351 pounds solids	9.76	10.42	11.07	11.73	12.37	13.03
Casing, warehousing, and selling cost per case	3.80	3.80	3.80	3.80	3.80	3.80
FOB cost per case at Florida plant	13.56	14.22	14.87	15.53	16.17	16.83
FOB cost per dozen 6-ounce	3.39	3.56	3.72	3.88	4.04	4.21

SOURCE: Department of Citrus, University of Florida.

TABLE 20-6 Brazilian FCOJ Price Quotes, Units of Measure, and Cost Factors

I. *Units used for quoting Brazilian FCOJ prices*
- U.S. $/tonne FOB Santos
- U.S. $/gallon FOB Santos
- U.S. $/tonne C.I.F. Florida port
- U.S. $/gallon C.I.F. Florida port

II. *Relationships between units of measure for FCOJ*

1 tonne	= 2204.6 pounds
1 tonne 65° brix	= 1433 pounds solids (p.s.)
1 tonne 65° brix	= 200.84 gallons 65° brix
1 tonne 65° brix	= 344.8 gallons 42° brix
1 gallon 65° brix = 7.135 pounds solids	= 1.717 gallons 42° brix
FCOJ/case (6- and 12-ounce cans)	= 2.25 gallons
1 gallon 42° brix	= 4.156 pounds solids
1 55-gallon drum 65° brix (contains about 52 gallons)	= 370 pounds solids and weighs about 625 pounds

III. *Additional costs for Brazilian product delivered to Florida plants*

Add to FOB Santos price

1. Transportation to Florida port	10¢/p.s.
2. Handling and transport to plant	2.0¢/p.s.
3. Equalization tax (Florida Citrus Advertising Tax)	2.6¢/p.s.
4. Tariff	34¢/p.s.
5. Reprocessing costs to convert to 48 6-oz. cans	$3.80/can 48 6-ounce

SOURCE: Department of Citrus, University of Florida.

CONSUMPTION

Concentrate consumption has soared along with production. In 1960–61, 84 million gallons of FCOJ were shipped while in the 1979–80 season over 230 million gallons were moved. In recent years, the increasing popularity of single strength, ready-to-drink chilled juice, in cartons and bottles, has provided a growing outlet for bulk concentrate which can then be reconstituted into single-strength juice.

The Florida industry has made great efforts to promote its product, stressing its nutritional and flavorful qualities. This has contributed to increasing the consumption base for FCOJ, as has population growth. In brief, the market can be characterized as having a steadily growing consumption base with a fluctuating supply.

FCOJ is marketed under three categories: retail sizes, institutional sizes, and bulk concentrate. Retail FCOJ is packed in three sizes: 6-, 12-, and 16-ounce sizes. The 6-ounce size is the standard, but over the years the 12-ounce container has become the most popular. Retail FCOJ is sold either under a manufacturer's label, such as Tropicana or Minute Maid, or the private label of a supermarket. The wholesale, or card price, is the relevant price for a retailer, representing the price for a dozen 6-ounce cans. Institutional concentrate is packed in 32-ounce containers for military use, cafeterias, and schools. Bulk FCOJ is packed in 55-gallon drums which can then be reprocessed. The increasing popularity of chilled single-strength orange juice has increased consumption of FCOJ which is shipped in bulk to a reprocessor.

ASSESSMENT OF THE SUPPLY-AND-DEMAND BALANCE

To estimate FCOJ production in gallons, we must first multiply the USDA Florida orange estimate by the percentage of oranges utilized for FCOJ. In the early 1970s, approximately 75 to 77 percent of Florida's oranges were utilized for FCOJ; in recent seasons, closer to 81 percent have been used for concentrate. The number of boxes utilized multiplied by the indicated yield per box gives FCOJ production in gallons. For example, an estimated 200 million boxes of Florida oranges with a yield of 1.3 gallons per box would mean 162 million boxes for FCOJ, based on 81 percent utilization, multiplied by the yield per box, would project FCOJ production at 210.6 million gallons. The major obstacle to this realization is a freeze, which would reduce both box count and yield per box.

FCOJ consumption is measured by weekly movement figures which are released by the Florida Citrus Processors' Association (see Table 20-7). In addition, this report will also give production, imports, and inventory levels. Brazilian imports are becoming increasingly important, as their output and exports to U.S. markets increase yearly.

The first question to be asked when analyzing the FCOJ market, as in many other markets, is whether there will be a stock decrease or increase this season. Total supply consists of carry-over stocks, production, and imports. Demand is measured by movement. The remainder, carry-out stocks, when related to projected movement, is an excellent measure of tightness in the market. A 10-week supply of FCOJ (end-year movement multiplied by 10) is normally considered adequate inventory until new crop juice comes in. The important price-determining factors then become a matter of what price is necessary to move a certain amount of product. A general formula is that price at retail will have to drop proportionally more than the desired increases in gallons to be moved, unless real income and the price of milk (a close substitute) are projected to offset the desired increase in movement. Some crude parameters are: (1) prices must be dropped at first more than the desired percentage increase in movement; and (2) prices can then be adjusted upward on a percentage basis by the same anticipated increase in real income and further adjusted upward by the same anticipated increase in milk prices. Further analysis is obtained by Table 20-8 which illustrates seasonal characteristics of prices. Delivered-in fruit prices are roughly aligned with futures, allowing for processing costs and a freeze premium that futures command over cash during the freeze season. This

TABLE 20-7 Pack and Movement of Florida FCOJ with Beginning and Ending Stocks *(1000 gallons)**

Season	Beginning stocks	Net season pack	Imports	FCOJ movement, Dec. to Nov.	Carry-over† ending stocks
1951–52	7,324	44,031	N.A.	43,066	8,289
1952–53	8,289	46,779	N.A.	50,514	4,554
1953–54	4,554	65,531	N.A.	53,711	16,417
1954–55	16,417	65,481	N.A.	72,184	9,713
1955–56	9,713	69,592	N.A.	66,462	12,843
1956–57	12,843	72,455	N.A.	73,742	11,556
1957–58	11,566	56,764	N.A.	61,601	6,719
1958–59	6,719	79,981	N.A.	70,096	16,605
1959–60	16,605	77,999	N.A.	84,941	9,663
1960–61	9,663	84,374	N.A.	80,405	13,631
1961–62	13,631	115,866	N.A.	95,748	33,750
1962–63	33,750	51,648	N.A.	69,998	15,399
1963–64	15,399	56,124	1,739	61,386	10,136
1964–65	10,136	90,342	1,473	78,665	21,814
1965–66	21,814	77,577	888	86,563	12,828
1966–67	12,828	132,155	400	117,758	27,225
1967–68	27,225	87,341	3,644	101,681	12,885
1968–69	12,885	108,043	2,460	103,528	17,400
1969–70	17,400	126,402	162	117,236	26,566
1970–71	26,566	133,744	3,981	137,743	22,568
1971–72	22,568	145,897	6,564	140,715	27,750
1972–73	27,750	180,174	1,230	160,552	47,372
1973–74	47,371	176,445	3,465	174,956	48,861
1974–75	48,861	178,174	5,778	187,216	50,759
1975–76	50,759	186,265	6,473	191,728	53,709
1976–77	53,709	158,035	9,456	199,025	25,526
1977–78	25,526	161,204	23,940	180,182	30,909
1978–79	30,909	173,053	28,735	200,790	37,385
1979–80	37,385	256,400	16,534	232,774	54,856‡
1980–81	57,280†	174,537	56,851	228,403	60,107§
1981–82	66,353	133,294	70,325	223,144	53,379

*Figures may not add because of recent conversions of various components to new 42° brix equivalent. Carry-over figures are final numbers.

†Statistical discrepancies cause the ratio of supply to utilization to be unbalanced.

‡Carry-over of 54.8 million gallons of 45° brix is equivalent to 57.3 million gallons at 43.4° brix.

§Revised 1980–81 carry out at 42° brix, effective December 1, 1981.

can be considered the "basis," representing the difference between cash and futures. In the winter, the futures premium to cash has gone to over 20¢ per pound, subsequently narrowing into only a slight premium in the spring. For instance, in December 1979, delivered-in prices averaged 84¢ per pound while the nearby January contract averaged close to 95¢ per pound. In April, delivered-in prices averaged 86¢ per pound and the nearby May averaged 89¢ per pound. This narrowing of the basis relationship provides the opportunity for

TABLE 20-8 U.S. Wholesale Prices of FCOJ by Months, 1975–1983
(Dollars per case of twelve 6-ounce cans)

	Jan.	Feb.	Mar.	Apr.	May	June	July	Aug.	Sept.	Oct.	Nov.	Dec.
1975	2.244	2.254	2.254	2.254	2.254	2.254	2.246	2.246	2.358	2.383	2.383	2.383
1976	2.383	2.352	2.352	2.383	2.383	2.383	2.187	2.187	2.187	2.187	2.187	2.089
1977	2.040	2.776	2.752	2.752	2.752	2.910	2.910	3.101	3.223	3.223	3.459	3.508
1978	3.508	3.508	3.514	3.514	3.514	3.514	3.514	3.514	3.514	3.514	3.649	3.787
1979	3.787	3.787	3.787	3.787	3.787	3.787	3.787	3.787	3.787	3.787	3.787	3.787
1980	3.787	3.787	3.787	3.700	3.700	3.626	3.626	3.626	3.626	3.626	3.441	3.441
1981	3.373	4.077	4.543	4.920	4.920	4.920	4.920	4.920	4.874	3.350	3.263	3.138
1982	3.129	3.288	3.364	3.282	3.165	3.095	3.094	3.071	3.078	3.077	3.075	3.032
1983	3.040	3.008	2.996	2.991	3.023	3.007	3.010	3.008				

SOURCE: Bureau of Labor Statistics, Department of Labor.

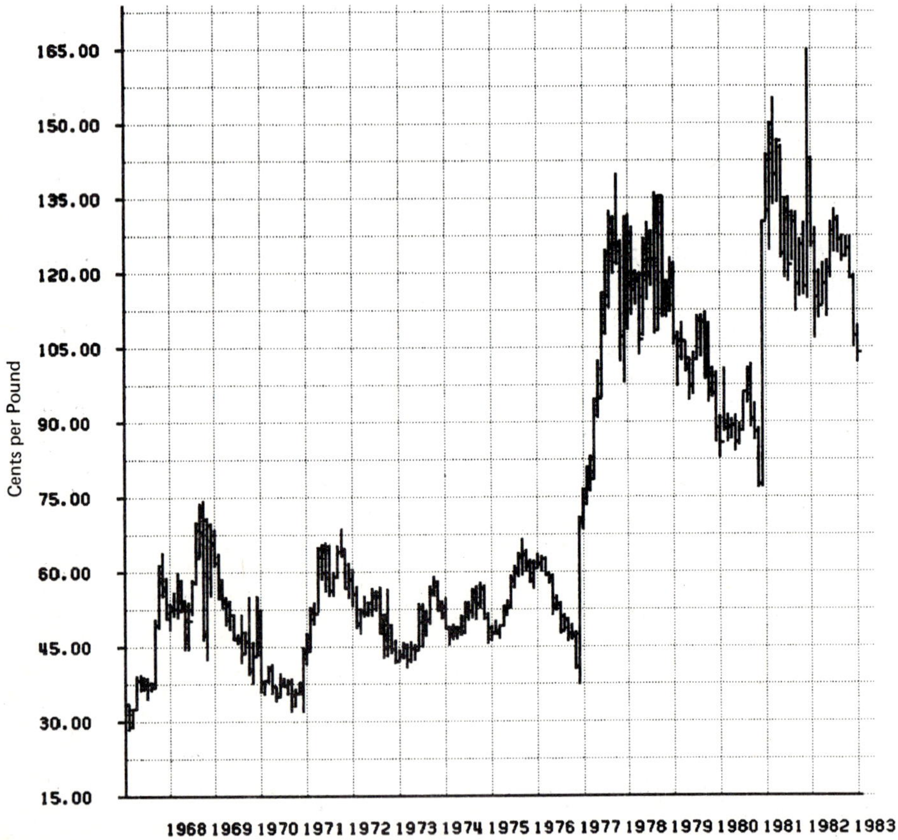

Figure 20-1 Monthly continuation, orange juice. *(ContiCommodity Research Division)*

processors or growers to hedge part of their production by selling futures. Figure 20-1 depicts the FCOJ price movements from 1968 to 1983.

The other side of pricing FCOJ is the card price for a dozen 6-ounce cans. This price typically does not fluctuate very much over the course of the season, so it gives only a rough indication of market conditions.

In seasons of surplus production, processors will offer premiums of discounts off the card price in an effort to stimulate movement and draw down inventories. This can have a bullish impact on futures, especially if it has been preceded by a slide in prices through the spring since offtake is likely to be increased and carry-out stocks are then potentially reduced.

SUMMARY AND TRADING CONSIDERATIONS

I. Critical factors affecting the orange juice supply-and-demand relationship

- **a.** USDA crop production estimates
- **b.** Weekly movement figures
- **c.** Brazilian imports

II. Leading indicators of orange juice price trends

- **a.** It is a bullish sign when nearby options rise at a faster rate than distant contracts (and vice versa).
- **b.** It is a bullish sign when forecasted crop year and world or U.S. stocks start to fall after many months of a rising trend (and vice-versa).

III. Avoiding common mistakes made by investors and traders

- **a.** Be particularly cautious when trading orange juice near delivery periods, especially during the week preceding each First Notice Day (FND), because the market is very volatile.
- **b.** Be aware of seasonal trends.
- **c.** Avoid trading in contract months when there is a small open interest.
- **d.** Be aware of the freeze period because the market tends to move seasonally upward irrespective of market fundamentals.

IV. What to look for at bull market peaks

- **a.** Prices have been running up sharply for several months in anticipation of, or because of, a freeze.
- **b.** Feature stories on the network news or the front page of newspapers describing pandemonium in the markets and traders expecting prices to go much higher.
- **c.** An exponentially rising trend in daily volume and open interest on the exchange.

V. What to look for at major troughs: Prices have been falling sharply and predictions of even lower prices abound.

CONTRACT DATA

Traded New York Cotton Exchange

Trading hours	10:15 A.M. to 2:45 p.m. Eastern Standard Time.
Contract unit	15,000 pounds orange solids.
Delivery point	Licensed warehouse in the state of Florida
Price quotation	Cents per pound of solids.
Minimum daily price fluctuation	0.05¢/pound ($5/contract).
Maximum daily price fluctuation	5¢/pounds of solids ($750/contract). Limit is expanded to 10¢/pound above or below the previous settlement for the spot contract only, during the final 3 days before the final trading day. All other contracts continue to trade with a 5¢/pound of solids daily limit.
Delivery months	January, March, May, July, September, and November. Contracts are traded up to 18 months out from the spot contract (i.e., as of November 1984 trading commences through the March 1986 delivery).
Product specifications:	
Quantity	15,000 pounds of orange solids (with permitted variation of 3 percent above or below), of U.S. grade A concentrated orange juice.
Brix value	51° to 66° (brix range may not exceed 3° from the average for the lot delivered).
Brix value to acid ratio	Not less than 13 to 1, not more than 19 to 1.
Minimum score and component factors	Total minimum score 94 Flavor component 37 Color component 37 Maximum score for defects 19
Bottom (sinking) pulp permitted	12 percent maximum on initial test.
Recoverable oil	Not less than 0.005 percent nor more than 0.02 percent
Packaging	Concentrate for delivery must be packed in 55-gallon rated capacity steel drums, with a double liner, and stored in licensed warehouses located in the state of Florida, designated as delivery points by the exchange.

SOURCES OF INFORMATION

Department of Citrus at the University of Florida—Gainesville, *Brazilian FCOJ Prices and Import Cost Information*, economic research report published annually each January.

Florida Citrus Processors Association, Winter Haven, Florida, *Frozen Concentrate Orange Juice Pack and Movement Summary*, weekly, available by subscription. Also contains cash price information.

Florida Citrus Reporter, Nancy Gurnett Hardy, Editor, weekly independent citrus newsletter.

Roy A. Goldberg, *Agribusiness Coordination*, Boston, 1968.

Roger W. Gray, *Futures Trading and Hedging in Frozen Concentrated Orange Juice*, 1970.

Clarence H. Rosenbaum, *How to Analyze the Orange Juice Futures Market*, 1976.

USDA Florida Crop and Livestock Reporting Service, monthly estimates of citrus crop production and yield.

CHAPTER

21

Cotton

Thomas Bell and Steven Gilson

INTRODUCTION

This chapter examines the supply and demand relationship of U.S. cotton, taking into consideration both domestic and international factors. The demand for cotton produced in the United States is split roughly in half between domestic consumption and exports. Production has gradually shifted westward with the Southwest and West now accounting for roughly 70 percent of total producton.

U.S. PRODUCTION

Acreage

U.S. acreage of upland cotton has fluctuated widely since the 1974 crop year. The fluctuations have resulted mainly from economic factors—principally, changes in the costs and returns from cotton production relative to those from competing crops, such as soybeans and sorghum. Also, the acreages of cotton and other crops are no longer as tightly controlled or influenced by government programs as they once were.

Before the 1974 crop year, cotton acreage was heavily influenced by government programs; in fact, during the 1960s, changes in the programs were primarily responsible for yearly variations in cotton acreage. When marketing quotas were removed for the 1971 and subsequent crops, cotton producers became more responsive to market prices, although the direct payment provisions of the 1971–1973 programs tended to moderate this response. With the adoption of the target-price programs in 1974, and with market prices generally above target prices, cotton producers are now almost wholly responsive to market conditions.

Crops competing for acreage are: (1) soybeans in the delta states of Arkansas, Louisiana, Mississippi, Missouri, and Tennessee; (2) corn and soybeans in the southeastern region, consisting mainly of Alabama, Georgia, North Carolina, and South Carolina; (3) grain sorghum, cotton's chief competitor in the southwestern states of Texas and Oklahoma; and (4) barley, the competitor in the western states of California, Arizona, and New Mexico. The major producing areas and their share of both acreage and production are shown in Table 21-1 and Figure 21-1.

Trends in cotton yields are similar in the Delta and Southeast. No discernible trend is evident in the Southwest, while the western region exhibited a significant trend effect in only the early to middle 1950s. Deflated cotton price has a significant effect in the Southeast and West, but not in the Delta and Southwest. In the Southwest, an area of relatively low cotton yields, producers apply fertilizer and other additives less intensively than producers elsewhere. Thus, the price variable is expected to be insignificant here.

Economic Factors

Changes in prices and production costs have both positive and negative impacts on cotton yields. For example, if higher cotton prices were expected, producers would increase the use of fertilizer and other yield-boosting inputs. They would also increase acreage planted to cotton, which would affect yield adversely because land that is inferior for raising cotton would then come into production.

In the delta region, greater cotton acreage usually means more planting in mixed or heavy soils, which are markedly less suited for cotton than are the finer soils. In the southwest region, increased cotton acreage is highly correlated with increased nonirrigated acreage. Cotton yields on such acreage may be one-third to one-half lower than on irrigated acreage.

Impact of Weather on Yield

Cotton is an adaptable plant, which may be rain-grown or irrigated, depending upon the area of growth and the variety desired. Regarding yield, there are several weather factors that determine the quality of fiber and the size of the yield. The most important of these are temperature, rainfall, and the length of the growing season. Important, but not as critical, is the amount of direct sunshine available to the plant.

Other climatic factors that affect final production are environmental phenomena such as hurricanes, which occur along the Atlantic and Gulf coasts, and hailstorms, which plague some parts of the Texas High Plains. Both can devastate the crops in these areas and, while they can significantly influence local yields, they still do not affect the great bulk of U.S. cotton production. In fact, producers in areas susceptible to such occurrences tend to diversify their plantings, choosing a secondary crop that, although it may not be as profitable, still suffers less damage than cotton in the event of extreme weather. This

TABLE 21-1 U.S. Harvested Acreage and Production (All Kinds) by Regions, and Each Region as a Percentage of Total Harvested Acreage

	Acreage								
Year beginning August 1	West[a]		Southwest[b]		Delta[c]		Southeast[d]		United States, 1,000 acres
	1,000 acres	percent	1,000 acres	Percent	1,000 acres	Percent	1,000 acres	Percent	
1974	1,821	14.5	4,980	39.7	4,320	34.4	1,426	11.4	12,547
1975	1,271	14.5	4,219	48.0	2,616	29.7	690	7.8	8,796
1976	1,562	14.3	4,843	44.4	3,611	33.1	898	8.2	10,914
1977	2,086	15.7	6,992	52.6	3,388	25.6	808	6.1	13,275
1978	2,151	17.4	6,813	54.9	2,862	23.1	574	4.6	12,400
1979	2,395	18.7	7,411	57.8	2,412	18.7	613	4.8	12,831
1980	2,259	17.1	7,438	56.3	2,846	21.5	672	5.1	13,215
1981	2,276	16.4	7,858	56.8	2,943	21.3	765	5.5	13,842
1982	1,954	20.1	4,770	49.0	2,381	24.5	624	6.4	9,729
1983	1,304	17.7	3,850	52.1	1,778	24.1	456	6.1	7,388

(Continued)

TABLE 21-1 *(Continued)*

	Production								
	West[a]		Southwest[b]		Delta[c]		Southeast[d]		United States, 1,000 acres
Year beginning August 1	1,000 acres	percent	1,000 acres	Percent	1,000 acres	Percent	1,000 acres	Percent	
1974	3,806	33.0	2,796	24.2	3,576	31.0	1,362	11.8	11,540
1975	2,640	31.8	2,563	30.9	2,491	30.0	607	7.3	8,302
1976	3,444	32.6	3,489	33.0	2,874	27.2	773	7.3	10,581
1977	4,100	28.6	5,936	41.3	3,827	26.6	527	3.7	14,389
1978	3,177	29.3	4,174	38.4	2,939	27.1	566	5.2	10,856
1979	4,868	33.3	6,061	41.4	3,061	20.9	639	4.4	14,629
1980	4,650	41.8	3,550	31.9	2,424	21.8	498	4.5	11,122
1981	5,286	33.8	6,103	39.0	3,394	21.7	863	5.5	15,646
1982	4,322	36.1	2,961	24.8	3,707	30.1	973	8.0	11,963
1983[f]	2,721	35.4	2,510	32.6	2,011	26.1	452	5.9	7,694

[a]California, Arizona, New Mexico, and Nevada.

[b]Texas, Oklahoma, and Kansas.

[c]Missouri, Arkansas, Tennessee, Mississippi, Louisiana, Illinois, and Kentucky.

[d]Virginia, North Carolina, South Carolina, Georgia, Florida, and Alabama.

[e]480 pounds, net weight.

[f]Preliminary; excludes 62,000 acres and 81,000 bales of pima cotton production.

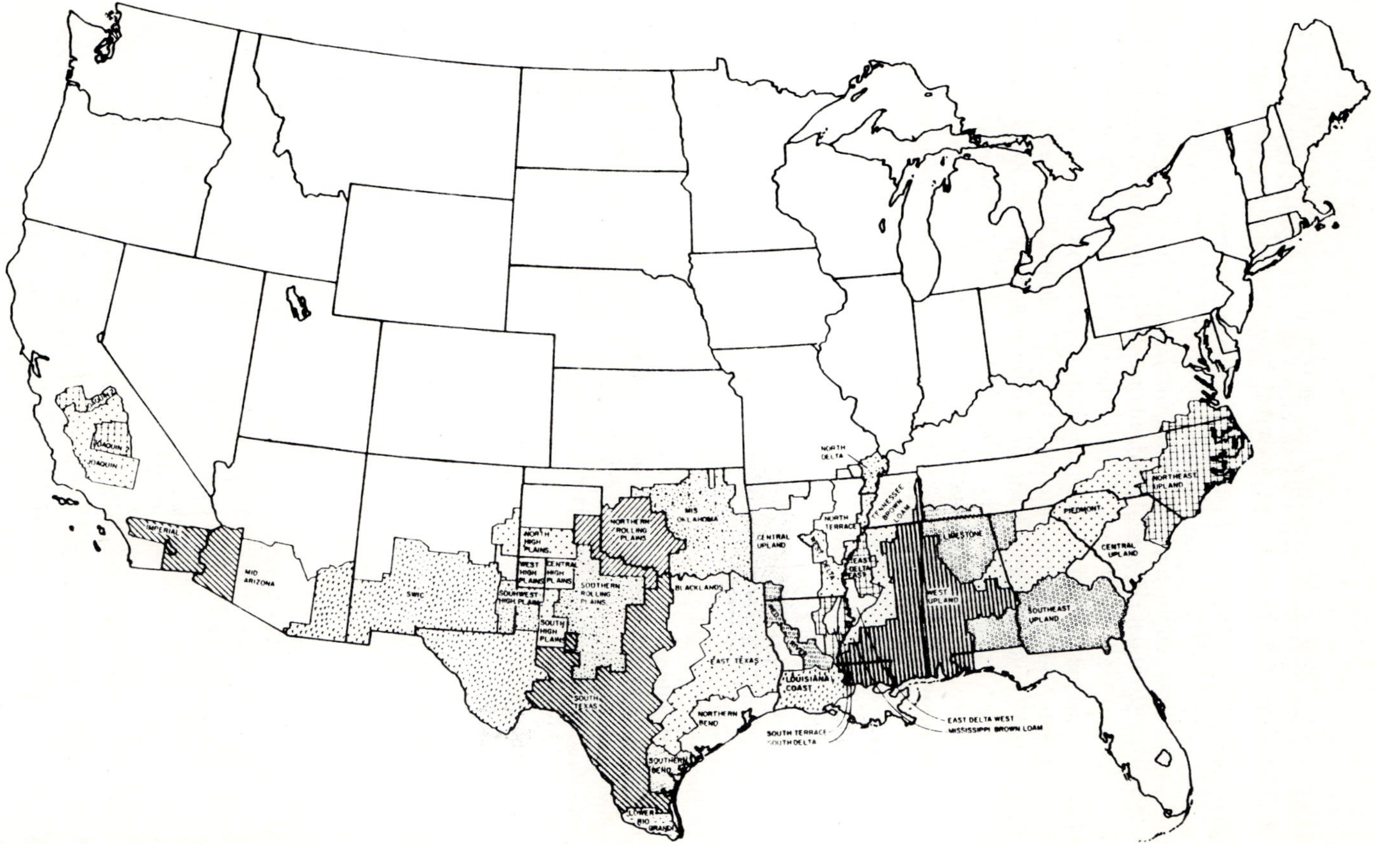

Figure 21-1 Cotton-producing areas of the United States.

causes an historically lower density of cotton in these areas. Also, since the secondary crop is usually well established on most farms in these areas, cotton is very susceptible to competition from it when price changes occur.

Temperature. Cotton is a hot-weather plant that thrives best in temperatures between 95° and 72° F. This is understood to refer to the peak growing season, when the plants are well along in their development. Temperature is most critical to yield during the emergence stage, when soil temperature must be maintained above 60° F at a depth of 8 inches to ensure optimum growth, and during the blooming and maturation stages, when fiber characteristics are determined.

Within 1 week after planting, the seedling should have a root system at least 8 inches below the surface of the soil to reach the water it will need later on when rainfall and surface moisture become less plentiful. Below 60° F growth slows, or even ceases, and a plant that fails to achieve the 8-inch depth on time becomes susceptible to drought and heat stress as the season progresses.

During the peak bloom and boll-forming stages, temperature becomes even more important. Excessively high temperatures accompanied by low moisture can cause shedding of blooms. Excessively cool temperatures during boll formation and maturation can retard the deposits of cellulose layers on the fiber wall, translating into a less mature, finer (lower micronaire), and weaker fiber. A fiber of improper thickness has undesirable strength characteristics and can mean too many or too few fibers will be used in spinning and weaving operations.

In the Texas High Plains, the August-September period is usually the most crucial for determining fiber thickness. Table 21-2 shows the relationship between the departure from the normal temperature and the yield in that area. Simply stated, higher-than-normal temperatures mean higher yields, lower-than-normal temperatures mean lower yields. The exception to this, excessive shedding due to heat stress, occurred during the 1978–79 crop year in California and Arizona.

Rainfall. Rainfall is by far the most critical factor in the development of the cotton plant. Although the growing plant needs all available rainfall, too much moisture in the soil at planting can interfere with soil temperature. The emerging seedling needs heat more than any other stage of the cotton plant in order

TABLE 21-2 Temperature Deviation from Normal on Texas High Plains, August to September

Year	Departure from normal (°F)	Yield (pound per acre)*	Weather
1971	−3.875	264	Coldest August average temperature, maximum 80.8°; September snow
1974	−7.000	264	Coldest September average temperature, maximum 72.5°
1975	−3.875	279	September temperature extremes (i.e., record lows followed record highs)

*Ten-year average yield: 358 pounds per acre.

to develop a deep root system. As the growing season progresses, soil moisture decreases because of evaporation. As Figure 21-2 illustrates, the developing plant is at the same time accelerating its use of water, requiring more and more each day until the peak blooming stage. Timely rainfall is crucial at this stage because the length of the fiber is determined to a large extent by moisture. Also, since the plant will only set as many bolls as it can bring to maturation, inadequate moisture will result in fewer bolls. If rains become more generous later in the season, as occasionally happens in the Texas High Plains, the plant's mechanism may be fooled into setting additional fruit at the expense of further maturation of existing bolls. In its effort to catch up, the plant will produce a large number of bolls, but few of desired quality.

Most cotton in east Texas and in the Delta and Gulf states is rain-grown, so rainfall concerns are most important to these areas. In the zone between Dallas and the Texas–New Mexico border, the crop is irrigated whenever feasible, and yield can be controlled somewhat. West of the Texas–New Mexico border, the entire crop is irrigated, and rainfall is not as much of a factor, except in times of drought or water shortages.

To demonstrate the impact of moisture upon yield, it has been shown in previous studies that a 1-inch departure from normal precipitation in the Texas High Plains in the January-March period changes yield by 24 pounds per acre. Also, a 1-inch departure from normal in the June-July period changes yield by 11 pounds per acre. In the southeastern gulf states, a 1-inch departure from normal precipitation in the summer months changes yield by 12 pounds per acre.

Water impacts in the Delta are more difficult to ascertain precisely. Early in the season, relative dryness may be beneficial from the aspect of soil temperature, since the soil requires less heat to maintain optimum growing temperatures for the young plants. But as the growing season advances, and the plants move into the squaring and blooming stages, much more rainfall is required to meet the increasing moisture needs of the plants during the accompanying rise in temperature (see Figure 21-2). Unfortunately, rainfall in the delta region is usually heaviest in the spring. The most crucial stage for the plant is a 90-day

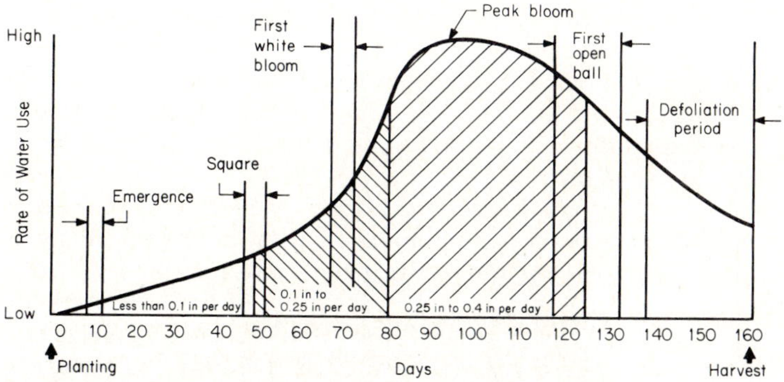

Figure 21-2 Plant and irrigation water requirements. (Commodity Year Book, *1979, Commodity Research Bureau, Inc.*)

period from June through August. If we define a drought as 20 days with no more than 0.5 inches cumulative precipitation in either 10-day period, there is a 25 to 50 percent probability of drought in June, 40 to 75 percent in July, and 35 to 90 percent in August.

Length of Growing Season. Most varieties of cotton require a minimum period of 160 days to grow from seed to maturity, given ideal conditions. Cooler-than-normal weather during planting and early growth stages tends to lengthen the time required for the plant to develop properly. Therefore, allowing for a delayed start, or an early minor disaster (such as the destruction of portions of the Texas High Plains crop by hail, which would necessitate replanting), it is generally believed that cotton is best grown in areas where there are at least 200 days between killing frosts to ensure a successful crop. This is illustrated by the events in Texas, where the replanted crop should be in the ground by June 10 to June 15 at the latest, or a decent harvest from that area will be doubtful. Since the first frost in that area usually occurs between November 1 and November 20, the crop planted on or after June 15 would be on an extremely tight schedule, with little room for further setbacks.

Sunshine. Although it is difficult to establish qualitative relationships, the amount of sunshine received by the plant certainly affects yield. The percentage of possible direct sunshine varies across the cotton belt, regardless of whether or not it is accompanied by precipitation.

FOREIGN COTTON PRODUCTION

General

The cotton production and potential export competition of ten countries exert a significant impact upon the U.S. cotton export market. These ten countries and their relative standings in the world cotton market are summarized in Table 21-3.

Cotton grown outside the United States is subject to the same environmental factors as domestically grown cotton. Slight differences do exist, however, in the lengths of the growing seasons in Central America, India, and Egypt because of the longer days and higher temperatures encountered nearer to the equator. Where the growing season is longer, the plant has more time to develop, and harvesting operations, which are still performed by hand in many countries, may be spread out over a period lasting from 3 to 8 months to give late-forming bolls a chance to mature.

Water availability is a determinant of yield regardless of where the crop is grown. Where rainfall is sparse or all but nonexistent, as in Egypt or in some cotton areas of the Soviet Union, the crop is irrigated. In tropical and subtropical regions, such as those in the southern growing areas of India, monsoonal rains supply most of the water for crops and are supplemented by irrigation and underground wells. In these areas, the crop is planted after the monsoon and is keyed intimately to the monsoon's performance. If the monsoon fails to

TABLE 21-3 Cotton Production by Country
(In thousand 480-pound bales)

Country	1982 Production	Percentage of world total	1982 Exports	Percent of world total
World	67,744		18,345	
Mexico	840	1.24	354	1.93
Guatemala	220	0.32	209	1.14
El Salvador	186	0.27	149	0.81
Nicaragua	365	0.54	313	1.71
Turkey	2,241	3.31	862	4.70
Soviet Unon	11.950	17.64	3,200	17.44
Pakistan	3,775	5.57	1,133	6.18
India	6,174	9.11	909	4.96
China*	16,531	24.40	−200	—
Egypt	2,117	3.13	747	4.07
United States	11,963	17.66	5,200	28.35
Australia	464	0.68	523	2.85
Sudan	944	1.39	950	5.18
French West Africa†	1,260	1.86	909	4.96
South America‡	4,531	6.69	1,260	689

*The People's Republic of China is a net importer of cotton.

†Includes Ivory Coast, Upper Volta, Mali, Niger, Senegal, Togo, Cameroon, Central African Republic, Chad, Burundi, Guinea, Bissar, Madagascar, and Zaire.

‡Major countries are Argentina, Brazil, Colombia, Paraguay, and Peru.

provide enough water one year, it will cause a decreased availability of water for irrigation. It will also cause the rivers to be too low to provide the hydroelectric power necessary to drive the irrigation pumps. Too much rain during the monsoon will leach soils of what little applied fertilizer exists in the seedbeds, and produce increased pest populations.

Another problem associated with poor monsoonal activity is extreme heat. In a typical year, the hottest time of the year is the spring, before the monsoon's onset. Extensive cloud cover is frequent during the monsoon season, decreasing sunshine and lowering daytime temperature. In India, a week during the summer with little cloudiness may cause temperatures in the northern areas to soar to 110° F. In such an environment, plants' water needs exceed available moisture supplies and yield prospects suffer.

The Soviet Union is our strongest competitor in terms of the share of its cotton production exported. The People's Republic of China is now the world's largest cotton producer.

Soviet Union

The Soviet Union is the world's second largest producer of cotton. Figure 21-3 shows the principal growing areas. The Soviet cotton belt extends from the Fergana basin in the east, continuing westward through the Tashkent-Golodnaya Steppe, and on into Samarkand, Bukhara, and Karakul. These areas produce about 60 percent of the total Russian crop. The remainder comes from Turkmenistan, near the border with Iran, and from the Azerbaidzhan region on the western shore of the Caspian Sea. (See Tables 21-4 and 21-5.)

Annual precipitation over the belt totals only 3 to 15 inches per year, with only light amounts falling during the main part of the growing season. This necessitates irrigation of all Soviet cotton.

Cotton enjoys a long growing season in the Azerbaidzhan region. The frost-free period lasts from late March through late November. Cotton is typically sown there in late April. Picking operations begin in mid-September and continue through late November.

In the central region, from Turkmenistan to Kirigzia, the season is much shorter. Cotton is sown in early May but is ripe and ready for picking at about the same time as in Azerbaidzhan. The crop here is highly dependent upon weather during September and October. Warm temperatures during these two months can result in the maturation of late-opening bolls, contributing to higher yields. Such warm temperatures are needed especially when spring thunderstorms produce locally heavy rains and wash out some of the acreage. Replanted acreage in this case is susceptible to earlier-than-normal cold temperatures, which cause substantial problems in the maturing process.

Table 21-6 shows monthly temperatures and precipitation at selected locations in the Soviet cotton belt. Rainfall may delay planting operations somewhat and interfere with soil temperatures during the crucial germination stage. In early May, flooding occurs and acreage may have to be replanted. If this happens, the crop may get off to a slow start, and the replanted acreage will require a sustained period of above-normal temperatures during the summer if an average yield is to be achieved

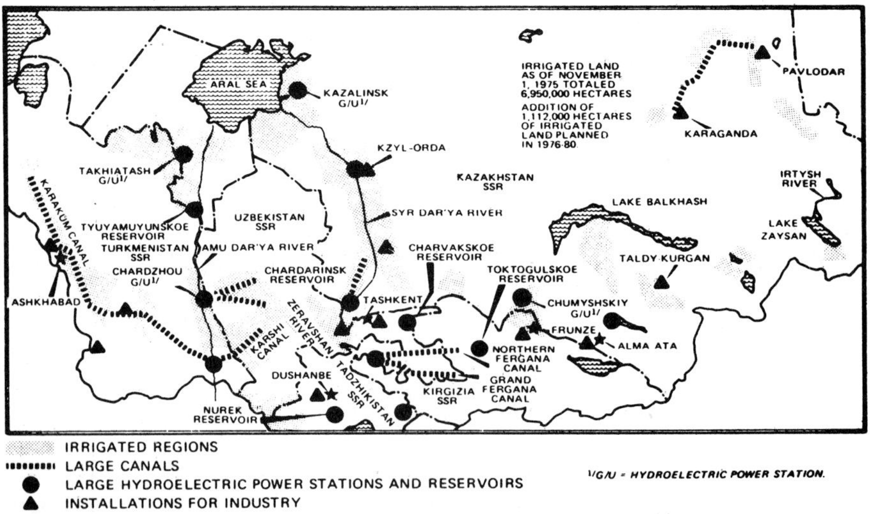

Figure 21-3 Irrigation in Central Asia and Kazakhistan. *(U.S. Department of Agriculture)*

TABLE 21-4 Cotton Production, Area, and Yield in the Soviet Union, 1979–80 to 1982–83

Region	1979–80 Area, 1,000 acres	1979–80 yield, pounds per acre	1979–80 Production, 1,000 480-pound bales*	1980–81 Area, 1,000 acres	1980–81 yield, pounds per acre	1980–81 Production, 1,000 480-pound bales*	1981–82 Area, 1,000 acres	1981–82 yield, pounds per acre	1981–82 Production, 1,000 480-pound bales*	1982–83 Area, 1,000 acres	1982–83 yield, pounds per acre	1982–83 Production, 1000 480-pound bales*
Uzbekistan	4,554	823	7,806	4,641	852	8,241	4,628	841	8,111	4,658	796	7,725
Turkmenistan	1,255	629	1,646	1,255	636	1,662	1,255	591	1,545	1,255	580	1,516
Tadzhikistan	751	782	1,223	761	843	1,336	756	794	1,251	756	742	1,169
Azerbaidzhan	596	810	1,005	618	908	1,168	699	938	1,367	761	677	1,073
Kazakhstan	294	730	447	314	722	472	311	716	465	311	561	364
Kirigzia	185	730	282	188	726	284	178	643	238	106	453	100
Total Soviet Union	7,635	780	12,410	7,776	813	13,164	7,828	796	12,976	7,848	731	11,948

*Production figures are arrived at by multiplying seed cotton production by a ginning percentage.

TABLE 21-5 Soviet Union Cotton Supply and Demand

Year	Planted (1,000 acres)	Yield (pounds per acre)	Beginning stocks	Production	Imports	Consumption	Exports	Ending stocks
1978	7,506	756	2,523	11,830	398	8,888	3,635	2,229
1979	7,635	780	2,229	12,410	229	8,916	3,884	2,026
1980	7,776	813	2,069	13,165	103	8,971	4,207	2,139
1981	7,828	796	2,159	12,975	118	8,984	4,358	1,910
1982	7,878	728	1,910	11,950	500	9,039	3,200	2,121
1983*	7,900	790	2,121	13,000	260	9,100	3,720	2,521

*International Cotton Advisory Committee estimates.

Finally, it should be realized that the entire Soviet cotton belt is located in a region that is highly prone to earthquake activity. Quakes periodically occur which are intense enough to cause structural damage to irrigation facilities. Since the Soviet crop is 100 percent irrigated, the implications of a strong earthquake in the region are obvious.

The People's Republic of China

The People's Republic of China (P.R.C.) is now the world's largest cotton producer and importer.

Cotton production in China is labor-intensive, and acreage and yield fluctuations are common (see Table 21-7). Increased availability of fertilizers, continued improvement of irrigation systems, and the ratio of cotton prices to grain prices are important factors in determining acreage and yield.

About 75 percent of China's cotton area is irrigated; this area is almost evenly divided between the northern and central areas (see Figure 21-4 and Table 21-7). Rainfall varies considerably between the two areas, however, and is seasonal in nature (i.e., summer rains result from typhoons, spring dryness results from pressure areas centered over Mongolia). High deviations from normal are commonplace. In the far northern provinces, annual rainfalls are only some 20 inches. Hence, spring rains that arrive later than usual, or large deviations from normal rainfall can create tremendous yield variations, because irrigation depends on water availability. Most early irrigation is done with buckets, although a few wells do exist and some areas are flooded later.

Unlike the northern provinces, the central provinces are generally faced with excessive seasonal rains and the topography of land makes water control the major problem. Depending on when it occurs, untimely rainfall can delay plantings, cause root rot, or cause the plant to put on vegetative growth at the expense of developing bolls. Flood control problems have to a large degree been alleviated and irrigation is much more sophisticated in this area.

Temperature extremes rarely cause significant problems in China, and weather is generally ideal at harvesting time. Since most cotton is hand-picked twice, little is left in the field.

Optimal yield, after the monsoon season ends, depends on avoiding substan-

TABLE 21-6 Monthly Average Temperature and Rainfall in the Soviet Union, 1981
(Selected locations in Soviet cotton areas)

	January		February		March		April		May		June	
	°F	Inches	°F	Inches	°F	Inches	°F	Inches	°F	Inches	°F	Inches
Tblisi	40	0.09	42	1.18	45	1.30	52	0.63	58	2.76	70	3.50
Kirovabad	38	0.16	41	0.55	45	0.24	54	0.47	60	2.32	69	0.91
Aralsk	16	0.39	18	0.31	33	0.67	48	0.91	61	2.28	72	2.80
Kzyl-Orda	25	0.26	26	0.83	42	1.38	53	1.57	63	1.77	71	2.52
Tashkent	40	2.09	41	1.46	53	3.58	58	1.97	69	2.05	76	0.51
Samarkand	39	N.A.*	3	Trace	50	0.35	57	N.A.	67	0.08	73	0.04
Chardzhou	40	0.67	42	0.94	53	1.97	62	1.57	72	0.87	78	Trace
Tedzen	42	Trace	42	0.31	49	0	63	0	70	0.01	76	0
Ashkhabad	41	0.98	43	1.54	53	1..89	59	2.99	67	2.80	78	Trace

*Not available.

TABLE 21-7 Cotton Production in the People's Republic of China

Province	1979–80 Planted, 1,000 acres	1979–80 yield, pounds per acre	1979–80 Production, 1,000 480-pound bales	1980–81 Planted, 1,000 acres	1980–81 yield, pounds per acre	1980–81 Production, 1,000 480-pound bales	1981–82 Planted, 1,000 acres	1981–82 yield, pounds per acre	1981–82 Production, 1,000 480-pound bales	1982–83 Planted, 1,000 acres	1982–83 yield, pounds acre	1982–83 Production, 1,000 480-pound bales
North												
Shandong	1,342	274	766	1,821	650	2,468	2,305	622	2,985	3,294	643	4,409
Hebei	1,376	185	531	1,324	411	1,135	1,295	383	1,033	1,727	497	1,787
Henan	1,371	319	911	1,490	601	1,866	1,483	520	1,608	1,646	429	1,470
Shaanxi (Shensi)	618	364	468	610	292	371	625	268	349	625*	335*	436
Xinjiang	398	294	243	445	393	364	610	379	482	610*	538*	684
Liaoning	89	394	73	89	529	98	91	506	96	99*	513*	106
Shanxi	546	262	298	610	280	356	593	268	331	625	353	459
Other	47	176	17	47	200	20	47	235	23	49	223	23
Total	5,787	274	3,309	6,437	498	6,677	7,050	470	6,908	8,676	519	9,374
Central:												
Hubei	1,428	691	2,056	1,436	486	1,453	1,433	554	1,653	1,347	557	1,562
Jiangsu	1,453	807	2,442	1,483	622	1,920	1,564	746	2,430	1,730	734	2,646
Anhui	739	290	447	823	327	561	791	399	657	791*	413*	680
Sichuan	625	392	511	697	299	434	630	297	390	427	423	377
Hunan	398	519	430	415	511	442	427	516	459	413	524	450
Jiangxi	245	392	200	259	366	198	272	365	207	255	485	257
Shanghai	245	806	411	250	674	350	282	485	285	282*	634*	372
Zheijiang	213	720	319	240	763	381	230	672	322	230*	844*	404
Other	20	279	11	20	268	11	20	335	14	20	335	14
Total	5,365	611	6,827	5,622	491	5,750	5,649	545	6,416	5,493	591	6,761
Total North and Central	11,152	436	10,135	12,058	495	12,427	12,698	—	13,324	14,169	—	16,135
Reported total	11,152	436	10,135	12,058	495	12,427	12,698	516	13,643†	14,169	560	16,531†

*Either estimated or left unchanged from last year's level.

†These figures are official reported figures.

SOURCES: Data compiled from official sources in the People's Republic of China, the U.S. Department of Agriculture, and the International Cotton Advisory Committee files.

tial wilt problems, which are brought on by a combination of excessive rainfall and high temperatures.

END USAGE

Mill Demand

In order to evaluate the mill demand for cotton, it is necessary to look at final goods demands for various end-use categories. Essentially, these trends in retail cotton consumption are very closely linked to the business cycle, as can be seen from Figure 21-5 which shows the relationship between the Department of Commerce's leading indicators, cotton use, and total fiber use. Figure 21-5 also shows that the leading indicators tend to foreshadow trends in total fiber consumption and therefore changes in the final demand for cotton.

U.S. domestic consumption of cotton has fallen steadily since 1950, when it was 31 million bales, or approximately 30 percent of the world's total, to around 6 million bales annually. The impact of synthetic fibers has been largely responsible for this trend; by 1981 cotton's share of total U.S. mill fiber con-

Figure 21-4 Map of The People's Republic of China.

sumption had fallen to around 25 percent from 75 percent in the early 1950s. The relationship between cotton and man-made U.S. fiber consumption in 1980 is shown in the following table.

Category	Percentage of cotton consumption	Cotton's percentage of total materials
Apparel	52.4	34.7
Home furnishings	25.8	22.0
Industrial uses	13.5	13.6
Exports	8.3	41.8

In assessing trends of cotton consumption, it is clearly important to try to estimate its competitive position vis-a-vis synthetic products. In this respect, the changes in the price of oil—a commodity from which synthetics are largely derived—is a very important factor. Rising oil prices will boost the cost of synthetics and, other things being equal, will encourage cotton usage. Conversely, a sharp decline in oil prices will encourage the substitution of synthetics for cotton, thereby having a depressing effect on the price of this agricultural commodity. These shifting consumption patterns are explained in more detail in Figure 21-6 and Table 21-8.

In the short run, cotton prices are very volatile for any given crop year and vary inversely by approximately 1¢ per pound for every 100,000-bale variation in supply. Consequently, it is not unusual to see cotton prices vary by 10¢ to 20¢ per pound during a crop year.

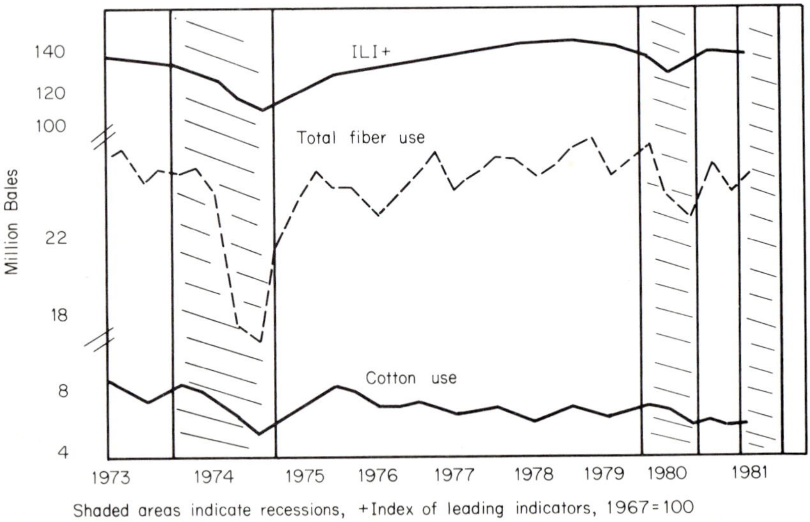

Figure 21-5 Economic activity and annual rate of mill use.

U.S. Cotton Exports

U.S. exports of cotton are not so much a function of the U.S. ability to export cotton as they are a function of demand. This function of demand is primarily a derivative of the country's economic status. Country-by-country analysis is very similar to that suggested for the United States. World demand is then aggregated. World trade-flow patterns are then combined with world availability. From this U.S. exports are determined, since the United States is essentially a residual supplier of the world's cotton needs. (Table 21-9 shows the major importers of U.S. cotton.)

The European Economic Community (EEC), while not now a major U.S. customer, is expected to become a substantial one in the future, because of new measures being negotiated in the International Multifiber Agreement between the EEC and the United States.

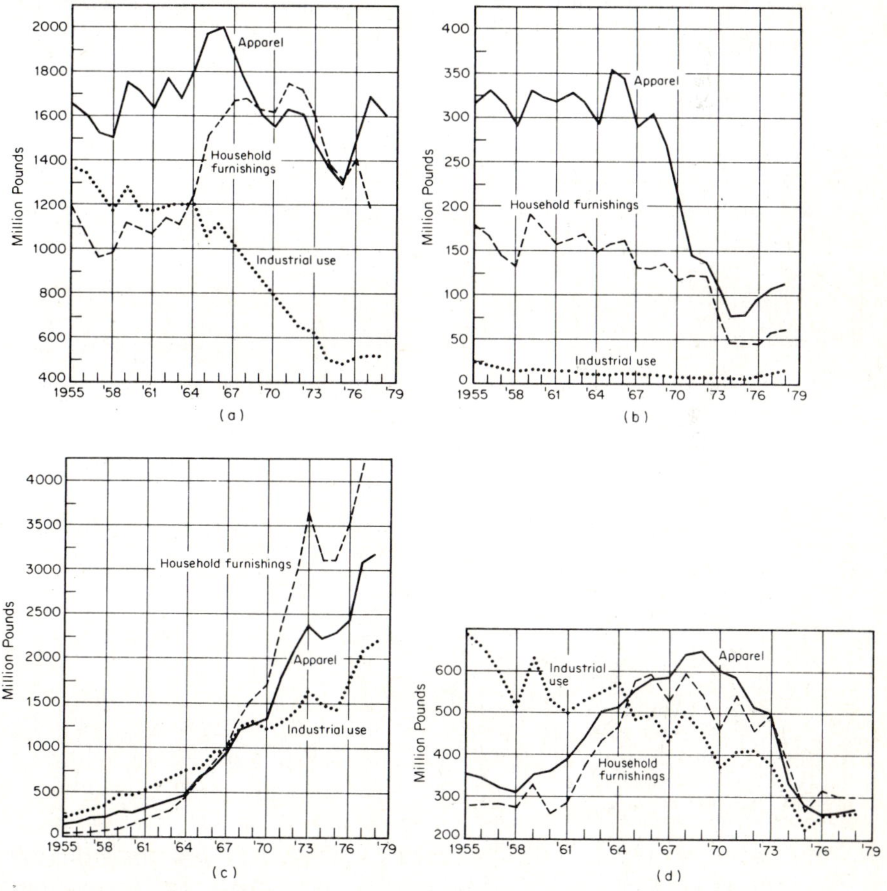

Figure 21-6 (*a*) Cotton fiber end use. (*b*) Wool fiber end use. (*c*) Noncellulosic fiber end use. (*d*) Cellulosic fiber end use.

TABLE 21-8 U.S. End Use Summary
(Million pounds and Percent)

End Use	Grand total			Cotton			Wool			Man-made fibers		
	Pounds	Percent*	Percent†	Pounds	Percent*	Percent†	Pounds	Percent*	Percent†	Pounds	Percent*	Percent†
1975	4,656	100	43.0	1,563	33.6	48.9	105	2.2	67.3	2,988	64.2	40.0
1976	4,831	100	41.0	1,736	35.9	49.7	127	2.6	72.6	2,968	61.5	36.5
1977	5,135	100	40.9	1,735	33.8	51.2	132	2.6	75.0	3,268	63.6	36.4
1978	5,053	100	39.2	1,683	33.5	52.0	139	2.8	73.9	3,201	63.7	34.2
1979	4,825	100	37.0	1,696	35.2	51.3	132	2.7	76.3	2,997	62.1	31.4
1980	4,823	100	39.5	1,727	35.8	53.8	125	2.6	74.4	2,971	61.6	33.6
1981	4,603	100	38.5	1,603	34.8	54.6	148	3.2	76.3	2,852	62.0	32.3
					Home Furnishings							
1975	3,232	100	29.9	906	28.0	28.4	32	1.0	20.5	2,294	71.0	30.7
1976	3,526	100	29.9	920	26.1	26.3	33	0.9	18.8	2,573	73.0	31.7
1977	3,842	100	30.6	905	23.6	26.7	32	0.8	18.2	2.905	75.6	32.3
1978	3,996	100	31.2	863	21.6	26.6	36	0.9	19.2	3,097	77.5	33.0
1979	4,092	100	31.4	848	20.7	25.6	27	0.7	15.6	3,217	78.6	33.7
1980	3,657	100	29.9	803	22.0	25.0	26	0.7	15.5	2,828	77.3	32.0
1981	3,540	100	29.6	774	21.9	26.4	29	0.8	14.9	2,737	77.3	31.0
				Indusrial and other consumer-type products								
1975	2,494	100	23.0	491	19.7	15.4	6	0.2	3.9	1,997	80.1	26.7
1976	2,963	100	25.1	569	19.2	16.3	8	0.3	4.6	2,386	80.5	29.3
1977	3,155	100	25.2	528	16.7	15.6	8	0.3	4.5	2,619	83.0	29.2
1978	3,334	100	26.1	472	14.1	14.6	9	0.3	4.8	2,853	85.6	30.4

1979	3,486	*100*	*26.8*	462	*13.3*	*14.0*	8	*0.2*	*4.6*	3,016	*86.5*	*31.6*
1980	3,120	*100*	*25.5*	423	*13.6*	*13.2*	11	*0.3*	*6.5*	2,686	*86.1*	*30.4*
1981	3,317	*100*	*27.8*	391	*11.8*	*13.3*	12	*0.4*	*6.2*	2,914	*87.8*	*33.1*
					Exports of domestic products							
1975	441	*100*	*4.1*	234	*53.1*	*7.3*	13	*2.9*	*8.3*	194	*44.0*	*2.6*
1976	476	*100*	*4.0*	267	*56.1*	*7.7*	7	*1.5*	*4.0*	202	*42.4*	*2.5*
1977	418	*100*	*3.3*	221	*52.9*	*6.5*	4	*0.9*	*2.3*	193	*46.2*	*2.1*
1978	449	*100*	*3.5*	220	*49.0*	*6.8*	4	*0.9*	*2.1*	225	*50.1*	*2.4*
1979	620	*100*	*4.8*	301	*48.5*	*9.1*	6	*1.0*	*3.5*	313	*50.5*	*3.3*
1980	617	*100*	*5.1*	259	*42.0*	*8.0*	6	*1.0*	*3.6*	352	*57.0*	*4.0*
1981	490	*100*	*4.1*	166	*33.9*	*5.7*	5	*1.0*	*2.6*	319	*65.1*	*3.6*
						Total end use						
1975	10,823	*100*	*100*	3,194	*29.5*	*100*	156	*1.5*	*100*	7,473	*69.0*	*100*
1976	11,796	*100*	*100*	3,492	*29.6*	*100*	175	*1.5*	*100*	8,129	*68.9*	*100*
1977	12,550	*100*	*100*	3,389	*27.0*	*100*	176	*1.4*	*100*	8,985	*71.6*	*100*
1978	12,802	*100*	*100*	3,238	*25.3*	*100*	188	*1.5*	*100*	9,376	*73.2*	*100*
1979	13,023	*100*	*100*	3,307	*25.4*	*100*	173	*1.3*	*100*	9,543	*73.3*	*100*
1980	12,217	*100*	*100*	3,212	*26.3*	*100*	168	*1.4*	*100*	8,837	*72.3*	*100*
1981	11,950	*100*	*100*	2,934	*24.6*	*100*	194	*1.6*	*100*	8,822	*73.8*	*100*

*The percentages in these columns show the share of each fiber in the specified end use each year. They add horizontally to the 100 percent shown in each of the "Grand total" columns.

†The percentages in these columns show the usage of each type of fiber by its major end use categories. They add vertically to the 100 percent shown under "Total end use."

SOURCE: *Textile Organon*, November 1982, p. 214.

TABLE 21-9 U.S. Cotton Exports to Key Industrial Countries
(480-pound bales)

Year	South Korea	China	Japan	Taiwan	Hong Kong	EEC
1975–76	938,656	8,569	672,352	521,712	131,588	404,000
1976–77	958,530	0	1,019,929	451,006	379,179	273,000
1977–78	1,231,030	442,567	1,077,051	511,917	503,452	327,000
1978–79	1,277,817	647,903	1,342,209	454,497	426,817	427,000
1979–80	1,483,718	2,267,525	1,588,033	727,670	636,166	640,000
1980–81	1,303,000	1,375,000	1,139,000	351,000	205,000	387,000
1981–82	1,412,000	847,000	1,626,000	777,000	243,000	538,000
1982–83	1,322,000	20,000	1,286,000	378,000	158,000	559,000

Japan is one of the world's largest importers of cotton, utilizing 80 percent of these imports for domestic use.

The ever-expanding potential for U.S. exporting markets, according to the U.S. Department of Agriculture's (USDA) long-range projections, is indicated by the huge populations of the textile-producing countries in the Far East, namely the Republic of South Korea, Hong Kong, and Taiwan.

During a 5-year period ending July 1980, the Republic of South Korea was the most rapidly expanding market for cotton in the world. South Korea is unique as a major importer in that it purchases all but 2 to 5 percent of its cotton requirements annually from the United States.

Most of the cotton imported by South Korea is financed under U.S government programs. South Korea probably can produce cotton textiles at a lower cost than any other country in the world. Its rapidly expanding textile industry is characterized by large units of new machinery working at full capacity, and efficient labor workng at relatively low wage rates. There is no other major cotton import market in which U.S. cotton has so predominate a share as South Korea. A few thousand bales are imported annually from Egypt and the Sudan, probably longer-staple cotton for special uses. Much of the remainder is from various countries in Latin America. The Korean government estimates that its cotton requirements will grow over the next decade. South Korea as yet supplies very little of the world trade in cotton textiles. Thus Korean textiles have worlds to conquer, particularly since South Korea can set export prices by fiat. A principal concern of South Korea is the rising competition from the People's Republic of China.

The advent of China as a major purchaser of U.S. cotton is not likely to be one of the most influential pricing factors for the future. China is undertaking a major modernization program, having enunciated its future economic policy in the "four-point modernization" plan proclaimed by Chou En-Lai at the Fourth National People's Congress in 1975. This "grand new plan" placed heavy emphasis on oil and textile exports to earn foreign exchange for the purchase of capital equipment and technology to expand and modernize its industrial base and complex, which in turn can produce products for the improvement of its agricultural output.

China's light industry, which includes the textile industry, supplies over 70 percent of all the consumer goods to the domestic market as well as the all-important foreign exchange-earning textile projects for the export market.

At present, textile imports are the fourth largest import commodity in terms of U.S. dollars, and it is obvious that the Chinese cotton industry cannot meet internal demand. Since textile yarn and fabrics represent approximately 50 to 60 percent of total manufactured goods, cotton cloth is rationed at about 4 to 6 meters per person per year in order to maintain export levels.

In 1979 and 1980, China's cotton imports from the United States rose dramatically. The reasons for this were twofold. First, the "four-point modernization" program, with its recent increased emphasis on consumer goods and disposable income, has significantly increased per capita consumption. Second, the emphasis Beijing (Peking) has placed on increasing exports has resulted in increased textile exports. In order to encourage exports, China has permitted some companies that are engaged in importing and exporting activities to use an internal exchange rate of 2.8 yen to the dollar, well above the official exchange rate of 1.5 yen to the dollar. The purpose of a higher internal exchange rate is to make exporting more attractive to Chinese firms, and make Chinese goods more competitive in the world market. Chinese businesses that are losing money in the export trade would essentially be subsidized, and exports would therefore be encouraged. The increased concern for the improvement of the standard of living, with its commensurate increase in output of consumer goods, together with the increased production and export of textile products as a result of the newly negotiated bilateral textile agreement between the United States and Peking will be the primary causes of expected increases in China's consumption of cotton. China's imports of United States cotton declined significantly during 1982–83 as China's production rose to record levels.

THE COTTON MARKET—AN OVERVIEW

A number of variables affect cotton's price at any given time, but the magnitude of their impact on the price structure (and industry) can differ considerably. General economic conditions and competition from synthetic fibers are among the important variables affecting the textile industry over the longer term, a time frame that typically is more relevant to hedgers in the futures market than to speculative traders, whose outlooks tend to be short-term.

Cotton market futures developments over the short run are generally more sensitive to supply considerations, specifically crop conditions and/or their prospects, the availability of quality-grade cotton, and especially the latter's relation to maturing futures. The supply factors are often more readily discernible than demand parameters. Market participants tend to be more speculative in respect to the influence on the market's price direction and momentum.

Cash Markets

The use of the supply utilization ratio as a price forecasting method is based on the major fundamental factors in the market. A frequent update of these vari-

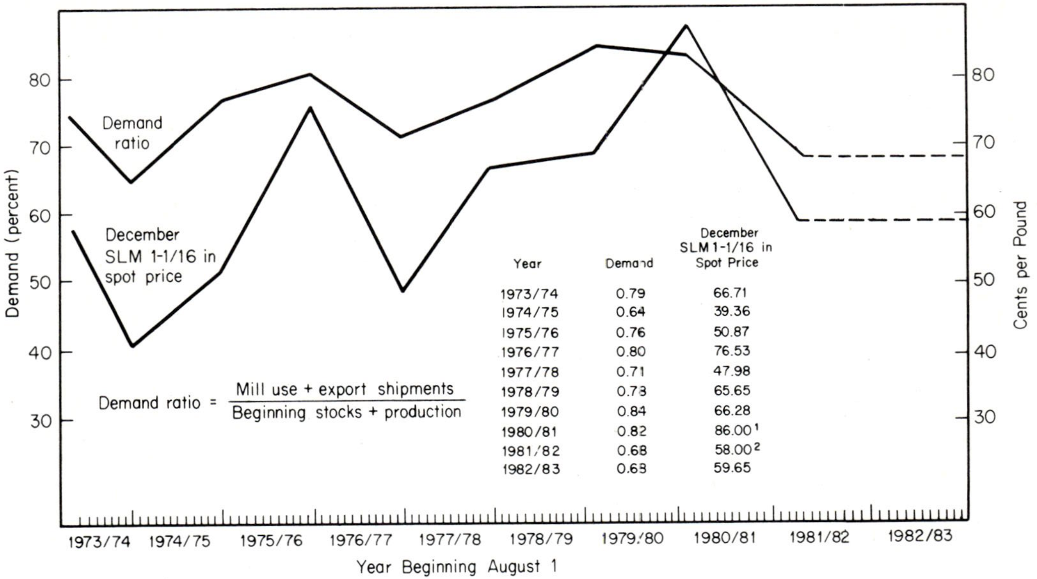

1. Average for March 1980 is 79.24, the increased offtake coupled with tenderability problems was not obvious until the December contract expired.

2. Tenderability problems became obvious early as the market outran the fundamentals.

--- Preliminary

Figure 21-7 Cotton demand ratio and price.

ables, based on historical data and knowledge of projections, will establish as nearly as possible a price forecast of the new crop cash price. Anticipated disappearance (mill use and exports) is placed in the numerator of a ratio that has as its denominator beginning stocks and forecast production. Over the long term, this is a forecast of an equilibrium price that constantly changes. Cotton (both mill and export) can be characterized as having three levels of price uncertainty, which are determined by such traditional variables as income, the price of polyester, and foreign production. There is also the yield uncertainty, that is, the uncertainty of production when the planted acreage is known. Finally, there is the remaining demand uncertainty after production is known, coupled with the new information assimilated. These factors are used within the supply-and-demand framework to compare analogous years in every respect, except for the changes from inflation. The ratio is used as a basis for a long-term forecast of new crop cash price. The stocks-to-usage ratio appears to work equally well as a forecasting mechanism. The supply-utilization ratio and the stocks-to-usage ratio are shown in Figures 21-7 and 21-8 and Table 21-10. Monthly changes in the USDA's supply-and-demand estimates are given in Table 21-10. Other considerations for present price are basis analysis, spread differences, and simultaneous analysis of all commodities.

Basis

Basis is an analysis of short-term distribution of supply and demand. Seasonal basis can be understood and somewhat predicted by looking at the historical seasonal tendencies. Within these seasonals, merchants tend to move the basis according to their positions. If the majority of merchants go into a month-long cash and short futures with an abundance of cotton available, basis is apt to weaken until a point at which the merchant could buy cotton and sell futures and deliver against the nearby contract. On the other hand, if the merchants have made forward sales and futures are long, these positions have to be covered as needed according to the delivery time specified in the contract. Basis then would tend to narrow, or strengthen. Therefore, to determine the present demand and its influence on price, periodic assessments of the likelihood of positions of the trade must be made.

Mention has to be made also, in relation to demand, of the strength of the

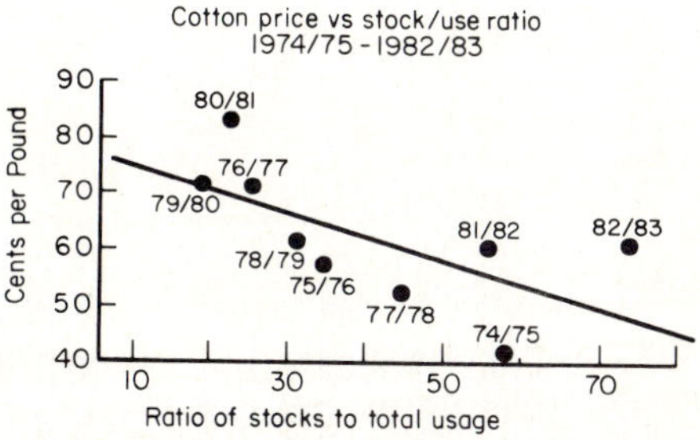

Figure 21-8 Stocks-to-use ratio and cotton price, 1974–75 to 1982–83.

TABLE 21-10 Supply-Utilization Ratio, 480-Pound Bales
(All figures in millions, except ratio)

1976	Jan.	Feb.	Mar.	Apr.	May	June	July*	Aug.	Sept.	Oct.	Nov.	Dec.
Beginning stocks	—	—	—	—	—	—	3.5	3.5	3.7	3.7	3.7	3.6
Production	—	—	—	—	—	—	11.0	10.7	10.7	10.2	9.8	10.2
U.S. exports	—	—	—	—	—	—	4.0	4.0	4.5	4.5	4.4	4.4
Mill use	—	—	—	—	—	—	7.0	7.0	7.0	7.0	6.6	6.6
Ratio	—	—	—	—	—	—	0.75	0.77	0.79	0.82	0.79	0.78
1977												
Beginning stocks	3.0	3.1	3.1	2.8	2.8	2.8	2.7	2.7	3.0	3.0	2.9	2.9
Production	12.0	12.0	12.9	12.7	12.7	12.5	12.7	13.5	13.2	13.3	13.8	14.4
U.S. exports	4.9	9.9	4.9	4.8	4.8	4.8	4.5	4.5	4.6	4.6	4.4	4.4
Mill use	6.8	6.8	6.8	7.0	7.0	7.0	7.0	6.7	6.7	6.7	6.7	6.7
Ratio	0.78	0.77	0.73	0.76	0.76	0.77	0.75	0.71	0.70	0.69	0.66	0.640
1978												
Beginning stocks	6.2	5.7	5.7	5.7	5.5	5.5	5.1	5.1	5.1	5.1	5.1	5.3
Production	11.8	11.9	12.4	12.4	12.4	12.3	12.3	11.8	10.8	10.8	10.9	10.9
U.S. exports	5.5	5.5	5.5	5.5	5.5	5.5	5.5	5.7	5.7	5.7	5.7	5.8
Mill use	7.0	7.0	7.0	7.0	6.75	6.75	6.75	6.75	6.75	6.75	6.75	6.25
Ratio	0.69	0.71	0.68	0.68	0.68	0.68	0.68	0.72	0.72	0.72	0.72	0.74
1979												
Beginning stocks	4.1	4.1	4.1	4.1	3.7	3.7	3.7	3.7	40.	4.0	4.0	4.0
Production	13.2	13.2	13.5	13.5	13.4	13.0	13.0	13.7	14.2	14.5	14.5	14.5
U.S. exports	5.3	5.3	5.3	5.3	6.0	6.0	6.0	6.0	6.0	6.2	6.8	7.0
Mill use	6.25	6.3	6.3	6.3	6.0	6.0	6.0	6.0	6.2	6.2	6.2	6.3
Ratio	0.66	0.67	0.66	0.66	0.70	0.72	0.72	0.69	0.67	0.67	0.70	0.71

Beginning stocks	4.0	4.0	4.0	4.0	3.2	3.2	3.2	3.0	3.0	3.0	3.0	3.0
Production	14.0	14.0	14.0	14.6	14.6	14.6	14.6	12.8	12.8	11.6	11.2	11.0
U.S. exports	8.0	8.0	8.0	8.5	7.3	7.3	7.3	6.8	6.8	6.0	5.7	5.5
Mill use	6.4	6.4	6.4	6.5	6.3	6.3	6.3	6.0	6.0	5.9	5.9	6.0
Ratio	0.76	0.76	0.76	0.801	0.76	0.76	0.76	0.81	0.81	0.82	0.82	0.82
1981												
Beginning stocks	3.0	3.0	3.0	3.0	3.0	3.0	3.0	2.5	2.7	2.7	3.0	3.0
Production	11.1	11.1	11.1	11.1	11.1	11.1	11.1	14.8	15.5	15.5	15.6	15.6
U.S. exports	5.5	5.7	5.7	6.0	6.0	6.1	5.9	7.0	7.0	7.0	6.8	6.8
Mill use	6.0	5.9	5.9	5.8	5.8	5.8	5.8	6.2	6.2	6.2	5.9	5.9
Ratio	0.82	0.82	0.82	0.84	0.84	0.84	0.83	0.76	0.73	0.73	0.68	0.68
1982												
Beginning stocks	2.70	2.70	2.70	2.70	2.70	2.70	2.70	6.60	6.50	6.60	6.60	6.60
Current production	15.70	15.70	15.70	15.70	15.70	15.70	15.60	11.10	11.00	11.40	11.90	12.10
U.S. exports	6.80	6.80	6.70	6.70	6.70	6.70	6.60	6.50	6.30	6.00	5.80	5.40
Mill use	5.80	5.60	5.40	5.40	5.40	5.30	5.30	5.50	5.60	5.60	5.40	5.40
Ratio	0.68	0.67	0.66	0.66	0.66	0.65	0.65	0.68	0.68	0.64	0.61	0.58
1983												
Beginning stocks	6.60	6.60	6.60	6.60	6.60	6.60	6.60	8.00	7.90			
Current production	12.10	12.00	12.00	12.00	12.00	12.00	12.00	7.80	7.80			
U.S. exports	5.40	5.00	5.00	5.40	5.50	5.10	5.10	5.30	5.20			
Mill use	5.40	5.00	5.40	5.40	5.30	5.50	5.50	5.90	5.90			
Ratio	0.58	0.54	0.56	0.58	0.58	0.57	0.57	0.71	0.71			

*July is final.

U.S. dollar relative to foreign currencies. For the United States, a strong dollar is both bullish and bearish. The bullish effect is that it holds down the price of imports and competing products manufactured in the United States. The bearish effect is that a stronger dollar makes U.S. products less competitive in weakened economies abroad.

Spreads

The relationship between delivery months is as important an analyzing tool for price forecasting as any that can be considered. The differences reflect the expectations of demand and relative supply. The dominant factor causing the spread difference in the cotton market is the certificated stocks. This is the cotton suitable for tenderability against the near month. Any tenderability problems reflecting lower quality than the contract specifies tend to produce a tightness in the spreads between delivery months. Someone has to pay the cost of carry. The certificated stocks represent cost of carry shifted from the seller to buyer. Theoretically, the larger the stocks, the wider the spread difference will be, and vice versa.

Seasonal Factors

One of the most important considerations for price forecasting is the seasonality of cotton prices based on a continuation series of monthly averages of futures prices. This movement is important for producers, merchants, and mills trying

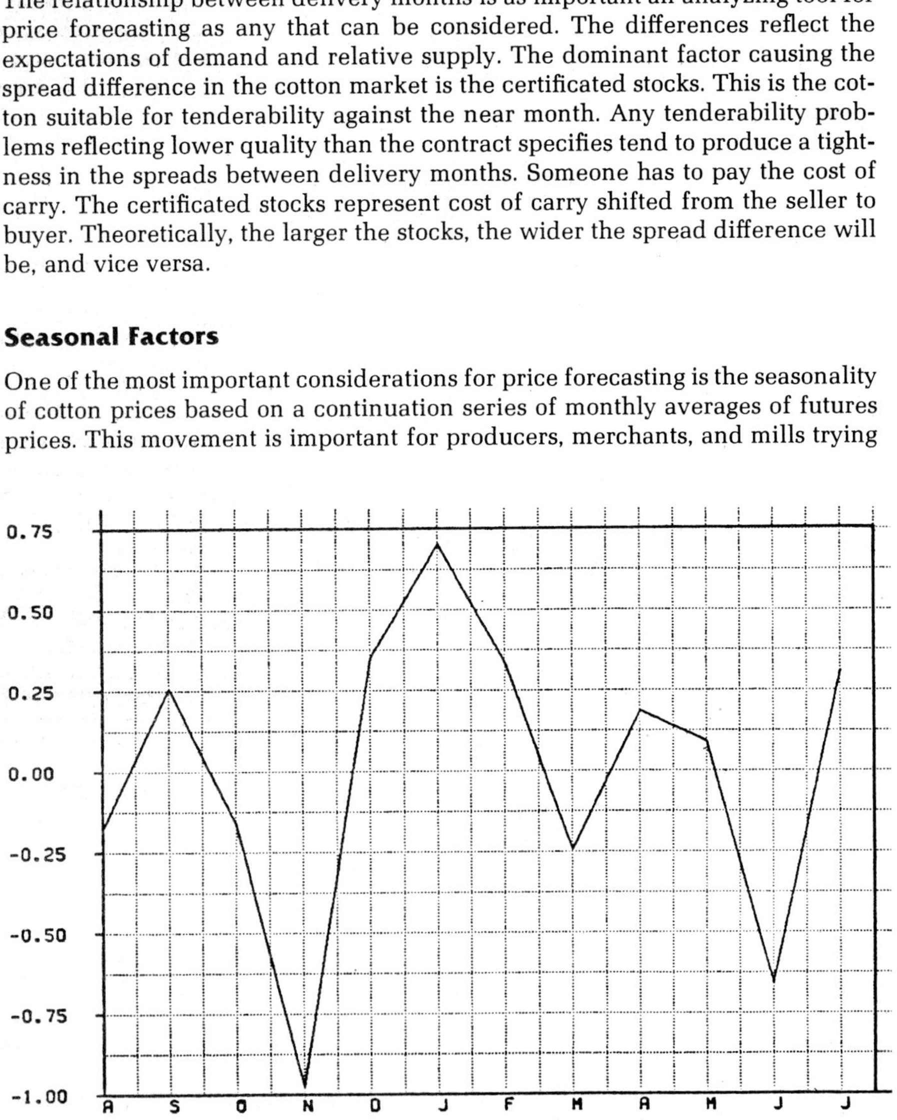

Figure 21-9 Seasonality of cotton prices. *(ContiCommodity Research Division)*

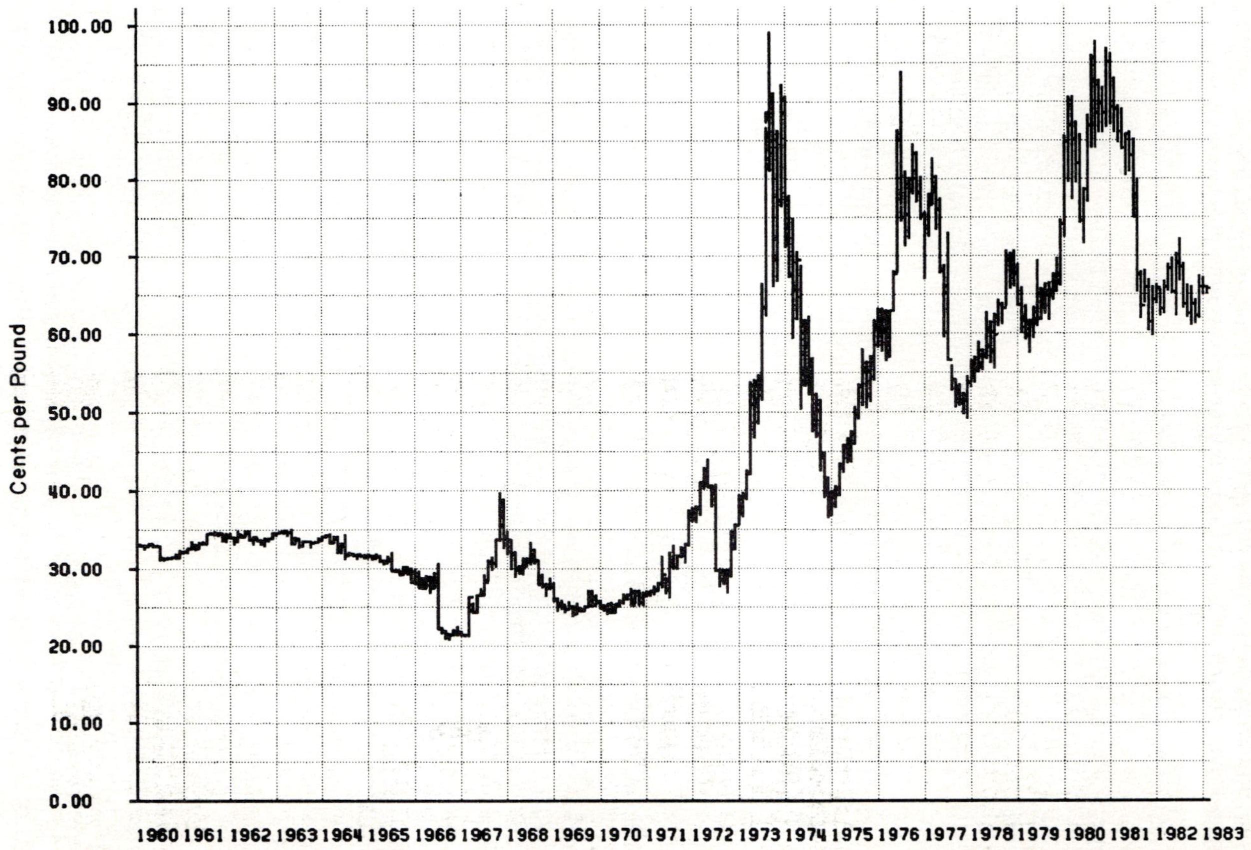

Figure 21-10 Monthly continuation, cotton. *(ContiCommodity Research Division)*

to best utilize the most opportune time of the year to make purchases or sales. Completion of harvest and the awareness that someone has to pay the cost of carrying the cotton to the market are factors partially responsible for the November low. March deliveries after mill fixations create lows again in February. Expectations of new crop planting difficulties usually cause prices to rise from March until May. After May, when the extent of actual planted acreage becomes known, prices decline. Expectations of the condition of the planted acreage or supply left from the old crop tend to push prices up in July and August. In September prices usually decline due to harvest pressure. A postharvest rally is usually apparent late in the year as mill fixations occur.

Figure 21-9 illustrates this seasonality in cotton prices; the movement of cotton prices over the past twenty years can be seen in Fig. 21-10. The astute reader will note from the seasonal price figure that price generally declines as the first notice day (FND) approaches, i.e., it declines with deliveries against the expiring contract month. The opposite is also generally true, i.e., most seasonal price advances occur at different times from deliveries against the expiring contract. Note that this figure portrays seasonals only (i.e., the original series has been detrended). These removed trends, if present, can add to and negate the effect of the seasonals, depending on their strength. Students of cycle price theory would do well to explore the cotton price cycles present in Figure 21-10, even though this chapter doesn't address this issue.

UNFIXED CALL PURCHASES

Unfixed call purchases and sales are generated by merchants whose primary concern is to move as much cotton as they can from the farmer to the mill and to generate enough profit from each transaction to cover expenses and provide an operating profit. Because they trade on the basis, flat price will affect their volume of business more than it will affect their profit margin on each transaction. Their transactions are almost always hedged, and these hedges may entail a fixed or unfixed price depending upon whether they have offsetting hedged business on the other side of their books.

For instance, a merchant will try to generate forward sales to mills first. Whether these sales involve a fixed price may depend on the merchant's customer. An unfixed call sale guarantees business to the merchant; at the same time, it affords the mill an opportunity to buy the cotton cheaper if the mill feels that prices are headed lower. Since a mill usually waits until it has a sale of cloth in advance before it actually buys its cotton, it will sell the cloth at a price predicated upon what it will pay for the raw cotton. The mill will then fix the price according to its needs. Meanwhile it has a guaranteed supply of cotton to meet its requirements.

But merchants must acquire cotton to meet their mill commitments. If they have no advance forward sales, they tend to fix the price of their cotton purchases from the farmer as each is transacted; their basis bids will be made to guarantee a profit. If a hedged forward sale exists already, the merchants can then afford to buy their cotton on a forward basis from the producer unfixed. That is, they will make bids to the farmer at a basis that they feel will guarantee an operating profit on their sales, allowing the farmer or producer the opportunity to hold out for a higher flat price.

For example, a merchant who has sold cotton to a mill at 500 off December (500 points below the price of the December contract) and later buys cotton from a farmer for 600 off December, will still make 100 points profit on the transaction whether the price is ultimately fixed at 60¢ per pound for the mill or 80¢ per pound for the producer. The mill will get its cotton for 60¢, the farmer will receive 80¢ for the crop, and the merchant has still made 100 points. It could easily happen that the transaction was initiated in June and scheduled for delivery in November, the mill fixed its price in July, and the farmer's price was fixed, in late October. Thus, this mechanism and the firming of it affords all participants the flexibility to transact business to their best advantage.

All cotton is certainly not traded in this manner. At times, conditions in the marketplace make this method of trading unprofitable, and merchants will switch to a different strategy of forward contracting.

It is beyond the scope of this chapter to explain the details of this widespread practice of the trade, but the important feature to be aware of when analyzing the unfixed call sales and purchases is that an unfixed call sale, which represents a sale to a mill, always entails a short position in futures, which must ultimately be resolved by either offset or delivery. On the other hand, an unfixed call purchase, which is a forward purchase from a producer, may or may not entail a long futures position. When the farmer fixes the price, the merchant will sell the corresponding futures, converting to a short hedge with a fixed price and basis, and wait only to deliver to the mill customer. Therefore, the merchant is not constrained to sell futures when a call purchase is on the merchant's books. However, the simple existence of the short position represented by an unfixed call sale ensures that the potential buying power is in the market to whatever extent the level of call sales outweighs call purchases. This figure can be established by determining the difference between call sales and purchases in the report from the cotton exchange (released weekly) which summarizes the outstanding transactions. All positions must be covered either by offset or delivery before the nearby contract expires.

CONSUMPTION AND STOCK STATISTICS

The following figures are reported in running bales and are released monthly with the exception of certificated stocks, which are reported daily. Average daily use means the average number of bales used by U.S. mills per day for the month. The seasonally adjusted (SA) annual rate is a monthly estimate of the number of bales to be consumed in the crop year by U.S. mills, based on that particular month's figures only. The cotton year begins August 1 and closes July 31. Mill stocks are the supply at the mills (i.e., the cotton which is physically at the mills). Public storage refers to cotton actually stored in warehouses. It has been ginned and probably compressed. The mills-week supply is an estimate of the number of weeks that mill stocks will last. Certificated stocks (released daily) are cotton that is deliverable against futures contracts. (See Table 21-11.)

TABLE 21-11 Certificated Stocks, Deliverable

Last business day of each month	1977	1978	1979	1980	1981	1982	1983
January	54,297	47,724	199,461	45,171	48,942	37,055	129,780
February	44,918	71,100	203,219	51,731	52,440	67,280	142,149
March	43,949	99,226	208,448	57,373	58,145	107,491	89,122
April	43,519	123,119	207,181	43,022	34,833	120,079	93,703
May	66,394	143,821	180,969	77,474	33,472	126,147	95,697
June	42,784	161,786	135,430	82,868	11,991	119,633	91,937
July	31,735	186,867	154,295	80,020	11,364	116,115	78,788
August	27,472	187,002	153,804	77,053	21,967	115,924	68,305
September	27,572	183,823	103,884	67,842	18,248	107,544	
October	37,553	186,283	40,659	70,561	17,745	107,176	
November	37,887	193,140	20,317	67,763	18,336	116,172	
December	40,761	196,720	34,824	64,443	26,953	124,168	

SOURCE: U.S. Census Bureau.

Production Estimates

This provides acreage, yield, and production (480-pound bales) estimates by state. When we use the term "bales," we are implying 480-pound bales. This information is released monthly before and during harvest. (See Table 21-12.)

Cotton Classing

Cotton classification, or classing, is a means of describing the quality of cotton in terms of grade and staple length. This information is released routinely during the ginning season by the USDA. The aggregate amounts tenderable give an indication of the overall quality of a particular year's crop. (See Table 21-13.)

Cotton Ginnings

This information serves as an aid in production forecasting and also helps determine how early or late the crop is as well as how fast the harvest is progressing. The reports are issued biweekly during harvesting. (See Table 21-14.)

Planting Intentions

These numbers are released two or three times each year before the growing seasons. They have tremendous market impact. (See Table 21-15.)

Export Data

These figures are also published as the number of running bales and are released weekly. Cumulative exports are the number of bales actually shipped

TABLE 21-12 Forecasts of and Final Report on Yield per Harvested Acre and Pounds per Acre Yield*

Crop year	Yield August 1	Production August 1	Yield September 1	Production September 1	Yield October 1	Production October 1	Yield November 1	Production November 1	Yield December 1	Production December 1	Yield January 1	Production January 1	Actual yield	Actual crop (May 1)
1960		14,471		14,581		14,553		14,298		14,309				14,272
1961	427	13,918	437	14,262	440	14,334	446	14,538	438	14,304			438	14,318
1962	461	15,102	449	14,687	448	14,675	444	14,533	455	14,723			457	14,867
1963	471	13,984	482	14,310	500	14,847	516	15,322	524	15,548			491	15,334
1964	506	14,785	511	14,945	522	15,274	528	15,444	524	15,356			517	15,182
1965	525	14,916	532	15,134	534	15,159	531	15,079	531	15,059			527	14,973
1966	530	10,820	539	10,992	524	10,688	504	10,290	482	9,627			480	9,575
1967	468	8,332	460	8,185	454	8,089	448	7,969	452	7,618			447	7,458
1968	511	10,976	521	11,197	515	11,071	508	10,912	511	10,822			516	10,948
1969	504	11,779	474	11,088	450	10,528	429	10,036	436	10,080			434	10,009
1970	470	11,079	456	10,752	450	10,618	442	10,429	441	10,270			437	10,166
1971	452	10,931	453	10,952	443	10,700	444	10,718	440	10,557		10,548	438	10,477
1972	452	13,343	471	13,582	493	13,670	497	13,955	502	13,469	495	13,567	507	13,702
1973	493	12,740	502	12,938	509	13,123	512	13,189	508	13,067	519	12,961	520	12,958
1974	470	12,758	485	13,200	471	12,818	450	12,080	442	11,877	443	11,702	441	11,450
1975	484	9,415	479	9,309	467	9,059	466	9,034	441	8,476	441	8,327	453	8,247
1976	466	10,730	451	10,375	445	10,251	435	9,891	451	10,264	465	10,557	465	10,517
1977	506	13,544	495	13,200	500	13,300	503	13,820	523	14,420	525	14,389	520	14,277
1978	462	11,820	436	11,155	425	10,873	429	10,980	418	10,964	421	10,841	421	10,762
1979	497	13,710	525	14,245	528	14,356	535	14,544	534	14,529	551	14,873	548	14,629
1980	461	12,812	421	11,689	419	11,589	408	11,224	401	10,938	411	11,125	404	11,122
1981	515	14,789	540	15,507	540	15,476	543	15,560	543	15,570	540	15,627	543	15,646
1982	563	11,143	569	11,029	587	11,365	605	11,947	605	12,102	582	12,019	590	11,963

*In thousands of 500-pound gross weight bales, linters not included, before 1971; after 1971, in thousands of 480-pound net weight bales.

SOURCE: U.S. Department of Agriculture.

TABLE 21-13 Tenderability of Cotton Crop

	Tenderable*		Untenderable		Total crop†	
Year	Bales	Percentage	Bales	Percentage	Bales	Percentage
1961	11,655,270	81.7	2,608,095	18.3	14,263,365	100.0
1962	11,373,949	77.1	3,380,447	22.9	14,754,396	100.0
1963	12,395,120	81.9	2,733,655	18.1	15,128,775	100.0
1964	10,154,264	67.5	4,878,050	32.5	15,032,314	100.0
1965	9,540,115	64.3	5,307,177	35.7	14,847,292	100.0
1966	4,902,137	51.6	4,589,060	48.4	9,491,197	100.0
1967	4,011,329	54.4	3,358,964	45.6	7,370,293	100.0
1968	6,714,407	62.0	4,123,977	38.0	10,838,384	100.0
1969	5,511,908	55.9	4,348,322	44.1	9,860,230	100.0
1970	6,342,53	63.1	3,712,684	36.9	10,055,237	100.0
1971	5,638,379	55.6	4,495,040	44.4	10,133,419	100.0
1972	7,279,575	55.3	5,895,947	44.7	13,175,522	100.0
1973	8,367,010	66.8	4,165,891	33.2	12,532,901	100.0
1974	6,651,985	59.2	4,587,750	40.8	11,239,735	100.0
1975	4,503,214	55.6	3,594,338	44.4	8,097,552	100.0
1976	5,767,782	56.1	4,516,274	43.9	10,284,056	100.0
1977	8,853,834	63.7	5,055,287	36.3	13,909,121	100.0
1978	5,711,866	54.6	4,747,335	45.4	10,459,201	100.0
1979	6,996,723	49.1	7,168,941	50.6	14,165,664	100.0
1980	5,405,563	50.4	5,316,703	49.6	10,722,266	100.0
1981	6,361,406	42.2	8,711,848	57.8	15,072,854	100.0
1982	7,166,579	62.7	4,263,069	37.3	11,429,648	100.0

*Beginning in 1965, tenderable with respect to grade, staple, and mike in settlement of futures contracts. Before 1965, tenderability was based on grade and staple only.

†As reported by the U.S. Census Bureau, in running bales.

SOURCE: U.S. Census Bureau.

to date, that is, the cotton that is no longer in the United States. Unshipped commitments means the number of bales that have been sold but not shipped. Next season's sales is new crop cotton that has been sold.

Export Target Information

This weekly information presents sales and shipments in running bales and must be converted to 480-pound bales. The export shipment target in 480-pound bales comes from the supply and utilization table. One running bale equals 1.056 480-pound bales. A conversion factor between sales and shipments is used in this calculation. An example of this would be: sales equals 1.15 times shipments, which means approximately 85 percent of sales are actually shipped. The weekly average required to meet the target is a function of the number of weeks remaining in the marketing year. The shipment weekly average required to meet the export target (in running bales) equals the shipment target minus cumulative exports divided by the number of weeks remaining.

TABLE 21-14 Cotton Ginning in the U.S. to Specified Dates
(Linters not included)

Crop year	Aug. 1	Sept. 1	Sept. 15	Oct. 1	Oct. 15	Nov. 1	Nov. 15	Dec. 1	Dec. 15	Jan. 1	Jan. 15	Feb. 1	Total	480-pound bales equiv.*
1972	40.2	520.7	784.1	1820.7	4438.6	6844.7	8242.1	9307.8	10442.0	11602.0	11878.9	12268.5	13269.4	13703.8
1973	2.7	135.0	245.7	496.1	1826.1	5014.1	7069.9	9196.7	10712.2	11601.1	12023.2	12373.4	12611.0	12973.5
1974	144.6	543.2	625.9	827.3	2314.8	4943.9	6509.4	8291.4	9687.2	10598.4	10898.9	11195.4	11328.4	11536.5
1975	29.8	168.6	228.2	373.2	1060.5	2766.7	4168.7	5793.6	7012.8	7602.6	7877.2	8054.9	8151.2	8296.5
1976	47.2	373.1	442.2	572.6	1563.9	3703.2	5951.5	7657.8	9114.6	9886.7	10109.6	10250.7	10347.1	10576.6
1977	85.5	693.6	1168.6	2353.2	4343.3	7493.4	9722.8	11710.6	12963.1	13513.3	13741.7	13858.6	14017.9	14388.3
1978	143.8	671.8	788.3	1490.4	2903.6	4658.6	5889.8	6668.2	8096.3	9316.9	9722.9	10048.8	10549.2	10850.7
1979†	72.3	538.5	697.4	916.4	2105.4	4798.5	7287.2	9937.2	11772.4	12727.7	13438.6	13831.8	13438.0	14261.9
1980	199.6	582.2	745.1	1312.0	2566.0	4599.5	6698.4	7840.5	8807.8	9872.8	10429.9	10675.7	10824.2	11115.2
1981	44.4	426.5	645.2	1724.8	3300.9	5528.6	7682.9	10156.1	12023.2	13460.1	14275.9	14777.8	15150.3	15627.5
1982	39.8	453.3	578.3	1531.6	2660.2	5299.2	7214.3	8825.8	9639.9	10580.1	10979.6	11301.0	11526.0	11940.5

*Data taken from U.S. Census Bureau reports, *Annual Cotton Ginning in the United States.*

†Release dates for U.S. Census Bureau reports, (1979): August 10, September 12, September 27, October 12, October 26, November 21, December 11, and December 21.

TABLE 21-15 U.S. Planted Cotton Acreage Estimates, All Kinds
(In thousands of acres)

Crop year	January intentions (upland only)	March and April intentions to plant	Preliminary estimate issued in June–July	Latest revised estimate
1961		No estimate	16,561	16,588
1962		16,412	16,427	16,293
1963		14,818	14,856	14,843
1964		14,833	14,754	14,836
1965		14,294	14,205	14,152
1966		10,868	10,567	10,349
1967		9,975	9,724	9,448
1968		11,108	11,051	10,912
1969		12,012	11,961	11,882
1970		12,224	2,138	11,945
1971		12,061	12,399	12,355
1972	13,213	13,529	13,831	14,001
1973	12,955	13,081	13,128	12,501
1974	13,979	13,979	13,699	13,699
1975	9,500	9,952	10,205	9,493
1976	11,225	11,256	11,711	11,656
1977	12,807	13,689	13,354	13,695
1978	12,516	13,147	13,048	13,360
1979	13,900	14,395	13,913	14,070
1980	13,755	14,843	14,338	14,361
1981	14,128	14,484	14,204	14,330.1
1982	12,598.8*	No estimate	11,568	11,340
1983	9,281.2†	8,125.2	8,299	8,299

*Issued February 1982.

†Issued February 1983.

SOURCE: U.S. Department of Agriculture.

The sales weekly average required to meet the export target (in running bales) equals the target minus cumulative exports plus unshipped commitments divided by the number of weeks remaining. The current week's net shipments can be calculated as the current week's shipments minus the previous week's shipments. The current week's net sales figures are released by the USDA.

Latest Forecast Supply and Utilization

Beginning stocks are an estimate of the carry-over. This estimate is revised monthly by the USDA. Current production is the estimate of U.S. production as shown in Table 21-15. Total available supply is the sum of beginning stocks and current production. U.S. exports are the estimate of annual shipments. Domestic use is an estimate of annual mill use. Total disappearance is the sum of exports plus mill use. Ending stocks are the difference between total available supply and total disappearance. They become beginning stocks for the next crop year.

A BRIEF HISTORY OF THE DECEMBER CONTRACT

December 1975 A low acreage number brought on by the 1974–75 recession was followed by decreasing production estimates and increasing mill use.

December 1976 A year of weather problems occurred, coupled with increasing exports. Relatively low acreage intentions were followed by dry Texas High Plains weather that delayed or prevented planting of 300,000 acres. Cold, dry Delta weather necessitated replanting, and a subsequent shortage of rainfall after July resulted in a Delta yield of 382 pounds per harvested acre.

December 1977 Low acreage intentions were followed by late plantings. South Texas had too much rain early in the season. Cool, dry weather in the Texas high plains and far west caused higher December futures prices followed by predictably higher acreage intentions the following April. Weather remained excellent during the summer and anticipated utilization decreased.

December 1978 An early spring with low subsoil moisture in the Texas High Plains and in Oklahoma, coupled with wet weather in the Mississippi valley, delayed plantings. The spring continued dry in Texas, followed by a low-moisture, high-temperature summer. Southwest yields were 294 pounds per acre. Extreme heat caused shedding in California, which (coupled with insect problem), caused the yield to fall to 708 pounds per harvested acre, compared to a 5-year average of 928 pounds per acre.

December 1979 The crop was late, although large. Tenderability problems associated with the Texas High Plains crop became apparent after the December contract expired. The Southwest and West accounted for three-fourths of U.S. production. Exports were much greater than originally anticipated.

December 1980 The drought scenario and reduced production resulted in a price run-up.

December 1981 Abundant production and reduced offtake resulted in a price decline that almost reached U.S. government support levels.

December 1982 Recession conditions resulted in weaker prices.

SUMMARY AND TRADING CONSIDERATIONS

Critical Factors Affecting the Cotton Supply-and-Demand Relationship

1. Estimate whether the carryover next year is above or below normal. (Source: USDA *Agricultural Supply/Demand Estimates*)
2. Establish the approximate acreage to be planted based on competing crops and government programs. (The trade is generally a good source.)
3. Estimate the domestic mill consumption of cotton. (The USDA is generally a good source.)
4. Estimate the exports. (The USDA is generally the best source.)

Leading Indicators of Cotton Price Trends

1. It is a bullish sign when nearby options rise at a faster rate than distant contracts (and vice versa).
2. It is bullish when forecasted crop-year-end world or U.S. stocks start to fall after many months of a rising trend (and vice versa).

Most Common Mistakes Made by Investors and Traders

1. Just because gold or soybeans have risen sharply in price it does not mean that cotton will follow.
2. When trading cotton, be particularly aware when the delivery periods and First Notice Day (FND) approach, because the market is very volatile then.
3. Be aware of seasonal trends.
4. Avoid trading contracts with a small open interest.

What to Look for at Bull Market Peaks

1. Prices have been running up sharply for several months on China buying and/or a poor harvest occurs there, especially if these reports fail to move prices higher when announced.
2. Rumors of shortages abound.
3. Significantly higher prices are forecast for the months ahead, following a sharp run up.
4. Feature stories appear on the network news or the front pages of newspapers describing pandemonium in the markets and traders' expectations that prices will go much higher.

5. A exponentially rising trend is seen in daily volume and open interest on the exchange.
6. Is the basis weakening, or are certificated stocks rebuilding?

What to Look for at Major Troughs

1. Prices have been falling sharply and predictions of even lower prices abound.
2. Major news stories about farm bankruptcies circulate, and appeals are made to the President and Congress to bail the farmers out.
3. Introduction of new support programs as a result of falling prices. These usually occur at 4-year intervals.
4. There are forecasts of bumper harvests around the world failing to push prices any lower.
5. Low "consensus" percentages and oversold conditions indicated by the relative strength index.
6. Is the basis strengthening, or are certificated stocks falling?

CONTRACT DATA

Base quality deliverable on Contract 2:	Strict low middlings 1 1/16 inch
Quantity	50,000 pounds (100 bales)
Staples Deliverable:	1 1/32 inch and longer on Contract 2.
Micronaire test:	Cotton must be Micronaire not less than 3.5 nor more than 4.9 to be tenderable on contract.
Price differences:	Premiums and discounts for the various grades and staples may be found in the Exchange's *Daily Market Report*.

Grades and Code Numbers for Tenderable Grades of U.S. Upland Cotton:

White grades	Code no.	Light spotted grades	Code no.
Good middling	11	Good middling light spotted	12
Strict middling	21	Strict midling light spotted	22
Middling plus	30	Middling light spotted	32
Middling	31		
Strict low middling plus	40		
Strict low middling	41		
Low middling plus	50		
Low middling	51		

Contract #2 Staple Lengths:	1 1/32	1 1/16	1 3/32 and up
Contract #2 Code Numbers:	33	34	35 and up

Rain-grown and non-rain-grown:	Non-rain-grown cotton shall be tenderable on contract without discrimination, but must be so identified.
Maximum price move:	Daily limit 2¢/pound = $1000 except when the nearby contract is in delivery and no limits apply. Expanded limits under other conditions. Minimum price fluctuation $\frac{1}{100¢}$/pound = $5.
Months traded:	March, May, July, October, and December generally with 2 red, that is, two additional new crop months. Other months can be traded, but rarely are.
Delivery warehouses:	Mobile, Alabama; New Orleans, Louisiana; Houston, Texas; Glaveston, Texas; Memphis, Tennessee; Greenville, South Carolina.

PART

4

Financial Instruments and Precious Metals

CHAPTER

22

Guidelines on Interest-Rate Forecasting

Richard T. Coghlan*

INTRODUCTION

Interest rates represent the price of money and as such are very much affected by economic behavior generally. In turn, they have crucially important feedback effects on the rest of the economy. The extent and importance of these interrelationships is derived from the central role played by money and credit in all aspects of economic behavior. Barter trades are very rare, and the vast majority of economic transactions are made through a medium of exchange—that is, money. In addition, the continuing process of saving and investing requires sophisticated credit markets. The price of money, or credit, naturally has an important bearing on the decisions which lie behind these actions.

The extensive interrelationship between economic behavior and the cost of credit itself imparts a significant cyclicality to the economy. High real interest rates raise costs and lower demand, leading eventually to a decline in loan demand and a fall in interest rates. Low real interest rates stimulate spending, investment and borrowing leading to expansion, and if carried too far, inflation. At some point the process has to come to an end and interest rates are pushed up, possibly dramatically. If the authorities add reserves to prevent an automatic tightening of liquidity, then the ensuing inflation eventually causes inves-

*Editor of *The Financial Economist*, Bala Cynwyd, Pa. This contribution is based on a chapter on forecasting interest rates in a forthcoming book by Richard Coghlan entitled *An Investor's Guide to the Business Cycle*.

tors to lower their demand for bonds, and long-term yields are pushed up. Either way, automatic forces at work within the financial markets tend to bring excessive expansion under control. However, the monetary authorities can play a major role in the timing and precise details of the cyclical pattern through their control over the reserves of the financial system. It is therefore necessary to understand the motives of these authorities in order to understand cyclical movements in interest rates.

All too often, in discussing interest-rate movements, inadequate attention is given to the different maturities and types of assets that can be held. This makes such analysis extremely unhelpful, particularly for the investor. There are, in reality, many different interest rates, and for analysis to be of any use, it is important to make at least broad distinctions between short and long term and between high and low quality. Other concerns, such as different tax treatment and the effect of varying tax rates, which can be very important to particular individuals and institutions, are not dealt with here.

It is not only short-term interest rates and long-term bond yields that change over the business cycle, but also the yield curve, that is, the relationship between short-term interest rates and long-term bond yields. This relative movement in interest rates is a key relationship in the link between interest rates and the rest of the economy.

Another change in relative interest rates associated with the business cycle, which is also important to note, is quality rather than maturity. Spreads between high- and low-quality paper of similar maturity can change a great deal depending on economic conditions and the confidence of the financial community. A major factor affecting quality spreads is the growth of debt during good times; debt becomes top-heavy and fragile as the economy moves into recession, thereby changing the conditions and assumptions on which the debt was originally built up. Not only are borrowers less able to repay, but at such times lenders suddenly become risk-averse and see the advantages of liquidity as overwhelming.

Each flow of lending and borrowing may seem justified at the time, but too often the participants fail to take full cognizance of the buildup in the stock of debt and reduction in the quality of their investment. This buildup of debt has extended far beyond the business cycle, thereby adding a further complication. Such a buildup adds to the fragility of the financial system over time and contributes significantly to the conditions creating the super cycle.

It is clear, even from this brief overview, that the interrelationships between interest rates, debt, and the economy are wide-ranging and extremely involved. The discussion in this chapter will try to bring these out clearly, while emphasizing the effect on interest-rate movements. First there is a description and explanation of short-term interest-rate movements, followed by a similar analysis of long-term bond yields.

The next section brings together short-term interest rates and long-term bond yields taking a look at the yield curve and the way in which relative interest rates interact with the rest of the economy, which essentially explains cyclicality in interest rates and the economy. Finally, quality spreads are analyzed, emphasizing how they move across the economic cycle.

SHORT-TERM INTEREST RATES

It is impossible to discuss all the possible influences on short-term interest rates. Even to attempt such a task would prove extremely unhelpful, as the discussion would quickly become enveloped in a mass of false leads and qualifications. Rather, the important thing to do is identify and concentrate on the predominant influences.

The key element in determining the level of short-term interest rates is liquidity, which affects both demand and supply. On the demand side, liquidity is closely related to confidence about the continuing stability of the economic and financial system. In some countries the possibility of confiscation in the event of a major political disturbance adds another aspect to the demand for liquidity. In such cases liquidity has more to do with anonymity and portability than with maturity of assets, and thus it causes a demand for gold, Swiss bank accounts, and so forth. This discussion, however, concentrates on interest rates and the more conventional view of liquidity.

From the demand side, liquidity is affected by confidence and therefore can change as rapidly as the collective mind of the market, which changes very fast indeed. But in discussing the supply of liquidity, it is necessary to talk about something more concrete. Normally attention is concentrated on the reserves of the banking system—clearly a crucial factor in supporting the private financial system. In a liquidity crisis, however, when investors rush for liquidity they generally choose U.S. Treasury bills above all else, and Treasury bonds are likely to come a close second. Clearly, the supply of liquidity includes all government and Federal Reserve paper. In an emergency it may be necessary for the government to expand the supply of Treasury paper dramatically in order to recycle the money back to the financial institutions, and so avoid a complete collapse of confidence. In more normal circumstances it is reasonable to concentrate on the supply of reserves to the financial system, and that is the procedure followed here. The perception of which assets are considered liquid can change so dramatically and so quickly that talking in terms of a supply of liquidity becomes difficult if not impossible. Instead, it is easier to discuss the supply of reserves.

In each country the ultimate source of reserves in the money markets is the central bank, as a representative of the government. In a modern economy there are a vast number of monetary transactions each day. In 1981 in the United States, for example, the average turnover of demand deposits—that is, the average number of times each deposit changed hands—was 281, over the year. The sophistication and speed of such movement requires a steady supply of reserves to keep the system lubricated. Without that liquidity the financial system would seize up—and the whole structure would come crashing down. In the United States the Federal Reserve is responsible for ensuring that the momentum is kept going by maintaining sufficient liquidity.

When reserves are in short supply the price naturally rises: money is a commodity like anything else, and its price is the interest rate that must be paid. Throughout history a shortage, and a consequently high cost, of money has been seen as a major restraint on economic expansion, and indeed, an extreme shortage has been widely viewed as a major cause or ingredient (depending on the precise views of the proponents) in the great depression of the 1930s. The cost of money remained very high in the 1930s despite the low level of nominal interest rates, because prices were falling and thus the *real* cost of money was raised. During most of the postwar period governments in all the industrialized countries have accepted the task of ensuring sufficient reserves to promote expansion as a primary objective. However, with the enthusiasm of converts they have taken the policy too far, with the result that finance has been kept excessively cheap for extended periods, which in turn has resulted in a persistent high and accelerating rate of inflation.

It is natural for inflation itself to eliminate excess finance by raising the prices of the things that can be bought, while at the same time raising the real cost of money (that is, real interest rates). These natural forces have, however, been widely resisted. Whenever possible, politicians have actually done the opposite; they have held the nominal interest rate down below the rate of inflation—but they have done this only by pumping yet more money into the system. The realization that the real cost of money is the important factor has dawned only slowly and is, in fact, still far from universally accepted. Consequently, policies to *prevent* inflation have been inadequate, with emergency action taken only when inflation has reached crisis proportions. As a result, there have been sudden changes in policy, when governments have moved from excessive ease to excessive tightness. The effect on short-term interest rates has been magnified many times, as the effect is transmitted through changing perceptions of liquidity.

Liquidity is not a constant. It depends upon the beliefs of individuals, which in turn are closely related to economic conditions generally. During periods of expansion when money is cheap, confidence first improves, then reaches a high level, and if continued, usually turns into overconfidence. This last state is characterized by the belief that the formula of perpetual motion has been discovered; that scarce resources no longer provide a limit to man's achievement; and that growth and prosperity will continue to accelerate far into the distant future. At such times the demand for liquidity is low because confidence is high. People—including usually conservative bankers—see no risks ahead and are happy to commit extensive funds under the most optimistic assumptions.

The idea of rising prosperity suggests to others the prospect of expanding opportunities to make profits. They, therefore, raise their demand to borrow money, particularly at the short end of the market where most initial financing takes place, which tends to raise the cost of money. This is the point at which the monetary authorities have generally stepped in to ease the pressure at the short end by putting additional reserves into the system, or by making reserves available in other ways, such as by relaxing reserve requirements.

As long as short-term money remains cheap and below the expected returns available in the future (regardless of what the actual returns turn out to be), this policy is likely to encourage excessive demand for short-term money. The comparison between interest rates and returns is, of course, made in real terms. It is, however, impossible to hold the real cost of money low for an indefinite period without extensive controls, and even with controls it can prove very difficult.

Excessive expansion changes expectations from real growth to inflation, and gradually increases the demand for liquidity—a development which tends to exaggerate the growth of both short-term deposits and the money supply, at the same time that the authorities have actually started to apply pressure on reserves. Excessive ease inevitably leads to excessive tightness to bring the expansionary psychology back under control. It is not sufficient simply to return to the more conservative path which should never have been left; instead, it is necessary to impose excessive tightness in order to change expectations.

The pressure created by a shortage of money pushes many firms and countries toward and into bankruptcy. As this happens, the risk of present and past lending increases, and the perception of that risk rises even faster. To begin with risks increase gradually, but some event—some surprise bankruptcy or announcement, such as the potential Mexican default in the summer of 1982—accelerates the process dramatically. Suddenly fear takes hold and dictates the actions of normally conservative individuals, who can now see that destruction of their wealth is possible.

What follows is a scramble for liquidity, but that is like chasing a ghost. If everyone desires liquidity, there is no liquidity. Liquidity, which represents the immediate spendability of one's assets, can be maintained only as long as it is passed along; once it stops moving, there is a danger that the whole financial structure may collapse. Instant repayment of all short-term debts cannot be achieved, and the attempt to demand it will only destroy all liquidity by bringing the financial superstructure crashing down, and the economy with it.

Fortunately, events rarely get pushed that far, and a major reason is the intervention of large governments operating through a range of supports and guarantees. The rush for liquidity does, however, result in a fall in short-term interest rates which is often quite sharp. (See Figure 22-1.) This important feature of the economic cycle occurs after the onset of recession, when it becomes clear that continued restraint will jeopardize the very existence of the economic system. Not only is there a heightened demand for liquidity, but also the monetary authorities are likely to relax the tourniquet on the supply of reserves.

There has been much discussion in recent years about the role of investors' expectations, but it should be remembered that the authorities are also learning from history and adapting their behavior accordingly. The significance of past events may well be misinterpreted, but the interpretation of the authorities is generally not very different from that of the majority of market participants.

Each cycle has its own unique characteristics, but there is a persistent pattern to short-term rates. Interest rates rise gradually to start with, often resisted by government which holds down the official discount rate. Toward the end of the cycle, the rise in rates accelerates sharply. Frequently, there is a false peak in short-term interest rates, when the authorities panic before conditions have really changed. Consequently, short-term interest rates have to run up again until economic activity has been well and truly depressed and optimism is destroyed. The longer the previous expansion has been under way, the longer this process takes. Finally, as optimism turns to pessimism and then to fear, short-term interest rates collapse. Once the conditions have been established, the trigger is generally supplied by some domestic or international event which suddenly focuses attention on the new reality. The state of the economy and, as discussed below, the yield curve are useful indicators of when the risk of rising interest rates is overtaken by the risk of falling interest rates.

LONG-TERM BOND YIELDS

The first of the two parts of this section deals with the effect of inflationary expectations on the long-run trend of long-term bond yields. Important cyclical influences around this trend provide major investment opportunities. The second and main part of this section deals with these cyclical influences. The discussion is in terms of specific indicators which have been specially constructed to identify cyclical turning points in interest rates, for use in *The Financial Economist.**

Inflationary Expectations

The overriding long-run influence on bond market yields is provided by expectations about inflation. Economic journals are full of attempts to explain exactly how inflationary expectations are formed, but there are many problems. It would be naive to believe that a single factor determines expectations of infla-

*Published monthly by the Financial Economist Publications Ltd., Bala Cynwyd, Pa.

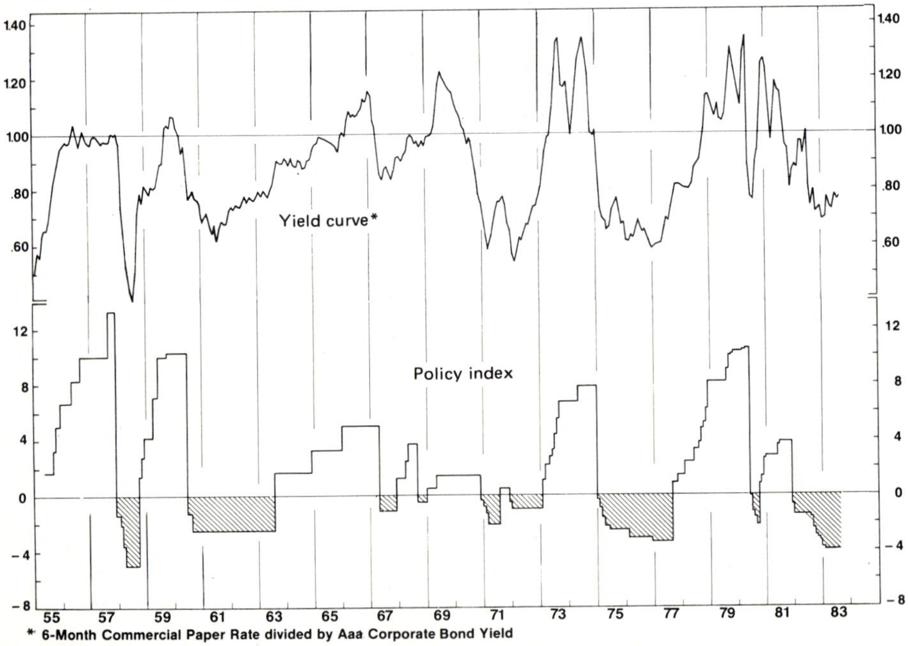

Figure 22-1 Liquidity indicators for the bond market. (© *The Financial Economist*)

tion, or for that matter expectations about anything; but people do learn from the past. Bond yields until recently have typically undershot the actual rate of inflation, clearly suggesting that the view of investors about the future course of inflation was too optimistic. Over time the persistence of inflation has gradually pushed up the trend of long-term bond yields, as shown in Figure 22-2.

The process is cumulative. Eventually investors will demand a real return on their assets—to compensate them not only for current lending but also for losses on past lending. Long-term bond yields tend not to rise as fast as inflation when inflation is accelerating, nor do they fall as fast when inflation is decelerating. Irving Fisher argued that the lags in the full adjustment of inflationary expectations could be as long as 20 years.* That may be the case, but the majority of the adjustment is likely to take place more quickly, say in 4–5 years. The point to note, however, is that the lags far exceed anything normally assumed.

The expected bond yield shown in Figure 22-2 has been constructed on the basis of adaptive expectations of past inflation plus a constant to measure the desired real interest rate. It can be seen that the trend of the actual bond yield has closely followed this expected rate. Any major deviation, as in 1957–58, when expected and actual yields went sharply in opposite directions, was soon followed by a period of readjustment during which the actual yield caught up with the expected yield. Later, in the 1975 to 1977 period, the two yields traced out similar patterns, but the actual yield was clearly too low, suggesting that investors were much too optimistic about the future course of inflation. What followed was a catchup, followed by overshooting to compensate for the earlier overoptimism.

Simply telling people that inflation will fall and that the right policies are being taken, will bring down neither inflationary expectations nor long-term bond yields. It would be strange if they did, and yet that is what some economists and politicians argued on both sides of the Atlantic, as the United States and the United Kingdom embarked on their "fight against inflation" in the early 1980s. Events proved otherwise; only a sharp fall in inflation *and* a deep recession were capable of bringing down yields, as indeed should have been expected after the years of persistent monetary ease and inflation.

It is also important to take account of the level of government expenditure, and the size of the budget deficit. Government spending has been a major factor contributing to the pressure of excess demand, which has led to accelerating and sustained inflation. Consequently, government spending has now become an important factor in influencing expectations about inflation. The pressure on financial markets coming from massive government demands for funds has also directly resulted in higher interest rates than would otherwise have been necessary—although that has not prevented interest rates from falling at times of very weak private sector financial demands.

Cyclical Influences

Liquidity Trends. This brings us to the cyclical influences on bond yields, which operate about the longer-run trend of inflation. First, there is the impact

*Irving Fisher, *The Theory of Interest*, Macmillan, New York, 1930.

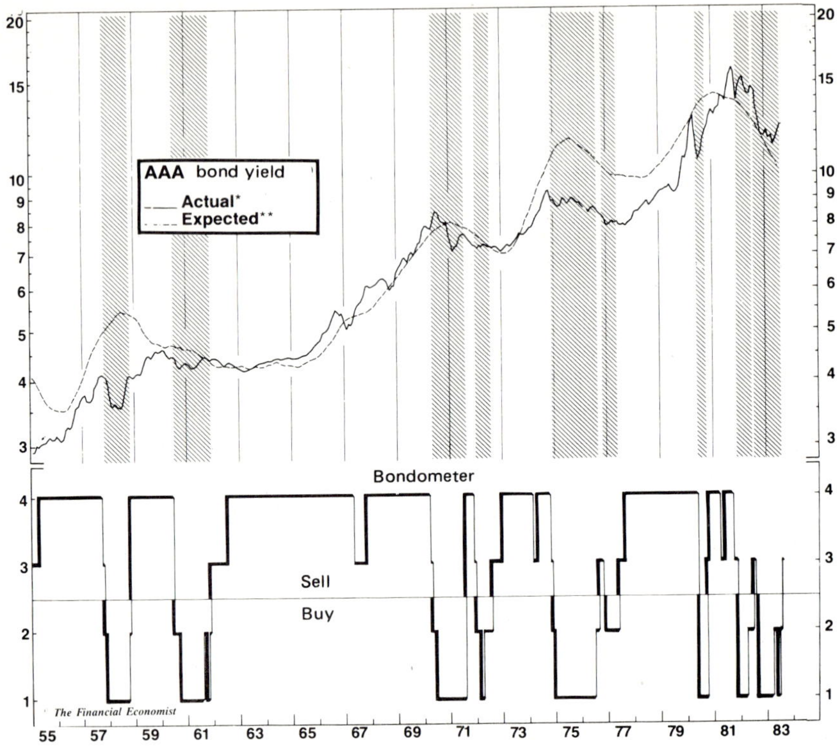

*Moody's corporate AAA bond yield.

**Based on inflation expectations.

BONDOMETER

The BONDOMETER is a unique indicator developed by **The Financial Economist** in order to identify the major turning points in the bond market. There is no one economic or monetary variable which will satisfactorily explain all turning points, and for this reason the BONDOMETER includes a variety of influences in the form of a composite index.

(1) ECONOMIC ACTIVITY INDEX - combines economic indicators into a composite index, measured as a deviation from trend. The index has consistently provided early warning of the strength or weakness of the economy.

(2) LOAN DEMAND - helps explain the pressure on the financial markets. A fall in the growth of loan demand below a certain level takes pressure off the credit markets, allowing interest rates to fall, and vice versa.

(3) CREDIT SUPPLY CONDITIONS - the availability of credit, as well as the demand for loans, is also important in determining the level of interest rates. This depends upon the supply of liquidity onto the market, and will be reflected in a rising trend of short-term interest rates.

(4) YIELD CURVE - tightening credit conditions are also reflected in movements in relative interest rates, as measured by the yield curve.

(5) POLICY INDEX - designed to measure the monetary policy actions of the Federal Reserve. Policy reactions continue to provide a timely indicator of credit pressures.

EXPECTED BOND YIELD

While the turning points in the bond market are identified by the BONDOMETER the underlying trend is given by the expected yield. This has been developed by **The Financial Economist** using a specially constructed measure of expected inflation. Generally, the correspondence between the actual and expected has been very close. However, there have been times of over-optimism in the market, as for example over the 1974-1978 period, and these have been followed by a turn towards pessimism.

Figure 22-2 Inflation and bond yields. (© *The Financial Economist*) of liquidity conditions on short-term interest rates and the relationship between short- and long-term rates, as measured by the yield curve. The process of tightening monetary policy by raising short-term rates and inverting the yield curve (when short rates are above long) will have an adverse effect on bond prices by restricting the liquidity of the market. Such a move will, however, help to establish the conditions under which bond yields will actually fall in the future. Obviously, continued easy money and rising inflation will eventually accelerate inflationary expectations, which will also cause bond prices to fall. However, a standard feature of the cyclical behavior of bond yields is that they are forced higher by attempts to correct the inflationary forces which account for the longer-term deterioration and fixed-interest asset values.

If investors had complete confidence in government policy, their confidence would help greatly to offset the negative impact of reduced market liquidity. In fact, quite the opposite generally occurs, and government action to stop inflation actually seems to increase investors' awareness of the problem. A number of indicators can be used to measure the influence of tightness or ease of monetary policy. Two measures are shown in Figure 22-1; the yield curve, and a specially constructed policy index. Liquidity can tighten if demand increases for a given supply, or if supply is restricted for any given demand. The later indicator is designed to measure periods when the Federal Reserve is deliberately tightening policy.

The market is liquid when there are ample reserves to finance the loans the financial system wishes to make. The market is highly liquid when the supply of funds exceeds the demand at the short end of the market. It is impossible to measure demand and supply directly, although attempts are still made to do so, but certain indicators are helpful in judging the situation. For example, when supply exceeds demand for any commodity the price should fall; the price in this case is short-term interest rates. As pressure comes off the short end, short-term interest rates should fall, not only relative to their recent trend but also relative to long-term bond yields. In addition, bank liquidity should also provide some guide to the ease or tightness of credit conditions. These then, very briefly, are the kinds of indicators to keep an eye on.

Economic Trends. A second way of approaching the bond market is to look directly at the strength of the economy. Again it is useful to employ a composite index based on more than one indicator, so as to include a broad range of possible scenarios. Such an indicator is useful on the grounds that a weak economy tends to bring down interest rates. In fact, history shows that it is a weakening economy, rather than one which is simply weak, that is most important. (See Figure 22-3.)

In constructing the composite measure, particular weight was given to the labor market. The resulting index is shown in Figure 22-4. The Economic Activity Index (EAI) provides early warning of decisive moves by the economy into recession and back to recovery. This indicator is important in triggering buy signals, but generally returns to strength at a time when there is still the potential for further improvement in the bond market. That is because loan demand does not pick up so quickly in the early stages of recovery, and the initial strengthening of the EAI should be treated as an early warning signal. The EAI

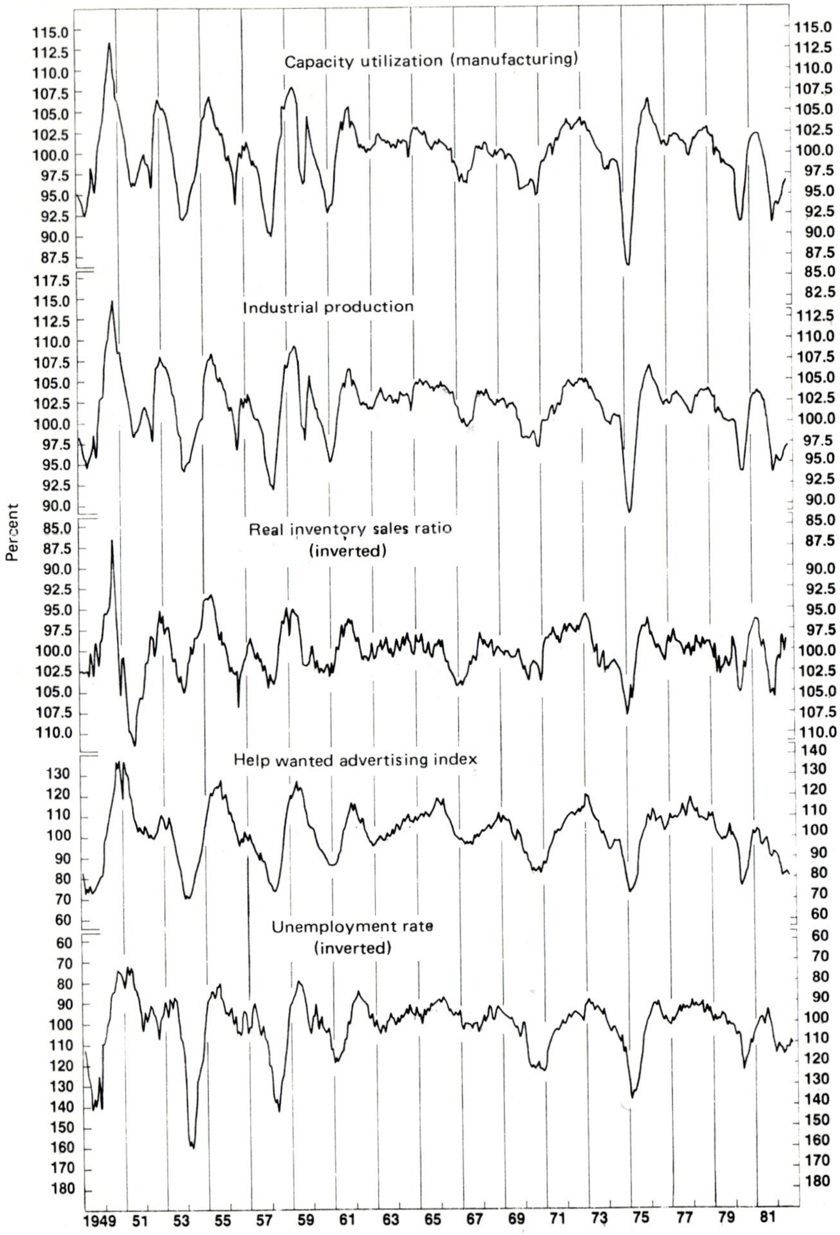

Figure 22-3 Cyclical economic indicators. (All indicators are seasonally adjusted and shown as a deviation from trend.) (© *Bank Credit Analyst*)

represents a highly conservative measure, and from 1949 to 1982, it would have kept investors short more than 80 percent of the time. This was very fortunate since long-term bond yields rose from 2½ to 15½ percent over this time period. In addition, the buy signals would also have shown a profit. No broad cyclical measure can ever hope to pick up all the intracyclical swings in prices, but knowing the condition of the economy is crucial for investment decisions.

An example of how this indicator can be too early giving a sell signal, if used on its own, occurred in 1975, while the bull market remained intact for another 2 years. It was clearly too early to sell in 1975, although the major part of the bull move had already taken place by then. Interest rates kept falling, as liquidity conditions were kept easy, and this was continued until the inevitable inflation forced a reversal of policy. However, precisely for such reasons it is important to take account of other available information, such as liquidity conditions and loan demand, discussed below.

The bull market that ended in 1977 extended much further than was justified, because it was fed on easy money, as reflected by the liquidity indicator. This overshooting on the up side by the bond market in part explains the subsequent extreme disillusionment felt by investors as well as explaining the depth of pessimism reflected in bond markets in the 1980s. The high level of interest rates reached then reflected the normal swing of the pendulum from one extreme to the other.

Trends in Credit Demands. The final fundamental indicator to be discussed here is a measure of private-sector short-term credit demands, which approaches the problem from yet another direction. In a period of economic expansion private-sector credit demands grow rapidly. After a time this results in a tightening of monetary policy, which pushes up interest rates as liquidity is drained out of the system, and interest rates remain high as long as demands for bank credit are excessive. Not until these demands fall are interest rates able to come down in a sustainable fashion. The method employed here is to combine business and consumer short-term credit into a single indicator, as shown in Figure 22-5.

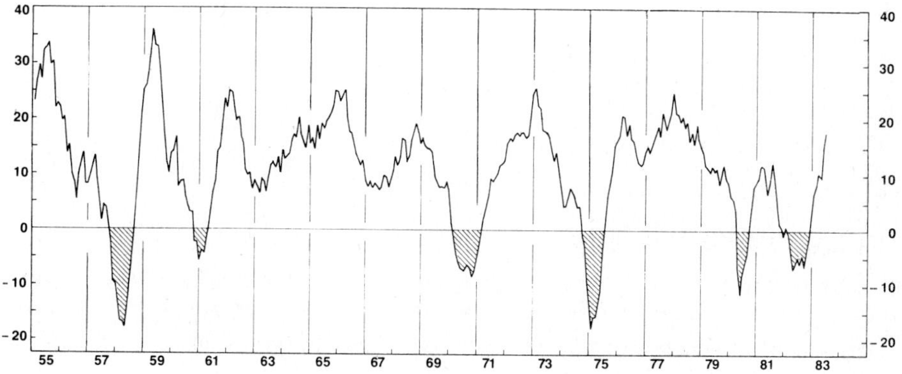

Figure 22-4 Economic activity index. (© *The Financial Economist*)

The typical pattern is that the rate of increase of consumer credit demands declines before the onset of recession, whereas corporate short-term credit demands first rise and then fall, as the economy actually moves into recession. The initial tendency for corporate short-term credit demands to rise results from the fall in consumer demand. Thus, there is an unintended rise in inventories and an unexpected fall in labor productivity, and these have to be financed in the short term. The recession deepens when companies react to their deteriorating financial positions by cutting inventory and laying off labor. At this point short-term credit demands also ease.

The three indicators discussed above are all different ways of looking at the same set of circumstances. The combination of events creates certain economic and financial conditions, and together these indicators should tell a consistent story: the story of bond price movements over the cycle. These indicators, however, do not constitute an exhaustive catalog. Other indicators that can and should be studied are the money supply and, when monetarist policies are in force, the growth rate relative to the target.

The most that such indicators can do is explain broad cyclical movements, and in this they have been very successful, as can be seen from Figure 22-2. Further support for identifying cyclical turning points, and for some of the intercyclical swings in bond prices, can be obtained by looking at the technical signals of the market. When making investment decisions, the objective should be to obtain as much information as possible from as many different sources as possible.

THE YIELD CURVE

The yield curve was introduced above as one of the ingredients in analysing market liquidity. A discussion of the yield curve in slightly more detail should help to clarify the argument. The yield curve is a valuable summary of a great deal of behavior and information. It is important both in explaining the cyclical behavior of the economy and as a basic guideline to the bond market.

A simple rule which has made a lot of money for investors, while enabling

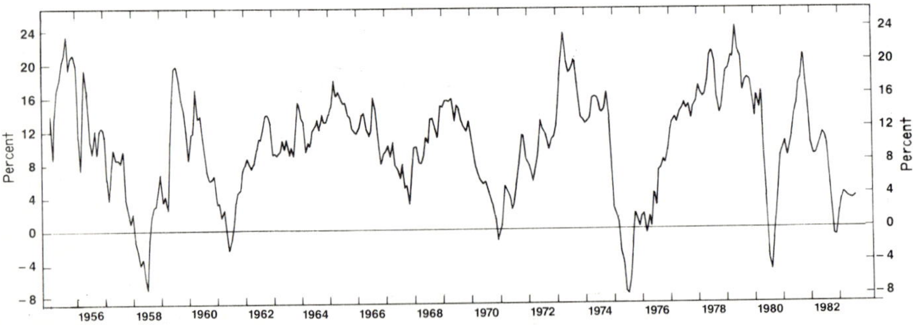

Figure 22-5 Business and consumer short-term credit and interest rates. (© *The Financial Economist*

them to avoid substantial risks during the postwar period: Stay in bonds as long as the yield curve is positive, and go short as soon as the yield curve becomes inverted, that is, as soon as short rates rise above long bond yields. This rough rule of thumb is very crude, but it has proved very effective. It has allowed investors to earn the higher bond yield as long as short rates were lower, but still to avoid the worst of the bond market crashes that have occurred. With a little fine tuning, and using indicators like those described above, performance could have been still further improved.

The yield curve is like a snapshot measuring the relationship between short- and long-term interest rates at a particular point in time. In an important sense it reflects expectations about what will happen to short-term interest rates in the future. For example, an increase in inflation will result in an increase in long-term interest rates, as lenders seek compensation for the loss of principal and real interest income resulting from the higher inflation rate. If short rates do not change, borrowers will turn to the short end of the market where costs are cheaper. This in turn will push up short rates. Short-term rates will be held down only if the monetary authorities pump in large amounts of additional reserves, and there are limits to how long that can continue in the face of a deteriorating bond market. Once tightening is under way, short-term interest rates will rise even further, in the attempt to bring inflation under control.

The extent to which short rates rise relative to long yields will depend on the resolve of the monetary authorities, while the level interest rates will have to reach will be determined by the rate of inflation itself. The level of nominal interest rates is generally meaningless as a measure of tightness or ease. An interest rate of 20 percent has very different implications for policy and the future course of inflation, depending whether inflation is running at 5 percent or 40 percent. But that is where the importance of the yield curve comes in, for relative interest rates reveal a great deal about the tightness of monetary policy.

Within a market environment, operating monetary policy means squeezing reserves in order to put up the price of money at the short end of the market. This squeeze on reserves may or may not be reflected in changes in the measured reserves of the banking system. Distortions are created particularly in the short term when—as now—rapid institutional changes are taking place within the financial system, and when transfers between different deposit categories imply different reserve requirements. Under such circumstances the most reliable guide to monetary policy is the price of money, and in particular the price of short-term money relative to the rate of inflation and the long-term bond yield (as a rough measure of the expected rate of inflation). The relationship between money growth, the yield curve, and economic growth, as measured by the change in industrial production, is shown in Figure 22-6. The yield curve here is measured by the ratio between the 4- to 6-month commercial paper rate and the Aaa corporate bond yield, and thus can be plotted as a single line.

Two major advantages of the yield curve as a measure of policy and indicator of the future are (1) the speed with which the information becomes available (that is, instantly for the yield curve and with a lag for the money supply and other statistics) and (2) the reliability of the information. There are no seasonal adjustment problems and the data are not continually being revised, misinter-

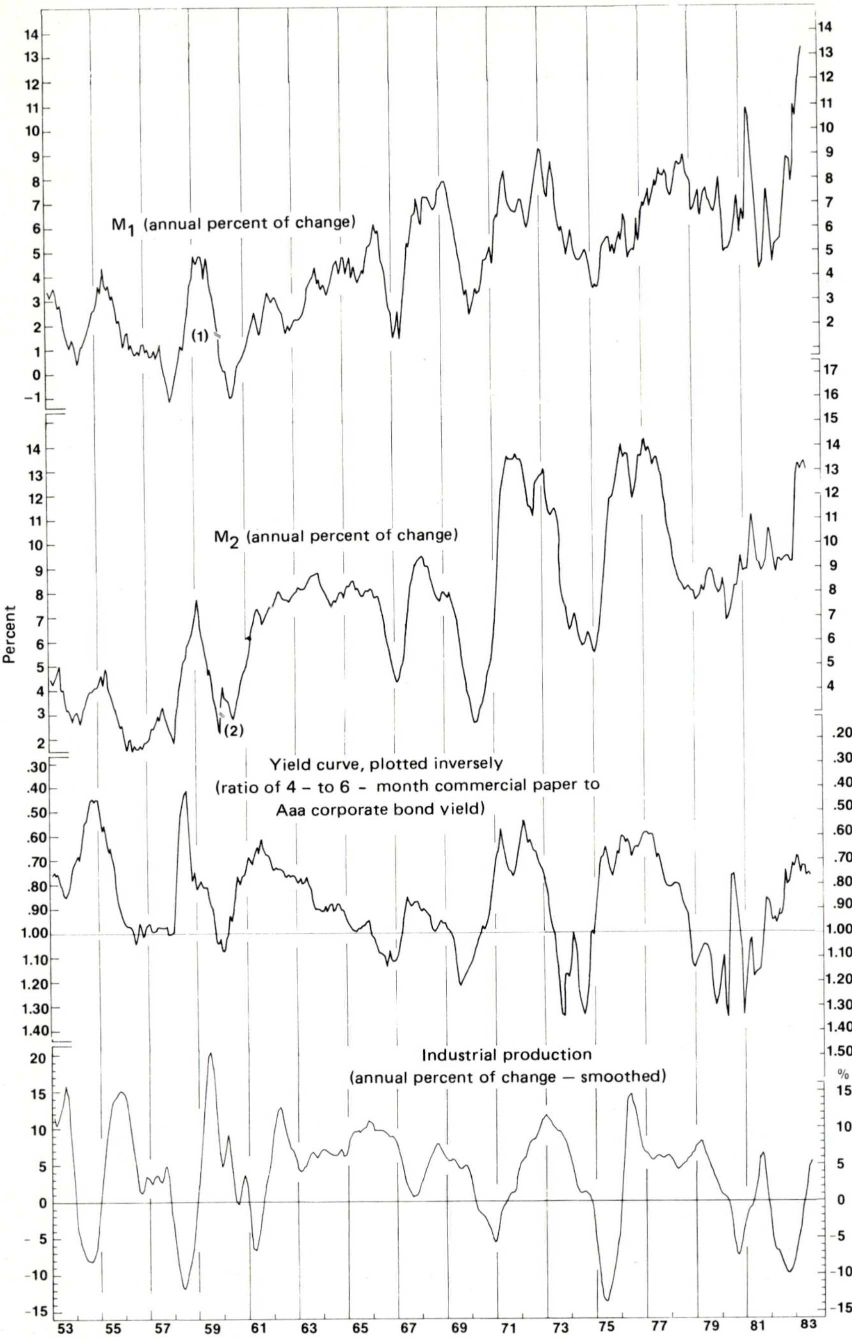

(1) Annual percent of change of old M1 before 1960.
(2) Annual percent of change of old M2 before 1960.

Figure 22-6 Measuring monetary policy in the United States. (© *The Financial Economist*) preted, misunderstood, and amended, as are other statistics on money and the economy.

When short-term interest rates rise significantly above long-term rates and remain there, they make short-term credit expensive and raise doubts about whether the increased cost can be passed on. As long as rates are expected to fall quickly, the contractionary effect is slight. Short-term interest rates have to remain high and the yield curve has to remain inverted long enough to create the expectation that they will stay that way for a long time. At some point there will be a sharp rise in risk and uncertainty, credit demands will be slashed, and demand for certain goods and services will evaporate. Then, in a domino effect, the decline in activity and disruption of balance sheets is transmitted through the rest of the economy, setting up a deflationary spiral. It is important to recognize that monetary policy will only put downward pressure on demand and inflation by first creating a recession—there is no other way. And it is only then that interest rates can be allowed to come down and the yield curve can unwind.

How much time it takes to reach this position, in which expectations in the private sector are turned around and demand and output are lowered, depends on many different factors. Three major influences are discussed briefly below.

First, inflation itself delays the process. The longer inflation has been a problem, the more persistent it becomes and therefore the harder reversing the trend becomes. Inflationary expectations become built more strongly into the decisions of government, workers, businesspeople, and investors. New contracts are structured in such a way as to provide protection from the inflation expected in the future, and this increases downward resistance and puts a floor under the rate of inflation. As a result, it becomes harder and harder to break expectations and get the economy to turn down.

Second, the more quickly policy has been reversed in the past, leaving inflation unscathed, the harder it becomes to reverse expectations. Rates cannot fall until they are expected not to fall, and weakness on the part of the monetary authorities in the past will only increase the problems of achieving control in the future. The situation is analogous to that of the little boy who cried "Wolf!" so many times that finally when a wolf did appear no one came to his rescue. Monetary authorities may start with a good deal of credibility, but once credibility is lost it is hard to win back. In fact, winning it back may well require excessively tight policies.

Third, credit controls, interest-rate ceilings, and restraints on competition have been gradually dismantled in recent years. This process has been speeded up in the 1980s, putting more pressure on interest rates to clear the financial markets. The overall effects on demand may be the same, but the process will be different and the visible signs of stress will also change. With more emphasis on the price of credit, interest rates will have to be pushed higher and stay there longer.

In sum, all these forces are working in the same direction, to make the yield curve more inverted and to keep it that way for longer. The main periods of tight money are clearly visible in Figure 22-6, in each case *preceding* the major downturns in the economic activity that have occurred since 1952. During this time, the peaks and troughs of money supply growth have tended to move higher, while the yield curve has become less positive during periods of monetary ease and more negative when monetary policy has been tightened. These trends are related to the gradual acceleration of the underlying rate of inflation which has become embedded in expectations, as well as to disillusionment with official policy and the removal of constraints on competition between financial institutions.

QUALITY SPREADS

Another aspect of interest rates which investors should take into account is the movement of the spread between high- and low-quality financial instruments. Liquidity, as discussed above, is a function of confidence, dependent basically on the perceptions of investors and potential investors. The trouble is that these perceptions can change dramatically over the economic cycle. Confidence is generally built up only gradually, but it breaks suddenly. At such times the mass of investors demand only the highest quality, and the spread between high- and low-risk paper can widen dramatically. Even without actual bankruptcy and repudiation of debt, the investor in low-quality paper is likely to see the value of the investment decline sharply, even as the price of high-quality paper is increasing. When this happens, investors who took lower-quality paper in order to earn a higher return will remember what they really always knew—that return and risk are positively correlated.

It is not simply that expectations change against a constant background. Typically, what happens is that debts accumulate during periods of easy money and favorable expectations of the future. Creditors are inclined to see their own claim in isolation from the many other claims that are also mounting up. However, when money tightens and liquidity becomes more highly valued, individuals lower their expectations about the future and a closer examination reveals the huge stock of debt which has been built up.

Then two things happen which together make creditors very nervous. First, the economic assumptions which were made to justify the original loan are found to be excessively optimistic. An example is the widespread assumption in 1980 that the price of oil would rise continuously, in both nominal and real terms, throughout the 1980s. It is one thing to lend to oil producers under that assumption, but quite another if there is a glut of oil and the real price starts to fall. Second, the situation is made far worse by the huge buildup of debt, and often a problem of gigantic proportions is created. Each individual loan becomes lost in a sea of credit, which only adds to the cash-flow problems of the debtors. Under these circumstances, creditors' concerns about relative returns are replaced by a deep-seated fear for the safety of their capital.

The monthly average quality spread for the United States is shown in Figure 22-7, along with the Aaa corporate bond yield and the *inverted* growth of industrial production. Two versions are presented, one in terms of the straight difference between Baa and Aaa and the second as the ratio of Baa to Aaa yields. These fairly conservative measures of the quality spread show that the pattern of both series has been broadly similar from 1964 to 1982, although the series based on the difference of yields did rise significantly above the ratio series at the start of the 1980s.

On the basis of differences alone, it was possible to argue that there had been a significant increase in risk over this period. However, it should be recognized that the level of interest rates had also risen strongly at that time. Consequently, for any given percentage difference, the absolute difference would be greatly expanded. It is not possible to say how investors actually perceive quality spreads, but it is likely that the absolute difference overrates expectations at times of high nominal interest rates such as those recently experienced.

Figure 22-8 gives the quality spreads on the same base, but with annual averages going back to 1920. Up until 1979 the ratio was always above the difference, at times very substantially. One thing that this suggests is that at times of low interest rates the ratio series probably overstates the degree of perceived risk. The true measure most likely lies somewhere in between, but at least the direction of movement in both series is the same. Also it would clearly be wrong to suggest that the quality spread so far in the early 1980s has been at all comparable to what happened in the 1930s.

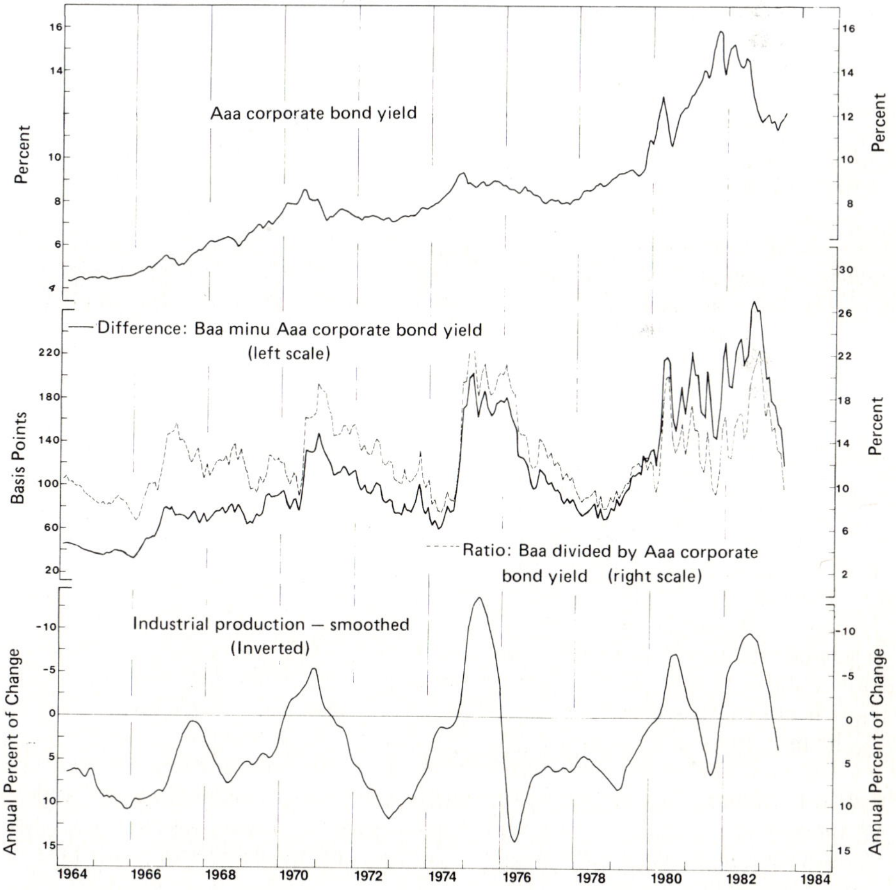

Figure 22-7 Quality spreads and economic activity. (© *The Financial Economist*)

The clear cyclicality in quality spreads, as shown in the figures is closely related to the level of rates at the high-quality end. Quality spreads are narrowest when interest rates are low *and* the economy is growing—basically when liquidity and confidence are both running at a high level. The existence of only one of these conditions is not enough. In the 1930s, as shown in Figure 22-8, the rate on high-quality bonds was very low but the quality spreads rose to astronomical levels because of the perceived risk of default. Also, even with high growth, quality spreads start to widen, if only gradually, as interest rates begin to firm up.

While the early widening of spreads is only gradual, the final move up at the end of the cycle is usually explosive. This last convulsive move is closely associated with a crack in the market, the collapse of loan demand, and a sharp, often dramatic, fall in interest rates at the high-quality end. At this point risks of a cumulative collapse, which could prove uncontrollable, seem highest. At the furthest end of the quality spectrum, yields rise while yields on medium-quality paper do not change much either way (always assuming that a major collapse is avoided), whereas the high-quality end shows sharp improvement. This divergence widens the spreads dramatically, just when rates start down, and the movement can be clearly seen in a close study of Figures 22-7 and 22-8.

Quality spreads can be used in two ways: first, as a guide to investment, either in staying with quality or in playing the spread, and second, as a confirming indicator of a turning point in the economic cycle and of the level of yields.

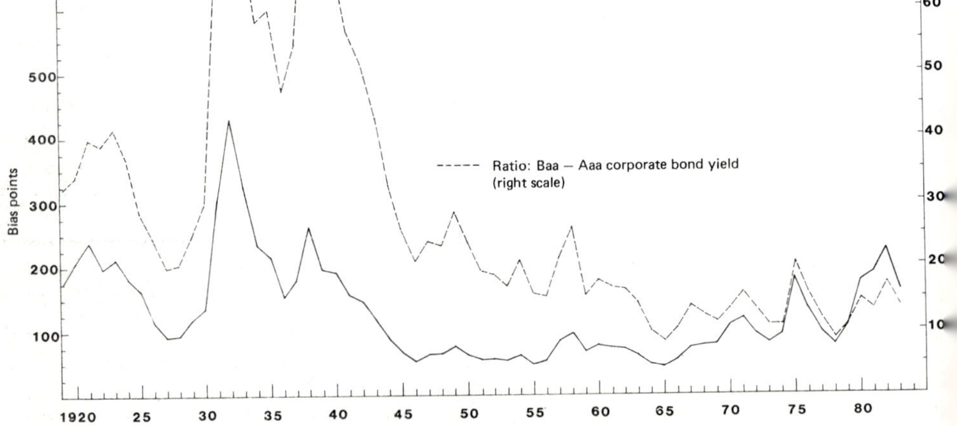

Figure 22-8 The long-term trend of quality spreads. (© *The Financial Economist*)

CONCLUSION

The underlying trend in the level of interest rates is related to inflation, while the shorter-term movements are clearly determined by the business cycle. The yield curve is also cyclical in its behavior, with short rates moving below long-term yields during periods of easy money and rising above when monetary policy is tightened. These movements create some excellent investment opportunities for investors, particularly those prepared to take a 2- to 3-year view when making decisions. This does not mean that holding periods have to cover 2 to 3 years, however; even short-term traders should try to look beyond their own trading horizon to establish the underlying trend.

Cyclical and secular trends may also be discerned in quality spreads. The sharp rise in the quality spread at the end of the cycle becomes potentially more dangerous as the outstanding stock of debt rises in real terms over time. A mass of defaults would result in an explosion in the quality spreads on a scale not seen since the 1930s, and the whole invested capital of many investors would be wiped out. This is an important consideration for investors when evaluating the relative risk and return they are willing to accept, and becomes a matter for major concern as the economy moves toward the terminal stages of the cycle.

There is a good chance that the underlying rate of inflation will gradually come down through the 1980s, but nothing is certain. Moreover, the decline will not be in a straight line, and it is virtually certain that cyclical fluctuations will continue to occur. Given that inflationary expectations should fall more slowly than the actual rate of inflation, sharp fluctuations in interest rates will probably continue to occur, even against a gradually declining trend. A permanent reduction in the rate of inflation will eventually result in substantial capital gains in long-term bonds—or to put it another way, continuing high yields at times of low current interest rates. However, because the outcome remains uncertain, investors should buy bonds when they are cheap, with emphasis on value. For this reason the cyclical movement in interest rates remains the key guide to investment decisions.

CHAPTER

23

The Business Cycle and the Yield Curve

Geraldine L. Szymanski

THE INFLUENCE OF THE BUSINESS CYCLE ON INTEREST RATES

General

Interest rates, which are properly viewed as the price of credit, reflect the demand and supply conditions in the market for credit. Accurate forecasts of interest rates and futures prices, therefore, depend on the ability to correctly anticipate and analyze the various factors that influence demand and the supply of credit. Demand is composed of the borrowing requirements of the private and public sectors, and is affected by the economic and political developments that cause borrowing by individuals, businesses, and governments—federal, state, and local—to fluctuate. The supply of credit is determined by the willingness of the private sector to supply funds to the credit markets and by monetary policy. Credit supply, therefore, is affected by a combination of economic conditions and the policy objectives of the Federal Reserve.

Private borrowing is largely a function of the business cycle. Businesses borrow short-term to even out their day-to-day cash flow, and they borrow long-term to finance expenditures for new plant and equipment. Individuals borrow to finance the purchase of homes, appliances, automobiles, and consumption items such as clothing and vacations. Investment and consumption expenditures, and hence private-sector borrowing, rise when business sales and income increase and fall when business sales and income decrease. In other words, private borrowing moves procyclically, rising during economic expansions and falling during economic contractions.

Because state and local governments are constrained by the necessity to balance their budgets, government borrowing at these levels also moves with the business cycle, increasing during expansions, when tax revenues rise, and decreasing during recessions, when tax revenues fall. Federal borrowing, however, moves countercyclically. During economic downturns, tax revenues decline while expenditures for social programs such as unemployment assistance increase. The federal deficit widens as a result, and the Treasury is forced to increase the amount that it borrows in the credit markets. During economic expansions, tax revenues rise, reflecting the overall improvement in income, and social spending falls. This causes a narrowing of the deficit, and Treasury borrowing diminishes.

It is important to note that high federal deficits and large borrowing requirements do not in themselves cause high interest rates. Because of the countercyclical nature of government borrowing, interest rates can be observed to decline during periods of economic weakness, when government deficits are high, and to rise during periods of economic strength, when government deficits are low. High interest rates are caused by the combined demand of both government and private borrowers; if one or the other significantly reduces its presence in the credit markets, than a decline in interest rates is likely to follow.

Keeping this in mind, it is possible to use Figure 23-1 as a useful framework for studying the relationship between interest rates and the business cycle. Moving from left to right, the curved line shows the economy rising from a

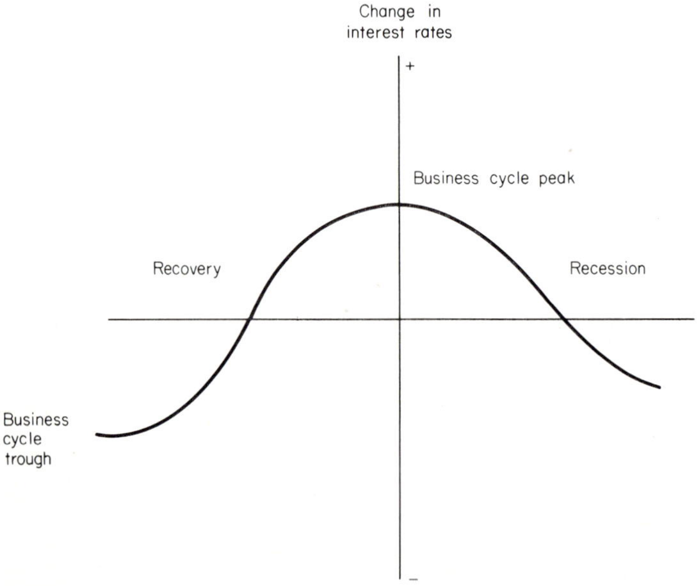

Figure 23-1 The relationship between interest rates and the business cycle.

business-cycle trough through a recovery to a business-cycle peak and then turning down again into a recession. The horizontal line can be thought of as the level of economic activity above which interest rates are rising and below which they are falling. What this diagram demonstrates is that changes in interest rates lag behind changes in economic conditions. During the early stages of a recovery, interest rates are still declining. Income has begun to increase, raising tax revenues and reducing the need for social spending. This causes deficit financing to shrink. Since the economy has only just begun to recover, private credit demand is relatively light, and the reduction in government borrowing and small private-sector borrowing allow interest rates to decline further.

As the economy strengthens, government borrowing declines further but private-sector borrowing picks up, which eventually places upward pressure on interest rates. This upward interest-rate pressure extends through the business-cycle peak and into the early stages of the downturn that follows. When the economy first begins to weaken, government deficits widen and government borrowing increases. Private borrowing also increases as business and individuals attempt to maintain their old spending and investment levels. With both the government and the private sector competing for credit, interest rates rise.

As the economy contracts further and income drops, the demand for credit by businesses and individuals decreases, and the federal government becomes the major borrower in the credit markets. Interest rates begin to fall once the decline in private borrowing is large enough to offset the increase in government borrowing.

The Economic Indicators

On a monthly basis, the government releases economic indicators that are used to track the general level of economic activity. Credit market participants try to anticipate each month what the announced numbers will be. Day-to-day bill and bond prices are effected by the announcements only to the extent that the actual numbers deviate from the amounts expected. However, the basic trend of debt market prices is influenced by the general trend of these economic indicators. Some of the more important monthly indicators are listed and explained below.

Construction Expenditures

Released monthly by the Bureau of Census, U.S. Department of Commerce, usually on the first business day of each month for the month previous to the preceding month.

Measures new construction put in place within three major categories:

1. Private residential construction
2. Private nonresidential construction (industrial, office, hospital, institutional, and educational)
3. Public construction (educational facilities, sewer systems, conservation structures, and highways and streets)

Consumer Credit

Released monthly by the Federal Reserve Board, usually early in each month for the previous month.

Measures short- and intermediate-term credit extended to individuals through regular business channels. Such credit is usually extended to finance the purchase of consumer goods and services, or to be repaid in two or more installments (or there may be an option to repay). Included are automobile credit, revolving credit (issued by commercial banks, retailers, and gasoline companies), and credit extended for mobile homes.

Consumer Price Index

Released monthly by the Bureau of Labor Statistics, U.S. Department of Labor, usually near the end of each month for the preceding month.

Measures the price level of a selected market basket of consumer goods and services. Included are food, home ownership, fuel and utilities, household furnishings, apparel, transportation (both private and public), and medical care. The categories that receive the most weight are food, home ownership, and transportation.

Durable Goods Orders

Released monthly by the Bureau of Census, U.S. Department of Commerce, usually during the third or fourth week of each month for the preceding month.

Measures new orders for durable goods under five major categories:

1. Primary metals (including blast furnaces, steel mills, and nonferrous and other primary metals)
2. Fabricated metal products
3. Machinery (except electrical)
4. Electrical machinery
5. Transportation equipment (including aircraft, missiles, and parts)

The inclusion of big-ticket items, such as aircraft, makes this series highly volatile since one or two large orders can produce wide swings in the month-to-month figure.

Housing Starts

Released monthly by the Bureau of Census, U.S. Department of Commerce, usually during the third week of each month for the preceding month.

Represents the number of housing units for which ground was broken during the month. It includes single-family units and structures with two units or more. Mobile homes are not included. The housing industry accounts for approximately 8 percent of real GNP.

Gross National Product (GNP)

Released quarterly by the Bureau of Economic Analysis, U.S. Department of Commerce, usually in the third week of the month for the preceding quarter. The preliminary figure appears in the month that follows the end of the quarter. One month after the preliminary figure is issued, a first revision is announced. A second revision appears 2 months after the preliminary figure is issued, and the figure is subject to further revisions for the following 3 years, usually in July.

Measures the total market value of the nation's output of goods and services. When adjusted for rising prices, the figure measures real output and is referred to as real GNP. Although it covers activity for the quarter, GNP is always expressed in annualized terms.

Industrial Production

Released monthly by the Federal Reserve Board, usually around the fifteenth of each month for the preceding month.

Measures the physical output of the nation's factories, mines, and electric and gas utilities.

Leading Indicators

Released monthly by the Bureau of Economic Analysis, U.S. Department of Commerce, usually late in each month for the preceding month.

An index of twelve economic indicators that historically have reached their cyclical peaks and troughs earlier than corresponding business-cycle turns. The twelve component indicators are:

1. Average workweek of production workers, manufacturing (in hours)
2. Layoff rate, manufacturing (per 100 workers)
3. New orders for consumer goods and materials (in 1972 dollars)
4. Vendor performance, percentage of companies receiving slower deliveries
5. Net business formation (index: 1967 = 100)
6. Contracts and orders for plant and equipment (in 1972 dollars)
7. New building permits, private housing units (index: 1967 = 100)
8. Net change in inventories on hand and on order (in 1972 dollars, a weighted four-term moving average)
9. Change in sensitive crude-materials prices (a weighted four-term moving average)
10. Change in total liquid assets (percent, a weighted moving average). Defined as M3 plus nonpersonal time deposits, short-term Treasury securities, commercial paper, bankers' acceptances, term Eurodollars held by United States residents other than banks, and money market mutual fund shares.
11. Stock prices, 500 common stocks (index: 1941–1943 = 100)
12. Money supply (M2 in 1972 dollars)

Manufacturing and Trade

Released monthly by the Bureau of Census, U.S. Department of Commerce, usually at the end of the second week of each month for the month previous to the preceding month.

Total Business Sales

Composed of value of shipments by manufacturers of durable and nondurable goods, retail sales, and sales by merchant wholesalers of durable and nondurable goods.

Total Business Inventories

Represents book value at end of month of inventories of nondurable and durable goods held by manufacturers, retailers, and wholesalers.

Personal Income

Released monthly by the Bureau of Economic Analysis, U.S. Department of Commerce, usually in the third week of each month for the previous month.

Includes wages and salaries, proprietors' income, rental income, dividends, personal interest income, and transfer payments, minus personal contributions for social insurance.

Producer Price Index (PPI)

Released monthly by the Bureau of Labor Statistics, U.S. Department of Labor, usually in the first week of each month for the preceding month.

Measures the average change in prices received for finished goods (goods that will be sold to final users or business firms and not processed further). Included are trucks, machine tools, foods, clothing, and gasoline.

Retail Sales

Released monthly by the Bureau of Census, U.S. Department of Commerce, usually in the second week of each month for the preceding month.

Represents total sales at the retail level. Included are sales by hardware stores, automobile dealers, furniture stores, department stores, food stores, gasoline service stations, and restaurants.

Unemployment

Released monthly by the Bureau of Labor Statistics, U.S. Department of Commerce, usually in the first week of each month for the preceding month.

Measures percentage of unemployed people in civilian labor force. This number is based on a household survey conducted during the calendar week containing the twelfth day of the month. Released at the same time are the results of an establishment survey that reports employment conditions (average workweek and average overtime hours) at business firms. The establishment survey is conducted for the pay period that includes the twelfth day of the month, but it may not correspond to the calendar week that contains the twelfth.

U.S. Trade Balance

Released monthly by the Bureau of Census, U.S. Department of Commerce, usually at the end of each month for the preceding month.

Measures net exports: government and nongovernment shipments abroad (excluding Department of Defense Military Assistance Program Grant-Aid shipments) minus imports.

THE INFLUENCE OF FEDERAL RESERVE POLICY ON INTEREST RATES

Federal Reserve policy, which currently emphasizes controlling the money supply, tends to reinforce this cyclical rise and fall in interest rates. The demand for money—and hence money growth—increases during periods of economic expansion and decreases during periods of economic contraction. In the initial stages of an expansion, the money supply has only begun to grow, the Fed is largely concerned with not choking off recovery, and monetary policy is relatively easy. When recovery is well under way, concern that continued high rates of money growth may be inflationary will cause the Fed to follow a more restrictive policy, and this will put upward pressure on interest rates. Monetary policy becomes easier only after monetary growth has declined to what the Fed considers to be less inflationary levels, and usually this does not occur until after economic activity has peaked and a contraction has begun. Once the Fed does ease monetary policy, however, interest rates decline.

INFLATION AND INTEREST RATES

The market rate of interest on government securities reflects the investor's expected rate of inflation plus the real rate of return that must be paid to induce individuals to buy and hold Treasury bonds. The inflation rate, therefore, is also a major factor influencing the level of interest rates. Inflation tends to turn up shortly after the economy has begun a recovery, and to turn down generally around, or just before, the time the economy begins to decline. Because expectations about inflation frequently lag behind changes in the actual inflation rate, expected inflation tends to turn up after a business-cycle upturn and to decline after a business-cycle downturn. This lagging pattern in expected inflation is another reason why turns in interest rates lag behind turning points in the economy.

THE YIELD CURVE

Although long- and short-term interest rates usually move in the same direction, short-term rates are much more volatile than long-term rates. When interest rates are rising, short-term rates rise faster and farther than long-term rates, and when interest rates are falling, short-term rates decline faster and fall further than long-term rates. Short-term borrowing to smooth fluctuations in the cash flow of day-to-day business operations and to finance credit purchases by consumers responds more quickly to variations in business conditions than does long-term borrowing to finance capital investment, which once begun can be difficult and costly to halt. Thus, at business-cycle peaks or troughs, short-term interest rates turn first. Treasury-bill rates, for example, turn 1 or 2 months after, and sometimes before, a cyclical peak or trough, while bond yields will turn later, especially at business-cycle troughs.

The relationship between short- and long-term interest rates is graphically represented by the yield curve. Because quality and liquidity differences in addition to differences in maturity will also affect interest-rate differentials, the yield curve refers to interest rates on the same type of securities. These are almost always U.S. government securities because they most satisfy the requirement that quality and liquidity be the same.

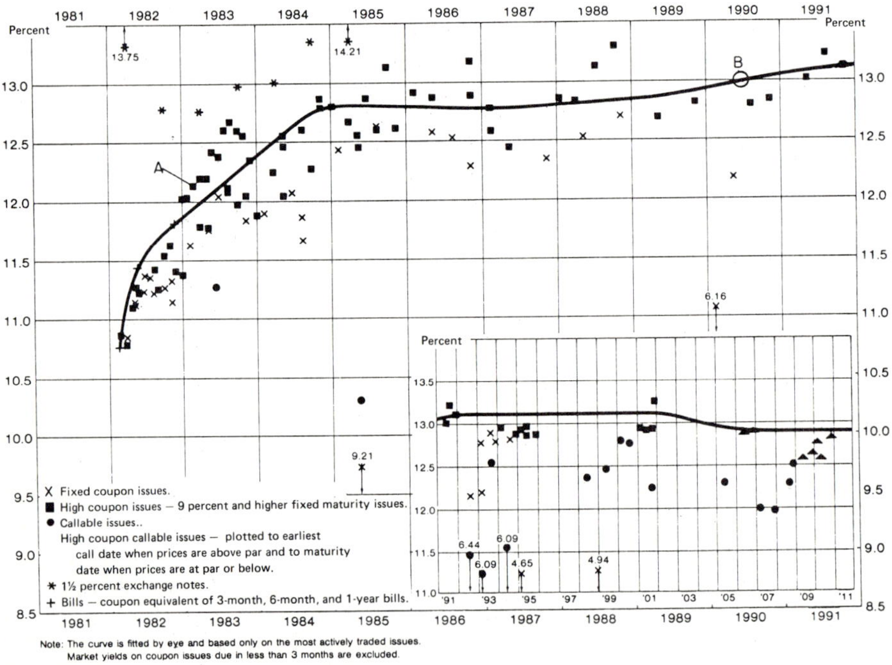

Figure 23-2 A normal yield curve. (Yields of Treasury securities, November 30, 1981. Based on closing bid quotations.)

The most commonly observed shape since the 1930s has been an upward-sloping yield curve, with short-term rates lower than long-term rates. The upward-sloping yield curve is also referred to as a normal yield curve, an example of which appears in Figure 23-2. Notice that a note maturing in 1983 (point A) has a yield of 12 percent, lower than the 13 percent yield on the bond that matures in 1990. At times the yield curve assumes an inverted shape, with short-term rates higher than long-term rates, as shown in Figure 23-3; at other times it is flat; and occasionally it takes on a humped shape.

At the beginning of a recovery, the shape of the yield curve will be normal. As the economy continues to strengthen, and interest rates begin to rise, short-term rates will rise faster than long-term rates, causing the yield curve to flatten. Near the peak of an expansion, when credit demand is strong, short-term interest rates will push above long-term rates, and the yield curve will invert. When the economy first turns down, short-term rates will begin to decline even though long-term rates are still rising, and this will cause a flattening of the yield curve. As short-term rates continue to decline and fall below long-term rates, the slope of the yield curve will once again become positive. Because short-term rates fall faster than long-term rates, this process will continue even after long-term interest rates start to decline.

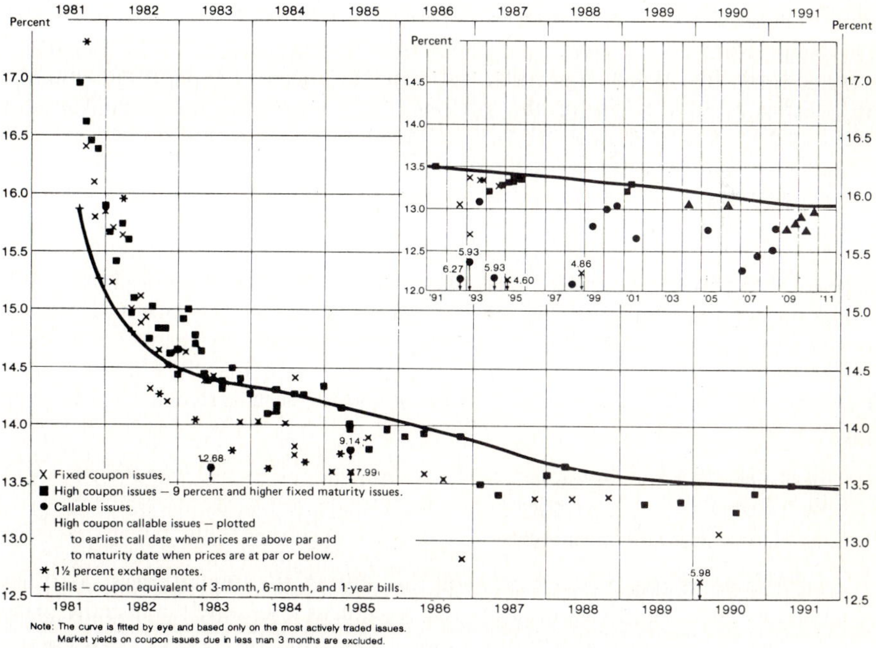

Figure 23-3 An inverted yield curve. (Yields of Treasury securities. May 29, 1981. Based on closing bid quotations.)

Basis and Spread Relationships: A Function of the Yield Curve

In the T-bond and Government National Mortgage Association (GNMA) markets, both the basis (the difference between the cash and futures prices) and the intramarket spreads are largely driven by fluctuations in short-term interest rates relative to long-term interest rates. An intramarket spread is a simultaneous long and short position in two different contract months of the same futures market. Government securities dealers and arbitrageurs usually finance their cash positions by borrowing the necessary funds and putting up the cash security as collateral. This is accomplished via a repurchase agreement (repo), in which the borrower of the funds "sells" the security to the lender of the funds with the borrower's agreement to "buy" the security back at a fixed date in the future. The term of the repo can be overnight, several days, several weeks, or occasionally, several months. Longer-term repurchase agreements are called "term repos." The repo rate is the interest rate charged by the lender to the borrower, and it varies depending on the term of the repo and the specific security being offered as collateral. Positive carry occurs when the interest earned on the cash instrument exceeds its financing cost (that is, its repo rate), and the carry is negative when the interest earned on the cash instrument is less than its financing cost.

Arbitrageurs in the financial instruments will buy the cash and sell the futures until all profit opportunity has been eliminated. When the carry is positive, this occurs at a point where the futures price is below the cash price. If the two prices were the same, a profit opportunity would still exist, for the arbritrageur could buy the cash securtiy, sell it in the futures for the same amount, and earn a positive return on the differential between the interest paid by the bond and its financing cost. Thus, arbitrageurs will continue to buy the cash and sell the futures until the price of the cash instrument has risen above the futures price by an amount that just permits the transaction to break even.

Suppose the repo rate for the September 5 to December 5 holding period for an 8 percent 20-year T-bond is 6 percent. Assume this bond pays interest twice a year, on February 15 and August 15. Further assume that bond yields are 8 percent and that both the cash 8 percent T-bond and the December bond futures are priced at par. An arbitrageur could earn a 2 percent annualized return by simply buying the cash bond at par, financing it at the 6 percent repo rate, and then selling it in the futures market at the same price at which it was purchased:

Coupon income	8 percent
Financing rate	−6 percent
Net interest income	2 percent

As arbitrageurs buy the cash and sell the futures, the buying pressure in the cash market and the selling pressure in the futures market will cause the price of the cash bond to rise above the futures price until the profit opportunity is eliminated.

When the carry is negative, the break-even level for the arbitrage is reached after the cash price has fallen below the futures price. The cash, or purchase, price must be far enough below the futures, or selling, price so that the profit earned on the differential between the two prices just offsets the negative net income that occurs when the financing charges exceed the interest income on the security. If the futures price were to rise above the cash price by too much, the resulting profit opportunity would be quickly eliminated by arbitrageurs who, by buying the cash and selling the futures, would cause the futures price to fall relative to the cash price. If the futures price falls too low, arbitrageurs will buy the futures and sell the cash until the difference between the two prices again reaches break-even.

If the basis is defined as the difference between the cash price and the futures price, during periods when the yield curve is positive (with short-term interest rates lower than long-term interest rates) and the carry is positive, the basis will be positive. That is, the cash price of the security will be higher than its futures prices. As the yield curve flattens and turns negative (with short-term interest rates rising above long-term interest rates), the carry will become negative. This will cause cash prices to fall below futures prices, and the basis will turn negative. Thus, a positive basis is generally associated with a positive carry and a positive yield curve, and a negative basis is generally associated with a negative carry and a negative yield curve.

Intramarket spreads in the financial futures, like the relationship between cash and futures prices, are driven largely by short-term financing costs. A bond futures trader who holds a long position in a nearby month and a short position in a back month can take delivery of the nearby contract, financing it via the repo market, and then redeliver the bond when the back contract expires. If the repo rate for the cash bond is less than its interest income, this strategy reaches break-even at a point where the price of the nearby contract is higher than the price of the back contract. When the price of the nearby contract relative to the price of the back month is lower than this, the resulting profit opportunity will attract arbitrageurs, who will buy the nearby month and sell the back month until the price of the nearby month is again far enough above the price of the back month for the trade to just break even. If the price of the nearby month rises too much higher than the price of the back month, then selling the nearby and buying the back contract will be profitable, and spread arbitrageurs, taking advantage of this profit opportunity, will again cause the spread to move toward break-even.

When the repo rate for the cash bond is greater than its interest income, the spread arbitrage reaches break-even at a point where the price of the nearby contract is lower than the price of the back contract. If the negative net financing costs that arise during the interval between the 2 delivery months are to be offset, then the bond must be redelivered into the futures at a higher price than the price at which delivery was taken.

On September 14, 1981, the repo rate for government securities was around 15.5 percent, considerably higher than the highest coupon deliverable T-bond, which was the 13 7/8s of May 2006–2011. The negative carry was reflected in the structure of the bond futures on September 14, where the price of each succeeding contract month was higher than the price of the preceding month. (See Table 23-1.)

Generally, the lower the repo rate is below the interest earned on the cash

TABLE 23-1 Treasury Bonds, Chicago Board of Trade

Contract month	Settle price
September 1981	58-12
December 1981	59-01
March 1982	59-18
June 1982	60-00
September 1982	60-10
December 1982	60-19
March 1983	60-27
June 1983	61-02
September 1983	61-09
December 1983	61-15
March 1984	61-21
June 1984	61-26
September 1984	61-31
December 1984	62-04

TABLE 23-2 Treasury-Bill Futures, International Monetary Market

Contract month	Settle price
March 1982	87.23
June 1982	86.87
September 1982	86.76
December 1982	86.67
March 1983	86.59
June 1983	86.59
September 1983	86.59
December 1983	86.59

security, the lower cash prices will be relative to futures prices and, in the futures market, the lower the price of the nearby month will be relative to the price of the back month. The higher the repo rate is above the interest earned on the cash security, the higher cash prices will be relative to futures prices, and in the futures market, the higher the price of the nearby month will be relative to the price of the back month.

For Treasury bills, the relationship of the deliverable cash T-bill to the nearby futures contract is also explained by the difference between the interest earned on the bill and its financing cost. However, because a deliverable bill does not exist beyond the first option, it is not possible to arbitrage either the spreads or the cash market against the back contract months. Thus, the T-bill spreads are not closely tied to the repo rate, and will show much more day-to-day volatility than either the repo rate or the bond and GNMA spreads.

However, the structure of the bill spreads will generally reflect the relationship between very short-term rates, such as the repo rate, and bill rates. That is, when the repo rate is lower than the cash 3-month bill rate, the International Monetary Market (IMM) price of a bill futures contract will usually be higher than the price of the contract month that follows it. Conversely, when the repo rate is higher than the cash 3-month bill rate, the IMM price of a bill futures contract will be lower than the price of the contract month that follows it.

On January 6, 1982, the discount on 3-month T-bills was 11.6 percent and the repo rate for government securities was around 11.375 percent. As a result, the carry in the bill market was positive, and except for the last four options, the price of the near month in the futures was higher than the prices of the back months that followed it. (See Table 23-2.)

CHAPTER

24

The Importance of the Federal Reserve to the Interest-Rate Market

Geraldine L. Szymanski

The better the forecast of where interest rates are going, the more successful the trading of financial futures. Obviously, changes in business activity influence the interest-rate markets, and this is what the newcomer to the market tends to look at first. The average investor knows that interest rates rise during economic upswings and fall when the economy weakens. However, near-term, the most influential force in the market, especially the Treasury-bill market, is the Federal Reserve. It is responsible for both setting and conducting monetary policy, activities that have a powerful effect on Treasury-bill rates. Thus, it is extremely important for traders of T-bill futures to acquire a basic understanding of the Federal Reserve System and how it manages monetary policy.

HOW THE FEDERAL RESERVE IS ORGANIZED AND OPERATES

The Federal Reserve System was established with the passage by Congress of the Federal Reserve Act of 1913. Its primary function is to contribute to a stable domestic economy by managing money and credit. The immediate goals mandated to the Fed are price stability, a high level of employment, and economic growth. The Federal Reserve also seeks to facilitate the flow of goods and money between the United States and foreign markets. Meeting all four of these goals simultaneously is always extremely difficult and frequently impossible. For example, rising prices often accompany high levels of employment, and thus it becomes necessary to choose between reducing inflation (by dampening economic activity and employment) and maintaining high employment (thus exacerbating inflation).

The organizational structure of the Federal Reserve System includes the Board of Governors, the Federal Open Market Committee (FOMC), the twelve Federal Reserve Banks and their branches, and the member commercial banks. The Board of Governors consists of seven members appointed to 14-year terms by the President of the United States and approved by the Senate. Only one governor at a time can be appointed from each Federal Reserve district. The chairman and vice-chairman of the Board each serve a 4-year term and are selected from among the seven governors by the President. It is the responsibility of the Board of Governors to formulate monetary policy consistent with the economic goals listed above, to oversee the operations of the Federal Reserve Banks, to regulate member banks, and to interpret and issue regulations under the Federal Reserve Act.

The Federal Open Market Committee has twelve members, including the seven members of the Board of Governors and the presidents of five of the Federal Reserve Banks. The president of the New York Federal Reserve Bank is a permanent member and vice-chairman of the FOMC, reflecting the critical role of the New York Bank in conducting monetary policy. The remaining four positions are rotated among the eleven other Federal Reserve Bank presidents. The chairman of the Board of Governors also serves as the chairman of the FOMC.

The Federal Open Market Committee is officially charged with directing open market operations, that is, the purchase and sale of securities—generally U.S. Treasury securities—for the Federal Reserve, but in recent years a wide range of policy-related matters have been discussed at FOMC meetings. Among these are changes in the discount rate (the rate charged to depository institutions that borrow reserves from the Fed) and the reserve requirement (the percentage of a depository institution's deposits that must be held aside in accordance with Federal Reserve regulations). The committee meets ten times a year at 4- to 5-week intervals. If unexpected market conditions develop between regularly scheduled meetings, the committee members hold telephone conferences to determine what, if any, adjustments in policy should be made.

There are twelve Federal Reserve districts in the United States, each with its own Federal Reserve Bank. In addition, twenty-four branch offices and two bank facilities are variously spread throughout the twelve districts in the system. The cities in which Federal Reserve Banks are located are Boston, New York, Philadelphia, Cleveland, Richmond, Atlanta, Chicago, St. Louis, Minneapolis, Kansas City, Dallas, and San Francisco.

Each Federal Reserve Bank is a federally chartered corporation. The stockholders are member banks of that district. Currently, member banks are required to subscribe to an amount of federal Reserve Bank stock equal to 6 percent of their capital accounts. Dividend payments are limited by law to 6 percent of the subscription value of the Federal Reserve stock. All remaining profits are turned over to the U.S. Treasury.

Reserve Requirements

Member banks of the Federal Reserve System are private, profit-seeking corporations in the commercial banking business. Historically, these have included the largest, most prestigious banks in the United States. In recent years, however, the number of banks in the system began to decline, as more and more commercial banks opted for state charters. The reason was that reserve requirements set by state banking regulators were lower than the reserve requirements of the Fed, and were sometimes eliminated altogether. Thus, by dropping out of the Federal Reserve System a commercial bank could reduce the amount of non-interest-earning funds it had to hold in reserve.

As the number of banks and the percentage of total deposits within the Federal Reserve System declined, controlling the money supply—already a hard task—became even more difficult. This situation was corrected in 1980 by a provision in the Monetary Control Act (also passed in 1980) that authorized the Federal Reserve to establish reserve requirements for all depository institutions. Not only member banks would be subject to reserve requirements, but also state-chartered commercial banks, savings and loan associations, mutual savings banks, and credit unions. In order to ease the burden on institutions that were meeting reserve requirements for the first time, the Fed announced a 5-year period over which the program would be fully phased in.

Money Supply

The Federal Reserve has defined several measures of the money supply, or monetary aggregates, listed in Table 24-1. In working down the list from M1 through L, the concept of what constitutes money broadens. Money is used in payment for goods and services, thus M1, the amount of currency, demand, and other checkable deposits outstanding, is an obvious measure of the money sup-

TABLE 24-1

Money aggregate	Definition
M1	Currency plus travelers checks plus demand deposits (negotiable order of withdrawal or NOW accounts) and automatic transfer service (ATS) plus other checkable deposit accounts at banks and thrift institutions, credit union share draft accounts, and demand deposits at thrift institutions
M2	M1 plus overnight RPs and Eurodollars, money-market mutual fund shares, and savings and small time deposits (time deposits in amounts of less than $100,000)
M3	M2 plus large time deposits, term repurchase agreements, and institutions-only money market mutual fund balances
L	M3 plus other liquid assets (nonbank public holdings of U.S. savings bonds, short-term Treasury securities, commercial paper, bankers' acceptances and term Eurodollars net of money-market mutual fund holdings of these assets)

ply. Highly liquid assets (or assets that can be readily converted to cash) are included in the broadest aggregate at the bottom of the list.

There is no one perfect measure of the money supply. The most commonly watched aggregates are M1 and M2, but it certainly can be argued that at times these measures understate the potential transactions balances of the economy.

How the Availability of Bank Reserves Affects the Money Supply

The Federal Reserve does not control the money supply directly, but exercises an indirect control through the level of bank reserves it supplies to the banking system. Banks create demand deposits (which are, in effect, money) whenever they make a loan. For example, when an individual borrows from a bank, the check is issued to the borrower, who then deposits the check in a demand deposit account in order to pay for goods to be purchased. Theoretically, a bank can continue to make loans up to the point where the amount of funds it must set aside to satisfy the Fed's reserve requirements is equal to the amount of reserves it holds. In actual practice, however, some banks will make fewer loans, thereby creating fewer demand deposits than their reserve holdings will support. These excess reserves (excess reserves = total reserves − required reserves) are then loaned to banks whose reserves fall short of the amount needed to support the level of demand deposits on their books.

If the banking system's deposit accounts are expanded to the maximum amount possible and the total level of reserves in the banking system is then reduced, there must be a reduction in total deposits outstanding. This is accomplished by not replacing maturing loans with new ones, by calling in some loans early, or both. This is the mechanism on which the Federal Reserve largely relies in its efforts to control the money supply.

However, the relationship between bank reserves and the money supply is not perfect. For example, if some reserves are held in excess, a reduction in total reserves to the system may not necessarily induce a reduction in deposit balances. Conversely, if bankers decide to hold more excess reserves, an increase in bank reserves may result in virtually no increase in deposit balances and therefore no increase in the money supply.

Even if the relationship between bank reserves and deposit accounts were perfect, there is a further obstacle to monetary control in that the Fed cannot manage precisely the amount of reserves in the banking system.

There are two sources of bank reserves: (1) open market operations and (2) borrowing from the Fed's discount window. The Federal Reserve conducts open market operations and by this means exerts direct control over the amount of nonborrowed reserves supplied to the system. However, the amount that banks borrow can only be indirectly controlled through the level of the discount rate (the interest rate charged by the Fed to borrowing banks), since banks can almost always borrow reserves from their Federal Reserve district bank if they meet the announced qualifications. The Fed encourages or discourages borrowing at the discount window by raising or lowering the discount rate, but the banks and depository institutions decide how much they will actually borrow.

Open Market Operations: The Most Frequently Used Method of Monetary Control

Altogether there are five means by which the Fed can influence the money supply: (1) moral suasion, or jawboning, (2) selective credit controls, (3) changes in reserve requirements, (4) changes in the discount rate, and (5) open market operations. Moral suasion involves public pronouncements by Federal Reserve authorities, such as the chairman of the Board of Governors, that banks should exercise restraint, or that they should reduce their loan activities. This approach is generally ineffective. Selective credit controls include regulating interest rates and the terms of various kinds of bank loans. Though not a major policy tool, credit controls are occassionally called into use. The most recent example is the credit-control program that was in effect for 4 months, from March through July 1980. Changes in the reserve requirement are made infrequently; the reserve requirement can have dramatic effects on banks' loans and investment activities. This is especially true of an increase in the reserve requirement, which can have strong contractionary effects on the banking system. Discount-rate adjustments, on the other hand, occur fairly often, several times a year.

But the most important tool of monetary control is open market operations. A daily activity of bill and bond traders in both the cash and the futures markets is to anticipate and interpret the Fed's open market activities. Depending on the size of the operation, bill prices are frequently affected directly by Fed market intervention. The effect on bond prices is indirect, but Federal Reserve activity has an important bearing on this market too.

Open market operations involve the purchase and sale of securities, primarily government securities, by the manager of the open market desk at the Federal Reserve Bank of New York. These purchases and sales alter the level of nonborrowed reserves in the banking system and are undertaken in accordance with the most recent policy directive of the Federal Open Market Committee.

The level of nonborrowed bank reserves increases when the Fed buys securities. For example, suppose T-bills are purchased by the Fed from a government securities dealer. The Fed pays the dealer, who deposits the funds into a checking account; this causes bank reserves to rise. Conversely, the level of nonborrowed reserves declines when the Fed sells securities. In this case the securities dealer pays the Fed, and the transfer of funds from the dealer's checking account to the Federal Reserve causes bank reserves to fall.

These adjustments to bank reserves can be made on either a permanent or a temporary basis. A permanent addition to bank reserves is achieved by an outright purchase of Treasury bonds or Treasury bills. When this happens, the Fed is said to have executed a coupon pass, in the case of a T-bond purchase, or a bill pass, in the case of a T-bill purchase. A permanent reserve drain occurs when the Fed sells Treasury bonds or Treasury bills. The market refers to these operations as "selling all coupons" and "selling all bills," respectively.

It is much more common for the Fed to make a temporary adjustment to bank reserves by executing system repurchase agreements (repos), in the case of a temporary addition to bank reserves, and by executing reverse repos (also called matched sales), in the event of a temporary reserve drain. When the Fed does a system repo, or simply a repo, it purchases T-bills and simultaneously agrees to sell them back on a fixed date in the future. In overnight repos, the bills are sold back the next day. On occasion, a term repo is executed, which extends the Fed's holding period to 2 or more days. The purchase of the bills by the Fed results in an increase in nonborrowed reserves during the time the Fed holds the bills, there having been a transfer of funds from the Federal Reserve to the securities dealer and hence the banking system. When the bills are sold back to the bond dealer, either the next day or as long as several days later, nonborrowed reserves decline, there being a transfer of funds from the bond dealer, and hence the banking system, to the Fed.

There is one other category of open market operations, the purchase and sale of bills for a customer's account. The customers in these operations are generally foreign central banks that have accounts at the Fed. From time to time these banks increase or decrease their holdings of U.S. Treasury bills and ask the Fed to execute the trade. Usually the Fed provides the securities out of its own holdings of T-bills, but sometimes it chooses to go to a dealer for a customer's sale or purchase order.

As with trades for its own account, the Fed can and does execute these transactions on either a temporary or a permanent basis, depending on what the customer has requested. Thus, it is not uncommon for an overnight customer's repos to be announced or for the Fed to purchase, say, $350 million in bills for a customer's account. There is never any question about whether the Fed's intervention in the market is for its own or a customer's account, for the Fed always announces at the time whether the operation is for the system, the Fed's account or a customer.

The Effect of Open Market Operations on the Federal Funds Rate

Besides adjusting the supply of nonborrowed reserves to the banking system, open market operations also influence the level of interest rates through the direct effect on the federal funds rate. Federal funds are reserves that banks hold above the amount necessary to meet their reserve requirements at the Fed. Interest is earned on these extra reserves by lending them out to other banks whose reserve holdings, given the level of their deposit accounts, fall short of the amount required by the Fed. Reserves available for lending between banks are called federal funds, and the federal funds rate is the interest rate charged by the lending to the borrowing bank. Common market usage is to refer to lending and borrowing as the sale and purchase of federal funds, respectively. Thus, a borrowing bank would be called a purchaser of federal funds, and a lending bank would be called a seller.

Because of the demand for funds by the banks, a reserve draining operation by the open market desk will put upward pressure on the Federal funds rate. Conversely, an addition to bank reserves will tend to push the funds rate lower.

The Federal Funds Rate versus the 3-Month T-Bill Rate

There is a fairly close relationship between the interest rate on 3-month cash T-bills and the federal funds rate. The open market operation itself provides one reason for this close connection. For example, when the Fed is buying T-bills and adding reserves to the banking system, the increase in demand for the available supply of bills may temporarily raise bill prices and depress their interest rates. Thus, an increase in bank reserves through open market operations tends to lower directly not only the federal funds rate, but also the interest rate on 3-month T-bills. When the Fed is selling bills in order to drain reserves from the banking system, the reverse happens; that is, T-bill prices tend to fall, and bill rates and the Federal funds rate tend to rise.

A more lasting tie between the two interest rates is generated by the way depository institutions manage their reserve balances. In addition to borrowing from the discount window and purchasing reserves in the Federal funds market, it is also possible for a bank to obtain reserves by selling T-bills out of its portfolio. Conversely, a bank with excess reserves to invest may choose to buy T-bills instead of loaning them out in the federal funds market. A sharp divergence between the federal funds rate and the rate on 3-month T-bills (that is, if the funds rate is much higher than the bill rate) cannot last for long. Banks in need of reserves will increasingly choose to sell T-bills, thereby reducing the demand for reserves in the federal funds market, and banks with extra reserves to invest will be more likely to sell them in the federal funds market, thereby increasing the supply. The combined effect of reduced demand and increased supply will be to lower the interest rate charged on federal funds relative to the 3-month bill rate. Thus, the process in which banks that need reserves seek out the lowest cost source of funds and banks with extra reserves place them in the highest-yielding market will keep the federal funds rate and the 3-month T-bill rate from moving far apart.

Because the risk of default on a U.S. Treasury bill is virtually zero, and the sale of funds on the federal funds market is an unsecured loan to a bank, the 3-month T-bill rate is generally lower than the rate on federal funds. Since October 1979, when the Federal Reserve announced a change in its operating procedure, the spread between the two rates has been as narrow as 50 basis points, and as wide as 500. The spread can widen whether interest rates are rising or falling. During periods of rising rates, the spread widens when the funds rate is pushed sharply higher by sudden Federal Reserve tightening. When rates are declining rapidly, the bill rate tends to fall more than the Fed funds rate, and this also causes the spread to widen. During periods of relatively moderate interest-rate movements, the spread narrows to 200 basis points or less.

An important exception to this spread relationship occurs every Wednesday. Depository institutions are required to meet their reserve requirements on a weekly, not a daily, basis. Wednesday is the last day of the bank statement week and, as a result, either there is a scramble for reserves by banks needing reserves, or a large amount of reserves may become available because most banks have already satisfied their reserve requirements. Thus, it is not unusual on Wednesdays to observe wide swings in the funds rate from the trading range observed earlier in the week. Because the funds rate can be expected to return to more normal levels on Thursday, the 3-month T-bill rate does not closely track sharp Wednesday moves in the federal funds rate.

MONETARY POLICY

The Fed's Choice between Controlling Bank Reserves and Stabilizing Interest Rates

The federal funds rate is determined by both supply and demand factors. A decline in the funds rate, for example, could come about because of an increase in the supply of bank reserves, a decrease in the demand for reserves by depository institutions, or both. However, the Fed can affect only the supply of bank reserves, for the demand for reserves rises and falls as loan activity at the various depository institutions rises and falls. Thus, it is not possible for the Fed to control simultaneously both the level of reserves in the banking system and the federal funds rate. Suppose, for example, the Federal Reserve wants to hold interest rates stable. If the demand for reserves by banks increases, the open market desk will have to accommodate this higher demand by adding reserves to the banking system or else risk having the federal funds rate, and eventually all interest rates, trade higher.

From World War II up to the fall of 1979, the Federal Reserve had set as its first priority maintaining rate stability in the credit markets. Demand shifts for federal funds were accommodated by the Fed to prevent sharp fluctuations in interest rates. Reserve and money supply targets were not ignored, but meeting them took second place to moderating movements in the funds rate. During the 1970s the Fed was increasingly criticized for its efforts at interest-rate stabilization. It was argued that because the Fed would increase bank reserves in response to demand pressures in the Federal funds market, it would overstimulate the economy during times of high economic activity and fuel inflation. If economic activity is weak, and bank loans and demand deposits decline, banks will need to borrow less in the federal funds market and the funds rate will slide. However, if the Fed drains reserves in order to limit the federal funds rate decline, all other interest rates are prevented from declining as they would otherwise, and this will prolong the slowdown. In other words, a policy of interest-rate stabilization is inflationary during times of heightened business activity, and will delay a recovery when business is poor.

The inflation rate rose sharply in 1974 and again in 1980. In both instances, the initial cause was accelerating oil prices, but the Fed was also held partly responsible for having allowed credit and hence the money supply to expand too rapidly. Thus on October 6, 1979, Federal Reserve Board Chairman Paul Volcker announced that henceforth the Fed would focus more on achieving its reserve targets, and that less emphasis would be placed on stabilizing the federal funds rate. The effect on movements in the federal funds rate was predictable. Whereas before a ½-percentage-point trading range from one week to the next had been common, since the Fed's policy change federal funds will easily move 2 full percentage points in 1 day.

Anticipating Federal Reserve Policy

Correctly anticipating Federal Reserve policy actions is one of the keys to trading the financial instruments successfully. A shift by the Fed toward easier credit conditions will cause interest rates to decline and bill and bond prices to rise, but if the Fed tightens, interest rates will rise and bill and bond prices will decline. To anticipate these policy shifts, first identify the Fed's targets with respect to monetary growth and the prefered near-term trading range of the Federal funds rate. Then, by tracking the money and reserve figures reported each week, you can assess how closely the Fed is coming to hitting these targets and whether additional credit tightening or easing is required.

Ever since Congress passed the Humphrey Hawkins Act (formally called the Full Employment and Balanced Growth Act of 1978), the Federal Reserve has been required to announce each year annual fourth-quarter-to-fourth-quarter monetary growth targets.

These numbers are widely reported in newspapers when they are announced by the Fed, and frequent reference to them is made throughout the year in *The Wall Street Journal* and *The New York Times* coverage of the interest-rate markets.

In order to keep near-term money growth from causing the year-over-year targets to be missed, quarterly targets are set and reviewed at every FOMC meeting. The minutes of these meetings are not released to the public until almost a month later. Complete copies of the minutes can be obtained at any of the Federal Reserve Banks, and summaries are carried in both *The Wall Street Journal* and *The New York Times*.

Although the information is released 1 month late, both parameters can be of assistance in identifying the near-term course of monetary policy. For example, if recent growth has exceeded the near-term FOMC targets, and if the federal funds rate has been trading below the desired range, it can be expected that further tightening and hence higher interest rates are imminent. If the signals are mixed, such as higher-than-desired money growth and a higher federal funds rate than is being targeted by the FOMC, whether the Fed will tighten (to reduce money growth) or ease (to reduce the federal funds rate) will depend on which target it deems more important. If the Fed decides that the economy will be better served by controlling interest rates, then it will be reasonable to expect monetary policy to be eased and interest rates to fall. However, if the Fed is focusing on reining in money growth, then monetary policy should be tightened and interest rates will rise.

Information about the importance that the Fed places on monetary control versus interest-rate stabilization can be obtained from FOMC minutes, public statements made by the chairman of the Board of Governors and the other members of the FOMC, and the chairman's testimony in appearances before Congress. These statements are reported in both *The Wall Street Journal* and *The New York Times*.

The Fed's success in hitting its monetary targets can be tracked on a week-to-week basis. Every Thursday afternoon at 4 P.M. Eastern time the Federal Reserve Bank of New York holds a press conference at which it releases weekly money supply and bank reserve figures. In addition to being carried over the various financial news services—such as Telerate, Reuters, and Commodities News Service—these figures are published in the Saturday edition of *The New York Times* and in the Monday edition of *The Wall Street Journal*. The "Federal Reserve Data" column that appeared in *The Wall Street Journal* on June 22, 1981, is reproduced in Table 24-2.

Money supply and reserve figures are given in Table 24-2 under "Monetary and Reserve Aggregates." The degree of current Federal Reserve tightness or ease is indicated by the amount of nonborrowed reserves supplied by the Fed and by the amount obtained by borrowing from the Federal Reserve discount window. The figure for borrowed reserves can be easily calculated by subtracting nonborrowed reserves from total reserves:

Total reserves − nonborrowed reserves = borrowed reserves

For example, using the reserve numbers reported for June 17, total reserves were $40.15 billion, nonborrowed reserves were $38.259 billion, and borrowed reserves were $1.891 billion ($40.15 billion − $38.259 billion = $1.891 billion).

The tighter the Federal Reserve policy toward credit, the higher will be the percentage of total reserves obtained by borrowing at the discount window. Money market analysts carry this analysis one step further by subtracting required reserves from nonborrowed reserves to get the amount of free reserves when the number is positive, or the amount of nonborrowed reserves when the number is negative:

Nonborrowed reserves − required reserves = free reserves (if positive) or net borrowed reserves (if negative)

Referring to the June 17 reserve numbers and subtracting $39.981 billion in required reserves from $38.259 billion in nonborrowed reserves, the result is −$1.722 billion. On June 17, net borrowed reserves totaled $1.722 billion. The more negative this number is, or the larger net borrowed reserves are, the more banks have had to borrow from the discount window in order to meet their reserve requirements, indicating credit tightness. When this number is positive, on the other hand, there are enough nonborrowed reserves in the banking system to meet the level of required reserves, which indicates the Fed is following an easier policy toward credit.

The monetary base is equal to the sum of bank reserves and currency held by the public. It too is tracked by Fed watchers as a measure of the system's current potential for monetary growth. Currency is included in this measure because once deposited in the banking system, it becomes part of bank reserves and can support much more than that amount in checkable deposit accounts. A rapidly expanding monetary base portends rapid monetary growth in the future; a slower increase in the base suggests a more moderate rise in the money supply.

TABLE 24-2 Federal Reserve Data
Key assets and liabilities of ten weekly reporting member banks in New York City (in millions of dollars)

	Level	change from
	June 10, 1981	June 3, 1980
Assets		
Total assets	218,434	+871
Total loans and investments—includes:	129,038	+1,721
Commercial and industrial loans	50,342	−548
Domestic	47,663	−659
Foreign	2,679	+111
Acceptances, commercial paper	1,387	+128
Finance company loans	3,982	−55
Personal loans	9,914	+24
Loan loss reserve	1,953	+21
U.S. Treasury securities	9,164	−75
Federal agency securities	2,643	−20
Municipal issues	11,423	+163
Due in 1 year or less	2,007	+59
Longer-term	9,416	+104
Liabilities		
Demand deposits	128,687	+679
Demand deposits adjusted*	23,228	+1,247
Time and savings deposits	58,450	−315
Negotiable CDs ($100,000 and up)	27,991	−372
Borrowings	48,772	+1,532

Member bank reserve changes (in millions of dollars)

Changes in weekly averages of member bank reserves and related items during the week and year ended June 17, 1981, were as follows:

		Change from week ended	
	June 17, 1981	June 10, 1981	June 18, 1980
Reserve bank credit: U.S. government securities			
Bought outright	120,655	+1,755	+596
Held under repurchase agreement			−1,082
Federal agency issues			
Bought outright	8,707	−11	−168
Held under repurchase agreement			−251
Acceptances			
Bought outright			
Held under repurchase agreement			−245
Borrowings from Fed	1,894	− 312	+1,499
Seasonal borrowings	279	+2	+268

TABLE 24-2 Federal Reserve Data (*Continued*)

	June 17, 1981	Change from week ended June 10, 1981	Change from week ended June 18, 1980
Float	3,538	−109	−304
Other Federal Reserve assets	9,760	+342	+4,314
Total reserve bank credit	144,556	+1,667	+4,359
Gold stock	11,154		−18
Special Drawing Rights (SDR) certificates	2,818		−150
Treasury currency outstanding	13,567	+6	+289
Total	172,095	+1,673	+4,480
Currency in circulation	136,969	+316	+10,433
Treasury cash holdings	505	−1	−41
Treasury deposits with federal reserve banks	3,196	+583	+1,173
Foreign deposits with federal reserve banks	258	−65	−18
Other deposits with federal reserve banks	391	+45	−964
Other federal reserve liabilities and capital	4,638	+270	−442
Total	145,957	+1,147	+10,141
Reserves			
With Federal Reserve Banks	26,138	+526	−5,661
Total incumbent cash	40,396	+885	−3,026
Required reserves	40,223	+961	−3,045
Excess reserves	173	−76	+19
Free reserves	− 1,442	+9	

Monetary and reserve aggregates (daily average in billions of dollars)

	1 week ended June 10, 1981	1 week ended June 3, 1980
Money supply (M1-A)‡	360.5	361.3
Money supply (M1-8)‡	425.4	424.9

	1 week ended June 17, 1981	1 week ended June 10, 1980
Monetary base	163.73	162.99
Total reserves	40.15	39.981
Nonborrowed reserves	38.259	37.774
Required reserves	39.981	39.73

	4 weeks ended June 10, 1981	4 weeks ended May 13, 1980
Money supply (M1-A)†	362.3	365.3
Money supply (M1-B)†	426.3	430.0

Key interest rates (weekly average)

	June 17, 1981	June 10, 1980
Federal funds	19.10	19.33
Treasury bill (90-day)	14.16	15.30
Commercial paper (dealer, 90-day)	15.86	16.68
Certificates of deposit (resale, 90-day)	16.35	17.13
Eurodollars (90-day)	17.35	18.0

*Excludes government and bank deposits and cash items being collected.

†The figures reflect adjustment for new Federal Reserve rules that impose reserve requirements on most deposit-taking institutions, including nonmember commercial banks, mutual savings banks, and savings and loan associations.

‡Seasonally adjusted.

SOURCE: *The Wall Street Journal*, June 22, 1981.

SOURCES OF INFORMATION

A good place to obtain information about the rate of growth of M1, bank reserves, the monetary base, and various other money measures is from the weekly St. Louis Federal Reserve Bank publication *U.S. Financial Data.* Using the latest figures available, this publication reports various annual rates of change, beginning with the most recent 8 weeks and extending back for 1 year.

M2 is released monthly. The best source of information about this aggregate is the H.6 report, which can be obtained by writing or calling the Board of Governors of the Federal Reserve System in Washington.

CHAPTER

25

Money Market Futures

Geraldine L. Szymanski

FIXED-INCOME SECURITIES AND THE CASH MARKET

The Treasury bill (T-bill), Treasury bond (T-bond), and Government National Mortgage Association Collateralized Depository Receipt (GNMA CDR) futures are based on fixed-income securities. Unlike corporate stocks, which represent shares in a business, a fixed-income security is a debt instrument. The issuer of the security is a debtor, or owes money, to the purchaser of the security, who in turn is a creditor of the issuer. These instruments pay a stated rate of interest over the life of the security, and at maturity the face value, or par value, is paid.

The term "fixed-income security" means that the future stream of interest income and the par value payment at maturity are known at the time the instrument is purchased. Compare this with the uncertain flow of dividend income associated with the ownership of stock shares.

The credit market—that is, the cash market in which fixed-income securities are issued and traded—can be thought of as three markets differentiated by the maturity of the securities involved. Maturities of 1 year or less are called money market instruments, and price changes in these securities reflect changes in short-term interest rates. Money market instruments include Treasury bills, corporate commercial paper, negotiable bank certificates of deposits, and bankers' acceptances. Intermediate-term interest rates are reflected in the prices of securities with maturities more than 1 year and up to 10 years from the original date of issue. Treasury notes and some corporate and utility bond issues fall into this classification. The long end of the maturity spectrum encompasses bonds with maturities of over 10 years. This includes U.S. Treasury bonds, which have been issued in maturities of up to 30 years; corporate bonds, whose initial maturity may be as long as 40 years; and public utility bonds.

The credit market is an over-the-telephone market in which dealers, brokers, and traders at large banks and other financial institutions sit in their various offices and conduct trading via the telephone. Not only are new corporate issues bought and sold in this manner, but so are securities that are being retendered for sale by current owners in what is called the secondary market. Thus, the cash market for fixed-income securities differs markedly from the financial futures market, where trading is conducted on an exchange floor with members arriving at prices by open outcry.

TREASURY BILLS

Characteristics

U.S. Treasury bills are discount securities. That is, they are sold at a discount to par, and at maturity the full face value, or par value, is paid to the investor. The difference between par value and the discounted price at which the security was purchased is the amount of interest earned. T-bills are quoted in terms of discount rate, which is an annualized interest rate based on a 360-day year.

Purchasers of T-bills are in effect buying the right to receive the bill's face value when it matures. The price of the bill is determined by both the interest rate and the number of days to maturity:

$$\text{T-bill issue price} = \text{face value} - \frac{\text{days to maturity} \times \text{T-bill discount} \times \text{face value}}{360}$$

Given the discount rate and the bill's face value, the fewer the number of days to maturity, the higher will be its price. In other words, the shorter the time period the funds are to be loaned to the U.S. Treasury, the more investors are willing to pay in return for a fixed amount of money when the bill matures. For example, when the discount rate is 10 percent, a 180-day $1 million T-bill will sell for $950,000, while a 90-day $1 million T-bill quoted at the same rate will sell for $975,000.

It is also important to note the inverse relationship between the discount rate and the price of the T-bill. That is to say, the higher the discount rate, the lower the bill's price, and the lower the discount rate, the higher the bill's price. The 90-day T-bill that is priced at $975,000 when the discount rate is 10 percent will sell for only $970,000 if the 90-day T-bill rate is 2 percentage points higher, or 12 percent.

The convention in the cash market is for dealers to quote T-bills in terms of their discount, or interest rate. The spread between the bid and the ask quotes reflects the dealer's desire to buy securities at a lower price (the bid) than the price at which they are sold (the ask). For T-bills, the discount quoted on the bid side will be higher than the one quoted on the ask side, which, because of the inverse relationship between interest rates and bill prices, is consistent with the principle of buying the security at a lower price than it is being sold for.

TABLE 25-1 Results of Treasury's June 29, 1981, 3-Month, 6-Month Bill Auction*
(000 omitted in dollar figures)

	3-month bills	6-month bills
Average price	96.484	93.114
Discounted rate	13.909%	13.621%
Coupon yield	14.62%	14.83%
Low price	96.467	93.105
Discounted rate	13.977%	13.638%
Coupon yield	14.69%	14.85%
High price	96.512	93.126
Discounted rate	13.799%	13.597%
Coupon yield	14.50%	14.80%
Accepted at low	68%	62%
Total applied for	$8,425,510	$9,783,750
Accepted	$4,000,060	$4,003,545
New York applied for	$6,824,380	$8,225,305
New York accepted	$3,093,505	$3,540,475
Noncompetitive	$765,695	$550,720

*Both these issues are dated July 2. The 3-month bills mature October 1, the 6-month bills December 31.

The "Treasury Issues; Bonds, Notes, and Bills" column from the June 30, 1981, edition of *The Wall Street Journal* is reproduced in Table 25-1. In the bottom section of that column the previous day's T-bill rates are quoted. On the far left-hand side each bill is identified according to its maturity date. The first bill listed, for example, matures on July 2, 1981. This is followed by the discount rates for the bid (13.74 percent), the ask (13.50 percent), and, in the far right-hand column, the bond equivalent yield (13.69 percent).

The bond equivalent yield adjusts the bill's return to reflect the longer, 365-day year that is used to calculate bond yields, and it provides the investor with a way to compare the returns on bonds and bills. Because the bond equivalent yield is based on a 365-day year, as contrasted to the 360-day year of the discount rate, the return as indicated by the bond equivalent yield is always higher than the bill's discount.

The Weekly T-Bill Auction

A new issue of both 13- and 16-week T-bills is sold every Monday (if Monday is a holiday, the bill sale is held on the preceding Friday) at an auction conducted by the Federal Reserve. These bills are the debt of the U.S. Treasury and not the Federal Reserve, which is acting only as the Treasury's fiscal agent. Bids must be submitted at a Federal Reserve Bank no later than 1:30 P.M. New York time on the day of the auction. Large investors submit competitive bids, and the highest-price bids are accepted first. Small investors can purchase up to $500,000 of T-bills by submitting noncompetitive bids which the Treasury fills at the weighted average price of the competitive bids accepted. T-bills are sold in minimum amounts of $10,000, and purchasers include individuals as well as bond dealers, banks, and corporations.

On the Tuesday before each auction, the Treasury announces the number of 3- and 6-month bills that will be sold the following Monday. The bills then trade on what is called the gray market during the week preceding the auction, up to the time the auction results are announced, usually after 5:00 P.M. New York time on the day of the auction. Positions taken in the gray market are based on some expectation of what the lowest auction price (highest rate) will be. After the auction results are announced on Monday and up to the following

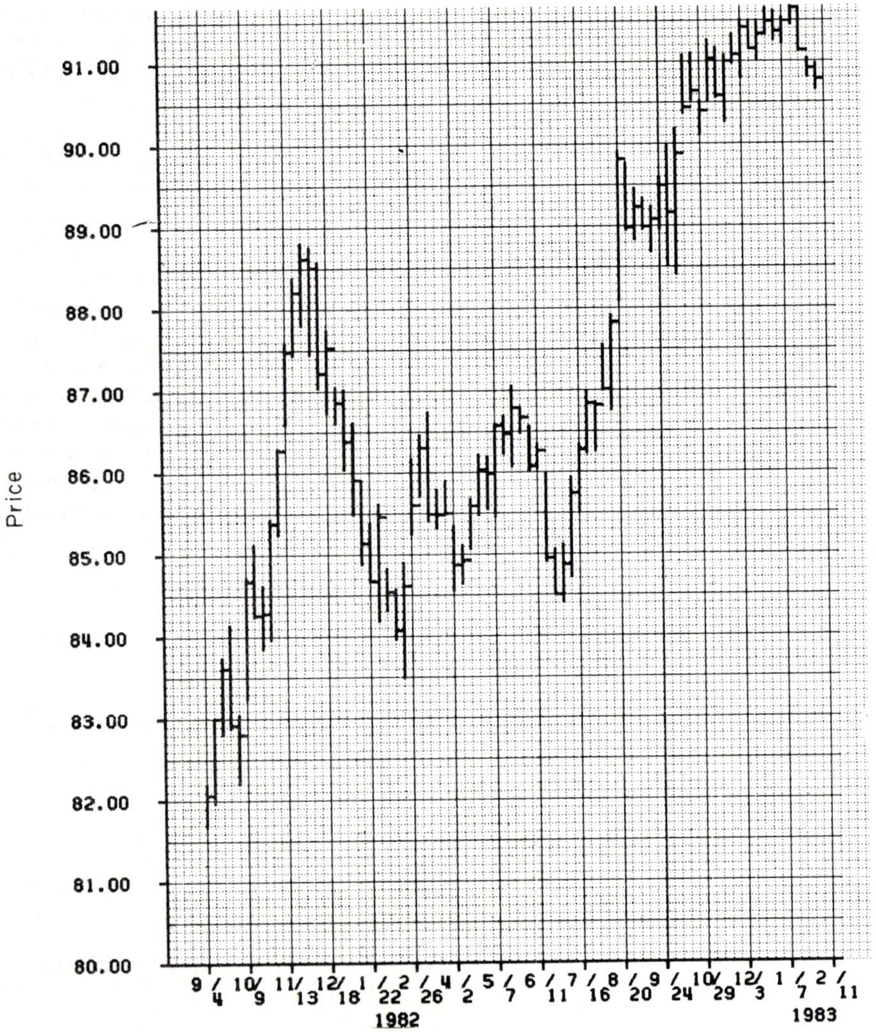

Figure 25-1 Monthly continuation, T-bills. *(ContiCommodity Research Division)*

Thursday, when the bills are finally delivered by the Treasury, trading in the newly auctioned bills proceeds on a when-issued (WI) basis. Notice that WI trading is unlike the gray market in that auction prices are known during WI trading.

The auction results are published on the day following the auction in *The Wall Street Journal, The New York Times,* and other newspapers. Tables 25-2 and 25-3 give the results of the Treasury auction held on June 29, 1981. Market traders follow these auction results as an indicator of the credit market's tone. Figure 25-1 illustrates the price swings in International Monetary Market T-bills from 1982 to 1983.

TABLE 25-2 U.S. Treasury Issues: Bonds and Notes, Monday, June 29, 1981

Rate	Maturity	Date	Bid*	Asked*	Change*	Yield
6 3/4s	1981	June n†	99.27	99.31		00.00
9 1/8s	1981	June n	99.28	100		00.00
9 3/8s	1981	July n	99.18	99.17	+0.5	14.53
7s	1981	Aug.	98.18	99.2		14.30
7 5/8s	1981	Aug. n	98.26	98.30	+0.2	15.88
8 3/8s	1981	Aug. n	98.29	99.1	+0.3	15.82
9 5/8s	1981	Aug. n	98.29	99.1	+0.1	15.13
6 3/4s	1981	Sept. n	97.26	97.3	+0.4	15.10
10 1/8s	1981	Sept. n	98.21	98.25	+0.3	14.83
12 5/8s	1981	Oct. n	98.30	99.2	+0.2	15.27
7s	1981	Nov. n	96.24	96.28	+0.2	15.75
7 3/4s	1981	Nov. n	97.4	97.8	+0.2	14.41
12 1/8s	1981	Nov. n	98.2	98.24	+0.4	15.19
7 1/4s	1981	Dec. n	96.6	96.1	+0.2	15.22
11 3/8s	1981	Dec. n	98.4	98.8	+0.3	15.15
11 1/2s	1982	Jan. n	97.28	98	+0.3	15.20
6 1/8s	1982	Feb. n	94.28	95.4	+0.2	14.53
6 3/8s	1982	Feb.	94.26	95.2	+0.4	14.90
13 7/8s	1982	Feb. n	99.6	99.1	+0.2	14.99
7 7/8s	1982	Mar. n	94.31	95.3	+0.3	15.00
15s	1982	Mar. n	100	100.4	+0.1	14.82
11 3/8s	1982	Apr. n	97.6	97.1	+0.2	14.91
7s	1982	May n	93.28	94.4	+0.2	14.38
8s	1982	May n	94.2	94.28	+0.4	14.44
9 1/4s	1982	May n	95.18	95.22	+0.2	14.68
9 3/8s	1982	May n	95.16	95.2	+0.2	14.64
8 1/4s	1982	June n	94.12	94.16	+0.4	14.36
8 5/8s	1982	June n	94.18	94.22	+0.2	14.54
8 7/8s	1982	July n	94.1	94.14	+0.3	14.60
8 1/8s	1982	Aug. n	93.22	93.3	+0.2	14.13
9s	1982	Aug. n	94.9	94.13	+0.3	14.55
11 1/8s	1982	Aug. n	96.16	96.2	+0.4	14.36
8 3/8s	1982	Sept. n	93.6	93.1	+0.4	14.40
11 7/8s	1982	Sept. n	96.3	97.2	+0.2	14.52
12 1/8s	1982	Oct. n	97.5	97.9	+0.2	14.44
7 1/8s	1982	Nov. n	91.4	91.12	+0.4	14.25
7 7/8s	1982	Nov. n	92	92.8	+0.4	14.28
13 7/8s	1982	Nov. n	98.3	99.2	+0.5	14.63

TABLE 25-2 U.S. Treasury Issues: Bonds and Notes, Monday, June 29, 1981 (*Continued*)

Rate	Maturity	Date	Bid*	Asked*	Change*	Yield
9 3/8s	1982	Dec. n	93.1	93.18	+0.9	14.30
15 1/8s	1982	Dec. n	100.12	100.16	+0.5	14.74
13 5/8s	1982	Jan. n	98.1	98.14	+0.4	14.77
8s	1983	Feb. n	90.28	91.4	+0.6	14.30
13 7/8s	1983	Feb. n	98.18	98.22	+0.5	14.79
9 1/4s	1983	Mar. n	92.4	92.8	+0.6	14.41
12 5/8s	1983	Mar. n	96.23	96.27	+0.6	14.73
14 1/2s	1983	Apr. n	99.22	99.24	+0.8	14.66
7 7/8s	1983	May n	89.3	90.6	+0.9	14.00
11 5/8s	1983	May n	95.26	96.2	+0.6	14.09
15 5/8s	1983*	May n	101.18	101.22	+0.4	14.59
3 1/4s	1978–1983	June	84.15	84.31	+0.7	12.10
8 7/8s	1983	June n	90.24	91	+0.4	14.21
14 5/8s	1983	June n	100.8	100.1	+0.6	14.44
9 1/4s	1983	Aug. n	90.28	91.4	+0.4	14.23
11 7/8s	1983	Aug. n	95.24	96	+0.8	14.12
9 3/4s	1983	Sept. n	91.16	91.24	+0.1	14.16
7s	1983	Nov. n	86.2	86.28	+0.4	13.66
9 7/8s	1983	Nov. n	91.12	91.2	+0.6	14.15
10 1/2s	1983	Dec. n	92.28	93.4	+1.17	13.85
7 1/4s	1984	Feb. n	86	86.8	+0.9	13.65
14 1/4s	1984	Mar. n	100.2	100.18	+0.3	13.85
9 1/4s	1984	May n	89.6	89.14	+0.2	13.83
13 1/4s	1984	May n	97.3	98.6	+0.5	14.04
15 3/4s	1984	May n	103.2	103.6		14.36
8 7/8s	1984	June n	87.2	87.28	+0.1	13.96
6 3/8s	1984	Aug.	82.12	83.12	+0.8	13.01
7 1/4s	1984	Aug. n	84.3	84.11	+0.3	13.55
13 1/4s	1984	Aug. n	97.14	97.18	+0.4	14.24
12 1/8s	1984	Sept. n	94.19	94.27		14.15
14s	1984	Dec. n	99.17	99.25	+0.1	14.08
8s	1985	Feb. n	84.4	84.12	+0.4	13.59
13 3/8s	1985	Mar. n	97.2	97.24	+0.5	14.16
3 1/4s	1985	May	84.12	84.28	+0.8	7.85
4 1/4s	1975–1985	May	84.8	84.24	+0.1	9.00
10 3/8s	1985	May n	89.24	90	+0.4	13.79
14 3/8s	1985	May n	101.4	101.12	+0.16	13.90
8 1/4s	1985	Aug. n	83.3	83.11		13.66
9 5/8s	1985	Aug. n	87.2	87.1	+0.4	13.75
11 3/4s	1985	Nov. n	92.2	92.28	+0.4	13.98
13 1/2s	1986	Feb. n	98.6	98.14	+0.6	13.97
7 7/8s	1986	May n	80.2	80.1	+0.11	13.52
13 3/4s	1986	May n	98.31	99.3	+0.5	14.02
8s	1986	Aug. n	79.3	80.6	+0.5	13.48
6 1/8s	1986	Nov.	75.4	76.4	+0.11	12.33
13 7/8s	1986	Nov. n	99.18	99.22	+0.8	13.95
9s	1987	Feb. n	82.4	82.12	−0.2	13.58
12s	1987	May n	93.22	93.3	+0.2	13.53
7 5/8s	1987	Nov. n	75.14	75.22	+0.2	13.42
12 3/8s	1988	Jan. n	93.3	94.6	+0.1	13.75

TABLE 25-2 U.S. Treasury Issues: Bonds and Notes, Monday, June 29, 1981 (*Continued*)

Rate	Maturity	Date	Bid*	Asked*	Change*	Yield
13 1/4s	1988	Apr. n	97.12	97.16		13.83
8 1/4s	1988	May n	77.6	77.14		13.37
8 3/4s	1988	Nov. n	78	78.8	−0.3	13.50
9 1/4s	1989	May n	79.3	80.6	+0.1	13.40
10 3/4s	1989	Nov. n	86	86.8	+0.1	13.54
3 1/2s	1990	Feb.	83.3	84.3	+0.1	5.74
8 1/4s	1990	May	75	76	+0.16	12.86
10 3/4s	1990	Aug. n	85.2	85.28	+0.1	13.49
13s	1990	Nov. n	96.28	97	+0.4	13.58
14 1/2s	1991	May n	104.12	104.14	+0.1	13.67
4 1/4s	1987–1992	Aug.	83.3	84.3	−0.2	6.14
7 1/4s	1992	Aug.	65.28	66.28	−0.4	12.95
4s	1988–1993	Feb.	84.1	85.1	−0.19	5.79
6 3/4s	1993	Feb.	63.6	64.6	+0.8	12.74
7 7/8s	1993	Feb.	68.16	69	+0.26	13.15
7 1/2s	1988–1993	Aug.	66.18	67.18	+0.8	12.85
8 5/8s	1993	Aug.	71.22	71.3	+0.12	13.36
8 5/8s	1993	Nov.	71.18	71.3	+0.1	13.36
9s	1994	Feb.	73.19	73.27	+0.7	13.34
4 1/8s	1989–1994	May	84.3	85.3	−0.7	5.78
8 3/4s	1994	Aug.	71.22	72.6	+0.8	13.28
10 1/8s	1994	Nov.	79.28	80.4	+0.1	13.25
3s	1995	Feb.	84.1	85.1	+0.1	4.58
10 1/2s	1995	Feb.	81.23	81.31		13.42
10 3/8s	1995	May	80.29	81.5	+0.3	13.40
12 5/8s	1995	May	95.6	95.15	+0.4	13.36
11 1/2s	1995	Nov.	87.26	88.2	+0.8	13.39
7s	1993–1998	May	61.26	62.26	+0.14	12.27
3 1/2s	1998	Nov.	84.7	85.7	−0.1	4.76
8 1/2s	1994–1999	May	70.11	70.27	+0.8	12.65
7 7/8s	1995–2000	Feb.	64.4	64.12	+0.18	13.00
8 3/8s	1995–2000	Aug.	67.8	67.16	+0.22	13.02
11 3/4s	2001	Feb.	89.6	89.14	+0.18	13.27
13 1/8s	2001	May	98.6	98.14	+0.7	13.35
8s	1996–2001	Aug.	65.12	65.2	+0.24	12.79
13 3/8s	2001	Aug.	99.2	99.24		13.41
8 1/4s	2000–2005	May	66.11	66.27	+0.1	12.69
7 5/8s	2002–2007	Feb.	63.2	63.1	+0.14	12.39
7 7/8s	2002–2007	Nov.	65.2	65.28	+0.28	12.24
8 3/8s	2003–2008	Aug.	67.14	67.22	+0.12	12.60
8 3/4s	2003–2008	Nov.	69.24	70	+0.12	12.69
9 1/8s	2004–2008	May	72.7	72.15	+0.5	12.75
10 3/8s	2004–2009	Nov.	81	81.8	+0.1	12.86
11 3/4s	2005–2010	Feb.	90.16	90.24	+0.4	12.98
10s	2005–2010	May	78.16	78.24	+0.6	12.80
12 3/4s	2005–2010	Nov.	97.22	97.30	+0.6	13.03
13 7/8s	2006–2011	May	105.22	105.25	+0.8	13.08

*Decimals represent thirty-seconds; 101.1 means 101 1/32.

†Treasury notes.

TABLE 25-3 U.S. Treasury Issues: Bills, Monday, June 29, 1981

Maturity	Bid	Asked discount	Yield
1981			
7-2	13.74	13.50	13.69
7-9	14.00	13.80	14.04
7-16	14.01	13.75	14.03
7-23	14.00	13.80	14.11
7-30	13.99	13.81	14.16
8-6	14.40	13.881	14.27
8-13	14.13	13.91	14.34
8-20	14.13	13.91	14.38
8-27	14.13	13.91	14.42
9-3	14.09	13.89	14.44
9-10	14.05	13.83	14.41
9-17	14.03	13.87	14.50
9-24	13.94	13.88	14.55
10-1	14.00	13.80	14.50
10-8	14.07	13.82	14.57
10-15	14.02	13.82	14.61
10-22	14.02	13.82	14.64
10-29	14.03	13.83	14.70
11-5	14.02	13.82	14.73
11-12	14.01	13.79	14.78
11-19	13.99	13.79	14.78
11-27	13.99	13.79	14.83
12-3	13.95	13.77	14.84
12-10	13.95	13.75	14.86
12-17	13.91	13.73	14.89
12-24	13.75	13.69	14.88
12-31	13.76	13.60	14.81
1982			
1-28	13.40	13.24	14.41
2-25	13.49	13.33	14.58
3-25	13.36	13.20	14.50
4-22	13.42	13.28	14.70
5-20	13.19	13.03	14.50
6-17	13.02	12.98	14.56

For example, the amount tendered, or the cover, should be noted. At an average auction, twice as many bids are submitted as the number of bills sold. More bids than that were submitted at the June 29, 1981 auction, which suggests that it may have gone well. However, it is also important to watch the tail, that is, the spread between the highest discount (the lowest price) and the average discount (the average price) at which the bill is sold. The difference between the two rates should be no more than 4 basis points. The tail for the auction reported above was 6.8 basis points (13.977 − 13.909), which is a bit wide. Thus, although the June 29 auction had fairly good cover, it was not well bid.

90-DAY TREASURY-BILL FUTURES: CONTRACT SPECIFICATIONS

The 90-day bill futures contract at the International Monetary Market (IMM) calls for delivery of $1 million of 90-, 91-, or 92-day Treasury bills. For trading purposes, however, a 90-day maturity is assumed. Instead of adopting the cash market convention of quoting bill prices in terms of their discount, the IMM has devised an index that reflects that bill prices rise when interest rates fall and fall when interest rates rise. The index is based on 100.00, and the discount rate is subtracted from it. For example, a discount rate of 14.25 percent in the 90-day bill futures would be a price quote at the IMM of 85.75. If the interest rate rises to 14.26 percent, the futures price will fall to 85.74, and if the rate falls to 14.2 percent, the futures price will rise to 85.76.

The minimum price fluctuation is 1 basis point, or 0.01 percent and 60 basis points is a limit move. A price change to 85.74 from 85.75, for example, is a 1-basis-point move; and from an 85.74 closing price, a rise the next day to 86.34, or a decline to 85.14, would be a limit move. If in *any* contract month prices move the limit in the same direction for 2 successive days, the limit move for *all* contract months is expanded to 90 basis points. If on the third day the contract moves the limit in the same direction as before, the limit move for all contract months is expanded to 120 basis points, and it will remain there as long as any contract month closes at that limit. When no contract month closes the limit in the same direction that triggered and maintained the expanded price limit, the regular 60-basis-point price limit is reinstated.

For each contract held, a 1-basis-point move represents $25 ($0.0001 \times 90/360 \times \$1,000,000 = \$25$). It is important to realize that the price indicated by the IMM index is not the amount paid for a bill contract at delivery. That sum is given by the T-bill formula and is based on the futures discount rate (which is 100.00 − the futures index price) and the maturity of the bill delivered. A bill futures price of 85.95 corresponds to a 14.95 discount ($100.00 - 85.95 = 14.05$), and if a 91-day bill were delivered at this interest rate $964,484.72 would have to be paid ($\$1,000,000 - 0.1495 \times 91/360 \times \$1,000,000 = \$964,484.72$).

The main delivery months are March, June, September, and December, and they extend for eight options, or 2 years into the future. Trading in the expiring option ends on the second business day following the third weekly bill auction in the delivery month, which almost always occurs on a Wednesday. Delivery then begins on the following business day, usually a Thursday, and T-bills must have 90, 91, or 92 days to maturity at the time delivery is made.

Treasury Bill Futures Trading Volume

Active trading in 90-day T-bill futures developed quickly after the contract was introduced at the IMM. Between January 6, 1976, when they were first listed, and the close of trading on December 31 of that year, 110,223 contracts changed hands. In 1977, volume jumped to 321,703 contracts traded, and in 1978 total contracts traded rose to 768,980. By 1980 over 2 million contracts were trading annually, and volume has continued to rise.

Volume figures in the bill futures are especially impressive when compared with trading in the cash market. In December 1980, the cash market was averaging $13.840 billion of bills traded daily. At that time the futures were averaging 19,000 contracts traded daily, which (at $1 million per contract) is equivalent to $19 billion of T-bill futures traded each day. Thus, by the end of 1980 the bill futures were exceeding the cash market volume by over 30 percent.

Commercial traders, or hedgers, in the bill futures include commercial banks, securities dealers, savings and loan associations, mortgage bankers, pension funds, and nonfinancial corporations. On March 30, 1979, the Commodity Futures Trading Commission (CFTC) conducted a fairly comprehensive survey of the participants in the financial futures markets and published the results in a paper entitled "Survey of Interest-Rate Futures Markets." According to that study, commercial traders composed 14.5 percent of all traders in the market, and speculators, or noncommercial traders, composed 85.5 percent. Table 25-4 shows the various categories of traders.

Volume figures are published each month by the CFTC in *Commitments of Traders*. According to the May 31, 1981, edition, hedgers held 12.4 percent of the long and 32.6 percent of the short open interest. Table 25-5 also reports hedging activity for the wheat contract at the Chicago Board of Trade (CBT) and the frozen pork bellies at the Chicago Mercantile Exchange (CME). These

TABLE 25-4 Occupational Groups of Traders, March 30, 1979

90-day T-bills (Contracts of $1 million)		
Occupations	Number	Percent
Commercial traders		
Commercial banks	24	2.0
Securities dealers, non-Fom	18	1.5
Securities dealers, Fom	11	0.9
Savings and loan associations	6	0.5
Mortgage bankers	4	0.3
Pension funds, insurance firms	4	0.3
Other financial firms	58	4.9
Real estate interests	12	1.0
Other nonfinancial commercial	37	3.1
Subtotals	174	14.5
Noncommercial traders		
Futures industry	132	11.3
Commodity pools and funds	98	8.4
Individual traders	774	65.8
Subtotals	1004	85.5
Grand totals	1178	100.0

SOURCE: Taken from Tables II-b and II-d in Naomi L. Jaffee and Ronald B. Hobson, "Survey of Interest-Rate Futures Markets," Division of Economics and Education, Commodity Futures Trading Commission, Chicago, December 1979.

TABLE 25-5 Total Open Interest Held by Large Hedgers*

Commodity	Percent of long open interest	Percent of short open interest
90-Day (IMM)	12.4	32.6
Wheat (CBT)	42.2	24.0
Frozen pork bellies (CME)	4.1	20.3

*Large positions are defined as 50 contracts or more for 90-day T-bills, 1 million bushels or more for wheat, and 25 contracts or more for frozen pork bellies.

SOURCE: *Commitments of Traders*, May 31, 1981.

figures show that a larger percentage of the open interest in wheat than T-bills is held by hedgers, and that a smaller percentage of the open interest is held by hedgers in pork bellies futures. It is apparent that although T-bill futures is a relatively new market, cash market participants are using the bill futures to protect themselves against the risk of adverse interest-rate movements.

BANK CERTIFICATES OF DEPOSIT

Cash Markets

Certificates of deposit (CDs) are negotiable bank instruments. Although some CDs are issued at a discount, as are Treasury bills, most are issued at face value, usually in denominations of $1 million, and pay a fixed rate of interest at maturity. When the CD matures the investor receives the face amount plus interest for the actual number of days the CD was outstanding. Interest calculations are based on a 360-day year, and coupon-bearing CDs are quoted on an interest-bearing, or a bank add-on yield, basis rather than the discount basis that is used in the T-bill market. The price of a CD is determined by using the following formula:

Market price in dollars = 1 + (coupon × days from issue to maturity)/360 × face amount 1 + (bank add-on yield × days from purchase to maturity/360)

Figure 25-2 shows CD prices from 1976 to 1982.

Negotiable bank certificates of deposit were first sold in the early 1960s by the large New York banks in order to tap the nationwide market for deposits. Although CDs were originally used to fund unexpected surges in loan demand and deposit drains, they have since become a regular feature of bank asset-liability management.

Major investors are money market funds, corporations, state and local governments, and other financial institutions. Commercial banks are limited buyers of certificates of deposit, since CD holdings are not deductible from reservable deposits, as are demand deposits with other banks. In addition, reserve requirements are incurred if the CDs are held in a repurchase agreement (repoed) with a nonbank entity. It should also be noted that banks are prohibited from buying back or investing in their own certificates of deposit.

Bank CDs are issued in initial maturities of 30, 60, 90, and 180 days. Although some CDs have been issued with maturities of over a year, the market for these longer-term CDs is relatively thin. Most CDs are issued in the 1- to 3-month maturity range.

Futures Market

Three-month certificate-of-deposit futures are traded on the International Monetary Market, which is part of the Chicago Mercantile Exchange. The contract size is $1 million of bank CDs. Prices are quoted in terms of the IMM index, which is 100.00 minus the bank add-on yield. For example, if the bank add-on yield is 11.85 percent, the corresponding IMM quote would be 88.15. A

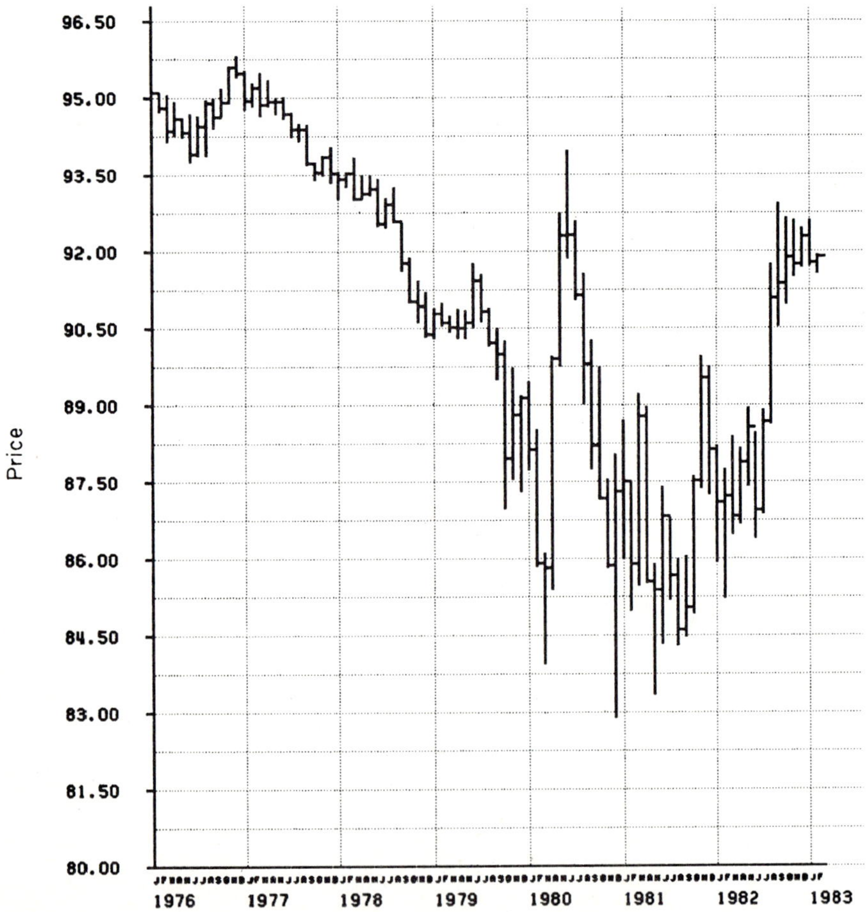

Figure 25-2 Weekly continuation, International Monetary Market *(ContiCommodity Research Division)*

minimum price move is 1 basis point. From 88.15, this would be a move to 88.16 in the case of an increase, or to 88.14 in the case of a decline. The value of a 1-basis-point move is $25.00. A limit move is 80 basis points.

March, June, September, and December are the delivery months, and delivery begins on the fifteenth day of the contract month and extends through the last business day of the month. Banks whose CDs are acceptable for delivery are based on a random sample of at least seven dealers from a list of at least ten dealers who are active participants in the domestic certificate of deposit market. This sample is taken in the delivery month, 2 business days before the fifteenth. Each dealer polled submits a list of banks with CDs of highest liquidity and lowest credit risk and which trade at identical yields. Banks that appear on at least five lists and have agreed to be deliverable on the contract constitute that month's list of deliverable CD issues.

In addition to appearing on the list of deliverable banks, a deliverable CD must meet the following conditions:

1. Maturity value of $1,000,000 to $1,200,000, where maturity value means principal value for discount CDs and principal plus interest payable at maturity for add-on CDs
2. No interest payments between the delivery date and the maturity date
3. Maturity date between the sixteenth and the last day of the month, 3 months after the delivery month
4. Maturity date on a business day that is not a bank holiday in either New York or Chicago
5. No more than 185-day accrued interest payable at maturity

CHAPTER

26

Treasury-Bond and GNMA Futures

Geraldine L. Szymanski

INTRODUCTION

The Government National Mortgage Association Collateralized Depository Receipt (GNMA CDR), the U.S. Treasury-bond (T-bond) futures at the Chicago Board of Trade (CBT), and the 90-day Treasury-bill (T-bill) futures at the International Monetary Market (IMM) of the Chicago Mercantile Exchange (CME) are the three most actively traded financial futures contracts. The GNMA CDR was introduced on October 20, 1975, which makes it the oldest contract of the three. Shortly thereafter, on January 6, 1976, the 90-day T-bill futures began trading at the IMM, and on August 22, 1977, the bond futures were introduced at the Chicago Board of Trade.

It was no accident that the GNMA CDR was the first financial instrument contract to be introduced to the futures market. The contract is based on the GNMA pass-through (or Ginnie Mae), a coupon-bearing security that represents a share in a pool of home mortgages insured by the Federal Housing Administration (FHA) or guaranteed by the Veterans Administration (VA). Timely payment of interest and principal to the security owner are guaranteed by the Government National Mortgage Association—and the guarantee is backed by the full faith and credit of the U.S. government. Cash market trading in Ginnie Maes began in 1970, and a forward delivery market evolved shortly thereafter. For years, sellers of mortgages had been protecting themselves against adverse interest-rate movements by making both advance and standby commitments, and forward trading in GNMA pass-throughs was a logical extension of this practice.

Once the cash forward market was established, the idea of trading a contract based on the GNMA pass-through in the futures market gained wider acceptance. It also became apparent that a GNMA futures market would avoid some of the problems inherent in forward trading. Because the exchange clearinghouse automatically assumes the opposite side of every trade, buyers and sellers of futures contracts do not have to know the identity or (more important) the financial standing of the individuals with whom they deal. In the forward market, however, there is no one to guarantee performance and traders must determine one another's financial viability.

Another drawback of the cash forward market is that reversing an earlier commitment is both difficult and costly. The agreement of the person on the other side of the transaction must be obtained, and seldom are market conditions and individual circumstances such that both parties can simultaneously profit from an early termination of the trade. Thus, those who want early termination have to pay a stiff premium to reverse their forward positions.

In the futures market, however, knowing the identity of the individual taking the other side of a trade is not necessary, and reversing a position is a simple matter of executing an opposite trade of equal size in the market.

CHARACTERISTICS OF A BOND

Bonds are debt instruments that represent the obligation of the issuer (1) to make regularly scheduled fixed-interest payments, and (2) to pay the face, or par, value of the bond when it matures or, in the case of a callable bond, is called. The face value, which appears on the front of the bond certificate, is also referred to as the principal amount, the par value, or the denomination of the bond.

The coupon rate is the stated rate of interest on the front of the bond. The bondholder is paid this percentage of face value every year, usually in two semiannual installments. For example, a bond with a face value of $1000 and a 6 percent coupon will pay $60 a year, or $30 every 6 months.

Callable bonds have an additional feature which permits the issuer to call the bond and pay off the face amount before its maturity date. When a bond is called, the issuer must also pay the bondholder a call premium, generally equal to 1 year's interest.

Price Quotes

Bond prices are quoted in thirty-seconds as a percentage of par. For instance, a price of 86 $\frac{8}{32}$ corresponds to 86 $\frac{8}{32}$ percent of the bond's face value. Using this price quote, a $1000 bond would sell for $862.50, a $10,000 bond would sell for $8625, and a $100,000 bond would sell for $86,250.

Bonds are like short-term fixed-income securities in that there is an inverse relationship between bond prices and interest rates. That is, bond prices rise when interest rates fall, and bond prices fall when interest rates rise. The amount by which prices move for a given change in interest rates depends upon the bond's coupon rate, its term to maturity, and the current level of market yields.

Calculation of the relationship between bond prices and interest rates is complex. The formula, which is based on the concept of present value, is given below.

Fortunately, bond tables, such as *Bond Yield Book** and bond calculators are available which will give investors the price of a bond if its coupon, maturity date, and market yield are known. Alternatively, if the bond's price, coupon rate, and maturity are known, the market yield can be calculated.

U.S. TREASURY BONDS

Treasury bonds are coupon-bearing securities with initial maturities of over 10 years that are issued by the U.S. Treasury. They come in denominations of $1000, $5000, $10,000, $100,000, and $1 million.

New issues are auctioned by the Federal Reserve, which acts as fiscal agent for the Treasury. These auctions are generally announced 1 to 3 weeks in advance, at which time the Treasury states the maturity and the amount of the issue to be sold. All bids must be submitted at a Federal Reserve Bank no later than 1:30 P.M., New York time, on the day of the auction, and investors can submit either competitive or noncompetitive tenders, as at Treasury-bill auctions.

After the auction closes at 1:30 P.M., New York time, and before the auction results are announced late that same afternoon, the bond is traded in the gray market. While trading in the gray market, bond dealers and traders have only an approximate idea of the price range that will be accepted by the Treasury. After the auction results are announced, and before the bond is delivered to the successful bidders a week or so later, it trades on a *(WI)* or when-issued basis.

Unless the auction is a reopening of an already outstanding issue, the auction is bid in terms of market yield. After the bids are opened, the Treasury sets the coupon rate. The bonds are then allocated to the highest bidder (the one submitting the lowest yield) first and then to each successively higher bidder until all of the bonds, except for the number required to fill the noncompetitive tenders, are sold.

The auction results are announced late that afternoon and appear the following morning in *The Wall Street Journal* and *The New York Times*. The outcome of each bond auction, like the outcome of each T-bill auction, is studied by market traders who want to identify the strength of the current demand for government securities. The three most important items to watch are average yield, cover, and tail. Observing the yield quotes on the bond during trading in the gray market makes it possible to determine what average yield the market expects. An announced average yield that is lower than market expectations tends to be viewed favorably and is one sign that the auction went well. The

**Bond Yield Book*, Financial Publishing Company, Boston.

cover is the ratio of tenders submitted to the bids accepted, and in a good auction it should be 2 to 1. A cover of 1.5 to 1 or less would indicate that the buying interest was relatively low. The tail is the difference between the high and the average yield, and it should be no larger than 3 basis points. Determining when an auction has gone well or poorly can be difficult when the signals are mixed—for example, when the average yield is higher than expected, the cover is good, and the tail is narrow. At such times experience and knowledge of current market conditions are indispensable.

Quarterly Treasury Refunding

During the first week of the middle month of each quarter, the Treasury undertakes a major refunding of its debt. (Treasury issues maturing during other parts of the quarter are also refunded.) The quarterly refundings are notable for their large size, which tends to have a depressing effect on bond prices.

From the end of World War II until the late 1970s, the Federal Reserve followed a policy of "even keeling" during periods of major Treasury refundings. The desired outcome was the stabilization of interest rates and bond and bill prices. The undesired side effect was the monetization of the federal debt by the Federal Reserve, which had to increase its open market purchases of government securities at these times in order to keep the additional supply of Treasury debt from depressing bond prices and forcing interest rates higher.

The Federal Reserve no longer attempts to hold interest rates stable during Treasury refundings. As a result, the market price of Treasury securities falls (and interest rates rise) to whatever level is necessary to attract a sufficient number of buyers to absorb the debt being issued by the Treasury at that time. The quarterly refundings are particularly stressful because not just one Treasury issue but as many as three may be sold during the week, in addition to the regular Monday 3-month and 6-month bill auctions.

The issues to be sold are generally announced by the Treasury on the Wednesday of the week that precedes the auctions. A three-pronged package is standard, consisting of a 3-year note, a 10-year note, and a 30-year bond. The auctions are held on Tuesday, Wednesday, and Thursday. The shortest maturity is sold first, followed by the intermediate-term security and finally by the long-term bond.

Crucial to the performance of bond prices during this time is the amount of the 30-year issue that will be sold. The long-term end of the maturity spectrum is not nearly as liquid as the market for short-term securities. This is especially true when short-term interest rates are higher than long-term interest rates, for at such times investors are reluctant to invest their funds in the lower-yielding, longer-term security. In 1981, the size of the long bond issue was running at $2 billion.

There is an active secondary market in which outstanding T-bond issues are bought and sold. Trades are arranged by telephone, with government securities dealers, banks, and customers—both individuals and institutions, such as pension funds and insurance companies—participating. *The Wall Street Journal* and *The New York Times* report the price quotes in these markets on a day-to-day basis. Reproduced in Table 26-1 is a portion of the "Treasury Issues: Bonds,

TABLE 26-1 Treasury Issues: Bonds, Notes, and Bills, Wednesday, September 30, 1981
(Midafternoon over-the-counter quotations, sources on request)

Rate	Maturity	Date	Bid*	Asked*	Change*	Yield
12⅝s	1981	Oct. n†	99.23	99.27	+0.1	13.89
7s	1981	Nov. n	99	99.4	+0.2	14.06
13⅜s	2001	Aug.	86.8	86.16	−0.2	15.59
8¼s	2000–2005	May	57.6	57.22	−0.2	14.69
7⅝s	2002–2007	Feb.	54.2	54.18	+0.16	14.34
7⅞s	2002–2007	Nov.	55.30	56.14	−0.7	14.26
8⅜s	2003–2008	Aug.	57.30	58.14	+0.12	14.51
8¾s	2003–2008	Nov.	59.30	60.6		14.75
9⅛s	2004–2009	May	62.10	62.18	+0.4	14.76
10⅜s	2004–2009	Nov.	69.28	70.4	+0.4	14.91
11¾s	2005–2010	Feb.	78.14	78.22	+0.6	15.00
10s	2005–2010	May	67.12	67.20		14.90
12¾s	2005–2010	Nov.	84.10	84.18	+0.2	15.12
13⅞s	2006–2011	May	91.14	91.12	+0.2	15.16

*Decimals represent thirty-seconds; 101.1 means 101 1/32.
†Treasury notes.

Notes, and Bills" column in the form in which it typically appears in the back pages of *The Wall Street Journal.*

The first two columns identify the bond according to its coupon and the month and year in which the bond matures. For a callable bond, both the year the bond becomes callable and the year it matures are given. For example, the last bond listed is the 13 ⅞s of 2011. Because it is callable in 2006, the year is given as 2006–11.

The bid and ask prices are also shown in Table 26-1. The bid is the price at which the bond dealer is willing to purchase the security, and it is always less than the ask, or the price for which the dealer is willing to sell that same security. In the far right column is the market yield that corresponds to the ask price.

U.S. Treasury-Bond Futures

On August 22, 1977, Treasury-bond futures began trading at the Chicago Board of Trade. Volume jumped from 3274 contracts traded during the first month to over 1.5 million contracts traded per month in 1983. Figure 26-1 shows T-bond futures trading from 1979 to 1982, which surpasses the trading volume in the cash market. In bond futures, hedgers hold a little less than a third of the total open interest. Included among the hedge accounts are bond dealers, corporations, pension funds, and insurance companies.

Contract Data

The bond futures contract at the Chicago Board of Trade calls for delivery of $100,000 face value of U.S. Treasury bonds that have at least 15 years to run to maturity. If the bonds are callable, they cannot be called sooner than 15 years after delivery. Any coupon that satisfies the maturity requirement is delivera-

Figure 26-1 Weekly continuation, Chicago Board of Trade T-bonds. *(ContiCommodity Research Division)*

TABLE 26-2 U.S. Treasury Bond Futures *(Conversion factor to yield 8.000)*

	Coupon rate, percent		
Term	8⅝	8¾	8⅞
21	1.0631	1.0757	1.0883
21-3	1.0632	1.0758	1.0885
21-6	1.0637	1.0764	1.0891
21-9	1.0637	1.0765	1.0893
22	1.0642	1.0771	1.0899
22-3	1.0643	1.0772	1.0901
22-6	1.0648	1.0777	1.0907
22-9	1.0648	1.0778	1.0908

SOURCE: *Treasury Bond Futures and Treasury Notes Futures Conversion Factors,* No. 765, Financial Publishing Company, Boston.

ble, but for day-to-day pricing purposes, the bond that trades on the exchange floor is assumed to bear an 8 percent coupon.

As in the cash bond market, prices are quoted in thirty-seconds as a percentage of par. For example, a futures price quote of 65.27 is interpreted to mean 65²⁷⁄₃₂ percent of the par value of an 8 percent T-bond. This price by itself does not, however, give the value of the contract at delivery. The amount of cash exchanged at that time will depend on the coupon and maturity of the bond that is delivered. The sum is adjusted upward for T-bonds that have a higher coupon, a lower maturity, or both. It is adjusted downward for T-bonds that have a lower coupon, a higher maturity, or both.

The minimum price fluctuation is ¹⁄₃₂, which is equal to $31.25 per contract ($100,000 × ¹⁄₃₂ percent = $31.25). A full-point move, such as a price decline from 65.21 to 64.21, is ³²⁄₃₂, which is equal to $1000 per contract ($31.25 × 32 = $1000). A limit move is ⁶⁴⁄₃₂, or 2 full points. Delivery begins on the first business day and continues through the end of the delivery month. The last day of trading is between the eighth and the last business day of the month. Contract months are March, June, September, and December, and they extend 2½ years into the future.

As of September 1981, fourteen different Treasury bonds qualified for delivery at the Chicago Board of Trade. To determine the last deliverable day for any issue, subtract 15 years from its computation date: the call date for callable bonds and the maturity date for noncallable bonds. Bonds delivered against a single contract must be of the same issue.

Regardless of what specific issue is delivered, the face, or par, value of the bonds must total $100,000 per contract. For invoicing purposes, the settlement price is then adjusted by a conversion factor: which is, the price of the coupon being delivered that will yield 8 percent at its current term to maturity. These factors are available in *Treasury Bond Futures and Treasury Note Futures Conversion Factors.** An excerpt is reproduced in Table 26-2.

**Treasury Bond Futures and Treasury Note Futures Conversion Factors,* No. 765, Financial Publishing Company, Boston.

Suppose, for example, the short notifies the Clearing Corporation on September 16 of an intention to make delivery in the September T-bond futures. Delivery would then occur 2 days later on September 18. For invoicing purposes the settlement price would be the closing price on the September contract at the end of trading on September 16. The invoice amount would then be determined by making the following calculations:

Invoice amount = (settlement price × $100,000 × conversion factor) + accrued interest

Assume further that the short plans to deliver the 8¾s of 2008. This bond matures on November 15, 2008, and becomes callable on November 15, 2003. On September 18, 1981, when delivery is made, the bond's term to call would be 20 years 0 months, rounding down to the nearest 3 months. The conversion factor for an 8¾s coupon that at delivery has 22 years 0 months before it becomes callable is 1.0771. On September 16 the September bond futures closed at 58²⁵⁄₃₂. Thus, the principal invoice amount will be:

0.5878125	Decimal equivalent of 58²⁵⁄₃₂ percent
× $100,000	Contract size
$58,781.25	
× 1.0771	Conversion factor
$63,313.28	Principal invoice amount

Accrued interest is calculated by multiplying tbe daily interest earned on the bond by the number of days during the interval since the last interest payment was made to the delivery date:

$$\text{Daily interest} = \frac{\text{semiannual coupon amount}}{\text{number of days during the half year}}$$

where the semiannual coupon amount is equal to

$$\text{Semiannual coupon amount} = \frac{\text{coupon rate} \times \text{face value}}{2}$$

In the case of the 8¾s of 2008,

$$\text{Semiannual coupon amount} = \frac{0.0875 \times \$100{,}000}{2} = \$4{,}375.00$$

$$\text{Daily interest} = \frac{\$4375.00}{184} = \$23.777173$$

Total accrued interest is $2972.15:

$23.777173	Daily interest
× 125	Number of days from May 16 through September 18 (including both May 16 and September 18)
$2972.15	Total accrued interest per contract

Adding together the principal invoice amount and the total accrued interest gives the invoice amount of $66,291.31:

Invoice amount = $63,313.28 + $2972.15 + $66,285.43

GNMA PASS-THROUGHS

GNMA pass-throughs are coupon-bearing securities backed by a pool of FHA-insured on VA-guaranteed home mortgages. Interest and principal are paid monthly to the security owner, reflecting the normal repayment schedule of the underlying loans and prepayments by those paying off their mortgages early. These securities thus differ from Treasury bonds, which pay interest semi-annually and return the principal only at maturity.

The term "pass-through" comes from the practice of passing through all principal payments to the security holder immediately, as the payments are received. GNMA pass-throughs carry the Government National Mortgage Association's guarantee of timely payment each month of principal and interest of those holding the security. Furthermore, this guarantee is backed by the full faith and credit of the U.S. government.

Each security represents an undivided share in a pool of FHA-insured or VA-guaranteed home mortgages. All mortgages in a pool must (1) carry the same rate of interest, (2) have been made for the same number of years, and (3) finance the same type of residence—such as single-family dwellings. Although the original term of the underlying mortgages in a pool is frequently 30 years, the life of the GNMA pass-through is much shorter than this because of the early repayment of many of the mortgages.

Most GNMA pass-throughs are originated by mortgage bankers who bring together FHA and VA mortgages in pools of $1 million or more, complete the necessary documentation, and obtain the approval of the GNMA. Mortgage bankers purchase some mortgages, but most of the mortgages packaged are ones they themselves make to home buyers. The coupon rate on a GNMA pass-through is ½ percentage point less than the interest rate on the underlying mortgages. For example, GNMA pass-throughs backed by a pool of 13 percent mortgages will carry a 12.5 percent coupon. The remaining 0.5 percent is divided between the mortgage banker, who receives 0.44 percent as a servicing fee, and GNMA, which receives 0.06 percent.

Pass-Through Origination and the Forward Market

Mortgage bankers' main sources of income are the servicing fees on the outstanding pass-throughs that they have originated. Government-mandated FHA and VA ceiling mortgage rates are usually lower than the rates on conventional mortgages. This means that the mortgage banker frequently takes a loss on the sale of mortgages in the cash market, since market yields tend to be higher than the FHA or VA mortgage rate. By charging the seller of the house a percentage of the amount borrowed (usually referred to as "points") at the time the home sale is closed, the mortgage banker can recoup part of the losses. The banker expects the balance of the losses to be more than covered by the servicing fees collected on the original mortgage. Thus loan origination is simply the means to a profitable end: the acquisition of a mortgage-servicing portfolio. Since the servicing fee for GNMA securities is 0.44 percent per annum, as compared with 0.375 percent per annum on conventional mortgages, mortgage bankers seem even less averse to incurring front-end losses in order to add to the volume of GNMA pass-throughs they issue and service.

Several months usually elapse between the time the mortgage banker agrees to finance a home purchase and the time the resulting pass-throughs, whose underlying pool includes that mortgage, are sold in the cash market. If interest rates rise during this interval, the mortgage banker may find that the price at which the pass-throughs are finally sold is so low that, even with the income from the servicing fees, the opportunity for profit has been eliminated. To avoid exposing pass-through production to this kind of price risk, GNMA dealers developed a cash forward delivery market. This has allowed the mortgage banker to fix beforehand the price, amount, and delivery date of the pass-throughs to be originated. Like the cash market for government securities, the GNMA forward market is an informal over-the-counter (that is, over-the-telephone) market.

Initially, firms that were approved by GNMA dealers were allowed to make substantial purchases and sales by telephone. These commitments were not accompanied by good-faith deposits, and abuses developed. For instance, if interest rates rose after the forward commitment was made, the investor would suffer an immediate portfolio loss when the GNMA was delivered. Most investors fulfilled the terms of their agreements, but there were some who reneged and refused to take delivery. The most notable case was Reliance Mortgage Corporation of Denver, which in May 1979 refused delivery on $350 million of GNMA pass-throughs it had earlier contracted to buy.

The Government National Mortgage Association has asked, as a result, that all forward commitments of 150 days or longer be marked to market. This applies to both the buyer and the seller, since the possibility of the seller's reneging arises when fewer mortgages than anticipated are originated. However, the failure of sellers to meet commitments has been much less of a problem than nonperformance by buyers. In addition, GNMA has asked each dealer to ensure that customers follow sound and prudent business practices. Thus a dealer may require some form of collateral, such as a letter of credit, from a customer's bank.

These safeguards are not mandatory, and dealer compliance is voluntary. Although most dealers would like to enforce such safeguards, they are reluctant to act independently for fear of losing customers to dealers who do not enforce safeguards. Marking to market, therefore, is still not practiced in the forward market.

Standby Commitment

As an alternative, the GNMA originator who seeks price protection for a production can purchase a standby commitment, more formally called an Optional Delivery Commitment for Purchase of GNMA Securities. The mortgage banker pays a nonrefundable commitment fee which, depending on the time period, varies from 1 percent to 1½ percent of the amount committed. The standby is then issued at the ask price of the current market. Delivery is not mandatory. If interest rates decline, the GNMA originator has the option of selling the production at the higher cash market price. Because of the large commitment fee, standbys are used infrequently by mortgage bankers. Pass-through production, therefore, is usually hedged in either the forward or the futures market.

Sale of Pass-Throughs to Final Investors

In general, mortgage bankers do not sell the pass-throughs they originate directly to final investors. First the securities are sold to dealers, usually investment banking firms, who then sell them to investors. Some of the larger dealer firms include Merrill Lynch Government Securities; First Boston Corporation; Salomon Brothers; and Paine, Webber, Jackson, & Curtis. Some banks, such as Citibank, Bankers Trust, First National of Chicago, and Bank of America, also have dealer operations in GNMAs.

The earliest investors in GNMA pass-throughs were savings banks and savings and loan associations. By keeping a high percentage of their assets in mortgage loans, such firms receive preferred federal income tax status. These institutions became enthusiastic GNMA purchasers when the IRS ruled that for federal income tax purposes, GNMA pass-throughs are considered an investment in mortgages. Now the list of investors also includes privately administered pension funds, insurance companies, public retirement funds, bank trust departments, bank portfolio investments, and fire and casualty companies.

Price Quotes and Yields

GNMA pass-throughs can be purchased in face values as low as $25,000. Their price, like that of bonds, is expressed in thirty-seconds and is quoted as a percentage of par. For instance, a price of 95⁸⁄₃₂ for a 15 percent GNMA means that, in order to purchase $25,000 face value of these securities, the investor would have to pay $23,812.50 (0.9525 × $25,000 = $23,812.50).

Although the stated maturity on the pass-through is the same as the maturity on the underlying mortgage, the yield is calculated under the assumption that the security will be prepaid in 12 years. This convention exists as a convenience and, contrary to popular belief, does not reflect the specific FHA experience rate, which is actually closer to 7 to 9 years. Pass-through yield is not strictly comparable to bond yield. Because payments on pass-throughs are made monthly, interest is compounded monthly. Bond interest is paid and compounded semiannually, however, Thus, if both securities have the same nominal rate, the additional compounding on the pass-through makes its actual return higher than the return paid by the bond.

GNMA pass-throughs are actively traded in the secondary market. Daily price and yield quotes can be obtained from the "Government Agency and Miscellaneous Securities" column, under GNMA issues, which appears in the back pages of *The Wall Street Journal*.

GNMA CDR Futures

The GNMA Collateralized Depository Receipt, which trades at the Chicago Board of Trade, was the first financial instruments contract introduced to the futures market. Trading began on October 20, 1975, and volume during that month was 6240 contracts. The market has continued to grow, and by 1983 trading volume was averaging around 200,000 contracts per month. The amount of GNMA-guaranteed, mortgage-backed securities outstanding in 1980 on cash markets was $93.874 billion. Around 33 percent of the open interest in GNMA CDR futures is held by hedgers. This includes dealers in GNMA pass-throughs, mortgage bankers, savings and loan associations, and some pension funds and insurance companies. Figures 26-2 and 26-3 show GNMA price charts.

Contract Data

The basic trading unit is $100,000 principal balance of a GNMA 8 percent coupon or its equivalent. Prices are quoted as a percentage of par in thirty-seconds.

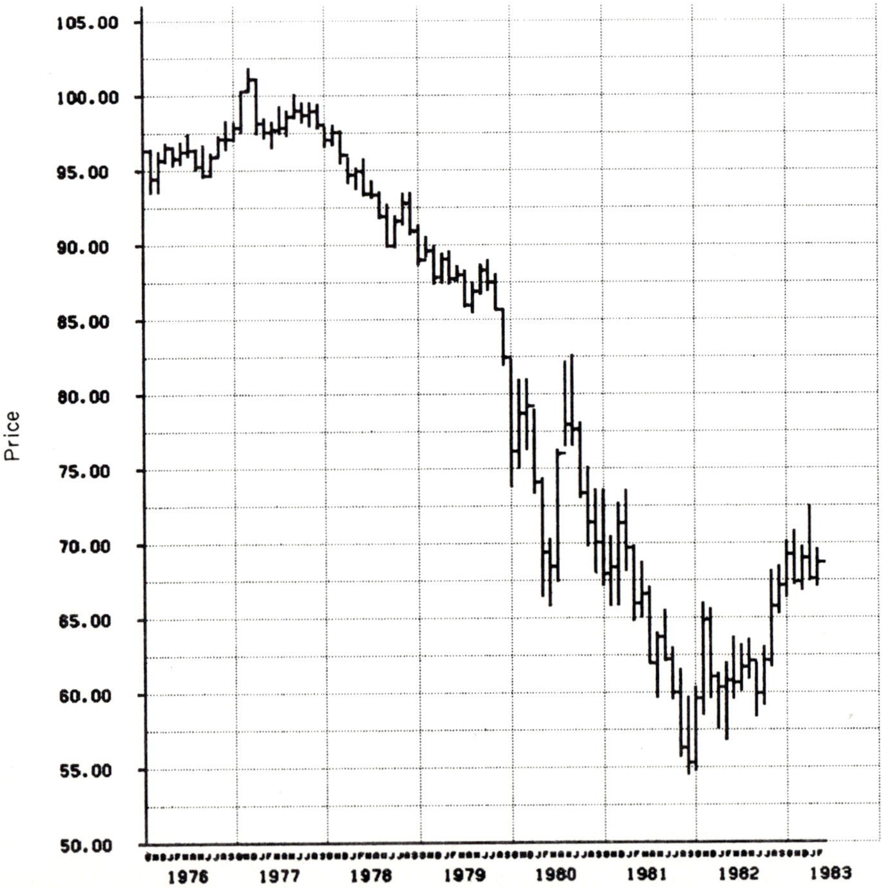

Figure 26-2 Monthly continuation, Chicago Board of Trade 8 percent GNMA. *(ContiCommodity Research Division)*

For example, a price of 64.06 is actually 64$\frac{6}{32}$ percent of $100,000. The minimum price fluctuation is $\frac{1}{32}$ point, which is equal to $31.25 per contract ($\frac{1}{32}$ percent × $100,000 = 0.0003125 × $100,000 = $31.25). A limit price move is $\frac{64}{32}$ above or below the previous day's settlement price, equal to $2000 per contract (64 × $31.25 = $2000). Trading hours are from 8 A.M. to 2 P.M., Chicago time.

Delivery

Delivery is made via a collateralized depository receipt which signifies that GNMA pass-throughs are being held in safekeeping at an authorized bank (Depository). The long receiving delivery can either hold the CDR and be paid $635 interest every month, or surrender the receipt to the Depository and receive the actual pass-throughs. At the time the CDR is returned to the Depository, between $97,500 and $102,500 principal balance of GNMA 8s, or the equivalent principal balance of another coupon, must be provided. Notice that there is a 2.5 percent tolerance limit of $100,000 of GNMA 8s. Discrepancies within the limit are settled with a cash sum based on 8s priced at par.

Listed in Table 26-3 are the principal balance factors for the various GNMA pass-through coupon rates. As the coupon rate rises, the principal amount that must be delivered declines.

Figure 26-3 Weekly continuation Chicago Board of Trade GNMA (new). *(ContiCommodity Research Division)*

TABLE 26-3 Official GNMA CDR Principal Factors

GNMA interest rate	Amount equivalent to $100,000 principal balance of GNMA 8s	GNMA interest rate	Amount equivalent to $100,000 principal balance of GNMA 8s
9¼	0.916031	12½	0.747664
9⅜	0.908403	12¾	0.736920
9½	0.900322	13	0.726744
9¾	0.885609	13¼	0.716846
10	0.871460	13½	0.707214
10⅛	0.863931	13¾	0.697350
10¼	0.857143	14	0.688231
10⅜	0.850461	14¼	0.679117
10½	0.843289	14½	0.670578
10⅝	0.836820	14¾	0.661888
10¾	0.830450	15	0.653595
10⅞	0.823723	15¼	0.645507
$10\frac{9}{10}$	0.822481	15½	0.637450
11	0.817439	15¾	0.629921
11⅛	0.811359	16	0.622084
11¼	0.804829	16¼	0.614753
11⅜	0.798935	16½	0.607441
11½	0.793021	16¾	0.600601
11⅝	0.786885	17	0.593472
11¾	0.781250	17¼	0.586941
11⅞	0.775194	17½	0.580131
12	0.769724	17¾	0.573888
12¼	0.758534	18	0.567376

The contract invoice amount at delivery is the settlement price multiplied by $100,000, plus accrued interest:

Total invoice amount = (settlement price × $100,000) + accrued interest

In other words, the sum paid at delivery is determined by the settlement price, whereas the amount of the principal balance delivered is adjusted according to the coupon rate on the pass-through backing the CDR. This differs from the delivery mechanism in the T-bond futures, where the face amount of the bonds delivered must always equal $100,000, but the invoice amount is adjusted according to the coupon and the maturity of the bond being delivered.

Suppose, for example, that on September 8 the short notifies the Clearing Corporation of intention to make delivery on September 10. The settlement price for invoicing purposes will be the closing price of the September option on September 8.

Assume that this price is 76.07 or $76\frac{7}{32}$ percent of par. The decimal equivalent of $76\frac{7}{32}$ percent is 0.7621875, and multiplying 0.7621875 by $100,000 gives the principle invoice amount:

0.7621875	Decimal equivalent of position day settlement price
×$100,000	Contract size
$76,218.75	Principal invoice amount

The registered holder of the CDR is paid $635 in interest on the second-to-last business day of each month. To calculate accrued interest, simply divide $635 by the number of days in the delivery month and multiply the result by the number of days from the first day of the month to the delivery day:

$21.166667	Daily interest ($635 divided by 30)
×10	Days to delivery
$211.66667	Total accrued interest

The total invoice amount is obtained by adding the principal invoice amount to the total accrued interest:

$76,218.75	Principal invoice amount
211.67	Total accrued interest
$76,430.42	Total invoice amount

The short making delivery can obtain a CDR from an originator, or can originate the CDR. To qualify as an originator certain Chicago Board of Trade requirements must be satisfied first, and time must be allowed for the CBT approval process. Before the CDR is delivered, it must be registered with the CBT Registrar and signed by the originator, the Depository, and the clearing member making delivery. Each time the CDR is transferred, both the Depository and the holder sign the back of the CDR: the Depository to certify the amount of GNMAs in safekeeping, and the holder to guarantee that the CDR is genuine.

CHAPTER

27

Foreign Currency Futures

James Leatherberry

INTRODUCTION

Many people consider foreign currencies an arcane "commodity." This is unfortunate, because currencies provide excellent speculative opportunities. Exchange rates react to virtually all significant world political and economic developments. Currencies are thus somewhat more volatile than many other commodities, because they are always responding to international events, but the increased risks are amply matched by increased profit opportunities.

Even traders who do not want to trade currencies per se should understand what makes them move, because currency movements can have profound effects on other commodities. Ask any soybean trader if changes in the Japanese yen have an impact on bean price; you'll certainly receive an affirmative answer.

Historical Background

Currency movements have not always been exciting. Before August 1971, currency values were essentially fixed. Exchange rates (an "exchange rate" is simply the price of one currency expressed in terms of another—that is, $2 in U.S. currency buys £1 in British currency) could fluctuate only 1 percent above and below the par values assigned by governments. In addition, the dollar was pegged to gold at a rate of $35 per ounce. The U.S. government was prepared to buy or sell gold at this price in unlimited quantities. Because other currencies were fixed to the dollar, they also had an indirect value in terms of gold. For example, if \$2 was equal to £1 and \$35 was equal to 1 ounce of gold, then £17½ would buy 1 ounce of gold (\$35 ÷ 2).

This scheme, often called the Bretton Woods system after the resort in New Hampshire where it was established in 1944, worked reasonably well throughout the post-World War II period, until 1971. The system began to break down because foreigners' faith in the dollar was shaken by U.S. economic policies that were producing inflation and balance-of-payments deficits. Foreigners no longer wanted to hold dollars because they felt the dollar was overvalued—not worth its current price in gold and other currencies. They began demanding gold for their dollars. In the summer of 1971, this process had reached a pace that if maintained would have depleted United States gold reserves in a relatively short time. To avoid this, President Nixon temporarily severed the dollar's link with other currencies and let the market determine new currency relationships. He also announced a suspension of gold sales and purchases. Exchange rates "floated" or moved in response to market forces until the end of 1971, when fixed rates were reimposed. By this time the dollar had declined in value as compared with most major currencies, particularly the German mark and the Japanese yen (a 12 percent decline in relation to each). The new fixed rates did not work well. By the spring of 1973 they were abandoned altogether, and we were left with the present system of floating exchange rates.

How the Market Works and Who Uses It

Foreign exchange markets are needed to facilitate international trade and investment. Let's take a simple example: Suppose you are a U.S. producer of machine tools and you want to sell your product in France. If you are paid in French francs, you can do little with the francs unless you have obligations in French currency. You cannot pay your U.S. employees in francs, nor can you use them for U.S. taxes or U.S. goods and services. You need to convert the francs to dollars. To do this you must utilize the foreign exchange market.

Most exchange activity takes place in the bank or cash market, which is not a market in the physical sense but rather a collection of market participants linked together by sophisticated communications equipment. Most participants are large banks, and they derive profits from exchange in two ways: First, they buy and sell currencies to their customers—mainly large corporations—and mark up their prices. For example, a bank might be willing to buy pounds at \$1.8550 (foreign exchange quotations are commonly carried out four places to the right of the decimal) and sell them at \$1.8560. The difference between the bid and offer prices is the bank's spread—not to be confused with spreads in the futures markets. This spread varies according to the level of uncertainty in the market, as well as the quality of the customer. A large oil company might be quoted a spread of \$1.8550–\$1.8560 for pounds, whereas a tourist might be quoted a spread of \$1.800–\$1.900.

Second, the more important source of bank profits is position taking. A bank will develop an attitude about where a particular currency rate is going and adjust its "book" or portfolio of currency positions accordingly.

There are three basic types of transactions in the bank market. First, in a spot transaction, currencies are bought or sold for immediate delivery. Second, in a forward transaction, currencies are bought or sold for a future date, ranging from 2 days to (in rare instances) 10 years. The most common transactions are 1-, 3-, 6-, and 12-month maturities. The prices paid for forward contracts are almost entirely a function of relative interest rates in the two countries involved. If a country has short-term interest rates below U.S. rates, that country's currency will sell for a premium in the forward market—in other words, it will be worth more in the future. If another country has interest rates above U.S. rates, that country's currency will sell at a discount—or be worth less in the future. An example is given below.

U.S. 12-month deposit rate	16⅛
French 12-month deposit rate	16¾
British 12-month deposit rate	14¾

The franc will be at a discount in the 12-month forward rate:

Spot francs	$0.1663
12-month forward	$0.1655

The pound will be at a premium in the 12-month maturity:

Spot pound	$1.8493
12-month forward	$1.8758

The third type of transaction in the bank market is a swap—a simultaneous spot and forward transaction. For example, a U.S. investor who wanted to make an investment in France for a year but not bear any exchange risk could buy francs in the spot market and purchase a 1-year French franc certificate of deposit (CD). At the same time, the investor would sell francs forward 1 year to guarantee the dollar amount of his investment. The simultaneous spot purchase of francs and forward sale is a common transaction in the bank market.

It is important to understand how prices are quoted in the bank market. By convention, most currencies are quoted in indirect or "European" terms. This means they are expressed in *foreign currency units* per U.S. dollar, for example, 2 Swiss francs per $1 U.S. A few currencies, most notably the British pound, are quoted in direct or "U.S." terms. This means they are expressed in *U.S. dollars* per unit of foreign currency, for example, $2 per £1. Only currencies with a value greater than $1 are expressed in these terms in the bank market. In the futures market (discussed below in greater detail), however, *all* currencies are quoted in direct terms. To convert from one price method to the other, you simply take the reciprocal of the quotation, for example, 40¢ = 1 German mark or 1 mark/40¢ = 2.5 marks/U.S. dollar.

An important characteristic of the exchange market is that it is a 24-hour market. Trading is almost always going on, although certain times are much more important than others. The most active period occurs when both U.S. and European markets are open, which is roughly 8 to 12 A.M., EST. Continuous trading means positions can move dramatically overnight and stops in the market will not always be effective. Although there is no one center for exchange trading, certain cities have greater relative importance. London and New York are by far the most important locales. Other important cities are Zurich, Frankfurt, Paris, Tokyo, Hong Kong, and Singapore.

The bank market is basically a wholesale market. The common unit of transactions is $1 million. Smaller transactions are handled but are generally discouraged.

Banks also prefer to deal with corporations rather than individuals. This preference caused some individuals to come up with an alternative mechanism for speculating in foreign currencies during the early days of floating rates. The International Monetary Market (IMM), a division of the Chicago Mercantile Exchange, was created in May 1972 to trade currency futures and is still the dominant currency futures market. Contracts are also traded in New York on the New York Futures Exchange (NYFE) and in Australia on the Sydney Futures Exchange. Currency futures have recently been introduced in the London futures market as well.

Currency futures contracts are closely analogous to bank market forward contracts, but there are several important differences. As mentioned earlier, futures prices are quoted in dollar or direct terms, whereas the bank forward market uses European or indirect terms. Amount and delivery date are standardized in futures contracts. A March Swiss franc contract is 125,000 francs and is to be delivered in mid-March. In the bank market, any date or amount may be dealt. Bank market positions do not have margin as such but are generally backed up by lines of credit. Futures positions do require margin and "mark-to-market" every day. In the bank market, gains or losses are not realized until the contract is closed out or matures.

Although the trading volume on the IMM has grown dramatically and 30,000 contracts per day (roughly $1.5 billion, face amount) is a common level of activity, the futures market is still dwarfed by the bank market. Precise volume estimates are difficult to obtain, but in the United States alone several hundred billion dollars of foreign exchange is probably traded every day. As a consequence, the bank market generally sets the trend for price movements and the IMM follows. In certain circumstances and currencies, however, the IMM can exert a significant influence on the bank market. This is particularly true on days which are holidays in one or more exchange centers and in the early afternoon (New York time) after the European market has closed.

Prices in the futures market and the cash market are kept closely in line by traders called arbitrageurs. Arbitrage is the simultaneous purchase and sale of the same or a similar item in two different markets. For example, if French francs sold for 17¢ in London and 19¢ in New York, an arbitrageur could simultaneously buy in London and sell in New York, earning a 2¢/franc profit. Similarly, traders buy and sell between the bank market and the IMM, keeping prices closely aligned.

Other participants in futures markets include "locals" or independent speculators on the floor of the exchange, as well as commission houses executing orders for the public.

FUNDAMENTAL FACTORS IN CURRENCY FORECASTING

The price of foreign currencies, like the price of any other commodity, is determined by the interplay of supply and demand. However, the factors that determine supply and demand of currencies are more changeable and less easily measurable than those of physical goods. Some knowledge of basic economics as well as financial markets is needed to understand the workings of currency markets.

Inflation

Inflation and inflationary expectations are very important in determining currency values. A change in the level of prices of a nation's goods and services affects the country's competitiveness. If we assumed that exchange rates were stable over time, the goods of countries with higher inflation rates would be priced out of world markets. For example, suppose that a good California wine costs $12 and a good French Bordeaux costs 72 francs, or (at a current exchange rate of 6 francs/$1) the equivalent of $12. If, after 1 year, inflation had been 5 percent in the United States but 15 percent in France, then (assuming constant exchange rates) the U.S. wine should cost $12.60 ($12.00 × 1.05) and the French wine should cost 82.8 francs (72 × 1.15) or $13.80 (82.8 ÷ 6). If this occurred, consumers in France, the United States, and other countries would probably buy more U.S. and less French wine. This would also mean there would be greater demand for dollars with which to purchase American wine and less demand for francs to purchase French wine.

An economic theory called purchasing-power parity attempts to predict currency values based upon differences in inflation rates of traded goods. According to this theory, all other things being equal (which they never are), currency rates should move an amount equal to the inflation differential. In the wine example above, this would mean that the franc should have declined by 10 percent (the difference between the two inflation rates of 15 and 5 percent) to a value of 6.6 francs/$1.

Purchasing-power parity is only useful in explaining currency movements over the long term (3 to 4 years) because in the short run very significant deviations from expected currency movements can occur. It is important to note that most market participants have at least a casual knowledge of purchasing-power parity theory and will at times react accordingly to the release of inflation indices.

By what measure should we gauge inflation? According to purchasing-power theory, we should look at the prices of traded goods or at an export price index. Unfortunately, this measure is not available for many countries or is slow in coming for those that do have one. A more commonly used indicator is the consumer price index (CPI), which is available for nearly all countries and is quickly disseminated. In some countries, however, notably France and the United Kingdom, a retail price index is released instead. The disadvantage of the CPI is that it contains many goods and services which are not traded, and thus it tends to distort comparisons between countries. Apartment rental costs and telephone calls, for example, are not traded across borders. Other commonly used inflation measures are wholesale prices (the producer price index in the United States) and the gross national product (GNP) deflator.

Balance of Payments

The balance of payments is a system of accounting which attempts to measure one nation's economic dealings against those of the rest of the world. The balance of payments is a flow concept—it measures transactions which use or acquire foreign exchange over an interval of time. It is analogous to the sources and uses of funds statements for a corporation.

The balance of payments has three major components, which are frequently mislabeled by the press. The first component is the trade account, which encompasses imports and exports of physical goods. The trade account is the most timely balance-of-payments statistic; most countries issue monthly figures with a 2- to 4-week lag.

The second component is the balance on invisibles, including investment income, tourism, royalties, freight, and insurance. All items may represent either inflows or outflows of funds. The net balance of the trade account and the invisibles produces the current account. Many countries have sharply differing performance on goods and services. The United States, for example, has a persistent trade deficit but a large invisibles surplus. Current-account figures, particularly for the United States, are slower than the trade account in being released.

The third major component of the balance of payments is capital movements, including items such as loans, deposits, purchases of stocks and bonds, and outright purchases of companies. The capital account is the most volatile and difficult to measure of the three major components. Netting the current account with the capital account yields a country's overall balance-of-payments position.

Exchange markets can react to the release of any of these statistics, although trade and current account information generally receives the most attention. The balance of payments is really an after-the-fact reflection of the supply of and demand for a nation's currency. Currencies tend to decline in reaction to news of balance-of-payments deficits and to strengthen in reaction to news of surpluses—but these tendencies do not always hold true.

Interest Rates

Over the past several years, the most crucial indicator affecting currency values has been interest-rate levels. In trading currencies, it is important to realize what interest rates are influential and to recognize that relative interest-rate movements are more important than the absolute level of rates.

Short-term interest rates are far more important for foreign exchange than long-term rates. The market most frequently looks at 3-month-maturity Eurocurrency rates as a benchmark. A Eurodollar or Euromark, for example, is a currency on deposit outside its country of issue. For example, a dollar deposit in London or Hong Kong is a Eurodollar (note that the prefix "Euro" is actually a misnomer, since the funds need not necessarily reside in Europe). Eurocurrency deposit rates are closely tied to domestic rates but tend to be somewhat higher because such funds are generally free from government regulation.

All the closely watched indicators of monetary policy—money supply figures, open market operations, and so forth—tend to have an effect on currency markets because of their impact on short-term interest rates. Another important item to monitor is interest-rate differentials. Investors look at relative interest-rate levels in deciding where to place their funds. If U.S. rates decline by 1 percent but Canadian rates also decline by 1 percent, there is likely to be little effect on the exchange rate. However, that one nation's interest rates are higher than another's does not mean its currency will be strong. Usually a significant margin (2 to 3 percent) is needed to induce capital flows and to affect exchange rates.

Political Developments

Political developments can have an important impact on currency values. Political events can be divided into two broad categories. The first is dramatic events such as assassinations and terrorist acts. Such events usually have a very brief and transitory effect on currency markets. The kidnapping of Prime Minister Aldo Moro in Italy, for example, had little impact on the lira.

What can have a more long-lasting effect on markets is an actual or prospective shift in a country's leadership. With respect to currency values, markets generally view conservative governments favorably and liberal ones negatively. Consequently, both Margaret Thatcher's election in the United Kingdom and Ronald Reagan's election in the United States had strong impacts on currency markets which lasted many months.

Economic Growth

News of national economic growth also affects foreign exchange values. Usually markets react favorably to news of rapid economic growth and favorably to indications of a slowdown in growth. This happens because many economies' balances of payments deteriorate when growth is high. Particularly in countries like the United States, the United Kingdom, and Italy, imports tend to rise as incomes rise. Faster growth is also usually associated with higher inflation, and as noted earlier, inflation is viewed unfavorably.

The market can, however, be perverse and interpret higher growth as favorable for a currency. This is because higher inflation is viewed as requiring higher interest rates to contain price pressures. This effect has been particularly noticeable in the United States in recent years.

TRADING CHARACTERISTICS OF THE MAJOR CURRENCIES

Deutsche Mark

Next to the dollar, the deutsche mark (DM) is the most important of all currencies. The dollar-DM exchange rate is pivotal in the world monetary system, for many other currencies take their cue from this relationship. The DM is widely traded around the world and has an extremely liquid market.

Announcements concerning interest rates, inflation, and balance of payments can have a large impact on the mark. Changes in monetary policy and interest rates are signaled by governmental adjustments in the discount and Lombard rates—rates at which commercial banks can borrow from central banks. Inflation rates (both consumer and wholesale) are issued on a timely basis by Germany. Trade and current account balances also are announced every month. Figure 27-1 shows a deutsche mark price chart from 1972 to 1982.

Domestic political developments such as key local elections, votes of no confidence in the prime minister, and changing party coalitions can all have an impact on the mark. Foreign political developments in eastern Europe and the Middle East have a big influence on the mark because of strong trade ties between Germany and those regions.

Swiss Franc

The Swiss franc is probably the most volatile currency traded on futures markets. It responds more to external world political and economic developments

Figure 27-1 Monthly continuation, International Monetary Market Deutsche marks. *(ContiCommodity Research Division)*

than to domestic events. Switzerland does not issue a great deal of economic data, and what is issued is not particularly timely. Markets do react to Swiss interest-rate changes. Effects of discount and Lombard rates are analogous to those in Germany. Figure 27-2 shows a Swiss franc price chart from 1972 to 1982.

Domestic political developments tend to be unimportant because of Switzerland's neutral foreign policy and because the Swiss central government has very little power. Most political power is decentralized and resides in the cantons or states.

Futures trading in Swiss francs tends to be a relatively higher proportion of total trading than in other currencies. At times the futures franc market will affect the bank market, a situation which is opposite to that which prevails in other currencies.

Canadian Dollar

The Canadian dollar is probably the least volatile of the major currencies on the futures market. It is traded primarily in North America in the bank market, with little European activity. As a consequence, overnight moves are less dramatic than in other currencies.

The single most crucial factor in forecasting the Canadian dollar is the interest-rate differential with the United States. If short-term Canadian rates are 2 to 3 percent higher than U.S. rates, the Canadian dollar will not generally be under pressure. The reason interest rates are so crucial is that the U.S. and Canadian capital markets are closely integrated and funds flow back and forth across the border quite easily. Figure 27-3 shows a Canadian dollar price chart from 1972 to 1982.

Timely data on inflation and balance-of-payments performance are available for Canada. These indicators, however, tend to have a much less profound effect on the dollar than do interest rates.

Political developments in Canada sometimes play a role in currency markets. In particular, the issues of separatism, labor disputes, and foreign investment rules may have impacts.

British Pound

Unlike most of the other major currencies, the pound is quoted in dollars per pound in the bank market—for example $1.70 per pound. The pound is influenced by a wide range of factors. Interest rates are a key influence, and the London money market rivals that of New York in depth and sophistication. Both money supply figures (M3; see Chapter 24) and Bank of England open market operations can influence currency movements. Inflation (retail prices in the United Kingdom) and balance-of-payments statistics are also important. In recent years, release of these indicators has been disrupted by various civil-servant work stoppages. Figure 27-4 shows a British pound price chart from 1972 to 1982.

Due to the role of the United Kingdom as an oil producer, Organization of Petroleum Exporting Countries (OPEC) and oil market developments can have

Figure 27-2 Monthly continuation, International Monetary Market Swiss francs. *(Conti-Commodity Research Division)*

Figure 27-3 Monthly continuation, International Monetary Market Canadian dollars. *(ContiCommodity Research Division)*

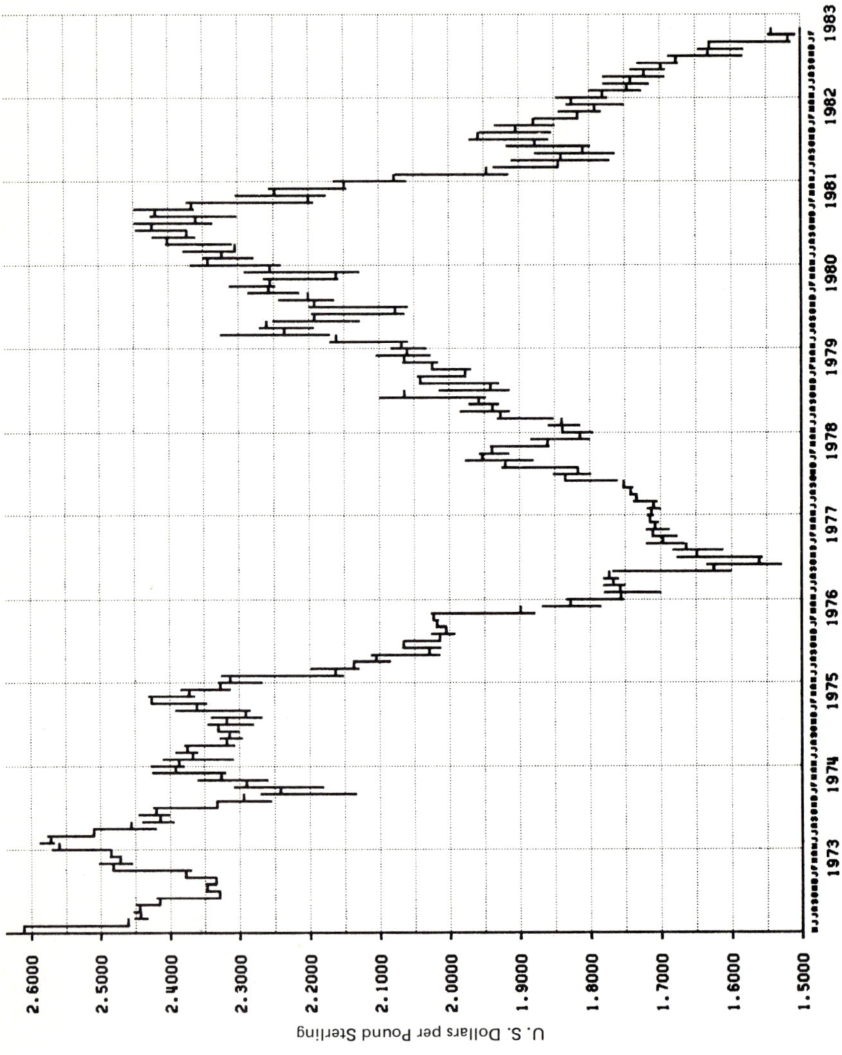

Figure 27-4 Monthly continuation, International Monetary Market British pounds. *(ContiCommodity Research Division)*

Figure 27-5 Monthly continuation, International Monetary Market Japanese yens. *(ContiCommodity Research Division)*

a profound impact on the British pound. Domestic political developments are also influential, and labor strife is a bigger factor in the United Kingdom than in most other countries.

The pound is very liquid and is just behind the mark in importance.

Japanese Yen

Several factors differentiate the yen from European currencies. First, because of time differences the Tokyo market does not overlap bank market trading in the United States. Since the yen market is much larger in Tokyo than in the United States or Europe, futures positions initiated in the United States frequently have their biggest moves in Tokyo overnight, rather than during the U.S. trading day. In addition, estimates of yen trading volume are available for Tokyo, whereas other foreign exchange trading centers do not provide them.

Japanese trade performance is very important for the yen. Statistics on this measure are abundant—perhaps too abundant. There are three ways of measuring trade; each is given in both yen and dollars and is also stated as both seasonally adjusted and not seasonally adjusted. The customs clearance figures in dollars are probably the most often used benchmark.

Inflation has somewhat less effect on the yen than on other currency, although it can be of interest on occasion. Interest rates are also less important in Japan than in other countries because they are tightly regulated by the government and because they change infrequently. One measure that can sometimes be useful in predicting the yen is the performance of the Tokyo stock market. Figure 27-5 shows a Japanese yen price chart from 1972 to 1982.

Japanese domestic politics rarely influence the yen because the same political party, the Liberal Democrats, have ruled throughout the entire postwar period. External developments do have an impact, however. News about oil market disruptions and trade protectionism have a big influence on the yen.

SOURCES OF INFORMATION

The most timely sources of information on currency markets are the Reuters and Telerate screens, but these are too expensive for most individual traders. The screens give current price quotations from major market participants, the latest news headlines, and economic statistics.

Several newspapers can be useful. The best for currency markets is probably *The Financial Times of London. The Wall Street Journal* and *The New York Times* are also useful.

Magazines which can provide background information are *The Economist, Euromoney*, and the international edition of *The Institutional Investor*.

Another source of information is the free publications on the various national economies distributed by many banks. The IMM division of the Chicago Mercantile Exchange also offers a number of free publications on currency futures.

CHAPTER

28

Gold

Robert Menzies

INTRODUCTION

Gold has been utilized in monetary, hedging, and fabrication roles for centuries. Despite occasional attempts by governments to devalue gold it retains in the early 1980s a key position as a financial asset. The major producers of gold are South Africa and the Soviet Union, but as a composite category the minor producers are also significant. The annual supply pattern has been varied because of such situations as the Soviet Union's need to finance grain purchases. Demand patterns have varied sharply according to price, political, and inflation hedge considerations, which naturally have shown differing trends in individual countries.

The key markets for physical gold are London, Zurich, Hong Kong, and New York; these four markets together cover a large portion of the world's daily time span. Other markets include Luxembourg, Paris, Frankfort, Singapore, São Paulo, and Tokyo, but these can in no sense be called significant international markets. Since the end of 1974, when it became legal for U.S. citizens to own gold, the futures market has spiraled in size and has become more important than physical trading as an overall price determinant and an investment or hedging mechanism. The key world futures markets are the International Monetary Market (IMM) in Chicago and the Commodity Exchange (COMEX) in New York.

Gold futures are also traded in Singapore, Hong Kong, Tokyo, Sydney, and Winnipeg. In Europe, futures trading on the U.S. system does not exist, but a considerable amount of undated gold is carried, creating an equivalent situation. Futures trading along U.S. lines commenced in London in April 1982, with a contract denominated by pounds sterling. Subsequently this has been replaced by a contract in U.S. dollars. Volume has so far only been moderate in this market.

USES OF GOLD

Gold purities vary but each market clearly stipulates acceptable levels and refinery marks. In New York, London, and Chicago, the acceptable purities are 0.995 fineness. The main uses of gold are for fabrication and hoarding. Gold is used in fabrication for official coins, jewelry, medallions, and nonmonetary coins, as well as in dentistry, and electronics, and other decorative and industrial applications. Hoarding is the purchase and retention of gold bullion in bar form as an investment vehicle.

Both of these major consuming sectors are price-sensitive. Traditionally, retail jewelry is particularly sensitive to gold prices, but because of the extremes seen recently in price, hoarders have also become much more price-sensitive.

New uses for gold have occasionally emerged in industry—electronics is an example—but even so, industry has not developed as a high-quantity gold consumer. Price has been a major constraint on the development of new uses of gold, along with developments in plastics and other materials.

MAJOR MARKET PARTICIPANTS

The major direct participants in the cash market for gold are banks, and even today a very restricted number of banks are involved in substantial worldwide trading. The major sales by producers of newly mined gold are largely made in the European market through the three gold-pool banks in Zurich (led by the Union Bank) and the bullion banks in London (of which Mocatta is probably the largest). As well as operating for the producers and on their own accounts, the bullion banks deal worldwide for a wide spectrum of purchasers—consumers, hoarders, and speculators. Customers include major jewelry groups, Middle East hoarders, Central Banks, and small-scale speculators. The element of delivery is much larger in the cash markets than in the futures markets, but the carrying angle is also significant and an artificial futures market has been created. As an estimate, at least 50 percent of transactions in the cash market result in delivery. Participation in the futures market is very varied and includes a large proportion of short-term speculators with local traders operating from the floors especially important. Bullion banks, important in the cash market, are key hedgers and speculators in the futures market, both on their own behalf and to varying degrees for clients. Commission house business also plays a vital role in creating liquidity in gold futures, supplying business to the floors from a variety of clients ranging from very large to extremely small. This category is mainly dominated by speculators. Delivery in the futures markets is normally limited to about 2 percent of total contracts, with no immediate change in prospect.

TECHNICAL INFORMATION

In recent years contract size in worldwide gold futures trading has become standardized on the 100-ounce unit, which is satisfactory for small, medium, and large purchasers. In the cash market in London and Zurich, however, the 400-ounce contract (historically the normal bar size) is still the key unit; 400 ounces is also still the normal refined size initially supplied by major producers. There are no signs that this situation will be quickly altered, but 100-ounce bars are now more readily available.

In futures trading on an organized basis under a clearinghouse system, U.S. markets dominate the world completely, and the only effective competition is the artificial futures market created in Europe. Within the United States, volume in Chicago is currently running at one-third the New York volume. Although arbitrage opportunities in gold exist between individual markets, particularly within the United States in futures and between U.S. futures and London cash, a more successful London futures market would clearly give new opportunites in this sphere.

FUNDAMENTALS

Gold Production

The world gold production picture has changed very little since 1970. (See Table 28-1.) South Africa has dominated, consistently mining more than all other countries together. The annual totals of South African production have been in a downtrend since the early 1970s, as mines have encountered lower-quality ore or have run out and closed. This underlying downtrend is expected to accelerate after 1985. Among minor producers, levels of mining higher than

TABLE 28-1 World Gold Production, 1977 to 1982 *(Tonnes)*

Area	1977	1978	1979	1980	1981	1982
South Africa	700	706	705	675	658	664
Ghana	17	14	12	11	12	12
Other Africa	21	17	16	22	27	31
Canada	54	54	51	51	53	63
United States	32	31	30	30	43	44
Brazil	16	22	25	35	35	35
Other Latin American countries	40	41	41	53	65	71
Philippines	19	20	19	22	25	26
Papua New Guinea	22	23	20	14	17	18
Australia	19	20	19	17	18	27
Other Asia and Oceania countries	10	9	8	8	8	9
Europe	13	13	10	9	9	11
Total (excluding the Soviet Union)	963	970	956	947	970	1011
South Africa percent	73	73	74	71	68	66

SOURCE: M. L. M. Da Boulay, *Gold*, Consolidated Goldfields PLC, London, 1983.

those of 1970 were only achieved in 1980 in Brazil, the Philippines, and Papua New Guinea. Longer term, the main change expected in the supply pattern relates to Brazil, where major discoveries were made in 1981 and 1982 that should boost yearly output to between 150 and 200 tonnes by 1985. Potential for higher production also exists in Papua New Guinea. Supplementing Western production is that of the Soviet Union, which is the second largest producer worldwide. No official figures are published for the Soviet Union, but reliable Western estimates put the annual production in the range of 200 to 250 tonnes.

Consumption of Gold

Fabrication is the hard-core feature in physical use of gold, including carat jewelry, electronics, dentistry, decorative uses, and other minor categories. Jewelry is by far the most important use, normally accounting for well over 50 percent of fabrication consumption. This important sector is very price-sensitive, moving in a close relationship to trends in important consuming countries. In other fabrication uses, there is less of a cyclical pattern demand. See Table 28-2 for information on demand for gold and Table 28-3 for information on supply.

Besides fabrication, the key elements of demand for gold are coin and bar hoarding. These two significant forms of investment purchasing are easily returnable to the markets. Coins have risen in significance since 1974, with the aggressive buildup in Kruggerand marketing by South Africa the key element. Essentially, an enlarged retail market for gold, in the form of coins at a price the small investor can afford, has evolved. This market has enabled South Africa to sell less gold in the form of bullion bars to the cash markets. The demand for bar investment is crucial in the market.

Purchasers of gold for hoarding vary considerably, from wealthy individuals

TABLE 28-2 Demand for Gold, 1970 to 1982 ***(Tonnes)***

Year	Jewelry and industrial use	Coins and medals	Bar investment including official purchases	Total
1970	1276	100	236	1612
1971	1282	106	000	1388
1972	1240	104	144	1488
1973	785	75	532	1392
1974	441	294	501	1236
1975	711	272	120	1103
1976	1152	232	50	1234
1977	1227	193	213	1633
1978	1269	288	185	1742
1979	1005	290	404	1699
1980	346	186	505	1037
1981	813	191	312	1316
1982	914	133	171	1218

SOURCE: Consolidated Goldfields PLC and ContiCommodity Research Division.

TABLE 28-3 Supply of Gold, 1970 to 1982 ***(Tonnes)***

Year	New production	Trade with Communist bloc	Net official sales	Net private dishoarding	Total
1970	1274	−3	0	341	1612
1971	1236	54	96	2	1388
1972	1177	213	0	98	1488
1973	1111	275	6	0	1392
1974	996	220	20	0	1236
1975	945	149	9	0	1103
1976	964	412	58	0	1434
1977	963	401	269	0	1633
1978	970	410	362	0	1742
1979	956	199	544	0	1699
1980	947	90	0	0	1037
1981	970	280	0	6	1316
1982	1011	207	0	0	1218

SOURCE: Consolidated Gold Fields PLC and ContiCommodity Research Division.

to central banks. Gold for hoarding, the key residual item in the market, is very sensitive to trends in world economics and politics. The development of futures markets on a world scale and the emergence of gold as much more of a financial commodity than it used to be have made seasonal patterns in gold prices much less obvious. The traditional buying periods of the cash market were in the early spring and in the autumn, and there was usually a quiet period in the summer; these patterns have largely been overwhelmed by market moves in response to financial or political developments.

Statistics on Gold

The statistics produced on gold futures turnover, open interest, and so forth are very good indeed, but few reliable statistics are produced on the cash market. In practice, a great deal of reliance has to be placed on trade estimates when compiling cash market statistics. By far the best source of gold statistics is the annual publication *Gold.** Data available monthly include reserves from the International Monetary Fund (IMF); revenues; Kruggerand sales and production from the Reserve Bank of South Africa; production from the United States; and imports and exports from Japan, Hong Kong, and the United States. Other data appear on a random basis. In general, gold is poorly covered statistically, in comparison with other markets. Crucial in this lack of information is the wish by both buyers and sellers to retain secrecy for many reasons. Recently both Switzerland and the United Kingdom stopped publishing detailed trade data at the request of certain selling and buying central banks, particularly from the Middle East and the Communist trading bloc countries.

*M. L. M. Da Boulay, *Gold,* Consolidated Goldfields PLC, London, 1983.

TACTICS IN GOLD TRADING

Tactics in gold trading vary greatly, depending on the point in the economic cycle. Precious metals tend to perform well in the acceleration phase of the economic cycle, as inflationary pressures mount and many major currencies experience weakness. Conversely, periods of deflation are likely to have a negative effect on prices. Figures 28-1 and 28-2 show price charts for gold in London and New York.

Traders should carefully watch the crucial relationship between precious-metal prices, movements in the U.S. dollar, and interest-rate developments in cash and futures markets. Particularly significant in this context is the relation-

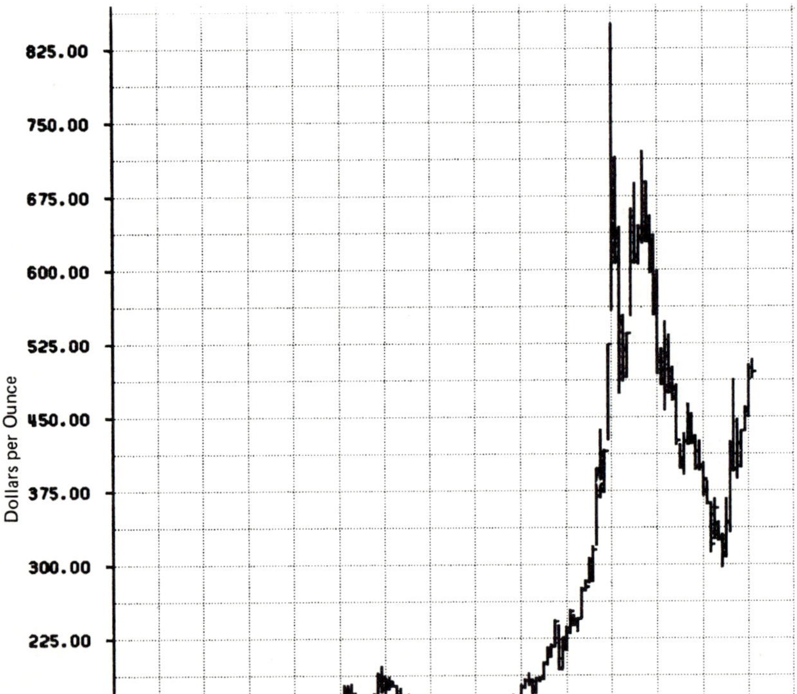

Figure 28-1 Monthly continuation, London gold bullion (London P.M. fix, in dollars per ounce), 1969 to 1983. *(ContiCommodity Research Division)*

ship between the dollar and the Swiss franc. For much of the time these key relationships hold up well, but at times (as in the first quarter of 1982) they may be overridden by other considerations—oil price trends, special supply distortions, and political factors. Political factors must be watched carefully, for often they can be traps (an example is fears about Poland in 1981 and 1982). Essentially, for a rising price a durable factor (increasing in seriousness over a worthwhile period of time) is needed. This type of factor will recur, and constant vigilance in watching for a switch of market attention from financial to political factors and vice versa will be rewarding.

Another area to watch carefully for effects upon the gold market is economic and political developments in the Soviet Union and South Africa. These give vital clues to marketing-policy tactics, which can have a strong impact on price

Figure 28-2 Monthly continuation, COMEX gold. *(ContiCommodity Research Division)*

levels. South Africa tends to arrange swaps in periods of balance-of-payments weakness and to withhold supplies in periods of strength. In the Soviet Union, the major factor that influences selling trends is import financing needs. Large purchases of agricultural products are particularly crucial and nearly always lead to a heavy gold sales campaign. It is important to spot heavy Soviet selling as soon as it starts, which is often difficult since the Soviet Union makes a major effort to keep its selling secret. South Africa is similarly secretive.

Finally, even the trader whose primary interest is the gold market should watch all precious-metals markets. Both on a given day and over lengthy periods, gold can be heavily influenced by the silver price in times of strength and weakness.

CHAPTER

29

Silver

Alan Davison

INTRODUCTION

Silver has been used in ornaments and utensils since records began. The ancient Romans adopted silver as the basis for their monetary system, and in the sixteenth and seventeenth centuries, the Spanish conquistadores found large supplies of silver in Mexico, Peru, and Bolivia. The United States became the predominant producer in the nineteenth century.

In recent years the supply of primary silver from mines has been insufficient to provide for worldwide industrial consumption. The result has been a drawdown of supplies from secondary sources, that is, scrap metal which has been remelted and refined.

PRODUCTION

Mining

All silver has to be refined electrolytically. Bullion markets and commodity exchanges require grades of 99.9 percent silver.

Primary Producers

Until recently the Eastern bloc countries have been exporters to the West although net trade has amounted to only around 10 million ounces per annum as compared with Western world consumption of about 400 million ounces. In

1982 the position turned around, with the Socialist countries becoming net importers. The major western primary mined silver producers in 1981 are shown in Table 29-1.

Only about 30 percent of the production by these countries is main-product silver, in which silver is the most valuable product and if the price of silver is too low, mining becomes economically unviable and production ceases. In the other 70 percent of world production, silver is a by-product and production of silver continues as long as the mine can make money from the main products, which are usually varying combinations of lead, zinc, and copper. Thus, silver production is relatively unresponsive to short-term changes in silver prices. New silver from Canada and Australia is mostly a by-product of large base-metal mines, whereas Mexican, American, and Peruvian production is usually a main product from smaller silver or combined silver and gold mines. Typical direct production costs in 1982 were about $1 to $3 per ounce for by-product silver and $5 to $10 for main-product silver.

Secondary Supplies

The most important constituent of secondary silver supply and also one of the most widely fluctuating, is old scrap. Normally scrap is largely made up of used photographic liquids, old electrical contacts, and spent catalysts, but in the silver boom of early 1980, this supply was supplemented by large amounts of melted-down sterling tableware and jewelry. It is estimated that production from old scrap in 1980 may have been double the level of the previous year, as price-sensitive supplies came to the market. In 1981, when prices fell sharply, silver recovered from old scrap is estimated to have dropped by as much as 50 percent, thus illustrating the volatile nature of this sector.

Indian Dishoarding

A large hoard of above-ground silver, which is usually placed in a separate category because of its size, exists in the Indian subcontinent. India mines no silver and imports none, but maintains exports of between 10 and 55 million ounces per annum, as well as consuming in recent years some 15 to 20 million ounces per annum. This would imply a rate of recovery of secondary silver of between 25 and 80 million ounces per year. Since February 1979, Indian

TABLE 29-1 Major Producers of Silver, 1981

Country	Millions of ounces	Percent of Western mine production
Mexico	53.2	18.0
Canada	37.4	12.7
United States	40.7	13.8
Peru	66.9	15.9
Australia	25.0	8.5
Total	223.2	68.9

SOURCE: U.S. Bureau of Mines.

exports of silver have been officially banned, but it has been impossible to prevent smuggling. In 1979 total exports were estimated at 22.5 million ounces, and even in 1980 probably some 15 to 20 million ounces were illegally exported. As prices fell in 1981 and 1982, exports dropped to 12.5 and 7 million ounces, respectively.

This large hoard of silver has been accumulated in India because of the underdeveloped economy. With no stable paper currency and an underdeveloped social security system, saving for old age or in case of famine due to crop failure has been necessary.

Melting of Coins

Another source of secondary silver is melted coins. There is large-scale trading in coins, and melting takes place in the United States as well as in Switzerland, Italy, the United Kingdom, and throughout the rest of western Europe.

This sector is also extremely volatile; during 1980, for instance, the quantity of melted coins doubled to around 70 million ounces from the 1979 figure of approximately 35 million ounces. These coins had been minted by various countries. Large numbers of U.S. silver coins and Austrian Maria Thresa thalers are still retained in private hoards, besides various Mexican, German, French, and Swiss coins. By 1982 the quantity of silver recovered from melted coins had fallen to approximately 7 million ounces.

Government and Eastern Bloc Sales

Official government silver stocks are not large compared with official gold stocks. The largest official stocks of silver are held by the U.S. government. The U.S. Treasury has stocks of around 39.4 million ounces, and the General Services Administration (GSA) in January 1982 had stocks of 139 million ounces. All the GSA stockpile has been declared surplus, and the GSA has made attempts to sell silver, but the moves have met substantial opposition by Congress and by other silver-producing countries.

The Mexican government has publicly stated a wish to hold silver in reserve as backing for Mexican currency in the same way that other countries hold gold. No other countries are expected to follow suit at present.

PRICE HISTORY

In recent years there have been three cyclical silver booms—in 1968, 1974, and 1979 to 1980—which suggests that there may be a 5- to 6-year long-run price cycle. A partial explanation for this phenomenon may be that during a boom there has always been a tremendous stimulus to production and a cutback in consumption, which has caused a surplus of silver and therefore an increase in private hoarding. When the price fell back there was a gradual rise in consumption and a reduction in production, especially from recycled material and above-ground supplies.

This has meant that the supply-demand surplus has gradually turned around, requiring a drawdown from private hoards and forcing prices to rise. The result has been an increase in speculator activity (this was especially true in the boom of 1979 to 1980) and a sharp increase in price. Figures 29-1 and 29-2 show price charts for silver in London and New York.

In quiet markets the silver price is often dependent upon the gold market, with the gold-silver price ratio usually fairly stable in the short term. In the long term, however, because the silver market is smaller than the gold market, silver is often more volatile than gold, with the result that substantial fluctuations in the gold-silver price ratio take place.

CONSUMPTION

End Uses

There are no published breakdowns by end use of silver, either worldwide or in the free world, and there are probably very few accurate private estimates. The United States Bureau of Mines does, however, publish figures on consumption of silver in the United States. The effect of large price rises in late 1979 and early 1980 on consumption can be seen from the figures for 1979 to 1982 shown in Table 29-2.

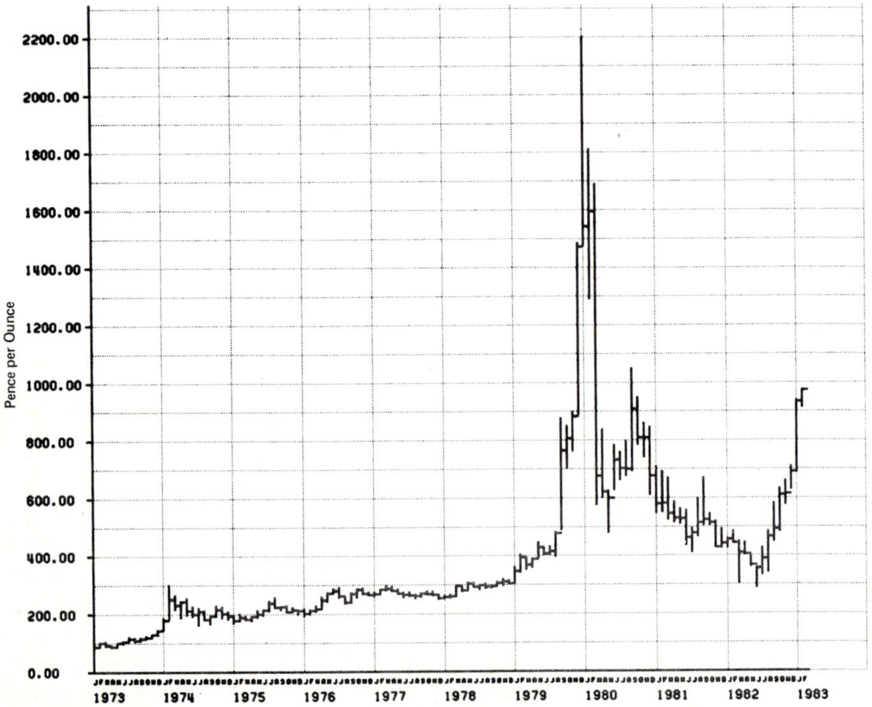

Figure 29-1 Monthly continuation, 3-month London silver. *(Conti-Commodity Research Division)*

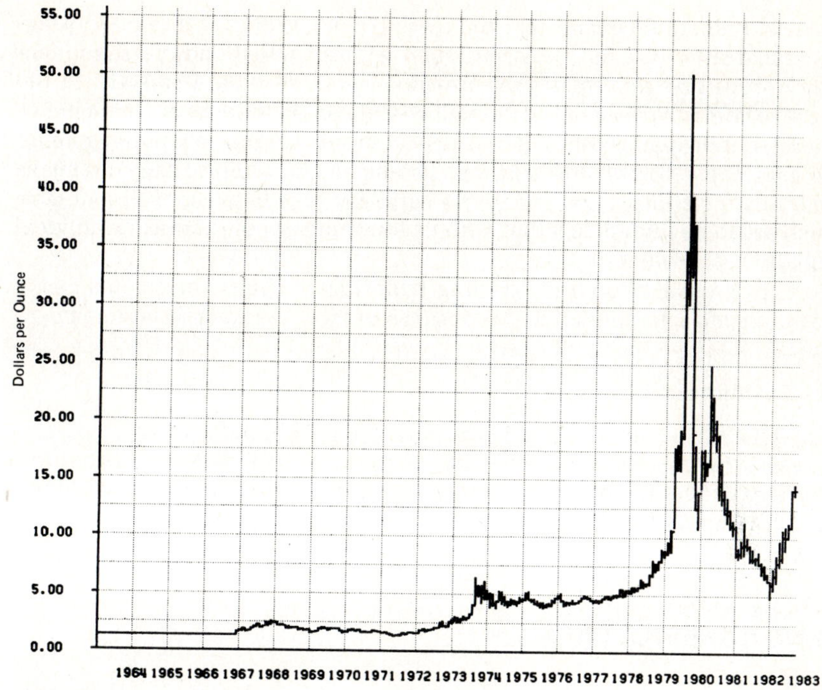

Figure 29-2 Monthly continuation, COMEX silver. *(ContiCommodity Research Division)*

TABLE 29-2 Silver Consumption, 1979 to 1982
(Millions of troy ounces)

Use	1979	1980	1981	1982
Photographic materials	66.0	49.8	53.0	51.8
Sterling tableware	13.1	9.1	4.4	6.6
Electroplated tableware	8.1	4.4	3.9	3.4
Jewelry	5.4	5.9	5.4	7.1
Dental and medical uses	2.3	2.2	1.7	1.7
Mirrors	1.9	0.7	0.6	1.0
Brazing alloys and solders	10.0	8.5	7.7	7.9
Electrical and electronic products				
Batteries	4.6	6.0	3.8	4.5
Contacts and conductors	33.5	27.8	26.4	28.9
Bearings	0.3	0.5	0.2	0.2
Catalysts	5.6	3.0	3.8	2.4
Coins, medallions, and commemoratives	4.7	4.7	2.6	1.5
Miscellaneous	1.0	5.5	5.0	4.6
Total*	157.3	124.7	116.8	121.7

*Columns may not sum to total because of rounding.
SOURCE: U.S. Bureau of Mines.

The main industrial consumer is the photographic sector, where no satisfactory chemical substitute has yet been found with an added "amplification factor" to improve or even equal that provided by silver halide crystals. In the electrical sector, silver has the highest electrical conductivity of any element or compound, but its use is restricted because of its cost and its low melting point, as well as because it tarnishes and thus its efficiency in low-voltage circuits is reduced. Silver's ability to penetrate the capillary gaps between different metals which are to be joined, together with its low melting point, makes it an ideal brazing alloy and solder.

Finally, it is used to produce sterling tableware, jewelry, and coins partly because of its attractiveness but also because of its value as an investment.

Major Consumers

As would be expected of a metal whose demand is based on industrial and leisure uses, the greatest silver consumption takes place in the industrialized Western world. The figures for 1979 to 1982 for the non-Communist world are shown in Tables 29-3 and 29-4.

SUMMARY AND TRADING CONSIDERATIONS

The silver market, like the gold market, tends to peak in the later stages of economic cycles. Silver, however, is really an industrial metal, so that a high level of commercial use is as important as speculator activity in providing depth and liquidity to the market.

Consistent failure by successive Western governments to eliminate price inflation and to stabilize paper currencies means that the role of silver as a store of value will also help to keep the silver market active and reasonably buoyant in the 1980s. That the silver market is so much smaller than the gold market means that prices should remain volatile and that it will continue to be an excellent vehicle for speculator activity.

TABLE 29-3 Silver Consumption by Area, 1979 to 1982
(Millions of troy ounces)

Area	1979	1980	1981	1982
United States	157.3	124.7	116.8	121.7
Europe	163.3	120.0	119.3	127.5
Japan	62.4	53.6	52.8	55.6
India	22.5	22.5	26.5	31.0
Canada	9.2	7.4	8.5	9.3
Mexico	6.2	5.0	3.4	4.5
Other Central and South American	17.0	13.0	12.5	14.5
Other	13.5	13.0	12.5	14.0
Total	451.4	359.2	352.3	378.1

SOURCES: Sumitomo Metals and Handy & Harmon.

TABLE 29-4 Silver: Balance of Supply and Demand for Silver in the Western World, 1975 to 1982
(Millions of troy ounces)

Year	Primary production	Secondary supplies	Net exports from Eastern bloc	Total silver supply
1975	241	188	3	432
1976	240	222	7	469
1977	259	165	5	429
1978	260	165	7	432
1979	265	183	5	453
1980	254	288	13	555
1981	279	165	8	452
1982	290	135	(10)	415

Year	Consumption: Industrial	Consumption: Coinage	Consumption: Total	Net increase or decrease in private and commercial hoards
1975	395	32	427	+5
1976	439	30	469	0
1977	424	27	451	−22
1978	436	39	475	−43
1979	451	27	478	−25
1980	363	15	378	+177
1981	352	10	362	+90
1982	378	12	390	+25

SOURCES: Metals and Minerals Research Services and ContiCommodity Research Division.

Certain industrial uses of silver are in danger from rival materials, and technological advances in electronics are especially likely to be detrimental to the silver market. But new markets, albeit small ones, are continually being sought by silver producers, and the expected growth in total Western industrial consumption should prevent the silver market from moving into continual oversupply in the 1980s.

SUBSTITUTION

Silver faces competition in various areas. In photography there is a possibility of an electronic counterpart to film based on silver halide crystals. In the home-movie sector, cinecameras will soon be totally replaced by electronic cameras that use celluloid tape similar to sound-recording tape and capable of being replayed on any domestic videotape recorder (VTR). Electronic counterparts to the still camera, which have recently come on the market, will store images on a disc, but silver-sensitive paper will still be needed to produce hard copies. No light-sensitive chemical substitute for silver in film has yet been found.

In the electronic sector, miniature silver batteries which have found widespread use in cameras, watches, and other equipment are encountering competition by cheaper, longer-lasting, and smaller batteries that do not utilize silver.

Silver electrical contacts in such uses as telephone exchanges are being replaced by solid-state circuits that do not use silver—and these solid-state circuits are themselves being replaced by microchips.

Use of silver in brazing alloys and solders has been diluted by the addition of alloying agents to the silver; however, the switch back from aluminum to copper in domestic heating and refrigeration systems has been beneficial to the brazing alloy sector.

CONTRACT DATA

Spot silver is traded primarily in London, New York, and Zurich. There are also futures markets in London (London Metal Exchange or LME), New York (Commodity Exchange, or COMEX), and Chicago (Chicago Board of Trade or CBT). Silver is traded in dollars in all markets except London, where it is traded solely in sterling on the LME and in both dollars and sterling in the London bullion market.

Contract sizes vary between markets. The specifications for each are:

Market	**Specifications**
COMEX	1000 and 5000 ounces
LME	2000 and 10,000 ounces
CBT	1000 and 5000 ounces
London spot	5000 ounces

All silver traded on commodity exchanges must be of a minimum 99.9 percent quality and must be in bars between 16 and 40 kilos in weight. Each bar must be marked with a serial number and the stamp of an acceptable refiner or assayer.

On COMEX, silver futures are traded for delivery during the current calendar month; the next two calendar months; and any January, March, May, September, and December for 23 months into the future. The market trading hours are 9:05 to 14:25, New York time. The daily limit move is presently 50¢/ounce. CBT hours of trading are 8:05 to 13:25, Chicago time.

LME silver is traded on any market days between prompt and 3 months (forward) delivery. Trading takes place from approximately 8:30 A.M. until the close of COMEX, with the bulk of business taking place in the four daily rings and two official curbs.

The London bullion market holds a fixing every market day at 12:15 P.M. in camera, for which all orders must be received by 12:00, London time.

SOURCES OF INFORMATION

Commodities Research Unit
31 Mount Pleasant
London WC1X OAD England

Monthly monitor and large-scale reports

Metals and Minerals Research Services
222 The Strand
London WC2R 1BA England

Quarterly data and large-scale reports

The Silver Institute
1001 Connecticut Avenue, N.W.
Suite 1138
Washington, DC 20036

Monthly newsletter and annual coinage and mine output figures

U.S. Bureau of Mines
2401 East Street, N.W.
Washington, DC 20241

U.S. monthly, quarterly, and annual data

CHAPTER

30

Platinum and Palladium

Alan Davison

INTRODUCTION

Platinum and palladium are the two major platinum-group metals (PGMs). Platinum is derived from the Spanish word *platina,* meaning "little silver." The earliest documented uses of platinum were by pre-Columbian Indians of Ecuador and Colombia who alloyed platinum with gold to form crude jewelry. In recent years, new industrial uses have been found for platinum, especially as a catalyst in the automotive, petrochemical, and chemical industries.

Palladium, less well known than platinum, is also used as a catalyst. Its major use is in the electrical industry, where it has impressive properties as an electrical contact.

Production of PGMs

The quantity of world output of platinum and palladium is very small as compared with other precious metals, but on a value basis the platinum market is almost half the size of the silver market. Table 30-1 compares world PGM production with production of other precious metals. Table 30-2 shows PGM reserves by country, and Table 30-3 breaks down PGM production by country.

Virtually all the South African production of PGMs comes from the Merensky Reef, discovered about 50 years ago. Two major firms, Impala and Rustenburg, mine platinum as a main product, although the deposits also contain commercially recoverable quantities of nickel.

Conversely, in the Soviet Union, platinum and palladium are mined as a by-

TABLE 30-1 World Production of Precious Metals, 1980

Metal	Annual mine output		Assumed value, dollars per ounce	Total, billions of dollars	Percent of world production
	Tonnes	Percent			
Gold	1200	10	400	15.4	78
Silver	10,600	88	8	2.7	14
Platinum	90	1	450	1.3	7
Palladium	80	1	75	0.2	1
Total	11,970	100		19.6	100

SOURCE: U.S. Bureau of Mines.

TABLE 30-2 Platinum-Group Metal Reserves by Country

	Percent		
	Platinum	Palladium	Total
Canada	1	1.1	1.1
Soviet Union	14	31.6	15.2
South Africa	83	66.5	73.3
Others	2	0.8	10.4
Total	100	100.0	100.0

SOURCE: U.S. Bureau of Mines.

TABLE 30-3 Production of Platinum-Group Metals by Country, 1978 to 1981

	Tonnes			
	1978	1979	1980	1981
South Africa	89	94	96	93.3
Soviet Union	95	99	101	104.2
Canada	11	6	13	12.4
Others	2	2	2	2.1
Total	197	201	212	212.0

SOURCE: U.S. Bureau of Mines.

TABLE 30-4 Estimated Breakdown of PGM Ores by Metal Percentage

	South Africa	Soviet Union	Canada	Colombia	United States
Platinum	61	30	43	93	19
Palladium	26	60	42	1	78
Other PGMs	13	10	15	6	3

SOURCE: U.S. Bureau of Mines.

product of nickel and copper mines in the Norilsk area, the country's main PGM-producing district.

In Canada, 80 percent of PGM output comes from the INCO nickel deposits, with other nickel producers accounting for the remainder. INCO material is refined in London, and the output of Falconbridge is sent to Norway for further processing.

Table 30-4 shows the considerable variation in the ratio of platinum to palladium throughout the world.

Although there is no official joint market agreement about PGMs (or gold) by South Africa and the Soviet Union, there has been considerable speculation in the press about whether the two countries do attempt at least partial coordination of sales policies.

Government Stockpiles

Tables 30-5 and 30-6 show the world balances of supply and demand for platinum and palladium. Only the United States holds significant quantities of PGMs, unlike gold and silver. PGM stocks are not held by the U.S. Treasury for monetary reasons but are held by the General Services Administration (GSA) for strategic purposes, in case supplies from either of the two major producing nations, South Africa and the Soviet Union, are suddenly halted. The geographical concentration of PGM reserves, coupled with the political instability of South Africa and the potentially hostile nature of the Soviet Union,

TABLE 30-5 World Balance of Supply of and Demand for Platinum, 1976 to 1982 (Tonnes)

	1976	1977	1978	1979	1980	1981	1982
Supply							
Free-world mine production	59.30	62.35	61.50	68.95	75.75	76.50	61.30
Secondary supplies	6.15	5.90	6.00	6.00	8.00	9.00	9.00
Net exports from Communist countries	20.50	17.50	7.00	10.50	10.50	10.00	11.00
Total	85.95	85.75	74.50	85.45	94.25	95.50	81.30
Demand							
U.S. and Japanese fabrication	62.50	58.80	73.90	72.70	61.55	62.80	56.70
Other fabrication	15.00	15.00	16.20	16.25	15.50	14.00	12.50
Total	77.50	73.80	90.10	88.95	77.05	76.80	69.20
Net increase (or decrease) in refined stocks	8.45	11.95	(15.60)	(3.5)	17.20	18.70	12.10

SOURCE: Metals and Minerals Research Services, Sumitomo Metals.

TABLE 30-6 World Balance of Supply of and Demand for Palladium, 1973 to 1982 ***(Thousands of ounces)***

	1973	1974	1975	1976	1977	1978	1979	1980	1981*	1982*
Total supply (including scrap)	2450	2800	2750	2807	2956	2765	2900	3000	2800	2900
Demand										
United States	1012	886	542	657	700	918	1133	910	890	925
Japan	915	643	490	663	566	804	929	883	1050	1145
Other	900	875	850	900	900	900	900	900	900	900
Total	2827	2404	1882	2220	2166	2622	2962	2693	2840	2970
Increase [or decrease†] in stocks	[377]	396	868	587	790	143	62	307	[400]	[70]

*ContiCommodity Research Division estimates.

†Figures in brackets are negative.

SOURCE: Sumitomo Metals.

means that a PGM stockpile is essential to the United States. As of September 1982, the status of U.S. stockpiling of PGMs is as follows:

	Tonnes	
	Platinum	Palladium
Present stockpile levels	14	39
Objective	41	93
Shortfall	27	54

SOURCE: U.S. Bureau of Mines.

Because of the shortage of funds at the disposal of the GSA, large-scale purchases of either platinum or palladium seem unlikely in the near future.

The Japanese government has stated its intention to stockpile palladium, but no figures or dates have been published.

CONSUMPTION

The major industrial use of platinum—and an extremely important use of palladium—is as a catalyst in the refining of petroleum and in the conversion of poisonous automobile exhaust fumes to harmless gases. Platinum or palladium converters oxidize carbon monoxide and hydrocarbon emissions to carbon dioxide and water vapour, whereas the alternative platinum or rhodium converters reduce nitrous oxides to nitrogen and oxygen.

Platinum also is used widely in jewelry. Its attractive appearance and rarity make it an eminently suitable substitute for gold, and its hardness has made it a popular medium with goldsmiths and silversmiths. In addition, an international marketing campaign, emphasizing that platinum often trades at a premium to gold, has been successful in promoting platinum as an alternative hedge against inflation and as a hoarding medium.

On the industrial front, the need to utilize crude oil fully has brought additional pressure to bear on refiners to improve their cracking techniques. This has led to greater use of PGM catalysts, even though total oil consumption has not been rising.

OUTLOOK

An important new market for platinum may arise. Platinum is being tested for use as a catalyst in fuel cells which would generate electricity directly by combining hydrogen and oxygen chemically. The hydrogen would be derived from natural gas, coal, or naptha and the oxygen would be provided by air. The power of these fuel cells would be supposedly up to 30 percent more efficient than other methods of using fuel and would also have the advantages of being quiet and pollution-free.

In agriculture, synthetic nitrogenous fertilizers are produced from nitric acid using rhodium-platinum-alloy wires.

There is also the possibility of further use of PGMs in pollution-control equipment areas other than automobiles. Certainly consumption of PGMs in this sector could rise substantially if further pollution legislation were approved by advanced industrialized economies.

PGMs are also used in health care to produce antibiotics and vitamins and are the basis of a drug used in the treatment of various cancers, although only microscopic amounts are consumed. The ability of PGMs to conduct electricity has led to use of palladium-alloy electrical contacts in telephone exchanges, and inks made from platinum and palladium provide a conducting track for printed circuits. However, technological advances are replacing electrical circuits with microprocessors, introducing multiplexing in telephones, leading to general miniaturization of components, and thus reducing consumption of palladium and platinum. At present, however, growth areas outnumber the potential for economies in platinum consumption. Demand for PGMs will no doubt remain highly price-elastic.

Tables 30-7 and 30-8 give breakdowns by end use for the two major platinum-consuming countries, the United States and Japan. Tables 30-9 and 30-10 give similar breakdowns for palladium.

As can be seen, the jewelry industry is far more important in Japan than in the United States. Demand is far more responsive to price in this sector than in other sectors.

Automotive demand for platinum can be expected to grow rapidly in both countries as antipollution legislation continues to be passed.

Palladium is far more dependent upon the electrical sector than platinum, and use of palladium in jewelry is far less important, in both Japan and the United States. Further strong growth in use of palladium in the automotive and petrochemical sectors is expected in the next decade in both countries.

Both platinum and palladium prices are influenced strongly by gold in the

TABLE 30-7 Pattern of Demand for Platinum in the United States, 1974 to 1982 *(Tonnes)*

Use	1974	1975	1976	1977	1978	1979	1980	1981	1982
Automotive	10.9	8.5	15.0	11.0	18.6	25.0	16.1	13.9	14.9
Chemical	6.7	4.6	2.6	2.6	4.6	3.0	3.7	2.4	2.0
Petroleum	4.3	3.4	1.8	2.3	3.3	5.3	4.5	2.7	0.7
Ceramics and glass	2.3	1.1	1.3	1.8	3.0	2.8	1.6	0.9	0.6
Electrical	3.1	2.3	2.8	2.5	3.3	3.6	4.7	3.5	2.8
Dental	0.8	0.5	0.8	0.6	1.4	0.8	0.8	0.6	0.7
Jewelry and arts	0.7	0.7	0.7	1.0	0.8	0.9	1.6	0.9	0.5
Other	0.5	0.6	1.4	1.9	2.0	2.4	1.8	2.2	2.1
Total	29.3	21.7	26.4	23.7	37.0	43.8	34.8	27.1	24.3

SOURCE: U.S. Bureau of Mines.

TABLE 30-8 Pattern of Demand for Platinum in Japan, 1974 to 1982 *(Tonnes)*

Use	1974	1975	1976	1977	1978	1979	1980	1981	1982
Jewelry	26.1	33.0	26.0	24.7	25.0	18.0	17.5	20.0	19.0
Automotive*								4.5	4.3
Chemical*	4.3	6.3	5.6	5.6	7.0	6.9	7.9	3.5	3.4
Electrical	2.1	1.8	1.4	1.2	1.2	1.0	1.1	4.0	3.5
Glass	2.2	1.3	1.1	1.0	1.4	1.2	1.2	1.5	1.2
Other	0.3	2.1	1.6	1.8	2.6	1.9	2.8	3.4	2.0
Total	35.0	44.5	35.7	34.3	37.2	29.0	30.5	36.9	33.4

*"Automotive" was included in "Chemical" before 1981. Petrochemical use is included in "Chemical" for all years.

SOURCE: Sumitomo Metals.

TABLE 30-9 Pattern of Demand for Palladium in the United States, 1974 to 1982 *(Tonnes)*

Use	1974	1975	1976	1977	1978	1979	1980	1981	1982
Automotive	4.6	3.0	6.0	3.9	6.2	6.9	5.5	4.0	3.7
Chemical	5.1	4.4	4.0	5.1	4.5	6.2	3.7	2.8	4.0
Petroleum Refining	0.5	*	0.2	0.2	0.6	0.7	0.7	0.6	0.6
Electrical	12.1	4.1	4.7	6.2	8.9	12.1	9.7	10.7	9.7
Dental	3.9	3.6	4.3	2.5	6.4	7.6	7.6	7.9	9.7
Jewelry	0.7	0.7	0.2	0.5	0.4	0.4	0.4	0.5	0.2
Other	0.7	1.0	0.9	1.4	1.5	1.2	0.7	1.0	0.8
Total	27.6	16.8	20.3	19.8	28.5	35.1	28.3	27.5	28.7

*Included in "Other."

SOURCE: U.S. Bureau of Mines.

TABLE 30-10 Pattern of Demand for Palladium in Japan, 1974 to 1982 ***(Tonnes)***

Use	1974	1975	1976	1977	1978	1979	1980	1981	1982
Electrical	8.5	4.5	6.2	5.5	5.5	6.5	5.5	12.0	13.0
Automotive*								2.5	2.8
Chemical*	5.9	5.2	6.9	6.3	10.5	13.5	12.5	9.0	10.0
Dental	3.5	3.5	5.5	3.7	6.5	8.0	7.0	5.0	6.0
Jewelry	1.5	1.8	1.5	1.5	1.5	2.0	1.5	2.0	1.9
Miscellaneous	0.7	0.3	0.6	0.6	1.0	2.0	1.1	2.2	1.9
Total	20.1	15.3	20.7	17.6	25.0	32.0	27.6	32.7	35.6

*"Automotive" was included in "Chemical" before 1981. "Chemical" includes electroplating.

SOURCE: Sumitomo Metals.

short term. The greater use of PGMs in industrial applications means that platinum and palladium do relatively worse than gold in times of low industrial activity and accordingly benefit more than gold in times of high activity. The industrial markets of both platinum and palladium look reasonably secure for the 1980s, with healthy growth prospects visible in most sectors, except for use of palladium as an electrical contact. The trend toward substitution of palladium for platinum in industrial uses is likely to continue in the future.

CONTRACT DATA

The major markets for platinum and palladium are in London, New York, and Zurich. London and Zurich have spot and forward markets for both metals. The London contract sizes are 50 ounces for platinum and 100 ounces for palladium. Market hours in London are approximately 9:30 to 17:30, London time, with two daily fixes in both metals at 10:20 and 16:15. The platinum and palladium fixes differ from gold fixes in that any price can be traded while the fixing price is being reduced.

In New York platinum and palladium are traded on the New York Merchantile Exchange. Platinum was introduced in 1965, and palladium trading started in 1968. Contract sizes are the same as in London, with a minimum purity of 99.5 percent for platinum and 99.8 percent for palladium.

Trading months are January, April, July, and October for platinum and March, June, September, and December for palladium. Maximum daily fluctuations in New York are $20 for platinum and $6 for palladium. (There are no limits to daily price movements in London and Zurich.)

New York markets tend to be more liquid than London, where a normal spread between bid and offer prices may be $2 or more in platinum and $1 in palladium.

SUMMARY AND TRADING CONSIDERATIONS

Gold is the main influence on platinum and palladium prices, although both metals are unlike gold in that they have a strong industrial base. The relatively small size of the platinum and palladium free markets often means that price fluctuations are greater than gold price fluctuations. Generally speaking, PGMs fare better than gold during periods of higher economic activity and conversely fall further than gold in depressed economic conditions. Figures 30-1 and 30-2 show price charts for platinum and palladium.

Even though platinum is extremely popular in Japan for jewelry and as a hoarding medium, its major use is as a catalytic converter in automobile exhaust systems. Palladium's major use is as a conductor in the electrical and electronic sector. Industrial demand for both metals seems likely to grow in the future. The only sector which could be in jeopardy from technological advances is the use of palladium as an electrical contact.

On the production side, mine output of both metals is heavily concentrated in the Soviet Union and South Africa. These two countries account for around 93 to 95 percent of world mine production. For this reason, the U.S. government holds a strategic stockpile of both metals.

Figure 30-1 Monthly continuation, New York Mercantile Exchange platinum. *(ContiCommodity Research Division)*

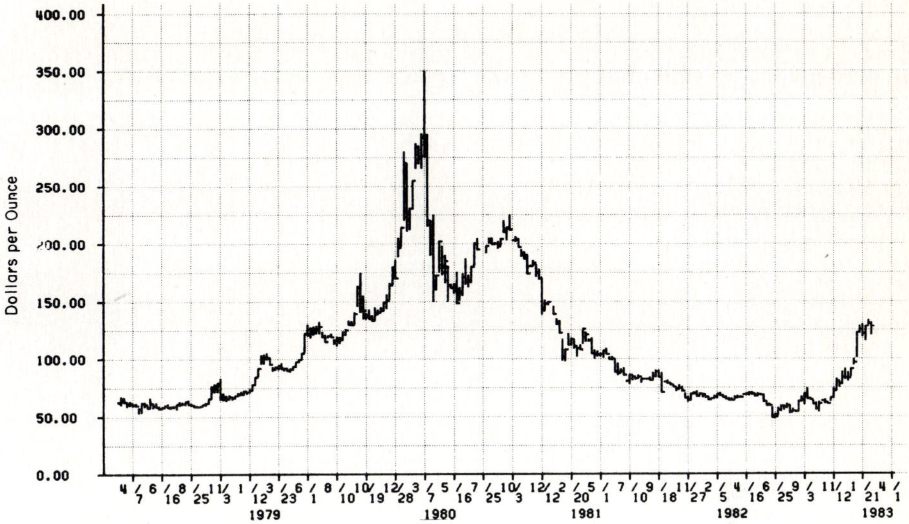

Figure 30-2 Monthly continuation, New York Mercantile Exchange palladium. *(ContiCommodity Research Division)*

Free-market platinum and palladium are traded in Zurich, London and New York, usually in lots of 50 ounces of platinum and 100 ounces of palladium.

SOURCES OF INFORMATION

Published information on platinum and palladium is difficult to find. However, the U.S. Bureau of Mines does produce monthly reports and occasional longer-term studies. J. Aron publishes an extremely comprehensive annual review of the market, and Sumitomo Metals publishes data on Japanese consumption and information on world markets in general.

PART

5

Industrial Commodities

CHAPTER

31

Copper

Marc Rivalland

HISTORICAL BACKGROUND

Copper and tin are generally considered the oldest known metals. The alloy of copper and tin gave its name to an entire age of civilization—the bronze age. Brass, the alloy of copper and zinc, has been used for about 2000 years. The first recorded discovery of copper was in what is now Anatolia. Early mining operations were developed in Cyprus, and it is not clear whether copper gave its name to the island of Cyprus or vice versa.

PRODUCTION

Major Types

Copper is generally classified according to the method by which it is refined:

Electrolytic copper is refined by electrolysis.

Fire-refined copper (or *lake* copper) is refined from smelted copper by using only a pyrometallurgical process.

Electrowon copper is directly deposited as a cathode from copper-bearing solutions.

The Technological Process

Most of the ores currently processed are sulphides. Once ore has been mined, it is subject to milling—crushing, fine grinding, and concentration by chemical flotation (or leaching, in the case of oxide ores). Typically, the ore might contain 0.5 to 15 percent pure copper and the concentrate 25 to 60 percent pure copper.

The copper concentrate is then smelted in a furnace. The impurities float to the top and combine as slag, while the copper, the iron, and most of the sulphur collect and form a product known as matte. The molten matte is transferred to a converter, where the airflow burns off the sulphur, oxidizes the iron, and yields a 99 percent pure "blister" copper. Most of the blister copper, after partial refining, is cast into copper anodes for electrolytic refining.

Thereafter the copper is often melted and cast into various shapes for consumer use. Recently there has been increased direct consumption of cathodes, bypassing the refinery casting step.

Major Producers

The major free-world copper *ore* producers are:

United States	23.0%
Chile	17.8%
Canada	11.8%
Zambia	9.9%
Zaire	7.7%
Peru	6.3%

Free-world mine production in 1982 totaled 6.2 million tonnes. Communist bloc production is estimated at 1.9 million tonnes, to which the Soviet Union (1.1 million tonnes) and Poland (0.35 million tonnes) are the major contributors.

The major free-world *refined* copper producers are:

United States	25.8%
Japan	14.3%
Chile	11.4%
Zambia	8.5%
Canada	7.1%
Belgium	5.3%
Germany	5.3%

The Communist bloc refines approximately 2.0 million tonnes. The Soviet Union and Poland are the major refiners.

It is important to note that, whereas the above figures seem to indicate that the United States dominates the world copper market, actually the United States consumes most of its copper domestically and is thus not a major factor in the world copper market. Instead, a select band of countries dominate world copper trade and have formed a cartel known as CIPEC (Intergovernmental Council of Copper Exporting Countries). CIPEC was established in 1967 by Chile, Peru, Zambia, and Zaire. Other small producers have since joined. CIPEC claims to control nearly three-quarters of the export trade of mine and smelter production. However, the only real attempt by CIPEC to influence the world copper market took place in late 1974, when it announced a plan to reduce export shipments by 15 percent in an attempt to bolster falling prices. The plan expired in June 1976 and cannot be regarded as a success.

Secondary production consists of new scrap and old scrap. New scrap consists of industrial discards such as shavings and end cuts, and old scrap is material that has already served its intended purpose and is now obsolete. The ratio of secondary copper production to primary production is declining, probably because of the decreased rate of investment in capital goods.

Smelters (refiners who specialize in recycling) normally purchase scrap on the basis of a discount to the futures price. Watching this discount, which normally ranges between 18 and 25 percent, can be most instructive; a wide discount suggests that the secondary producer has sufficient feed and material and is not a keen buyer. Either the producer believes prices will fall, or the capacity is fully utilized because demand is higher. The converse applies to a narrowing discount.

In 1982 the following figures* constituted the percentage of secondary productions to total consumption:

Western Europe	16.7
Japan	9.6
United States	26.9

CONSUMPTION

End Uses of Copper

The U.S. demand pattern for copper is as follows:

Electrical	54%
Construction	19%
Nonelectrical machinery	11%
Transport	11%

With minor variations, this pattern is typical of most industrialized countries.

In electrical equipment, copper is used in the manufacture of electrical motors, power generators, fans and blowers, electrical instruments, switch gear, and lighting equipment. It is also used in sophisticated electronic navigation and communication systems. Although aluminum is now used in virtually all high-voltage overhead power-transmission lines, copper is still widely used in underground lines. In addition, it dominates the smaller-gauge wire market.

Because of the corrosion resistance of copper, it has many uses in the construction industry, principally in roofing and plumbing.

Copper is also widely used in the transportation industry—for example, in diesel locomotives, passenger trains, signal devices, radiators, heaters, and carburetors and bearings in automobiles. It is used, as an alloy with nickel, in many marine applications. In fact, the end uses of copper are so manifold that copper consumption is often regarded as a good barometer of the industrial health of an economy.

*Morris Ronek, "World Copper Analysis and Outlook," *CRU Metal Monitor*.

Major Consumers

The major consumers of copper are the large industrial countries of the world:

United States	26.1%
Japan	18.2%
European Economic Community	36.0%

The Communist bloc consumes nearly all its production of copper, so that the impact at the margin of Communist production and consumption is negligible. As a whole, the Communist countries are net exporters of roughly 50,000 tonnes of refined copper per annum (less that 0.7 percent of the free-world supply).

Shifts in Usage

By far the most important future shift in copper usage will be in the telecommunications industry. This is true for two reasons:

First, copper is being more efficiently used in telephone cables. There has been roughly a 40 percent reduction in the weight of copper used in telephone cables over the last 20 years, and the gauge is getting thinner all the time. The introduction of pulse code modulation (pcm) to improve the transmission of sound waves has also stunted a potential increase in copper consumption. One U.S. copper producer has estimated that the equivalent of 45,000 tonnes per year of copper wire is being "lost" by additions to pcm circuits in the United States.

Second, *fiberoptics* are the real cause for concern. Glass fibers as conductors have many advantages over copper. They are immune to electromagnetic interference, and they are far more compact. Transmission losses are also less with fiberoptics. They also have the advantage of compactness. The frequency of light is thousands of times higher than that of radio waves, which have been conventionally used in telecommunications. The fiberoptic cable, relying on light pulses instead of electrical pulses, is thus much smaller than a copper cable of equivalent capacity. However, the extensive use of fiberoptics as a replacement for copper is expected to become a threat only in the 1990s. To illustrate this point, the following table shows the prospective loss of copper cable consumption by the U.S. telecommunications industry in 1985. It is the central forecast of the Copper Development Association (CDA).

Wire gauge change	44,000 tonnes
Multiplexing	19,500 tonnes
Fiberoptics	1,400 tonnes

However, the main overall substitute for copper is, and will continue to be, *aluminum*. The CDA has forecast no increased penetration by aluminum into the telecommunications industry. It is really only in the automobile industry, and to a small extent in the construction industry, that aluminum is likely to make relative gains against copper, and these gains will probably be made primarily because of the weight and price advantages of aluminum.

In conclusion, no major reductions in usage and no major substitutions are expected to have a serious effect on copper consumption in the 1980s. On the other hand, no significant new uses for copper are anticipated. Thus copper consumption should, on average, continue to grow at a normal rate.

COPPER STOCKS

The balance of supply of and demand for copper in the Western world is shown in Table 31-1.

The Inventory Cycle

The correlation between industrial production and actual raw material consumption can be distorted by consumer destocking and restocking. Where consumers destock, reported consumption will be less than actual consumption. In contrast, restocking may cause a rise in reported consumption, even though there has been no actual increase in consumption. Thus an important indicator to watch is not only industrial production but also consumer stocks in the United States. Data on consumer stocks are released monthly by the American Bureau of Metal Statistics (ABMS) in the form of refined copper stocks at wire mills and brass mills.

Seasonal Tendencies

There are recurring seasonal tendencies in the copper market. Consumption tends to be strong in the first 2 months of the calendar year, as consumers and merchants buy forward to meet their needs until the summer shutdown. In July and August, production and consumption tend to fall sharply because plants are closed for vacations. Then, in September and early October, there is often a surge in consumption as activity picks up. Thus copper prices have a tendency to strengthen in the first quarter and fall in the second quarter of the year.

MARKET SUMMARY

The two principal futures markets for copper are the Commodity Exchange of New York (COMEX) and the London Metal Exchange (LME).

Comex

COMEX, founded in 1933, is the world's largest metals futures exchange (taking precious metals into account). A COMEX copper futures contract calls for the delivery of one of several listed grades of copper during each of the specified future months. Trading is continuous between the hours of 9:50 A.M. and 2:00 P.M., New York time. The contract size is 25,000 pounds (2 percent more or less) of electrolytic, lake, or certain other types of fire-refined copper. The basis grade is electrolytic copper *cathodes*. Lake copper is deliverable at a premium which varies according to the refinery shape, and fire-refined copper is deliverable at a small discount.

TABLE 31-1 Western World Copper Supply and Demand Balance *(Tonnes)*

	Mine production	Primary refined production	Secondary refined production	Total refined production	Refined consumption	Net refined input, eastern block	Implied increase in metal inventory	Published stock levels
1977	6275	5920	939	6850	6875	20	−5	1960
1978	6100	5890	1010	6900	7275	10	−365	1535
1979	6135	5860	1155	7015	7520	40	−465	1090
1980	6060	5860	1200	7040	7110	60	−10	1030
1981	6515	6255	1105	7360	7235	55	+180	1090
1982	6240	6010	1120	7130	6760	40	+410	1500

SOURCE: World Bureau of Metal Statistics.

Delivery is made at one of the specified warehouses at the seller's option during any business day of the month specified in the contract. Trading is conducted for delivery during the current calendar month; the next 2 calendar months; and any January, March, May, July, September, and December falling within a 23-month period beginning with the current month.

Price changes are registered in multiples of $\frac{5}{100}$¢/pound, which is equivalent to $12.50/contract. During any one market day, price fluctuations are limited to 5¢/pound above or below the settlement price of the previous day. This is equivalent to $1250/contract. Limits do not apply to prices for the current delivery month.

LME

The LME was formally established in 1876. Initial trading took place principally in copper and tin. Formalized contracts for trading in these metals had been established in 1883, when the basis grade was Chile wirebars assaying not less than 96 percent copper.

The former copper wirebar contract ceased trading on a 3-month basis beginning September 1, 1981. A new contract for higher-grade copper started trading on that date. The change was not dramatic, since wirebars that were deliverable under the old contract are still deliverable under the new contract. The only real change is that higher-grade *cathodes* are also now deliverable. The LME committee has already approved over thirty cathode brands, which will constitute good delivery. The illiquid LME copper cathode contract is continuing in its present form but has been renamed "copper-standard cathodes." Under the new contract, it is the seller's option whether to deliver cathodes or wirebars.

Delivery takes place on the prompt date at one of the specified warehouses at the seller's option. The contract size is 25 tonnes (55,115 pounds).

The LME does not have a clearinghouse mechanism. The metals quoted on the market are traded for a prompt date some time in the future. Prices are generally quoted for a cash and 3-month basis. The 3-month date is simply the nearest trading day to the date 3 months after the current trading day. It is the most liquid (actively traded) position, and new transactions are normally entered on a 3-month basis. However, trading for any specific prompt date within 3 months, if desired, is possible. To liquidate a position, it is necessary to liquidate for the specific prompt date already dealt in. For example, suppose that on August 1 a trader buys 1 contract of 3-month copper; the prompt date will be November 1.

CONTRACT DATA

Trading does not take place continously on the LME. Each morning between 8:30 and 11:45 there is a "premarket," over-the-counter market. At 11:50 a series of 5-minute "rings" starts; during each ring, one metal is exclusively traded. Each metal has two morning rings. After the morning rings end at 1:10 P.M., there is a 20-minute kerb during which all the metals are freely traded. The market then closes until 3:30 P.M., after which time the whole cycle of rings and a final kerb is complete. The official closing time is 5 P.M. and the COMEX close is at 7:00 P.M. This market is very illiquid. The times of the various rings are shown below.

Morning Market

	First morning ring
Silver	11:50–11:55
Aluminum	11:55–12:00
Copper	12:00–12:05
Tin	12:05–12:10
Lead	12:10–12:15
Zinc	12:15–12:20
Nickel	12:20–12:25

Interval

	12:25–12:30 Second morning ring
Copper high-grade cathode	12:30–12:35
Copper cathodes and fire-refined	12:35–12:40
Tin	12:40–12:45
Lead	12:45–12:50
Zinc	12:50–12:55
Aluminum	12:55–13:00
Nickel	13:00–13:05
Silver	13:05–13:10

Afternoon Market

	First Afternoon Ring
Lead	3:20–3:25
Zinc	3:25–3:30
Copper	3:30–3:35
Tin	3:35–3:40
Aluminum	3:40–3:45
Nickel	3:45–3:50
Silver	3:50–3:55

Interval

	3:55–4:00 Second Afternoon Ring
Lead	4:00–4:05
Zinc	4:05–4:10
Copper high-grade cathodes	4:10–4:15
Copper cathodes and fire-refined	4:15–4:20
Tin	4:20–4:25
Aluminum	4:25–4:30
Nickel	4:30–4:35
Silver	4:35–4:40

SUMMARY AND TRADING CONSIDERATIONS

As copper is mainly an industrial material, demand for the metal is largely determined by the level of industrial production throughout the world. The price of copper, however, depends upon the balance of supply and demand and the level of inventories. Although these factors are influenced by the level of demand, they are also dependent upon the supplies of new material from mines and recycled metal from secondary smelters. The balance between supply and demand can be altered suddenly by production from new mines, the closing of old mines, accidents that temporarily reduce output from existing mines, and strikes that cause producers to suspend production and declare *force majeure*. Figures 31-1 and 31-2 show price charts for copper in London and New York.

The effect on prices of any of these possible events depends on whether the market is expecting the event. Companies publicize the start-up dates of new mines months ahead, but strike announcements or accidents such as explosions can be unexpected and often do provide a considerable spur in a thin market.

Demand forecasts are usually compiled from estimates of leading indicators relating to major world economics. For instance, a rise in U.S. housing starts would signify an increase in demand for copper pipes. A rise in real personal income would suggest that consumers would have more money to spend on

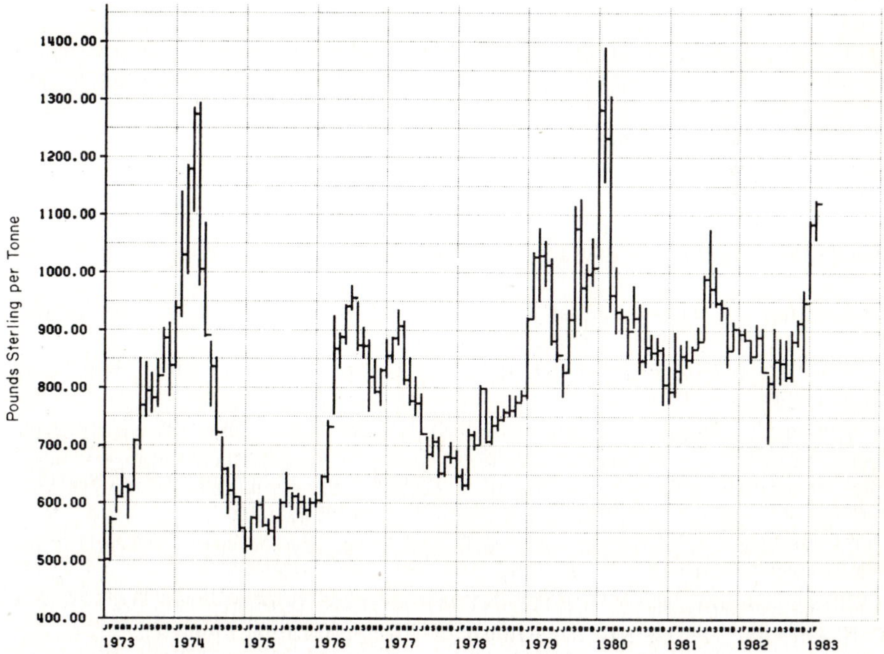

Figure 31-1 Monthly continuation, three-month London copper wirebar. *(ContiCommodity Research Division)*

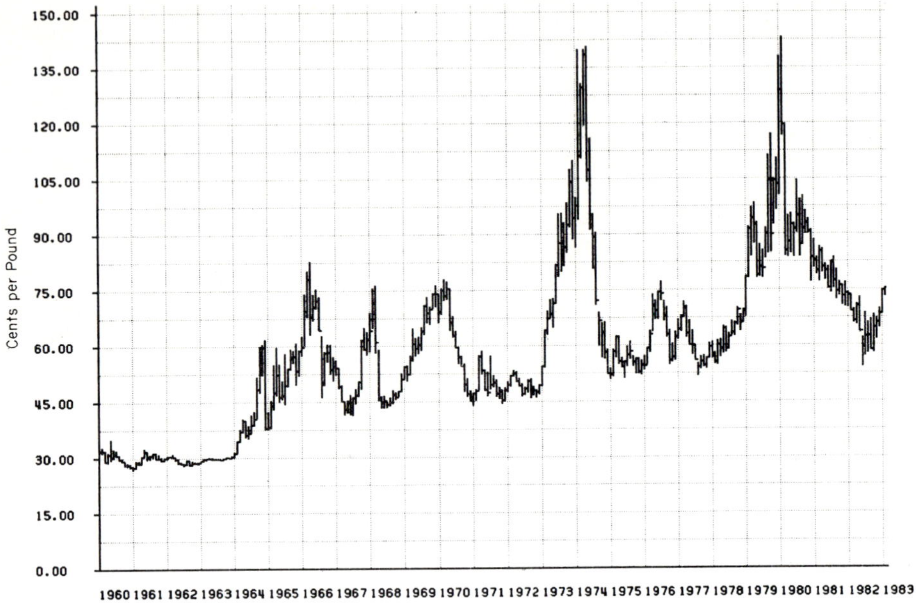

Figure 31-2 Monthly continuation, COMEX copper. *(ContiCommodity Research Division)*

cars, refrigerators, and other consumer durables containing copper. Conversely, a rise in interest rates or restrictions on credit or money supply would imply a fall in demand for copper and would encourage holders of copper stocks to reduce their inventories by either selling material back to the market or refraining from buying more material.

SOURCES OF INFORMATION

Information on developments in copper usage is available from the Copper Development Association in London. Data on the availability of scrap material in the United States is published by the National Association of Recycling Industries (NARI).

Information on mine supplies—including news and rumors of mine closures, both temporary and permanent—is available from mining company annual reports, and the various mining and trading journals, such as *Mining Journal, Mining Annual Review, Metals Week,* and *Metal Bulletin.*

Statistics on copper supply, demand, and inventory levels in the world market are published by the World Bureau of Metal Statistics in London. Japanese statistics are collected by MITI. U.S. statistics are published monthly by the U.S. Bureau of Mines and the American Bureau of Metal Statistics.

Short-term copper prices tend to fluctuate in sympathy with gold and silver, especially on the COMEX. In London, copper is also affected by other metal prices and by the dollar-sterling exchange rate; rallies in the base metals also encourage speculative buying of copper. Copper producers and traders use rallies of this sort to unload surplus metal, with the result that, even if other metals continue to rise in value, copper can fall back if the demand-supply situation does not improve. A sustained rise in copper prices occurs only when the demand for copper improves relative to the supply.

CHAPTER

32

Aluminum

Alan Davison

INTRODUCTION

Aluminum is the most abundant structural metal element in the earth's crust. Such has been the growth of demand that, measured either in quantity or in value, the use of aluminum now exceeds that of any other metal except iron. The metal only became available in real commercial quantities just over 90 years ago when electrolytic smelting processes became commercially viable.

PRODUCTION

Technological Process

Bauxite is the main ore of aluminum. Briefly, the production process consists of the surface mining of bauxite, followed by hydrometallurgical processing to produce alumina.

Alumina is aluminum oxide (AL_2O_3). The alumina is then reduced to metal by fused-salt electrolysis in a molten bath of fluoride salts. This relatively simple process has encouraged the strong increase in world aluminum production in recent years. The major cost in the processing of aluminum is *energy*. Even though relatively cheap hydroelectric power is usually used, the production process is so energy-intensive that production problems arise not so much because of the cost of the energy as because of the huge quantities of energy consumed.

The following examples illustrate this:

Example: In the United States, 35 percent of total aluminum capacity is located in the Northwestern states of Washington, Oregon, and Montana, having been originally attracted there by cheap hydroelectric power. However, the Bonneville Power Authority, which supplies the area, is having difficulty coping with demand for energy. It periodically cuts off a portion of the power to aluminum producers, especially in winter months if inadequate snowfall causes power shortages. Substantial price increases were enforced at the end of 1979 and again in 1982, and these have reduced the competitiveness of the producers relying on Bonneville electricity.

Example: In Norway and Greece, aluminum projects have been canceled because of power supply problems.

Example: In Japan, the power problem has become so critical that the government has forced aluminum refiners to scrap productive capacity of 600,000 tonnes, leaving Japan with only 1 million tons of production capacity. Further cutbacks are planned, and it is estimated that by the end of June 1983 Japanese capacity will have fallen to 625,000 tonnes.

All these changes have led to a concentrated move to relocate expansion projects to Australia, where power is plentiful and inexpensive. Australia could emerge as a major aluminum producer by the late 1980s, but even here some projects have been mothballed or scrapped because of the downturn in the world economy.

The hope is that eventually these power problems may be curbed by the addition of lithium and other compounds to the electrolyte, which will reduce power consumption during the reduction process. Even if marginal savings become possible, however, the cost and availability of energy will still be the prime consideration, in choosing locations for new refineries.

Major Producers

The major bauxite producers in 1981* were:

Australia	35.5%
Guinea	17.2%
Jamaica	12.5%
Brazil	6.3%
Surinam	6.9%

The major free-world producers of primary aluminum in 1981* were:

United States	36.0%
Canada	9.0%

*World Bureau of Metal Statistics.
†U.S. Bureau of Mines.

Japan	6.2%
Germany	5.8%
Norway	5.1%

Production in the Western world totaled 10.75 million tonnes in 1981. The impact of the Eastern bloc countries at the margin is not great both because they have sufficient supplies of bauxite to supply their own needs and because they consume domestically a large part of the 3.2 million tonnes they produce annually. Net exports to the Western world are normally between 100,000 and 200,000 tonnes a year.

The sharp fall in Japanese capacity in recent years, mentioned above, is reflected in production data: Japanese primary output fell over 400,000 tonnes between 1977 and 1981, to a level of only 770,000 tonnes, and then halved again in 1982, falling to only 350,000 tonnes.

The aluminum industry is dominated by six corporate groups and their affiliates—Alcan, Alcoa, Reynolds, Kaiser, Pechiney, and Alusuisse—which operate about 40–45 percent of world productive capacity for bauxite and 40 percent of primary aluminum capacity. So far this noteworthy fact appears to have neither helped nor hindered market traders. Although these companies operate a producer pricing system, their list prices are discounted in times of surplus to match free market quotes.

CONSUMPTION

End Uses

The following is the U.S. demand pattern for primary aluminum metal*:

Construction	25%
Cans and containers	21%
Transportation	18%
Electrical	12%

Typical end uses for aluminum in the construction industry include residential sidings, windows, roofing, mobile homes, bridge rails, and guardrails.

In the container and packaging industry, aluminum competes with steel and other materials. It has increased its market share substantially. More than 52 percent of U.S. beverage cans are now aluminum, and aluminum's market share is also rising rapidly in other countries. Aluminum beverage cans are easy to recycle, which makes them popular with environmentalists.

Passenger cars account for 50 percent of transportation uses of aluminum—and whereas in 1955 an average of 30 pounds of aluminum was used per car, 1978 models contained an average of 115 pounds. Forecasts for 1984 suggest consumption of 133 pounds per car. The trend is expected to continue. The high strength-to-weight ratio of aluminum makes it suitable for any carrier. The

*U.S. Bureau of Mines.

growth in aluminum usage has to some extent been at the expense of other base metals such as copper and zinc.

In the electrical industry, steel-reinforced aluminum cable has entirely replaced copper in overhead power transmission lines.

Aluminum is also used in a wide range of consumer durable goods and as tubing in agricultural and special industrial machinery.

Major Consumers

The industrialized Western world accounts for the greatest share of aluminum consumption. The major consumers of primary aluminum in 1981 were:

United States	33.6%
Japan	15.1%
Germany	9.2%
Rest of European Economic Community	16.2%
Total	76.1%

Shifts in Usage

The strong increase in aluminum consumption over the last decade has mainly been the result of its penetration of additional markets. It has been substituted for steel and wood in the construction industry, for steel and tin in the packaging industry, and for copper in the electrical industry. This trend may continue to some extent, but it seems that the bulk of substitution possibilities have already been exploited and the rate of growth of aluminum consumption will be slower in the 1980s. Table 32-1 shows the balance of supply and demand for primary aluminum.

TABLE 32-1 Balance of Supply and Demand for Primary Aluminum, 1973 to 1982
(Million tonnes)

	Refined production	Refined consumption	Net imports from Eastern bloc	Net increase in stocks	IPAI free-world year-end primary inventories	Primary stocks as a percent of consumption
1973	10.2	11.2	0.2	(0.8)	1.4	13
1974	11.1	11.2	0.2	0.1	2.0	18
1975	9.9	8.6	(0.2)	1.1	3.1	36
1976	9.9	11.1	0.1	(1.1)	2.3	21
1977	11.3	11.4	0.1	0	2.5	22
1978	11.6	12.0	0.1	(0.3)	2.1	18
1979	12.0	12.6	0.1	(0.5)	1.5	12
1980	12.8	12.1	0.1	0.9	2.1	18
1981	12.5	11.2	0.2	1.5	3.1	28
1982*	10.7	10.8	0.1	—	2.9	27

*Conticommodity Research Division estimates.

SOURCE: World Bureau of Metal Statistics and International Primary Aluminium Institute.

In fact, in some instances substitution of other metals for aluminum could occur, because aluminum is more difficult to work than other metals. In domestic piping, for example, where brazing has to be carried out on site, it is far simpler to braze copper than aluminum. The savings in labor costs outweigh the additional material cost of copper.

ALUMINUM STOCKS

Inventory Cycle

As an industrial raw material, and particularly as a substitute for copper, aluminum has the same inventory cycle as copper. It may have a slightly closer linkage to the construction industry than does copper, but this linkage has not been particularly significant in the past.

Seasonal Tendencies

Aluminum has the same seasonal pattern as the other base metals: strong demand and strong prices in the first quarter of the year, low demand and low-volume trading during the holiday period of July and August, and strong demand in September and October. In some years the traditional first-quarter strength of aluminum has been accentuated by reports of production disruption in the United States, where power shortages have been caused by lack of adequate snowfall in January.

SUMMARY AND TRADING CONSIDERATIONS

At present* the only futures market for aluminum is the London Metal Exchange (LME), where dates up to 3 months forward from the prompt delivery date are actively traded. Although the LME aluminum contract was only introduced in 1978, it has gained greatly in popularity among speculators, consumers, and merchants in the last few years, with consequent improvement in market depth and liquidity. The contract has also had a bearing on producer realized prices. Aluminum consumption, like copper consumption, is closely tied to the level of industrial demand in the world economy, especially in the construction industry. Aluminum production is dependent upon the level of both primary and secondary smelter output. Fluctuations in aluminum prices are primarily caused by envisaged improvement or deterioration in the supply-demand balance, which shows up as a decrease or increase in reported stocks. Rallies in other base metals may cause sympathetic movements in aluminum prices, but no rally will be sustained unless the market sees an improvement in the overall aluminum supply-demand balance. Figure 32-1 shows a price chart for aluminum in London.

*The COMEX is soon to commence trading in aluminum futures.

Statistics on world supply, demand, and inventory levels of both primary and secondary aluminum are published monthly by the U.S. Bureau of Mines and the American Bureau of Metal Statistics. Because the LME quote for aluminum is in sterling and aluminum prices worldwide are normally quoted in dollars, LME price movements can be caused by fluctuations in the sterling-dollar exchange rate alone. Speculators must therefore be aware that an improvement in world aluminum prices may not lead to a rise in LME prices if sterling strengthens at the same time. However, trading aluminum in dollars causes little or no extra inconvenience when dealing with most LME brokers.

CONTRACT DATA

The only futures market for aluminum is the LME. The market specifications are as follows:

Contract size

- 25 tonnes (55,115 pounds)

Quotation

Figure 32-1 Weekly continuation, 3-month London aluminum. *(Conti-Commodity Research Division)*

- Pounds sterling per tonne

  Minimum fluctuation
- 50 pence per tonne

  Equals per contract
- £12.50

  Maximum fluctuation
- None

  Trading position
- *Cash* (for prompt delivery and payment on the day following the transaction) *3 months* (forward) and *any* market days between cash and 3 months.

  Settlement

  Difference payable on prompt dates (expiration dates)

  Market hours

• Morning	11:55–12:00
	12:55–13:00
Official A.M. kerb	13:15–13:25
Afternoon	15:45–15:50
	16:25–16:30
Official P.M. kerb	16:40–16:55

Trading is permitted outside these times.

Tenderable grades

- 99.5 percent aluminum

Maximum iron content	0.4 percent
Maximum silicon content	0.3 percent

Each ingot must weigh between 12 and 26 kilograms

SOURCES OF INFORMATION

American Bureau of Metal Statistics (ABMS)
420 Lexington Avenue
New York, NY 10017

International Primary Aluminium Institute (IPAI)
New Zealand House
Haymarket
London SW1 England

U.S. Bureau of Mines (USBM)
2401 E Street, N.W.
Washington, DC 20241

World Bureau of Metal Statistics (WBMS)
42 Doughty Street
London WC1N 2LF England

CHAPTER

33

Lead and Zinc

Alan Davison

LEAD

INTRODUCTION

History does not record the earliest discovery of lead, but we do know that it was extracted by smelting in the days of the ancient Egyptians and used for the manufacture of coins and medallions. Later the Romans used it for ornaments and water pipes, examples of which have been discovered, still in serviceable condition, in Roman ruins.

The lead market differs from other base-metal markets in that a large part of metal production each year (between 35 and 50 percent) is derived from scrap rather than mines. The major reason for this is the predominance of the automobile battery market, which accounts for about 50 percent of lead use. Automobile batteries last for only 2 to 3 years, but at the end of that time, virtually none of the lead within the battery has been lost. To break open the battery and recycle the lead is a simple task.

PRODUCTION

Major Producers

Lead and zinc deposits are usually found together, and the two are commonly known as the "sister metals." The major ore and concentrate producers by continent in 1982 can be found in Table 33-1. The largest individual-country producers of ore in 1982 are shown in Table 33-2.

Because a large part of the lead consumed each year is from secondary

TABLE 33-1 Major Lead Producers by Continent, 1982

Continent	Percent	Thousands of tonnes
Europe	16	416
Africa	10	263
America	52	1338
Asia	4	125
Australia	17	444
Total non-Communist world	100*	2586

*Numbers do not sum to 100 percent because of rounding.

sources, many of the major refineries are located in the industrialized Western world rather than near the mines. Total metal production by continent in 1982 is shown in Table 33-3.

The Soviet Union is a net importer of lead from the Western world.

Technical Processes

There are two ways of smelting lead ores, the blast furnace and the open hearth. High-grade galena ores and concentrates can be smelted by the open-hearth method as long as there are low levels of impurities in the concentrate, especially silica, iron and zinc sulphides, antimony, arsenic, silver, and gold. If significant amounts of these contaminants are present they can be recovered when refining the bullion after initial smelting in a blast furnace.

Scrap

A large proportion of the lead consumed each year is refined from secondary sources because, in many end uses, lead is consumed in a relatively pure form and thus can be recycled. In a fairly simple process, a scrap dealer can break open spent batteries, neutralise the acid, and recycle the lead. The process of recycling lead roofing, guttering, and cable sheathing is even simpler. Lead can also be recovered from alloys by distilling, as lead often melts at a lower tem-

TABLE 33-2 Major Lead Producers by Country, 1982

Country	Thousands of tonnes
United States	543
Australia	444
Canada	341
Peru	201
Mexico	168
South Africa	125
Yugoslavia	113
Morocco	100

SOURCE: International Lead and Zinc Study Group.

TABLE 33-3 Metal Production by Continent, 1982

Continent	Thousands of tonnes	Percent
Europe	1493	38
Africa	167	4
America	1597	41
Asia	408	10
Australia	261	7
Total non-Communist world	3926	100

SOURCE: International Lead and Zinc Study Group.

perature than its alloying elements. The lead in tetraethyl lead (TEL), ammunition, chemicals, and pigments, however, cannot be recovered.

In the short term, secondary lead production is far more price-sensitive than primary production. This factor helps the industry to be quickly self-adjusting, reducing supply in times of low price and increasing supply as prices rise.

CONSUMPTION

The industrialized Western world accounts for the greater part of free-world lead consumption, as could be predicted from a knowledge of the major end uses. The breakdown by continent in 1982 was as shown in Table 33-4.

The four largest consumers—the United States, Japan, the United Kingdom, and Germany—accounted for over 50 percent of total Western world lead consumption. The consumption of these countries in 1982 broke down as shown in Table 33-5. The balance of lead supply and demand from 1977 to 1982 is shown in Table 33-6.

In the chemical sector, lead is used to add clarity and brilliance to glass, porcelain, ceramic glazes, and enamels. Use of lead in paints has been cut back in many domestic areas in recent years because of the threat of lead poisoning.

TABLE 33-4 Major Lead-Consuming Continents, 1982

Continent	Thousands of tonnes	Percent
Europe	1583	42
Africa	119	3
America	1414	37
Asia	604	16
Australia	69	2
Total	3789	100

SOURCE: International Lead and Zinc Study Group.

TABLE 33-5 Lead Consumption, 1982

Use	Percent
Batteries	56
Pipe and sheet	7
Alloys	6
Tetraethyl lead	8
Cable sheathing	5
Chemicals	12
Ammunition	2
Miscellaneous	5
Total	100*

*Numbers do not sum to 100 percent because of rounding.

TABLE 33-6 Balance of Supply of and Demand for Lead
(Thousands of tonnes)

Year	Primary	Secondary	Total	Consumption
1977	2310	1790	4100	4100
1978	2370	1760	4130	4130
1979	2390	1900	4290	4150
1980	2300	1810	4110	3950
1981	2240	1800	4040	3890
1982	2310	1620	3930	3790

Year	Net refined exports to Eastern bloc	Implied increase (or decrease) in refined stocks	Year-end reported stock levels	Stocks as a percent of consumption
1977	50	(40)	470	11.4
1978	120	(120)	400	9.7
1979	220	(80)	460	11.1
1980	120	(40)	530	13.5
1981	130	20	518	13.3
1982	120	(20)	560	14.8

SOURCE: International Lead and Zinc Study Group.

However, lead has retained most of its anticorrosion markets in industrial uses, and many steel fabrications are coated in red lead as soon as they are completed. Lead chemicals are also used in yellow pigment for road markings and plastics. Lead sheeting also has uses in x-ray and gamma-radiation shielding which, in addition to domestic and industrial uses, also has potential for military and civil defense purposes. Soundproofing and sound deadening is another possible growth sector. Tin can be alloyed with lead to produce a nontoxic solder with a low melting point for use in tin cans. Lead alloys are also used in type metal.

End Users

Lead remains unchallenged by other materials in its main market: starting, lighting, and ignition automobile batteries. Technological advances have reduced the weight of the average battery, and reduction in weight and engine size, especially in the United States, has allowed a further reduction in the sizes of batteries. However, the advent of the diesel-powered family car means an increase in battery size, for diesel engines require larger batteries than do conventional petrol engines.

There have been attempts to produce an alternative to the lead battery, using varying combinations of nickel, zinc, and iron, but no commercially viable alternative has yet been found. Increased use of plastic lattices to support lead plates has led to use of thinner lead plates and a consequent reduction in lead content.

Lead producers have for some time hoped that car manufacturers would develop a practical electrical car, which would stimulate lead demand. No such car has yet gone beyond the prototype stage, and none seems likely to do so in the near future.

The market for tetraethyl lead, which is used as an antiknock additive in petrol, is diminishing rapidly. For instance, consumption in the United States for the period 1977 to 1981 fell sharply, as shown in Table 33-7. The major reason for this decline is the antipollution legislation being passed by the U.S. government. High-compression gasoline engines give better performance than their diesel counterparts but tend to be less efficient and to expel more pollutants. This problem has led to the introduction of platinum and palladium catalytic converters, which have reduced automobile pollution. Unfortunately for the lead industry, these converters become quickly polluted by lead, with the result that lead-free gasoline has had to be introduced. In Europe also, lead emission limits are being lowered and the lead content of gasoline has had to be reduced.

Use of lead for roofing and piping fell during the 1960s and 1970s because of a trend away from constructing durable buildings and toward constructing low-cost, less durable buildings. Lead was replaced by cheaper concrete tiles, plastic guttering, and pipes. In the 1980s a return to more extensive use of lead in roofing and guttering is possible, especially in Europe where government regulations about the refurbishing and demolition of old buildings may curb the use of inferior or different materials, forcing builders to use lead, zinc, or copper in roofing and zinc or lead in guttering.

Use of lead in cable sheathing has fallen because of its replacement by polyvinylchloride (PVC). In the 1980s lead consumption in cable sheathing may also be adversely affected by the switch from copper cable to fiberoptics. However, because total cable usage is expected to accelerate, total lead consumption in cable sheathing should continue to grow.

Lead ammunition is little used by the military now but has retained most of its practice and sporting market, although the danger of lead poisoning by contamination of fowl to be used as food has meant that use of lead in wildfowl hunting is being phased out.

TABLE 33-7 U.S. Tetraethyl Lead Consumption, 1977 to 1982

Year	Thousands of tonnes
1977	211
1978	178
1979	187
1980	128
1981	111
1982	119

SOURCE: International Lead and Zinc Study Group.

Seasonal Tendencies

Demand for lead tends to rise in winter and early spring, when automobile batteries fail because of cold, damp weather and have to be replaced. Refinery workers take their summer vacation in July, August, and September, and refineries use the opportunity to repair plants. Thus there is often a fall in lead output during these months.

FACTORS AFFECTING THE PRICE OF LEAD

Because the battery sector is the largest consumer of lead, any factor which affects demand for batteries will in turn affect the price of lead. An increase in car production or spell of very cold or very hot weather boosts demand for batteries and thus boosts lead consumption. As mentioned above, there is a tendency for demand for batteries to rise in the late winter and early spring. Other uses of lead are fairly evenly spread throughout industry, although the con-

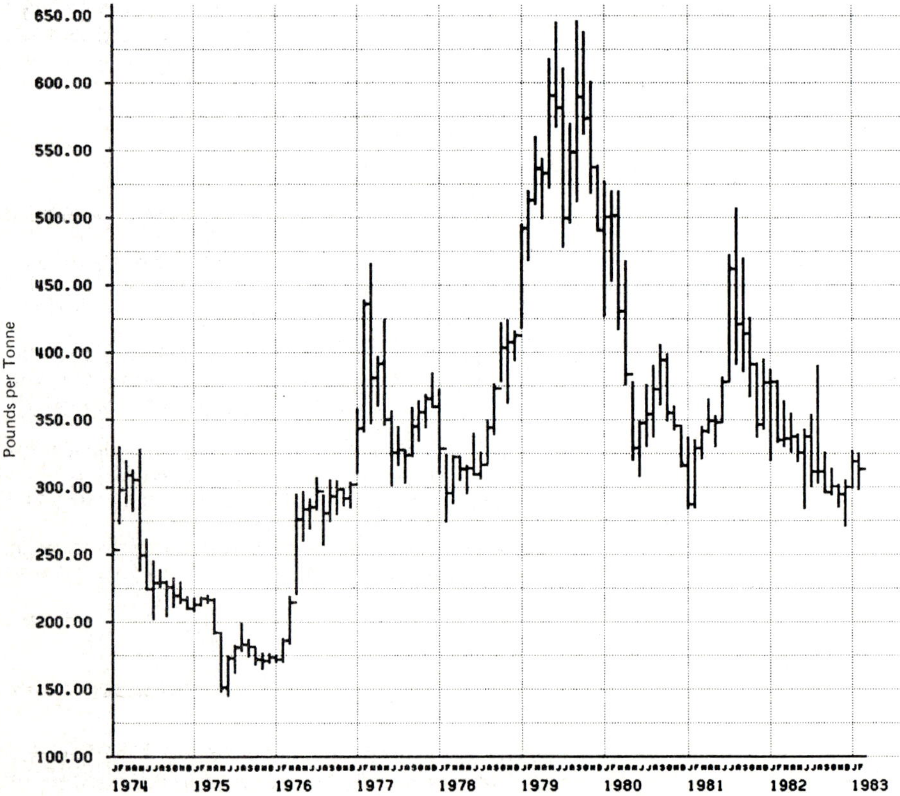

Figure 33-1 Monthly continuation, 3-month London lead. *(ContiCommodity Research Division)*

struction sector is an important lead consumer and its level of economic activity should be monitored accordingly.

Cycles in lead prices tend to be much shorter than cycles in prices of base metals as a whole, because of the highly price-sensitive nature of the scrap lead market. Secondary or scrap producers are able to close plants and cut back costs far more quickly and effectively than primary producrs, who often have contracts to smelt concentrates from certain mines on a long-term basis. The result is that both low prices (that is, prices below around 20¢/pound) and high prices (that is, prices about 50¢/pound) are difficult to sustain for more than 6 months. No long-term shortage of lead is forecast, and it is likely that lead prices will continue to be closely tied to average production costs. Figure 33-1 shows a London price chart for lead.

SUMMARY AND TRADING CONSIDERATIONS

Lead consumption is primarily determined by demand for batteries, which is dependent upon vehicle production in the Western world.

Technological advances have caused a reduction in lead used per battery in recent years, but expected shifts from gasoline to diesel engines in the next decade should negate these reductions.

Any successful attempt to market battery-powered cars would give the lead market a strong boost. However, no market breakthrough is thought to be imminent at present.

The secondary or scrap sector is very large, because of the ease with which batteries can be recycled. This large sector tends to have a stabilising effect on lead prices.

Most of the major lead-mining countries are located in North and South America, and these countries account for over 50 percent of mine production. The geographical breakdown of smelters, however, is more even; many small secondary smelters are located throughout the world. At present Communist countries are net importers of lead and do most of their buying on the London Metal Exchange (LME), where lead is traded for dates up to 3 months forward. In the short term, lead prices tend to fluctuate in line with copper, gold, and zinc, but longer-term lead prices are determined by the supply-and-demand situation of the industry and the availability of nearby material.

CONTRACT DATA

The only futures market for lead is the London Metal Exchange. The market specifications are shown below.

Contract size	25 tonnes (55,115 pounds)
Quotation	Pounds sterling per tonne
Minimum fluctuation	25 pence per tonne
Equals per contract	£6.25

Maximum fluctuation	None	
Trading positions	*Cash* (for prompt delivery and payment on the day following the transaction)	
	3 *months* (forward) and *any* market days between cash and 3 months	
Settlement	Difference payable on prompt dates (expiration dates)	
Market hours	Morning rings	12:10–12:15
		12:45–12:50
	Official A.M. kerb	13:15–13:25
	Afternoon rings	15:20–15:25
		16:00–16:05
	Official P.M. kerb	16:40–16:55

Interoffice trading is permitted outside these hours.

ZINC

INTRODUCTION

Zinc was first called "false silver" about 2000 years ago. Zinc-filled bracelets dating back to 500 B.C. have been found on the island of Rhodes, and the Romans, who were well acquainted with brass as early as 200 B.C., used a zinc alloy to make coins. In terms of annual tonnage consumed, zinc is the fourth most important metal, being surpassed only by steel, copper, and aluminum.

PRODUCTION

Grades

The basis grade for refined zinc on the LME is 98 percent pure zinc, also known as good own-brand zinc. In recent years the standard output of smelters has become high-grade zinc with a purity of 99.9 percent—and in fact, the main U.S. producer quote has now become high-grade zinc.

Commercial zinc, cast in various shapes and sizes, is known as *slab zinc.*

The grade and producer of each slab are identified by the registered brand name cast into the metal.

Prices

Four main prices are quoted by the zinc industry:

1. The North America producer price is quoted in U.S. or Canadian cents per pound and is a producer-delivered price.
2. The European producer price is quoted in dollars per tonne and is also a producer-delivered price.

3. London Metal Exchange cash and 3-month prices are quoted in sterling per tonne and are FOB LME European warehouses. As zinc is usually thought of as a dollar commodity, LME prices will (ceteris paribus) move inversely with the strength of sterling against the U.S. dollar.
4. The *Metals Week* U.S. merchant's price is quoted in U.S. cents per pound and excludes transport costs.

Producers may often maintain their list prices in public but will in actual fact give customers substantial discounts either by charging below list prices or by offering advantageous credit terms. Producer prices are normally at a premium to the free market prices because the quote, besides including transport costs, can also include favorable payment terms. Consumers are often willing to pay a premium to free market prices in order to obtain less volatile price movements and improved security of supply, both of which are offered by producer pricing systems.

Technological Process

Zinc is often derived from compound ores and is most frequently mined together with lead, as mentioned above. For example, in the United States in 1977, zinc ores alone contributed 53 percent of total mine output, combined zinc and lead ores contributed 22 percent, lead ores contributed 18 percent, and all other ores contributed 7 percent.

The processing of zinc goes through the normal stages of milling (crushing), concentration by flotation, roasting (to eliminate sulfur), bleaching with sulfuric acid, and finally electrolytic deposition on aluminium cathodes. The cathodes are lifted from the tanks at intervals, and the zinc is stripped off, melted in a furnace, and cast into slabs.

Major Producers

The major free-world producers of zinc ore are shown in Table 33-8. In 1981 free-world production of zinc ore totaled 4.43 million tonnes. The Communist bloc produced 1.65 million tonnes; the Soviet Union's contribution was just over 1 million tonnes, making it the second largest producer in the world. The major free-world producers of slab zinc are shown in Table 33-9. Free-world

TABLE 33-8 Major Free-World Producers of Zinc, 1982

Country	Percent
Canada	24.5
Australia	13.2
Peru	11.2
United States	6.9
Japan	5.2
Mexico	5.1

SOURCE: International Lead and Zinc Study Group.

TABLE 33-9 Major Free-World Producers of Slab Zinc, 1982

Area	Percent
European Economic Community	28.5
Japan	15.3
Canada	11.8
United States	6.6
Australia	6.8

production of slab zinc in 1981 totaled 4.52 million tonnes, and Communist bloc production was 1.67 million tonnes.

CONSUMPTION

End Uses

The three main end uses of zinc are galvanizing, which accounts for 45 to 50 percent of consumption; die casting, which accounts for 15 to 20 percent; and the brass industry, which accounts for 15 to 20 percent.

Galvanized steel sheeting is used principally in the construction industry in the nonresidential sector. The zinc is used as a protective coating for structural steel, roofing, siding, and guttering. Galvanized sheet is the standard duct material for air-conditioning, ventilating, and heating systems. Galvanized steel is also used in the automobile industry and in electrical equipment and appliances. Zinc die castings are used as components and parts for the transportation industry, in industrial and agricultural machinery, and in consumer durables.

Alloy copper, or brass, as it is commonly known, is used for decorative purposes, in the construction and automobile industries, and in industry in general.

Major Consumers

The major free-world consumers of zinc are:

European Economic Community	32.6%
United States	18.4%
Japan	17.1%

In recent years the Eastern bloc countries have been significant importers of zinc concentrates and zinc metal from the Western world.

SUBSTITUTES

In the 1970s zinc lost a number of its markets. Competition from aluminum and plastics forced producers to develop new markets for zinc to replace those that had been lost and to augment those that survived. The major losses came in the die casting sector, especially in the automobile industry, where zinc consumption per car shrank dramatically and even now shows little sign of improving.

The main culprits have been the lighter and more fashionable substitutes, aluminum and plastics. Some markets have been regained by the development of "thin-wall" die casting of zinc, but even so, zinc use has been adversely affected. Any significant long-term increases in the price of zinc relative to its substitutes would lead to further moves away from the use of zinc, probably for good.

In the galvanizing sector, zinc use is rising, for emphasis on corrosion resistance is leading steel producers to increase zinc coatings rather than reduce them.

There have been some attempts to replace galvanized coatings with *galvalume*—a mixture of zinc and aluminum. These experiments have not been totally successful, especially in Europe, which has a far more corrosive atmosphere than North America. Recently an alternative method using another alloy, *zincrometal*, has proved successful. Since the main constituent of zincrometal is zinc, and since introduction of zincrometal has led to development of new markets for zinc protective coatings, the affect of zincrometal on total zinc consumption will probably be beneficial.

In the brass industry in the 1960s and 1970s, zinc lost some of its market to aluminum and stainless steel, but most substitution has now been completed and further such losses are unlikely.

Finally, the use of zinc oxide powder in tires has been reduced by the switch from cross-ply to radial tires, which last twice as long. A large part of this transition also is now complete, and further losses by the zinc industry seem unlikely.

NEW APPLICATIONS

The major new end use for zinc could be zinc batteries. Several types have been developed but none have yet gone beyond the prototype stage. If, however, a zinc-based battery came into general use, either for power-peak smoothing uses or in electric cars, the zinc industry would have difficulty for a few years in supplying sufficient material.

OUTLOOK

The bull market for zinc in 1973 and 1974 was a double-edged sword because, besides forcing prices up to £875/tonne on the LME, it also started a spate of zinc exploration activities which have led to development of a large number of new mine and smelter projects since 1973. The recessions of 1974 to 1975 and the early 1980s, combined with the low level of industrial growth in the intervening period, have meant that zinc consumption since 1973 has grown at far lower rates than the historical norm. Low consumption in turn led to an excess of supply over demand and caused the consequent low price of zinc between 1974 and 1980. Only in the early 1980s has the zinc price risen above its floor price. The result has been a dearth of investment in new zinc mine projects, planned to come into production in the mid to late 1980s.

If the zinc market can maintain at least a small level of growth, then zinc prices can probably remain buoyant during the 1980s, for supply growth is likely to be lower than demand. In fact, if growth rates approach historical levels of over 4 percent, there could well be a shortage of zinc. Table 33-10 shows the balance of supply and demand for zinc.

TABLE 33-10 Balance of Supply of and Demand for Zinc, 1976 to 1982
(Million tonnes)

Year	Metal consumption	Net exports of metal to socialist countries	Releases from national stockpile	Increases in stocks	Reported metal stocks	As a percent of consumption
1976	4.16	−0.04	−0.01	−0.01	1.14	27
1977	4.24	−0.04	−0.05	+0.02	1.20	28
1978	4.66	0.03	−0.08	−0.48	0.82	18
1979	4.74	0.05	0	−0.08	0.85	18
1980	4.48	0.02	0.03	0	0.79	18
1981	4.42	0.06	0.03	0.11	0.88	20
1982	4.20	0.18	0.02	−0.04	0.80	19

Year	Mine production	Change in concentrate or ore stocks*	Net exports of concentrates to Eastern bloc	Direct use of zinc oxide	Total metal production	Secondary production
1976	4.55	0.20	0.09	0.10	4.12	0.25
1977	4.84	0.22	0.19	0.10	4.27	0.26
1978	4.69	0.01	0.18	0.11	4.29	0.21
1979	4.61	−0.41	0.17	0.10	4.71	0.26
1980	4.52	−0.19	0.14	0.07	4.47	0.28
1981	4.46	−0.32	0.13	0.07	4.56	0.28
1982	4.83	−0.01	0.12	0.07	4.32	0.28

*The change in concentrate stocks implies a 93 percent rate of recovery of zinc metal from zinc concentrates.

SOURCE: International Lead and Zinc Study Group.

SOURCES OF INFORMATION

The major leading indicators of zinc consumption are the levels of activity in the construction industry (which, as discussed above, accounts for a large proportion of zinc consumption in galvanizing) and in automobile production (which uses zinc in die casting, brass, and galvanizing).

Other uses of zinc are spread fairly evenly throughout industry, so that total Organization for Economic Cooperation and Development (OECD) industrial production or GNP would give a positive correlation with zinc consumption. Figures on stocks, trends in demand and supply, and trade with Communist countries are available from the International Lead and Zinc Study Group in London and the World Bureau of Metal Statistics in the United Kingdom. European studies on the zinc industry are published occasionally by the European Economic Community. The American Bureau of Metal Statistics and the U.S. Bureau of Mines publish monthly, quarterly, annual, and long-term insights into the U.S. and sometimes the world zinc industry. The Ministry of International Trade Industry (MITI) publishes statistics on Japanese use of zinc.

New uses for zinc are promoted by the Lead and Zinc Development Association in London.

The addresses of these sources are given under "Sources of Information" at the end of this chapter.

SUMMARY AND TRADING CONSIDERATIONS

Zinc is an industrial material which has its main end uses in the galvanizing and die-casting industries. The only liquid futures market for zinc is the London Metals Exchange, where prices up to 3 months forward are traded daily. LME contracts are for 25 tonnes of 98 percent zinc, and the market is quoted in sterling, although a trader who wants to eliminate fluctuations in prices due to exchange-rate movements can normally arrange to trade in dollars. Short-term fluctuations in zinc prices are often caused by movements in the lead and copper markets, but no sustained increase in zinc prices can be seen unless the

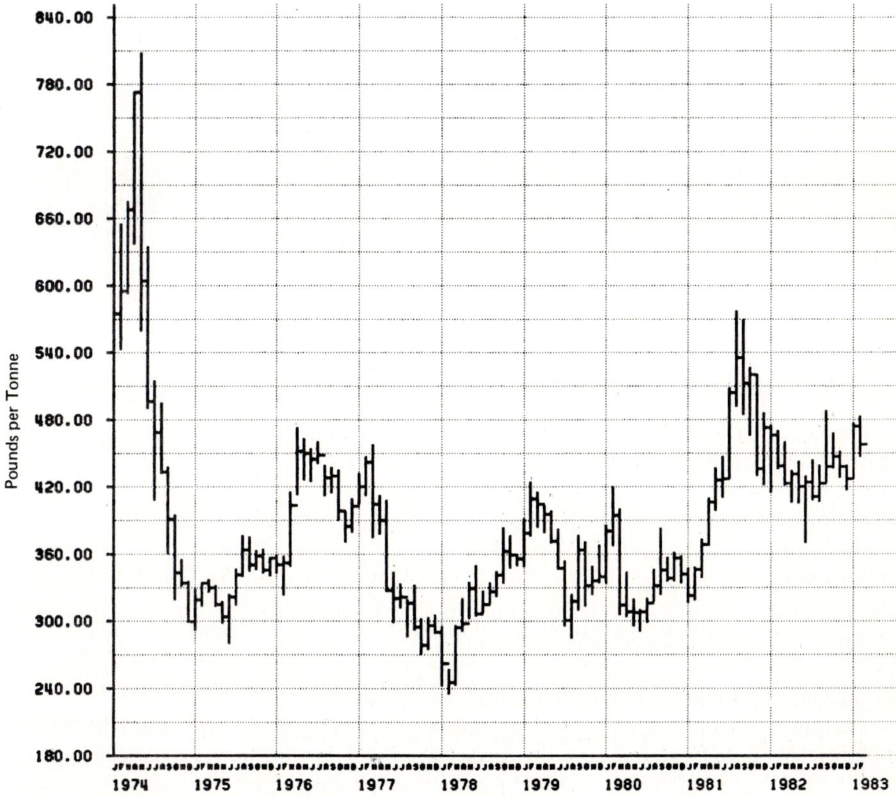

Figure 33-2 Monthly continuation, 3-month London zinc. *(ContiCommodity Research Division)*

fundamental outlook for zinc itself changes. Although the zinc sector went through a difficult, depressed period in the 1970s, the industry has reemerged in a fitter, leaner shape, having sponsored research into new commercial uses for zinc which is gradually beginning to pay dividends. Figure 33-2 shows a London price chart for zinc.

The market is solely dependent upon industrial uses and thus is closely tied to world economic activity.

CONTRACT DATA

Contract size	25 tonnes (55,115 pounds)	
Quotation	Pounds sterling per tonne	
Minimum fluctuation	25 pence per tonne	
Equals per contract	£6.25	
Maximum fluctuation	None	
Trading position	*Cash* (for prompt delivery and payment on the day following the transaction)	
	3 months (forward) and *any* market days between cash and 3 months	
Settlement	Differences payable on prompt dates (expiration dates)	
Market hours	Morning	12:15–12:20
		12:50–12:55
	Official A.M. kerb	13:15–13:25
	Afternoon	15:25–15:30
		16:05–16:10
	Official P.M. kerb	16:40–16:55

Premarket trading takes place on an interoffice basis between the approximate hours of 8:30 and 12:00 each morning, local time.

SOURCES OF INFORMATION

American Bureau of Metal Statistics (ABMS)
420 Lexington Avenue
New York, NY 10017

International Lead and Zinc Study Group
Metro House
58 St. James Street
London SW1A ILD England

Lead Development Association (LDA)
34 Berkeley Square
London W1Y 6AJ England

U.S. Bureau of Mines (USBM)
2401 E Street, N.W.
Washington, DC 20241

World Bureau of Metal Statistics (WBMS)
41 Doughty Street
London WC1N 2LF England

USEFUL PUBLICATIONS

Lead and Zinc Statistics

International Lead and Zinc Study Group
Metro House
58 St. James Street
London SW1A 1LD England

Metal Bulletin

Metal Bulletin PLC
45/46 Lower Marsh
London SE1 7RG England

Metals Analysis and Outlook

Metals and Minerals Publications Limited
222 The Strand
London WC2R 1BA England

Metals Week

McGraw Hill, Inc.
1221 Avenue of the Americas
New York, NY 10020

World Metal Statistics

World Bureau of Metal Statistics
41 Doughty Street
London WC1N 2LF England

CHAPTER

34

Tin

Alan Davison

INTRODUCTION

Tin is one of the oldest metals known to humankind. Its use initially flourished because of its capacity to combine with other metals to form alloys. Probably most significant was its ability to mix with copper to form bronze, used in the earliest stages of human development for the manufacture of cutting tools and weapons. More recently it has been used in the plating of steel to form metal containers and in mixtures with lead to form solder.

Various qualities of tin, such as its nontoxicity, electrical conductivity, resistance to corrosion, ability to be cold-worked, and low melting point, make it difficult to replace in modern industrial society.

PRODUCTION

World Production

Over two-thirds of the world's tin is mined in Malaysia, Indonesia, Thailand, and Bolivia. The balance is produced by China, the Soviet Union, Australia, the United Kingdom, Burma, Japan, Canada, Portugal, and Spain. Tables 34-1 and 34-2 show production figures for mined and refined tin.

Figures are not readily available from the Communist bloc. However, estimated production is around 34,000 tonnes, with China and the Soviet Union accounting for almost all the production.

Table 34-1 Mined Tin Production in the Non-Communist World, 1982

Continent	Thousands of tonnes	Percent
Europe	5.0	3
Africa	10.7	6
Asia	124.9	66
North and South America	37.4	20
Australia	12.3	6
Total	190.3	100

SOURCE: International Tin Council.

TABLE 34-2 Refined Tin Production in the Non-Communist World, 1982

Continent	Thousands of tonnes	Percent
Europe	14.1	8
Africa	6.4	4
Asia	123.8	69
North and South America	30.9	17
Australia	3.1	2
Total	178.3	100

SOURCE: International Tin Council.

Methods of Production

Mined Production. The various methods for mining tin are listed below.

1. Lode mining. Tin-bearing deposits are mined at depth underground by means of adits, tunnels, or shafts.
2. Surface mining. Overlying ground is removed and the deposits are worked:
   a. By dredges, or large raft platforms with a chain of either buckets or suction pumps to elevate and wash alluvial deposits
   b. By gravel pumping, using water and pressure pumps
   c. By open cast mining, or excavation performed from the surface
3. Offshore mining. Deposits are extracted from the continental platform by buckets or suction dredges.
4. Suction boats. Converted fishing vessels are used as suction dredges. This method is used in Thailand.
5. Dubang washing. Concentrates are mined with pans from stream beds. This method is mainly used in Malaysia.

Recycled Tin. Tin can be recovered from the trimmings of tinplate sheets, from strips of tinplate scrap, and from residues arising from tinplating and alloying processes.

Technological Process. Tin can be smelted in three ways:

1. Reduction. Tin concentrates are reduced in a process involving the use of oil-fired furnaces operating at a temperature of about 1200°C.
2. Cleaning slags. The charge, consisting of tin concentrates with 10 to 15 percent anthracite coal for reduction and a limestone flux, is mixed and charged for the furnace through openings in the roof. The smelting then takes between 10 and 12 hours.
3. Refining impure tin. Metal smelted from alluvial deposits normally requires very little refining, as the main impurity is usually only a small amount of iron. Tin smelted from lode concentrates, however, contains varying amounts of iron, antimony, lead, arsenic, bismuth, and sometimes copper; it must be further refined using a combination of liquidation, boiling, and electrolysis.

CONSUMPTION AND END USES

Consumption of refined tin in the free world is shown in Table 34-3.

Estimates from the Communist bloc show consumption of around 51,000 tonnes for 1981, with China and the Soviet Union the largest consumers. This would imply net exports to the Eastern bloc in the range of 20,000 to 35,000 tonnes per annum.

Tinplate accounts for some 40 percent of total world consumption. About 90 percent of tinplate is used in manufacture of metal containers, mostly for beverages and human and pet foods. A smaller percentage is used in containers for paint, oil, chemicals, and cosmetics. The balance of tinplate produced is used for screw caps and crown corks; kitchen and dairy equipment; and (in the engineering and electrical industry) gas meters, automobiles, radios, and electrical appliances.

Solder accounts for the second largest portion of world tin consumption, around 25 percent. Solder is widely used in electronics equipment, automobile radiators, heat exchangers, and the joining of metals. In the domestic sector, solder is essential for the installation of central heating and plumbing.

TABLE 34-3 Consumption of Refined Tin in the Free World, 1982

Continent	Thousands of tonnes	Percent
Europe	46.70	31.9
Africa	3.65	2.5
Asia	40.14	27.4
America	53.02	36.2
Australia	2.95	2.0
Total	146.46	100.0

SOURCE: International Tin Council.

TABLE 34-4 Balance of Supply of and Demand for Tin, 1975 to 1982
(Thousands of tonnes)

Year	Refined production	Refined consumption	Net exports to the Eastern bloc
1975	178	164	7
1976	182	185	11
1977	180	172	16
1978	194	172	23
1979	201	173	25
1980	197	161	26
1981	197	152	22
1982	170	148	18

Year	General Services Administration disposals	International Tin Council disposals†	Implied increase in commercial stocks†
1975	0.5	(2)	(5.5)
1976	3.5	19.5	9
1977	2.5	1.0	(4.5)
1978	0	0	(1)
1979	0	0	3
1980	0	0	10
1981	6	(3)	26
1982	4.0	(50)‡	(42)

†Figures in parentheses are negative.

‡This implies that the 23,294 tonnes of tin in the International Tin Council (ITC) buffer stock on June 30, 1982, but not carried over to the sixth ITC buffer stock does not come back on to the market by year end.

SOURCES: International Tin Council, Metals and Minerals Research Services, and ContiCommodity Services Limited.

Most of the remaining 35 percent of tin consumption is split between bearing alloys (8 percent), tin bronzes (7 percent), and tin chemicals (8 percent). A small percentage is used in pewter, tin and tin-alloy coatings, and other metallurgical applications.

Table 34-4 shows the balance of supply and demand for tin.

SUBSTITUTES

The increasing real price of tin in recent years has led consumers to search for substitutes for tin and to economize on its use where no suitable substitutes are available. In the canning industry there has been a trend toward two-piece cans rather than three-piece cans, because the two-piece can requires fewer soldering operations and thus less tin.

Alternatives to tinplate include aluminum, blackplate (chromium plated steel), and plastic. So far, aluminum has been the main competitor; it has had great success especially in the soft-drink industry because of its low density and ease of recycling.

Production of tinplate, however, is a widespread and substantial industry. Any moves away from tinplate will be gradual, and with the packaging industry still expanding, the overall use of tinplate could continue to rise rather than fall.

At present few alternatives to use of tin in solder are in widespread use. The rapid growth of the electronics industry should provide further markets for solder, though increased miniaturization will eventually reduce the use of tin.

SEASONAL TENDENCIES

Two-thirds of the world's tin is produced in Asia, and hence ore production is likely to fall in the monsoon season. Because this seasonal factor is anticipated, it usually has no effect on the futures market. In the industrialized West, smelter production is likely to fall between July and September, when workers take their summer vacation and smelters do repairs. Workers in tin-consuming industries take vacations during the same period, and thus consumption also falls; the net result is often zero.

INTERNATIONAL TIN AGREEMENT

The tin market is partially controlled by the International Tin Council (ITC), which is presently made up of six producing nations and eighteen consuming nations. These nations have signed the sixth International Tin Agreement, which took effect in July 1982. Currently the two major functions of the ITC are to control member countries' exports and to manage a buffer stock designed to stabilize tin prices.

The ITC buffer stock manager (BSM) has orders to sell tin from the buffer stock when the Penang price reaches a predetermined level. Conversely, when the Penang price drops to a floor level the BSM must buy tin. Between these extreme levels, the BSM has discretionary power. The BSM may intervene in any market and has authority to raise funds on the world's capital markets if the need arises. In 1982 buffer stock buying has been a force to be reckoned with in the tin market. The BSM purchased over 50,000 tonnes of tin during the year, equivalent to 3 to 4 months of annual consumption. Without this support the tin price would have easily collapsed after an influential buyer, who had pushed prices up sharply in the first quarter of the year, withdrew from the market and started dumping surplus metal.

It is interesting to note that the United States does not participate in the Sixth International Tin Agreement, although the United States is the largest consuming country in the world. In fact, the U.S. government has a 190,000-tonne strategic stockpile of tin, controlled by the General Services Administration (GSA). Some 150,000 tonnes of this stockpile has been declared surplus, and Congress has given the GSA permission to dispose of 30,000 tonnes. Sales began in July 1980, and in the next 18 months the GSA sold only 3000 tonnes. Congress granted permission to ship stockpiled tin overseas in mid-December 1981, and subsequently sales accelerated. The stockpile auctions provided an alternative source of material when the LME and Penang markets came under strong buying pressure in the first quarter of 1982. Since the end of the squeeze on the LME in 1982, the GSA has sold only occasional packets of material.

SUMMARY AND TRADING CONSIDERATIONS

At present the only futures market for tin is the London Metal Exchange, but an alternative market is to be set up in Penang in the not-too-distant future. The main disadvantage of speculating in tin futures is that the small size of the tin industry combined with the relatively small number of tin producers leaves the market open to attempts to control prices.

The Sixth International Tin Agreement has so far proved successful in keeping Penang prices within their predetermined limits, although LME prices have tended to fluctuate more widely. The Sixth Agreement shows no sign of breaking down at present, but unless something is done to reduce the sizable surplus of metal on the market, more drastic steps may be needed to restore market equilibrium. Figure 34-1 shows a London price chart for tin.

The main problem for tin producers is that demand is growing very slowly because of substitution of competitive materials, primarily aluminum.

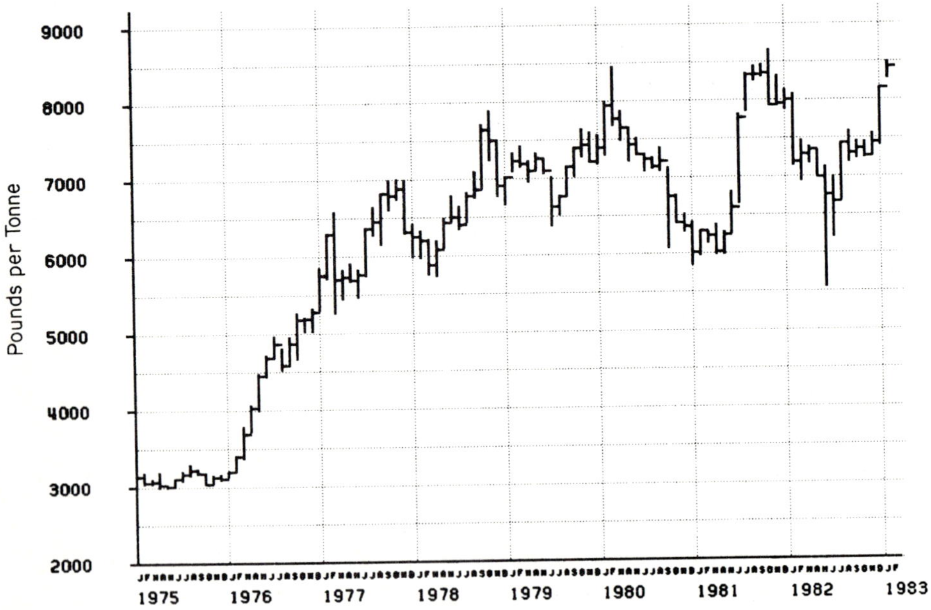

Figure 34-1 Monthly continuation, 3-month London tin (high grade). *(ContiCommodity Research Division)*

CONTRACT DATA

There are two principal markets for tin: the London Metal Exchange and Penang.

London

Contract size	5 tonnes (11,023 pounds)	
Quotation	Pounds sterling per tonne	
Minimum fluctuation	£1 per tonne	
Trading positions	*Cash* for prompt delivery against payment on the business day immediately following the day of transaction	
	Forward for delivery against payment on any business day between cash and 3 months	
Settlement	Cash difference between purchases and sales paid or received on expiration of contract	
Market hours, London time	Morning	12:05–12:10
		12:40–12:45
	Official A.M. kerb	13:15–13:25
	Afternoon	15:40–15:45
		16:20–16:25
	Official P.M. kerb	16:40–16:50

The times listed above are termed official rings and kerbs and are controlled by a market chairman. However, trading is permitted outside these times (from 08:30 until 19:00) on an interoffice basis, though it normally ceases at 17:00 local London time.

Two contracts are traded on the LME, standard tin and high-grade tin. Any tin delivered against a contract is strictly controlled by the LME and must be of minimum purity: standard tin must be not less than 99.75 percent pure and high-grade tin not less than 99.85 percent. In addition, only certain brands are permitted for fulfillment of contracts. Deliverable tin must be ingots or slabs between 12 and 50 kilograms in weight and must be delivered to a warehouse approved by the LME.

Penang

The Penang market is presently a straightforward physical market with no facility for futures trading. The market is traded in ringgits (Malaysian dollars) per kilogram, and delivery takes place within 2 weeks. There has been talk of establishing a futures market in Penang, and negotiations are currently under way. The latest information is that a 1-tonne contract may soon be traded on a new futures market.

SOURCES OF INFORMATION

Commodities Research Unit Ltd.
31 Mount Pleasant
London WC1X OD England

Publications: *Monthly reports and selective reports on the metals industry, including tin*

International Tin Council (ITC)
Haymarket House
1 Oxendon Street
London SW1Y 4EQ England

Publication: Monthly Statistical Bulletin

McGraw Hill
1221 Avenue of the Americas
New York, NY 10020

Publication: Metals Week

Metal Bulletin PLC
45/46 Lower Marsh
London SE1 7RG England

Publications: Metal Bulletin *(a biweekly publication) and* Metal Bulletin Monthly

Metals and Minerals Publications Ltd.
222 The Strand
London WC2R 1BA England

Publication: Metals Analysis and Outlook, *a quarterly fundamental outlook on and review of the metals markets, including tin*

CHAPTER

35

Nickel

Alan Davison

INTRODUCTION

Until 1870, nickel production was limited to small deposits in Germany, Greece, Scandinavia, and the United States. A nickel silicate ore was discovered in New Caledonia in 1864, and New Caledonia was the principal source of nickel from 1875 until 1905, when Canada became the leading producer. The Sudbury area of Canada is still the principal world source of nickel.

MAJOR TYPES

Depending upon the metallurgical processes involved in smelting the nickel ores, the final product of smelters or refiners may be nickel metal, nickel oxide, or ferronickel. There are established merchant markets for all these materials, but a futures market exists only for the metal. Nickel metal is sold in various shapes and forms; the two main grades are 99.9 percent plating nickel and the inferior 99.7 percent melting nickel.

PRODUCTION

Technical Process

Because each nickel ore body is different, there are many methods for processing nickel ores. The two main types of ores are the sulphide variety, found in Canada, Botswana, and parts of Australia, and the oxide or laterite ore bodies.

The laterites are complex ores, usually mined by surface methods, which require large energy inputs for smelting. Sulphides are usually mined underground but are far less energy-intensive to smelt because they can be concentrated before smelting, unlike laterite ores. Recovery of nickel from sulphide concentrates involves a wide variety of processes, including leaching and then matte smelting to refine the metal. Sulphide processors have been under pressure recently to reduce sulphur dioxide emissions, which would raise their costs.

The three basic methods for smelting ores are:

1. Acid leach. Nickel and cobalt are dissolved in sulphuric acid and then precipitated out, using hydrogen sulphide.
2. Ammonia leach. Best suited to the lower-grade limonitic laterites. The final product is usually nickel oxide.
3. Pyrotechnical. In general the pyrotechnical method, accounting for some 60 percent of laterite conversion, produces ferronickel and does not allow the independent recovery of cobalt. This is a serious deficiency because in recent years the cobalt recovered has sometimes been as valuable to the mines as the nickel.

Major Producers

Western nickel producers account for 70 to 75 percent of total world production. The major Western mine producers in 1980 are shown in Table 35-1.

The Canadian producers International Nickel Company (INCO) and Falconbridge are usually thought of as the market leaders. Both have expanded outside Canada in recent years; INCO has opened mines in Guatemala and Indonesia, and Falconbridge has opened the Falconbridge Dominican plant in the Dominican Republic.

Most of the smelters and refineries are vertically integrated with major producers carrying out mining, smelting, and refining, as well as operating their

TABLE 35-1 Major Western Producers of Nickel, 1981

Country	Percent
Canada	33.2
New Caledonia	15.5
Australia	15.4
Indonesia	5.4
Philippines	7.8
South Africa	5.5
Dominican Republic	4.1
Botswana	3.4
Zimbabwe	2.4
Greece	3.2
Others	4.1
Total	100.0

SOURCE: U.S. Bureau of Mines.

TABLE 35-2 Locations of Major Nickel Smelters and Refiners

Country	Percent
Canada	28.0
Japan	20.1
Australia	7.0
Norway	7.0
New Caladonia	6.0
United Kingdom	3.5
Total	71.6

SOURCE: U.S. Bureau of Mines.

TABLE 35-3 Major Uses of Nickel, 1980

Use	Percent
Stainless steels	47
Other alloy steels	9
Iron castings	8
Plating	9
Nickel-based alloys	18
Copper-based alloys	4
Miscellaneous	5
Total	100

SOURCE: U.S. Bureau of Mines and Conti-Commodity Research Division.

own sales forces. Table 35-2 shows the geographic locations of the major nickel smelters and refiners. INCO has the world's largest plant in Sudbury and another in Wales. Falconbridge has smelting and refining plants in Canada and Norway. There are also large smelting and refining plants in Japan, which mostly handle rough nickel mattes from New Caledonia, the Philippines, and Indonesia.

The Communist bloc is a net exporter of nickel.

CONSUMPTION

Major Consumers

Nickel has the ability to impart to other metals certain valuable qualities: high resistance to corrosion, malleability, and high strength over a range of temperatures. Hence it is most commonly used as an alloying agent. Because of its pleasing appearance it is also used in plating.

As shown in Table 35-3, alloys account for 86 percent of all nickel use. The miscellaneous category is mainly accounted for by use of nickel as a catalyst in various organic processes.

Substitution

Nickel could be replaced in many of its end uses if the need arose—for instance, if supplies were cut off. No large-scale substitutions for nickel are currently planned by the major end users, but more economizing and reduced intensity in use of nickel are likely in the future.

In stainless steel, for instance, nickel is used in all austenitic steels but in not in ferritic steels. Though moves from austenitic to ferritic steels are expected, austenitic steels will not be completely eliminated. In other alloy steels, nickel can be replaced by varying combinations of molybdenum, chromium, cobalt, vanadium, and columbium, though most substitutes are either inferior or more expensive. In the superalloy sector, cobalt-based alloys are superior to but have recently been far more expensive than nickel-based alloys.

Iron-based superalloys are inferior to but cheaper than nickel-based super-

TABLE 35-4 Balance of Supply and Demand for Nickel, 1974 to 1982

	Thousands of tonnes						As a percent of consumption
Year	Refined production	Consumption	Surplus (or deficit)	Net Communist exports*	Implied increase (or decrease) in stocks	Stocks at year end†	
1974	530	550	(20)	10	−10	85	15
1975	510	410	100	15	+115	200	49
1976	550	495	55	15	+70	270	55
1977	520	460	60	15	+75	345	75
1978	420	510	(90)	30	−60	285	56
1979	465	585	(120)	40	−80	205	35
1980	535	530	5	40	+45	250	47
1981	490	470	20	35	+55	305	49
1982	390	435	(45)	30	−15	290	66

*Exports to the West minus imports from the West.

†ContiCommodity Research Division estimates.

SOURCE: World Bureau of Metal Statistics.

alloys. Cobalt and chromium may be used as substitutes for nickel in plating but are not expected to make inroads into nickel usage unless there is a physical shortage of nickel.

Overall nickel can be expected to hold its own in most end uses, with large-scale substitution of other metals occurring only when there is a physical shortage of nickel that puts processors in the position of deciding whether to close down their plants or use a substitute for nickel. See Table 35-4 for a breakdown of the balance in supply and demand for nickel.

SEASONAL TENDENCIES

In July and August there is some curtailment of activity at nickel refineries and production levels usually fall. This decrease is expected by the market and usually has no effect on the price.

The major consuming industries of alloy steels are also the major market for nickel. These industries are varied, with the result that the demand for nickel tends to level out. For example, whereas there may be cutbacks in the automobile industry during summer vacations, the construction industry is usually working at full capacity in summer to take advantage of good weather conditions.

SUMMARY AND TRADING CONSIDERATIONS

Since the largest consumer of nickel is the steel industry, peaks in nickel consumption coincide with peaks in steel production, especially stainless steel. Statistics on free-world steel production are published monthly by the International Iron and Steel Institute (IISI), and weekly U.S. production figures are published by the American Iron and Steel Institute (AISI). Nickel demand and supply statistics are published monthly by the World Bureau of Metal Statistics and are often reported in the metals press. Unfortunately, because of the small size of the nickel industry the statistics are some months in arrears.

Stainless steel production is notoriously volatile, which makes the level of nickel consumption also very volatile. Wage negotiations at the large nickel plants in Canada take place every 3 years. When the market is in recession and stocks are high, the INCO management tend to take a tough line in wage negotiations, which usually leads to a prolonged strike. INCO uses this strike period to reduce surplus stocks, and nickel prices do tend to rise in anticipation of the strikes. Figure 35-1 gives a London price chart for nickel.

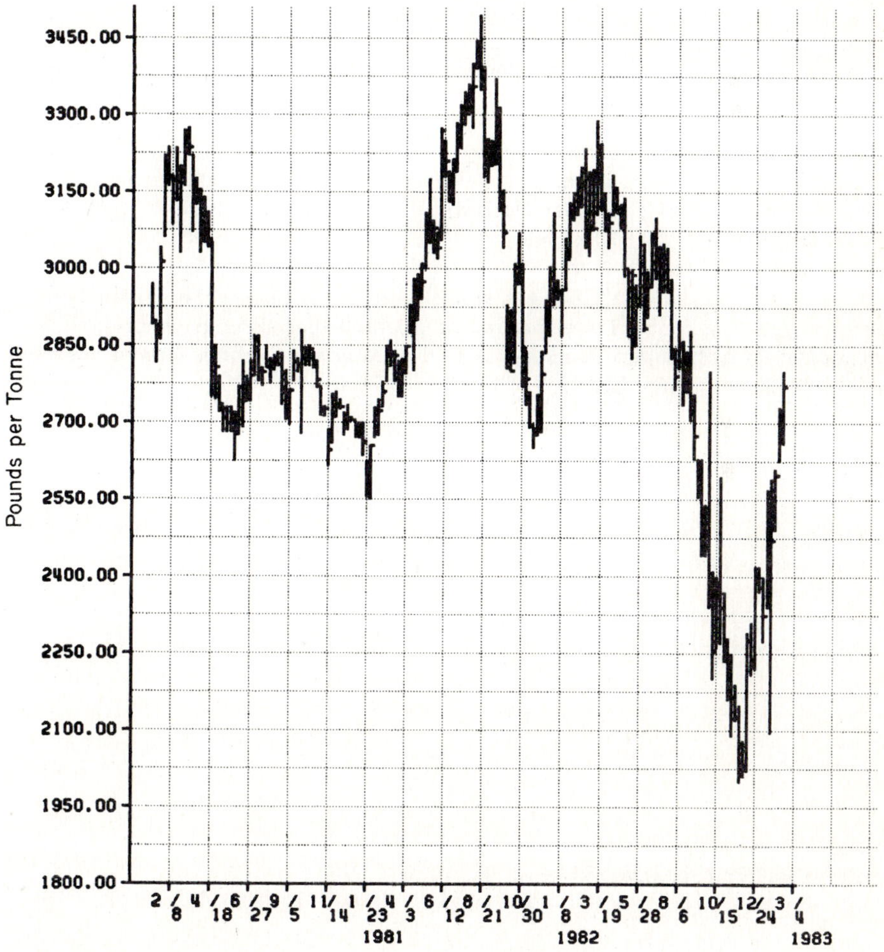

Figure 35-1 Weekly continuation, London Metal Exchange 3-month nickel. *(ContiCommodity Research Division)*

CONTRACT DATA

LME Nickel Specifications

Contract size	6 tonnes (13,288 pounds)
Quotation	Pounds sterling per tonne
Minimum fluctuations	1
Equals per contract	6
Maximum fluctuations	None
Trading position	Cash (for prompt delivery and payment on the day following the transaction)
Settlement	3 months (forward) and any market days between cash and 3 months
Market hours	Differences payable on prompt dates (expiration dates)

Morning	13:00–13:05	12:20–12:25
Official A.M. kerb		13:15–13:25
Afternoon		15:45–15:50
		16:30–16:35
Official P.M. kerb		16:45–16:50

Interoffice trading is permitted outside these hours

At present the LME futures market is often thin, as most major nickel producers have shunned it and will not place their surplus material on LME warrant. However, minor and Communist producers have found the market is a useful medium for disposing of surplus material, especially in recent depressed times.

CHAPTER

36

Lumber and Plywood

Richard Newbury

LUMBER

General Background

In the early 1960s the Chicago Mercantile Exchange (CME) and the Chicago Board of Trade (CBT) began considering lumber and plywood futures contracts and announced that trading would begin in 1969. Feasibility studies and correlation analysis were done. Cash prices were compared to determine species, grades, and dimensions which would correlate well with most other species, grades, and dimensions. It was determined that two-by-fours of white fir, standard, and better grade would be the bellwether item. The contract size was initially set at 40,000 board feet but later was revised three times both to attract speculative interest and to meet industry standards and practices. The trading unit eventually settled upon was 130,000 board feet.

Because of changes in the availability and usage of white fir, other species have been added to the contract. Spruce pine fir (SPF) is now the dominant species. In the early years of trading there were only a limited number of commercial users of the futures, but interest increased and now virtually all lumber producers, wholesalers, and retailers at least investigate hedging even if they do not not actively participate. Price levels, high interest rates, and very large and volatile swings in the cash markets forced commercials to look to futures as a means of managing price risks.

There are thousands of lumber producers in the United States and Canada, ranging in size from small independent stud mills to the huge, integrated operations of such Fortune 500 companies as Weyerhaueser, Boise Cascade, International Paper, and Georgia Pacific. It is interesting to note, however, that the largest producers combined have only a very small percentage of the total output. Lumber is still one of the most competitive of industries.

Because there are many species, grades, and dimensions of lumber as compared with other commodities, it is difficult to determine the direction of any one species at a given time relative to the overall market or to the contract species and grade. For example, SPF, now the dominant species in the futures contract, may be weak because of lack of demand, high inventories or mill production, or both—but Douglas fir of the same grade may be very strong because of mill shutdowns, large exports, or increased housing demand in California (which tends to use a good deal of Douglas fir).

Lumber is a highly complex commodity. Lumber grades in most softwood species include clears; No. 1, No. 2, and so forth; construction; standard and better; utility; and economy. Of these, only the clears and economy would not be readily hedgeable. Other grades of lumber used for industrial purposes and millwork are not hedgeable, nor are cedar, redwood, and hardwoods. Various grading agencies, such as the Western Wood Products Association (WWPA) and the West Coast Lumber Inspection have grading books that include hundreds of pages of rules. In periods of high housing starts, either high prices or lack of availability of lumber can force builders to substitute metal studs, plastic molding, asphalt shingles, metal windows, and so forth. Even so, most people prefer wood for its beauty.

Major Users

The major consumer of lumber is the home-building industry. Other major users are industry, firms that supply materials for remodeling, and the export business. Approximately 40 to 50 percent of lumber production goes into housing. Since housing is the major market, lumber (and plywood) prices respond primarily to the same economic forces that stimulate and depress housing starts, and only secondarily to influences generated by economic growth overseas or changes in dollar exchange rates.

In recent years the do-it-yourself trade has become a major consuming factor. Major firms—Wickes, Lowes, and Payless Cashways, among others—buy hundreds of cars of building materials at a time. Unlike the major wholesalers, these consumers usually buy continuously, rather than buying when they expect prices to go higher. The high cost of new housing has put many first-time buyers out of the market for new homes. Instead, these buyers purchase and fix up older homes. Such remodeling has spurred the growth of the home remodeling industry.

PLYWOOD

Plywood is used primarily for wall, roof, and floor sheathing. Plywood grading is much simpler than lumber grading. The contract grade CDX is the most common grade of sheathing and ½ inch is the most common thickness. Almost half the plywood produced goes into single- and multifamily housing. Other uses include concrete forms, furniture, aircraft and railcar manufacturing, crates, and boxes. Almost 20 billion feet of plywood are expected to be produced each year in the middle 1980s.

Much plywood in both the South and the West is now shipped by truck or is shipped by rail to reload centers. Traditionally, plywood is produced and shipped in one dimension and grade at a time. Reload centers buy these "straight" cars and mix the loads to meet retailer demand.

One of the biggest differences between plywood and lumber is that there are only a few producers of plywood, as compared with the large number of lumber producers. About twenty major U.S. firms produce most of the plywood used in this country. Softwood plywood is produced in Canada as well as in the United States, but there is no export trade to the United States because of tariff restrictions.

Until quite recently, most plywood production was in Western species, primarily Douglas fir, but Southern pine production has grown rapidly and now 30 to 40 percent of plywood now comes from the South. Marketing trends have changed as well. Builders and retailers that used to buy only "fir" plywood now find the price, quality, and availability of Southern plywood not only acceptable but also desirable.

Plywood is somewhat different from lumber in terms of contract grading. Douglas fir or Western plywood competes directly with Southern yellow pine. When one species gets too expensive for delivery, orders are placed for competitive species. Douglas fir is preferred for its quality. Futures correlate very well to yellow pine.

Plywood futures contracts call for a certificate delivery, as contrasted with "on-trade" delivery for lumber. An example is a plywood contract which has been proposed for trading on the Chicago Mercantile Exchange and is being considered by the Commodity Futures Trading Commission (CFTC). This contract calls for "on-trade" delivery. The delivery unit is to be two cars of plywood, or 152,064 square feet. It is believed that the larger contract (the Chicago Board of Trade contract is for 76,052 square feet) will attract more speculative interest. The plywood futures market is a "carrying-charge market," primarily because plywood is a storable commodity. Lumber is usually stored outdoors in separate lengths, dimensions, and species. Plywood, however, is stored in warehouses because of its susceptibility to warping in changeable weather and because it usually arrives at the retail yard in units of one size, grade, and dimension. Plywood futures have been traded as long as lumber futures but have not enjoyed the same popularity as lumber, partly because of the lack of diversity of participants from the cash markets.

Major Market Participants

The major buyers of plywood and lumber futures are the wholesaler and the retailer, but during bull markets the speculator also plays a large role. Because of relatively small volume and open interest, locals are very influential on a day-to-day basis. Wholesalers use the futures both to forward and to speculate, that is, to take uncovered positions in the markets. It is therefore common practice for large wholesalers to buy substantial quantities (100 cars) of cash lumber

Figure 36-1 Monthly continuation, Chicago Mercantile Exchange lumber. *(Conti-Commodity Research Division)*

if they believe that the market will go higher, even though it is not sold ahead. In this way they can increase their inventories without much additional capital. Large retail chains, particularly those that cater to builders, buy futures to lock in costs for materials they have already bid for. They may also be forward pricing to their customers by buying futures in the fall for spring delivery, so that they do not have to carry larger-than-normal inventories over the winter. Figures 36-1 and 36-2 show price charts for lumber and Western plywood.

Producers are the major sellers since it is their desire to lock in a certain basis

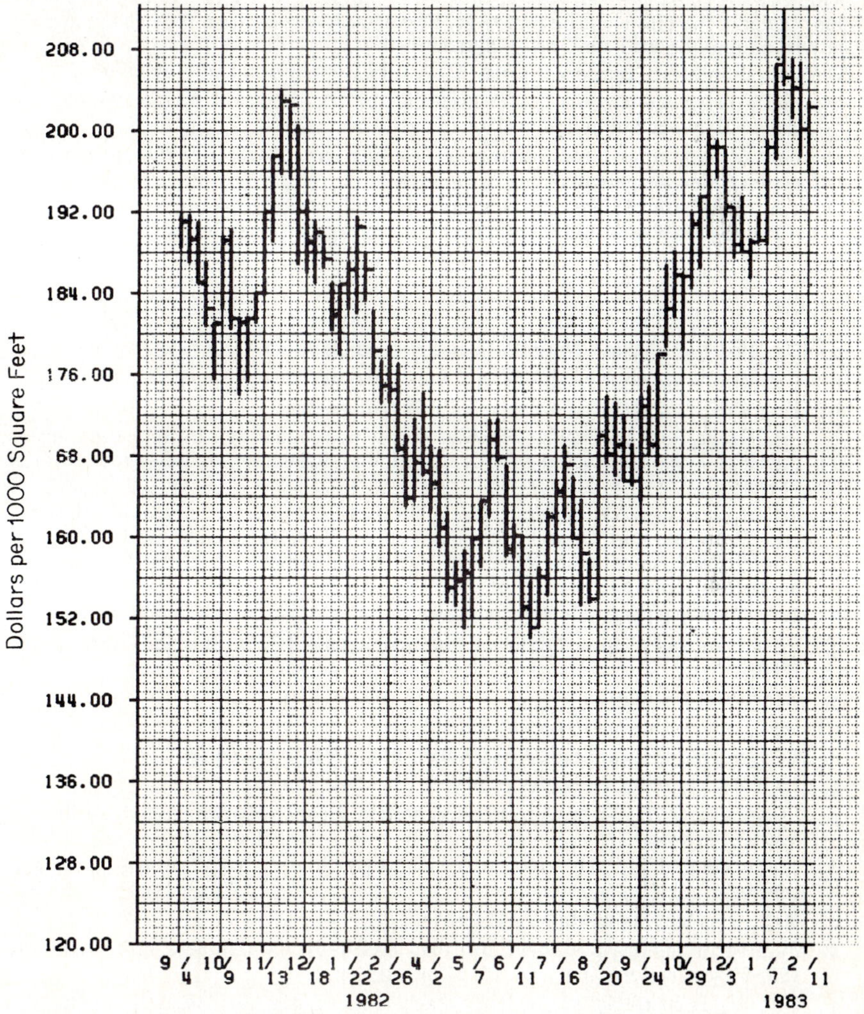

Figure 36-2 Weekly continuation, Chicago Board of Trade western plywood. *(ContiCommodity Research Division)*

level or price that will ensure a profit on some of their production. Wholesalers and retailers can also hedge-sell in order to protect the value of their inventory.

CONTRACT DATA

Lumber

1. The contract calls for delivery of 130,000 board feet of two-by-fours of random length—from 8 to 20 feet. Grade stamp shall be construction and standard, standard and better, or No. 1 or No. 2. Lumber must be manufactured in California, Idaho, Montana, Nevada, Oregon, Washington, or Wyoming, or in Alberta or British Columbia, Canada. Species shall be alpine fir, Englemann spruce, hem fir, lodgepole pine, or spruce-pine fir, and shall be grade-stamped.
2. Delivery months are January, March, May, July, September, and November.
3. Minimum price movements are in multiples of 10¢/thousand. Limits are $5/1000 board feet above or below the previous day's settlement.
4. Delivery is made after termination of the trading period, which is the business day before the sixteenth calendar day of the month.
5. Delivery shall be by flatcar, paper-wrapped. Lumber deliveries are on-track; that is, there are no certificates and warehouses are not regular for delivery.

Plywood

1. *Chicago Board of Trade—New Western Plywood Contract*
   - **a.** 1/2 cdx grade, exterior glue, 4 by 8 feet; four- or five-ply panel.
   - **b.** Unit size: 36 units, 66 pieces each (76,032 square feet).
   - **c.** Price basis: delivery FOB any regular mill or warehouse approved by the Chicago Board of Trade in Washington, Oregon, Idaho, Montana, or California, north of Fresno.
   - **d.** Produced under U.S. product standards PS-1-74. Softwood, plywood, construction, and industrial. Grading of the panels by the testing agencies of the American Plywood Association, Pittsburgh Testing Laboratories, and the Timber Engineering Company.
   - **e.** Deliveries may be made by rail or truck.
   - **f.** Prices are traded in multiples of $10/1000 square feet with a daily limit of $7/1000.
   - **g.** Certificate delivery.
2. *Chicago Mercantile Exchange—Plywood**
   - **a.** 1/2 cdx grade, exterior glue 4 by 8 feet; four- or five-ply panel.
   - **b.** Unit size: 72 units, 66 pieces each (152,064 square feet).
   - **c.** Price basis: FOB mill or warehouse located in Washington, Oregon, or California, north of Fresno.
   - **d.** Produced and graded under same standards and testing facilities as in cost contract.
   - **e.** Deliveries may be made by rail or truck.
   - **f.** Futures prices are traded in 10¢/1000 multiples, with futures unit of trading 150,000 square feet. Daily limit is $7.50/million.
   - **g.** Delivery is on-track; that is, while there is a provision for "tendering," the plywood is not stored but is delivered.

*Trading began August 1981.

h. Storage of the plywood is possible, however, by mutual agreement of buyer and seller.

SOURCES OF INFORMATION

1. *WWPA Basomette.* Production, orders, shipments, unfilled orders, and lumber inventory. Compiled from sawmills reporting to Western Wood Products Association (WWPA).
2. *Weekly FOB Price Summary Past Sales.* Inland mills, WWPA.
3. *Monthly FOB Price Summary Past Sales.* Coast mills, WWPA.
4. *Western Lumber Facts.* WWPA. Monthly industry estimates of production, orders, shipments, unfilled orders and lumber inventory, together with charts among trends of acreage prices received, relationship of orders, unfilled orders, inventory, housing starts, and end-use markets.
5. *Lumber Price Trends.* Inland Mills, WWPA. Reflects the trend of weighted prices for inland species.
6. *Statistical Yearbook.* WWPA.
7. U.S. Department of Agriculture, Forest Service.
8. *Weekly Trade Barometer.* Southern Pine Association (SPA).
9. U.S. Department of Commerce, *Construction Activity.* Value of new construction, by type.
10. *Housing Starts.* U.S. Department of Commerce, Bureau of the Census.
11. *Random Lengths.* Weekly lumber prices.
12. *Crowe's Weekly Digest.* Weekly lumber prices.
13. *F.W. Construction Bulletin.* McGraw-Hill, Inc., 1221 Avenue of the Americas, New York, NY 10020.
14. *Lumber Instant News Wire.* Commodities news service.
15. *Reuter's News Service.*
16. Commodity Research Bureau.
17. *Plywood Statistics* and *Monthly Market Report.* American Plywood Association (APA).

CHAPTER

37

Heating Oil

Thomas Bell, Brian Singer, and Steven Gilson

INTRODUCTION

Trading in No. 2 heating oil futures began on the New York Mercantile Exchange (NYME) in November 1978 and gained popularity rapidly. In addition, a London gas-oil and heating oil contract opened in April 1981, and a Gulf Coast delivery contract was approved in summer 1981 to trade on the NYME. Gasoline contracts also are now traded in the United States and are being studied in London, suggesting that the industry believes the energy futures market has begun. A liquid propane futures contract is occasionally traded on the New York Cotton Exchange. As a result of the extreme volatility of energy prices in the past decade, heating oil futures trading is particularly well suited to the needs and wants of hedgers and speculators alike. This chapter will review the crude oil situation, assess heating oil supply and demand, and offer an outlook on the relationship between political and economic developments and heating oil prices.

WORLD CRUDE OIL SITUATION

The Organization of Petroleum Exporting Countries (OPEC) was formed during the 1960s as a countercartel to the "seven sisters" (British Petroleum, Shell, Exxon, Gulf, Calso, Texaco, and Mobil). OPEC immediately demonstrated its potential by successfully rescinding the price reductions desired by the seven sisters. However, not until the 70¢/barrel price increase and supply cutbacks of 1973 did OPEC evince the full strength of its position in the oil world. Prices have since risen dramatically, placing a tremendous strain on the world economic situation. OPEC revenue more than tripled in less than 4 months in 1973 and 1974, helping to create a worldwide recession, together with a subsequent decline in the demand for oil. By 1977 the oil market was slack and production was only at approximately two-thirds of capacity. As the subsequent global recovery gained momentum, crude oil supplies once again became tight and oil prices again rose. Table 37-1 shows OPEC petroleum prices from 1964 to 1982.

By the early 1980s, this series of sharp increases in the price of oil had encouraged a significant amount of exploration and conservation of oil, leading to substantial overcapacity of crude oil production facilities. By 1982 only significant production cutbacks by OPEC and a disruption of supplies due to the Iran-Iraq war were sustaining oil prices at a high level relative to almost all other commodities. In 1982 another worldwide recession and global crude oil destocking reduced demand, forcing OPEC to decrease the benchmark price of Saudi light oil to $29 per barrel from $34 per barrel. Unless some unforeseen political or military event in the Middle East destroys a substantial portion of the world's oil production facilities, it is unlikely that the 1980s will witness the kind of oil price explosion that occurred in the 1970s.

Studying actual figures will help to make clear the trends discussed above: Table 37-2 summarizes world crude oil production from 1977 to 1982. Table 37-3 shows the sources of energy consumed in the United States in 1980 and 1981. Table 37-4 shows oil supply and consumption in the free world from 1977 to 1982. Table 37-5 shows average quarterly imports of crude oil by the United States from 1977 to 1983.

TABLE 37-1 OPEC Petroleum Prices, 1964 to 1982
(In current dollars per barrel)

Year	Price
1964–1970	$ 1.30
1971	1.70
1972	1.90
1973	2.70
1974	11.20
1975	10.90
1976	11.70
1977	12.80
1978	12.90
1979	18.60
1980	30.50
1981	34.30
1982	33.50
1983	29.80*

*ContiCommodity Research Division estimate.

TABLE 37-2 World Crude Oil Production, 1977 to 1982
(In millions of barrels per day)

Area	1977	1978	1979	1980	1981	1982
OPEC						
Saudi Arabia	9.2	8.8	9.5	10.0	9.9	6.3
Kuwait	2.0	2.1	2.5	1.6	1.4	0.7
Iran	5.7	5.2	3.1	1.55	1.4	2.0
Iraq	2.5	2.6	3.4	2.7	0.8	0.9
United Arab Emirates	2.0	1.8	1.8	1.7	1.5	1.8
Qatar	0.4	0.5	0.5	0.5	0.4	0.3
Venezuela	2.2	2.2	2.4	2.2	2.1	1.9
Nigeria	2.1	1.9	2.3	2.1	1.4	1.3
Libya	2.1	2.0	2.1	1.8	1.2	1.1
Indonesia	1.7	1.6	1.6	1.6	1.6	1.3
Algeria	1.7	1.2	1.2	1.1	0.8	0.7
Gabon	0.2	0.2	0.2	0.2	0.2	0.2
Ecuador	0.2	0.2	0.2	0.2	0.2	0.2
Total OPEC*	31.4	30.3	30.8	27.25	22.9	18.4
Free world						
United States	8.2	8.7	8.5	8.6	8.6	8.6
North Sea Oil Field	1.1	1.5	2.0	2.2	2.3	2.7
Mexico	1.0	1.2	1.6	1.9	2.4	2.7
Oman	0.3	0.3	0.3	0.3	0.3	0.3
Other	4.9	5.1	4.9	5.2	5.4	5.5
Total	15.5	16.8	17.3	18.2	19.0	19.9
Total free world*	46.9	47.1	48.1	45.45	41.19	41.5
Communist block						
Soviet Union	10.9	11.2	11.8	12.1	11.8	11.9
Other eastern Europe	0.4	0.4	0.4	0.4	0.4	0.4
China	1.8	2.0	2.1	2.1	2.0	2.0
Total*	13.1	13.6	14.3	14.0	14.2	14.3
Total world*	60.0	60.7	62.4	60.05	56.0	55.9

*Any discrepancies in totals are caused by rounding.

SOURCES: *Petroleum Intelligence Weekly*, *Petroleum Economist*, and American Petroleum Institute.

TABLE 37-3 Sources of Energy in the United States, 1980 and 1981
(In trillions of BTU)

Energy source	1980	1981*
Oil	34,100	31,987
Natural gas	20,495	20,119
Coal	15,553	16,109
Hydrothermal and geothermal	3,229	3,146
Nuclear	2,704	2,957
Total	76,081	74,318

*Preliminary estimates.

SOURCE: Independent Petroleum Association of America.

TABLE 37-4 Free-World Oil Supply and Consumption, 1977 to 1980
(In millions of barrels per day)

Year	Production	Other*	Supply	Consumption	Stock change
1977	46.9	2.4	49.3	49.5	−0.2
1978	47.1	1.9	49.0	51.0	−2.0
1979	48.1	3.2	51.3	51.3	—
1980	45.5	4.1	49.6	49.3	+0.3

*Other includes Communist imports and natural gas liquids production.

SOURCES: *Petroleum Economist, Oil Buyers Guide, and British Petroleum Statistical Review.*

TABLE 37-5 U.S. Quarterly Average Crude Oil Imports, 1977 to 1981
(In millions of barrels per day)

Period	1977	1978	1979	1980	1981	1982	1983
First quarter	6.4	5.8	6.4	6.0	4.8	3.2	2.4
Second quarter	6.8	5.6	6.1	5.2	4.1	3.1	3.1
Third quarter	6.6	6.4	6.5	4.9	3.4	3.8	3.9
Fourth quarter	6.1	6.9	6.4	4.8	3.9	3.4	
Year average	6.5	6.2	6.4	5.2	4.0	3.4	

SOURCE: American Petroleum Institute.

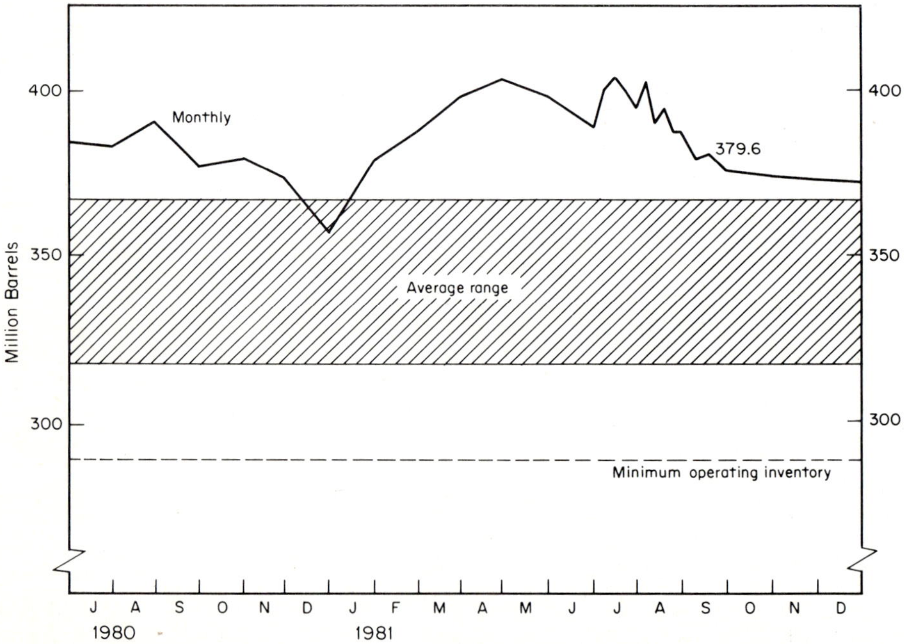

Figure 37-1 Stocks of crude oil, U.S. total. *(U.S. Department of Energy)*

REFINERY CAPACITY

Large oil companies have turned to refinery operation for the majority of their income. In late 1981 refinery capacity responded to oversupply, and North American refineries were operating at about 66 percent of capacity. In comparison, capacity utilization was 75 percent in 1980 and 85 percent in 1979. This is important because of the relative inflexibility of refinery operations. The product yield curve of a refinery operation dictates that limited volumes of each product can be distilled. A barrel of crude oil when refined yields approximately 45 percent gasoline, 20 percent distillate fuel (of which home heating oil is the largest component), 12 percent residual fuel, 6 percent jet fuel, and 17 percent assorted petrochemical products. Refiners can alter their yield, but only slightly, to produce a bit more of a product that is in season. For example, a refiner will produce more gasoline during the summer at the expense of distillates (heating oil), by using sophisticated cracking facilities. Figure 37-1 shows U.S. total stocks of crude oil in 1980 and 1981.

Several further considerations, which will not be discussed at length in this chapter but which are worthy of mention because of their probable impacts on the market, are:

1. The rate of U.S. crude oil production is brought on by higher prices or may result from decontrol. Drilling rigs in place are a good indicator of future production.
2. The U.S. Strategic Petroleum Reserve (SPR) capacity is 750,000 million barrels. Currently the SPR holds 355.7 million barrels and the filling rate is 250,000 barrels per day.
3. When oil companies draw down inventories, the number of tankers carrying oil typically increases dramatically.
4. Natural gas prices are being decontrolled in the United States.
5. Most oil company profits are made in refinery operations, and examination of growth and net margins as well as overall balance sheet performance aids in market analysis.

DISTILLATE FUELS

Distillate fuels include No. 2 heating oil, No. 1 and No. 4 fuel oils, and diesel fuels. No. 2 oil is the largest component. No. 4 oil is used for industrial operations. Distillate stocks are very seasonal, primarily because of demand for heating oil, as shown in Figures 37-2 and 37-3 and Table 37-6.

USERS OF FUTURES MARKETS

Fuel Oil Distributors

Fuel oil distributors have an inventory risk because of uncertain supply and the seasonality of demand for No. 2 heating oil. As a result, they build up stocks during the late summer months in anticipation of high fall and winter demand.

TABLE 37-6 Supply of and Demand for Distillate Fuel Oil, 1977 to 1982
(In thousands of 42-gallon barrels)

Year	Beginning stocks	Daily average production	Daily average imports	Average daily disappearance	Ending stocks	Days of supply†
1977–1978*	247,079	3,140	131	3,353	217,570	65
1978–1979*	217,570	3,194	178	3,340	230,771	69
1979–1980*	230,771	2,849	157	3,003	210,587	77
1980–1981*	232,079		145	2,891	210,587	73
1981–1982*	210,587	2,602‡	104‡	2,823‡	167,505‡	59‡
1977–1978						
Oct.–Mar.	247,079	3,146	146	3,894	137,564	35
Apr.–Sept.	137,564	3,134	117	2,812	217,570	77
1978–1979						
Oct–Mar.	217,570	3,193	170	3,940	113,908	29
Apr.–Sept.	113,908	3,196	185	2,739	230,771	84
1979–1980						
Oct.–Mar.	230,771	3,032	214	3,546	176,082	50
Apr.–Sept.	176,083	2,666	101	2,459	232,079	94
1980–1981						
Oct.–Mar.	232,079	2,805	115	3,303	162,414	49
Apr.–Sept.	162,414	2,566	175	2,479	209,978	85
1981–1982						
Oct.–Mar.	210,587	2,559†	121‡	3,147‡	125,645‡	40‡
Apr.–Sept.	125,645‡	2,644†	86‡	2,500‡	167,505‡	67‡

*October to September.

†One day of supply equals stocks ÷ disappearance.

‡ContiCommodity Research Division estimates.

A viable futures market gives a distributor the ability to predetermine demand to a great extent by entering into a future supply agreement with a local school board or hospital at a fixed price and then hedging this transaction with a long position in the futures market. Not only does this hedging possibility allow distributors to lock in adequate operating profits, but also it gives them the opportunity to reduce their need for cash financing during periods of low demand.

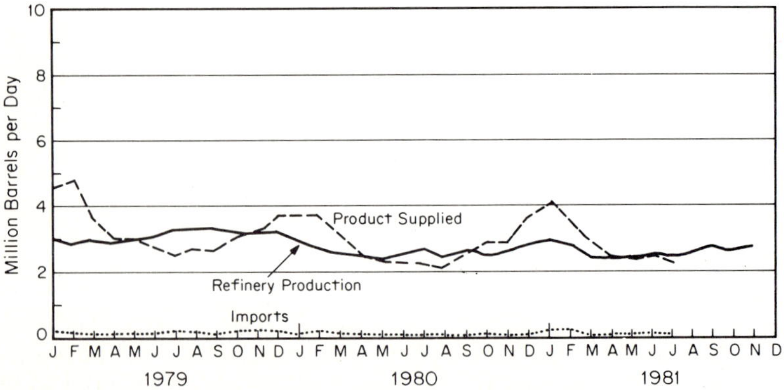

Figure 37-2 Distillate fuel. *(U.S. Department of Energy)*

Refiners

Before 1973, refiners entered into long-term oil delivery contracts based on a specified price. Long-term agreements are still used, but the majority of contracts do not have a stipulated price. Rather, the price remains negotiable until delivery time, when an agreement must be reached. It is obvious that under such circumstances the refiner is at the mercy of short- and long-term price fluctuations in the price of oil. On the futures market, however, a refiner can hedge against falls in refined product prices by selling futures contracts at a fixed price. Such contracts deny refiners additional profits if supplies tighten, but they do have the advantage of letting refiners know their refining margin in advance.

Jobbers

Jobbers perform the wholesale function within the petroleum distribution network. They receive shipments of refined products by truck or rail from refineries or terminals, and then redistribute the products by tank truck to large commercial accounts, home owners, farms, and gasoline stations. Jobbers, who are quite vulnerable to movement in the price of oil, can utilize the futures markets to execute either a buyer's or a seller's hedge.

Example—Buyer's Hedge. On November 1 a jobber enters into a supply agreement to deliver 10,000 barrels of heating oil on February 1 at a price of $1.10/gallon. The pricing decision is based on:

Spot	$ .95	(November 1)
Carry	.06	(3 months at 2¢/month)
Profit	.09	(Gross margin)
Price	$1.10	

To hedge this margin, the jobber buys 100 February contracts of No. 2 heating oil on November 1 at a price of $1.01. On January 1 the jobber buys 100,000

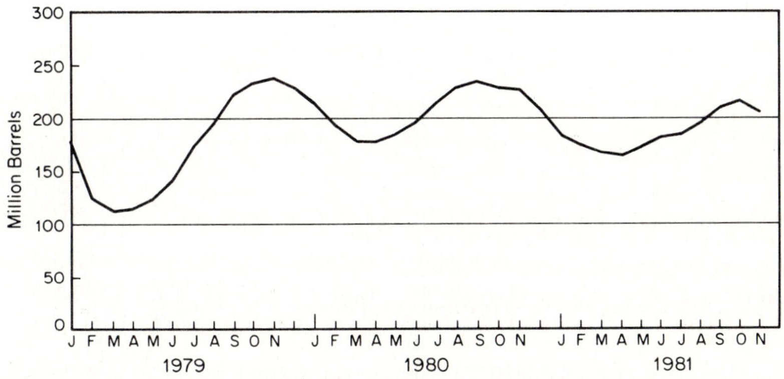

Figure 37-3 Stocks of distillate fuel. *(U.S. Department of Energy)*

barrels of heating oil on the spot market for the February 1 delivery commitment at $1.15 and at the same time liquidates the 100 futures contracts at $1.16.

	Spot	Futures
November 1		
Agrees to deliver product on February 1 at $1.10/gallon	$4,620,000	
Buys 100 February contracts at $1.01/gallon		$4,242,000
January 1		
Purchases heating oil at $1.15/gallon	4,830,000	
Sells 100 February contracts at $1.16/gallon		4,872,000
Loss	210,000	
Gain		630,000
Net gain		$420,000

Although the jobber paid more than expected for No. 2 heating oil, this loss was offset by a profit on the futures transactions, thereby protecting the gross margin and in this case making a profit as well.

Primary metal, chemical, and textile industries, which are large consumers of fuel oils, could also make use of the futures market to reduce their costs. Since contracts for heating oil seldom include a price provision, owners of

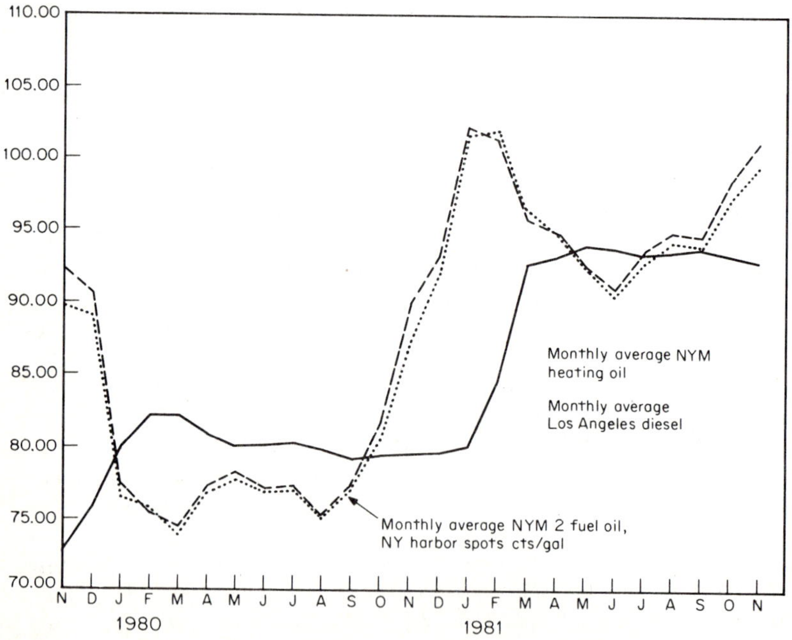

Figure 37-4 Price of heating oil, fuel oil, and diesel, 1980 to 1981.

apartment buildings, especially in the Northeastern United States, have to compete with everyone else in the cash market for supplies. The petroleum futures market offers these landlords, who use large quantities of heating oil, a hedging opportunity.

A tremendous opportunity exists for cross-hedging heating oil with other distillates. There is a reasonable correlation between jet fuel (spot Gulf Coast prices) and heating oil (spot New York prices). Since jet fuel consumption in the continental United States runs about 33.3 million barrels a year, opportunities for hedging could be substantial.

The correlation between prices of diesel fuel and heating oil is also close, as shown in Figure 37-4. Farmers and trucking companies sometimes run their vehicles with No. 2 heating oil, which can be substituted for diesel fuel. Thus, not only trucking companies but also large moving companies and bus lines could use the futures market to help offset rising costs of operation.

HEATING OIL

Heating oil, also known in Europe as gas-oil, represents between 20 and 30 percent of the total product mix obtained from refining a barrel of crude oil. This percentage can vary from 5 to 7 percent, depending upon the type of crude oil and the market requirements. Since heating oil is a derivative of crude oil, its price behavior is largely supply-oriented and is therefore affected by fluctuations in the availability of crude oil. The demand for heating oil is also an influential price determinant. The physical characteristics of heating oil make it suitable for use as a domestic and industrial fuel, as a chemical feed stock, and as a substitute for diesel fuel.

Recent Industry Changes

In the wake of the oil crisis of 1973 to 1974, the Iranian Revolution of 1978, and the more recent Gulf war, it is obvious that the oil supply cannot be guaranteed. These events have brought about a fundamental change in the way the petroleum industry conducts its business.

The major change has been a reduction in the domination of the petroleum industry by the major multinational oil companies. This domination has been replaced by direct producer and government control, and the most significant result has been the rise of the powerful oil cartel, OPEC. The effect has been to reduce the security of supply, which in turn leads to much greater price volatility in the world market for crude oil and related products.

During the preembargo days, the most profitable aspect of the oil industry was exploration and production. At that time, U.S. import quotas kept out cheap foreign oil. In addition, government programs such as depletion allowances and tax incentives made the production of crude oil enormously profitable. This system worked well for oil producers and equally well for jobbers and distributors. Oil companies, through their refinery operations, were able to absorb normal fluctuations in volume incurred by distributors. If distributors purchased too much oil, the oil companies would buy it back; conversely, a shortfall in supply was easily made up by the oil companies, with little or no penalty charge to distributors. This system allowed small jobbers to reduce their inventory risks.

By 1975, however, the major oil companies were forced to reassess their methods of doing business. One effect of the embargo was the lifting of import quotas; government subsidy programs were curtailed and domestic wells were working at capacity. In this climate, oil companies became less and less willing to allow small distributors to hedge their inventory without cost. As a result, distributors faced an inventory risk exposure that had been previously unknown.

While all these changes were taking place, wholesalers and independents were not sitting idly by, wondering who was going to bail them out; they also began to adjust and to turn their attention to the activity of the spot oil market. Some shrewd dealers became wholesale oil traders. Through daily contact with other dealers, they came to know who had too much inventory and who was in need. In response to this market activity, the New York Mercantile Exchange began trading a No. 2 heating oil futures contract in fall 1978. Early in 1981, the International Petroleum Exchange in London began trading a gas-oil contract.

Since 1974 there has been a shift in the role of the major oil companies away from distributing the products they produce. At present, independent, small, and medium-size jobbers handle about 50 percent of all distribution in the continental United States. Consequently, a great many distributors have an inventory risk exposure that they can hedge in only two ways. A distributor can either (1) enter the cash forward market or (2) buy or sell futures against inventory. Many distributors are still using the cash forward market to secure their inventories. Although this market functions well, opportunities and options in the futures market make the No. 2 heating oil futures contract very attractive. The futures market possesses a liquidity that the cash forward market lacks. It allows distributors to purchase forward their inventory, using only a fraction of the money required to purchase the forward contract. Finally, the futures option allows distributors to buy in either the cash or the futures market, depending on which offers the greatest profit potential.

Because of the volatility of petroleum prices since 1976, the heating oil futures contract is well suited to the needs of hedgers and speculators alike.

TABLE 37-7 Heating Degree-Days in New York City, as Measured in Central Park, 1977 to 1982

Month	1977–1978	1978–1979	1979–1980	1980–1981	Normal	1981–1982
October	307	311	271	305	209	320
November	524	510	373	602	528	495
December	903	802	734	1,000	915	883
January	1,140	969	963	1,194	1,017	1,224
February	1,051	1,100	969	715	885	
March	797	554	731	698	741	
Total	4,722	4,246	4,041	4,514	4,295	2,922

TABLE 37-8 Average Daily Disappearance of Distillate Fuel in the United States, 1977 to 1982 *(of 42-gallon barrels)*

Period	1977–1978	1978–1979	1979–1980	1980–1981	1981–1982
October to March	3874	3940	3546	3303	3089

Consumption

Weather affects the supply of most commodities, especially grains, but the opposite is true of heating oil—weather affects demand. (See Figure 37-3.) Heating oil usage shows a very strong seasonal pattern. Peak consumption occurs and stock levels are drawn down during the fall and winter; demand eases and stocks build up from spring through early fall. It follows that the more severe the winter, the greater the demand on existing stocks. To fully understand and measure the severity of a winter, it is necessary to be familiar with the concept of "heating degree-days." Heating degree-days are the number of degrees the daily average temperature is below 65°F. Heating is not normally required in a building when the outdoor average daily temperature is 65°F or above. A heating degree-day is determined by subtracting the average daily temperature from 65°F. Therefore, a day with an average temperature of 50°F has 15 heating degree-days.

The winter of 1980 to 1981 was much colder than the 1979 to 1980 winter. Using New York City as a basis, the 1980 to 1981 winter had 473 more heating degree-days than the previous winter, or an increase of 11.7 percent (see Table 37-7). The result should have been a corresponding increase in consumption, but that was not the case. Consumption during the winter of 1980 to 1981, as measured by distillate disappearance, was 7 percent lower than the year before. (See Table 37-8.) Consumption during the winter of 1979 to 1980 was 10 percent lower than 1978 to 1979 levels, and their trend continued into the 1980 to 1981 and the 1981 to 1982 heating seasons. The reasons cited for this trend are that a great many people are switching to other forms of heating, such as gas, and that programs to encourage improvements in home insulation and reduction in unnecessary oil consumption have largely worked. Consequently, the well-established linear relationships of previous years appear to be much less reliable indicators of either consumption or price movement than in the past.

Price Analysis

Any reliable forecast of heating oil prices is dependent first upon the price of crude oil. The crude oil price, in turn, is determined by underlying supply and demand factors, as well as by world political tensions, which can affect the supply of crude oil to consuming markets.

Information on the distillate components taken as a group, coupled with the supply-demand situation of heating oil in particular, serves as a guide to actual price projections. Even so, the complexity of the relationships makes forecasting extremely difficult.

For example, the forecast heating degree-days, the stocks of distillate fuel relative to the previous week and previous year, the industry rate of production expressed as a percentage of rated capacity, and the inherent seasonality of heating oil prices must be considered together for a short-term projection. The degree-day forecast must be compared with the normal level for the time of year in order to obtain an indication of potential demand in relation to normal consumption. Stocks and production figures give an indication of the ability and willingness of the refining industry to meet excess demand in an exceptionally cold winter. A low production rate suggests that the industry could easily meet such excess demand, which would alleviate any potential supply problems, whereas a high rate of production would indicate an inability to meet such demand, even at higher price levels.

Finally, the seasonal pattern of heating oil prices provides the "pointer." If the seasonal pattern at the time of year being examined favors lower prices during a period of potential supply problems, the forecast price direction may not develop on schedule, since seasonals are then counter to the actual equilibrium relationship. However, depending upon the urgency of the short-term demand requirements, the seasonal pattern, rather than being overcome by supply and demand considerations, may simply negate the counteracting

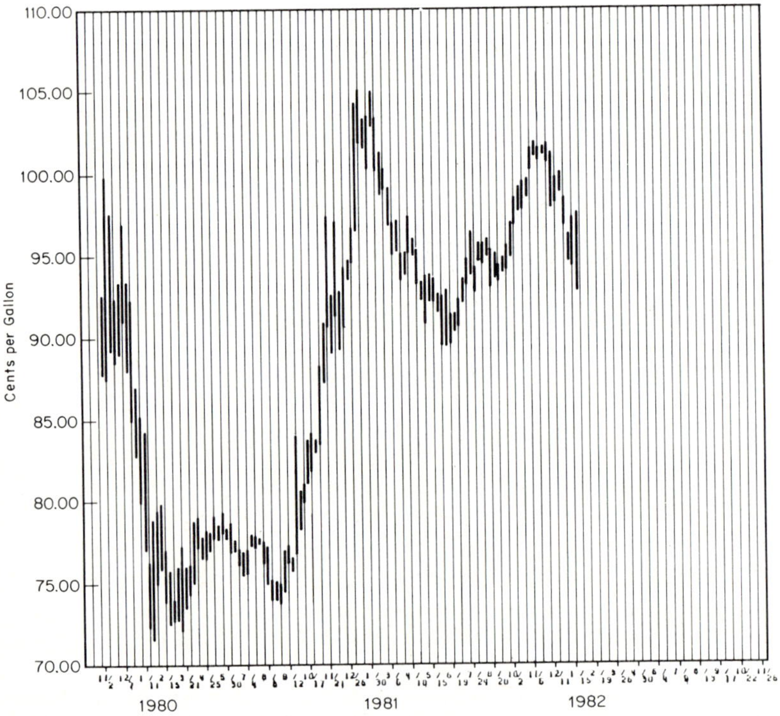

Figure 37-5 Weekly continuation, New York Mercantile Exchange heating oil, 1980 to 1983. *(ContiCommodity Research Division)*

effects of the supply squeeze, resulting in little or no price movement to the up side. A price forecast is much more credible therefore if the seasonals and the supply and demand considerations are in agreement. A decision to take a position on either side of the market should be made only after careful consideration of all these factors.

SUMMARY AND TRADING CONSIDERATIONS

Crucial trading considerations for the energy sector are summarized below. Also see Figures 37-5 to 37-8 for historical price charts.

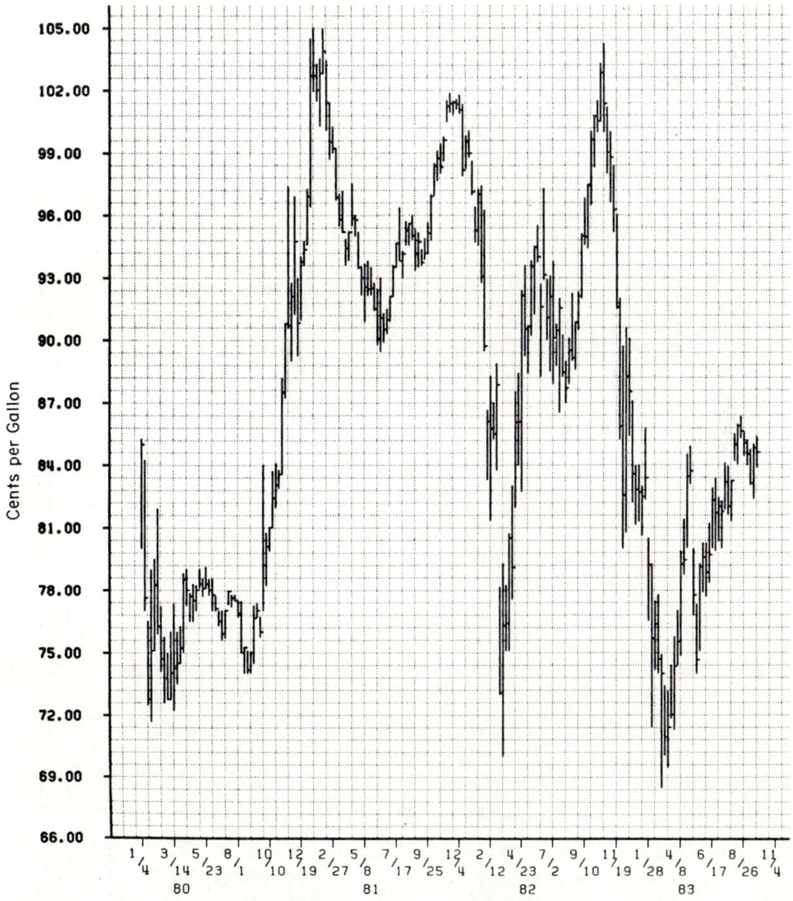

Figure 37-6 Weekly continuation, New York cash heating oil, 1973 to 1983. *(ContiCommodity Research Division)*

1. Critical factors affecting the heating oil supply-demand relationship:
   a. American Petroleum Institute (API) weekly trading figures (published in *The Wall Street Journal*)
   b. Winter temperatures and the subsequent effect on oil demand
   c. Political occurrences and uncertainties
   d. OPEC pricing and production decisions
   e. Overall world and U.S. economic considerations
2. Leading indicators of heating oil price trends:
   It is a bullish sign when nearby options rise at a faster rate than distant contracts, and vice versa.

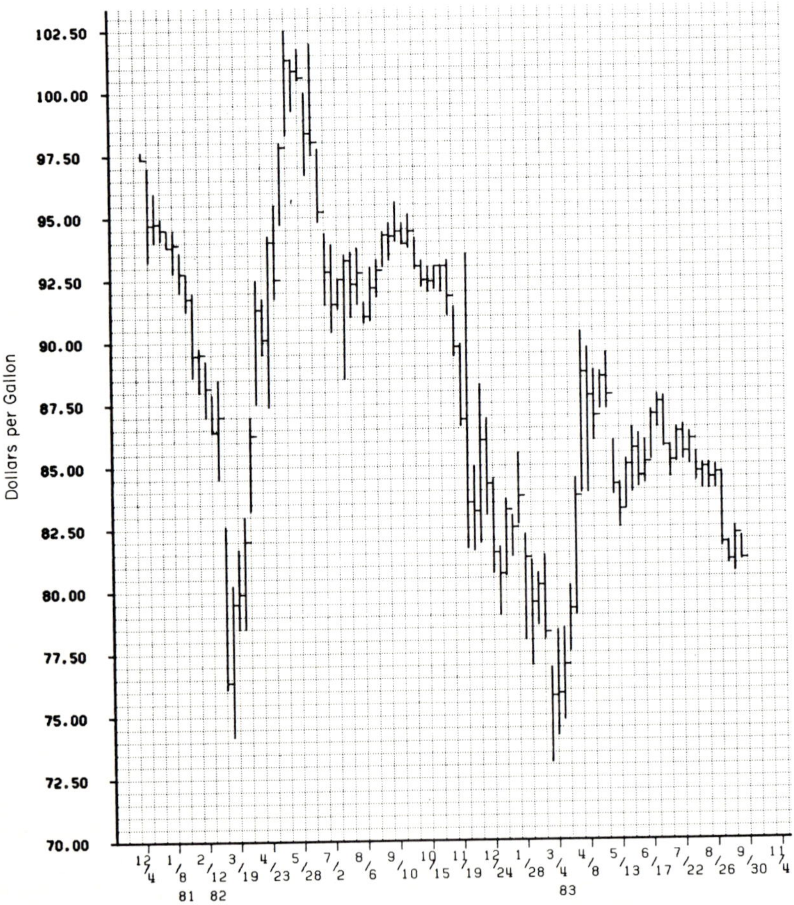

Figure 37-7 Weekly continuation, New York Mercantile Exchange leaded gas, 1981 to 1983. *(ContiCommodity Research Division)*

3. Important factors to consider:
   a. Be aware of first notice day (FND) and related price volatility.
   b. Be aware of seasonals.
   c. Avoid trading contract months with a small open interest.

CONTRACT DATA

Propane

Contract unit	42,000 U.S. gallons (1000 U.S. barrels)
Delivery point	Mont Belvieu, Texas (near Houston) Group 145, Conway, Kansas
Price quotation	Dollars and cents per gallon
Minimum daily price fluctuation	\$0.0001 (0.01¢) per gallon (equivalent to \$4.20/contract unit)

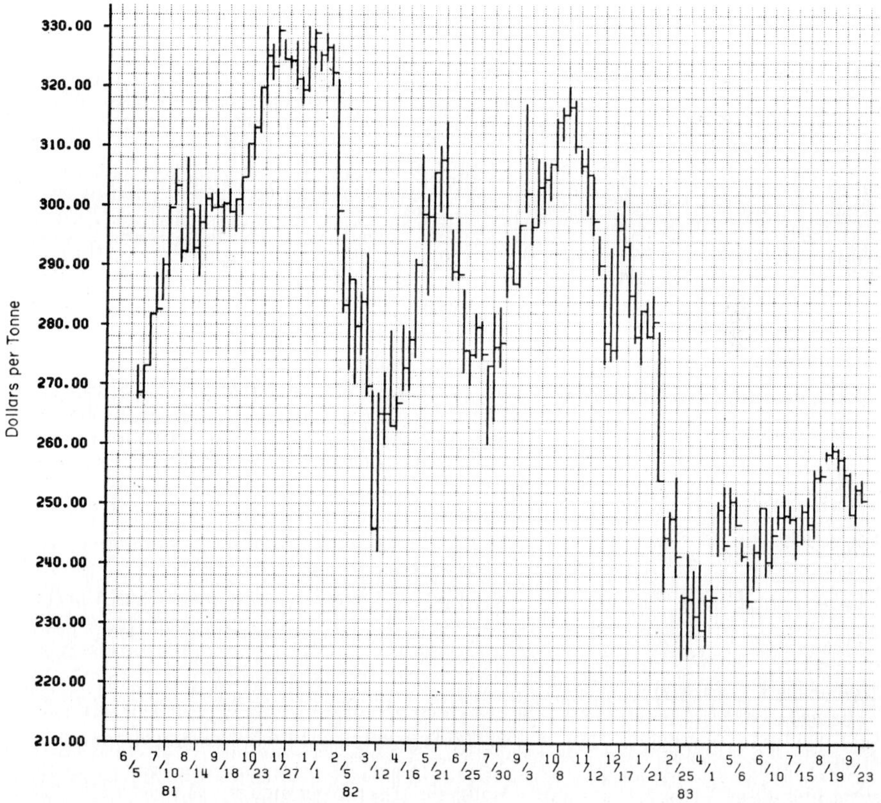

Figure 37-8 Weekly continuation, New York Mercantile Exchange gas oil, 1981 to 1983. *(ContiCommodity Research Division)*

Maximum daily price fluctuation	$0.03 (3¢)
Traded month	The current month and the 11 succeeding months
Trading hours	9:45 A.M. to 2:35 P.M., New York time, Monday through Friday
Product specification	Liquefied propane gas meeting the specification of NGPA-HW-5 (National Gas Producers Association publication 2140-68) effective January 1, 1968, or any subsequent revision thereof in effect at the date of the tender for delivery in the contract
Notice day	Five business days before the delivery date
Delivery day	The first business day of the contract month
Last trading day	The last business day prior to the notice day for the contract month

New York No. 2 Heating Oil

Contract unit	42,000 U.S. gallons (1000 U.S. barrels)
Delivery Point	New York Harbor
Price quotation	Dollars and cents per gallon
Minimum daily price fluctuation	$0.0001 (0.01¢)/gallon (equivalent to $4.20/contract unit)
Maximum daily price fluctuation	$0.02 (2¢); no limit during the month preceding the delivery month; subject to expanded limit rules (The maximum daily price limit is equivalent to $840/contract.)

IPE Gas-Oil

Contract unit	100 tonnes
Price quotation	U.S. dollars and cents per tonne
Minimum daily price fluctuation	25¢ tonne (equivalent to $25 per contract)
Maximum daily price fluctuation	U.S. $30/tonne above or below the previous day's close (equivalent to $3000/contract), after which trading shall cease for 30 minutes before reopening without limits for the rest of the trading day
Traded months	Nine consecutive months, commencing 1 month forward
Trading hours	9:30 to 12:30 and 14:45 to 17:15, London time, Monday through Friday
Delivery point	Amsterdam, Rotterdam, or Antwerp (ARA area)

Unleaded Gasoline

Contract unit	42,000 U.S. gallons (1000 U.S. barrels)
Delivery point	New York Harbor
Price quotation	Dollars and cents per gallon
Minimum daily price fluctuation	$0.0001 (0.01¢)/gallon (equivalent to $4.20/contract unit

Maximum daily price fluctuation	$0.02 (2¢)/gallon; no limit during the month preceding the delivery month (The maximum daily price fluctuation is equivalent to $840/contract for all contracts other than spot.)
Delivery month	All months
Product specification	

	Unleaded regular	Leaded regular
Octane (average)	87.0% minimum	89.0% minimum
Color	Undyed	Dyed yellow or bronze
Lead	0.04 gram/gallon	4.00 grams/gallon
Gravity	30° minimum	30° minimum
Corrosion	1 maximum	1 maximum
Doctor	Negative	Negative
Mercaptan sulfur	10 parts per million	10 parts per million

Both contracts	Class*
December, January, and February	E
March, April, October, and November	D
May and September	B
June, July, and August	C

	Class C			
Distillation	B	C	D	E
Evaporation, percent, (°F maximum)				
10	149	140	131	122
50	170	170	170	170
50	245	240	235	230
90	375	365	365	365
End point (°F maximum)	430	430	430	430
Reid vapor pressure Pounds maximum	10	11.5	13.5	14.5

*Class refers to vapor pressure. Vapor pressure varies in usage according to weather and area.

SOURCES OF INFORMATION

American Petroleum Institute Publications

Weekly Statistical Bulletin
Monthly Statistical Bulletin
Monthly Report of Heating Oil and Other Distillates

Contact: American Petroleum Institute, 2101 L Street, N.W., Washington, DC 20037

Oil Buyers' Guide

A weekly publication covering petroleum industry news, price trends, inventory situations, and so forth, concentrating mostly upon domestic markets.

Contact: Oil Buyers' Guide, P.O. Box 998, Lakewood, NJ 08701

Petroleum Intelligence Weekly

A weekly publication concentrating on international petroleum market developments.

Contact: Petroleum Intelligence Weekly, 1 Times Square Plaza, New York, NY 10036

Platt's Petroleum Series

Platt's Oil Gram Price Report. *Detailed daily information.*
Platt's Oil Price Handbook & Almanac. *Annual detailed price summary*
[*Data Resources, Inc. (DRI) has monthly updates available.*]

Contact: McGraw-Hill, Inc., 1221 Avenue of the Americas, New York, NY 10020

PART

6

Technical Analysis

CHAPTER

38

Technical versus Fundamental Analysis

Martin J. Pring

INTRODUCTION

Fundamental analysis is concerned with an appraisal of the goods in which the market deals. Technical analysis is a study of the action of the market itself. In fundamental analysis, described in Parts 1 to 5 of this handbook, the investor, speculator, or analyst tries to assess the interaction of the various components of the demand-and-supply relationship and their probable effect on future prices. For the technician, the problem with fundamental analysis is that no analyst, however adept and knowledgeable, can possibly know everything about the fundamentals of a specific financial market or commodity—nor is the technician in a position to assess the knowledge, hopes, fears, and psychological makeup of the various market participants, since these can change from day to day as new information becomes available.

Technical analysis studies the action of the market itself. Therefore it assumes that all the factors that influence all market participants are reflected in the price of a commodity. The technician does not need to know that a poor Russian grain crop is pushing up the price of grains, for this is reflected in the technical structure of the grain charts. Knowing that all possible information and attitudes are reflected in the price would not be of much practical use were it not true that prices generally move in trends. Technical analysis is the *art* of identifying such a trend at a relatively early stage and maintaining a position until it is apparent that a reversal is taking place. The word "art" is emphasized because technical analysis is not a science; its successful implementation requires judgment. Although technical analysis comprises various specific rules and principles, it is not infallible. The influences of many factors must be weighed before reaching a conclusion.

ADVANTAGES AND DRAWBACKS OF TECHNICAL ANALYSIS

Technicians point out the following advantages of a technical approach:

1. It permits market participants to make money without inside information and without the input of top fundamental research analysts.
2. Individual investors can easily follow a wide range of commodities, financial instruments, and currencies by using technical charts. To do a creditable job on so many investment opportunities with fundamental analysis would be nearly impossible.
3. Studying the principles of technical analysis makes it possible to obtain some idea of the probable magnitude and duration of a price move.
4. Because technical analysis involves a study of the past price behavior and proportionate swings of a commodity, it can also help to identify levels at which the odds would favor a successful purchase or sale transaction.
5. A quick glance at a chart can give vital clues to the trading characteristics of a commodity—for example, whether it is very volatile, moves in clearly defined cycles, or is prone to misleading whipsaws.

Fundamentalists argue that the price action of most commodities is so volatile that many of the principles of technical analysis fail to work successfully much of the time. Thus, they believe that the advantages of technical analysis are more than outweighed by its disadvantages.

This popular misconception is perhaps the most widely voiced criticism of technical analysis. It is based on the tendency of many technicians and market letter writers to be too free and specific in their opinions, which renders them extremely vulnerable to mistakes. Then too, many people base their expectations of exceptional results on too little knowledge and experience. When their expectations are disappointed, they blame technical analysis rather than their own inexperienced application of it.

The technical analyst, like the practitioner of any other art form, must acquire considerable practical experience before consistent results become possible—that is, before trading or investment can become profitable. This does not mean that the novice cannot be successful with technical analysis but rather that if beginning expectations are too high, there is much room for disappointment.

Another reason for the tendency of technical analysis to fall into disrepute is that many technicians have claimed to have found the "perfect indicator." It is highly unlikely that the perfect indicator exists, since the successful application of technical analysis depends on an objective interpretation of many data supplied by a variety of indicators. Narrowing the method to one indicator and excluding all others invites disaster.

Various indicators are designed to measure many changing market conditions and many specific aspects of market action, all of which must be taken into consideration. Valid and profitable conclusions can only be based on a broad view. Many indicators may work successfully for the short term, but all are subject to failure over longer periods. A dangerous trap that practitioners of the "perfect indicator" are liable to fall into is too heavy reliance on any one indicator. Many of the mechanistic techniques described in the chapters of Part 6 offer reliable indications of changing market conditions, but all may fail to operate at one time or another. This fact should not present an overriding stumbling block to serious and disciplined investors. A good working knowledge of the principles underlying major movement in commodity prices and a balanced view of their overall technical position offer a much superior framework in which to operate.

In this era of mass media and immediate communications, with its tendency to foster the herd instinct, there is no substitute for independent thought. Since the underlying characteristics of the market are reflected in the technical indicators, it is up to the individual to put the pieces of the jigsaw together and construct a working hypothesis.

Although technical analysis has a lot to offer, learning to apply it is no easy task. Initial—and possibly undeserved—success can easily lead to overconfidence and arrogance. Charles H. Dow, the father of technical analysis, is quoted as saying, "Pride of opinion caused the downfall of more men on Wall St. than all the other opinions put together."

Commodity trends are essentially a reflection of people in action. Normally, market activity develops along a reasonably predictable path. Just as people often reflect and change their minds, so price action in the market can deviate from an anticipated course. As changes in the technical position emerge, investors must consequently change their horizons and attitudes in order to avoid serious setbacks.

TECHNICAL ANALYSIS DEFINED

The technical approach to investment and speculation is essentially

> . . . a reflection of the idea that the commodity markets move in trends which are determined by the changing attitude of investors to a variety of economic, fundamental, monetary, political and psychological forces. The art of technical analysis . . . is to identify changes in such trends at an early stage and to maintain an investment posture until a reversal in that trend is indicated.*

Technical analysis assumes that human nature remains more or less constant and thus that people tend to react in a reasonably consistent manner to similar situations. Sharply falling prices, for example, stimulate fear and panic for investors with a long position, whereas an explosive rally leads to widespread optimism and misplaced overconfidence.

A study of the history of market turning points reveals many characteristics that help to identify major tops and bottoms. The technician tries to take advan-

*Adapted from *Technical Analysis Explained*, p. 2.

tage of the tendency of investors to make the same mistakes that they have made in the past. But human reactions are extremely complex and rarely repeated in identical fashion. Therefore, although the characteristics of major market turning points are often very similar, an exact reproduction is unlikely. The altered decisions made by investors are reflected in the price action of the commodity markets. The recurrence of several characteristics is sufficient, however, to give technical analysis its strength and to permit careful observers to identify major turning points.

THE DISCOUNTING MECHANISM OF FUTURES MARKETS

All price movements have one thing in common: They are a reflection of trends in the hopes, fears, knowledge, optimism, and greed of the investing and speculating public. In futures markets, the aggregate of these emotions is measured by the price level, which, as one prominent stock market technician noted, is "never what a [futures contract] is worth but what people think it is worth."

The process of market evaluation includes assessing not only the attitudes of traders who are actually buying and selling at any given moment, but also the attitudes of those who might be in the market if they perceived conditions as favorable. Movements in and out of a commodity futures contract are made at the margin as each participant—investor, speculator, commercial account arbitrageur, or hedger—digests new information. The price level of a particular commodity market incorporates all the available information in a way that no single individual could possibly hope to do.

The implication is that investors in the futures markets are looking ahead 3 to 9 months or more, and are buying or selling contracts now in order to make a profit in the future, when the anticipated news or development actually materializes. If the development is better or worse than original expectations, investors will sell either sooner or later, depending on the particular circumstances. Thus the familiar maxim "Sell on good news" applies only when the "good" news is equal to or below the market's expectations. If the news is good but less favorable than expected, a quick reassessment will take place and (other factors remaining the same) the market will fall. If the news is better than expected, the possibilities are clearly more positive. The reverse of course applies during a declining market. This process explains the paradox of markets turning down when conditions are favorable and turning up when the outlook is most gloomy.

In this context, the reactions of commodity markets to news events (such as crop reports or publication of economic statistics) can be most revealing when used in conjunction with the technical structure. For instance, if a market ignores what would otherwise be regarded as bullish news and sells off, the indications are fairly certain that the development has already been discounted by the market. A good example occurred in the gold market in September 1980, when the bullion price was around $700, having rallied from the mid-$400 area over the previous 4 months. The event that sparked the final portion of the rally was the outbreak of the Iran-Iraq war. The gold price hit its high on the day of the first damage to a major Iranian oil refinery. This news should have been super-bullish for gold; instead, after a brief flurry, the market sold off. Gold was not able to mount another major rally until March 1981, when the price was nearly $300 lower.

In retrospect, it can be seen that this bearish action of the gold bullion market was suggesting that not only were some of the worst fears of gold market participants already built into the price structure but also investors and other participants were already looking to other factors—a disinflationary environment and high U.S. interest rates.

SUMMARY

Technical and fundamental analysis use very different approaches to reach the same goal: forecasting the future prices of commodity and financial markets. Indiscriminate application of technical analysis can lead to disappointment, but cautious and conscientious use should produce significantly better results.

The most successful approach is to combine the two methods of analysis. Each discipline should be practised independently, and care must be taken not to distort the results of one to fit the conclusions of the other. For example, a bullish technical position should not be used to support fundamentals unless the fundamental case is itself strong. Similarly, a bearish opinion based on an analysis of fundamental aspects should not influence the analyst to interpret the technical position bearishly if the weight of technical evidence is pointing in the opposite direction. It is, of course, almost impossible to achieve a complete separation, since the implications of one approach will almost inevitably color the interpretation of the other. However, if a sincere effort is made to apply technical analysis and fundamental analysis separately and then to combine the two results, much greater success can be obtained than from use of either approach alone.

CHAPTER

39

Some Introductory Technical Perspectives

Martin J. Pring

The description in this chapter of some of the basic tenets of technical analysis will serve as background and provide a framework within which the more detailed concepts presented in later chapters can be explored.

THREE STAGES OF PRIMARY BULL AND BEAR MARKETS

All financial markets move in trends, of which there are three types: First, the *major* trend, often known as the primary or cyclical trend, lasts usually from 1 to 4 years. Second, the *intermediate*, or secondary, trend operates counter to the main trend and can last from 3 weeks to 6 months. Third, the *minor* trend is the day-to-day activity of the market and is probably the one commonly followed by most commodity speculators.

In most commodity markets the cyclical or primary trend consists of three distinct phases, separated by two intermediate or secondary corrections, as shown in Figure 39-1. The stage is set for a primary bull trend when the fundamentals for a given commodity are extremely bearish—when it seems that production will never stop increasing, consumption will never stop falling, and inventories are sufficient for the next decade. Some new substitute may have taken away much of the demand for the commodity, or some new process may have dramatically reduced the cost. Whatever the reason, there is usually tremendous pessimism about the specific commodity, or about commodities in general. At such a time, knowledgeable trade sources, investors, and speculators begin accumulating futures contracts in anticipation of higher prices in the months ahead. The first phase of the new bull market usually comes after a panic sell-off when undermargined participants are forced to liquidate and other institutional and technical factors cause prices to fall off sharply. This first phase is often regarded with widespread disbelief and is usually rationalized as a technical rally. People in general find it difficult to believe that the bull market has in fact begun.

Another way in which a bull market might start is for prices to fluctuate quietly and listlessly for several months or longer, while the bearish fundamentals are being digested. During this period, forecasts of ridiculously lower prices find their way into the financial press and the general expectation is that prices will break down. When they move in the opposite direction, the rally is therefore treated with disbelief.

Following the initial bull market rally, an intermediate correction sets in. This takes the form of either a retracement of much of the previous advance or a sideways trading band. Since the fundamentals are still bearish to most observers, forecasts call for a violation or at least a test of the old lows. That the market can hold together during this period is a good sign that a primary bull market is in force.

The second leg of the bull market is fueled by the fulfillment of the expectations of those who accumulated futures contracts when prices were at distressed levels. The overhanging level of inventories may start to decline, or consumption may start to pick up. Or for agricultural products, the weather may become adverse and a poor harvest may result. In this second leg of the bull market, the economy is usually picking up considerable strength, following its recessionary phase at the bear market low.

The second bull market leg is also followed by a correction of intermediate proportions. Doubts about the continuation of the bull market set in, quite often triggered by an announcement of some isolated incident or aberration in a statistical report.

The final phase of the bull market is usually based upon wild expectations that probably cannot materialize. On paper, speculators have been making a lot of money and therefore have the financial capacity to leverage up their positions even more. For agricultural commodities, bad weather may cause projec-

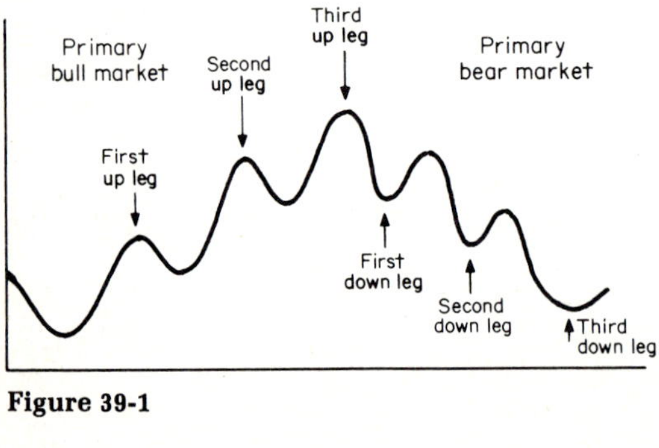

Figure 39-1

tions of tremendous shortages, encouraging speculators to bid up prices to extraordinary levels. In the metals market, the economy is usually extremely robust and producers are working at or near full capacity. This last stage of the bull market is usually accompanied by carelessness and overconfidence. Investors have been used to bull market conditions for a considerable period of time. Since this is a time when the fundamentals appear excellent, forecasts of substantial price increases abound.

Eventually it becomes clear that the overly optimistic expectations of investors cannot materialize; prices collapse sharply and overextended participants pull out of the market.

The first decline in the new bear market is followed by an intermediate rally. This rally is usually extremely deceptive in nature, since the fundamentals and news background are still reasonably bullish. The rally is usually quite sharp but soon peters out after profit taking from short covering is completed. As the fundamentals begin to turn more bearish, a second leg down in the market begins. This leg is also followed by an intermediate rally, which in turn gives way to the third down leg.

The third leg begins as the fundamentals deteriorate to a degree far worse than expected. Where crop shortages were anticipated, surplus supplies become apparent: Farmers, encouraged by higher prices, plant more; or consumers, discouraged by higher prices, look for cheaper substitutes. In the metals markets it is usually a slump in demand, caused by a weakening economy or sharply higher interest rates, that curtails the desire to hold high levels of inventory. Whatever the reason, the market usually sells off very sharply, liquidation takes place, and a new bull market begins.

Students of the market should remember this description of the three phases of bull and bear markets when they approach the commodity markets. The description, however, should be viewed only as a conceptual framework, not as an actual game plan—for, although many markets do operate as described much of the time, many others do not. The speculative phase, for example, may be absent in one cycle, or the panic phase may develop at the end of the second leg of the bear market rather than at the bear market low. Despite possible aberrations in the conceptual framework, it is useful to play the psychological guessing game of figuring out which phase of the primary bull and bear cycle a particular market may be in. This information, if accurate, can then serve as a basis for profitable action.

PRICE CHARTS

The price chart is the technician's basic work tool. Prices can be plotted in the form of bar charts, closing prices, or point and figure charts. The construction of point and figure charts is described in Chapter 50.

Price charts have two axes; the vertical axis measures price and the horizontal axis measures time. Charts can be daily, weekly, or monthly. Daily charts are used mainly for trading purposes, while monthly and weekly charts help set the perspective for longer-term movements. Prices on a bar chart are usually plotted on the basis of a range for the particular period being covered—day, week, or month. The chart therefore contains the high and the low for that period. The closing price is also usually indicated by a small horizontal line to the right of the bar. Sometimes an opening price is recorded, as a small horizontal line to the left of the bar. On a daily chart, if the price of a specific commodity opened the day at its low, the chart would show a horizontal bar at the bottom left of the vertical price bar. If it closed at its high, the horizontal line to the right of the price bar would be at the highest point of the price bar.

Since a bar chart shows intraperiod price swings, it is quite useful in judging the character of market action during the period in question.

On the other hand, because the price action can often move to unrealistic levels, especially within the course of a day's trading, bar charts sometimes give misleading technical signals. For this reason and others, many technicians prefer to use a price chart based on closing prices only, especially as intraday price swings can be subject to manipulation. A closing price chart is constructed by joining the closing price at the end of a day, week, or month. The resulting chart tends to give a much more subdued picture of the price action and is therefore usually more reliable for identifying changes in price trends.

Most price charts also include volume for the period and represent it by a vertical bar. Open interest (see Chapter 49) is normally represented by a solid line.

The principles described in subsequent chapters apply to both bar and closing charts, but the strict application of these principles in terms of trend breaks is more reliable for closing charts since price action during the day is more susceptible to manipulation by influential market participants.

SIMPLE TREND IDENTIFICATION

A rising market is usually interrupted by temporary setbacks or reactions, as shown in Figure 39-2. As long as each succeeding rally and reaction is higher than its predecessor, it should be assumed that the uptrend is still intact. A reaction that falls below a previous reaction low, however, alerts technicians to the probability of a reversal in trend, as indicated at point X in Figure 39-2a. A

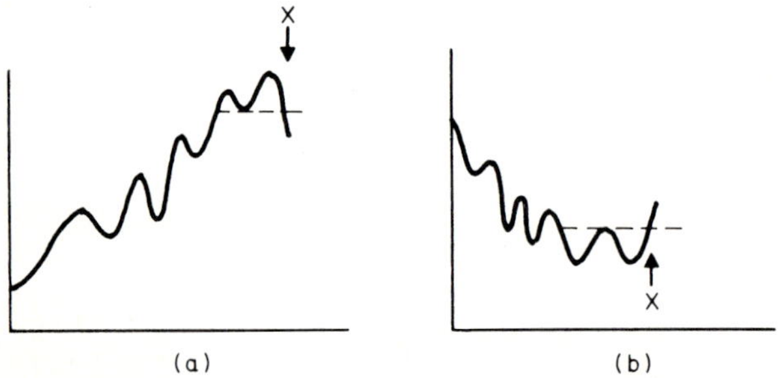

Figure 39-2

reversal to an uptrend would be signaled at point X in Figure 39-2b, where the first rally moves above the peak of the previous rally. There are more sophisticated ways of identifying trend reversals, but this brief outline illustrates one of the basic principles of technical analysis. Later chapters will explain price patterns, trend lines, and flag and pennant analysis, all of which are essentially based on this simple trend-identification principle.

CHAPTER

40

Price Patterns

Martin J. Pring

INTRODUCTION

Technical analysis is essentially the art of identifying a trend at a relatively early stage and following it until it is shown to be reversed. The most common method of identifying reversals involves the use of price patterns. Over the years technicians have noticed that a rising price trend does not usually reverse itself overnight but is separated from a declining trend by a period in which the price action takes the form of a trading range. During this trading action, the balance between buyers and sellers is fairly equally matched. Then, at some point, the trading area is breached, one side wins out, and prices proceed one way or the other.

Figure 40-1 shows the broad upsweep in prices, the sideways trading action, and the final breakdown. Figure 40-2 illustrates the kind of specific price action that may be expected during the period of horizontal trading. Lines AA and BB mark the outer ranges of this price action. As prices rise to AA, buyers become reluctant to make additional purchases, and as the price backs off, sellers decide to take profits. Eventually the price slips to line BB. At this point buyers come back into the market, especially those who missed earlier rallies and do not wish to be left out again. Conversely, sellers become less anxious to liquidate because of the lower prices, and so the price begins to rally once again. Quite clearly, this sort of thing cannot go on forever; eventually one side or the other must win out.

Movements above or below the trading range, known as *breakouts*, should be treated with respect. A price breakout below level BB (known as a *support*

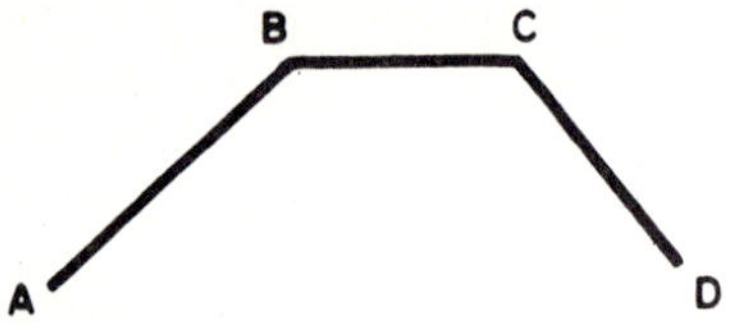

Figure 40-1 *(From Martin J. Pring,* Technical Analysis Explained, *© 1980 by McGraw-Hill, Inc. Used with permission)*

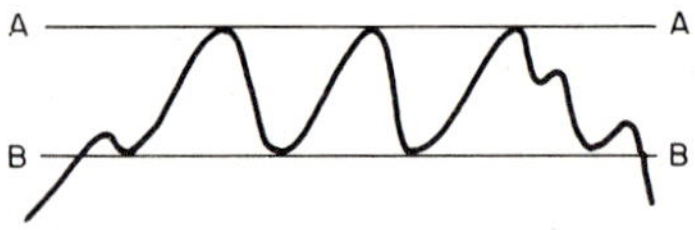

Figure 40-2 *(From Martin J. Pring,* Technical Analysis Explained, *© 1980 by McGraw-Hill, Inc. Used with permission)*

level) gives technicians a fairly reliable signal that the price trend has reversed. On the other hand, a price breakout above line AA (known as a *resistance* level) alerts technicians to the probability that prices will continue to rise.

A trading move that can be conveniently bounded between two parallel lines, as shown in Figure 40-2, represents a price pattern or formation known as a *rectangle*. In this very simple type of formation, it is relatively easy to ascertain when the boundaries have been exceeded. Some slightly more involved patterns are discussed later in this chapter. At this point, it is important to grasp certain basic terminology and principles affecting all price patterns and to understand why price patterns work.

In Figure 40-2 prices are shown breaking down from the rectangle. This trading action represents a *reversal* pattern, since it is a transitional period between the rising and declining trends. If prices broke up above line AA, the period of price action would represent a period of *consolidation* before prices worked their way higher, and the pattern would be called a *continuation* or consolidation pattern (see Figure 40-3a). A reversal formation that separates a rising from a falling trend, as shown in Figure 40-2, is known as a *distribution* pattern. If a rectangle forms at the bottom of a price decline, as in Figure 40-3b, the formation is termed an *accumulation* pattern.

An important technical principle is that *a trend should be assumed to be in force until it is shown to have been reversed.* It is normally safer to assume that a developing price pattern will ultimately turn out to be a consolidation rather than a reversal, but safest of all is to await the decision of the market (that is, a breakout one way or the other) rather than jump the gun. Since all trends are eventually reversed, the longer a trend has been in existence, the greater the odds that a potential price pattern will prove to be of the reversal type.

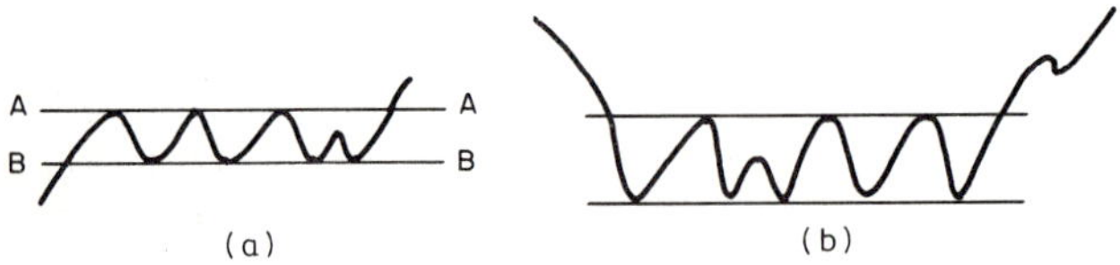

Figure 40-3 *(From Martin J. Pring,* Technical Analysis Explained, *© 1980 by McGraw-Hill, Inc. Used with permission)*

WHY PRICE PATTERNS WORK

Figure 40-4a represents two armies (AA and BB) fighting a trench war. The arrows between the two trenches mark the forays between the two combatants, but the lines of defense prove too strong to allow either army to win. In Figure 40-4b, on the other hand, army AA has been able to push through the BB defense and then to advance much further. Eventually AA is forced to stop again, either because of the difficulty of supplying an extended advance or because BB has reached a new line of defence. The advance is stalled and a new stalemate develops.

This analogy is similar to the battle between buyers and sellers within a trading level. The implications of a breakout, whether from a price pattern or a trench, are the same; that is, the price or the army is likely to continue for some time to move in the direction of the breakout. Just as an army can become overextended if it does not consolidate, so too a commodity price movement can become vulnerable to a reversal if it does not consolidate. Moreover, an army advance (in this case AA) is likely to be stopped at an old line of defense, in this case the old BB trench line which is now of course occupied by army AA. Just so, in the commodity markets the former level of resistance in Figure 40-3a will now become one of support.

Certain characteristics which apply to all price patterns will be discussed below, and later the various price patterns will be described.

SIGNIFICANCE OF PRICE PATTERNS

The significance of a price formation is a direct function of its size and depth. The longer it takes to complete a pattern and the wider the price fluctuations within that pattern, the more substantial the ensuing price move is likely to be. Referring again to the military analogy, the fighting and winning of a major battle is obviously much more significant in the course of the war than is a minor skirmish. Similarly, a price pattern that develops over a 6- to 12-month period following a 2-year decline is of far greater significance than one that is completed in 2 to 3 weeks. A breakout during either period indicates the probable future price trend, but the longer pattern represents a greater battle between buyers and sellers and thus means that the ensuing movement is likely to go further and last longer.

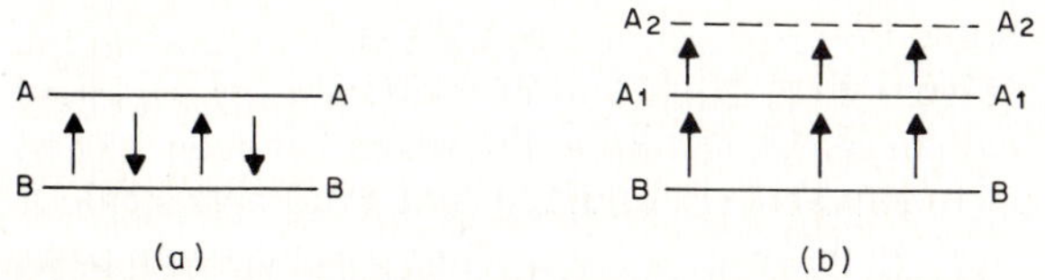

Figure 40-4 *(From Martin J. Pring,* Technical Analysis Explained, *© 1980 by McGraw-Hill, Inc. Used with permission)*

Just as a skyscraper must have a huge foundation so that it will not fall down, a bull market requires a long period of accumulation to serve as its foundation. The term "accumulation" is used because market bottoms always occur when news is bad. Bad news about a particular commodity stimulates sales by uninformed market participants who were not expecting adverse developments. During market bottoms, futures contracts are accumulated by more sophisticated participants who position, or accumulate, them in anticipation of improved conditions a few months later. The futures contracts therefore move from weak, undermargined, and uninformed participants into strong and knowledgeable hands.

At market tops the process is reversed, as participants who were formerly accumulating futures contracts now begin feeding them out. Unsophisticated participants become more and more attracted to the commodity as bullish reports continue and price forecasts are revised upward. The longer the period of accumulation or distribution, the greater the amount of a commodity that moves from the uninformed to the better informed and vice versa, and the greater the ensuing move.

How long it takes to complete a price pattern is important not only because of the amount of the commodity that changes hands but also because the outer boundaries of the pattern represent important psychological boundaries at which participants have been influenced to buy at one price and sell at another. A move beyond either limit therefore represents a fundamental change which has great psychological significance.

MEASURING IMPLICATIONS

Most techniques of technical analysis are useful in identifying a trend, but few of them can indicate the magnitude of a move. Price patterns, however, do offer some measuring implications.

There are two methods or scales of bar charting: (1) arithmetic and (2) ratio or logarithmic. The choice of the scale determines the significance of the measuring implications. Almost all the chart services that measure short-term (6- to 12-month) price history use the arithmetic scale. The logarithmic scale is more useful for the measurement of longer-term trends and movements.

Arithmetic Scale

Arithmetic charts have an arithmetic scale on the vertical axis and time on the horizontal axis, as shown in Figure 40-5. Each unit of measurement is plotted in the same amount of vertical space; for example, the space between 10 and 20 is the same size as the space between 110 and 120. The arithmetic scale is relatively satisfactory for measuring price action over short periods when price swings are not particularly great, but is apt to give exaggerated readings as prices push their way higher or lower. For example, a price move from 10 to 20 represents a doubling of price, but a move from 110 to 120 represents less than a 10 percent rise; yet the two are given identical treatment on the arithmetic scale.

Ratio Scale

On a ratio scale, in contrast to an arithmetic scale, commodity prices are plotted in such a way that identical percentage moves are given identical amounts of vertical space.

Figure 40-6 shows a ratio scale in which the vertical distance between 1 and 2 (a 2 to 1 ratio) is ½ inch. Similarly, the distance between 2 and 4, also a 2 to 1 ratio, is ½ inch. Consequently a 2 to 1 ratio is measured by ½ inch anywhere on the scale, a 4 to 1 ratio by 1 inch, and so on. (Graph paper for use in constructing ratio or logarithmic scales can be obtained from most large office supply stores.)

Figure 40-7 shows a completed rectangle formation of the distribution type. The measuring implication derived from this formation is the vertical distance between the two parallel boundaries projected downward from the breakout point, line BB. If AA represents 100 and BB represents 50, the down-side objective will be 50 percent on a ratio scale, that is, to 25. This measuring formula offers a rough guide, but remember that what is being measured is usually the *minimum* expectation and prices usually go much further. In a distribution pattern the minimum down-side objective will quite often prove to be a level of temporary support from which a rally takes place (and vice versa for an accumulation pattern). If the rectangle is of the accumulation or continuation type, the same measuring implications are derived as shown in Figure 40-7.

If the minimal objective proves to be the ultimate extension of the new trend, a substantial amount of accumulation or distribution, whichever is appropriate, will usually have to occur before prices move in their original direction. Thus, if the completion of a 2-year rectangle calls for a downward price objective which is reached relatively quickly even though a further price decline does not take place, it is usually necessary for a base (accumulation) of approximately the same size as the distribution (in this case 2 years) to develop before a sustainable upward move will take place.

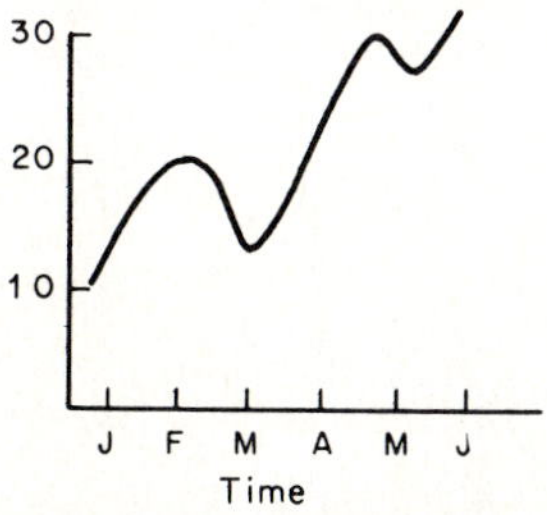

Figure 40-5 *(From Martin J. Pring, Technical Analysis Explained, © 1980 by McGraw-Hill, Inc. Used with permission)*

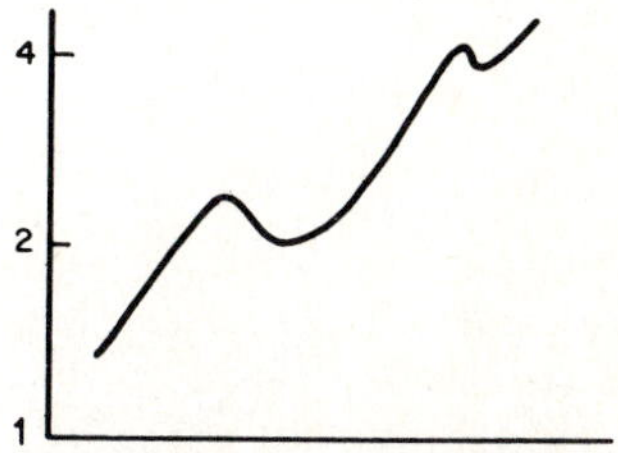

Figure 40-6 *(From Martin J. Pring, Technical Analysis Explained, © 1980 by McGraw-Hill, Inc. Used with permission)*

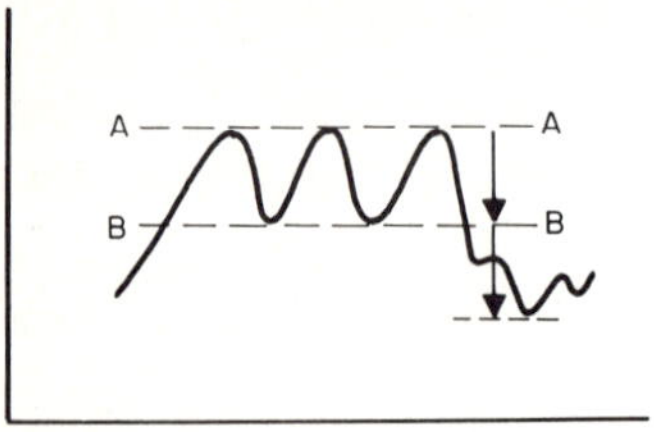

Figure 40-7 *(From Martin J. Pring, Technical Analysis Explained, © 1980 by McGraw-Hill, Inc. Used with permission)*

CONFIRMATION OF A VALID BREAKOUT

Price

It has been assumed so far that any price move out of the boundaries of a formation, however small, constitutes a valid signal. Because misleading moves known as *whipsaws* occur occasionally, technicians have found it more advantageous to await a 3 percent penetration of the boundaries before concluding that the breakout is valid. The adoption of this rule filters out a substantial number of misleading moves even though the results are less timely.

Because of the tremendous leverage associated with commodities and because about half the breakout moves are followed by "return" moves to the extremity of the pattern, it is often a good idea to await such a development before committing to an outright position. While the pullback results in some uncertainty about the breakout on the part of the investor or speculator, it does not negate the validity of the breakout. (If the return move does not materialize, an opportunity will of course have been missed, but it should never be forgotten that another opportunity will always occur.)

Figures 40-8a and 40-8b show a return move for both a positive and a negative breakout. As shown, it is often a good idea to draw a trend line joining the peaks in Figure 40-8a (or troughs in Figure 40-8b) of the rallies (or reactions) of a return move. The signal to buy (or sell) is given when the price breaks above (or below) the trend line, as marked by the arrows.

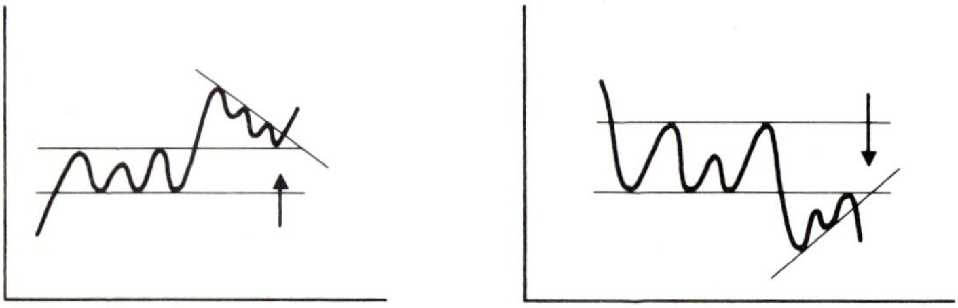

(a) (b)

Figure 40-8

Volume

An accepted technical principle is that volume goes with the trend. In other words, it is perfectly normal for volume to expand as prices rise and contract as they fall. Volume is always considered in a relative sense and is therefore compared with volume a few days, weeks, or even months ago because, over time, various contracts rise or fall in popularity. Long-term volume comparisons do not therefore reflect market enthusiasm for a particular price move. For example, in late 1979 the heating-oil contract was relatively new and volume was small. By 1981 volume had expanded enormously as the contract gained acceptance. The reverse happened with silver after 1980 because of the price collapse and because the IRS attacked silver straddles.* Consequently these changes in the level of volume were more a fundamental than a technical factor.

Volume comparisons therefore should take account of such developments. Anything different from the normal relationship—for example, volume moving in an opposite direction to the trend—should be regarded as suspect. Completion and breakout of various rectangles are shown in Figure 40-9, with daily volume shown in the vertical lines at the bottom. This figure shows that volume expands marginally as the commodity approaches its low. As accumulation pattern AA develops, selling pressure abates and the trend is toward a declining volume. Finally volume expands as prices begin their ascent out of the pattern. The breakout therefore should be accompanied by *expanding* volume; otherwise the move would be suspect since it would lack the enthusiasm that would indicate a reversal in psychology.

Following the sharp rise from rectangle AA in Figure 40-9, the excitement dies down during the return move as volume contracts with price. The next rally is accompanied by even greater volume and the price action then forms rectangle BB.

It is worth noting that, although the volume from the breakout of rectangle BB is high, it is less than that of the previous advance in relation to the overall cycle. This is a bearish factor since *volume usually leads price*. In this case volume made its peak just before entering rectangle BB, and the peak in prices is not observed until rectangle CC.

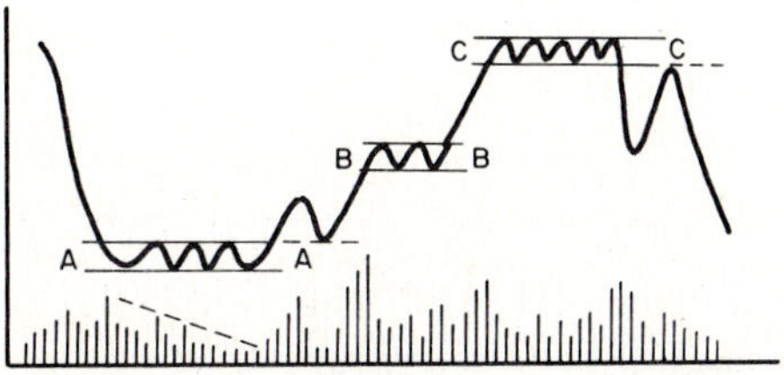

Figure 40-9 *(From Martin J. Pring, Technical Analysis Explained, © 1980 by McGraw-Hill, Inc. Used with permission)*

*For a full description of straddles, see Chapter 51.

During the completion of rectangle CC, volume again contracts and then expands, as prices break on the down side. The expanded level of activity associated with the violation of the support at the lower boundary of the rectangle emphasizes the bearish nature of the breakout, although expanding volume is not a prerequisite for a valid signal with a down-side breakout, as it is for an up-side move. The declining volume associated with the return move reinforces the bearish evidence of the pattern breakout.

HEAD AND SHOULDERS

Some of the more common price patterns are discussed below.

General

The head-and-shoulders (H-and-S) pattern is perhaps the most reliable of all patterns. It consists of a rally, the *head line*, surrounded by two smaller rallies, the *shoulders*. The reaction lows can be joined by a simple trend line. Figure 40-10 shows a perfectly symmetrical H-and-S distribution pattern. Volume is normally heaviest during the rallies that form the left shoulder and the head. The advance tip-off that a H and S is in the process of completion is offered by the uncharacteristically low volume in the rally forming the right shoulder. (See also Figure 40-11.)

The signal for the breakout is given as the price falls below the trend line joining the two reaction lows. This line is known as the *neckline*.

The minimum down-side price objective is obtained by projecting the vertical distance from the top of the head to the neckline downward from the neckline, as shown in Figure 40-10. Clearly, the deeper the pattern, the more serious the implications of its completion.

H-and-S patterns can be formed over a period as short as 2 to 3 weeks or as long as 2 to 3 years. Generally speaking, the longer the period of distribution, the greater the ensuing move is likely to be.

The larger H-and-S patterns are often complex and can consist of several shoulders or miniature H-and-S formations, as shown in Figure 40-12. Usually,

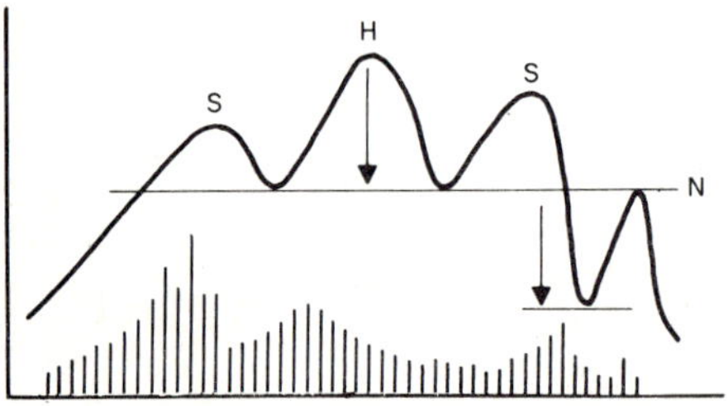

Figure 40-10 *(From Martin J. Pring, Technical Analysis Explained, © 1980 by McGraw-Hill, Inc. Used with permission)*

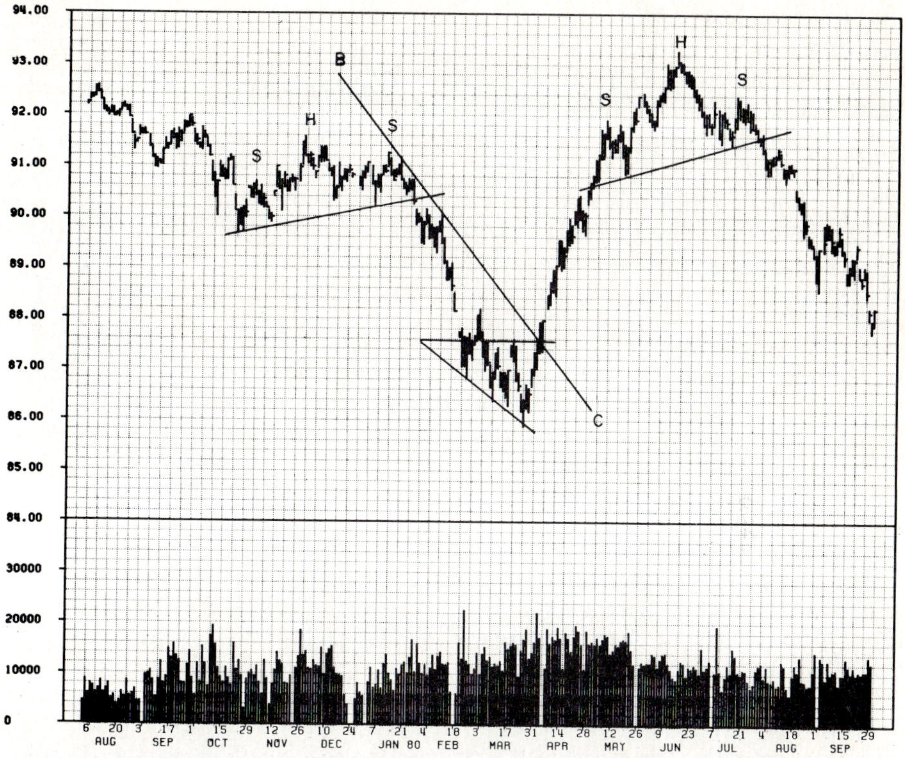

Figure 40-11 Thirteen-week continuation, International Monetary Market December 1980 T-bills. The price action of December 1980 T-bills offers some fine examples of price formations: first, the head-and-shoulders consolidation pattern traced out between November and January; second, the small broadening formation with a flat top in March; finally, the head-and-shoulders distribution pattern between May and July. It is also worth noting that the price broke out of the broadening formation at the same time that it broke the down trend line BC. This combination emphasized the reversal in trend which had taken place.

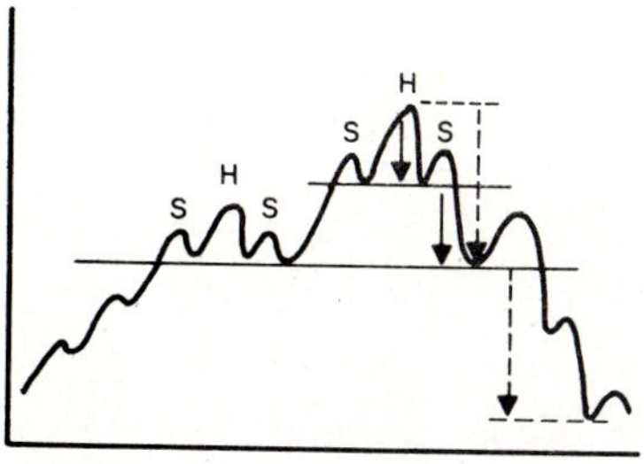

Figure 40-12 *(From Martin J. Pring,* Technical Analysis Explained, *© 1980 by McGraw-Hill, Inc. Used with permission)*

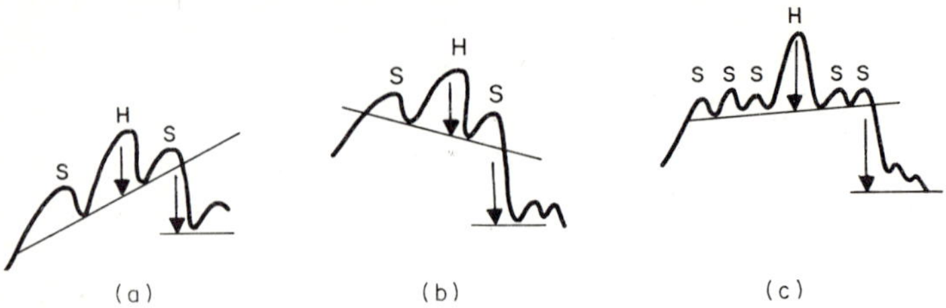

Figure 40-13 *(From Martin J. Pring,* Technical Analysis Explained, *© 1980 by McGraw-Hill, Inc. Used with permission)*

the greater the complexity, the more bearish the pattern, since the multiplicity of shoulders represents a considerable number of battles between buyers and sellers. It follows that the breakdown will have a tremendous psychological effect on the bulls when it occurs.

The H-and-S patterns so far considered have had horizontal necklines, but patterns with upward- and downward-sloping necklines are also valid. Examples are shown in Figure 40-13.

Head-and-shoulders patterns that occur at market bottoms are known as *inverse head and shoulders*, or *H-and-S Bottoms;* examples are shown in Figures 40-14 and 40-15. Volume is usually relatively high at the bottom of the left shoulder and during the formation of the head. The major factor to look out for is activity on the right shoulder, which should normally contract during the reaction that forms the right shoulder and then expand fairly dramatically on the breakout rally. The measuring formula is the reverse of that on the H-and-S distribution pattern, shown in Figure 40-14 by the arrows. There are also upward- and downward-sloping, as well as complex, varieties; some examples are illustrated in Figure 40-16.

H-and-S Failures

Sometimes the price action of a commodity exhibits all the characteristics of an H-and-S distribution pattern but either refuses to penetrate the neckline or

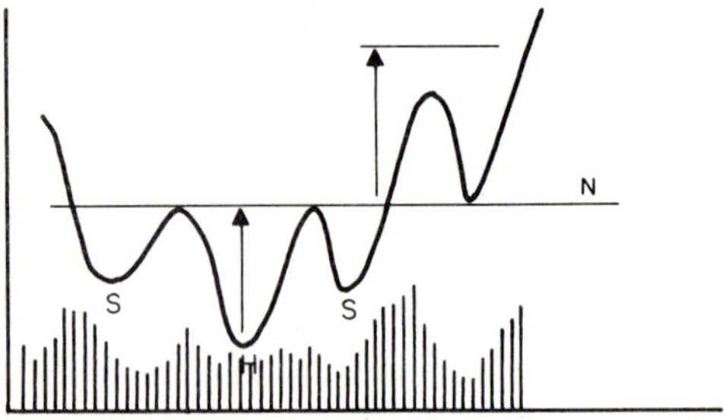

Figure 40-14 *(From Martin J. Pring,* Technical Analysis Explained, *© 1980 by McGraw-Hill, Inc. Used with permission)*

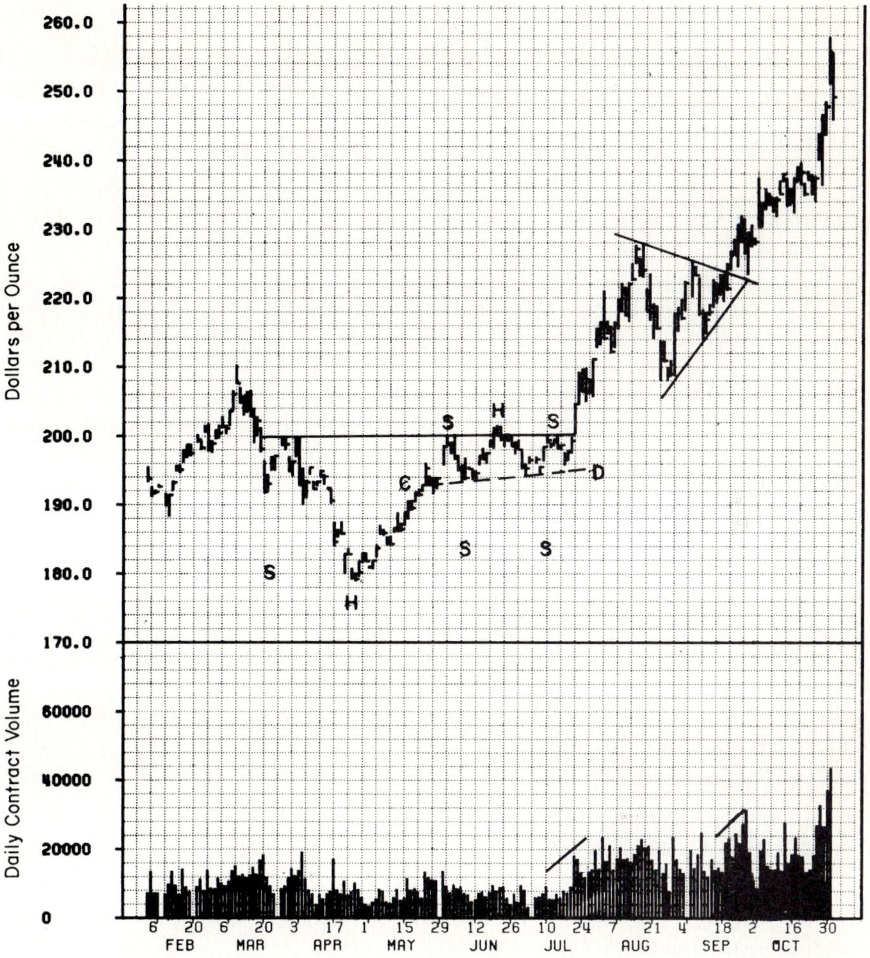

Figure 40-15 April 1979 gold. In July the price of the April gold contract broke out of a complex inverse head-and-shoulders pattern. The breakout is particularly noteworthy, not only because of the high volume but also because of the failure of a small head-and-shoulders pattern, the neckline of which would have been line CD. As so often happens when such failures occur, the resultant move is extremely sharp. Also worth noting is the triangle pattern formed between August and September, the breakout from which was accompanied by expanding volume.

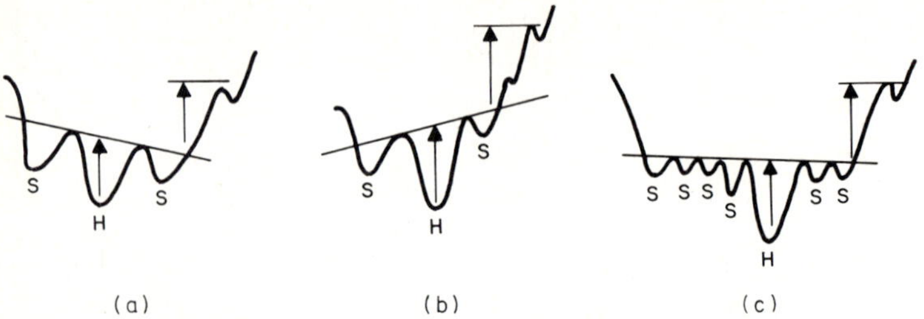

Figure 40-16 *(From Martin J. Pring,* Technical Analysis Explained, *© 1980 by McGraw-Hill, Inc. Used with permission)*

penetrates it temporarily and then starts to rally, as shown in Figure 40-17a. This represents an H-and-S failure and is usually followed by an explosive rally. Unfortunately, the pattern itself gives no indication that it is going to fail. Sometimes evidence in this direction can be gleaned from other technical factors. Such failures tend to be fairly rare but do point out the necessity of waiting for a decisive breakout on the down side. If any action is contemplated, it should be taken when the price of the commodity breaks above the right shoulder on heavy volume. Usually such signals offer substantial profits in a very short period of time and are well worth acting upon. Inverse H-and-S patterns can also fail; an example is shown in Figure 40-17b. Again, the failure is usually followed by an extremely sharp sell-off, as participants who bought in anticipation of an *upward* breakout are flushed out and the new bearish fundamentals become more widely known.

H and S as a Consolidation

H-and-S and inverse H-and-S formations occur as continuation as well as reversal patterns. The measuring implications are the same as for the accumulation or reversal type.

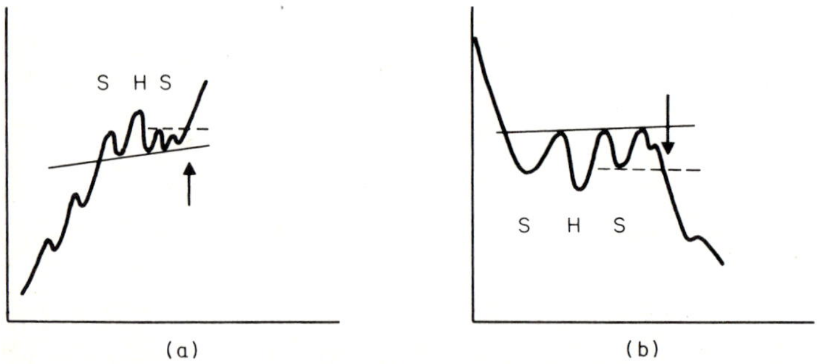

Figure 40-17

DOUBLE TOPS AND BOTTOMS

A double top consists of two peaks separated by a reaction in prices. The second top is usually associated with considerably lower volume than the first during the rally phase. The double-top formation is completed when prices break below the reaction low separating the two tops, as shown in Figures 40-18 and 40-19.

A typical double bottom is shown in Figure 40-20. The second bottom is accompanied by lower volume than the first, as compared with the breakout, which should be associated with rapidly expanding volume. Usually, the second bottom is formed slightly above the first, but such patterns are equally valid whether the second exceeds or is formed slightly below the first bottom.

Occasionally the double bottom or top extends into a triple, quadruple, or other complex formation. The principles and measuring implications for such patterns are the same; some examples are shown in Figure 40-21.

BROADENING FORMATIONS

A broadening formation occurs when a series of three or more price fluctuations widen in size so that peaks and troughs can be connected by two diverging trend lines. The *flattened-top* or *flattened-bottom* varieties are the easiest to detect and the most reliable of the broadening formations. Examples are given in Figures 40-22a and 40-22b.

The pattern in Figure 40-22a is sometimes referred to as a *right-angled broadening formation.* Volume patterns are difficult to characterize, since such formations are usually charged with extreme psychological and emotional crosscurrents. The patterns both at tops and bottoms are similar to the H-and-S variety except that the head is always the last to be formed. In a sense, broadening formations of this kind are really potential H-and-S patterns that fail to be completed because the price of the commodity is in such a hurry that it does

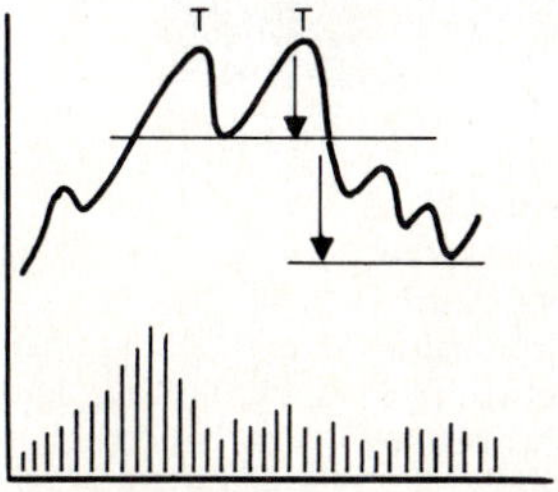

Figure 40-18 *(From Martin J. Pring,* Technical Analysis Explained, *© 1980 by McGraw-Hill, Inc. Used with permission)*

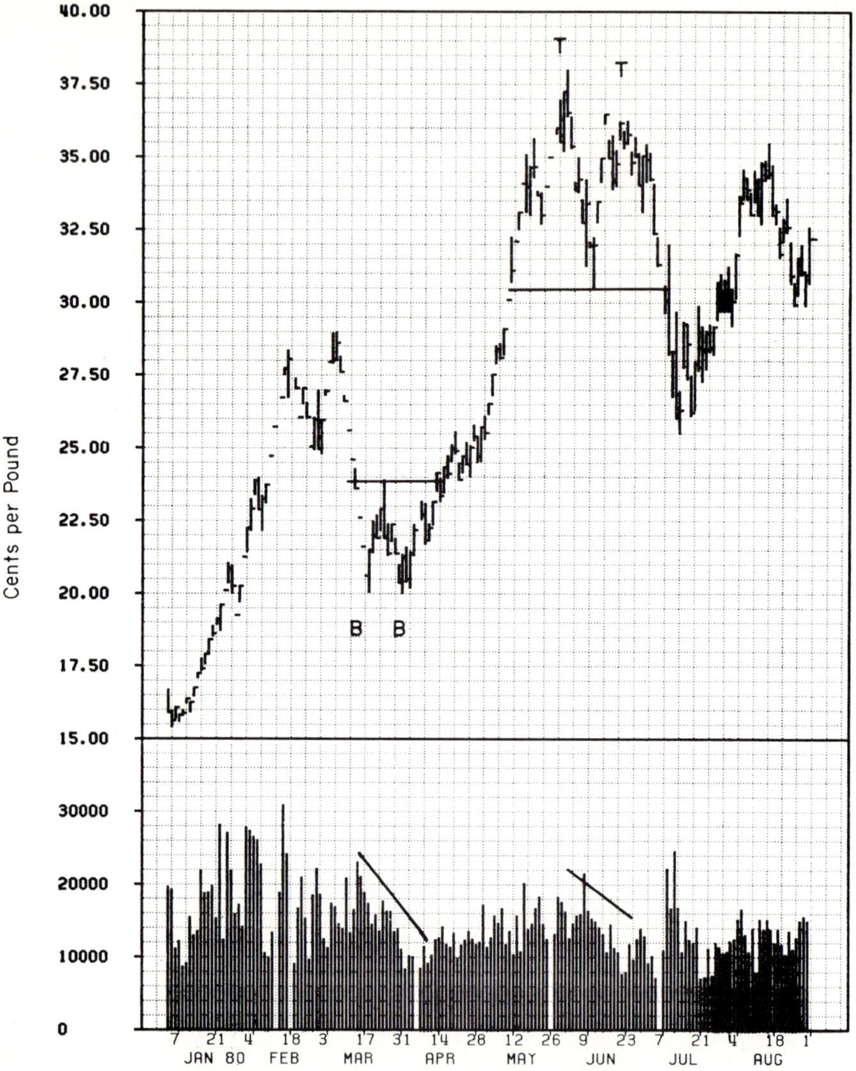

Figure 40-19 September sugar, world #11, 1980. This represents a fine example of both a double bottom in middle and late March and a double top in June and July. Note how the volume shrinks considerably on both the late March low and the late June high relative to the mid-March low and June high. It is also worth noting that the gap around the May 12 at the 30-cent level represented 50 percent of the March to June advance.

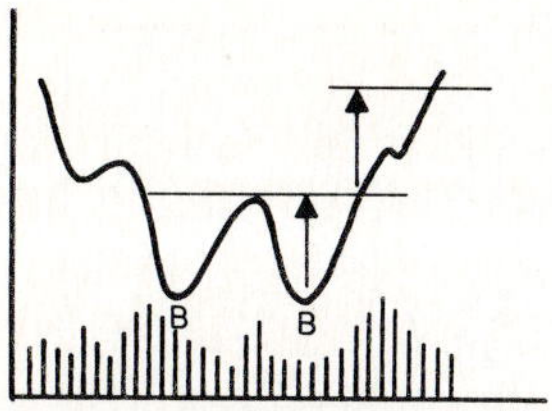

Figure 40-20 *(From Martin J. Pring, Technical Analysis Explained, © 1980 by McGraw-Hill, Inc. Used with permission)*

not have time to complete the right shoulder. Needless to say, the resulting move from a completed broadening formation with a flat top or bottom is usually extremely powerful. (See also Figure 40-23.)

Such patterns can also be of the continuation variety, as Figure 40-24 shows. Unfortunately, there does not appear to be an early point at which a decision can be made about whether the pattern will be a reversal or a continuation type. The best approach is to draw a trend line joining the peaks or troughs (depending on the pattern), using a 3 percent breakout above or below the trend line as a signaling point, as in Figures 40-24a and 40-24b.

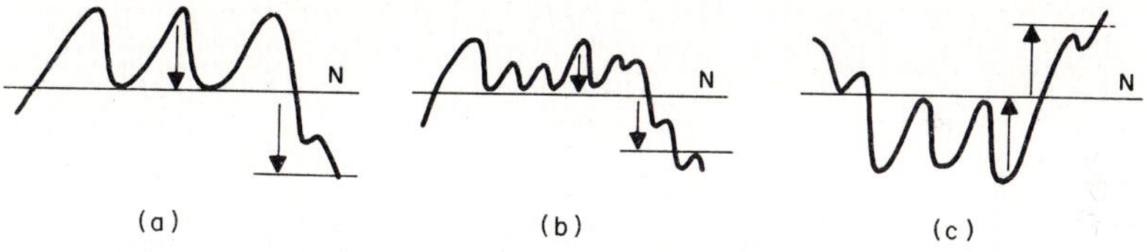

Figure 40-21 *(From Martin J. Pring, Technical Analysis Explained, © 1980 by McGraw-Hill, Inc. Used with permission)*

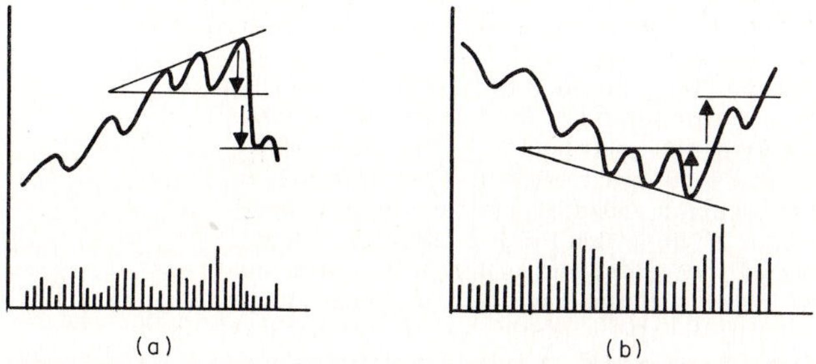

Figure 40-22 *(From Martin J. Pring, Technical Analysis Explained, © 1980 by McGraw-Hill, Inc. Used with permission)*

Figure 40-23 March 1979 cocoa. This chart of March cocoa shows some very interesting examples of price formations. First, the breaking of trend line AB alerted investors to a possible trend reversal. Second, this break was confirmed by the completion of the massive head-and-shoulders pattern formed between September and December. Also worth noting is the small triangle pattern formed in September. The implication of the down-side breakout was that prices would go significantly lower, especially as the triangle itself represented an island. However, as so often happens toward the end of a strong move, the breakout proved to be a whipsaw; the signal would have been given on October 15, for not only was the down trend line of the triangle formation bettered on the up side with high volume, but also the gap from the day's price action left a 5-day island. As so often happens when a pattern fails to "work," the move in the opposite direction to that indicated by the pattern (in this case an upward one) was very violent.

Figure 40-24 *(From Martin J. Pring,* Technical Analysis Explained, *© 1980 by McGraw-Hill, Inc. Used with permission)*

The *orthodox broadening top* is shown in Figures 40-25 and 40-26. This pattern consists of three rallies reaching successively higher levels and separated by two bottoms, with the second bottom lower than the first. This pattern is rarely found at market bottoms.

Unfortunately, there is no clearly definable level of support whose violation could serve as a useful benchmark. The violent and emotional nature of the price and volume trends makes the identification of these patterns even more difficult. Obviously, under such conditions a breakout is difficult to pinpoint, but if the formation is reasonably symmetrical, a 3 percent move below the descending trend line joining the two bottoms, or even a 3 percent decline below the second bottom, usually serves as a timely warning that an even greater decline lies ahead.

TRIANGLES

Triangles may be consolidation or reversal formations, and they generally fall into two categories, symmetrical and right-angled.

Symmetrical Triangles

A symmetrical triangle consists of a series of two or more rallies and reactions in which each succeeding peak is lower than its predecessor and the bottom of each reaction is higher than its predecessor, as in Figure 40-27. In a sense the price action is like a coil that gets tighter and tighter as time progresses until it

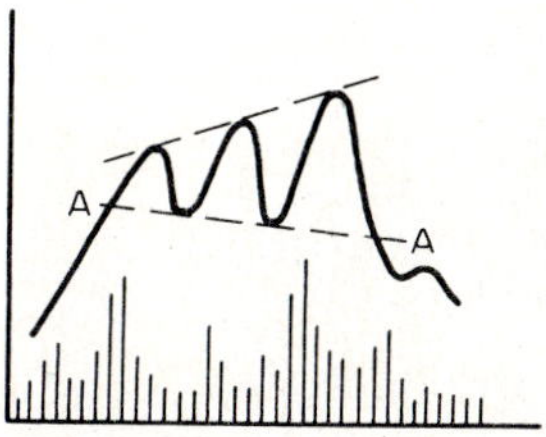

Figure 4-25 *(From Martin J. Pring,* Technical Analysis Explained, *© 1980 by McGraw-Hill, Inc. Used with permission)*

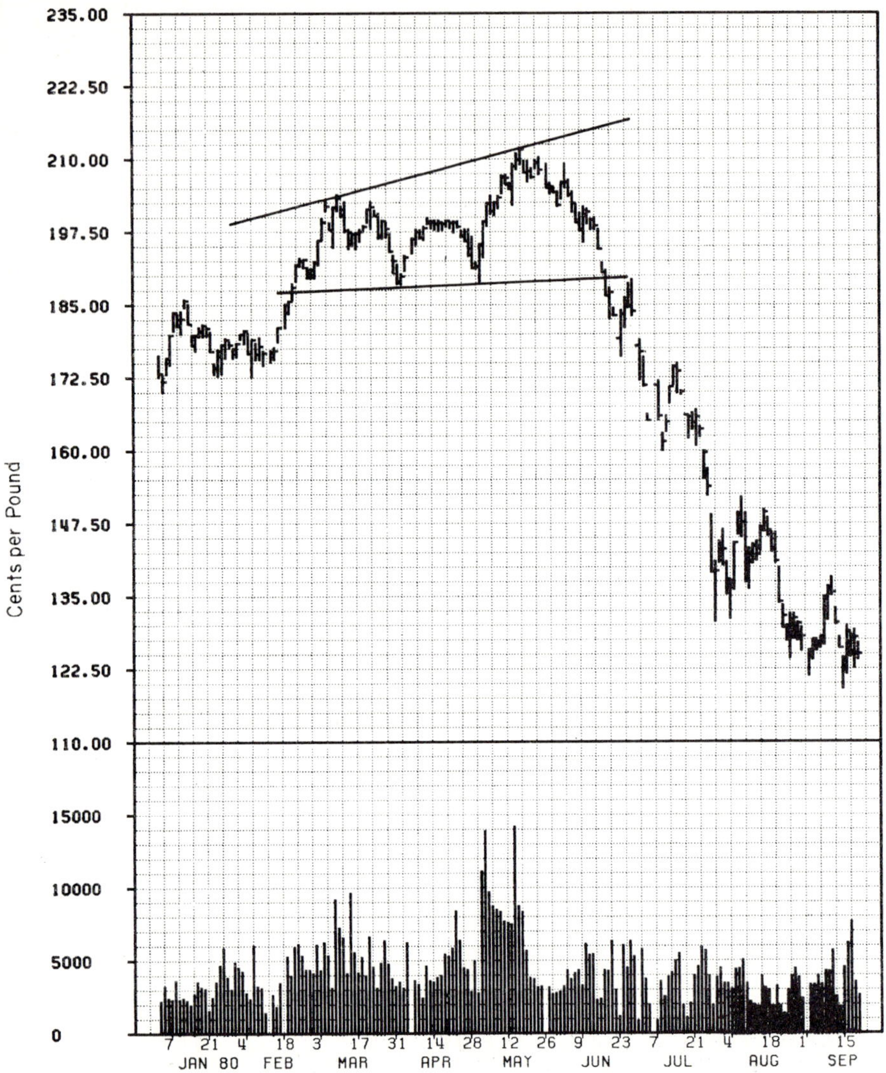

Figure 40-26 September 1980 coffee. The price action of September 1980 coffee is a good example of a broadening top with a flat bottom. Ideally, the April rally should have taken the price up to the ascending trend line to make the pattern symmetrical. Once the flat bottom was broken, prices fell sharply. Note also the 3-day retracement rally that took the price back to the lower reaches of the pattern.

finally explodes in one direction or another. Volume should contract as the triangle is formed. (See also Figure 40-28.) Generally speaking, triangles are reliable indicators of future trends when the breakout occurs somewhere between half and three-fourths of the distance from the widest peak and trough to the apex, as in Figure 40-29. The volume and 3 percent confirmation rules used for other patterns are also appropriate for triangles.

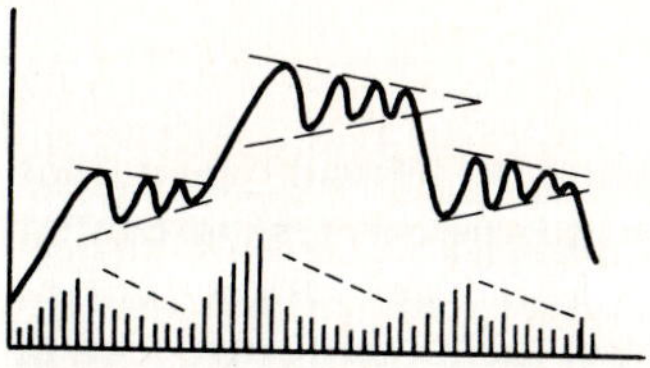

Figure 40-27 *(From Martin J. Pring,* Technical Analysis Explained, *© 1980 by McGraw-Hill, Inc. Used with permission)*

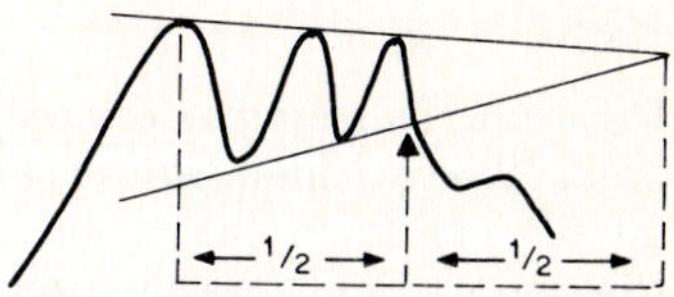

Figure 40-29 *(From Martin J. Pring,* Technical Analysis Explained, *© 1980 by McGraw-Hill, Inc. Used with permission)*

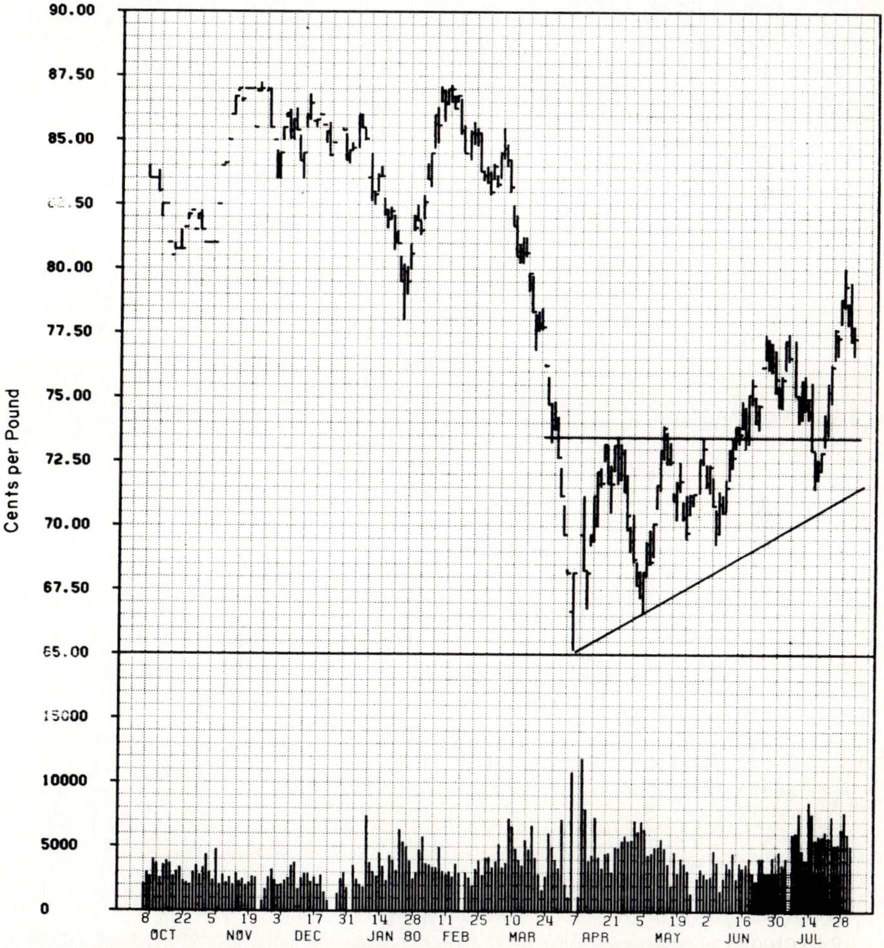

Figure 40-28 September 1980 cattle. The price action between March and May represents a good example of an ascending triangle. Quite often prices will become very volatile at important lows, but as a pattern progresses, the degree of volatility decreases. In this case the four successful tests of the 65-cent low washed out weak holders and served as a significant base for a substantial bull market in cattle prices.

Right-Angled Triangles

Right-angled triangles are really a special form of the symmetrical type in that one of the two boundaries is formed at an angle of 90 degrees, that is, horizontal to the vertical axis, as shown in Figures 40-30 and 40-31. These triangles, unlike the symmetrical type, give some advance indication of the ultimate direction of the breakout, because the sloping part of the pattern usually points in the direction of the breakout.

One drawback associated with all types of triangles is that many rectangles begin as triangles and therefore the breakouts often prove to be false. An example is shown in Figure 40-32.

Measuring objectives are obtained by drawing a line parallel to the base of the triangle through the peak of the first rally. This extended line (BB in Figures 40-33a and 40-33b) represents the objective which prices may be expected to reach or exceed. The reverse procedure should be used for a down-side breakout, as shown in Figures 40-33c and 40-33d.

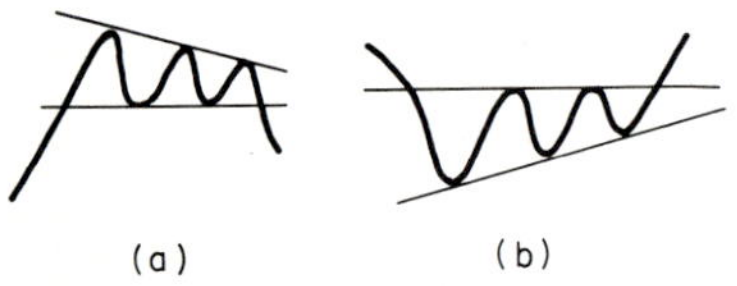

Figure 40-30 *(From Martin J. Pring,* Technical Analysis Explained, *© 1980 by McGraw-Hill, Inc. Used with permission)*

Figure 40-32 *(From Martin J. Pring,* Technical Analysis Explained, *© 1980 by McGraw-Hill, Inc. Used with permission)*

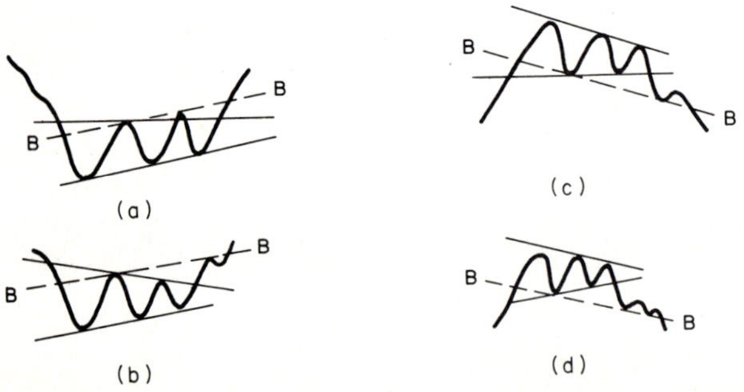

Figure 40-33 *(From Martin J. Pring,* Technical Analysis Explained, *© 1980 by McGraw-Hill, Inc. Used with permission)*

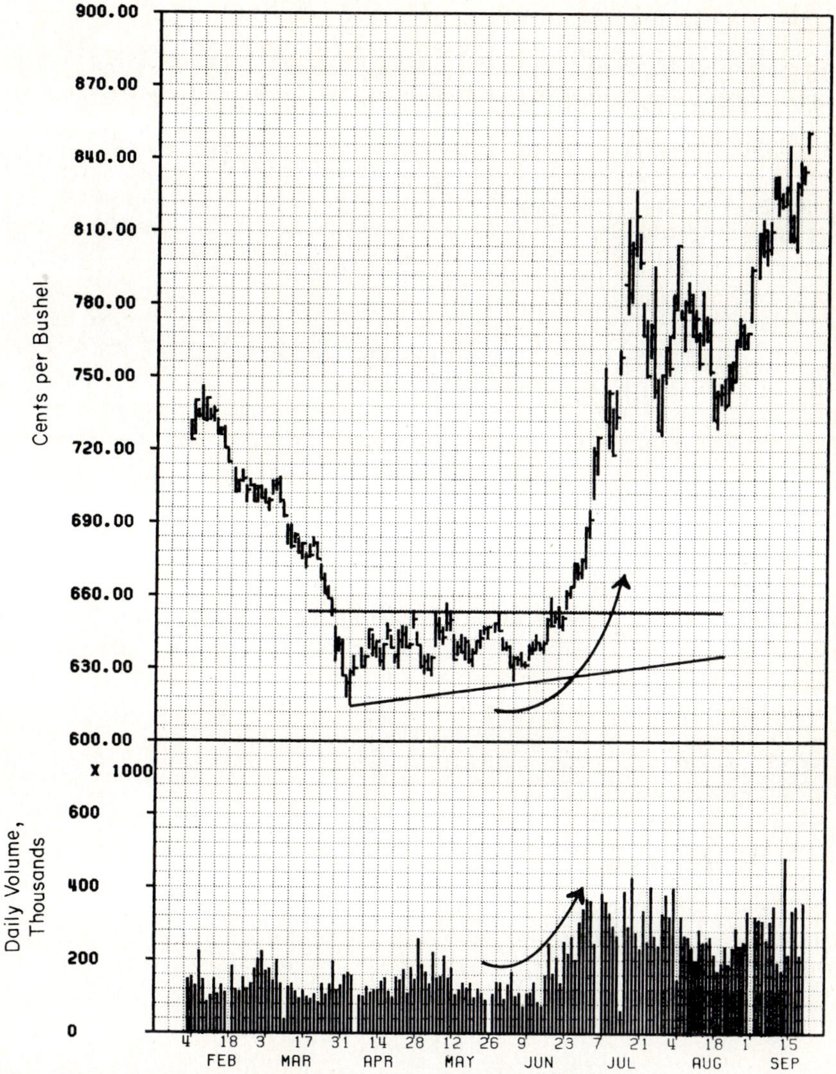

Figure 40-31 September 1980 soybeans. The summer rally in September 1980 was signaled by the breakout from an ascending right-angled triangle pattern. While this is not a classic formation in purely symmetrical terms, the simultaneous exponential increase in price and volume left little doubt about the true direction of the market.

CHAPTER

41

Trend Lines

Martin J. Pring

GENERAL

The trend line is probably the easiest technical tool to understand and undoubtedly the most widely used. A simple observation of any commodity price chart will reveal that a series of rising bottoms in an uptrend can be joined by a single line and that a series of declining peaks in a declining market can also be joined. These lines are known as trend lines (Figure 41-1). From a technical point of view, they are drawn as a rough approximation of a trend. When a trend line is violated, it is assumed that some kind of disturbance to that trend has taken place.

Trend lines can also be drawn horizontally, to follow sideways trends—the neckline of a head-and-shoulders pattern, for example, or the boundaries of a rectangle. The penetration of a head-and-shoulders pattern or a rectangle warns of a change in trend, just as the penetration of a trend line does.

A breakout from a price pattern can signify a reversal or a continuation of a trend, and the violation of a trend line has the same effect. Figure 41-2 illustrates this point in a rising trend. In Figure 41-2a the trend-line break signals a reversal in trend. The trend-line violation in Figure 41-2b is identical to that in Figure 41-2a, but the resulting action is entirely different. The violation in Figure 41-2b merely signals that the advance will continue but at a greatly reduced pace.

It is unfortunate that there is no reliable way of forecasting which possibility is likely to take place, but valuable clues can be obtained by using other techniques, described elsewhere in this section. A knowledge of price pattern con-

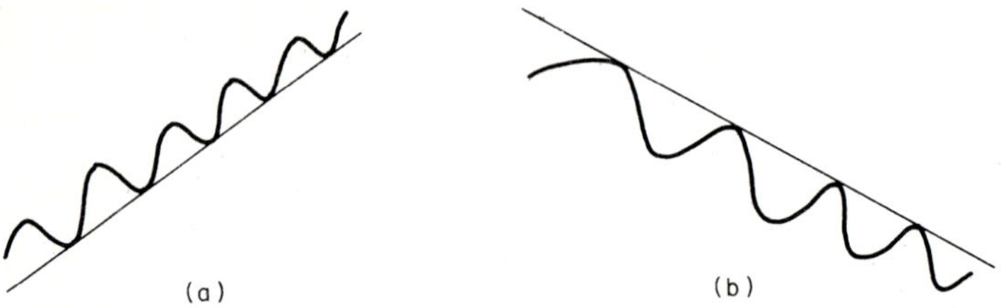

Figure 41-1 *(From Martin J. Pring,* Technical Analysis Explained, *© 1980 by McGraw-Hill, Inc. Used with permission)*

struction can also be helpful, since a trend-line penetration often occurs around the time of the successful completion of a reversal pattern, as shown in Figures 41-3 and 41-4.

In Figure 41-3a the last two reaction lows that touch the trend line represent the formation of an upward sloping head-and-shoulders pattern. Figure 41-3b shows the completion of a rectangle, and Figure 41-3c shows the breakout on the down side of a broadening formation with a flat bottom.

Quite clearly, if the trend-line break and the price pattern completion develop at the same time, they have the effect of reinforcing each other. Sometimes the trend line break develops before that of the price pattern, as in Figure 41-5. Since a trend is assumed to continue until a reversal has been proved, the violation should be regarded as a sign of an interruption of the prevailing movement rather than as a sign of a reversal. In an advance, it is therefore a good idea to wait for a decline in the price of a commodity below its previous trough before giving confirmation of an actual trend reversal. In such an instance the trend-line penetration should be treated as an alert, and additional evidence such as volume characteristics (discussed in Chapter 40) should be looked for. A series of rallies accompanied by less and less volume will clearly add to the bearish impetus of a down-side violation of an upward-sloping trend line, since volume is no longer going with the trend. While it is not necessary for volume to expand on a down-side breakout, the bearishness of the signal is clearly indicated if it does, since expansion of volume emphasizes a switch in the balance in favor of sellers.

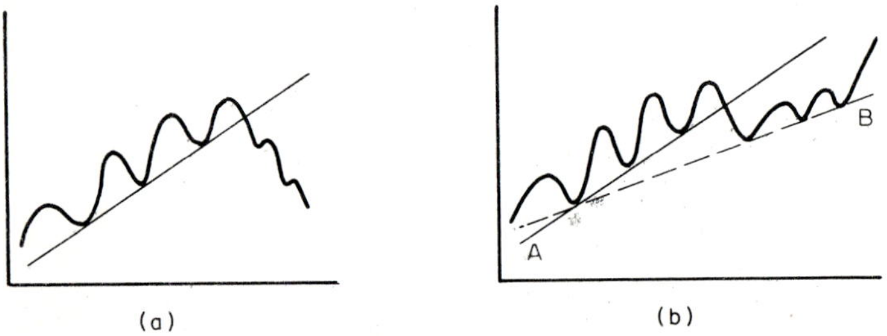

Figure 41-2 *(From Martin J. Pring,* Technical Analysis Explained, *© 1980 by McGraw-Hill, Inc. Used with permission)*

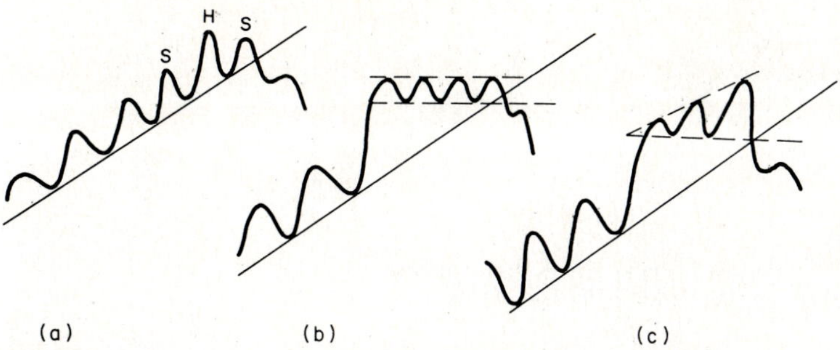

Figure 41-3 *(From Martin J. Pring,* Technical Analysis Explained, *© 1980 by McGraw-Hill, Inc. Used with permission)*

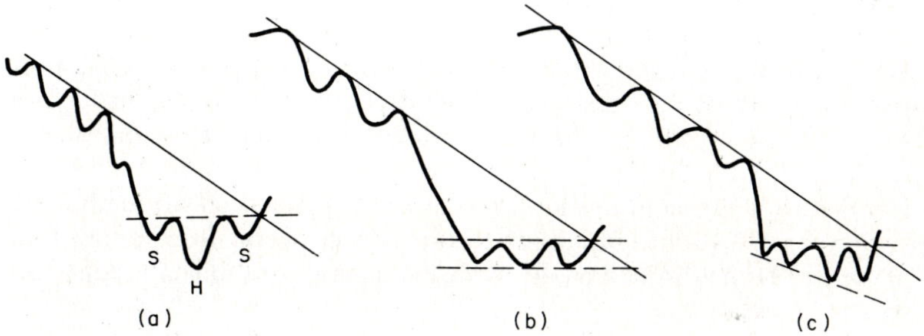

Figure 41-4 *(From Martin J. Pring,* Technical Analysis Explained, *© 1980 by McGraw-Hill, Inc. Used with permission)*

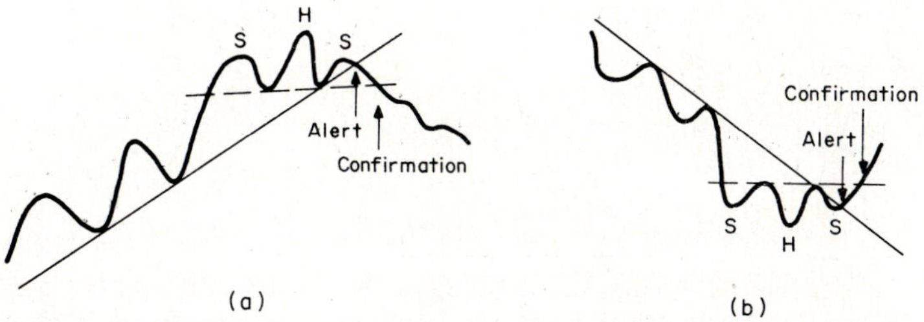

Figure 41-5 *(From Martin J. Pring,* Technical Analysis Explained, *© 1980 by McGraw-Hill, Inc. Used with permission)*

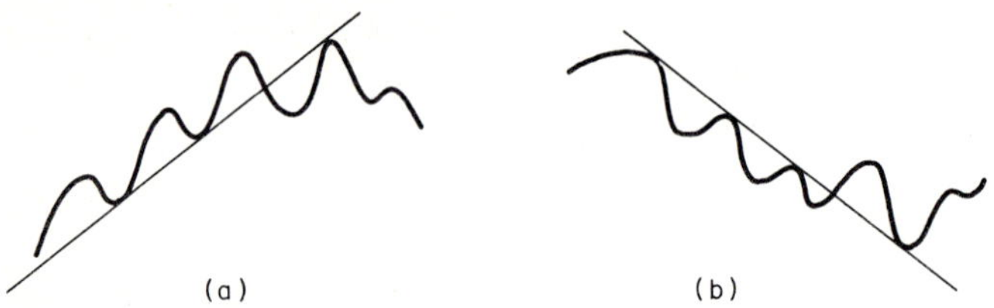

Figure 41-6 *(From Martin J. Pring,* Technical Analysis Explained, *© 1980 by McGraw-Hill, Inc. Used with permission)*

It was noted earlier that on a good many occasions a return move develops following a price pattern breakout. The same phenomenon, known as a *throwback,* also occurs with trend lines. Some possibilities are shown in Figure 41-6. In Figure 41-6a the trend line reverses its previous role of support, as the ensuing rally finds resistance at the trend line. The reverse situation for bear markets is shown in Figure 41-6b.

The advantages of ratio scale over arithmetic scale, discussed in Chapter 39, are especially critical in timely and accurate use of trend-line analysis. At the end of a major movement, prices tend to accelerate in the direction of the prevailing trend, that is, they rise faster at the end of a bull market and have a tendency to decline at a faster rate as a bear market reaches its terminal phase. Figure 41-7 shows how this exponential movement takes the price well away from the trend line if the commodity price is being plotted on an arithmetic scale. The price must therefore fall much faster before a trend-line penetration can take place on the arithmetic scale, which makes the ratio scale chart far more timely.

SIGNIFICANCE OF TREND LINES

It has been established that a trend-line break can result in either an actual price reversal or an interruption of a trend, followed by a resumption of the original trend. Although it is not always possible to determine which of these

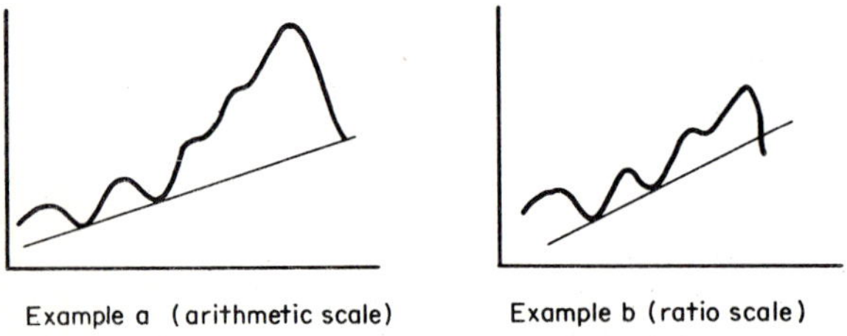

Figure 41-7 *(From Martin J. Pring,* Technical Analysis Explained, *© 1980 by McGraw-Hill, Inc. Used with permission)*

alternatives will develop, understanding the significance of a trend-line violation is still important. The principles discussed below are helpful.

Number of Times a Trend Line Has Been Touched

Since a rising trend line marks an area of support (and a falling trend line marks an area of resistance), the more often the trend line has been touched, the greater is its importance as a support (resistance) level and therefore the more important its violation will be.

Length of a Trend Line

A trend line is a technical tool designed to approximate a trend. Consequently, the longer a trend line, the longer the trend that it is measuring and the greater the significance of a break in the trend line. For example, a trend line joining a series of peaks and troughs that develops over a 3- to 4-week period has significance for only a small trend. On the other hand, a trend line that has been in existence for several years reflects a longer-term trend and its violation is much more important.

Slope of a Trend Line

Generally, the steeper the slope of a trend line, the less sustainable the price move will be. Consequently, the violation of a trend line loses importance the steeper its slope is.

TREND-LINE CONSTRUCTION

The ability to construct a trend line is based on individual judgment acquired through trial and error. Usually, the more obvious the construction, the more validity the trend line will have. In Figure 41-8, for example, the slope of trend line AA is relatively flat; by the time the line is violated, most of the price decline has already taken place and therefore the trend line is not of much

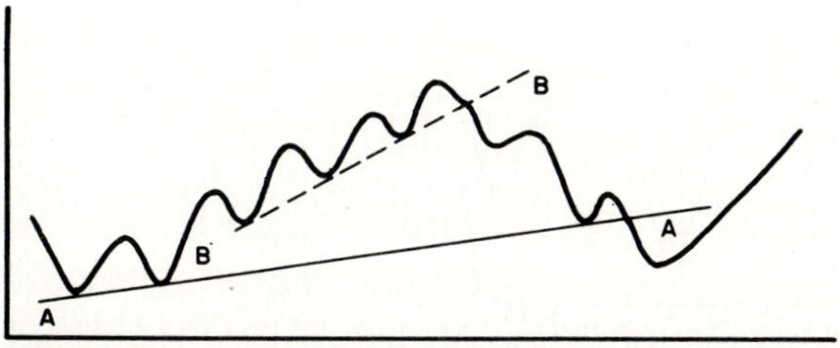

Figure 41-8 *(From Martin J. Pring,* Technical Analysis Explained, *© 1980 by McGraw-Hill, Inc. Used with permission)*

practical use. The slope of line BB is a little sharper and has been touched many times; therefore, although BB is a shorter line than AA, it more accurately reflects the trend.

On the other hand, a very sharply sloping trend line, like the one shown in Figure 41-9, is not usually so sustainable. Therefore, even though the line has been touched several times, its violation would be regarded as a temporary interruption of a trend that would later be resumed at a more sustainable pace.

MEASURING IMPLICATIONS

Measuring objectives can be obtained from trend-line violations in the same manner as described above for price patterns. For a rising trend line, the vertical distance (A_1 in Figure 41-10) between the peak in the commodity price and the trend line is projected downward from the point of violation (A_2 in Figure 41-10). When the violation is the reversal type, the price objective is usually well exceeded. Quite often, if prices fall below the objective, the subsequent rally is reversed at the level of the objective, as shown in Figure 41-11. The example in Figure 41-12 shows this principle operating in reverse for a falling trend line.

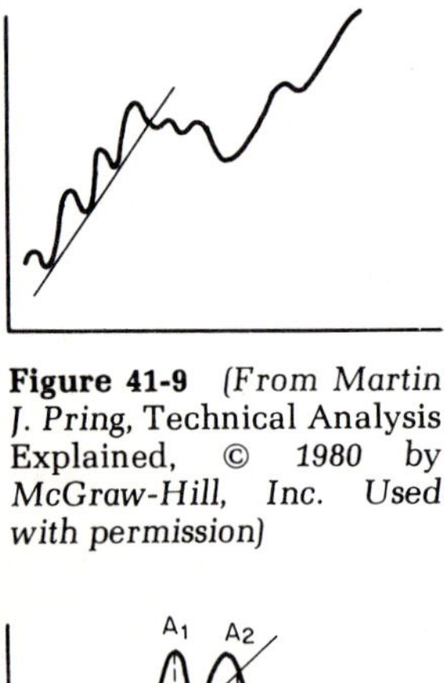

Figure 41-9 *(From Martin J. Pring, Technical Analysis Explained, © 1980 by McGraw-Hill, Inc. Used with permission)*

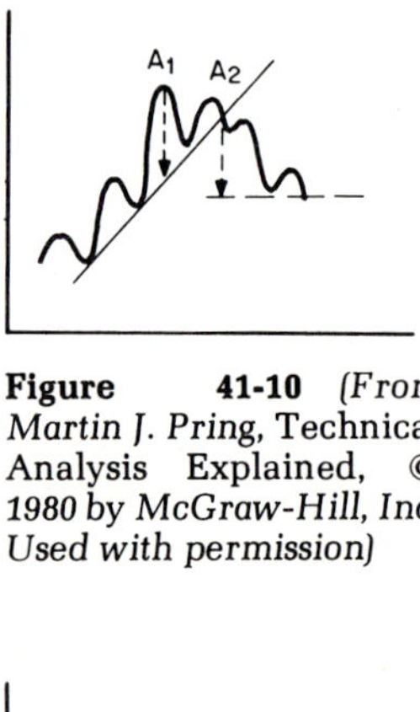

Figure 41-10 *(From Martin J. Pring, Technical Analysis Explained, © 1980 by McGraw-Hill, Inc. Used with permission)*

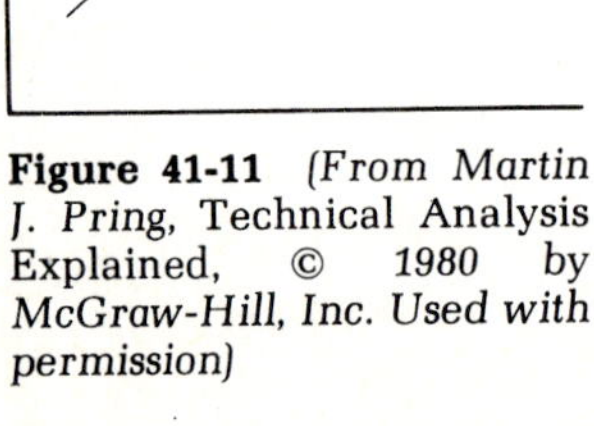

Figure 41-11 *(From Martin J. Pring, Technical Analysis Explained, © 1980 by McGraw-Hill, Inc. Used with permission)*

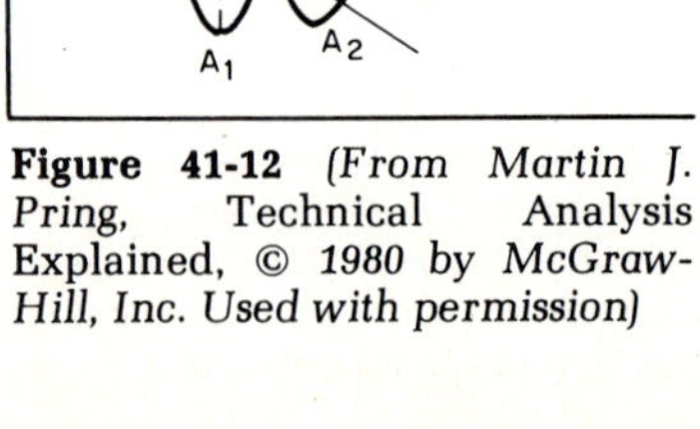

Figure 41-12 *(From Martin J. Pring, Technical Analysis Explained, © 1980 by McGraw-Hill, Inc. Used with permission)*

THE CORRECTIVE FAN PRINCIPLE

At the beginning of a new bull move, the first intermediate rally is usually quite strong and sharp. It often represents a technical reaction to the previous over-extended decline, as speculators with short positions rush to cover them. The ensuing trend line is therefore quickly violated on the down side, as represented by line AA in Figure 41-13. A new line joining the bear market low to the first intermediate low (AB) is then constructed. This trend is more sustainable because it is less steep, but even this line is eventually violated, requiring the construction of a third line (AC). The fan principle states that the termination of a bull move has been confirmed once the third line has been violated. The fan principle is just as valid for downtrends and can be used for identifying reversals in intermediate as well as cyclical movements. In an intermediate rally (or reaction), the three trend lines would be drawn against minor troughs (or peaks).

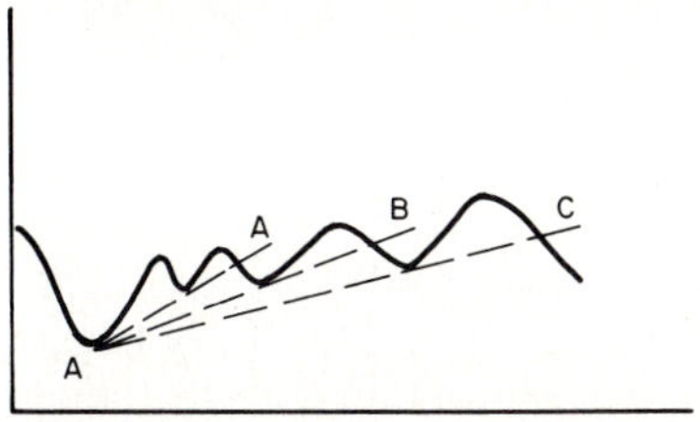

Figure 41-13 *(From Martin J. Pring,* Technical Analysis Explained, *© 1980 by McGraw-Hill, Inc. Used with permission)*

TREND CHANNELS

The description of trend lines so far has concentrated on joining troughs during advances and peaks during declines, but it is often possible to join peaks during advances and troughs during downtrends. The resulting price action is contained in a *trend channel.* Figure 41-14 shows some trend channels. The line parallel to the main trend line, represented by the dashed lines in Figure 41-14, is known as the *return trend line.*

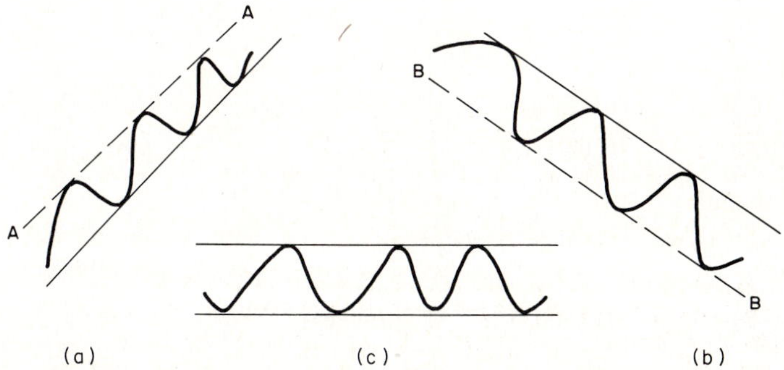

Figure 41-14 *(From Martin J. Pring,* Technical Analysis Explained, *© 1980 by McGraw-Hill, Inc. Used with permission)*

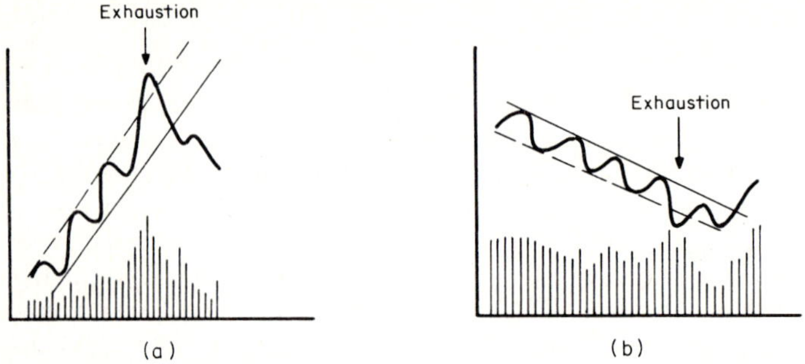

Figure 41-15 *(From Martin J. Pring,* Technical Analysis Explained, *© 1980 by McGraw-Hill, Inc. Used with permission)*

The return trend line is useful for two reasons. First, it represents a line of resistance during advances, or support during declines, at which the price is temporarily reversed. Second, penetration of the return trend line usually indicates that a basic reversal lies ahead. In Figure 41-15a prices work their way above the return trend line in an almost exponential manner, accompanied by sharply higher volume. This represents an *exhaustion move.*

Consider a man sawing a thick piece of wood; he gradually becomes frustrated as he realizes his task is going to take him some time. He slowly begins to increase the speed of his sawing strokes and then bursts into a frantic effort. Finally, he is forced to give up his task, at least temporarily, because he becomes completely exhausted. Figure 41-15b shows how a similar exhaustion move develops in a down market.

CHAPTER

42

Flags, Pennants, Wedges, and Gaps

Martin J. Pring

The price patterns discussed in Chapter 41 can develop as either reversal or continuation formations. Those discussed in this chapter are almost invariably continuation formations.

FLAGS

A *flag* formation, as the name implies, looks like a flag when charted. It represents a period of backing and filling following a sharp, almost vertical, rise or decline before an additional sharp rally (decline). Flags for up and down markets are shown in Figures 42-1a and 42-1b. Essentially, the flag formation takes the form of a parallelogram in which the rally peaks and reaction lows can be connected by two lines that run parallel to each other. In a rising market, the flag is usually formed with a slight downtrend, whereas in a falling market the flag has a slight upward bias. Flags may also be horizontal.

In a rising market a flag usually separates two halves of an almost vertical rise. Volume is extremely heavy just before the flag formation begins. As the pattern is completed, volume gradually dries up almost completely; then it explodes as the price works its way out of the completed formation. Flags can form in as short a time as 5 days, or they may take as long as 3 to 5 weeks. Essentially, in a rising market, a flag represents a period of controlled profit taking.

In a falling market, a flag is formed during a period of declining volume. However, since this type of flag represents a formation with an upward bias in price, the volume implication—that is, rising price with declining volume—is essentially bearish in nature.

It is extremely important to check on whether the price and volume characteristics agree. Following a sharp rise, for example, if the price consolidates in what appears to be a flag formation but volume fails to contract appreciably, much caution is indicated, for prices may react on the down side. Also suspect is a flag that takes more than 4 weeks to develop. Since a flag is a temporary interruption of a sharp uptrend, a 4-week or longer formation period represents an unduly long time for profit taking.

Flag formations can usually be relied upon in forecasting, for not only is the direction of the move well indicated but also the ensuing move is usually sharp and worthwhile from a trading point of view. Flags tend to form halfway up or down a particular move, and therefore, as far as measuring is concerned, the move out of the pattern should be regarded as being approximately the same size as the move from the original breakout.

Since flags take a relatively short period to develop, they do not show up on weekly or monthly charts.

PENNANTS

A pennant develops under exactly the same circumstances as a flag and has the same characteristics except that it is constructed by joining a series of rallies and peaks that converge as shown in Figure 42-2. In a sense, a flag corresponds to a rectangle, and a pennant to a triangle. Volume tends to contract even more during the formation of a pennant than of a flag. In every other way, however, pennants are identical to flags—measuring implications, time taken to develop, and so forth.

SAUCERS AND ROUNDING TOPS

Figures 42-3a and 42-3b show the formation of a saucer and a rounding top. Obviously, a saucer pattern occurs at a market bottom and a rounding top

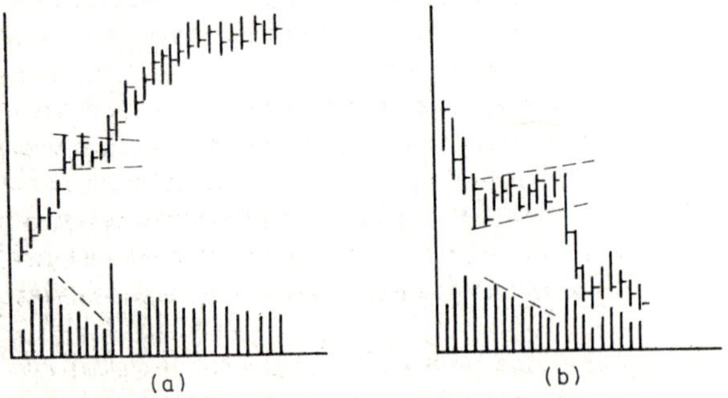

Figure 42-1

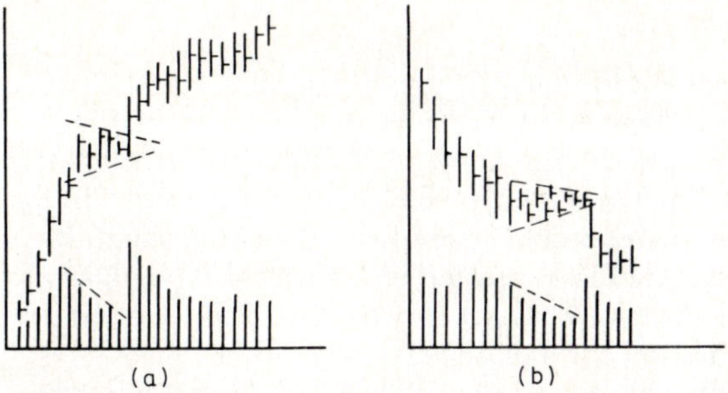

Figure 42-2

develops at a market peak. The price part of a saucer is constructed by drawing a line under the lows that roughly approximates a letter U, except that the lower portion of the formation is usually more elongated or saucer-shaped. As prices fall toward the low point, downward momentum dissipates. People lose interest in the commodity and volume almost dries up at the same time. Gradually both price and volume pick up until each explodes almost exponentially.

In terms of price, the rounded top is almost the exact opposite of the saucer. Volume characteristics are almost the same, however, with the result that if volume is plotted below price, it is almost possible to draw a complete circle, as shown in Figure 42-3b. The tip-off to the bearish implication of the rounded top is that volume shrinks as prices reach their highest levels and then expands as they fall, both of which are unnatural phenomena.

Rounding tops and saucers are fine examples of a gradual changeover in the supply-and-demand balance, as it slowly picks up momentum in the opposite direction to the previous trend. Quite clearly, it is difficult to obtain breakout levels for such patterns since they develop slowly and do not offer clear support or resistance levels on which to establish a breakout move. Even so, trying to identify such formations is worthwhile, for they are usually followed by substantial moves.

Saucers and rounding tops can also be observed as consolidation as well as reversal phenomena.

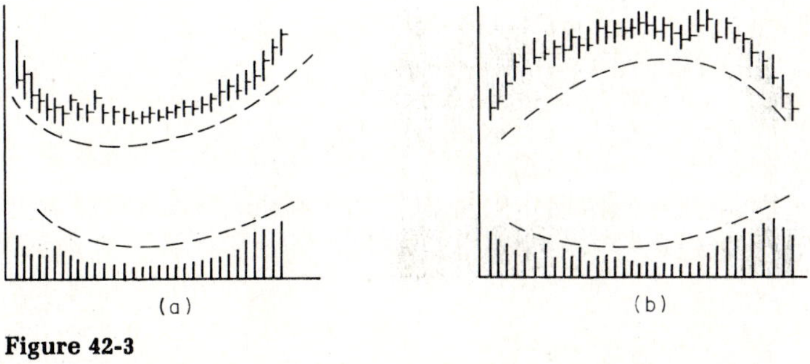

Figure 42-3

WEDGES

A wedge is very similar to a triangle in that two converging lines can be constructed from a series of peaks and troughs to form a wedge, as shown in Figure 42-4. However, a triangle consists of one rising and one falling line, or one horizontal line, but the converging lines in a wedge both move in the *same* direction. A falling wedge represents a temporary interruption of a rising trend. It is normal for volume to contract during the formation of both types of wedges.

Wedges can take anywhere from 2 to 8 weeks to complete. They sometimes show up on weekly charts but are too short to appear on monthly charts.

Rising wedges are fairly common as bear market rallies. Following their completion, prices usually break very sharply, especially if volume picks up noticeably on the down side.

KEY REVERSAL DAYS

A key reversal day usually occurs after a prolonged move. The term "key reversal" is used because, at the beginning of the day, prices move sharply in the direction of the previous trend, but by the end of the day, the prices have "key-reversed," and they close opposite to the direction in which they began the day. Key reversal days are usually associated with an explosion of volume well above levels of the recent past. They represent an exhaustion of buying power at peaks and an exhaustion of selling power or liquidation at troughs (see Figures 42-5a and 42-5b).

A key reversal is, in a sense, a 1-day price pattern. Therefore, it merely implies a short-term trend reversal. Since such patterns usually develop after a long and sustained move, however, they are often followed by important trend reversals.

The price range in a key reversal day usually dwarfs anything that has gone before. Often the price moves as much in the first 2 to 4 hours as it would in 2 to 5 normal trading days, usually opening well above or below the previous day's close.

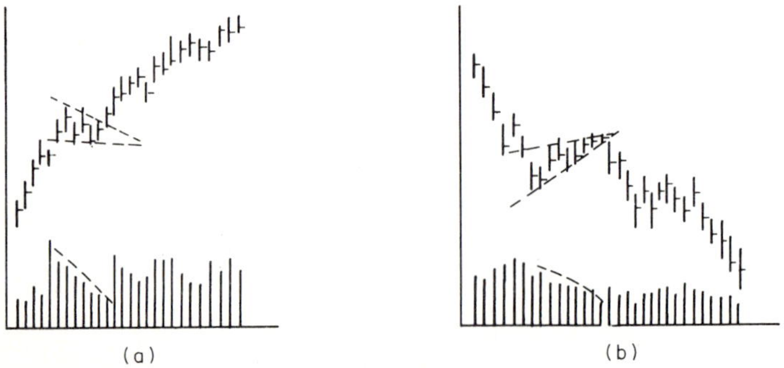

Figure 42-4

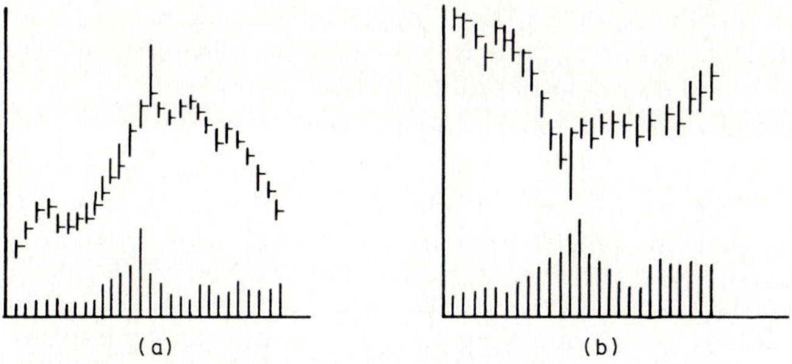

Figure 42-5

GAPS

A gap occurs when the lowest price at which a commodity trades on a specific day, week, or month is above the highest level on the previous day or month (Figure 42-6a) or when the highest price on a specific day, week, or month is below the lowest price of the previous day, week, or month (Figure 42-6b). It follows that gaps can only occur on bar charts on which intraday, intraweek, or intramonth prices are plotted, and that a gap is really an empty vertical space between one period of trading and another. Within a day's trading many gaps are made between ticks, but these do not show up on intraday charts. Daily gaps are far more common than weekly ones because a gap on a weekly chart must by definition fall between the close of Friday trading and the opening of Monday trading—that is, there is only a 5 to 1 chance of occurrence of a daily gap. Monthly gaps are even more rare because "holes" on the chart can only develop between month-end closings.

A gap can be closed only when price action comes back and retraces the whole range of the gap. This process may take a few days or a few months or weeks; more rarely, it never occurs. There is an old saying that the market abhors a vacuum and therefore all gaps are eventually filled. It is certainly true that *almost* all gaps are eventually closed; however, since an occasional gap is never closed and because it can take months or even years to fill a gap, trading strategies should not be implemented on the assumption that a gap will be filled in the immediate future.

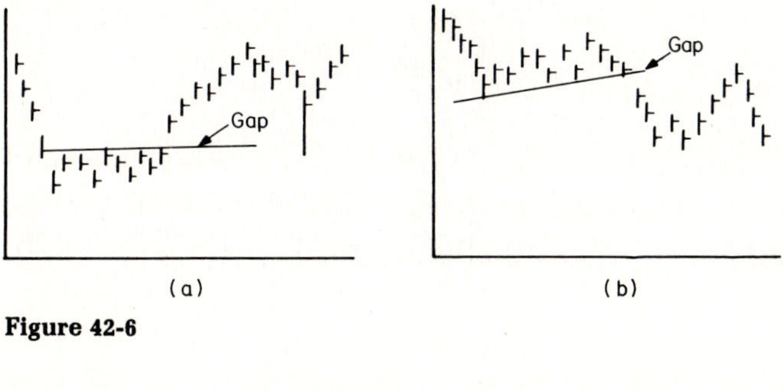

Figure 42-6

Gaps should be treated with respect, but their importance should not be overemphasized. Gaps which occur during the formation of a price pattern are usually closed fairly quickly and do not have much significance.

Three types of gaps are worthy of consideration: breakaway, runaway, and exhaustion gaps.

Breakaway Gaps

A breakaway gap is created when a price breaks out of a price pattern (as in Figures 42-6a and 42-6b). Generally speaking, the gap emphasizes the bullishness or bearishness of the breakout, depending on which direction it takes. Even when a gap occurs, however, it is still important for an up-side breakout to be accompanied by a relatively high level of volume. In other words, it is necessary for a change to bullish sentiment not only to develop in terms of price but to be backed up with money on the buying side; that is, there must be sufficient volume to justify the bullish sentiment. It should not be concluded that every gap breakout that takes place is always a valid one, since there is no such thing as absolute certainty in technical analysis. However a breakout that does develop with a gap is more likely to be valid than one that does not.

Continuation or Runaway Gaps

A runaway gap occurs during a straight-line advance or decline when price quotations are moving rapidly and emotions are running high (see Figure 42-7a. Such gaps are either closed very quickly (that is, within a day or so) or tend to remain open for much longer periods. The gap often occurs halfway between a breakout and the ultimate duration of the move. For this reason, they are sometimes called measuring gaps.

Exhaustion Gaps

A price move will often contain more than one runaway gap, indicating that a powerful trend is in force. A second or third runaway gap should also alert traders that the move will inevitably run out of steam sooner or later and that the second or third gap may be an exhaustion gap.

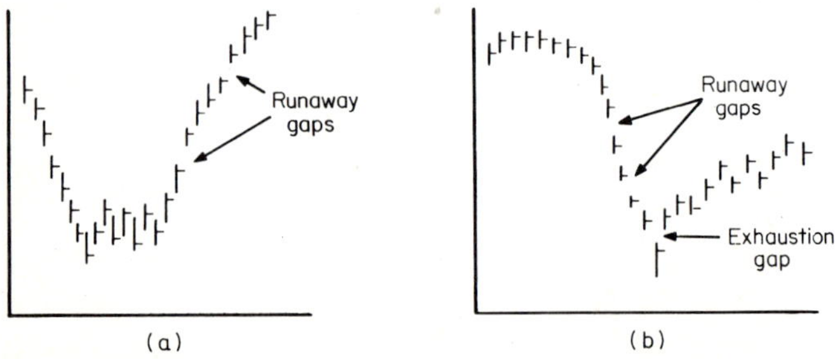

Figure 42-7

When a gap occurs, of course, it is not easy to ascertain whether it is another runaway gap or an exhaustion gap. One clue is unusually heavy volume in relation to the price change of that day. In an exhaustion gap, volume usually works up to a crescendo well above previous levels, which should have been expanding in any event. Sometimes the price will close near to the vacuum (or gap) and well away from its extreme reading. If the next day's trading creates an "island" on which the gap day is completely isolated by a vacuum from the previous day's trading, the gap day was probably in fact a key reversal day. Such exhaustion is only a sign of temporary reversal, but it should be sufficient to indicate to highly leveraged traders that they should sell out or should reverse from the long to the short side or vice versa.

CHAPTER

43

Moving Averages

Martin J. Pring

By now it will have become apparent that futures prices can be extremely volatile, and at times can appear to be almost haphazard. An approach that can be used to tone down these fluctuations and reduce distortions is the construction of a moving average. The three basic types of moving averages are *simple, weighted,* and *exponential.*

SIMPLE MOVING AVERAGES

Construction

Most chart services and technicians use a simple moving average (MA) in analysis because it is relatively easy to construct and use. An average is constructed by totalling up a series of observations and dividing the total by the number of observations. A 10-day average, for example, is obtained by adding up the price data for 10 days and dividing the total by 10. To get the average to "move", the first day's value is subtracted from the total and the eleventh's day's is added, so that there is still a total of 10 days' observations; the new total is then divided by 10. A 13-day MA would require a total of 13 days of observations, and so on.

Moving averages can be constructed for any time period—days, weeks, months, or even years. Clearly, the choice of construction will depend upon the time period under consideration. Short-term trends require MAs measured in days, and long-term trends are measured in weeks or months. Table 43-1 shows the calculation of a 10-period MA.

A 13-week MA is shown in Figure 43-1a by the dashed line. Generally speak-

TABLE 43-1 Calculation of Simple Moving Average

Date	Index	10-week total	Moving average
Jan. 8	101		
Jan. 15	100		
Jan. 22	103		
Jan. 29	99		
Feb. 5	96		
Feb. 12	99		
Feb. 19	95		
Feb. 26	91		
Mar. 5	93		
Mar. 12	89	966	96.6
Mar. 19	90	955	95.5
Mar. 26	95	950	95.0
Apr. 2	103	950	95.0

ing, a rising MA represents market strength, and a declining MA, market weakness. It can be seen from Figure 13-1a that the moving average changes direction some time after the peak or trough of the commodity price. This change occurs because the MA is plotted on the thirteenth week, whereas the average price of 13 weeks of observations actually occurs halfway through the observation period, in this case during the seventh week.

If the MA is to fit the actual trend correctly, it should therefore be centered—that is, plotted—on the seventh week. The problem with centering a moving average is the time delay involved, in this case 6 weeks. When analyzing economic or other slow-moving data, such time delays, while irritating, are not

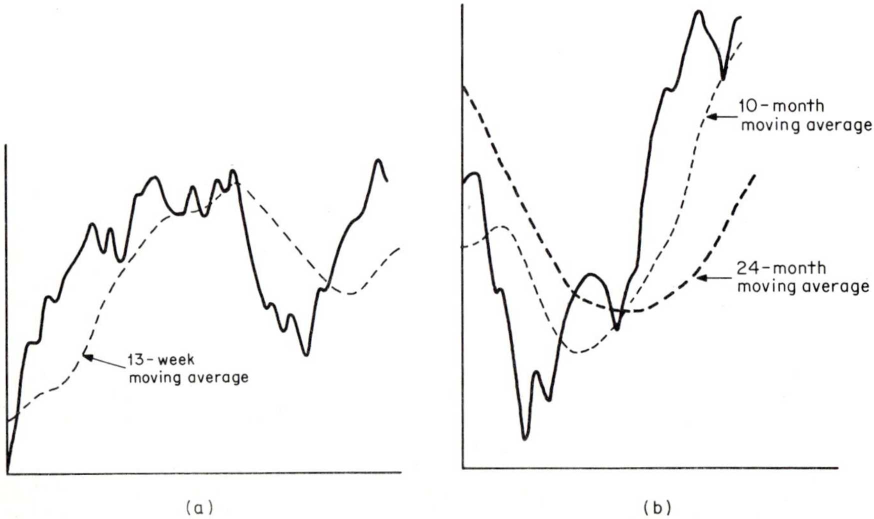

Figure 43-1 *(From Martin J. Pring,* Technical Analysis Explained, *© 1980 by McGraw-Hill, Inc. Used with permission)*

particularly critical. For commodity market timing, however, delays are important; they could cause the loss of many profitable opportunities. For this reason, most technicians choose to plot moving averages in the final period. As a result, timing signals are looked for not so much in reversals in the direction of a moving average as in *crossovers* between the price of the commodity and its MA. A change from a rising to a falling trend is confirmed when the price crosses below its MA, and vice versa.

Guidelines for Buying and Selling

Because the MA is a more objective tool than a trend line, it usually pays to heed a crossover signal, especially when a chart shows that similar reliable signals have occurred in the past. Some of the principles associated with MAs and MA crossovers are listed below.

1. Since a moving average is itself a reflection of a trend, prices often find support or resistance at the level of the average. The more often that this appears to be the case, the greater the significance of the MA crossover.
2. A moving-average crossover is often a vital clue that confirms a trend change. Greater emphasis should be placed on this kind of signal, however, if the MA either is flat or has already changed direction before the crossover.
3. If the violation occurs while the MA is still proceeding strongly in the direction of the prevailing trend, the crossover should be treated more as an alert than as a strong signal. Confirmation of the crossover should therefore be sought from other technical sources.
4. The longer the time span of a moving average, the greater the significance of any given crossover. It is highly unlikely that a crossover of a 10-day MA will signal anything other than reversal of a minor trend, for example, whereas a crossover of a 200-day MA is an indication of reversal of a relatively longer-term trend.

Choice of Time Span

As discussed above, moving averages can be constructed for any time period. However, over the years certain time spans have proved to be more reliable than others. Choice of length is therefore very important. For example if it is assumed that an intermediate uptrend lasts 13 weeks, a 40-week MA would be of little use, since theoretically it would smooth out all fluctuations during that period. In this instance a 6- or even 10-week MA would be a far more appropriate measurement. On the other hand a 10-day MA would catch virtually every move but would be of very little help in identifying a cyclical reversal in price. Bearing these factors in mind, the following time spans are suggested.

For fairly long trends, 52-week, 40-week (200-trading day), 30-week, and 13-week MAs have proved useful, probably because each spans a 3-month or longer period. Other averages that also offer good crossover signals are 10- and 6-week MAs. Shorter term, many technicians favor 30-, 25-, 15-, and 10-day periods as probably the most useful. The length of the trend being measured should always be the determining factor.

MULTIPLE MOVING AVERAGES

Some technicians prefer to use two MAs, one short and one long. When the shorter-term MA crosses over the longer-term MA, a signal is given. This technique has the advantage of further smoothing out the data, which reduces the possibility of a whipsaw but still gives a warning if a trend changes fairly quickly. This point serves to emphasize the continual trade-off in the choice of MA—that is, there is always a choice between possible lateness and possible oversensitivity.

By definition, MA crossovers always occur after a peak or trough in prices and therefore serve as a *confirmation* that a change in trend has taken place. Commodity markets can and often do trade in a broad sideways band and therefore several misleading whipsaw signals are inevitable; it is always wise to use MA crossovers in conjunction with other technical signals.

WEIGHTED MOVING AVERAGES

As mentioned above, in an ideal situation a MA should be centered. One way to speed up the turning points of a moving average is to "weight" one or more of the most recent observations instead of treating all the data equally. Weighting can be achieved in many ways; one of the most common is to weight the last period of data by the number of observations in the average and to reduce the weights proportionately until the first observation is not weighted at all. In a 6-week MA, for example, the latest observation would be multiplied by 6, yesterday's observation by 5, the observation of the day before yesterday by 4,

TABLE 43-2 Calculation of Weighted Moving Average

Date	Index (1)	6 × col. 1 (2)	5 × col. 1 1 week ago (3)	4 × col. 1 2 weeks ago (4)	3× col. 1 3 weeks ago (5)	2 × col. 1 4 weeks ago (6)	1 × col. 1 5 weeks ago (7)	Total cols. 2 to 7 (8)	Col. 8 ÷ 21 (9)
Jan. 8	101								
Jan. 15	100								
Jan. 22	103								
Jan. 29	99								
Feb. 5	96								
Feb. 12	99	594	480	396	309	200	101	2080	99.1
Feb. 19	95	570	495	384	297	206	100	2052	97.7
Feb. 26	91	546	475	396	288	198	103	2006	95.5
Mar. 5	93	558	455	380	297	192	99	1981	94.3
Mar. 12	89	534	465	364	285	198	96	1924	92.5

and so forth. The totals for each period are then added up, and the result is divided by the sum of the weights: 6 + 5 + 4 + 3 + 2 + 1 = 21. Table 43-2 shows the calculations for a 6-week weighted MA using this formula.

An easier approach to the calculation of a weighted MA is to treat all the data equally except the most recent period, which has twice the weight of the others. To start the calculation for a 5-week MA using this type of formula, first add the prices:

Week	Price
1	101
2	100
3	103
4	99
5	96
5	96
Total	595

Then use the following equation:

$$\frac{\text{Total}}{\text{Weeks}} = \frac{595}{6} = 99.2$$

Usually technicians treat a change in direction of a weighted MA as a signal of trend change rather than an actual crossover, because of the greater sensitivity of the weighted MA.

EXPONENTIAL MOVING AVERAGES

An exponential moving average (EMA), like a weighted MA, gives greater weight to the most recent data. It therefore changes direction much more quickly than a simple MA. From the viewpoint of physical calculation, however, the EMA is much easier and quicker to construct.

To calculate a 20-week EMA, it is necessary first to construct a simple 20-period MA—that is, the total of 20 periods of observation divided by 20. Table 43-3, column 6, shows this construction for the 20 weeks ending January 1. This

TABLE 43-3 Calculation of Exponential Moving Average

Date	Price (1)	EMA for previous week (2)	Difference (col. 1 − col. 2) (3)	Exponent (4)	Col. 3 × col. 4 +/− (5)	Col. 2 + col. 5 EMA (6)
Jan. 1						99.00
Jan. 8	100.00	99.00	1.00	0.1	+0.10	99.10
Jan. 15	103.00	99.10	3.90	0.1	+0.39	00.49
Jan. 22	102.00	99.49	2.51	0.1	+0.25	99.74
Jan. 29	99.00	99.64	(0.64)	0.1	−0.06	99.68

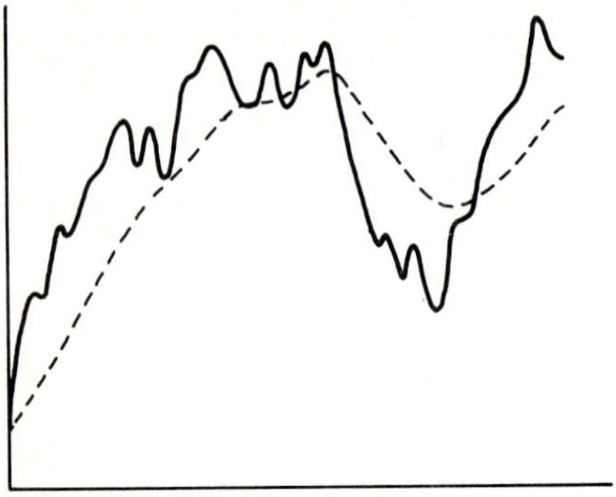

Figure 43-2 *(From Martin J. Pring,* Technical Analysis Explained, *© 1980 by McGraw-Hill, Inc. Used with permission)*

figure is used as the starting point and transferred to column 2 on the following week. Next, the observation for the twenty-first week (January 8 in Table 43-3) is compared to the MA (that is, 99). The difference is added or subtracted and posted in column 3: 100−99= 1.0. The difference is then multiplied by the exponent, which for a 20-period EMA is 0.1. This exponentially treated difference, 1.0 × 0.1, is added to or subtracted from the previous week's EMA. The calculation is then repeated. The figure in column 6 becomes the EMA and is therefore plotted. A 13-period EMA is shown in Figure 43-2.

The exponent to be used depends on the time period chosen. The relevant exponents for specific time spans are:

5-period	0.4
10-period	0.2
15-period	0.13
20-period	0.1
40-period	0.05
80-period	0.025

Whether the period is 5 days, 5 weeks, or 5 months, the same exponent, 0.4, should be used. The correct exponents for time spans not listed above can be

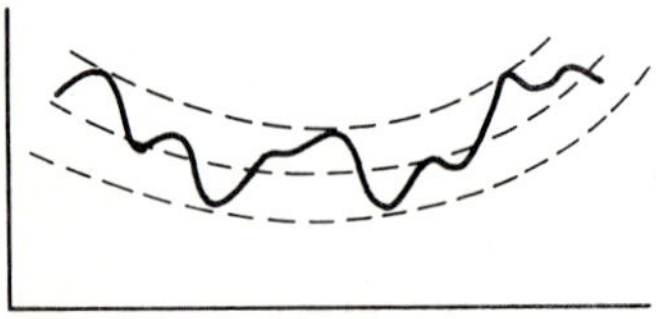

Figure 43-3 *(From Martin J. Pring,* Technical Analysis Explained, *© 1980 by McGraw-Hill, Inc. Used with permission)*

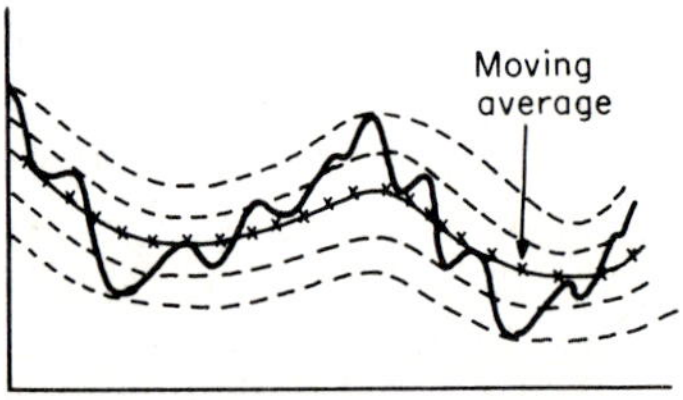

Figure 43-4 *(From Martin J. Pring,* Technical Analysis Explained, *© 1980 by McGraw-Hill, Inc. Used with permission)*

calculated by dividing 2 by the time span: 2 ÷ 20 = 0.1; 2 ÷ 10 = 0.2, and so forth.

If an EMA proves too sensitive for the trend being monitored, two solutions are possible: (1) use a longer time span or (2) smooth the first EMA with another EMA. The second method uses an EMA calculated in the manner described above and repeats the process using a further exponent.

ENVELOPES

The role of moving averages as important support and resistance points has already been described. It is also possible to draw lines, or *envelopes*, at certain equidistant points from a specific MA, which can also be used as support or resistance points. Figure 43-3 shows an example. This technique is based on the principle that prices fluctuate around a given trend. An analogy is a person walking a lively dog; the person must continously pull the dog back as it gets to the end of the leash and tries to pull away. When the commodity price moves a certain proportion above or below its MA, as marked by the envelope, it seems to meet resistance or support, and is "reined in" to the center of its trend, that is, back to the MA.

There are no hard-and-fast rules for deciding where to draw the envelope. It can only be drawn on a trial-and-error basis for a specific market. Indeed, as Figure 43-4 shows, several envelopes can often be drawn around a single moving average. This approach has a clear disadvantage: there is no way to know at exactly which envelope the price will turn. Thus the approach should be used on the basis that when an important envelope is reached, probabilities favor a temporary reversal in trend. The importance of those probabilities will always depend upon the positions of other technical indicators.

CHAPTER

44

Rate of Change and Momentum

Martin J. Pring

The technical approaches discussed in earlier chapters have involved ways to develop signals after peaks or troughs in prices have been achieved. The evaluation of momentum, on the other hand, may sometimes help to identify technical weaknesses ahead of time or may at least point out an underlying vulnerability while a price low or high is being reached.

MOMENTUM

The concept of momentum can probably best be explained by an analogy. A ball thrown into the air begins its trajectory at a very fast pace. Gradually the pace of its advance into the air is reduced and then stalled, and finally the ball begins to fall back to the ground. The ball's upward momentum is declining in the final stages of its rise, but the ball itself is still moving away from the ground. The decline in momentum is the tip-off that the ball is about to reach its highest peak. Similarly, in commodity price trends, momentum usually peaks and then falls before prices peak.

Unfortunately, this is not always the case since peaks in momentum measures often coincide with peaks in prices. (Similarly, in the ball analogy, the trajectory of the ball would be instantly reversed if the ball hit a ceiling before it finished its natural upward path.) No advance warning of a peak in prices is given in such cases, but the level of the momentum indicator can give some valuable clues that a price peak has been reached.

Another analogy can help explain changes in momentum during declining price trends: If a car is pushed up and over a hill, it will then begin to roll down the hill. As it rolls, its downward momentum increases. The downward momentum reaches its maximum at or before the car reaches the bottom of the hill. The car is still moving, but momentum dissipates as the road flattens out. Finally the car reaches its farthest point away from the top of the hill and stops.

Similarly, in most market declines the rate of price descent reaches its maximum well before prices stop falling. Consequently, momentum indexes normally reach their most extreme readings before the lowest prices are reached.

RATE OF CHANGE

The rate-of-change (ROC) technique is the simplest method of measuring momentum. Rate of change compares the price today with the price a given number of days ago. Thus a 10-day rate of change compares the price today with the price 10 days ago. (The number of days is usually measured in trading days, ignoring weekends and holidays.) If today's price is 110 and the price 10 days ago was 100, the plot for the ROC index would be about 1.1 (that is, 110 ÷ 100). If tomorrow's price is 90 and the price 9 days ago (that is, 10 days before tomorrow) was 100, the ROC index would be approximately 0.9 (that is, 90 ÷ 100). If the prices today and 10 days ago are identical, then the reading would be 100.

TABLE 44-1 Calculation of 10-Week Rate-of-Change Index of the Dow Jones Industrial Average

Date	DJIA (1)	DJIA 10 weeks ago (2)	10-week rate of change (col. 1 + col. 2) (3)
Jan. 1	985		
Jan. 8	980		
Jan. 15	972		
Jan. 22	975		
Jan. 29	965		
Feb. 5	967		
Feb. 12	972		
Feb. 19	965		
Feb. 26	974		
Mar. 5	980		
Mar. 12	965	985	98.0
Mar. 19	960	980	98.0
Mar. 26	950	972	97.7
Apr. 2	960	975	98.5
Apr. 9	965	965	100.0
Apr. 16	970	967	100.3
Apr. 23	974	972	100.2
Apr. 30	980	965	101.6
May 7	985	974	101.1

SOURCE: Martin J. Pring, *Technical Analysis Explained*, McGraw-Hill, New York, 1980.

The rate-of-change index is constructed by joining the various daily readings. The result is an oscillating index that continually crosses above and below the 100 level. Table 44-1 shows how a 10-week ROC index of the Dow Jones Industrial Average (DJIA) would be calculated.

When a 10-week momentum index is above its reference line, the commodity price which it is measuring is higher than it was 10 weeks ago. If the index is also rising, it is evident that the difference between the current reading of the price and its level 10 weeks ago is growing. If the index is above its central reference line and falling, then even though the price level is above that of 10 weeks ago, the difference, or momentum, is falling.

When the momentum index is below its reference line and falling downward, momentum is expanding; that is, the difference between current prices and prices 10 weeks ago is widening. Conversely, when the index is below its reference line and rising, the price is still below its level 10 weeks ago, but the rate of decline is slowing.

A rising ROC index implies a growth in momentum, and a falling ROC index implies a loss in momentum. Rising momentum should generally be regarded as a bullish factor and falling momentum as a bearish one.

PRINCIPLES AND APPLICATIONS OF MOMENTUM INDICATORS

The momentum index is usually plotted under the price index, which makes comparing the action of the two indexes easy. Figure 44-1 shows that the maximum rate of momentum is at point A, since the rallies at B and C are accompanied by declining peaks in the rate-of-change index. A negative divergence between the ROC index and the price index is generally regarded as a negative characteristic which emphasises the bearishness of the sell signal. In Figure 44-1 the sell signal occurs when the price itself falls below the dashed trend line joining the two reactions.

Whereas point E marks the ultimate low in prices, the momentum index reaches its lowest level at point D. This type of development, known as positive

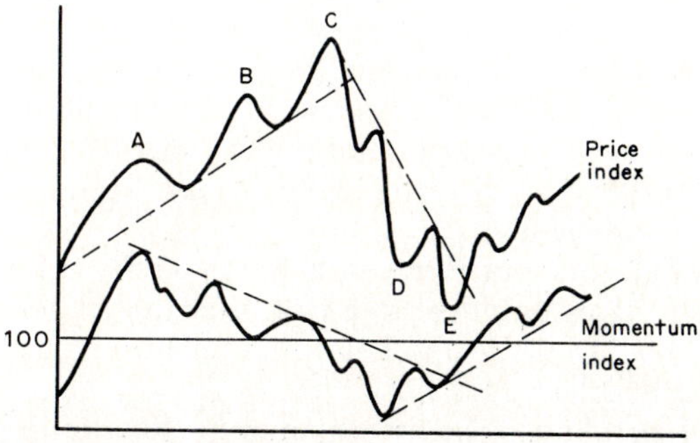

Figure 44-1 *(From Martin J. Pring,* Technical Analysis Explained, *© 1980 by McGraw-Hill, Inc. Used with permission)*

divergence, should be regarded as a bullish characteristic, but the actual signal to buy is a trend reversal in the index itself. In Figure 44-1 two areas determine the trend reversal: (1) an upward penetration of the declining (dashed) trend line on the ROC index and (2) an upward penetration of the declining (dashed) trend line in the price itself.

In Figure 44-1 the confirmation of a trend reversal in the price index is given by a trend-line violation, but a moving-average (MA) crossover or the completion of a price formation would have been equally valid. The main point to bear in mind is that, *however positive or negative the relationship between momentum and price index, a buy or sell signal can only be derived from a confirmation of a trend reversal in the price index itself.* Occasionally a commodity market can remain in a long, sustained uptrend or downtrend, in which the ROC index continually loses and gains momentum and in which the price trend itself does not break. Waiting for the confirmation is therefore a form of insurance well worth taking in order to avoid making a serious mistake.

Figure 44-2 shows a momentum index and a commodity price peaking simultaneously. In this case no positive or negative divergence develops, and so there is no advance warning of a trend reversal. In such a case, however, a joint trend-line break, such as that at point A, is sufficient to trigger a bearish warning.

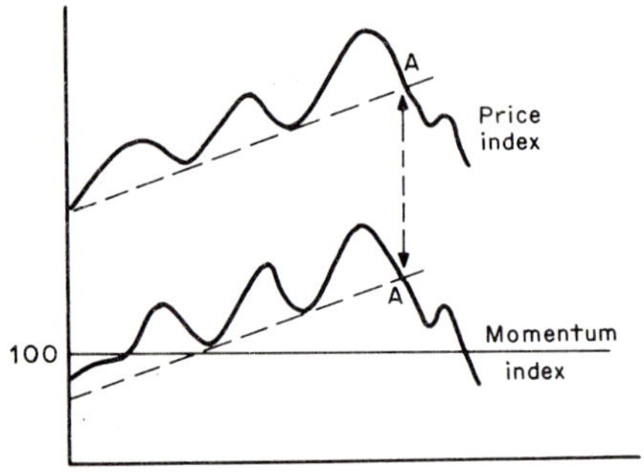

Figure 44-2 *(From Martin J. Pring, Technical Analysis Explained, © 1980 by McGraw-Hill, Inc. Used with permission)*

Momentum indexes are also capable of tracing out price patterns. Normally, momentum indexes used in this way are of the accumulation type, although distribution formations are not uncommon. Because of the shorter lead times normally associated with reversals of falling momentum (bear moves are usually shorter in time than bull moves), a breakout from an accumulation pattern, when accompanied by a reversal in the downward trend of the index itself, is usually a highly reliable indication that a worthwhile move has just begun. A breakout of this type is shown in Figure 44-3.

Another way in which the concept of momentum can help to identify price reversals is through observation of the actual level in a rate-of-change index. Since a ROC index is continually moving above and below the 100 level, there are clearly defined levels beyond which it does not normally go. The actual levels of these extreme readings depend upon the time span of the ROC index (the longer the time period, the greater the potential movement) and upon the volatility of the price of the commodity.

Figure 44-4 shows some of the principles discussed above as applied to the gold market between 1980 and 1982. It is usually possible, on a trial-and-error

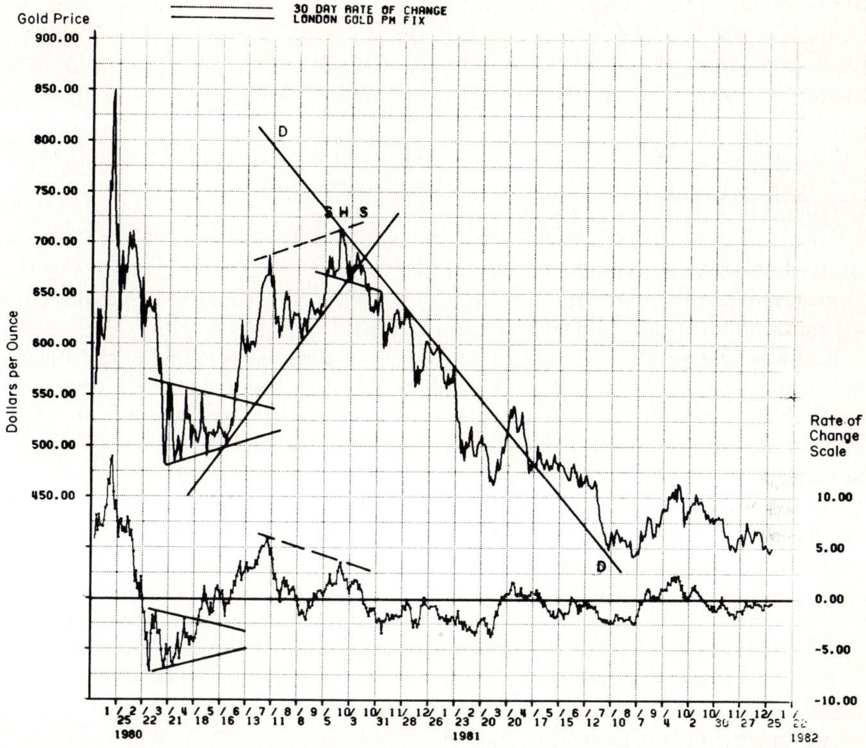

Figure 44-3 *(From Martin J. Pring,* Technical Analysis Explained, *© 1980 by McGraw-Hill, Inc. Used with permission)*

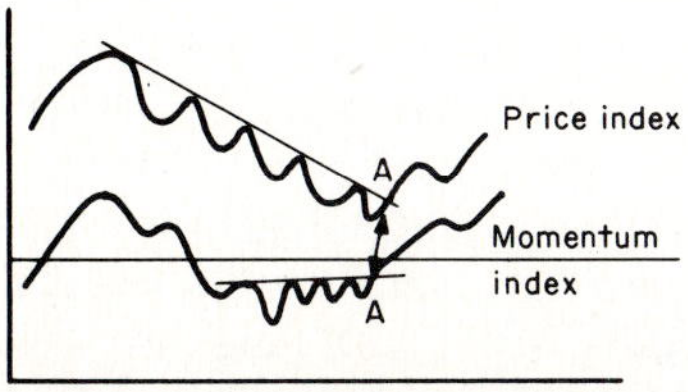

Figure 44-4 London gold fix, 1980 to 1981, and a 30-day rate of change. This chart vividly portrays a number of very important technical principles. First, in May 1980 the gold price began to test its low at the $500 level, but the rate-of-change index had by this time formed and broken out from a triangle pattern. This bullish sign would have alerted investors that, if the gold price did in fact complete a triangle formation by breaking above the $550 level, a significant price advance could be expected. The peak of this mini-bull market was also signaled by the ROC index, which refused to confirm the September high and thereby set up a positive divergence. This was quickly confirmed by the price itself, which not only broke below its bull market trend line but also broke down from a small head-and-shoulders pattern, as indicated on the chart. It is also worth noting that although the important trend line (DD) at the September peak did not signal a trend reversal, its violation on the up side represented an important indication that a major rally was about to unfold.

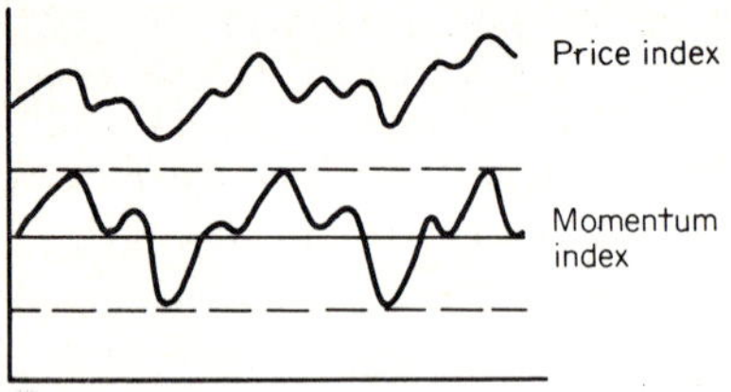

Figure 44-5 *(From Martin J. Pring,* Technical Analysis Explained, *© 1980 by McGraw-Hill, Inc. Used with permission)*

basis, to draw two dashed lines similar to those in Figure 44-5, which serve as "overbought" and "oversold" levels. There are therefore no hard-and-fast rules about what constitutes overbought and oversold readings.

If the overbought and oversold lines are constructed just inside the normal extremities of the ROC index, it is often a good idea to let the index move through the line, reverse direction, and then cross through it once again on its way toward the 100 level before taking any action. The second crossover serves as the signal.

At the beginning of a bull market, a momentum index usually remains in an extremely overbought position for a long time. At such times the price becomes very sensitive when an oversold or even the 100 level is reached, and it then turns around and rallies. When the move matures, prices find much more resistance at overbought levels and therefore are much more sensitive to them. Thus an oversold reading is usually a reliable signal of an imminent trend reversal in the early stages of a bull market, and an overbought reading tends to be more reliable as an indication of market frothiness either during the mature stages of a bull market or during a bear market.

A further indication of the maturity of a trend occurs when the momentum index moves strongly in one direction but the accompanying price move is much smaller. The examples shown in Figure 44-6 suggest that the price index is tired of moving in the direction of the prevailing trend, for despite the push (or drag in example b) of energy from the momentum index, prices are unable to respond.

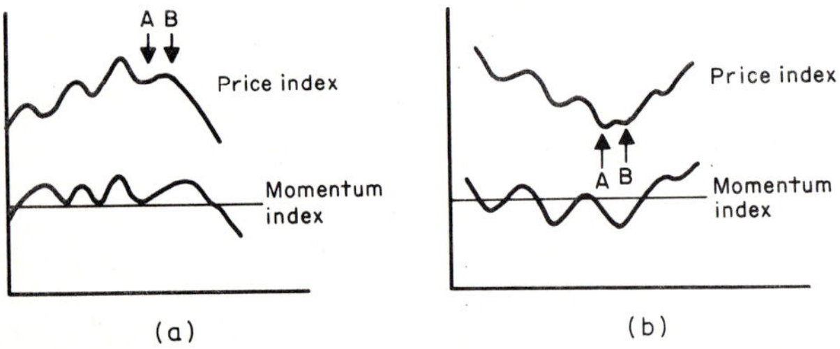

Figure 44-6 *(From Martin J. Pring,* Technical Analysis Explained, *© 1980 by McGraw-Hill, Inc. Used with permission)*

SMOOTHED MOMENTUM

Since the interpretation of rate-of-change indexes can be very subjective, some technicians prefer to run a moving average through the momentum index. The resulting line is much smoother than the raw data, and reversals in direction are very much delayed. Buy and sell signals from these smoothed indexes are given at the time they reverse direction, as shown by the arrows in Figure 44-7a. Reliance on these signals alone would of course create a risk, as discussed above, for the trend itself might be a very long and substantial one.

An alternative is to draw predesignated overbought and oversold levels which, when exceeded and violated, serve as buy and sell signals, as indicated in Figure 44-7b. Besides the drawback described above, this technique may sometimes fail to give the countervailing signal. For example, the smoothed ROC index may fall below the oversold line and then rally above it, thereby giving a buy signal, but may not reach the overbought level during the rally, with the result that no sell signal materializes.

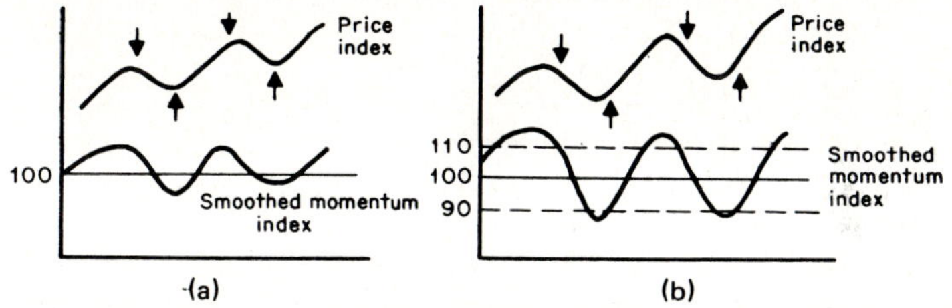

Figure 44-7 *(From Martin J. Pring,* Technical Analysis Explained, *© 1980 by McGraw-Hill, Inc. Used with permission)*

Another possible way to use momentum indexes is to combine several rate-of-change indexes into one index. This method has the advantage of combining two time cycles and, if done correctly, often gives better results than one index alone. (See Table 44-2.)

TABLE 44-2 Calculation of Smoothed Rate of Change, Dow Jones Industrial Average

Date	DJIA (1)	6-week rate of change (2)	10-week rate of change (3)	Col. 2 × 6 (4)	Col. 3 × 10 (5)	Col. 4 + col. 5 (6)	Col. 6 ÷ 16 (7)
Jan. 1	900						
Jan. 8	910						
Jan. 15	920						
Jan. 22	918						
Jan. 29	925						
Feb. 5	950						
Feb. 12	945	105		630			
Feb. 19	936	103		618			
Feb. 26	925	101		606			
Mar. 4	934	102		612			
Mar. 11	940	102	104	612	1040	1652	103
Mar. 18	945	100	104	600	1040	1640	103
Mar. 25	951	101	103	606	1030	1636	102

SOURCE: Martin J. Pring, *Technical Analysis Explained*, McGraw-Hill, New York, 1980.

INDEX TO TREND

This form of momentum index is constructed by dividing a commodity price by its own moving average. Since the moving average represents the trend of the index being monitored, the resulting momentum indicator shows how slowly or how quickly, the index is advancing, or declining, in relation to that trend.

This form of momentum index is really a horizontal representation of the envelope analysis discussed in Chapter 43, as can be seen by comparing Figures 44-8a and 44-8b. The upper and lower envelopes are both drawn at a level that is 10 percent above or below the MA; the same is true of the horizontal dashed lines in Figure 44-8b, since the MA is represented by the horizontal line at 100.

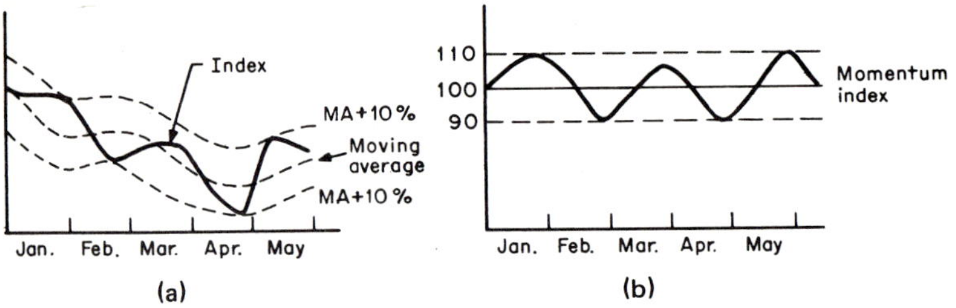

Figure 44-8 *(From Martin J. Pring,* Technical Analysis Explained, *© 1980 by McGraw-Hill, Inc. Used with permission)*

While this method of presentation offers essentially the same information as the envelope analysis, in many ways it can better illustrate the subtle changes in the latent strength or weakness of the price index being monitored.

CHOICE OF TIME SPAN

Rate-of-change indexes are really another way of bringing out the timing and magnitude of commodity cycles. Quite clearly, the choice of which ROC index to use should depend upon the kind of cycle under consideration. A short day-to-day cycle could quite well be handled by a 10- or 15-day ROC. On the other hand, rates of change based on 13 weeks, 26 weeks, or 12 months have proved useful in monitoring cycles of greater length.

CHAPTER

45

Miscellaneous Techniques

Martin J. Pring

This chapter will cover support and resistance, swings and proportion, and relative strength. Support and resistance, touched on in Chapters 40 and 41, will be discussed here in a little more detail. The principles of price swings and proportion offer some help in determining the possible magnitude of a move, and the concept of relative strength (RS) helps in comparing the price strengths of two commodities.

SUPPORT AND RESISTANCE

Support has been defined as "buying, actual or potential, sufficient in volume to halt a downtrend in prices for an appreciable period," and *resistance* has been defined as "selling, actual or potential, sufficient in volume to satisfy all bids and hence stop prices from going any higher for a time."*

A support level represents a concentration of buying power, and a resistance level represents a concentration of potential selling. The actual buying power and selling power are always equal at any price; their relative strength determines trends. Figure 45-1 shows the operation of support and resistance areas in both a rising and a falling market. The left-hand side of the figure shows a commodity in a declining price trend, with a selling "climax" at point B. The climax represents the juncture of maximum emotion, but the actual low in

*Robert D. Edwards and John Magee, *Technical Analysis of Stock Trends*, John Magee, Springfield, Mass., 1957.

prices comes later. A short while after the price falls below the level at B—that is, $20—it finds temporary support and forms a rectangle. Finally, even this ray of hope is dashed and the price breaks down to its ultimate low at $2.50. Prices rise to the lower end of the rectangle at line AA and are temporarily halted, for people who bought during the formation of the rectangle have lost hope and are trying to get back even. Consequently, what was once a support level now becomes a resistance level. Since volume was relatively low during the formation of the rectangle, the resistance does not prove to be formidable. The price is able to push through line AA on an explosion of volume. On the other hand, the setback in price is far greater following the advance in price to line BB, since this marks the point where a considerable amount of the commodity is changing hands during the selling climax.

1. Thus, the first rule for assessing a potential support or resistance area is to determine the number of transactions, or the volume, in that area.

The price also runs into a problem at BB; the advance is overextended at that point because the commodity had little chance to digest its price gains. The technical position at line BB is rather like that of a man trying to push open a trap door after having run 10 miles. The trap door (in this case the overhead resistance) would have been difficult to open (surmount) anyway, but following a long run (a sharp, uncorrected price advance) the man (the commodity price) is more or less forced to rest before proceeding.

2. Therefore, the second rule for assessing whether a potential support (or resistance) level will have a significant effect on prices is to determine the speed and extent of the previous decline or advance.

The more overextended the price move, the less the support or resistance required to reverse or halt it. In Figure 45-1 it can be seen that the price retreats after having unsuccessfully assaulted the resistance line at BB, and finds support at the former resistance line AA. The explanation is probably that traders who bought at or around the bear market low may have taken profits at $10. Then they got frustrated when they saw the price rise to $20, and the $10 price began to look like a bargain. Other traders who bought at $10 and sold at $20

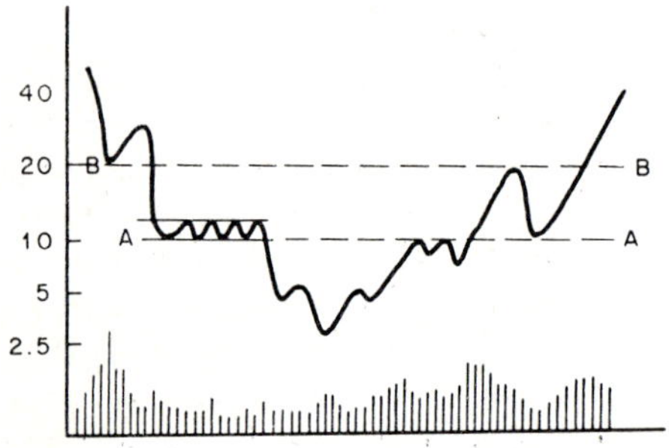

Figure 45-1 *(From Martin J. Pring, Technical Analysis Explained, © 1980 by McGraw-Hill, Inc. Used with permission)*

may want to try to repeat their shrewd maneuver. Still others may have shorted the commodity at $20 and decided to cover their short position at the $10 support level.

3. The third rule for establishing the significance of potential support and resistance levels is to assess the amount of time between the current period and when the congestion developed originally.

Generally speaking, the longer the period, the less important previous support (resistance) areas are likely to be. The chances that the same people bought a commodity at a certain price and then waited to break even are less over 3 years than over 3 months, and so forth. Even so, it is surprising how often the same support and resistance areas keep cropping up. Quite often they develop at a round number such as 10, 100, or 1000.

SWINGS AND PROPORTION

Swings

The law of physical motion is that for every action there is a reaction. Price action in commodity markets is really crowd psychology in motion and is subject to the same law.

Hence, no market move is a straight-up or straight-down affair. Each is subject to contratrend swings. Over the years technicians have noticed that these swings are often repeated in proportion. In a sense, the measuring rules applicable to trend lines and price patterns reflect the principle of proportion in action. Hence, if the distance between the top of a head and a neckline of a head-and shoulders pattern is 20 percent, a breakdown from that pattern will imply a decline of 20 percent from the neckline.

Chapter 40 pointed out that such moves often go much further than the measuring objectives indicates. If the original objective is exceeded, the ultimate move may carry the price by a multiple proportion beyond the indicated target; for example, if the measuring objective calls for a 10 percent move on the up side, the eventual high could be 20 percent, 30 percent, 40 percent, or more above the breakout—that is, 2, 3, 4, or more times the indicated objective.

Observation will reveal that almost every commodity price has a tendency to move in specific price units or multiples of the units on an arithmetic chart, or in certain percentage swings or multiple swings on a ratio chart. The key problem in assessing the size of a move is that, without the benefit of hindsight, only the probable turning points, not the actual ones, can be isolated, since whether the move will be a 2, 3, 4, or higher multiple of the indicated objective cannot be assessed beforehand.

Proportion

Application of the principle of proportion in contrast to the principle of swings, does indicate probable reversal points. The degree of emphasis to be placed on such points should then be determined by other technical tools, such as momentum, cycle analysis, or extended trend lines. Support and resistance areas do not exist when a commodity is moving into new high ground. In such cases, the principle of proportionate price movements can prove very helpful. First it can be used to establish the degree of probable price swings from previous price action. In addition, three proportions—usually called the 50 percent rule and the one-third and two-thirds proportions—appear to repeat themselves fairly consistently.

Figure 45-2 Relative strength of T-bonds versus gold, 1980 to 1982. This chart, which represents the nearby T-bond continuation contract divided by the nearby COMEX gold continuation, shows how relative-strength indexes can be used to trade markets. For example, after several years in a declining trend, the relationship between T-bonds and gold formed a massive triangle base between early 1980 and late 1981. Note also the pullback to the top of the base in summer 1982.

The 50 percent rule is probably the most widely known of these proportions. Many bear markets cut prices in half. The gold price, for example, fell from $200 in late 1974 to $100 in August 1976. And many bull markets increase prices by multiples of 50 percent.

The one-third and two-third proportions more often apply to corrections that move against the main trend. For example, if the price of a commodity rises from $6 to $12, it is normal for the ensuing correction to bring the price back to $8 (two-third correction) or $10 (one-third correction).

RELATIVE STRENGTH

Although there is a tendency for most commodities to move up and down with the business cycle, there are also many periods when, for specific fundamental reasons such as weather, strikes, or the introduction of new substitutes, specific commodity price trends move in a different direction from the main trend of the indexes (Figure 45-2). The relative-strength (RS) concept is helpful in identifying such situations, since RS measures the performance of one commodity against another.

RS is obtained by dividing one price by another. The denominator is usually the price of the commodity that the technician is interested in buying or selling, and the numerator is usually the commodity or commodity index against which performance is to be measured. Calculated in this way, a rising RS line denotes that the commodity in question is performing better than the one against which it is being measured, and vice versa. For example, if the grain complex as a whole is expected to advance, some RS analysis against the various grains or perhaps against the Commodity Research Bureau (CRB) Grain Index would clearly prove useful in isolating the best grain with which to play the bull market. Sometimes, however, the RS line will appear to move around at random and thus will not be particularly helpful; but more often a clear trend or trendline break will occur, which will give the investor or trader confidence in the relationship.

At other times the RS line may appear as a giant rectangle, as the relationship between two commodities continually oscillates between one extreme and another. At one extreme, traders might actually want to play the relationship by shorting one commodity and going long on the other. Then if the relationship got more into line or worked toward the other extreme, they might well take profits or even reverse positions.

One of the problems with using this technique is that, for some fundamental reason, the extreme levels of the RS line may one day be exceeded and the old relationship may no longer hold.

CHAPTER

46

Commodity Prices and Equities

Martin J. Pring

INTRODUCTION

Previous chapters have concentrated on the task of identifying trend reversals from the price action of the commodities themselves. Another useful approach is to consider the trading action of equities whose future profits are linked to commodity prices. This approach is not possible with such items as grains, cocoa, and coffee, but commodities such as gold, silver, and copper do have equities that are fairly closely related. The classic example is mining shares—especially shares of gold and silver mines whose profits tend to be closely linked to the prices of the precious metals.

The gold and silver equity-bullion relationship has proved very reliable. Other relationships—copper to copper shares, aluminum to aluminum shares, sugar to sugar shares—are also worth monitoring but do not appear to have the strength of the relationship between precious metal shares and bullion prices. The discussion in this chapter therefore applies primarily to gold and gold shares. The principles discussed below can be adopted for other equity-commodity relationships but will be less reliable.

In most instances, the prices of shares tend to lead the price of the commodity. Consequently, the breakout of a gold share or, more important, a gold share index from a price pattern gives some form of advance warning for the future price action of gold bullion. Even when there is no advance notice, it is still important to make sure that a specific move in the gold price is confirmed by a move in the share price, and vice versa. When no such confirmation exists, the move should be considered suspect.

THE RELATIONSHIP BETWEEN GOLD BULLION AND GOLD SHARES

There are several reasons for the close correlation between the prices of gold bullion and gold shares:

First, investors in gold shares are concerned about the flow of profits from those shares, and this flow is determined by the average price of gold bullion over a particular period. If investors in shares believe that the average price is going to fall, they sell well in advance of the expected drop.

Second, gold shares are more leveraged than bullion, not only because gold mines borrow money to go into production but also because, as the gold price rises or falls, the marginal ore deposits become commercially profitable or unprofitable. These changes have proportionately more effect upon the value of the mine than does the change in the actual price of the metal.

Third, the profits of gold mines are a function not only of the gold price but also of the cost of production. Because these costs are basically subject to the same influences as other corporations, trends in profits are also influenced by the business cycle. Since profits are a leading indicator, and inflation (which is discounted in the trend of bullion prices) is a lagging indicator, the net effect, other things being equal, is for gold shares to lead the price of bullion.

GOLD BULLION AND GOLD SHARES

This section gives some examples of the relationship between equity and bullion.

The top of Figure 46-1 shows the prices of the London P.M. fixes from 1970 to 1982. Underneath are two important gold share indexes, the Toronto Stock Exchange (TSE) Gold Share Index and the *Financial Times* (of London) Gold Share Index. The latter essentially consists of South African stocks, which are traded in London. Both indexes have been converted from local currencies to U.S. dollars to maintain consistency. The figure shows that the (TSE) index reached a cyclical high in March of 1974, whereas the bullion price topped out 9 months later, in December 1974. The *Financial Times* index also gave a warning signal by peaking out in early 1974, again failing to confirm the late 1974 high in bullion price. Until March 1974, all three indexes had been moving together, as each confirmed a new high made by the other two.

In addition, the two share indexes were actually making distributional tops in 1974; they later broke down from these tops. Thus, at the beginning of 1975, it became fairly clear that the technical structure of the gold asset markets was breaking down. Not only had the shares failed by a wide margin to confirm the bullion, but they had actually given important indications that they were going to lead the bullion price lower.

At the bottom of the bear market in mid-1976, this technical position had partly reversed itself. Whereas the bullion price made its low in August 1976, the TSE gold index refused to make a new low, thereby setting up a positive divergence. The South African index did confirm the low in the bullion price, but August 1976 marked the first time since late 1974 that the three indicators refused to confirm one another. Though this was clearly a positive sign, a truly bullish signal did not occur until later that year, when the bear market trend line (line AB in Figure 46-1) of each index was penetrated on the up side.

The relationship between equity and bullion is useful for assessing shorter-term as well as longer-term movements in the gold price, as Figure 46-2 shows. A close study of Figure 46-2 will reveal little relationship between the three series during much of the time covered. However, there are points at which the shares give a clear-cut lead for the bullion, either in terms of an actual divergence or in terms of clear-cut relative-strength superiority. In November 1979, for example, all three indicators were consolidating their October losses, but by the middle of the month the shares had begun to move up sharply. The United Kingdom index in particular had broken out of an inverse head-and-shoulders pattern. Although this lead given by the shares was a very powerful bullish sign, no action should have been taken until the bullion price itself had also broken out of its trading band.

It is very important for all the gold asset markets to be in gear. The cyclical peak in gold bullion in January 1980 is an interesting example. This was one of the few occasions when the shares *lagged behind* the bullion price. During the

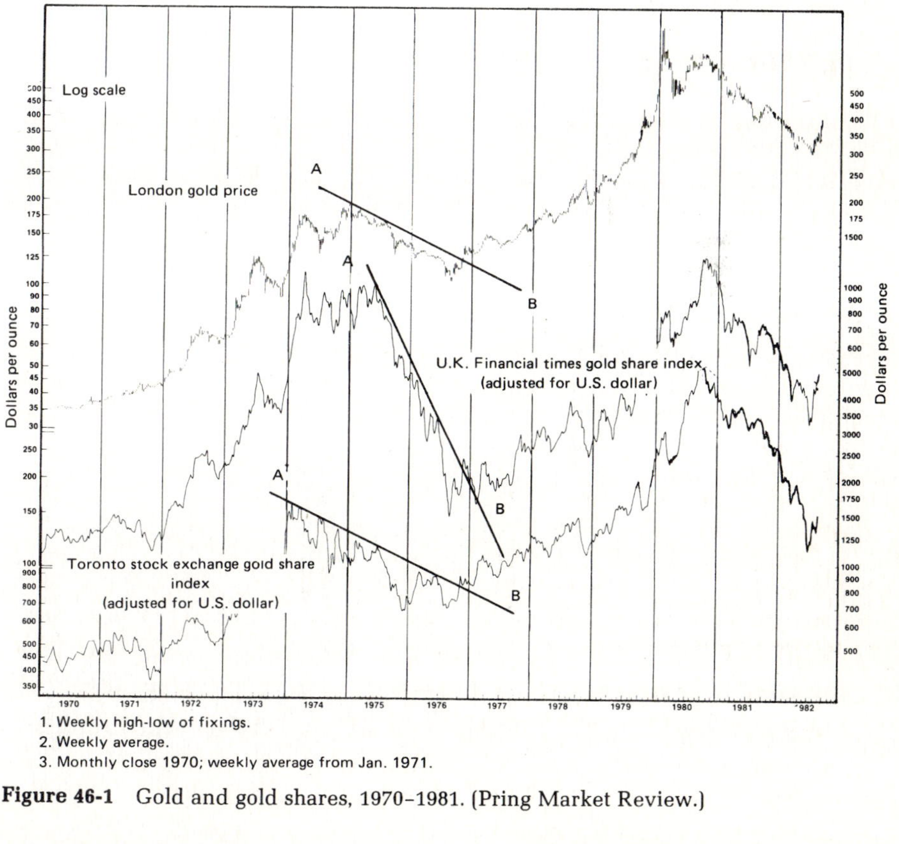

1. Weekly high-low of fixings.
2. Weekly average.
3. Monthly close 1970; weekly average from Jan. 1971.

Figure 46-1 Gold and gold shares, 1970–1981. (Pring Market Review.)

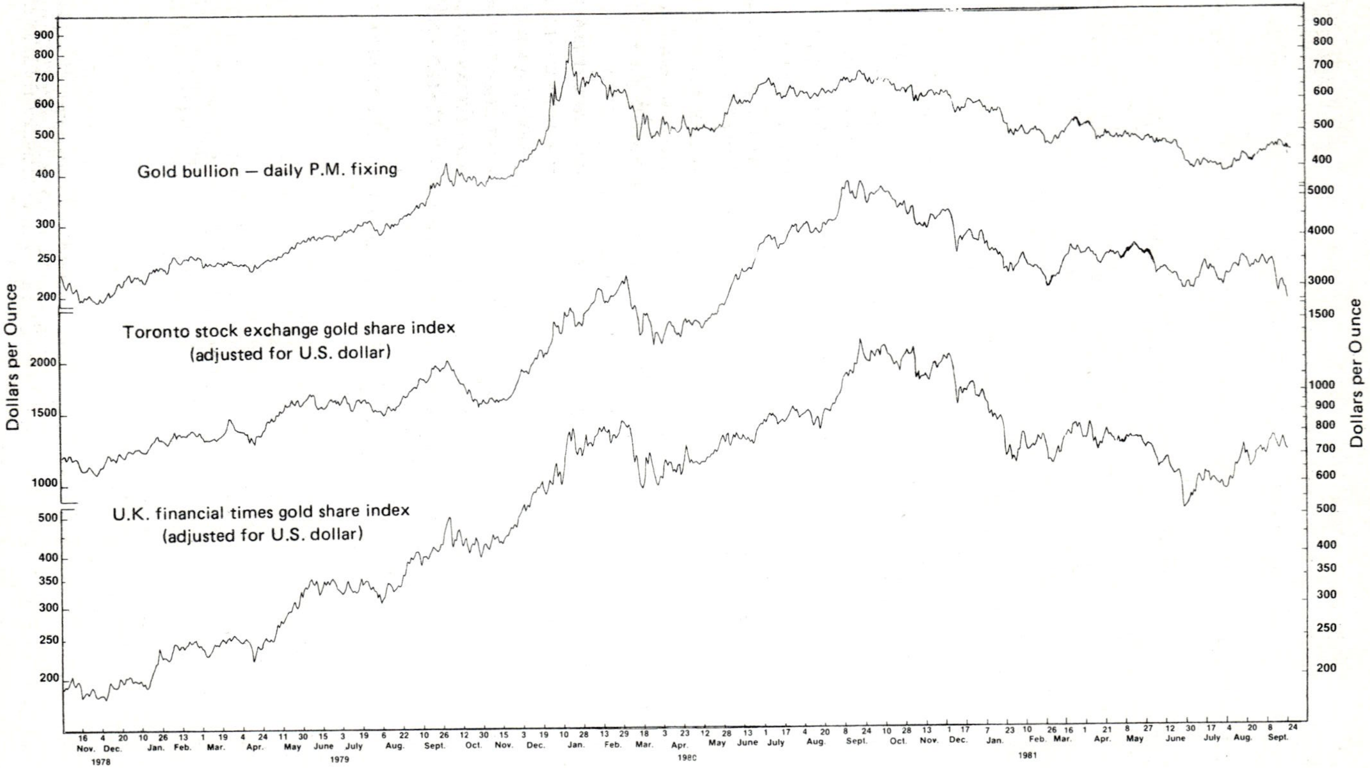

Figure 46-2 Gold and gold shares, 1978–1981. (Pring Market Review)

period from December 1979 to February 1980, the gold bullion price formed a small head-and-shoulders pattern in the face of rising share prices. Because of the leading characteristic of the gold share prices, it might have been expected that the distribution pattern being traced out by the bullion would "fail." Since it did not fail, and since investors and speculators in commodity markets take positions in the physical metal, not in shares, it would have been wise to exit from the market at the time of the trend break in the bullion price.

Although the shares tend to lead the bullion, there are occasions when they lag. A higher price move in bullion, which remains unconfirmed by the shares and vice versa, is almost always bearish in its implication. It is signaling that the gold asset markets are not in gear.

Another point worth noting is that the first index to move generally has the largest ensuing price swing. Gold bullion peaked at $850 in January 1980 and led the shares on a decline. The bullion lost almost half its value (it fell from $850 to $450), and the shares only lost about 30 percent to 40 percent of theirs.

By May 1980 the decline for all three series had run its course. The formation and completion of important bottoms in both share indexes before the bullion bottom was highly significant for two reasons: first, these bottoms gave advance warning of an imminent up-side breakout in the metal, and second, they added tremendous validity to the breakout when it did in fact occur.

The September peak in the gold price was also instructive, since it found the gold asset markets once again in a major disagreement. Gold shares reached a new cyclical peak, yet the bullion price was well below its January high. The ensuing decline was extreme for both the shares and the bullion. By December 1980 all three series were again in gear—this time in a bear trend, as head-and-shoulders distribution formations were completed almost simultaneously on the down side.

CONCLUSION

Analysis of the relationship between gold bullion and gold-related equities suggests that in most cases the equities lead the gold. However, a move by one that remains unconfirmed by the other is usually bearish. When the shares do lead the bullion, no action should be taken on the bullion until the bullion confirms. When the bullion does confirm the lead of the shares, the odds are very high that the leadership given by the shares is a valid one.

The relationship between gold shares and bullion is very reliable and is closely followed by the relationship between silver and silver shares. The gold relationship is also useful since it is easy to monitor, because of the widespread publication of gold-share indexes. A partial list of shares and their related commodities is given in Table 46-1.

As in the relationship between gold bullion and gold shares, confirmations and divergences between each commodity and its related equity should be looked for. In investigating individual shares it is important to make sure that specific fundamentals are not responsible for unusual strength or weakness. Suppose, for example, that the price of Phelps Dodge moved up significantly, while Noranda and other copper mines were unaffected. The price change in

TABLE 46-1

Shares	Commodity	Where Traded
ASA	Gold	New York
Homestake	Gold	New York
Campbell Redlake	Gold	New York
Dome Mines	Gold	New York
Hecla	Silver	New York
Day Mines	Silver	American Stock Exchange
Phelps Dodge	Copper	New York
Noranda	Copper	Toronto
INCO	Nickel	New York
Falconbridge Nickel	Nickel	Toronto
Alcan	Aluminum	New York
Alcoa	Aluminum	New York
Cominco	Lead and zinc	Toronto
Amstar	Sugar	New York
Iowa Beef	Beef	New York
Holly Sugar	Sugar	New York
Rustenberg	Platinum	South Africa
Impala	Platinum	South Africa

Phelps Dodge would therefore most likely be caused by a specific Phelps Dodge development rather than by investors' anticipation of a general increase in the copper price. In other words, a consensus among copper shares should be looked for; the more the copper shares agree, the greater the probability that their signals are valid. Similarly, if copper shares, other base metal shares, and precious metal shares were all in agreement on the bullish side, it could be concluded that the odds favored a bullish outlook for metal markets in general. And naturally, the converse would hold true for bearish signs.

CHAPTER

47

A Study of the Elliott Wave Principle

David Weis

BASIC ELLIOTT WAVE PRINCIPLE

Form

The wave principle developed by R. N. Elliott* is based on the repetitive form of price movement. The basic form consists of a 5-wave movement in the direction of the trend, followed by a 3-wave correction. This basic form is inherent in the building up and tearing down of prices which occurs over hourly, daily, weekly, and monthly intervals. Figure 47-1 shows the basic Elliott Wave form. Waves 1, 3, and 5 are impulses within the upwave. Wave 2 corrects wave 1, and wave 4 corrects wave 3. The total impulse from the bottom of wave 1 to the top of wave 5 is corrected by an a-b-c movement.

Degree

Five-wave movements in commodity prices are visible to the trained eye. Figures 47-2 to 47-4 show 5-wave movements on several different kinds of soybean charts. Figure 47-2 begins from the 1970 low shown in Figure 47-3, and Figure 47-4 reveals the details of a portion of the final up wave (shown later, in Figure 47-9).

Figure 47-3 shows waves labeled with Roman numerals enclosed in parentheses. These waves are of different degree than waves (1) through (5) shown in Figure 47-4; however, all of them have a 5-wave form. Elliott recognized that

*Refer to the books listed in "Sources of Information."

the very minute waves build into minor waves which combine to form intermediate waves which in turn create large cycle waves. He prepared a system of notation for waves of different degree that included nine classifications ranging from subminuette to grand supercycle. A wave of subminuette degree may only last an hour, whereas a grand supercycle wave may encompass 50 years of price work. For the purpose of dissecting and labeling waves in commodities, the following categorization has been found to be useful:

Degree:	*Notation*
Subminuette	a to e
Minuette	$\underline{1}$ to $\underline{5}$
Minute	i to v
Minor	1 to 5
Intermediate	(1) to (5)
Primary	I to V
Cycle	(I) to (V)

Waves (I) to (V) usually cover many years—as shown, for example, in the average monthly cash soybean chart which represents the up wave from 1937 to 1973 (Figure 47-3). Waves (I), (III), and (V) are each subdivided into wave movements of primary degree (Figure 47-5). Primary waves I, III, and V are composed of intermediate waves (Figure 47-6). Intermediate waves (1), (3), and (5) are composed of minor waves (Figure 47-7). Minor waves 1, 3, and 5 break down into minute waves i, ii, iii, iv, and v. The minute waves are comprised of minuette waves which in turn are formed from subminuette waves. The latter two categories of waves are not always discernible on a daily bar chart, but they do appear on intraday charts.

EXCEPTIONS TO THE 5-WAVE FORM

The one major exception to the 5-wave form occurs in elongated waves which Elliott called "extensions." As shown in Figure 47-8, extensions occur in waves 1, 3, and 5. Elliott discovered that most extensions are visible in the wave 3 position. In commodities, the wave 5 position is the most common area for extensions. Some waves do not have an elongated subwave, but break down into 9 waves of approximately the same length. Such a formation is an extension also, but there is no way of determining whether wave 1, wave 3, or wave 5 is the one being extended. (See Figure 47-9.)

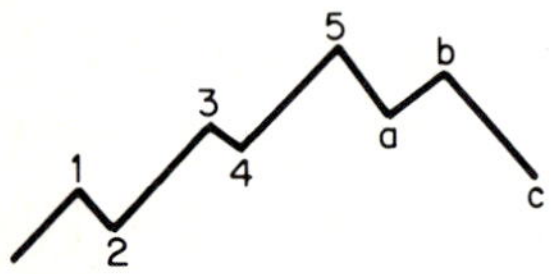

Figure 47-1

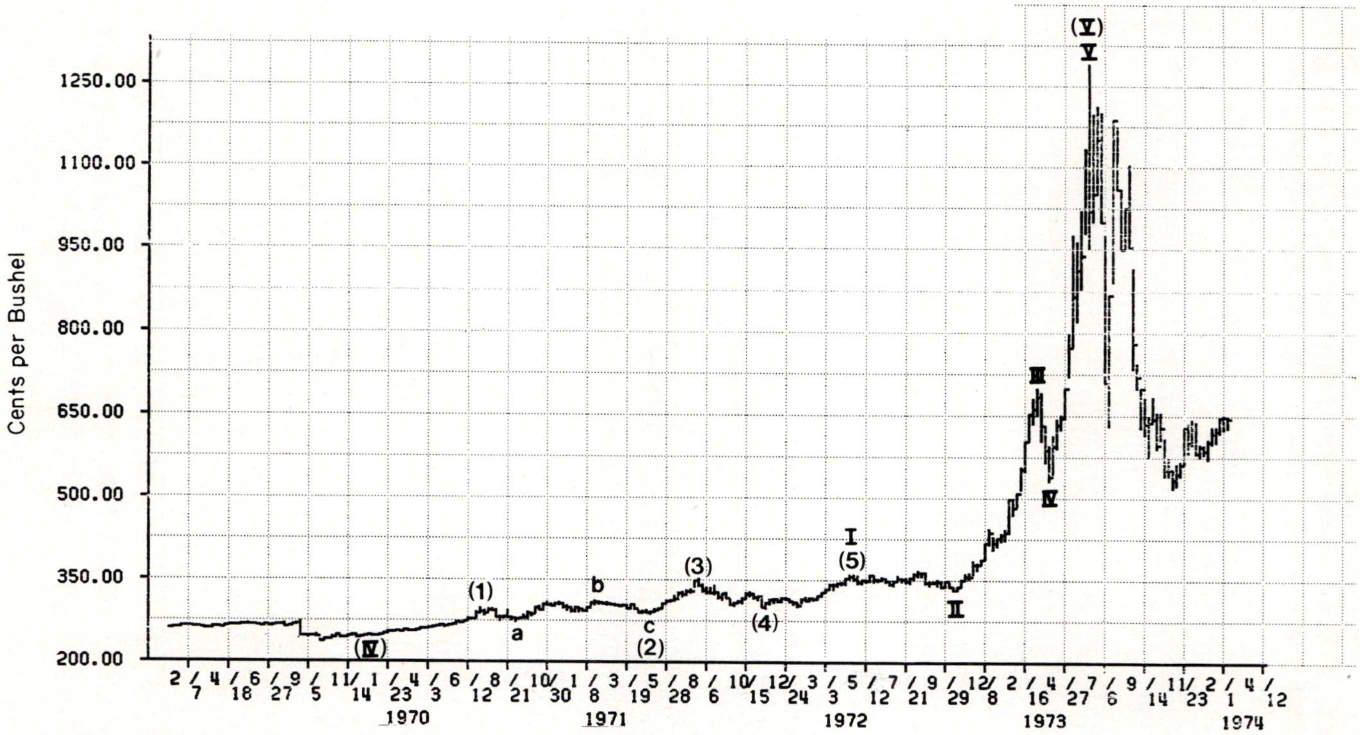

Figure 47-2 Weekly Chicago Board of Trade soybeans, 1970 to 1974. *(ContiCommodity Research Division)*

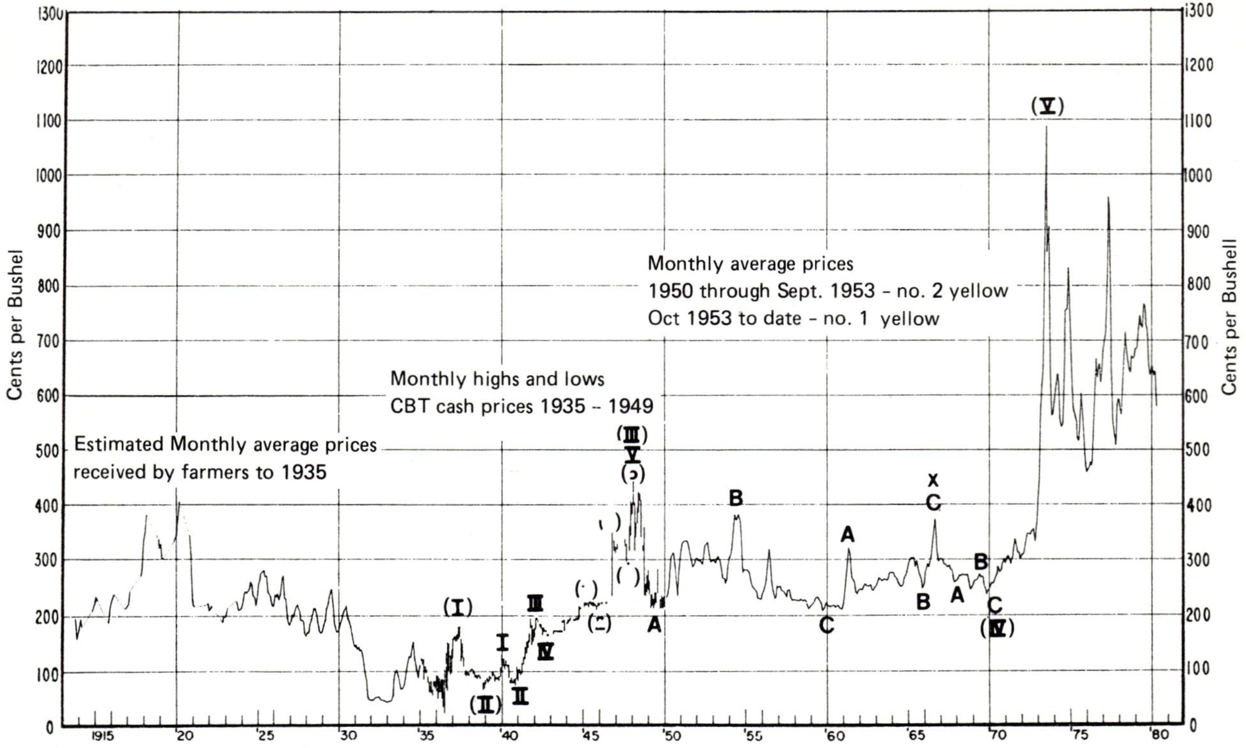

Figure 47-3 Chicago Cash prices for soybeans, monthly average, 1913 to 1982. *(Conti-Commodity Research Bureau)*

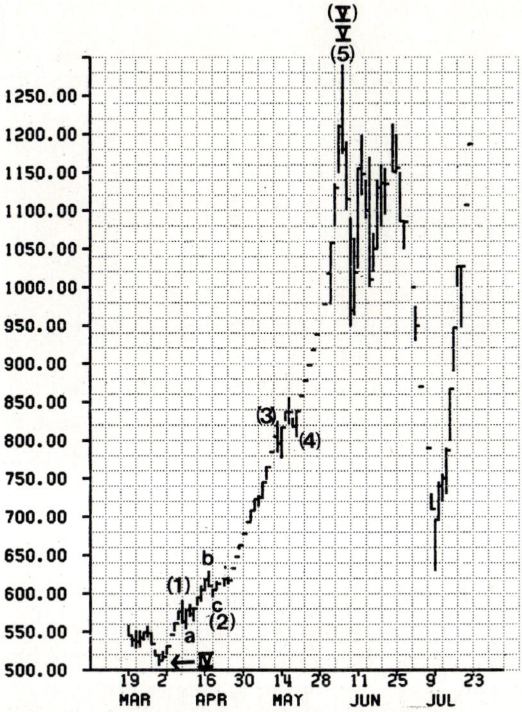

Figure 47-4 Chicago Board of Trade soybeans, July 1973. *(ContiCommodity Research Division)*

The characteristics of extensions are that they occur only as a commodity contract is making new highs for its immediate trading cycle. (Bear markets also have extensions; they occur as the down wave moves into lower territory but do not necessarily represent new contract lows.) Extensions are retraced twice, so that the first reaction is a 3-wave movement that reaches back to the point where the extensions occurred. The second retracement can exceed the

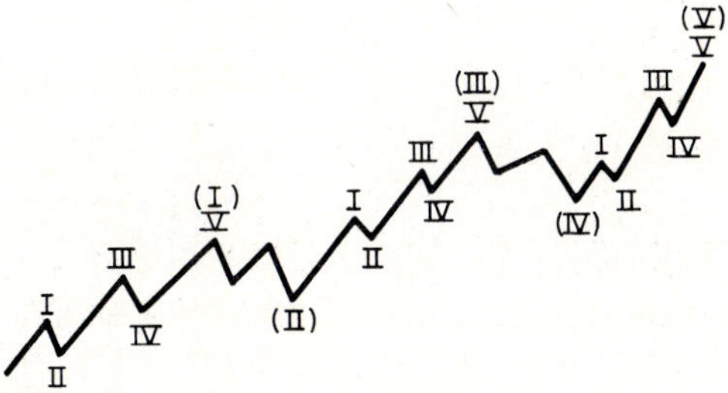

Figure 47-5

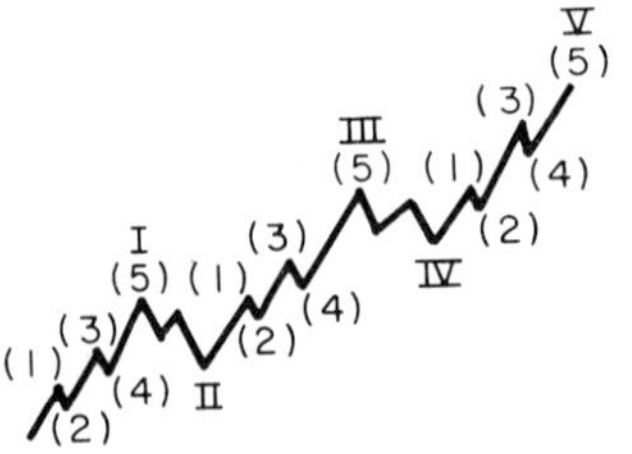

Figure 47-6

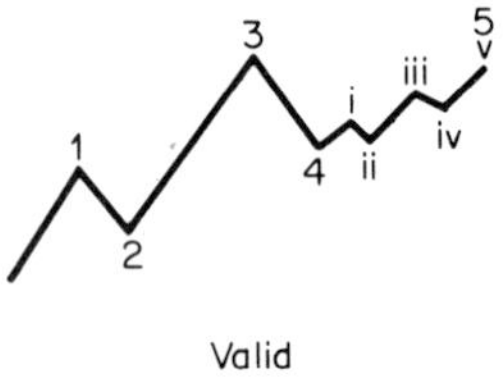

extremity of the extension, but will fail to follow through. This can be seen in Figure 47-10.

The second exception to the 5-wave movement is called a failure and is a nemesis for most Elliott practitioners. A failure occurs when the fifth wave of an impulse subdivides into a 5-wave form but does not exceed the top of wave 3. (See Figure 47-11.)

Characteristics of Waves 1, 3, and 5

In commodities, wave 1 is often characterized by sluggish, dull behavior. The volume is usually light, for little attention is focused on a market at this stage. Open interest may increase in the deferred contracts as professionals unobtrusively accumulate. There is no media hype for a bull market, and most traders do not believe the bearish fundamentals can be overcome. Wave 1 action can be compared to the gentle waves visible at sea on a calm day. Wave 3 is never the shortest impulse wave and has a greater tendency to be extended than does wave 1. It is also much looser than wave 1. The volume increases on this up wave as does open interest. Wave 3 can be very powerful, but this will signal a less volatile wave 5. In commodities, wave 5 is most often extended and may lead to an exponential increase in price. It is usually the fastest up wave. During wave 5, the daily limits are expanded or abandoned, initial margin rates are increased 500 percent or more, and public participation is greatest.

Another characteristic of impulse waves is described by the rule of equality, which states that a tendency exists for 2 of the 3 impulse waves to have approximately the same length. If waves 1 and 3 are about equal in length, wave 5

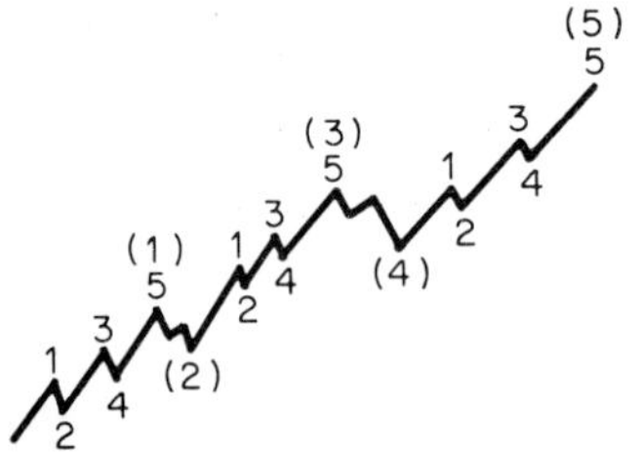

Figure 47-7

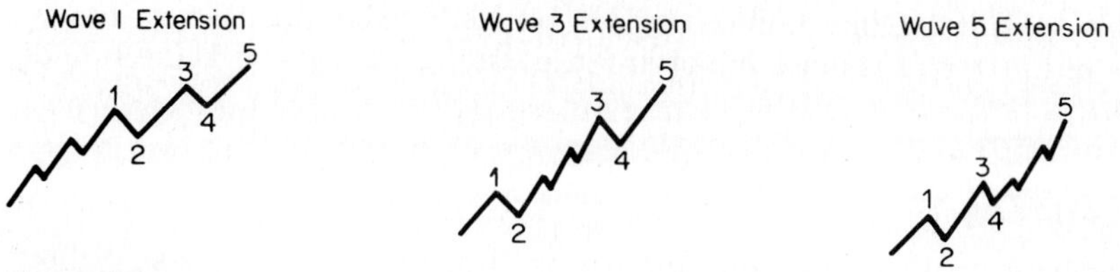

Figure 47-8

Figure 47-9

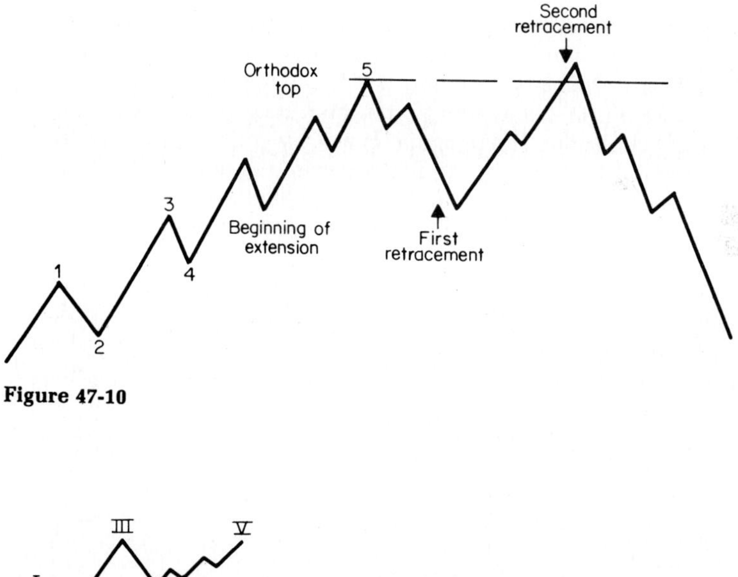

Figure 47-10

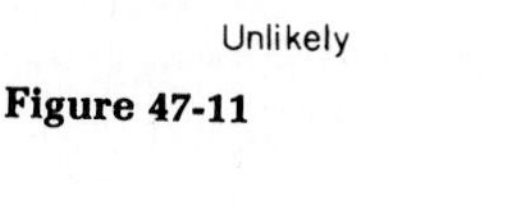

Figure 47-11

should be extended. Other deductions can be made using this rule; however, the form of the waves is more important in counting waves than is the rule of equality.

Wave Counting

The most important rule for counting waves is to adhere to the basic Elliott form. Therefore, impulse waves must have 5 subwaves when visible, and corrections must have 3 waves or other sideways structures (discussed below). Overlapping waves are not usually allowed (the diagonal triangle is the only exception). In other words, the low of wave 4 in an uptrend cannot fall below the top of wave 1 of the same degree.

Correct and incorrect forms are shown in Figure 47-12. The first example is incorrect, as labeled, but the waves labeled 3 and 4 could be waves i and ii of wave 3. Thus, they would not overlap; wave ii could occur below the top of wave 1 since they are of different degree. Another interpretation of this same structure anticipates the discussion on corrections. Corrections can exceed the orthodox top (OT) of an impulse, as described in the double retracement of an extension.

A-B-C Corrections

A-B-C corrections are 3-wave movements and are broken into two categories. The strongest A-B-C correction is a flat which has a 3-3-5 structure. The A wave has 3 waves, the B wave has 3 waves, and the C wave has 5 waves. In a flat correction, the bottom of the C wave will often hold near the bottom of the A wave. Some flat corrections have an irregular B wave which exceeds the orthodox top. A less common but very strong flat correction is one in which the B wave is irregular and the C wave holds around the high of the preceding orthodox top. This is a running correction. Figure 47-13 illustrates the 3-3-5 correction.

In bear markets, corrective rallies are merely inverted structures. It must also be noted that not every portion of the 3-3-5 or 5-3-5 structure will be visible on a daily bar chart. There are simple A-B-C corrections which have the shapes of their namesakes and which are of smaller degree than the ones outlined above. The second category of A-B-C corrections has a 5-3-5 structure and is called the "zigzag." In this case, the A wave is a 5-wave decline which corrects

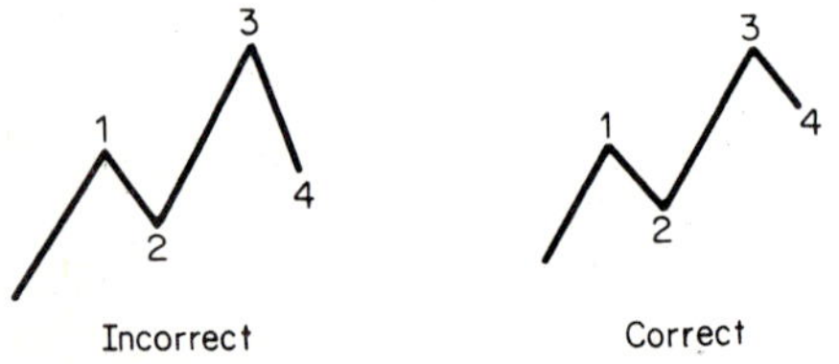

Figure 47-12

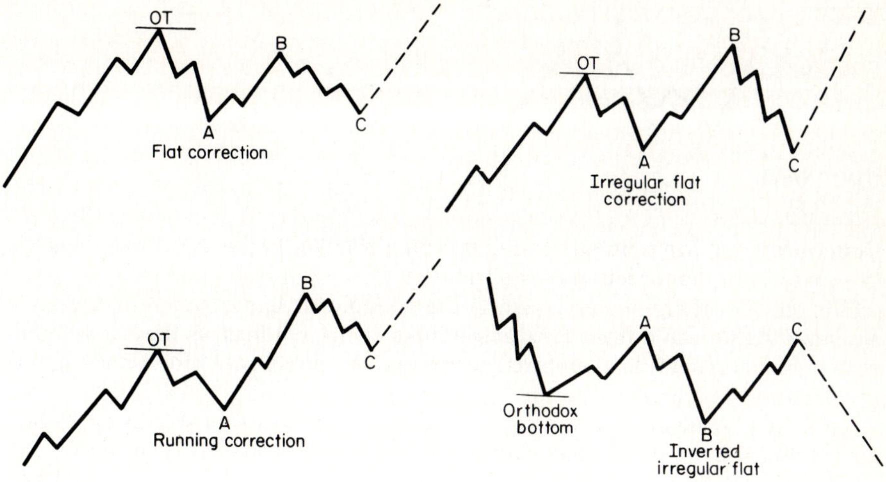

Figure 47-13

more deeply into the preceding impulse wave. The B wave rarely retraces to the top of wave A, and the C wave moves down farther. (See Figure 47-14.)

Complex Corrections

It was stated above that the repetitive form of price movement is a 5-wave impulse in the direction of the trend, followed by a 3-wave correction in the opposite direction. As shown above, this 3-wave form can have the structure of either a flat (3-3-5) or a zigzag (5-3-5). There are more complex corrective structures which do not conform to these patterns. The first is more apparent on long-term than on short-term charts and is referred to as a double-three correction. It is a chain of two a-b-c structures separated by a wave with a 3-wave pattern. The double-three correction is illustrated in Figure 47-15.

A variation of this structure (shown in Figure 47-16) is the triple-three correction, which is self-explanatory. The a-b-c structures in a double- or triple-

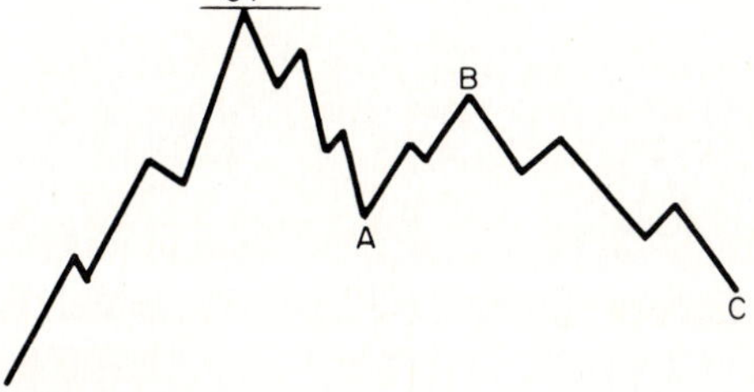

Figure 47-14

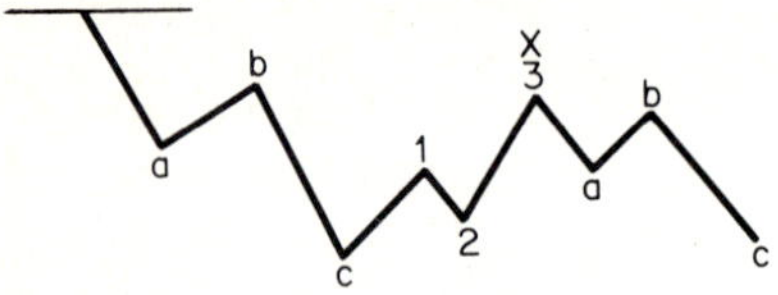

Figure 47-15

three formation are pointed in the opposite direction to the trend, whereas the "x wave" is in the direction of the trend.

The second complex correction is the triangle. It is composed of 5 waves, each having an a-b-c form. The extremities of these 5 legs, as they are called, may either narrow into a contracting triangle or widen out to form an expanding triangle. (See Figure 47-17.)

Triangles occur only in the fourth wave and in B waves within an A-B-C correction. A B-wave triangle is illustrated in Figure 47-18. In this example, the A-B-C correction is a combination of several structures. Wave A is a zigzag because its a-b-c substructure has a 5-3-5 form. The B wave is a 5-leg contracting triangle, and wave C has the normal 5-wave form.

Another triangle structure which Elliott noticed in price movement is the diagonal triangle (see Figure 47-19). This formation occurs at the end of a move, which means it can appear in wave 5 of an impulse or in wave C of a correction. The subwaves or legs of a diagonal triangle must have an a-b-c form, and overlapping should occur between legs 1 and 4.

TRADING WITH THE WAVE PRINCIPLE

The ideal way to trade with the Elliott wave principle is to recognize and take a position at the point in the cyclical movement of a stock or commodity where the fifth waves of several degrees come together to form an extremity. For example, on January 21, 1980, London gold traded at $850. Theoretically, a trader with an hourly chart could have recognized the completion of wave e of subminuette degree, which in turn completed wave 5 of minuette degree, wave v of minute degree, wave 5 of minor degree, wave (5) of intermediate degree, and wave V of primary degree. [This extremity also represented the top of a cycle wave, but in 1980 it appeared to be wave (III). The price action in Sep-

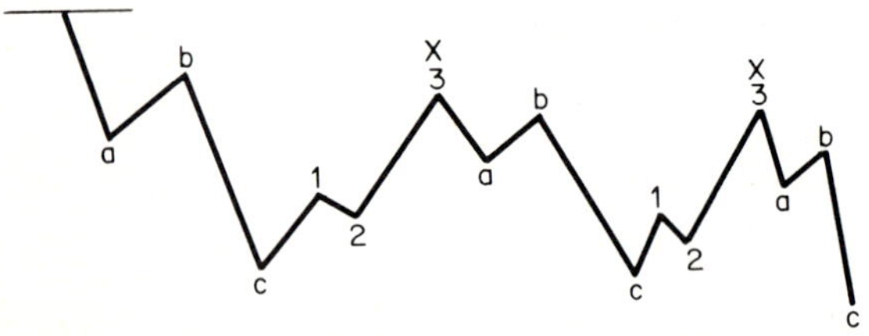

Figure 47-16

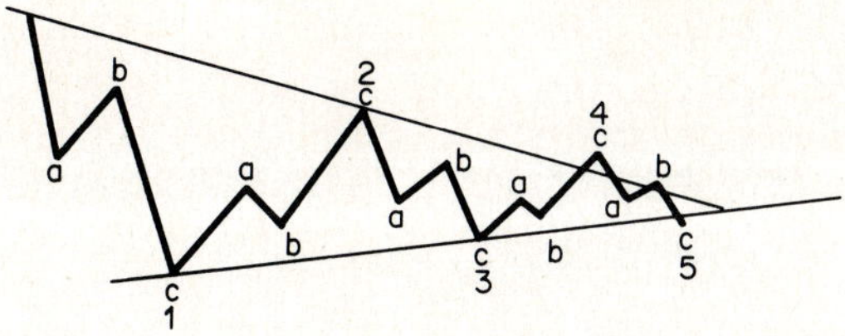

Contracting triangle

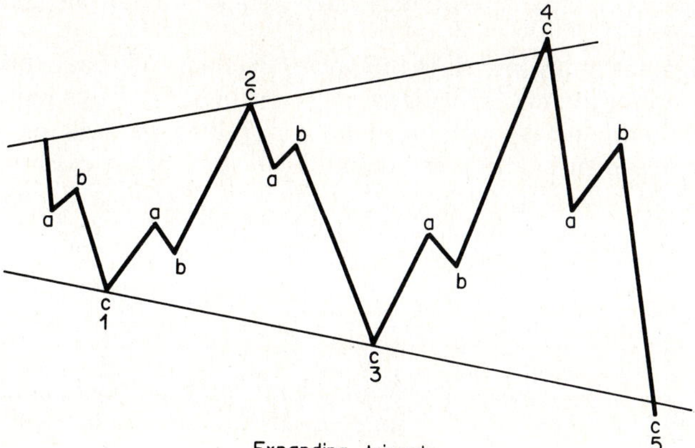

Expanding triangle

Figure 47-17

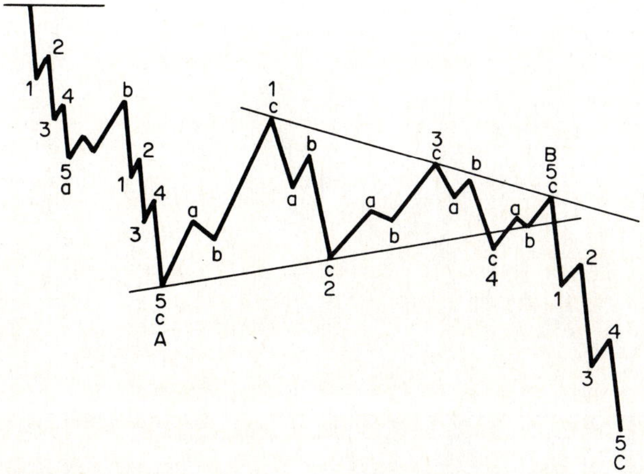

Figure 47-18

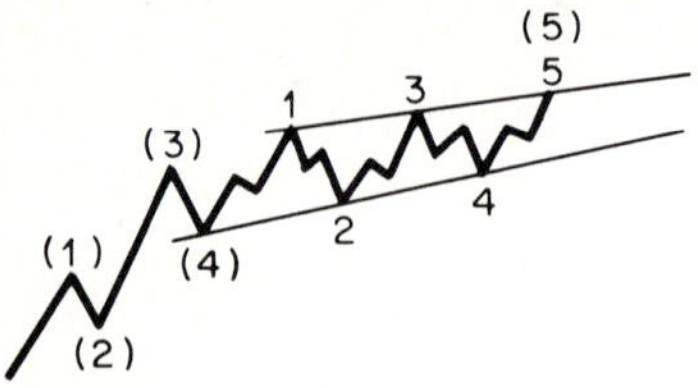

Figure 47-19

tember 1981 would eventually force an alternate interpretation: that $850 gold was the top of cycle wave (V).]

However, piecing together hours and days of wave movements within a 13-year advance is more than the average speculator may wish to undertake. Long-term wave analysis is valuable for recognizing major extremities, but a simpler way to trade using the wave principle is to follow the history of an existing commodity contract only. For example, the chart of October 1978 hogs (Figure 47-20) shows a number of 5-wave movements ranging in degree from minute to intermediate. The first impulse from 29.10 to 31.80 could not have been traded from this chart alone, but the near 50 percent retracement to 30.50 could have been purchased with a 140-point stop for at least a minute 5-wave advance. (See Figure 47-20.)

It would have been very difficult for a trader to go long and steadfastly hold the position from the low around 30.50 to the top. Some kind of automatic trend-

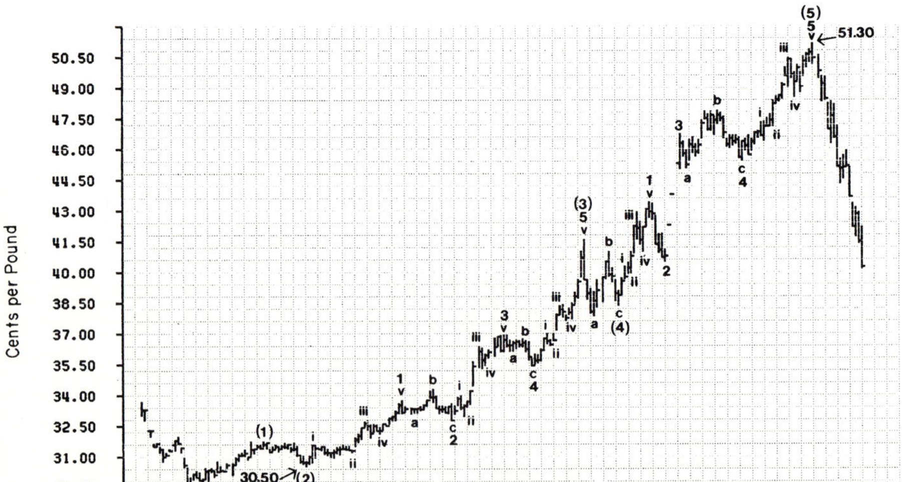

Figure 47-20 Chicago Mercantile Exchange live hogs, October 1978. *(Conti-Commodity Research Division)*

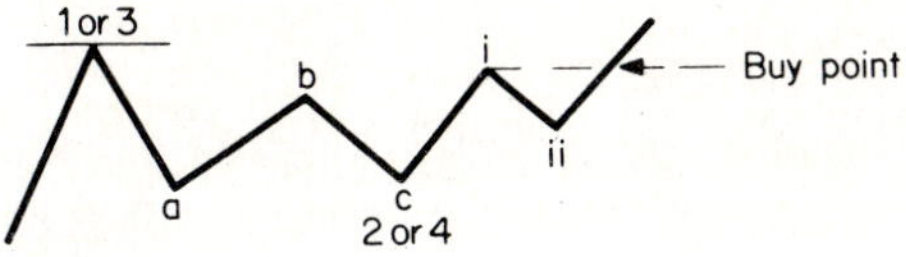

Figure 47-21

following system may be required to maintain objectivity. However, with a plan of trading for only the 5-wave moves of minute degree (that is, waves i to v), profits could have been made repeatedly. The first part of the plan should be that long positions are established on the second high after an a-b-c correction, as diagrammed in Figure 47-21. Stop-loss orders can be placed below the bottom of wave ii in case the move above wave i is part of an irregular formation. (See Figure 47-22.)

However, once the hog market moves 75 points above the top of wave i, the likelihood of an irregular wave ii is minimal at this degree of price movement. The sell-stop can then be raised to a few points below the top of wave i. If prices rally 75 points or more above wave i and then overlap below the top of wave i on the next decline, a v-wave move is not unfolding and buyers should offset their positions.

The second part of the plan is that as the hog market moves into wave v, stops will be raised so that they are always 50 points away from the previous day's closing. This is conservative trading, but it is a good way for a new student of the Elliott Wave principle to be exposed to the problems of analysis and trading. Figure 47-23 shows the buy and sell points; these points are based solely on counting minute waves i through v and recognizing the form of an a-b-c correction. (A similar trading method can be applied to other commodities as long as only the minute waves are its basis.) From the low at 30.50 to the top at 51.30, there were six trading opportunities, and only the last created a small loss. This conservative method would have earned 1070 points within a total move of 2080 points.

Dealing only with Figure 47-20, which shows October 1978 hogs, a clear 5-wave count can be made in retrospect. It would have been impossible to make this analysis correctly while each minute, minor, and intermediate wave was unfolding. The problem of where hog prices were in May 1978 is compounded tenfold by any attempt to fit this up wave into the price history that began with the 1975 top. The beginner should keep the analytical problem as simple as possible. (See Figure 47-23.)

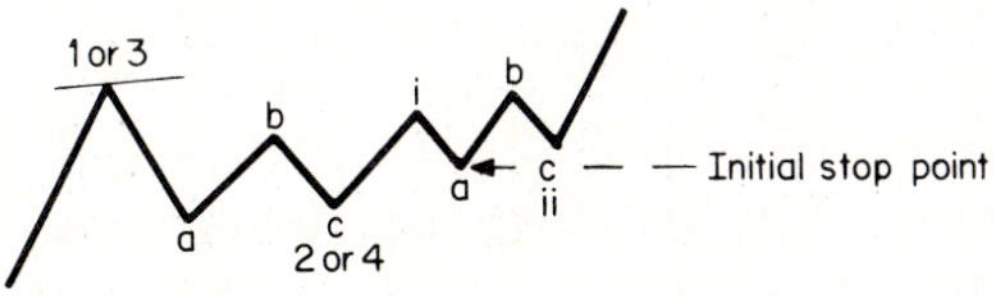

Figure 47-22

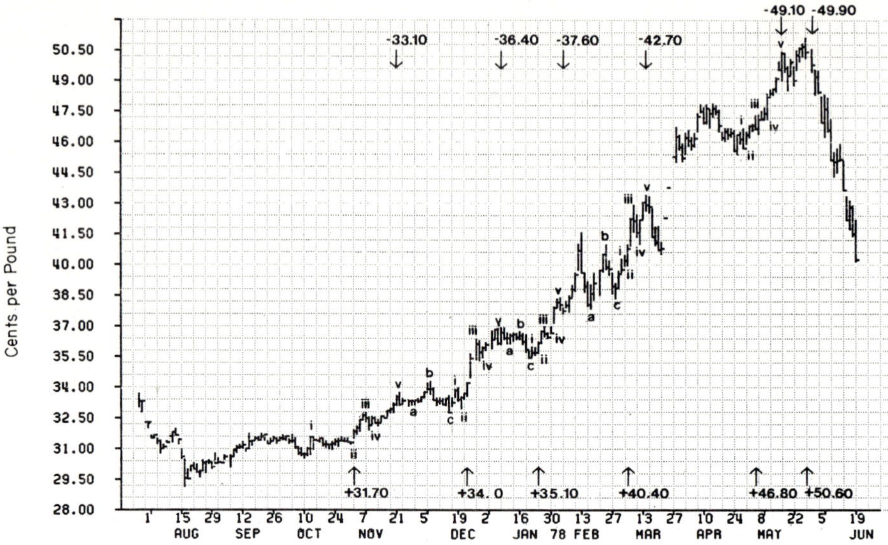

Figure 47-23 Chicago Mercantile Exchange live hogs, October 1978. *(Conti-Commodity Research Division)*

SOURCES OF INFORMATION

Bolton, A. Hamilton: *The Elliott Wave Principle, A Critical Appraisal,* Monetary Research, Ltd., Hamilton, Bermuda, 1960.

Frost, Alfred John, and Robert Prechter, Jr.: *Elliott Wave Principle, Key to Stock Market Profits,* New Classics Library, Chappaqua, N.Y., 1978.

Prechter, Robert R., Jr., ed.: *The Major Works of R. N. Elliott,* New Classics Library, Chappaqua, N.Y., 1980.

CHAPTER

48

Cycle Analysis

J. R. Stevenson

This chapter is intended to give an overview of and background in the use of cycles for the forecasting of commodity prices. The drawbacks and benefits of cycle analysis are also discussed.

DEFINITIONS

In this chapter the term *cycle* will be used to mean an event that recurs with some degree of regularity in a certain time interval. The phrase *time interval* can refer to such periods as seconds, minutes, days, weeks, months, years, and decades. The word *event* will be used to refer to a change in direction of the price movement in commodity prices. For example, when prices have been rising for 10 weeks and then change direction and go down for 10 weeks, the point of reversal is referred to as a cycle *high;* an "event" has occurred that produced more selling than buying. If another price rise develops and if, 20 weeks after the first event, prices go down again, there is some indication that a 20-week cycle is effective in this market. If prices also make a *low* every 20 weeks, this constitutes additional evidence of a 20-week cycle. The more events that occur with a certain time interval between them, the greater the probability that another change in price will occur in the future within the same time interval.

The use of cycles is concerned with a specific dimension of technical analysis.

HISTORY AND DEVELOPMENT

One of the first recorded use of cycles is found in the Bible, in the Book of Amos (Chapter 8, verse 5), which mentions the 28-day moon cycle. The existence of this cycle also seems to have a significant bullish effect on many commodities during the full moon cycles. It definitely has weight that cannot be ignored. This research has been further supported by the 20-market-day (28-calendar-day) cycle that many cycle analysts have found in a variety of markets.

One of the earliest, if not the first, cycle researchers in the United States, was an Ohio farmer named Arthur Benner, who published *Benner's Prophesies of Future Ups and Downs in Prices* in 1875. He based forecasts upon rhythmic cycles and discovered a 9-year cycle in pig-iron prices; on the basis of this cycle, he made a series of forecasts up to World War II, which proved highly reliable. If pig-iron prices had been traded on the basis of Benner's cycles from 1875 to 1935, 12 of the 14 transactions would have been profitable, and only 2 unprofitable. Benner also discovered cycles in corn, cotton, wheat, and pork prices. His 5½-year corn cycle was published by the Foundation for the Study of Cycles in 1955 and projected to the year 2000.

W. D. Gann was a gifted mathematician who, in the late nineteenth and early twentieth centuries devoted many years to studying and writing about cycles. He wrote,

> I soon began to note the periodical recurrence of the rise and fall in stocks and commodities. This led me to conclude that natural law was the basis of market movements. I then decided to devote ten years of my life to the study of natural law as applicable to the speculative markets and to devote my best energies toward making speculation a profitable profession. After exhaustive researches and investigations of the known sciences, I discovered that the Law of Vibration enabled me to accurately determine the exact points to which stocks or commodities should rise and fall within a given time. The working out of this law determines the cause and predicts the effect long before the Street is aware of either. Most speculators can testify to the fact that it is looking at the effect and ignoring the cause that has produced their losses.

Gann wrote many articles, study courses, and books on cycles in the commodity and stock markets. In 1909, under an appointed referee, Gann made 286 trades in the stock market, both on the long side and by selling short. Of the 286 trades, 264 resulted in profits, 22 in losses. His writings, study courses, and theory are still used extensively by market participants and analysts.

THEORY OF CYCLE ANALYSIS

Over the years several principles of cycle theory have been developed:

1. The longer the cycle, the greater the amplitude in price—for example, a 54-year cycle is likely to have a far greater price influence than a 10-week cycle.
2. The greater the number of cycles that reach their lows at about the same time, the greater the ensuing price movement is likely to be. This is known as the principle of "commonality." An example is the 1932 depression low

in commodity prices, which is thought to be a 54-year cycle low, as well as lows of the 27-year, 9-year, 6-year, and very short cycles.

3. Cycles tend to have harmonies of 2 to 1 or 3 to 1 ratio—that is, if a 5-week cycle exists, 10- 20-, 40-, and 80-week cycles should also exist.
4. The high point of a cycle is moved to the right if the major trend is up—a process known as "translation to the right." This principle helps to explain why cycle highs often do not come near the center of a time interval. Theoretically, this same effect occurs with cycle lows, but it is not as pronounced with lows as with highs.

SOME COMMODITY CYCLES

Some of the charts that should be considered when making a cyclic analysis are illustrated and discussed in this section.

The 54-Year Cycle—The Kondratieff Wave

Figure 48-1 shows the price of wheat in the United States from 1710 to 1972. A visual check of the times between the extreme peaks and valleys of this cycle

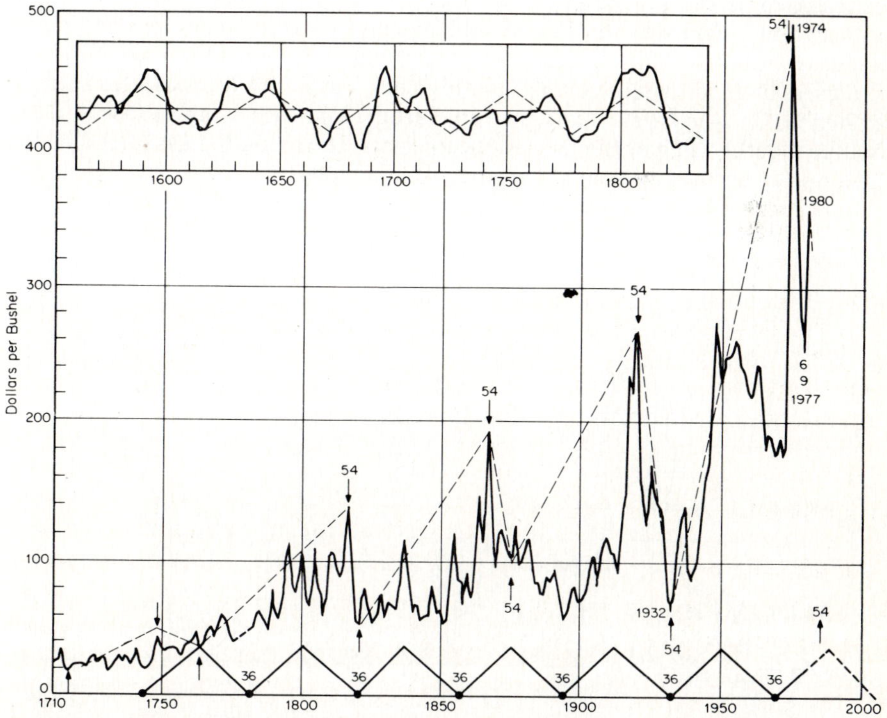

Figure 48-1 Wheat prices, 1710 to 1972. *(inset)* The 54-year cycle in wheat prices in western and central Europe.

indicates the probability that the cycle topped in 1973 to 1974. The Kondratieff cycle has been charted for the past 200 years. At each cycle high during this extensive period, many reasons were probably given to explain why conditions were different "this time" and the 54-year cycle would not work. However, a simple observation of the chart reveals that the peaks came about every 54 years. Currently, again, many reasons (price support, inflation, population, and so forth) are being given to explain why this cycle will not work this time. However, in 1974—almost exactly 54 years after the 1920 peak—wheat prices reached $6.44/bushel. This price was not exceeded during the inflation cycle of 1975 to 1980. Although there will continue to be times of strong prices, the Kondratieff Wave indicates that wheat prices will probably not reach a major low in price until 1986 or 1987.

The 5.6- to 6-Year and the 27-Year Cycles

The lower portion of Figure 48-2 shows the 5.6- to 6-year cycle that was discovered by Arthur Benner in 1875. Superimposed on this same chart is a 27-year cycle (note that 27 years is one-half of 54 years) that clearly shows a 13- to 15-year up-and-down cycle in prices. If this cycle is repeated, 1974 plus 13 years will mean that a low will occur in 1987, the same date that the 54-year cycle is expected to be at a low point.

Figure 48-3 shows Arthur Benner's ideal 5.6-year cycle. The upper portion of the chart indicates a low is expected in 1987 and a high in 1985, and so forth.

Figure 48-4, showing average monthly cotton cash prices, indicates further evidence of a 5- to 9-year cycle. The most recent high was made in 1980 to 1981, but the monthly high or the nearest future contract was made in 1974. A slightly lower price occurred 6 years later, in December 1980.

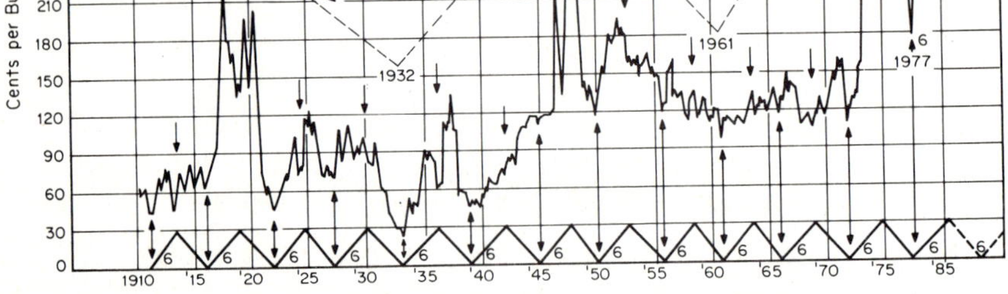

Figure 48-2 The 5½- to 6-year corn cycle (5.7-year average); Chicago corn cash price.

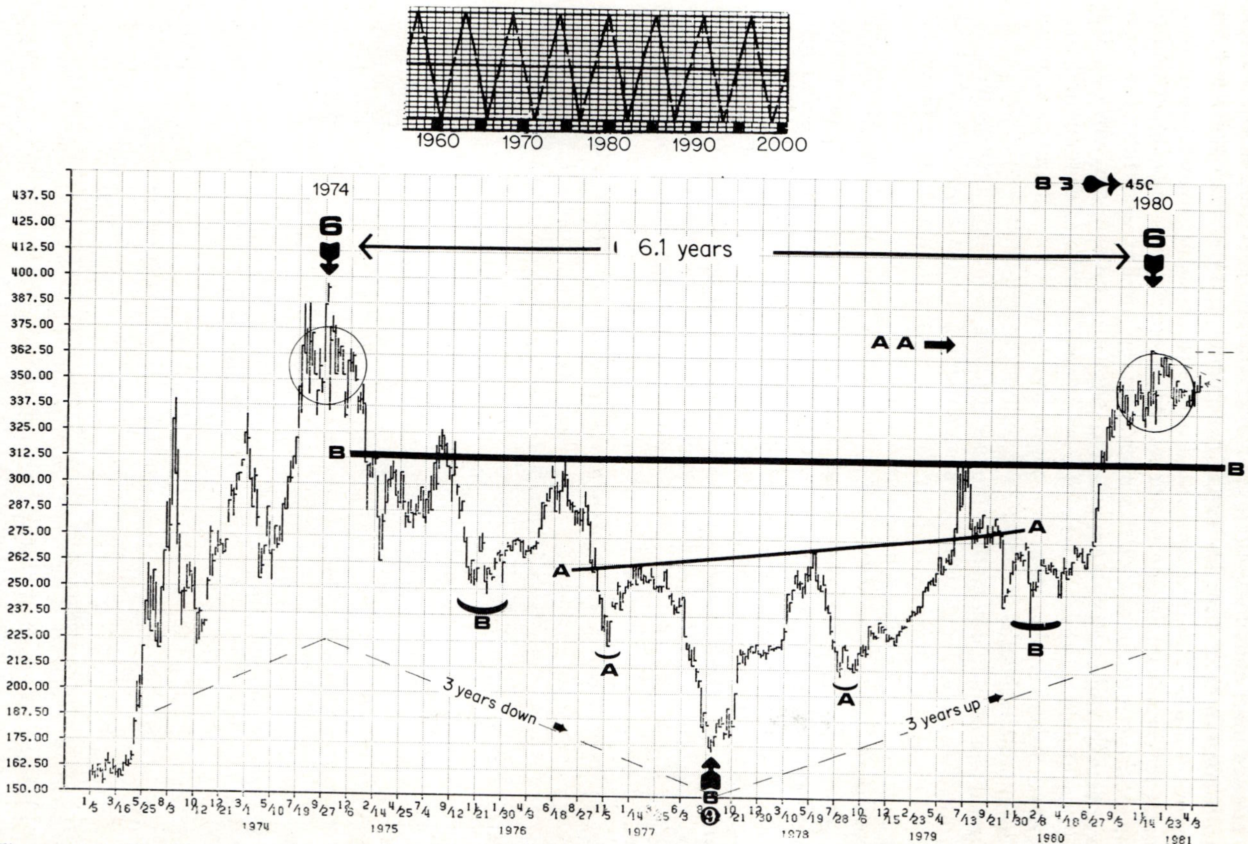

Figure 48-3 Weekly corn cash prices. *(ContiCommodity Research Division)*

METHODS FOR DETECTING CYCLES

The method most commonly used for identifying cycles is simple *observation:* The observer notices that an event has occurred, and when the event is repeated after a certain time interval, the observer becomes aware that a cycle is occurring. For example, the winter storms of 1982 seemed to be appearing at 7-day intervals (on weekends); this event was repeated several times, and so a 7-day cycle in winter storms appeared to exist. A technician may observe that the price of gold makes a low about every 8 weeks, time after time, and so a hint of an 8-week cycle exists. The charts presented in this chapter show that cycles of certain lengths occur and are continually repeated.

Cycles can also be detected by the use of *filters.* A moving average will "filter" out most cyclic fluctuations that are smaller (of shorter length) than the time span of the moving average that is used. The resultant average will show certain cyclic characteristics in a commodity price.

Systematic period reconnaisance is a technique that tests for all possible periods with the limits desired and results in a periodogram that shows the most dominant cycles. Another mathematical method, called *Fourier analysis,* reveals the existence of various cycle lengths, their amplitudes, and their phases. Some methods, called *detrending,* take the "trend" out of a price movement in order to find a cycle. Detrending is another use of a moving average. After a cycle is detrended, visual inspection generally becomes much easier.

It is not necessary to detect all the various cycles present in a price chart in order to forecast the probable future direction of prices. It is important, however, to have a belief and conviction that the price chart contains the past

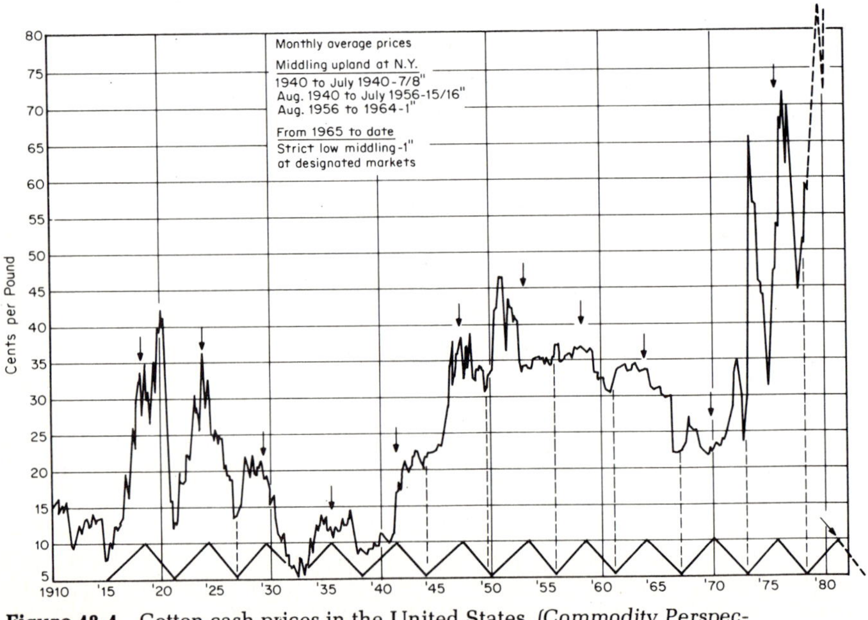

Figure 48-4 Cotton cash prices in the United States. *(Commodity Perspective Bureau)*

behavior patterns of all market participants and that these patterns will repeat, either in a regular time-interval pattern or in an expanding-contracting pattern. It is also important to study and research cycles in other related areas. It has been observed hundreds of times that political news, unusual weather, economic crises, and other phenomena in various fields occur at turning points previously indicated by cyclical analysis. For example, a market cycle high may be predicted to occur at a specific date and time in the future. On this specific date, a world news item causes market participants to act in such a manner as to make the projection work out. The reasons for the high were not known, nor could they have possibly been known, by any market participant, yet the charts reflected that "something" was going to happen to reverse the previous trend. It would appear that most cycles found in the price of any one commodity occur because of cyclical fundamental news items which occur outside the marketplace and are unrelated to any one commodity. The charts tell when and how much the market participants will react to the news, but cannot forecast what the news will be.

DRAWBACKS OF CYCLIC ANALYSIS

A problem that confronts all cycle analysts is the "apparent change" in the cycle period when least expected. A cycle may have been observed to make a low every 8 weeks and to repeat itself time after time. However, about the time that confidence is high that the cycle will repeat one more time, "something" causes the cycle to change or disappear completely. This has been explained as the result of a strong trend, or by the combination of several other cycles acting (mathematically) in such a way as to distort or replace this particular cycle. These explanations may be true; but when we realize that the actions and reactions of people make the market, then the explanations seem to fall short. Regardless of the reason for apparent changes in cycle periods, an analyst must be aware of these changes and not "bet the house" that the cycle will be repeated.

There are many other problems associated with cyclic analysis, such as time lows versus price lows, left and right translations, long- versus short-range cycles, and the many different cycles that are found in all commodities. Many of these problems have been partially solved by analysts to the point where a workable (profitable) method can be used. The one truism in cyclic analysis that is shared by all analysts is that "failure often leads to success." When a commodity cycle fails to perform as expected, much can be learned from the resulting cyclic configuration. Careful and knowledgeable adjustments can increase the probability that the next trade will be successful.

PUTTING CYCLES TO WORK

Whether you use your own analysis or that of someone else, you should never rely 100 percent on a cycle for an entry or exit point. Chart patterns, volume, open interest, support and resistance zones, and other technical or fundamental factors should be used to support cyclic timing. Further, it is highly recommended that a study of psychology be part of your study analysis. The habits and emotions of people, both individually and as a group, have cyclic characteristics. Remember that all market participants are part of a large group or crowd. The worldwide advent of instant quotes, instant news, instant charts, and instant communication has made the emotions of most participants "instant" also. However, people have changed very little over the centuries, and by studying their habits, emotions, and other characteristics, you can determine how they will act when an event occurs.

The two checklists presented below may help you keep your feet on the ground. They may enable you to avoid joining the crowd at the most bullish point (highest price), or they may give you courage to enter the market when others have lost interest. Timing is very important, not only for making money but also for peace of mind. Good cycle analysis can help, and these checklists can also help.

Indications of a Major Cycle Top

1. Is the news (on television, in newspapers, on commodity wire services, and in *The Wall Street Journal*) very bullish?
2. Has the bullish news campaign been going on for 3, 6, or 12 months or longer?
3. Is the bullish consensus (contrary opinion) climbing? Has it been high for several weeks?
4. Are the known fundamentals very bullish? (Is scarcity evident?) And are the fundamentals well published?
5. Are chart patterns predicting higher prices? Are the trend lines intact?
6. Are your logic, reasoning, and intellect convinced of yet higher prices?
7. Are your friends, customers, and co-workers bullish? Are they telling others to buy?
8. Are the feelings from the floor very bullish? Is there "electricity in the air"?
9. Do accounts have large profits? And are they adding to their positions?
10. If profits are taken, do you buy back on the next fast rally?
11. If you are a broker, are you very busy on the phone? Are you establishing new accounts? Are strangers calling?
12. Does going short seem to be the most risky action to take?
13. Are you impatient to make a trade? Do you think you missed the move and want to jump in?
14. Do you wish the market would stay open longer so you could continue to trade and make money? Are you glued to the quote machine?
15. Are you *absolutely* sure that you should be long this market?

Indications of a Major Cycle Low

1. Is the news nonexistent or bearish?
2. Is the tape very quiet? Is there little interest in trading?

3. Is the contrary opinion (bullish consensus) below 40 percent and falling?
4. Are all known fundamentals very bearish?
5. Would you be laughed at if you suggested a long position?
6. If you are a broker, is your telephone very quiet? Are you establishing no new accounts?
7. Are the boardrooms empty?
8. Has the bearish campaign been going on for 3, 6, or 12 months or longer?
9. If you are a broker, do you have any customers left? Have they decided that the only way to make money is to go short?
10. Has everyone on the floor lost hope? Do you hear no noise?
11. Have the chart patterns flattened? Do they show very little volatility?
12. If you are a broker, are your co-workers looking for other jobs? Is commodity trading "out of vogue"?

Humphrey Neill, author of *The Act of Contrary Thinking,* observed that "knowing what every one thinks about is not enough, when everybody *acts* alike, their actions are often wrong." Nothing could be more true at cycle tops, when the crowd takes over. By developing a knowledge that cycles do exist and will continue to exist in the future, you can also develop the confidence to go opposite to the crowd at the right time.

CHAPTER

49

Volume and Open Interest Analysis

Reid Hampton

The interpretive art of technical analysis incorporates three data series: price, volume, and open interest. Of these three, price is the most important and useful tool in the attempt to forecast commodity prices, and has been discussed at the most length in this book. This chapter will examine the other two tools of the technician, volume and open interest, with the intent of defining these statistics and exploring the ways in which they are used.

Volume is the number of contracts of any given commodity bought or sold during a single trading session. A simple measurement of market activity, it represents the intensity of the buying or selling taking place in the market for that particular trading session. *Open interest* is the number of open or outstanding contracts in a particular commodity market—or, in other words, the number of futures contracts that have not been closed out or offset by an opposite transaction. One short position (one contract sold) and one long position (one contract purchased) combine to make one open contract. During a trading session, if ten contracts are bought and ten sold by traders entering new positions, open interest increases by ten contracts. If ten contracts are bought and ten sold by traders closing out positions or completing trades, open interest decreases by ten contracts. The significance of this figure lies in changes in the relative level of open interest in relation to the direction of price movement.

The basis of technical analysis is that the psychology of the market is always reflected in price movement. Volume and open interest figures help technicians to determine changes in this psychology—preferably by identifying small changes before the more significant changes occur.

OPEN INTEREST

Following a market scenario should clarify the roles of volume and open interest. Let us start with a "strong" market, with the bulls "bidding up" for a given commodity, hereby advancing the price. As price increases, the bears grow apprehensive about their positions and begin to cover shorts. Short covering only serves to further fuel the rally and to reduce open interest. When advancing price is accompanied by shrinking open interest, the market is technically weak; new buying is drying up, and the only buying taking place seems to be short covering.

Once the short covering is over, there is no buying power to "support" price, or keep it up. Open interest is further declining as some of the longs are liquidating because of lack of confidence in the ability of the market to rally further. We now reach our first axiom: *Price up with open interest down indicates a forthcoming price reversal.* As prices begin to turn down, new sellers enter the market, aggressively forcing the market down. At some point, longs still in the market liquidate their positions, further pushing prices down and, at this point, also reducing open interest. Several things are changing in the complexion of the market. New sellers are not entering the market, and the selling that is taking place represents longs scrambling to liquidate. Shorts are now ready to take profits, and a second axiom may be reached: *Downward price direction and a decreasing open interest figure suggest to the technician that the downtrend may be near an end.* When price and open interest move together, a continuation of the existing price trend may be expected. If they move in opposite directions, a change in the complexion of the market may be forthcoming.

The relationship of price to open interest can be stated in eight basic rules:

1. Price up, open interest up: Bulls are buying; market is strong.
2. Price down, open interest down: Bulls are selling; market is strong.
3. Price flat, open interest up: New shorts and new longs; market is neutral.
4. Price flat, open interest down: Bulls are selling; bears are covering; market is neutral.
5. Price up, open interest down: Bears are covering; market is weak.
6. Price down, open interest up: Bears are selling; market is weak.
7. Price up, open interest flat: Bulls are buying; bears are covering; market is neutral.
8. Price down, open interest flat: Bulls are selling; market is neutral.

At this point in the use of open interest, complications cloud its usefulness. Many of these complications are connected with seasonal tendencies in open interest. For harvested commodities, such as grains and oilseeds, open interest generally rises considerably during harvesttime and immediately thereafter, because of heavy supplies and a rise in hedging activities. Because of these seasonal trends, only large, sharp changes in open interest have any significance. Even if a technician can accurately interpret these changes, they give no clue to the timing of price trend changes unless they are used with price charts. Unusual changes in open interest can occur, however, when price action diverges from normal seasonal tendencies because of trading-range behavior that may extend for several weeks. An example occurs when commercial interests are entering new short positions, causing an increase in open interest (which would normally be interpreted as new longs). When price then begins to exhibit trading-range behavior or a temporary equilibrium, the commercial hedges cover shorts, hoping for an opportunity to resell at a higher price. This type of buying will decrease open interest considerably, but price will not increase; these transactions take place quietly in the trading range because the commercials do not have to "chase" price upward to buy.

VOLUME

Volume is generally easier to interpret than open interest because it lacks the seasonality of open interest. Volume figures are normally expressed as a sum of the number of trades in all contracts in a particular commodity, although a per-contract breakdown is available. The general rule used by most technical analysts in interpreting volume statistics is that commodity prices will tend to move in the direction in which volume increases. If price is in an uptrend on high volume, the bull trend is expected to persist. If volume increases on drops in price, a downtrend exists and any rallies (on lighter volume) will be short-lived.

The urgency of trading, that is, the buying or selling pressure, is measured by volume in that the market temperament is reflected in changes in trading volume. Whereas open interest is generally viewed in terms of relative levels over longer time periods, volume is considered more important when studied as patterns of daily changes. It may be somewhat of a mistake, however, to try to interpret day-to-day changes in volume unless they are extraordinary—unless they represent either a particularly large increase or a particularly large decrease.

The following general characteristics of volume behavior have been observed over time:

1. In a major bull move, volume increases on rallies and subsides on downward reactions.
2. During a major decline in price, volume rises on weaknesses in price and lightens up on rallies.
3. Volume is reduced when a bottom is forming, and then it expands dramatically as the price makes its last downward thrusts. This is often called a "selling climax."

These characteristics are merely tendencies and are certainly not absolute necessities for advancing or declining markets. There have been both bull and bear markets that have not behaved in line with these characteristics, and there have also been markets whose behavior diverged considerably from these expected patterns of behavior.

The technician is really only looking at supply and demand and thus is trying only to measure the balance between these market forces rather than to analyze

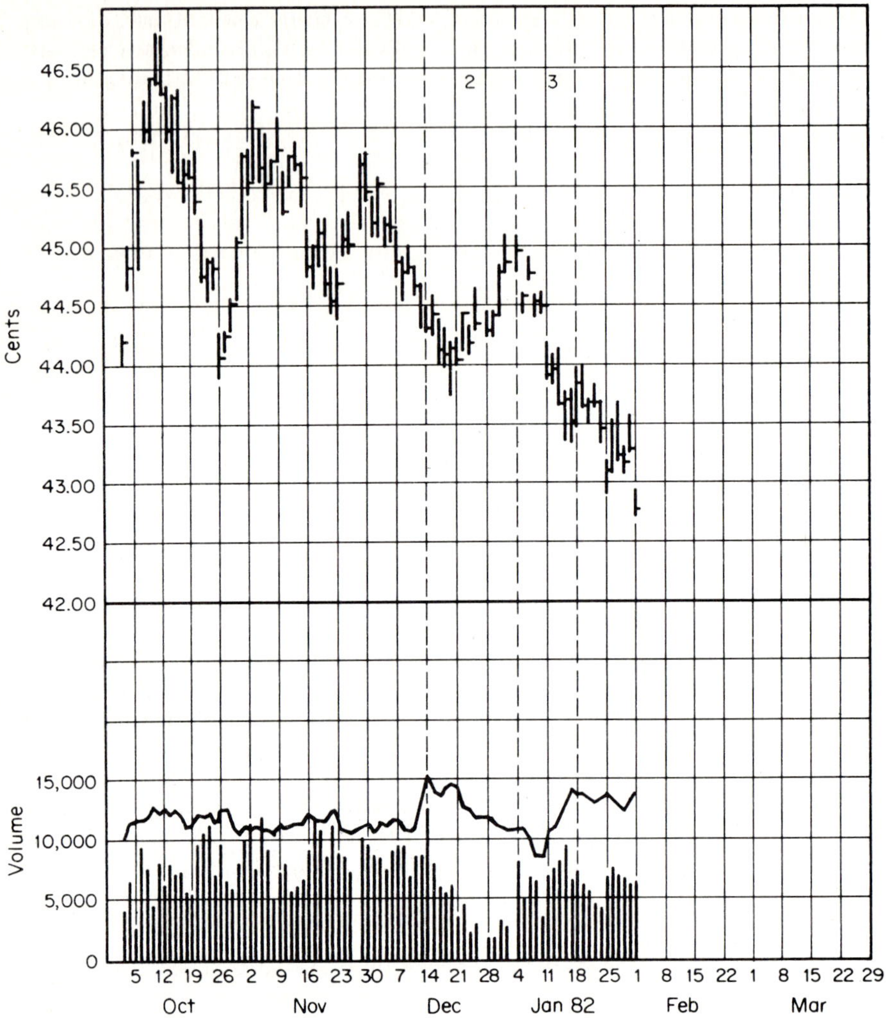

Figure 49-1 D-mark illustrating volume and open interest, March 1982. This figure illustrates rules 2 and 3 of the following general rules for the interpretation of volume and open interest. The time period from December 14 to January 4 is exemplary of rule 2, and the immediately following 2 weeks manifest rule 3. The subsequent weakness in this currency gives us a real-world situation in which the analyst can observe the validity of this set of rules: (1) Price up, volume up, open interest up: Weak market. (2) Price up, volume down, open interest down: Weak market. (3) Price down, volume up, open interest up: Weak market. (4) Price down, volume down, open interest down: Strong market.

the fundamentals. The relationships between the fundamentals are too numerous and complex to understand, much less forecast. The technician is looking at *the market only* and, accordingly, bases all decisions on the analysis of the balance between supply and demand.

SUMMARY

Although either volume or open interest can be considered in isolation, it is common practice to consider both when looking at price movement in order to obtain a more balanced view of the technical structure. The general rules for the interpretation of price, volume, and open interest are as follows:

1. Price up, volume up, open interest up: Strong market.
2. Price up, volume down, open interest down: Weak market.
3. Price down, volume up, open interest up: Weak market.
4. Price down, volume down, open interest down: Strong market.

Figure 49-1 illustrates these generally accepted rules for interpretation.

Although generalities cannot be blindly applied to today's market, any divergence between price, volume, and open interest may be a sign of changes in the market and may thus deserve a closer examination. When used as a portion of a total system of technical analysis, volume and open interest can be likened to the pulse and the heartbeat of the market, and can be used to diagnose whether the market is "sick" or "healthy" well before any "symptoms" begin to show up in price behavior.

SOURCES OF INFORMATION

Allan: *Price Momentum, Volume Pressure, Speculative Volume*, Institute for Technical Research.

Angrist, Stanley: *Sensible Speculating in Commodities*, Simon & Schuster, New York, 1974.

Gold, Gerald: *Modern Commodities Futures Trading*, Commodity Research Bureau, Inc., New York 1975.

Jiler, W. L.: "Volume and Open Interest: Analysis Is an Aid to Price Forecasting," *CRB Yearbook*, Commodity Research Bureau, Inc., New York, 1975.

Kent, W. A.: "The Volume Gambit," *Encyclopedia of Technicians*.

Weis, David: "Trading Volume Predicts Price Trend," *Commodities*, September 1981, pp. 50–51.

Weis, David, and J. R. Stevenson: "Open Interest Reconsidered," *Grain*.

Wyler, Joseph A.: *The Application of Scientific Principles to Stock Speculation*, Blooming Grove, Hawley, Pa., 1966.

1978 Futures Trading Course, Commodity Research Bureau, Inc., New York, 1978.

CHAPTER

50

Point and Figure Analysis

Amos Cohen

INTRODUCTION

The analysis of price movement with point and figure charting is based on the idea that filtering out many insignificant price fluctuations and looking at the more condensed picture can clarify the important battles between supply and demand. The bigger the cause for a coming move in prices, the bigger will be the effect or the larger the price change, as best recognized on the point and figure chart.

It should be noted that point and figure charts *do not* predict the direction in which prices will emerge from a congestion area. This kind of information can best be derived from an analysis of other indicators of the overall technical structure. Point and figure charts are solely concerned with price and do not therefore have a time or volume scale.

CONSTRUCTION OF POINT AND FIGURE CHARTS

The construction of a point and figure chart is basically simple. When prices go up, X's are plotted and when prices go down, 0s are recorded. As long as prices are rising, X's are continually recorded in the same column and vice versa. Thus the point and figure chart develops as alternating columns of X's and 0s. Before a point and figure chart is constructed, two principles must be established: (1) How much of a price change does each square marked with an X or a 0 represent? (That is, what is the sensitivity of the chart?) (2) When is a decision to start a new column of X's or 0s based on a reversal in prices being made? To a large extent, the answers to both questions are subjectively rather than scientifically determined.

How Much Price Change Should Each X or 0 Represent?

One popular way to answer this question is to use fluctuations for different commodities based on their "normal" behavior—in this case the minimum change in price that seems to be "significant." For example, in corn or wheat, 1¢; in pork bellies, 20 points; in metric cocoa, $10; and in orange juice, 50 points. The individual user must answer the question by exercising judgment for each commodity about what constitutes the minimum significant price change. Table 50-1 presents some guidelines based on price fluctuations in the early 1980s.

TABLE 50-1 Common Sensitivity Applicable to Several Markets, Feb. 1, 1982

Commodity	Sensitivity	Reversal
Corn	1	3
Oats	1	3
Beans	1	3
Meal	100	300
Oil	10	30
Wheat	1	3
Live cattle	20	60
Hogs	20	60
Pork bellies	20	60
Metric cocoa	10	30
Coffee	50	150
Cotton	20	60
Orange juice	50	150
Sugar	10	30
Copper	50	150
Gold	20	60
Silver	50	150
Lumber	1	3
T-bonds	$\frac{4}{32}$	$\frac{12}{32}$
T-bills	5	15
Swiss franc	20	60

For example, in a more volatile environment 2¢ should be used in wheat and soybeans with the appropriate reversal also multiplies by 2. That change will filter out all swings less than 6¢ in wheat or beans. A similar change in T-bonds would be from $\frac{4}{12}$ to $\frac{8}{24}$ ratio.

Deciding When to Start a New Column of X's or 0s

A new column, commonly referred to as the "reversal amount" or "reversal box" is expressed in multiples of the sensitivity unit. This number determines the amount of filtering that a particular point and figure chart accomplishes. The most popular ratio of reversal to sensitivity is 3 to 1 and is written as a 1 × 3 point and figure chart. Therefore, when using a scale of 1¢ × (or 0) for corn, a reversal would be 3¢. This means that all reversals less than 3¢ will be filtered out by the point and figure chart. Only after a reversal greater than 3¢ would a new column be started.

For example, in Figure 50-1, in order to change from the column of 0s to a new column of X's, the price of corn would first have to rise by 3¢ to 305 (3.02 + 0.03). Thus the minimum number of X's or 0s in each column in a 1 × 3 point and figure chart is 3. This is true for any chosen ratio—that is, the minimum number of X's or 0s is equal to the reversal size. The only exception would be a 1 × 1 chart where the minimum entry in each column would be fixed at 2.

Sources for Construction of Point and Figure Charts

Some technicians maintain that a bar chart is sufficient for construction of point and figure charts. In other words, a reversal is determined only when the high or low for the day is exceeded the next day by the minimum amount and the close is in the opposite direction to the previous day (all inside days are ignored). An inside day is a day on which high and low prices do not exceed the high and low of the previous day. However, in volatile markets, the intraday movement can be crucial to the proper usage of the point and figure chart. An example to that effect is given in Figures 50-2 and 50-3. Figures 50-2a and 50-3 represent an actual 16-day period in February 1982 pork bellies. Figure 50-2a is the bar chart, and Figure 50-3a shows the intraday tick-by-tick activity as copied from the actual tape. Only reversals greater than 60 points are marked. The point and figure charts derived from Figures 50-2a and 50-3a are presented in Figures 50-2b and 50-3b, respectively. Since a point and figure price projection is based on the number of price fluctuations within a given

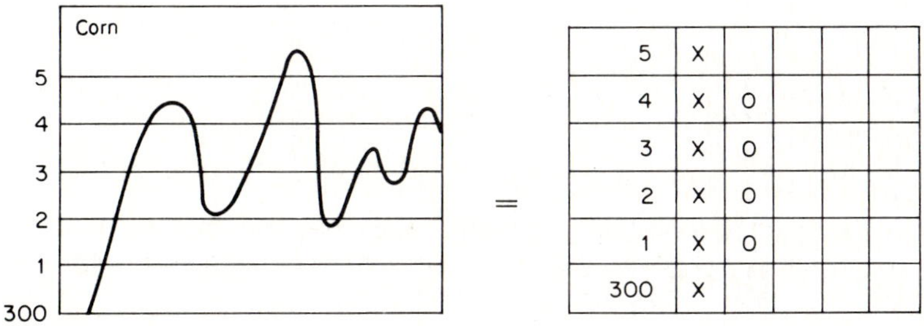

Figure 50-1

range, the information in Figure 50-3b calls for a much more substantial move than the one in Figure 50-2b. Consequently, reversals as reflected by the daily tick chart tend to be more reliable than those based on the information used in a bar chart. This is especially true because many volatile commodities make intraday moves presenting important areas in the distribution or accumulation process which would be lost in the daily bar chart.

Since a point and figure chart does not have a time scale, it is helpful to indicate dates so that each chart can be compared with other charts. One way to indicate the dates is to color the last price of each month and note the next month at the bottom of the chart. Another is to note the day of the week on the day's last price.

Continuation charts give a long-term perspective on price changes. Constructing the charts involves replacing one contract month with another on its expiry so that a continuous price chart results. It is reommended that liquidating contracts (contracts for settlement in the current month) not be used.

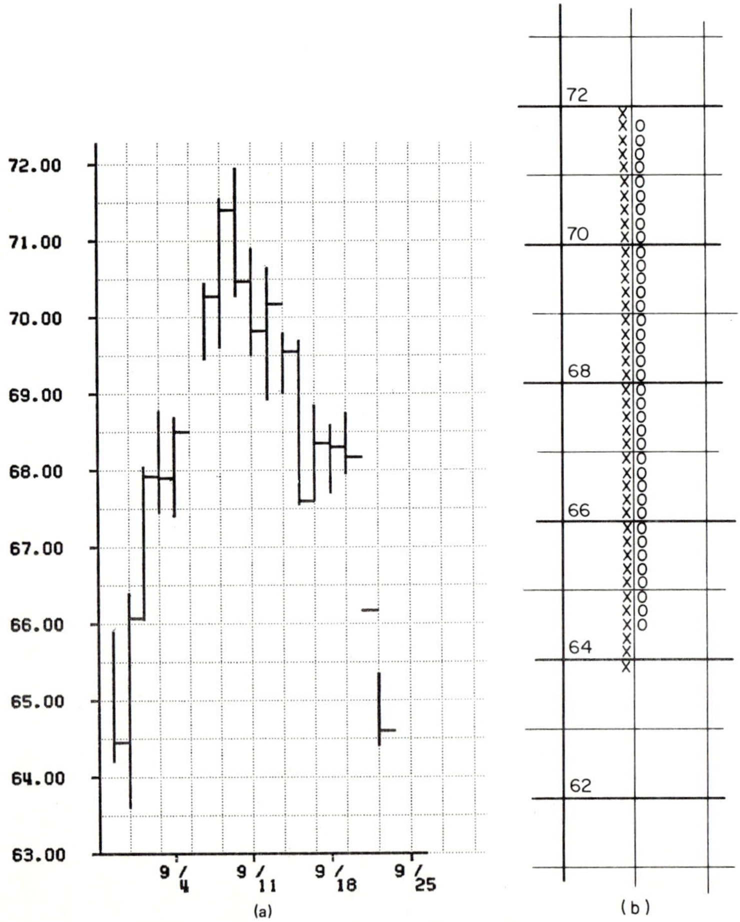

Figure 50-2

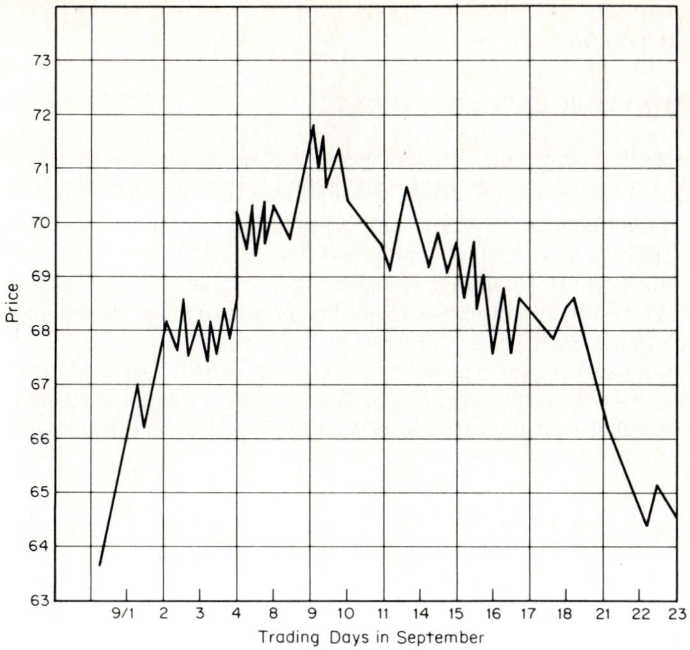

(a)

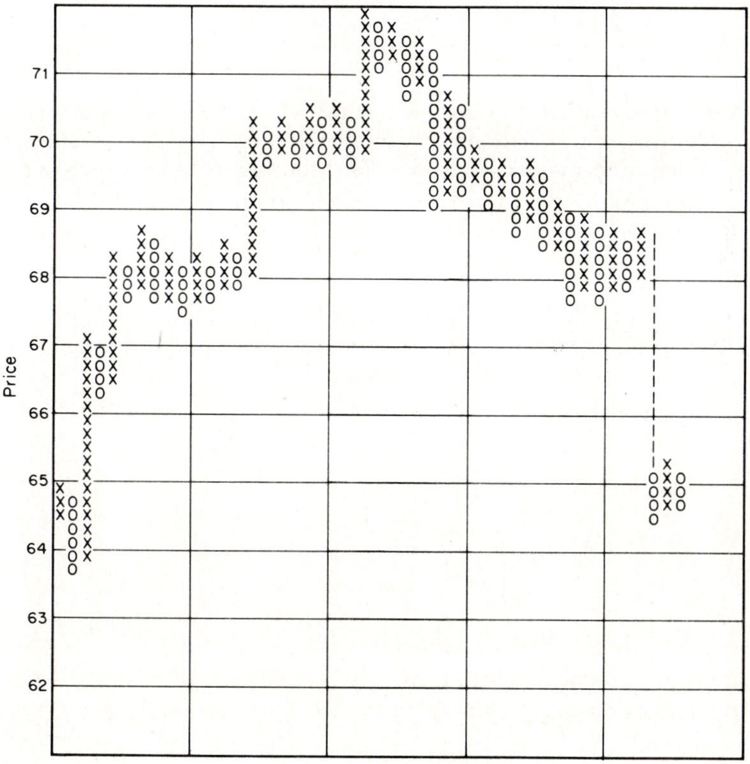

(b)

Figure 50-3

HOW TO USE POINT AND FIGURE CHARTS

Choosing the Charts

The problem is simply which combination of sensitivity box and reversal box to use. The choice depends primarily on the individual commodity and the past usefulness of particular charts. A major study by Charles C. Thiel and Robert E. Davis (see "Sources of Information") revealed that different combinations can lead to very wide results, especially when the charts are used mechanically. Other analysts advocate using the charts that count best (discussed below), but this leads to a circular argument since the count is determined by the combination. It is clear that there is no simple answer and that an automatic approach to this issue can be harmful. The values indicated in Table 50-1 are suggested as guidelines.

Mechanical Rules

The rules given below should not be followed blindly but should be used in conjunction with techniques described in other chapters in Part 6.

Basic Buy and Sell Signals. When the price of a commodity rises, then falls, and then rises by at least one square above the previous peak, a buy signal is indicated. The reverse succession of events indicates a sell signal. (See Figure 50-4.)

Triple Top and Triple Bottom. When a commodity price rises, falls, rises again, falls again, and on the next rise penetrates the previous top (hence the name "triple"), a triple formation is created. This formation is considered one of the most reliable point and figure signals. (See Figure 50-5) According to a statistical study quoted by Robert E. Davis,* this signal can result in a success rate of 88 percent.

45° Angle Lines. The use of 45° angle lines has special significance for mechanical usage of point and figure charts as they serve as both support and

*Robert E. Davis, *Profit and Profitability,* Dunn and Hargitt's Financial Service, West Lafayette, Ind., 1965, p. 94.

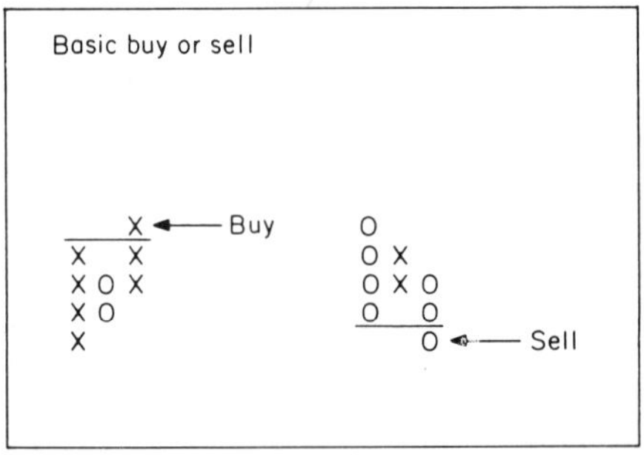

Figure 50-4

resistance. In addition to the normal use of support and resistance lines, similar to the way they are used on bar charts, two lines have been proposed. (See Figure 50-6). The bearish resistance line is a 45° line drawn toward the lower right-hand part of the chart. This should start from an exposed column of X's, and it can project the next support which would enter the market on the next sell-off. The bullish resistance line is just the opposite; it is a 45° line drawn toward the upper right-hand part of the chart from an exposed column of 0s. This line would indicate the next resistance to be encountered in an uptrend. (See Figure 50-7.)

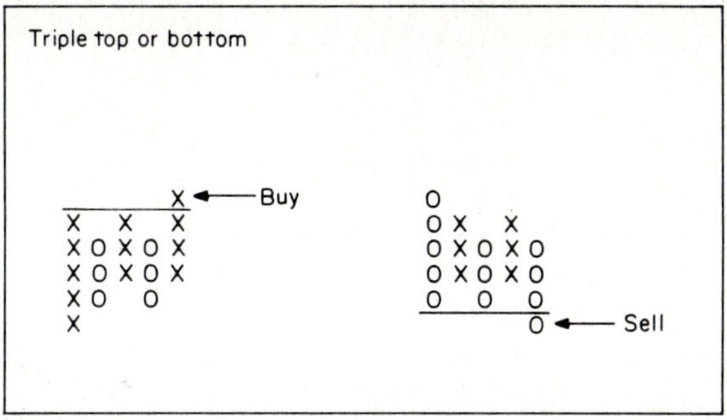

Figure 50-5

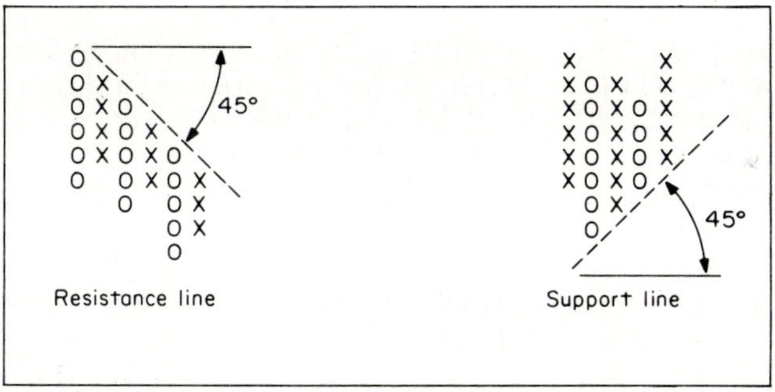

Figure 50-6

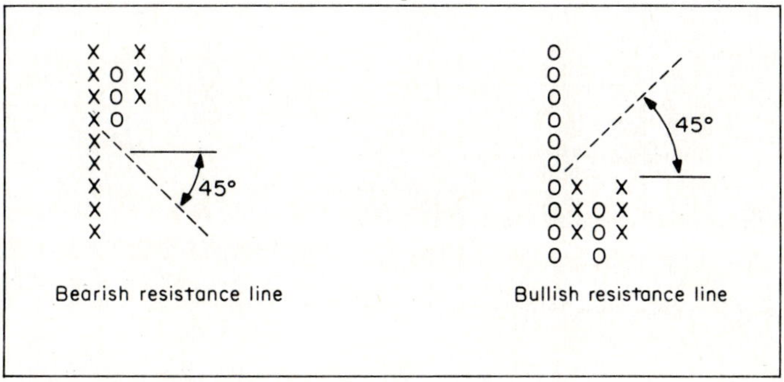

Figure 50-7

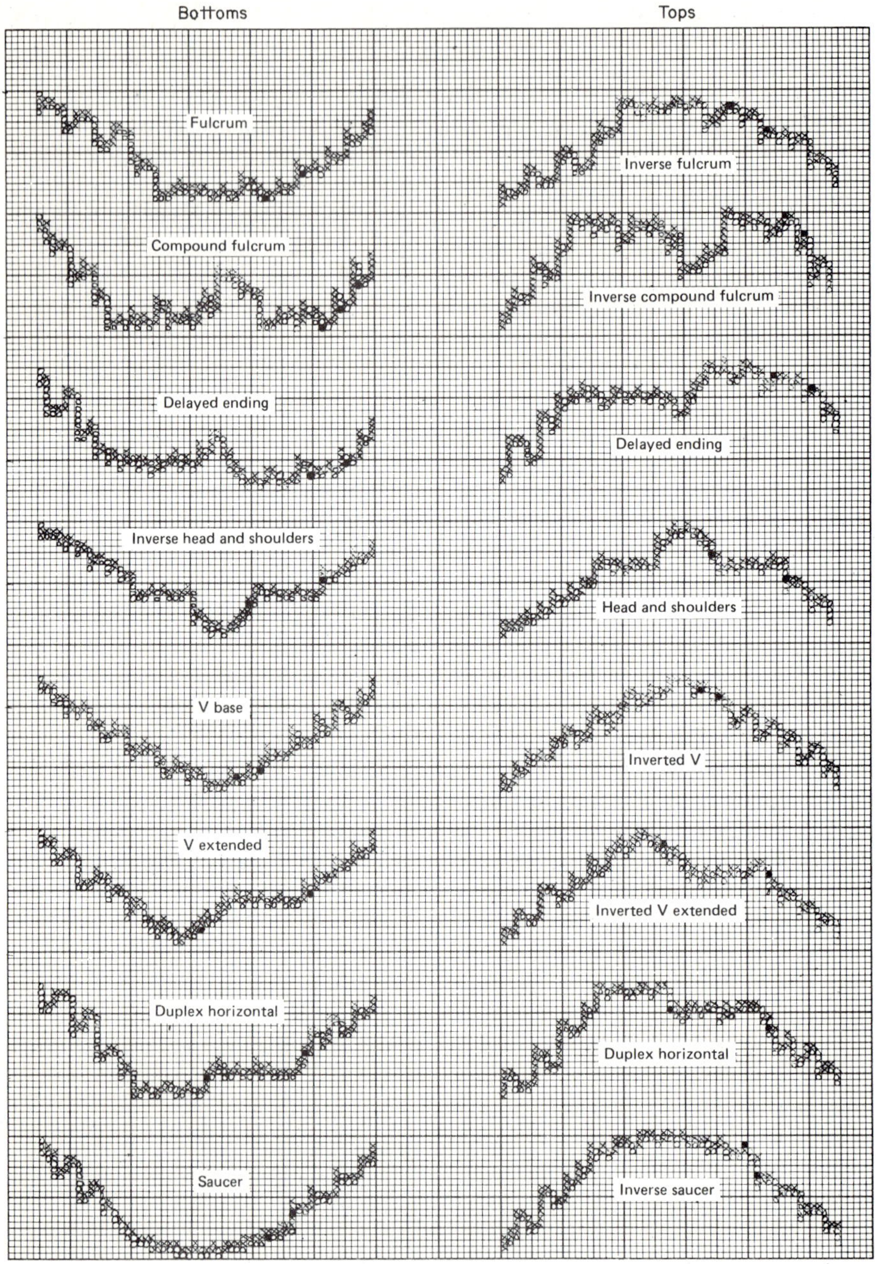

Copied from study helps in point and figure technique

Figure 50-8 *(Study Helps in Point and Figure Technique)*

Chart Patterns

Alexander H. Wheelan, in his classical discussion of point and figure technique (see "Sources of Information"), identified eight major chart patterns which are visible in commodity charts: the fulcrum, compound fulcrum, delayed ending, head and shoulder, V, V extended, duplex horizontal, and saucer. These patterns appear in bottoms, and in tops their inverse patterns can be recognized. (See Figure 50-8.) When such patterns are distinctly recognized, they can add validity to trading decisions. The darker squares are recommended buying and selling points.

Trend Lines

Point and figure charts should be used in conjunction with a bar chart and volume. Since they follow the price movement of a commodity, long-term trend lines drawn between significant points of support or resistance tend to serve as excellent check points for corrections in bull markets or rallies in bear markets. The tendency of price to stay within the boundary of a parallel channel can either support swing trading techniques or confirm the trend. Channel lines also serve as distinct locations at which to place stop-loss orders.

Point and Figure Counting

The count, which is the most important application of point and figure charts, is used as a basis for price projection. It is made by totaling the number of columns in a congestion area, or the number of times that prices reversed themselves within a congestion area.

There are several mechanical approaches to the counting method. When a congestion area is well defined between two vertical walls, the convention is to count between the two walls. The count must be taken across the same price line, and blank squares are included in the count. When such walls are not well defined, different mechanical approaches apply various rules such as using the line that has the lowest number of unoccupied squares, or using a line that represents the average between the top and bottom of a slanting side (this technique is not recommended).

Point and figure charts should be used in conjunction with a bar chart and volume. Only from such comparisons can the proper use of the point and figure count be determined. The rule for making the count is as follows: When a bear market has practically fulfilled its projected count and has gone through a consolidation period, the correct count for the potential upswing should start with identifying (on the bar chart) the last reaction before the beginning of an uptrend. After this point is identified on the point and figure chart, the count starts from right to left on the line to the column where support initially formed. The number of columns multiplied by the reversal box is the projected price change. For example, based on the guidelines in Table 50-1, a count of 17 columns in the Swiss franc would project a move of $17 \times 60 = 1020$ points; a count of 15 columns in orange juice would represent a move of 16.5¢. Conversely, after a long advance, prices will begin to stall, a congestion area will form, and prices will eventually break. The proper count to predict the extent of the decline should start from the last rally high and go across the top of the congestion area to the point where the advance stopped for the first time.

When a congestion area is composed of distinct phases, the proper way to count is to include the most recent phase alone. Only after the projected price has been exceeded is going back and adding other phases of the congestion area justified.

SOURCES OF INFORMATION

Davis, Robert E.: *Profit and Probability*, Dunn and Hargitt's Financial Service, West Lafayette, Ind., 1965.

Thiel, Charles C. and Robert E. Davis: *Point and Figure Commodity Trading: A Computer Evaluation*, Dunn and Hargitt's Financial Services, Inc., West Lafayette, Ind., 1970.

Wheelan, Alexander H.: *Study Helps in Point and Figure Technique*, Morgan, Rogers, and Roberts, Inc., New York, 1954.

"Point and Figure Procedure in Commodity Market Analysis," in Harry Jiles (ed.): *Guide to Commodity Price Forecasting*, Commodity Research Bureau, Inc., New York, 1967.

CHAPTER

51

A Review of Options

John Parry

HISTORICAL BACKGROUND

Options have been traded continuously on the London Metal Exchange (LME) and London Commodity Exchange (LCE) since the 1920s. In the United States during that time, option trading has had a sad stop-and-go history. The stops have resulted from congressional orders issued because of fraudulent practice and lack of control in the U.S. option markets.

In 1974 the Commodity Futures Trading Commission (CFTC) renewed U.S. trading in London options. By 1978 the CFTC, bowing to congressional pressure, was forced to ban U.S. trading in London options because of fraudulent practice in the retailing of the options. Contrary to opinion circulated in the United States and even in Europe at the time, the scandals were in no way the fault of the London authorities or the London brokers or the London options themselves, which gained an undeservedly poor image at the time. The fault lay with ineffective U.S. regulation of marketing of London options in the United States by certain U.S. brokers.

In 1982 the regularity authorities permitted trading in options on a limited number of commodities.

CURRENT REGULATIONS IN THE UNITED KINGDOM

Soft commodity options are controlled by the International Commodity Clearing House (ICCH), which acts as guarantor and clearing agent for all option contracts. The ICCH holds premium money paid on options, releasing the money to the seller of the option only on the maturity of that option.

Metal options are controlled by the LME. There is no clearing house on the LME, and trading for both futures and options is on the basis of principal to principal. The member companies on the LME carry financial responsibility for each contract and therefore must meet the most stringent financial requirements at all times. The LME committee can and does monitor the open position of any member and demand additional financial assurances when deemed prudent.

Traded options exist officially only in London on the sugar market. Commodity options are traded unofficially, as are metals options. The markets for metals options are made by individual London Metals Exchange dealers.

TERMINOLOGY

Option

A commodity option is an instrument that permits the buyer to purchase or sell a specific commodity contract at an agreed price over an agreed time period. The *buyer* of an option may also be referred to as a *taker*, the *seller* as a *grantor*.

A call option gives the purchaser the right to buy the commodity contract, and a put option gives the right to sell. Purchasers of calls believe the price is going to rise, whereas put buyers believe the price will fall.

Strike Price or Basis Price

The *strike price*, the agreed price on which the option is based, is the price at which the buyer of the option may choose to buy (exercise a call option) or sell (exercise a put option) the underlying commodity. The strike price may be either the price prevailing in the market (LME or soft options) at the time the deal was struck or a contrived price agreed upon by buyer and seller.

Premium

The buyer of an option is paying for time in which an idea may come to fruition. The grantor is willing to sell time, at a price. That price, which is subject to the normal laws of supply and demand, is called the *premium*. To an option buyer, the premium is the only cost of entering into an option. No margin or deposit is required, and there is no further financial risk once the premium has been paid.

The price of a premium is affected by two factors:

1. The length of time the option is to run—the more time, the more money.
2. The volatility or strength of a one-way trend—the more volatile or the stronger a trend, the higher the premium.

Declaration Date or Expiration Date

The date on which the time that has been bought expires is called the *declaration date* or the *expiration date*. On this date the buyers of an option must declare their intentions—whether or not they wish to exercise the rights that the option has given them. The buyer of an option may declare the option earlier than the declaration date, but as discussed below, this is an unwise move. By mutual agreement between buyer and seller, a choice of declaration dates is available for periods from 1 day to 2 years in the future. In practice, most options run from 1 to 6 months.

On the declaration date, a profitable option becomes part of the futures market by being converted into a long holding, in the case of a call option, or a short holding, in the case of a put option. The choices open to any holder of a profitable futures contract are then available.

Options

An option is a choice about whether or not to exercise a right that has been bought for a certain period of time. A commodity option gives the buyer a choice of whether to buy from (exercise a call option) or sell to (exercise a put option) the grantor at a previously agreed price (strike price) at any time up to the declaration date.

Three types of options are available:

1. *Call option.* The right to purchase a specified quantity of a commodity during an agreed time and at an agreed price.
2. *Put option.* The right to sell a specified quantity of a commodity during an agreed time and at an agreed price.
3. *Double option.* The right to purchase or sell a specified quantity of a commodity during an agreed time and at an agreed price.

The next two sections deal with "London" options as opposed to traded options. The theoretical concepts involved in the two types are much the same, and all the theories that are relevant to London options are also relevant to traded options. However, there are some additional refinements that apply exclusively to traded options, which will be discussed below in the section entitled "Traded Options in the United States."

The examples used below to illustrate the London options are all based on actual London commodities.

BUYING OPTIONS

Call Options

Assume that a trader held a view that prices would move higher but was uncertain about the timing of the rise. Also assume that the trader did not want to be stopped out or whipsawed in the market before that view was proved correct. Buying a call option would be the way to back the hunch with a strictly limited risk. The buyer would be looking for an opportunity to sell the commodity at a higher price than the sum of the strike price plus the premium.

Let us take sugar as an example (see Figure 51-1):

Example: Sugar Price: quoted in pounds per tonne
Contract size: 50 tonnes
Minimum fluctuation: 5 pence
Value per point: £1 = £50

If sugar stands at £300, a 3-month call option may cost £20 to buy. The buyer will establish a gross profit above £300 and a real net profit above £320 (£300 strike plus £20 premium). This is because the buyer has bought the right to buy sugar at £300/tonne from the grantor at any time until the declaration date, no matter what price prevails in the market at the time. If the price of sugar moved to £360, the option buyer could exercise the right to buy sugar at £300 from the grantor and sell it for £360 in the market. A profit of £60 would have been made for an outlay of £20.

On the other hand, if the price of sugar dropped and never again moved above £300 before the declaration date, there would be no point in exercising the right to buy sugar at £300 and the option would be allowed to expire. Remember, no matter how low sugar fell, the maximum exposure to the buyer was the £20 cost of the option.

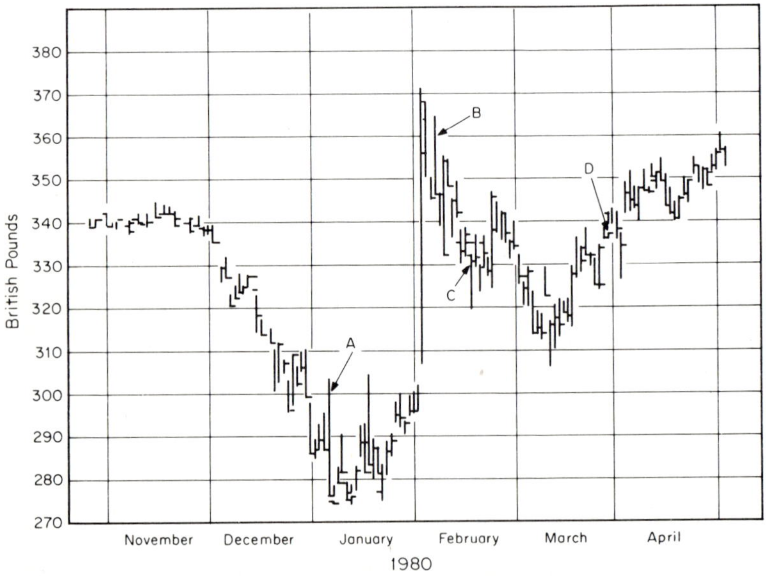

Figure 51-1 May sugar, 1980. *(ContiCommodity Research Division)*

Tricks of the Trade within the Life of an Option

As stated above, if a worthwhile profit was showing for the option taker, it would be unwise to declare the option early. Now let us see why this is true, taking the same sugar option as an example. (See Table 51-1.)

If prices rise to £360, after the option has been bought for a £20 premium, strike £300, a net £40 profit will be available. If the option is declared at that point, there can be no further profit. But if a sugar futures contract is sold at £360, there is a potential for increasing the profit. Once the future has been sold at £360, the position is proof against any further price rise because any loss on the short futures contract would be offset by the call option which is still running. However, if prices fell, the profit on the futures contract would offset the lessening profit from the call option. If prices subsequently fell from £360 to say £330, a £30 profit on the futures could be taken which would "pay" for the option premium with a £10 profit on top, and a "free" option could then be allowed to run. The lower the price fell before the futures position was covered, the more profit would be obtained with absolutely no further risk.

Put Options

Say the buyer of a put option holds the opinion that a commodity will move lower but again is uncertain of timing and does not want to be liquidated by an uptick which may precede the bearish move.

Again taking sugar as an example, if the put option buyer pays a £20 premium for a 3-month put option when the strike price was fixed at £300, the breakeven

TABLE 51-1 A Call Option Bought
Commodity: May sugar
Lot size: 50 tonnes
Declaration date: April 1

Date			Debit	Credit
January 6	**1.**	Buy one May sugar call option. Premium £20, strike £300 Premium paid (premium price × unit size): £1000	£1000	
February 8	**2.**	Decide to lock in profit. Sell one May sugar (futures contract) at £360.		
February 19	**3.**	Decide to take profit on short sell. Buy one May sugar (futures contract) at £330. Profit: £360 − £330 × 50 = £1500		£1500
April 1	**4.**	Declaration date: Declare option at market price of £340. Profit on option: £340 − £300 × 50 = £2000		£2000
		Net profit	£2500	
			£3500	£3500

With no extra risk, £2500 has been made, as opposed to the £2000 that would have been made if the option had been declared at £360.

point will be £280. The reason is that the option buyer is looking to exercise the right to require the grantor to buy sugar at £300 a ton. If the buyer can sell at £300 to the grantor and buy in the market for £280, the £20 cost of the option will be covered. Anything below £280 is all profit.

Double Options

A double option or straddle is an instrument which gives the purchaser the right to take *and* make delivery of a futures contract at an agreed price within an agreed time. After the premium for a double option has been paid, every move in the underlying strike price, either up or down, will reduce the cost of the outlay on the option. If prices move far enough in any direction, a gross profit will be made. How can this work?

A double option will normally cost twice as much as a single put or call option. Again using sugar as an example, with a strike at £300, say a 3-month double option will cost £40. The buyer has, in effect, bought both a put option and a call option. Why do that? Because conditions do occur in which it is not clear which way a market will move, even though it is felt that a substantial move one way or the other is imminent.

In the sugar example, if the price moves up, the buyer may exercise the right to buy sugar at £300. If the price moves down, the buyer may exercise the right to sell sugar at £300. The main thing to consider is that having paid £40 for a double option rather than £20 for a single option, the buyer must now look for a £40 move to clear a net profit, rather than a £20 move which would allow a profit with a single option.

Only if the price never moves at all during the life of a double option contract will the buyer not gain back some of the premium. Another advantage of owning a double option is the riskfree opportunities it affords for trading against the position in the futures market. Any futures contract opened against an option and therefore entirely riskfree will not be subject to any deposit or margin.

Besides sugar, the London option markets offer the following commodities in which options may be struck:

Gold	Cocoa
Copper	Coffee
Silver	Rubber
Aluminum	Sugar
Zinc	Soybean meal
Nickel	Wool
Lead	Potatoes
Tin	

In addition, Dutch bonds and gold options may easily be traded on the Amsterdam Option Exchange.

SELLING OPTIONS

General

How can profits be made from selling options? The question of granting non-traded (LME and soft) options will cause most credit controllers and most brokers to break out in a cold sweat.

However, a sensible, patient and disciplined program of option granting can provide steady growth for an option portfolio. This strategy must be monitored every second that the market is open and therefore would not be suitable for nonprofessionals, though much private equity is successfully handled through granted option portfolios under brokers' discretion.

Granting options is especially attractive when option premiums are high. Naturally, operators in options should seek to buy when prices (premiums in this case) are low and sell when they are high.

When options are granted, a known amount of money (the premium) will be raised, and on declaration dates, this money will be credited to the grantor. Thus there is a fixed financial target, namely protecting the money due. This can be accomplished by trading in the futures market, if necessary.

There are three golden rules for assuring as far as possible the safety and success of granted options. Each will be discussed below.

1. Always trade when the underlying commodity price moves through the strike price.

Let us take tin as an example (see Figure 51-2):

Example: Tin Contract size: 5 tonnes
Price: quoted in pounds per tonne
Minimum price fluctuation: £1
Value per point: £1 = £5

Imagine a grantor has sold a 3-month tin put option, premium £400, strike £7300. If the price rises between the time the option is sold and the declaration date, the grantor will retain the whole premium, or £400 × 5 = £2000. The reason is that at no time did tin fall below the strike price, where it would have been worthwhile for the buyer to exercise the right to sell tin at £7300 and then buy it back at the prevailing (cheaper) market price.

But what if the price falls and the grantor is in danger of being put upon? In theory, the grantor will retain a profit until the price reaches strike price minus option premium: £7300 − £400 = £6900. Below that level the grantor is at risk for every pound move. What should the grantor do? The answer is to sell a tin future if and when the price of tin moves just below strike price, in this case at say £7290. This short futures position will then protect any obligations that the grantor may face in having to buy tin at £7300, because any loss on the option will be offset by a corresponding profit on the short position.

Should prices subsequently rise above the strike price, the grantor *must* buy back the short position, at say £7310, because the cover is no longer needed and as a straight short position will start to lose money. A small loss of £100 will have to be taken, but there is £2000 coming due to the grantor on declaration date.

Thereafter the grantor must buy or sell every time the price moves through the strike price until the option expires. *Never take a view on what might happen. Always buy or sell when the price moves through the strike level.* The way in which this granted tin option may work is shown in Table 51-2.

It is obvious that, if prices moved up and down through the strike price in sufficient swings and enough times, more losses would accrue than the amount of money being raised through the sale of the premium, and a real loss would occur. This leads to the second golden rule of option granting:

2. Spread the levels at which options are granted.

If one granted option is being whipsawed, it must mean that options granted at another level are quite unaffected. Therefore it is essential to aim to establish different levels at which granted options are struck. The options should be sufficiently far apart to avoid two options being whipsawed at roughly the same time, but not so far apart that the strike prices are never reached and only one or two strike levels are established. The distance between the strike levels will vary from commodity to commodity and will vary on volatility. As a rough guide, we suggest tin strikes should be spread by £300, whereas sugar should be spread £20 or copper by £40. It does not matter whether puts or calls are sold at any one strike level. Figure 51-3 illustrates a well-managed option granting program in copper, with strike prices spread by £40.

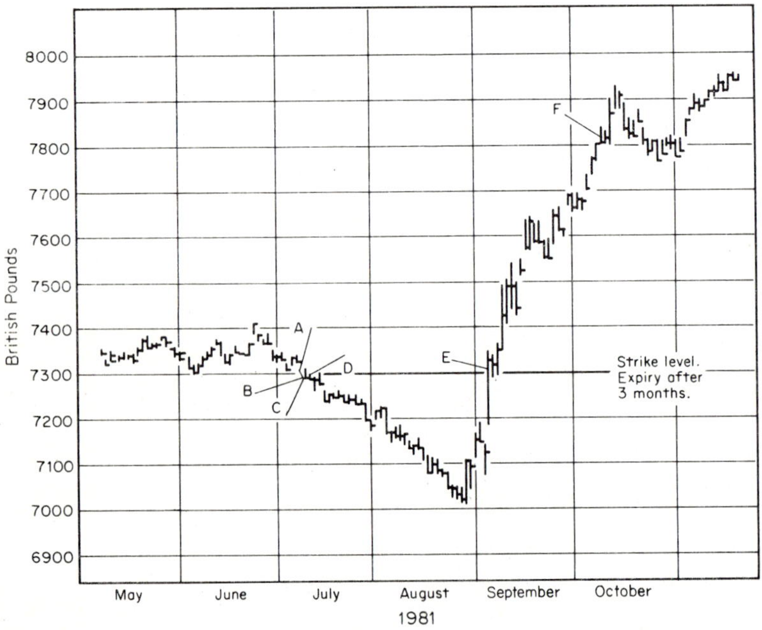

Figure 51-2 Three-month tin, 1981. *(ContiCommodity Research Division)*

TABLE 51-2 A Granted Option: Protecting the Premium
Commodity: 3-month tin
Lot size: 5 tonnes
Declaration date: October 9

Date			Debit	Credit
July 12	1.	Sell one 3-month tin put option. Premium £400, strike £7300 Premium raised (premium price × unit size): £2000		£2000
July 12	2.	Price moves down. Sell one 3-month tin at £7290.		
July 13	3.	Price moves up. Buy back one October 12 tin at £7310. Loss: £7310 minus £7290 × 5 = £1000	£100	
July 14	4.	Price moves down. Sell one October 12 tin at £7290.		
September 5	5.	Price moves up. Buy back one October 12 tin at £7310. Loss: £7310 minus £7290 × 5 = £100	£100	
October 9	6.	Declaration date: Option expires worthless. Net profit	£1800	
			£2000	£2000

Figure 51-3 Three-month copper, 1981. *(ContiCommodity Research Division)*

The third golden rule of option granting is a self-evident safety factor:

3. Spread the option-granting risk into more than one commodity.

Provided sufficient control can be exercised and provided premiums are not too low, the more different commodities that are carrying the option grantor's risk, the less the likelihood of being whipsawed in one market.

Selling Options as a Hedging Operation

The foregoing ideas about granting options all apply to the speculative grantor, but there are other traders to whom the granting of options acts as a hedging medium. Clearly, producers or holders of physical commodities can afford to grant options in the knowledge that, whatever happens, cash income will increase. Either the grantor will be called and will deliver physical holdings against the option, or the option will expire and the grantor will retain inventory, having boosted cash by the amount of the premium.

TRADED OPTIONS (U.S. STYLE)

Traded options exist on all London metals markets and on the London sugar market. However, the area of explosive growth is in the U.S. options futures market. In October 1982 traded options were introduced on the gold, T-bonds, and sugar markets. Subsequently, options have been introduced on currencies and stock indexes.

In time, probably all U.S. futures contracts will carry options, because they are perfect for use as a hedging or insurance medium. Some pundits are even predicting a larger volume in options than in the underlying futures markets during the late 1980s.

Traded Options Defined

As discussed above, soft and LME options give a buyer the right to buy or sell a commodity at a fixed price within an agreed time. A traded option gives the same rights in addition to the ability to close out the actual option itself. During the life of the option, its value may rise or fall according to the price movement of the underlying commodity and the length of time still to run on the option.

A traded option can be struck at various different levels no matter what commodity price is prevailing at the time. Thus, if copper were trading at £900, there would probably be options available at strike prices of £800, £900, £950, and £1000. Assume the date is early December, there is no backwardation (nearby premium) or contango (forward premium), and the price is £900/tonne. A small section of the copper option board would look like this:

Series	January		February		March	
	Call	Put	Call	Put	Call	Put
850	56	8	62	12	68	17
900	18	19	23	23	27	26
950	8	56	14	61	19	67

The first column shows the exercise price, and the other columns show actual market prices. Additional exercise prices and additional distant options would also be available.

In-the-Money and Out-of-the-Money

If the price of copper is £900 and a call option is bought for a strike price of £950, this option is termed "out-of-the-money." Because there is no hope of declaring the option profitably until copper rises about £950, the only attraction of this option to the buyer is the time that it buys, during which copper may rise to £950. The price of the option is based on *time value*. The longer the option is to run, the more must be paid.

In this case, with copper standing at £900, a 3-week £950 call option will probably only cost £1 or £2, whereas a 6-month £950 call option may cost £35, reflecting the extra time being bought during which copper may top £950.

On the other hand, if an option is bought with a strike of £850 when the prevailing market price is £900, this option is termed "in-the-money." The buyer could exercise the option immediately for a gross profit at £50 above strike, though of course the profit will not be immediate because the premium paid will reflect the intrinsic value of the option as well as the time element. Two components of an in-the-money option contribute to the price: time value and intrinsic value. The intrinsic value is a known constant, the difference between the strike price and the underlying market price. The time value, on the other hand, is constantly changing and will eventually erode to zero. At that point the only value (if any) left in the option will be intrinsic. Therefore, the passage of time works against buyers of options and in favor of sellers. Furthermore, time value erodes faster in the last half of an option's life than in the first half—a feature which those who straddle or spread options should bear in mind.

Advantages of Traded Options

One of the best features of traded options is the much reduced risk inherent in selling options, because of the ability to buy them back and close them down. Let us examine the advantage of selling trading options.

For example, suppose the price of gold stands at $410 and a grantor sells $450 call options, with 2 months to declaration, for $10; these are obviously out-of-the-money options. At the same time, the grantor sells $375 out-of-the-money put options for $9, with the same declaration date. If gold remains between $450 and $375 for 2 months, both options will expire worthless and the grantor will retain the whole premium. If prices rise, the grantor must be prepared to buy back the $450 call options. If gold rises by $20 to $430, the grantor will be able to buy back the options for about $14 and take a $4 loss. Note that, as long as the option remains out-of-the-money and has no intrinsic value, a move in the underlying price will not be reflected dollar for dollar in the premium price. In this instance, having lost money on the call option, it is evident that the put option granted at $375 for $9 is looking safer and safer. Having bought the $450 series back before they become in-the-money, the grantor should then attempt to sell the next higher out-of-the-money series (the 475 series) for, say, $8. The grantor would then be hoping that gold would stay between $475 and $375 until declaration date. In this case, if that happens, the grantor should retain $8 for the $475 calls, plus $9 for the $375 puts, less $4 lost on the $450 calls, or $13. How time erodes the premium and works for the grantor is obvious in this example.

Why Buy Traded Options?

In no other form of futures trading can the percentage of profit for outlay be geared as high as when buying traded options.

Suppose a speculator has a firm viewpoint on a market—is convinced, for example, that gold is about to rise substantially. The hunch should be backed by buying out-of-the-money call options. Say spot gold stands at $417 and the quotes on gold calls, in dollars per ounce, are as follows:

Series	Month	Last trade, $/ounce	Month	Last trade, $/ounce	Month	Last trade, $/ounce
380	Feb.	56	May	67	Aug.	80
400	Feb.	35	May	48	Aug.	62
620	Feb.	20	May	30	Aug.	50
440	Feb.	10.5	May	16.5	Aug.	27
460	Feb.	3.5	May	11	Aug.	14
500	Feb.	2	May	7	Aug.	9

If the buyer bought February 500 calls for $2, the outlay on 100 ounces of gold would be $200. If gold were to rise by the third Friday in February (declaration date) to $600, a profit of at least $100/ounce ($600 minus $500), or $10,000, could be realized on the option. This profit represents a fiftyfold increase for absolutely no risk beyond the $200 cost of the option, and no margin is required.

Clearly, for an outlay of $900 (by buying August 500 calls for $9), another 6 months could have been bought, to allow the hunch to reach fruition. If this idea had worked, the increase would still have been elevenfold.

It is true that if 100 ounces of gold futures had been bought at $417, a profit of $18,300 would have been made, but the trade would not have been riskfree and, on a deposit requirement of around $5000, would have represented only a 3.6-fold increase. With reference to the option, it is unlikely that a move of such magnitude will be accurately forecast. However, if the price moves up at all, the premium itself will gain in value and may be sold for a profit, and if it does not move up, only a very small amount of money will have been lost.

Another reason for buying traded options is as a hedge against a short-term move. Suppose that, one Friday afternoon, there is a tense political situation in, say, a copper-producing country. Everyone knows that if the situation blows up over the weekend, copper will open sharply higher, but that if there is no crisis, copper will drift lower. If a trader buys a short-term, out-of-the-money option—which may cost as little as £2 or £3—any dramatic rise will be covered, for an outlay of £50 or £75 per lot. This strategy may be particularly attractive to a bear trader who is trying to hold a long-term short position.

A final advantage of buying traded options is that a favorable move in the underlying futures price will always create a favorable move in the option price, which can then be traded out for a profit. In contrast, the premium for a London option remains static, and thus a move must occur in the underlying futures price over and above the premium before a net profit will be realized.

SPREADS AND STRADDLES

Traded Option Spreads

In an option spread, one option contract is bought and another is sold in the same commodity at the same time. Since buying a traded option requires payment and selling a trading option entails receiving money, a spread is always talked of in terms of the difference between the two—for example, a spread might be bought for a £4 debit. The two basic spreads are vertical and time (or horizontal) spreads. A vertical spread can be bullish or bearish, and it is used to back a market hunch for even lower cost and therefore less risk than the ordinary option. Time spreads are adopted when markets are moving sideways. Both are discussed below in more detail.

Vertical Spreads

In a vertical spread, two options have different exercise prices but the same expiry date. Let us see how a spread may work in a hypothetical example—a bull spread.

Example: London Copper: Contract size: 25 tonnes
Price: quoted in pounds per tonne
Minimum fluctuation: 50 pence
Value per point: £1 = £25

Call option series	Option price, £/tonne	Copper price, May 15
May 950	30	£970
May 1000	12	970

If a spread is created by simultaneously buying May 950 copper calls for £30 and selling May 1000 copper calls for £12, the cost of the spread will be £18 (£ 30 minus £12), or £450 total for one contract.

After time has passed and copper has risen, the options will look like this:

Call option series	Option price	Copper price
May 950	£60	£1000
May 1000	15	1000

The option price difference which cost £18 to buy can now be sold for £45 by "closing out" the spread, that is, selling the May 950 for £60 and buying the May 1000 for £15. The accounts would look like this:

Pay £450 to put on spread.

Receive £1125 on sale of spread.

Because £450 has been put on the spread and £1125 has been received on the sale, a net profit of £675 has been made, or 150 percent.

Why put on the spread for £18 to make £45, when £50 or more could have been made by buying the May 950 call? The answer is: to limit risk. If copper had failed to move up, £30 might have been lost by buying the call on its own, whereas no more than £18 can be lost by establishing the spread. The "cost" of this lessened exposure is lessened profit potential. The maximum that could have been made was the difference between the two strike prices: £1000 − £950 = £50.

Example: U.S. Treasury Bonds (CBT) Contract size: $1 million
Price quoted in percentage of $100
Minimum fluctuation: 1
Value per point: $\frac{1}{64}$ = 15.625

Put option series	Option price	Bond price
Dec. 60	0.$\frac{60}{64}$ (0.9375)	66 $\frac{60}{64}$
Dec. 65	2$\frac{16}{64}$ (2.25)	66 $\frac{60}{64}$

Buy the put spread:

Buy December 65 puts.

Sell December 60 puts. Debit 1. $\frac{20}{64}$ (1.3125) or $1312.50

Assume that bonds drop: then prices may look like this:

Put option series	Option price	Bond price
Dec. 60	2.$\frac{56}{64}$ (2.875)	61
Dec. 65	6.$\frac{48}{64}$ (6.750)	61

Sell the put spread:

Sell December 65 puts.

Buy December 60 puts. Credit 3. $^{56}/_{64}$ (3.875) or \$3875

Net profit = \$3875 − \$1312.50 = \$2562.50, for a total outlay and maximum exposure of \$1312.50.

A bear spread would be put on in exactly the same way by using put options instead of calls. The prices in the example below illustrate a bear spread using T-bond options.

The reason the straddle works is that when the December 65 put series became in-the-money (when December bonds moved below \$65), it gained in intrinsic value point for point with the decline in the underlying bond market. By contrast the December 60 put series gained more slowly, as it was always out-of-the-money and only had time value.

In both the preceding examples, no margin or deposit is required because the risk is entirely limited to the cost of establishing the spread which is paid for at the outset.

It is possible to put on a vertical spread for a credit and raise money at the outset of the operation, but in this case a deposit will be required. Below is an example using U.S. sugar options:

Example: New York Sugar Contract size: 50 tons
Price: quoted in cents per pound
Minimum price fluctuation = 1 point
Value per point = \$11.20
Date of trade: Mid-May

Assume the spreader is expecting the market to fall.

Call option series	Option price	Sugar price, July
July 14	0.80	14.50
July 15	0.10	

If the July 14 call is sold for 0.80 and the July 15 is bought for 0.10, a credit of 0.70 points, or \$784, is established. This is the maximum profit that could be retained—and it could be retained only if sugar was below 14¢ when the option expired, because both options would be worthless upon expiration. But any decline in the underlying sugar price will erode the premium on the in-the-money July 14 series faster than the out-of-the-money July 15 series, thus allowing the spread to be bought back profitably. The risk of the option is limited to the difference between the striking price (1¢) and the initial price received (0.70 points), which is 30 points or \$336.

Time or Horizontal Spreads

There is an option scheme for every eventuality, including very quiet market conditions. Apart from granting naked puts or calls, a time spread can be established for a known risk. Assume that the London lead market is expected to enter a quiet period.

Example: London lead Contract size: 25 tonnes
Price: quoted in pounds per tonne
Minimum price fluctuation 25 pence
Value per point £1 = £25
Date: Mid-January

Assume the following prices:

Call option series	April option price	July option price	Lead price
325	6	8	300

A time spread could be established for a £2 debit by selling the April 325 series for £6 and buying the July 325 series for £8. Assume the lead price is around £300 by the April expiration date, causing the April option to expire worthless. The July option should be worth considerably more than £2 with 3 months still to run, on the basis that with the 3 months to run the April was worth £6. Therefore the July option could be sold for say £6, yielding a £4 profit. £4 may not sound like much, but it is 100 percent profit on the £2 initial outlay.

CONCLUSION

Option markets can offer very attractive returns in terms of both the ratio of risk to reward and the percentage returns on the money staked. These markets are particularly suited to the speculator who would like to enter the fast-moving world of futures trading but does not want to be exposed to the degree of risk which is usually inherent in those markets.

However, it must be pointed out that even when buying options for a known risk, there is a possibility that not every option bought will make money. Money could be spent on buying options which could be worthless upon expiration, and all the capital would be lost.

CHAPTER

52

Spreading Strategies

Phillip E. Tiger

Spread trading has always played a major role in futures markets, and its role has expanded in recent years. Discussion of the nature of spreads and spread trading is particularly appropriate at this time. Recent expansion of price volatility coupled with wide fluctuations in interest rates have increased the attraction of spread trading to both hedgers and speculators alike.

This chapter provides a general definition of spread relationships, a brief description of the factors which affect spreads, an approach to spread analysis, and a few examples of popular spreads.

WHAT IS A SPREAD?

A commodity spread (or straddle) is the measure of the relationship between two things. Spreaders are concerned less with absolute value than with price differentials. They must, therefore, have the self-discipline to divorce their thinking from the bullish or bearish forces affecting the market. Instead, spread traders must be alert to relatively bullish or bearish influences as they relate in time to the two deliveries under scrutiny.

In spread trading, it is desirable for the bought commodity to gain on the commodity sold (that is, the "long" should gain on the "short"). Spreads are usually defined chronologically (for example, "December versus March soybean oil"). The trader can define the trading position by indicating "long" or "short." A "forward" spread in the above example would read "long December versus short March Oil." A "back" spread would read "short December versus long March Oil." Other terms sometimes used are "widening" and "narrowing"; traders should avoid these terms because they can create confusion about which commodity delivery has a premium or discount.

There are four categories of spreads: *interdelivery*, *intercommodity*, *intermarket*, and *source or product*.

Interdelivery Spreads

The interdelivery spread is the most popular type. It involves two different delivery months of the same commodity traded on the same exchange. Examples are May versus December Copper, July versus November soybeans, and June versus October cattle.

The so-called limited-risk or carrying-charge spread is a special type of interdelivery spread which can be used for all storable commodities. Carrying-charge spreads will be discussed in greater detail below.

Intercommodity Spreads

The intercommodity spread is a spread between two different but usually related commodities—usually on the same exchange and with the same delivery month. Examples are July corn versus July wheat, or February hogs versus February pork bellies.

Intermarket Spreads

The intermarket spread involves the same delivery months of the same commodity on different exchanges. This concept is applicable to relationships between wheat traded in Chicago, Minneapolis, and Kansas City. An example is March Kansas City wheat versus March Chicago wheat.

Source or Product Spreads

The source or product spread is applied to soybeans versus soybean products—soybean meal and soybean oil. This type of spread is usually described as a "crush" (in which soybeans are bought and the products are sold) or a "reverse crush" (in which the products are bought and soybeans are sold). The proper ratio for this relationship is 10 contracts of beans (50,000 bushels) to 9 contracts of soybean oil (540,000 pounds) plus 12 contracts of soybean meal (2,400,000 pounds). However, many traders simply trade one contract of beans versus one of meal and one of oil as a close approximation of the true relationship.

THE MAJOR FACTORS AFFECTING SPREADS

Supply-and-Demand Balances

Supply-and-demand balances are the primary focus for most traders. An accurate and constantly updated survey of both domestic and world supply is maintained by both government and private interests. The U.S. Department of Agriculture (USDA) and other organizations issue frequent reports on current and anticipated supplies of all grains and associated products, livestock, and metals, in addition to reviewing such important items as reserve stocks, grain under loan, anticipated crop yields, and weather.

An attempt is also made to define actual and anticipated demand, but this task is more difficult, particularly with regard to export demand. Demand can rarely be defined until after it has made itself known. Assessment of forthcoming supply is often accurate, and thus there is a time gap between knowledge of supply and knowledge of demand. This situation can often lead to significant price movement and accompanying spread movement.

However, a generalization that is often valid is that when supplies appear ample relative to demand and little tightness of supply is anticipated, the spread relationships will reflect the abundance by reflecting premiums for successive deliveries. That is, the nearest future month will be discounted to the next delivery, which will be discounted to the next, and so on—a structure which is termed a "normal" market. When tightness of supply is anticipated, or when a significant decline in carryover stocks from one crop year to the next is anticipated, or when both these conditions occur simultaneously, the spread relationships will shift the emphasis to the nearby contracts. This kind of shift will often generate a premium structure in which the nearest delivery will be at a premium to the next delivery, and so on—a structure which is termed an "inverted" market.

Most of the above influences will be greatest on interdelivery spreads, but commodities in tight supply can be expected to gain on those in abundance, and intercommodity and intermarket spreads can be expected to reflect such differences.

Seasonal Factors

Seasonal factors are recurring cycles usually caused by fundamental factors which have a consistent effect on the market regardless of tightness or abundance of supply. Domestic agricultural commodities reflect dominant seasonal factors based on the growing season as well as on the logistics of the opening and closing of the Great Lakes to shipping each year between mid-December and mid-April. Corn and soybeans have similar growing seasons, with planting occurring in the second quarter of the year and harvest beginning at the onset of the fourth quarter of the year. The "crop scare" season for corn and soybeans is therefore in midsummer, when weather may have the greatest effect on potential crops. Though cash lows and highs are often seen in November and June, respectively, the futures market generally anticipates price movement and therefore tends to make lows and highs in advance of the cash market. Futures lows for corn and soybeans are often made in August, while highs are often made in April and May. April and May highs are abetted by the opening of the lakes to shipping in mid-April, which can create a demand base for Chicago stocks going into the delivery period for the May contracts.

The increasing importance of the southern hemisphere soybean crop has had an effect on seasonals sold on the Chicago Board of Trade. Because the southern hemisphere crop is harvested in February and March, Brazilian or Argentine soybeans are available to the world market by April, if the crop is good. This has caused the seasonal highs to shift to an earlier time frame. Where highs previously might have been anticipated on the July soybean contract, the May contract has now assumed leadership as the primary old-crop month.

The wheat market has a different growing season. Wheat is planted in autumn for harvest in the spring (approximately 80 percent of all U.S. wheat is winter wheat). Therefore, though wheat is subject to the same logistic influences as soybeans when the Great Lakes are closed, the wheat market reflects the new crop beginning with the characteristically weak July contract, and the last old-crop month is the characteristically strong May delivery.

Seasonal factors affect virtually all other markets as well. Livestock marketings are heaviest before the crop planting and harvesting seasons, thereby exerting a negative influence on deliveries of live hogs and live cattle during March and April and again in October. The strongest livestock delivery months are typically midsummer.

The world agricultural commodities—coffee, cocoa, and sugar—also display seasonality, with strength at the end of the old crop and weakness at harvest. Even the industrial commodities—copper, plywood, and lumber—display seasonal tendencies based on the high demand for these materials going into summer as opposed to the weak demand period next year end.

Each commodity has characteristic strong or weak months based on seasonal factors. Table 52-1 gives general guidelines only, as any given year can involve exceptional factors which will change otherwise normal patterns.

Carrying Charges

Carrying charges affect the differential in so-called normal markets in that the distant delivery cannot exceed the value of the nearby delivery by more than the full carrying charges applicable to the market. If full carrying charges were reflected by the futures structure, traders would take delivery of the nearby

TABLE 52-1 Seasonal Tendencies

Commodity	Strong months	Weak months
Wheat	December and May	July
Corn	May and July	December
Beans	May and July	November and January
Meal	January and July	March
Oil	May and July	December
Hogs	February and June to July	April and October
Cattle	February and June	April and October
Pork bellies	February and July	March and August
Copper	May	December
Cocoa	July	December
Sugar	May	October
Cotton	May to July	October to December
Lumber	May to July	September to November
Plywood	May to July	September to November

contract and deliver the commodity against a later delivery at no cost—with the market paying for it. The marketplace rarely provides a "free ride," and therefore full carrying-charges differentials are rarely, if ever, seen. Predictably, the widest carrying-charge structures are seen in the most bearish situations, while inversions are seen usually only in a bullish context.

The carrying charge is made up of three cost components: storage, insurance, and money (as represented by the value of the commodity and current interest rates). Though storage costs vary, storage and insurance costs (in the early 1980's) can be approximated at 4½¢/bushel/month for grains and soybeans. Comparable figures for soybean oil are 13¢/pound/month, for soybean meal $2.25/ton/month.

Metals incur relatively low storage and insurance costs—usually about $50/contract/month, while the frozen commodities—orange juice and pork bellies—have high storage costs which can run over $200/contract/month because of the energy involved.

Some commodities, though storable, do not reflect true carrying-charge relationships because of the nature of the contract definition. These include world sugar, lumber, and the "live" markets such as cattle and hogs. Note that Treasury-bill futures are not redeliverable, as they have a 90-day term and there are 90 days between contracts. Therefore, the other financial future—Treasury bonds and GNMAs—tend to reflect more stability in their spread relationships.

The money-cost component of carrying charges can be approximated by multiplying the value of the commodity by the current prime rate. For example, the full carrying charge for soybeans, when they are trading at $10/bushel and the prime interest rate is at 15 percent would be:

$$\frac{\$10.00 \times 15\%}{12 \text{ months}} + 4\tfrac{1}{2}¢\text{/month (storage and insurance)}$$

or

$$12\tfrac{1}{2}¢ + 4\tfrac{1}{2}¢ = 17¢\text{/bushel/month}$$

Since the market rarely exceeds 85 percent of full carrying charges, the maximum differential that might be expected between soybean deliveries under the given conditions would be 14½¢/month. A spread—with the nearby contract long and the distant delivery short—might then be described as having limited risk. That is, the maximum risk would be the difference between the values where the spread was initiated and 85 to 100 percent of full carrying charges.

Interest rates have been very unstable since the mid-1970s, and this has negated most of the limited-risk aspects of the marketplace. Therefore, traders establishing forward spreads in carrying-charge markets must carefully examine the outlook for interest rates in addition to analyzing the commodity in question. Interest rate fluctuations have been seen to influence price movement to a greater degree than individual market supply-and-demand fundamentals.

When a market reflects nearly full carrying charges, hedgers can take advantage of the situation by committing their needs by forward spreads and concentrating their commitments to the nearest deliveries. This strategy not only allows hedgers to have the marketplace pay for some of their storage costs, but also allows for profit maximization when and if the market shifts to a more bullish posture and the nearby contracts begin to gain on the distant deliveries—moving toward an inverted situation under most bullish conditions.

SPREAD ANALYSIS

Market analysis has four components: fundamental, technical, historical and cyclic. Though there is obviously some overlap between these categories, it is preferable to have at least three out of the four components favorable to any trade. Hedgers should use this analytical approach to optimize the timing of their placement of hedge positions.

Fundamental analysis, which involves examination of supply-and-demand statistics has been discussed in detail in various chapters of this book. The other three components will be discussed below.

Technical Analysis

Technical analysis involves the examination of charts, or graphic histories of price movement. Some assumptions made by the chartist are that (1) the market tends to maintain momentum in a given direction for a measurable period of time (that is, prices tend to *trend*), (2) areas in which upward price movement has been restricted in the past will continue to have restricted upward price movement (that is, there will be areas of price resistance), and (3) areas in which downward price movement has been restricted in the past will act as price support levels in the future.

There are many charting methods and many aspects of technical analysis that go beyond simple definition of trend, support, and resistance. These matters have been discussed in other chapters of this book. Here it is enough to say that many authorities view technical analysis as an end in itself and have demonstrated an ability to trade successfully on the basis of technical analysis alone.

Spread charts are usually drawn as line charts connecting the closing price differentials between two items under study. Spread charts also indicate areas of support and resistance, cycle, and trends. However it is virtually impossible to generate a continuation (year-to-year) chart of a spread. Longer-term tendencies and cycles must be discerned by interpreting the compilation of previous years' spread charts, or by examining the long-term behavior of the market or markets in question, or by using a combination of these two techniques.

Historical Analysis

Historical analysis—the analysis of current prices relative to past prices, allowing for inflation—can indicate whether, on a historical price basis, a commodity's price level or spread differential is expensive or inexpensive. For example, in spring 1980, soybean prices were near $6/bushel. Allowing that a 1980 dollar was worth about 40¢ in 1971 buying power (when soybeans last established a major base area), then 40 percent of $6 should approximate that base level—and indeed it did just that, for 1971 soybeans were trading between $2.50/

bushel and $3/bushel. Subsequent price action demonstrated that area as a base: soybeans rallied to $10/bushel by the end of 1980 (the equivalent of about $4/bushel in 1971 terms). Historical analysis of spreads is also possible, for historical support areas (allowing for the significant change in carrying charges over the past decade) and resistance areas in given spread relationships can be similarly assessed.

Cyclic Analysis

The analysis of cycles is an esoteric discipline which has received significant attention only in recent years. The cyclic analyst assumes that all things (including commodity prices) moves in a wave pattern. Thus, the definition of wave patterns peculiar to a given item (in this case a specific commodity futures contract or spread relationship) can help to indicate the optimum time frame for price highs and lows, or can at least show when price momentum should be favored in a particular direction.

There are many wave theories. One of the most popular is the Elliott Wave theory, which holds that all prices move in five waves—three waves in the direction of the trend and two waves contrary to the trend. (See Chapter 47.) All the wave or cycle theories serve primarily to define long-term price cycles and short-term trading patterns. They are extremely useful in analysis of both long- and short-term anticipated price trends.

SELECTED SPREADS

Long-term study of the futures markets has highlighted the consistent behavior of certain spread relationships within each market, on both seasonal and historical bases. Though each year must be viewed as an anomaly, the spread trader should be alert to such relationships. The following list must be considered incomplete and is offered only as a guide.

Grains	Sell September corn and buy December corn on June 1.
	Buy July corn and sell July wheat on December 1.
	Buy December wheat and sell December corn on June 1.
	Buy May soybeans and sell August soybeans before January 30 if at 15¢, or in August if higher.
	Buy January soybean meal and sell March or May soybean meal by August 30.
Livestock	Buy June cattle and sell October cattle by January 20, particularly if October cattle are at a premium.
	Sell April hogs and buy July hogs by February 1, particularly if April hogs are even or at a premium to July hogs.

	Buy July hogs and sell July bellies by February 1; anticipate hogs at a premium to bellies.
	Buy February bellies and sell March bellies at 60 points or more above the March premium.
New York Markets	Buy July cocoa and sell December cocoa by February 15, if December cocoa is at a premium.
	Buy May sugar and sell October sugar if October sugar is at a premium on November 1.
	Sell October cotton and buy December cotton when October cotton is 300 points or more at a premium to December cotton.

The metals spreads tend to trade as carrying-charge functions, with the exception of copper. Long May copper and short December copper was an excellent seasonal spread until the interest rate rises of 1979 to 1981. Because of these rises, the cost of carrying copper became so high that seasonal inventory building—which in the past caused May to gain, often significantly, on December copper—was negated and the spread no longer performed as anticipated. Interest rates have similarly affected many other markets. Spreads should be viewed with caution as long as interest rates remain high and as long as commodity supplies are adequate. Conversely, if supplies of any storable commodity become short, the lack of inventory could cause significant moves in the forward spreads.

Spreads in financial instruments have earned much attention and should continue to provide trading opportunities. They have not traded long enough, nor have they traded enough within a framework of price or interest rate stability, to provide an indication of seasonal tendencies or well-defined cyclic behavior. If stability returns to the interest rate markets in the years ahead, a "normal" yield curve may return to the marketplace. This would result in nearby deliveries trading at premiums to the more distant deliveries; that is, higher yields would result for the more uncertain distant deliveries.

CONCLUSION

All futures markets afford a plethora of spread potential. The trader must anticipate the relationship changes within a market in order to participate, but the rewards of participation can be great. Indeed, because of the generally lower margin requirements for spreads, the gains (as measured by return on equity) can often be more significant than those for net positions. The risks are proportionate to the potential gains and should not be ignored. Even when risks are taken into account, however, spread will often protect against the liability of catastrophic price movement, such as an unforeseen limit move following a major report or news event.

Spreads can be dealt with as a separate trading entity or, as an adjunct to net futures trading. Either way, they can be a useful part of a diversified trading approach and can contribute significantly to trading performance.

PART

7

Glossary and Bibliography

CHAPTER

53

Glossary

arbitrage The simultaneous purchase and sale of a given commodity with the intent to profit from price differentials, usually the differentials between two or more locations. Thus, arbitrage often refers to intermarket spreading. Example: London sugar versus New York sugar.

backwardation A futures market condition in which the nearby months are premium to the distant months.

basis The difference between the cash price and the futures price of the same commodity. Basis equals the cash price less the futures price and can be a positive or a negative number.

bear One who believes that prices will decline.

bear market A market characterized by declining prices.

bear spread (back spread) A spread that consists of a short position in the nearby contract and a long position in the distant contract.

bull One who believes that prices will rise.

bull market A market characterized by rising prices.

bull spread (forward spread) A spread that consists of a long position in the nearby contract and a short position in the distant contract.

butterfly spread A three-position spread that consists of a body position and one wing position on each side of the body. Each wing position is half the number of contracts in the body position. Example: short 10 contracts of March soybeans/long 20 contracts of May soybeans/short 10 contracts of August soybeans.

carry order An order that simultaneously liquidates an existing position and initiates a new position in the same direction in a later contract month. This is used to roll over or switch a position that has matured into a new distant position. See "switch" and "roll."

carrying charges The cost incurred in storing the physical commodity, obtaining insurance on the stored product, financing the inventory, and foregoing interest for not having sold the commodity when it was procured (the opportunity cost of the capital).

cash market The market for the purchase and sale of actual physical commodities. The commodities that are bought or sold in the cash market are called cash commodities.

close only A day order to be executed at the market on the close.

commission The fee charged by a brokerage firm for its services.

contango A carrying charge market or a market that closely reflects full carry.

cover To exit a short position or a bear spread.

crop year The year based on the period from one harvest to the next harvest. The crop year is standardized for each commodity, although harvest may overlap several months between different regions where the crop is grown.

crush (1) The process by which soybeans are converted to soybean oil and soybean meal. A 60-pound bushel of soybeans yields 48 pounds of soybean meal and 11 pounds of soybean oil with 1 pound of waste. (2) A spread that consists of long soybeans, short soybean meal, and short soybean oil. An exact soybean crush is 10 soybean contracts versus 12 meal and nine oil contracts. (3) A spread that consists of long feeder cattle, long corn, and short live cattle. An exact cattle crush is three feeder cattle contracts and two corn contracts versus five live cattle contracts. See "reverse crush."

daily trading limits The maximum price fluctuations permitted a contract during one trading session. They are fixed by the exchanges and are different for different commodities.

deliverable stocks Stocks that are in storage and certified as deliverable against a short futures position. (Certificated in the case of cotton.)

delivery The tender and receipt of the physical commodity or warehouse receipts covering the commodity.

discount Less than the cash or regular price.

distant The contract of a spread that is the furthest in the future.

first notice day The first day on which notices are issued for delivery in the specified delivery months.

free supply The part of supply that is available to the market and not under the shelter of government programs. Producers are eligible to receive loans for their grain at specified loan levels. If the market price falls below the loan rate, producers are induced to turn their grain over to the government, reducing free supply.

fundamental analysis Analysis based on the economic factors affecting supply and demand and their influence on market prices.

futures contract A legal agreement to buy or sell a specified quantity of a standardized commodity at a given price at a specific future date.

hedging The sale of futures against the physical commodity as protection against a price decline, or the purchase of futures against forward sales as protection against a price advance. Hedging is often used to offset the risks associated with the fluctuating value of inventory.

intercommodity spread A spread that consists of a long position in one commodity and a short position in another commodity. Example: a corn/wheat spread.

intermarket spread A spread that consists of a position in one market and an opposite position for the same commodity in a different market. Example: Kansas City Board of Trade wheat/Chicago Board of Trade wheat.

intramarket spread (interdelivery spread) A spread that consists of opposite positions in different contract months of the same commodity. An intramarket spread can involve contracts of the same crop year or contracts of different crop years. Example: July cotton/December cotton is an old crop/new crop intramarket spread.

inverted market A market that does not reflect carrying charges; the nearby contract months are premium the deferred contract months. See "backwardation."

leg One side or position of a spread.

lifting a leg The act of closing out one leg of a spread, leaving an outright position open.

limit down The maximum daily downward movement of a commodity price, set by the individual exchanges.

limited risk spread A bull spread that is limited in its potential adverse movement against the trader by full carry. This possibility only occurs for storable commodities.

limit order An order that allows the

broker to pay a price that is less than a specified limit or to sell at a price above a specified limit.

limit up The maximum daily upward movement of a commodity price, set by the individual exchanges.

liquidate To exit a long position or bull spread.

long position A position in which the trader has bought a futures contract that does not offset a previously established short position.

margin The collateral that must be deposited by the trader with a commodities brokerage firm to protect the firm from a loss on the position.

narrowing Gains in a nearby contract relative to the distant contract in a normal market. Thus, the difference between the two contract prices becomes smaller.

nearby The contract (or leg) of a spread that is closest to expiration.

normal market A market that reflects carrying charges; the nearby contracts are discounted in relation to the distant contracts.

not held basis order An order whereby the price may trade through or better than the trader's desired level, but the broker is not held responsible if the order is not filled.

old crop/new crop spread (intercrop spread) A spread that consists of a position in the new crop year and an opposite position in the old crop year (a type of intramarket spread). Example: since the soybean crop year is September to August, an intercrop soybean spread would be long July soybeans/short November soybeans.

open interest The total purchase or sale commitments that are outstanding.

outright A long or short position in a futures contract.

point Usually the minimum unit in which changes in a futures price may be expressed.

position An initial, as opposed to offsetting, futures market commitment.

premium More than the cash or regular price.

prime rate The interest rate charged by major banks to their most credit-worthy customers.

ratio spread A spread that consists of the price of one commodity futures contract divided by the futures price of a different commodity. Example: November soybeans divided by December cotton.

reverse crush (1) A spread in which, for example, the trader is short soybeans, long soybean meal, and long soybean oil. (2) A spread in which, for example, the trader is short feeder cattle, short corn, and long live cattle. See "crush."

roll A switch that simultaneously liquidates an existing position and initiates a new position in a different contract month. See "switch" and "carry order."

roll back A roll from a distant futures contract into a nearer futures contract.

roll forward A roll from a nearer futures contract into a more distant futures contract.

seasonality Price patterns that occur at approximately the same time each year.

short position A position in which the trader has sold a futures contract that does not offset a previously established long position.

source/product spread A spread between a commodity and one or more of its products. Example: November soybeans/December soybean oil.

spot price The price at which the cash commodity is selling. For grains, the term is cash price.

spread (1) A trade that consists of the simultaneous initiation of opposite positions in futures contracts. (2) The difference between two contract prices in the same or different markets.

spread order An order that consists of the simultaneous initiation of two opposite positions.

stop limit order A stop order that is restricted by a range. If it is a buy stop limit order, the broker cannot buy a contract until the price rises above a certain level, but that level cannot be higher than another specified price level.

stop order A buy stop or sell stop order instructs the broker not to initiate a position unless the price of a commodity reaches a specified level.

straddle Used interchangeably with the term "spread." A straddle is often a spread initiated between two different commodities.

switch A roll from one month to another. A switch can be done at the market or at a specified difference. See "carry order" and "roll."

technical analysis Analysis based on market action through chart study, moving averages, volume, open interest, oscillators, formations, and other technical indicators.

unwinding Liquidating a spread.

volume The total number of commodity futures contracts traded in a given period.

widening Gains in a distant contract relative to the nearby contract in a normal market. Thus, the difference between the two contract prices becomes greater.

CHAPTER

54

Bibliography

1. Futures Trading and Commodity Exchanges

Bakken, H. H.: *Theory of Markets and Marketing*, Mimir, Madison, Wis., 1953.

Boyle, J. E.: *Speculation and the Chicago Board of Trade*, Macmillan, New York, 1920.

Gold, G.: *Modern Commodity Futures Trading*, Commodity Research Bureau, New York, 1966.

Hoffman, G. W.: *Future Trading upon Organized Commodity Markets in the United States*, University of Pennsylvania Press, Philadelphia, 1932.

New York Coffee and Sugar Exchange: *History and Operation of the New York Coffee and Sugar Exchange, Inc., 1882–1947*, New York, 1947.

2. Trading Psychology

Baruch, B.: *My Own Story*, Holt, New York, 1957.

Le Bon, G.: *The Crowd*, Viking, New York, 1960.

Lefevre, E.: *Reminiscences of a Stock Operator*, American Research Council, New York, 1923.

Longstreet, R. W.: *Viewpoints of a Commodity Trader*, Frederick Fell, New York, 1968.

Mackay, C.: *Extraordinary Popular Delusions and the Madness of Crowds*, Page, London, 1932.

Neill, Humphrey: *The Art of Contrary Thinking*, Caxton, Caldwell, Ohio, 1960.

Schwed, Fred, Jr.: *Where Are the Customers' Yachts*, John Magee, Springfield, Mass., 1955

3. Individual Commodities

Aronson, J. R.: *The Soybean Crushing Margin, 1953–62: An Economic Analysis of the Futures Market for Soybeans, Soybean Oil, and Soybean Meal,* Clark University, Worcester, Mass., 1964.

Atwood, E. C., Jr.: *Theory and Practice in the Coffee Futures Market,* Princeton University Press, Princeton, N.J., 1959.

Green, L.: *Understanding the Frozen Orange Juice Market,* in Harry Jiler (ed.), *Commodity Year Book,* Commodity Research Bureau, New York, 1968.

Harlow, A.: *Factors Affecting the Price and Supply of Hogs,* U.S. Department of Agriculture Technical Bulletin 1247, 1964.

Houck, J. P.: *Demand and Price Analysis of the U.S. Soybean Market,* Agricultural Experiment Station Bulletin 244, Minnesota, 1963.

———, M. E. Ryan, and A. Subotnick: *Soybeans and Their Products: Markets, Models and Policy,* University of Minnesota Press, Minneapolis, 1972.

Lowell, F. R.: *The Wheat Market,* Keltner Statistical Service, Kansas City, Mo., 1968.

Meinken, K. W.: *The Demand and Price Structure for Wheat,* U.S. Department of Agriculture Technical Bulletin 1136, November 1955.

Weymar, F. H.: *The Dynamics of the World Cocoa Market,* Massachusetts Institute of Technology, Cambridge, Mass., 1968

4. Technical

Appel, G.: *Winning Stock Market Systems,* Signalert Corp., Great Neck, N.Y., 1974.

Ayres, L. P.: *Turning Points in Business Cycles,* August M. Kelly, New York, 1967.

Benner, S.: *Benner's Prophecies of Future Ups and Downs in Prices,* Chase and Hall, Cincinnati, 1875. Reprinted in *Journal of Cycle Research,* vol. 8, no. 1, January 1959.

Bernstein, J.: *The Handbook of Commodity Cycles: A Window on Time,* John Wiley, New York, 1982.

Bretz, W. G.: *Juncture Recognition in the Stock Market,* Vantage Press, New York, 1972.

Coppock, E. S. C.: *Practical Relative Strength Charting,* Trendex Corp., San Antonio, Tex., 1960.

Dewey, E. R.: *Cycles: The Mysterious Forces that Trigger Events,* Hawthorne Books, New York, 1971.

——— and E. F. Dakin: *Cycles: The Science of Prediction,* Henry Holt, New York, 1947.

Drew, G.: *New Methods for Profit in the Stock Market,* Metcalfe, Boston, 1968.

Edwards, R. D., and John Magee: *Technical Analysis of Stock Trends,* John Magee, Springfield, Mass., 1957.

Eiteman, W. J., C. A. Dice, and D. K. Eiteman: *The Stock Market,* McGraw-Hill, New York, 1966.

Fosback, N. G.: *Stock Market Logic: A Sophisticated Approach to Profits on Wall Street,* The Institute for Econometric Research, Fort Lauderdale, Fla., 1976.

Frost, A. J., and Robert R. Prechter: *The Elliot Wave Principle—Key to Stock Market Profits,* New Classics Library, Chappaqua, N.Y., 1978.

Gann, W. D.: *Truth of the Stock Tape,* Financial Guardian, New York, 1932.

Gartley, H. M.: *Profits in the Stock Market,* Lambert Gann Publishing, Pomeroy, Wash.

Gordon, W.: *The Stock Market Indicators,* Investors Press, Palisades Park, N.J., 1968.

Granville, J.: *Strategy of Daily Stock Market Timing*, Prentice-Hall, Englewood Cliffs, N.J., 1960.

Greiner, P., and H. C. Whitcomb: *Dow Theory*, Investors' Intelligence, New York, 1969.

Hamilton, W. D.: *The Stock Market Barometer*, Harper Bros., New York, 1922.

Hurst, J. M.: *The Profit Magic of Stock Transaction Timing*, Prentice-Hall, Englewood Cliffs, N.J., 1970.

Jiler, W.: *How Charts Can Help You in the Stock Market*, Commodity Research Publishing Corp., New York, 1961.

Krow, H.: *Stock Market Behavior*, Random House, New York, 1969.

Merrill, A. A.: *Filtered Waves: Basic Theory*, Analysis Press, Chappaqua, N.Y., 1977.

Nelson, S.: *ABC of Stock Market Speculation*, Taylor, New York, 1934.

Pring, M. J.: *Technical Analysis Explained*, McGraw-Hill, New York, 1980.

———: *How to Forecast Interest Rates*, McGraw-Hill, New York, 1981.

———: *International Investing Made Easy*, McGraw-Hill, New York, 1981.

Rhea, Robert: *Dow Theory*, Barrons, New York, 1932.

Shuman, J. B., and D. Rosenau: *The Kondratieff Wave*, World Publishing, New York, 1972.

Smith, E. L.: *Common Stocks and Business Cycles*, William Frederick, New York, 1959.

Index